ACCA

Strategic Business Reporting (SBR)

Practice & Revision Kit

For exams in September 2022, December 2022, March 2023 and June 2023

Fourth edition March 2022

ISBN 9781509744114
e-ISBN 9781509745111

British Library Cataloguing-in-Publication Data
A catalogue record for this book is available
from the British Library

Published by

BPP Learning Media Ltd
BPP House, Aldine Place
142–144 Uxbridge Road
London W12 8AA

www.bpp.com/learningmedia

Printed in the United Kingdom

Your learning materials, published by BPP Learning Media
Ltd, are printed on paper obtained from traceable,
sustainable sources.

We are grateful to the Association of Chartered Certified
Accountants for permission to reproduce past examination
questions. The suggested solutions in the practice answer bank
have been prepared by BPP Learning Media Ltd, unless otherwise
stated.

BPP Learning Media is grateful to the IASB for permission to
reproduce extracts from the International Financial Reporting
Standards including all International Accounting Standards, SIC
and IFRIC Interpretations (the Standards). The Standards together
with their accompanying documents are issued by:

The International Accounting Standards Board (IASB) 30 Cannon
Street, London, EC4M 6XH, United Kingdom.

Email: info@ifrs.org Web: www.ifrs.org

Disclaimer: The IASB, the International Financial Reporting
Standards (IFRS) Foundation, the authors and the publishers do
not accept responsibility for any loss caused by acting or
refraining from acting in reliance on the material in this
publication, whether such loss is caused by negligence or otherwise
to the maximum extent permitted by law.

A note about copyright

Contents

	Page
Finding questions	
Question index	iv
Topic index	viii
The exam	xi
Helping you with your revision	xvii
Essential skill areas	xix

Section 1: Preparation questions

Questions	3
Answers	89

Section 2: Exam-standard questions

Questions	17
Answers	109

Section 3: Mock exams

Mock exam 1

• Questions	281
• Answers	291

Mock exam 2 (ACCA Specimen exam 1, amended)

• Questions	309
• Answers	319

Mock exam 3 (March/June 2021 exam)

• Questions	337
• Answers	347

Mock exam 4 (September/December 2021 exam)

• Questions	361
• Answers	369

Mathematical tables	383
Review form	

Finding questions

Question index

The questions in section 1 are preparation questions to help consolidate your knowledge before you move onto the exam-standard questions in section 2. The questions in section 2 are grouped according to the structure of the exam. Section A of the exam will contain two questions, the first on groups and the second on ethical and reporting issues. Section B of the exam will contain two 25-mark questions which could cover any area of the syllabus. Here we have generally categorised questions containing analysis/appraisal of information and current issues under 'Section B-type questions' however, these areas could be examined in either section of the exam.

Questions which require consideration of an issue from the perspective of an investor or other stakeholder are marked below with an asterisk *.

Many of these questions are based on past real SBR exam questions (or predecessor exams P2 and ACR), which have been updated for changes in the syllabus or accounting standards as appropriate, as indicated in the question index below.

The IASB's *Conceptual Framework for Financial Reporting* was substantially revised and reissued in March 2018. References to the *Conceptual Framework* or the revised *Conceptual Framework* throughout this Kit refer to the March 2018 version unless otherwise stated.

		Marks	Time allocation Mins	Page number Question	Page number Answer
Section 1: Preparation questions					
1	Financial instruments	6	12	3	89
2	Leases	10	20	4	89
3	Defined benefit plan	10	20	4	90
4	Sundry standards	30	59	6	91
5	Control	12	23	7	94
6	Associate	20	39	8	96
7	Part disposal	25	49	9	98
8	Step acquisition	15	29	11	101
9	Foreign operation	25	49	11	103
10	Consolidated statement of cash flows	20	39	13	106
Section 2: Exam-standard questions					
Groups questions					
11	Robby	30	59	17	109
12	Banana (SBR September 2018 (amended))	30	59	19	113
13	Hill (SBR Specimen exam 2)	30	59	21	116
14	Luploid (SBR September/December 2019)	30	59	22	120
15	Sugar Co (SBR September/December 2020)	30	59	24	124
16	Angel (Adapted from P2 December 2013)	30	59	26	128
17	Moyes (Adapted from SBR December 2018/P2 2015)	30	59	28	132
18	Hummings Co (SBR March 2020)	30	59	30	135
19	Carbise (SBR March/June 2019)	30	59	32	139

		Marks	Time allocation Mins	Page number Question	Page number Answer

Section 2: Exam-standard questions

Ethical issues questions

		Marks	Mins	Question	Answer
20	Bagshot Co (SBR March 2020)	20	39	33	142
21	Calibra Co (SBR September/December 2020)	20	39	34	145
22	Farham (SBR September 2018)	20	39	35	147
23	Gustoso* (SBR Specimen exam 2)	20	39	36	149
24	Fiskerton (SBR December 2018)	20	39	37	151
25	Hudson (SBR March/June 2019)	20	39	38	153
26	Stent (SBR September/December 2019)	20	39	39	156

Section-B-type questions

Current issues

		Marks	Mins	Question	Answer
27	Calendar Co (SBR Specimen exam 2)	25	49	40	159
28	Digiwire (SBR September/December 2019 (amended))	25	49	41	161
29	Ecoma Co (SBR March 2020)	25	49	43	165
30	Egin group	25	49	44	168
31	Alexandra* (Adapted from P2 June 2012/December 2011)	25	49	45	172
32	Yanong (Adapted from P2 June 2015)	25	49	46	175
33	Avco* (Adapted from P2 June 2014)	25	49	48	179
34	Lupin	25	49	49	182
35	Janne* (Adapted from P2 June 2013)	25	49	50	185
36	SunChem (P2 September/December 2015 (amended))	25	49	51	188

Question containing analysis

		Marks	Mins	Question	Answer
37	KiKi* (SBR Specimen exam 2)	25	49	52	192
38	Skizer* (SBR September 2018 (amended))	25	49	53	194
39	Toobasco (SBR September 2018)	25	49	55	197
40	Holls* (SBR December 2018)	25	49	56	199
41	Crypto (SBR March/June 2019)	25	49	58	203
42	Guidance* (SBR September/December 2019)	25	49	59	205
43	Handfood Co (SBR September/December 2020)	25	49	60	208
44	Moorland*	25	49	61	211
45	Amster* (P2 December 2017 (amended))	25	49	62	213
46	Havanna (Adapted from P2 December 2013)	25	49	63	216
47	Operating segments* (adapted from P2 December 2011/ June 2010)	25	49	65	219
48	Cloud (P2 December 2015 (amended))	25	49	66	223

		Marks	Time allocation Mins	Page number Question	Answer
Financial reporting issues					
49	Leria Co (SBR March 2020)	25	49	66	226
50	Corbel Co (SBR September/December 2020)	25	49	68	229
51	Fill (SBR December 2018)	25	49	69	231
52	Zedtech (SBR Mar/Jun 2019 (amended))	25	49	70	234
53	Kayte (SBR December 2018 (amended)/adapted from P2 December 2014)	25	49	71	236
54	Pensions (adapted from P2 December 2007/P2 June 2012)	25	49	72	240
55	Emcee (P2 Mar/Jun 2016 (amended))	25	49	74	242
56	Estoil (P2 December 2014 (amended))	25	49	75	245
57	Evolve (P2 Sep/Dec 2016 (amended))	25	49	75	248
58	Gasnature (P2 Sep/Dec 2015 (amended))	25	49	76	250
59	Complexity* (Adapted from P2 December 2009)	25	49	77	253
60	Carsoon (P2 Mar/Jun 2017 (amended))	25	49	78	256
61	Leigh (ACR June 2007 (amended))	25	49	79	258
62	Mehran (P2 March/June 2016 (amended))	25	49	80	261
63	Ethan (P2 December 2012 (amended))	25	49	82	263
64	Whitebirk (P2 December 2010 (amended))	22	43	83	266
65	Revenue recognition	25	49	83	268
66	Seltec (P2 June 2010 (amended))	25	49	84	271
67	Della Co	25	49	85	275

Mock exam 1

1   Joey
2   Ramsbury
3   Klancet*
4   Jayach

Mock exam 2 (ACCA Specimen exam 1, amended)

1   Kutchen Co
2   Abby Co
3   Africant Co*
4   Rationale Co

Mock exam 3 (March/June 2021 exam)

1   Columbia Co
2   Bismuth Co
3   Sitka Co
4   Colat Co*

Mock exam 4 (September/December 2021 exam)

1   Chuckle Co
2   Agency Co
3   Stem Co
4   Symbal Co*

Topic index

Listed below are the key SBR syllabus topics and the numbers of the questions in this Kit covering those topics. We have also included a reference to the relevant Chapter of the BPP SBR Workbook, the companion to the BPP SBR Practice and Revision Kit, in case you wish to revise the information on the topic you have covered.

If you need to concentrate your practice and revision on certain topics or if you want to attempt all available questions that refer to a particular subject, you will find this index useful.

Syllabus topic	Question numbers	Workbook chapter
Accounting policies (IAS 8)	27, 42 Mock exam 1: Q4	2
Alternative performance measures (APMs)	35, 39, 41, 42, 44 Mock exam 2: Q3 Mock exam 4: Q3	18
Associates	39, 41, 42, 61, Mock exam 4: Q1 Mock exam 4: Q3	
Business combinations (IFRS 3)	11 – 14, 36, Mock exam 1: Q1, Mock exam 2: Q1, Mock exam 3: Q1, Mock exam 4: Q1	11 – 13
Conceptual Framework	11, 28, 33, 34, 35, 38, 40, 48, 51, 52, 53 Mock exam 1: Q4, Mock exam 2: Q4	1
Consolidated statement of cash flows	15, 16, 17	17
Deferred tax (IAS 12)	13, 25, 34, 40, 57, 63 Mock exam 3: Q2	7
Disposals of investments	12, 13, 19 Mock exam 2: Q1, Mock exam 3: Q3 Mock exam 4: Q1	13
Ethics	20–26, Mock exam 1: Q2, Mock exam 2: Q2, Mock exam 3: Q2, Mock exam 4: Q2	2
Events after the reporting period (IAS 10)	13, 57, 58	6
Employee benefits (including pensions)	12, 15, 25, 29, 43, 54, Mock exam 2: Q1, Mock exam 3: Q1, Mock exam 4: Q4	5
Fair value measurement (IFRS 13)	14, 28, 32, 35, 36, 55, 60, 62, 63, Mock exam 1: Q4, Mock exam 2: Q3, Mock exam 3: Q3, Mock exam 4: Q1	4

Syllabus topic	Question numbers	Workbook chapter
Financial instruments (IFRS 9)	12, 13, 18, 23, 26, 28, 31, 33, 41, 45, 48, 57, 58, 59, 60, 62, 63, Mock exam 2: Q1, Mock exam 3: Q2, Mock exam 4: Q4	8
Foreign transactions and entities (IAS 21)	18, 19, Mock exam 4: Q2	16
IFRS for SMEs Standard	43, 64	19
IFRS Practice Statement 1 *Management Commentary*	40, 44	18
IFRS Practice Statement 2 *Making Materiality Judgments*	27, 30, 31, 35, 36, Mock exam 1: Q3, Mock exam 1: Q4, Mock exam 2: Q4	20
Impairment (IAS 36)	14, 22, 50, 51, 56, 63, Mock exam 3: Q2, Mock exam 3: Q4	4
Intangible assets (IAS 38)	27, 36, 38, 49, 50, 55, Mock exam 3: Q3, Mock exam 4: Q2, Mock exam 4: Q4	4
Integrated reporting	30, 38, 43, 48	18
Interim reporting (IAS 34)	53	18
Investment property (IAS 40)	24, 35, 57, 63	4
Joint arrangements (IFRS 11)	11, 28, 41, 58, Mock exam 4: Q3	15
Leases (IFRS 16)	24, 27, 28, 29, 34, 41, 46, 49, 60, Mock exam 3: Q3, Mock exam 4: Q3	9
Measurement	35, Mock exam 1: Q4, Mock exam 2: Q3	1
Non-current assets held for sale and discontinued operations (IFRS 5)	17, 18, 22, 46, 49, 50, 53, 55, 57	14
Operating segments (IFRS 8)	44, 47	18
Provisions, contingent liabilities and contingent assets	20, 23, 25, 29, 54, Mock exam 3: Q4, Mock exam 4: Q4	6
Related party transactions (IAS 24)	20, 26, 36, 30, 31, 55, Mock exam 2: Q2	2
Revenue recognition (IFRS 15)	21, 24, 27, 28, 37, 46, 52, 60, Mock exam 3: Q3	3
Segment reporting (IFRS 8)	44, 47, Mock exam 1: Q3, Mock exam 2: Q2	18

Syllabus topic	Question numbers	Workbook chapter
Share-based payment (IFRS 2)	14, 17, 34, 45, 61, Mock exam 1: Q1	10
Step acquisitions (IFRS 10)	11, 15, Mock exam 1: Q1, Mock exam 2: Q1, Mock exam 4: Q1	12
Sustainability	29, Mock exam 3: Q4	18, 20

The Exam

Computer-based exams

Strategic Professional exams are all computer-based exams (CBE).

ACCA CBE practice platform

ACCA has launched a free on-demand resource, the **ACCA CBE practice platform**, designed to mirror the live CBE experience. You can access the ACCA CBE practice platform via the Study Support Resources section of the ACCA website: navigate to the CBE question practice section and log in with your myACCA credentials.

If you are sitting SBR as a CBE, practising as many exam-style questions as possible in the **ACCA CBE practice platform** will be key to passing the exam.

Important note for UK students who are sitting the UK variant of Strategic Business Reporting

If you are sitting the UK variant of the Strategic Business Reporting exam you will be studying under International standards, but between 15 and 20 marks will be available for comparisons between International and UK GAAP.

This Practice & Revision Kit is based on IFRS Standards only. An online supplement covering the additional UK issues and providing additional illustrations and examples is available on the Exam Success Site; for details of how to access this, see the inside cover of this Kit.

Approach to examining the syllabus

The Strategic Business Reporting syllabus is assessed by a 3 hour and 15 minute exam. The pass mark is **50%**. All questions in the exam are **compulsory**.

At the revision stage, we advise students to revisit the following main syllabus requirements so that you have a good understanding of the overall objectives of this exam. Remember, ACCA's examining team expect you to be able to:

- Demonstrate **professional competences** within the business reporting environment. You will be examined on concepts, theories, and principles, and on your ability to question and comment on proposed accounting treatments.

- Relate professional issues to relevant concepts and practical situations. The **evaluation of alternative accounting practices** and the **identification and prioritisation** of issues will be a key element of the exam.

- Exercise **professional** and **ethical judgement**, and **integrate technical knowledge** when addressing business reporting issues in a business context.

- Adopt **either a stakeholder or an external focus** in answering questions and demonstrate personal skills such as **problem solving**, **dealing with information** and **decision making**. You will also have to demonstrate **communication skills** appropriate to the scenario.

- Demonstrate specific professional knowledge appropriate to the **preparation and presentation of consolidated and other financial statements** from accounting data, to conform with relevant accounting standards. Here, you may be required to interpret financial statements for different stakeholders and/or communicate the impact of changes in accounting regulation on financial reporting.

The ACCA website contains a useful explanation of the verbs used in exam questions. See: 'What is the examiner asking? 'available at www.accaglobal.com/uk/en/student/sa/study-skills/questions.html

Format of the exam

100 marks, two sections, each section 50 marks		Marks
Section A	Two compulsory scenario-based questions, totalling 50 marks Question 1 (30 marks): • Based on the financial statements of group entities, or extracts thereof (syllabus area D) • Also likely to require consideration of some financial reporting issues (syllabus area C) • Discussion and explanation of numerical aspects will be required Question 2 (20 marks): • Consideration of the reporting implications and the ethical implications of specific events in a contemporary scenario Two professional marks will be awarded in Section A. Further guidance will be given in the questions clarifying what these professional marks will be awarded for.	50 (incl. 2 professional marks)
Section B	Two compulsory 25-mark questions Questions: • May be scenario, case-study, or essay based • Will contain both discursive and computational elements • Could deal with any aspect of the syllabus • Will always include either a full or part question that requires the appraisal of financial and/or non-financial information from either the preparer's or another stakeholder's perspective Two professional marks will be awarded in Section B. Further guidance will be given in the questions clarifying what these professional marks will be awarded for.	50 (incl. 2 professional marks)
Current issues		
The current issues element of the syllabus (Syllabus area F) may be examined in Section A or B but will not be a full question; it is more likely to form part of another question.		

Analysis of past exams

The table below shows when each element of the syllabus has been examined and the section in which the element was examined.

Workbook chapter		Specimen exam 1	Specimen exam 2	Sept 2018	Dec 2018	Mar/Jun 2019	Sept/Dec 2019	Mar 2020	Sept/Dec 2020	Mar/June 2021	Sept/Dec 2021
	Fundamental ethical and professional principles										
2	Professional and ethical behaviour in corporate reporting	A	A	A	A	A	A	A	A	A	A
	The financial reporting framework										
1	The applications, strengths and weaknesses of an accounting framework	A, B	A	B	A, B	B	A, B	A			
	Reporting the financial performance of a range of entities										
3	Revenue		B	B	A	B	B		A	B	
4	Non-current assets		A, B	A, B	A, B			B	A, B	A, B	A, B
8	Financial instruments		A	A		B	A, B	A		A	B
9	Leases		B		A	B		B		B	B
5	Employee benefits	A				A	B	B	A, B	A	B
7	Income taxes		A		B	A	A				
6	Provisions, contingencies and events after the reporting period		A	B		A		A		B	B
10	Share-based payment						A				
4, 8	Fair value measurement	B					A			B	
19	Reporting requirements of small and medium-sized entities (SMEs)								B		
2, 4, 9, 18	Other reporting issues		B				B	A			

Workbook chapter		Specimen exam 1	Specimen exam 2	Sept 2018	Dec 2018	Mar/ Jun 2019	Sept/ Dec 2019	Mar 2020	Sept/ Dec 2020	Mar/ June 2021	Sept Dec 202
	Financial statements of groups of entities										
11, 14–17	Group accounting including statements of cash flows	A	A	A	A	A	A, B	A	A	A	A
11, 15	Associates and joint arrangements		A	A		B	B				A, E
12, 13	Changes in group structures	A	A	A	A	A		A	A	A, B	A
16	Foreign transactions and entities						A	A			A
	Interpreting financial statements for different stakeholders										
18	Analysis and interpretation of financial information and measurement of performance	A, B	B	B	B	B	B	B	B	B	B
	The impact of changes and potential changes in accounting regulation										
20	Discussion of solutions to current issues in financial reporting	A, B	B	A, B	A, B	B	B	B		B	

IMPORTANT!

The table above gives a broad idea of how frequently major topics in the syllabus are examined. It should **not be used to question spot** and predict, for example, that a certain topic will not be examined because it has been examined in the last two sittings. The examiner's reports indicate that they are well aware that some students try to question spot. The examining team avoid predictable patterns and may, for example, examine the same topic two sittings in a row, particularly if there has been a recent change in legislation. Equally, just because a topic has not been examined for a long time, this does not necessarily mean it will be examined in the next exam!

Syllabus and Study Guide

The complete SBR syllabus and study guide can be found by visiting the exam resource finder on the ACCA website.

Examinable documents

The following documents are examinable for sittings up from September 2021 to June 2022. Knowledge of new examinable regulations issued by 31 August will be required in examination sessions being held in the following exam year. Documents may be examinable even if the effective date is in the future.

The syllabus and study guide offers more detailed guidance on the depth and level at which the examinable documents will be examined.

	International Accounting Standards (IASs)/International Financial Reporting Standards (IFRSs)
IAS 1	Presentation of Financial Statements
IAS 2	Inventories
IAS 7	Statement of Cash Flows
IAS 8	Accounting Policies, Changes in Accounting Estimates and Errors
IAS 10	Events After the Reporting Period
IAS 12	Income Taxes
IAS 16	Property, Plant and Equipment
IAS 19	Employee Benefits
IAS 20	Accounting for Government Grants and Disclosure of Government Assistance
IAS 21	The Effects of Changes in Foreign Exchange Rates
IAS 23	Borrowing Costs
IAS 24	Related Party Disclosures
IAS 27	Separate Financial Statements
IAS 28	Investments in Associates and Joint Ventures
IAS 32	Financial Instruments: Presentation
IAS 33	Earnings per Share
IAS 34	Interim Financial Reporting
IAS 36	Impairment of Assets
IAS 37	Provisions, Contingent Liabilities and Contingent Assets
IAS 38	Intangible Assets
IAS 40	Investment Property
IAS 41	Agriculture
IFRS 1	First-time Adoption of International Financial Reporting Standards
IFRS 2	Share-based Payment
IFRS 3	Business Combinations
IFRS 5	Non-current Assets Held for Sale and Discontinued Operations
IFRS 7	Financial Instruments: Disclosures

	International Accounting Standards (IASs)/International Financial Reporting Standards (IFRSs)
IFRS 8	Operating Segments
IFRS 9	Financial Instruments
IFRS 10	Consolidated Financial Statements
IFRS 11	Joint Arrangements
IFRS 12	Disclosure of Interests in other Entities
IFRS 13	Fair Value Measurement
IFRS 15	Revenue from Contracts with Customers
IFRS 16	Leases
IFRS for SMEs	IFRS for Small and Medium-sized Entities

	Other Statements
	Conceptual Framework for Financial Reporting (March 2018)
	The International Integrated Reporting <IR> Framework
IFRS Practice Statement 1	Management Commentary
IFRS Practice Statement 2	Making Materiality Judgements

Important note

Many of these IFRS standards are also tested in Financial Reporting (FR). The technical knowledge required for SBR is **an extension** of that required for FR. The SBR examining team have commented that many student responses do not demonstrate a good technical FR knowledge. However, a good understanding of FR is vital to pass your SBR exam and you need to be able to demonstrate it. Before you begin your studies for SBR, be sure that you have revised all FR topics.

Helping you with your revision

BPP Learning Media – ACCA Approved Content Provider

As an ACCA **Approved Content Provider**, BPP Learning Media gives you the **opportunity** to use revision materials reviewed by the ACCA examining team. By incorporating the ACCA examining team's comments and suggestions regarding the depth and breadth of syllabus coverage, the BPP Learning Media Practice & Revision Kit provides excellent, **ACCA-approved** support for your revision.

These materials are reviewed by the ACCA examining team. The objective of the review is to ensure that the material properly covers the syllabus and study guide outcomes, used by the examining team in setting the exams, in the appropriate breadth and depth. The review does not ensure that every eventuality, combination or application of examinable topics is addressed by the ACCA Approved Content. Nor does the review comprise a detailed technical check of the content as the Approved Content Provider has its own quality assurance processes in place in this respect.

BPP Learning Media do everything possible to ensure the material is accurate and up to date when sending to print. In the event that any errors are found after the print date, they are uploaded to the following website: www.bpp.com/learningmedia/Errata.

The structure of this Practice & Revision Kit

This Practice & Revision Kit is divided into three sections. The questions in Section 1 are preparation questions to help develop your knowledge. Section 2 contains exam-standard questions which are of appropriate complexity and format to mimic the style of the final exam. Section 3 contains four mock exams. You should attempt all four mock exams, preferably under exam conditions, as this will provide excellent preparation before you take the real exam.

Question practice

Question practice is a core part of learning new topic areas. When you practice questions, you should focus on improving the Exam success skills – personal to your needs – by obtaining feedback or through a process of self-assessment.

Practising as many exam-style questions as possible (using the ACCA CBE practice platform as much as you can) will be the key to passing this exam. You should attempt questions under timed conditions and ensure you produce full answers to the discussion parts as well as doing the calculations. Also ensure that you attempt all mock exams under exam conditions.

ACCA have launched a free on-demand resource designed to mirror the live exam experience helping you to become more familiar with the exam format. You can access the platform via the Study Support Resources section of the ACCA website navigating to the CBE question practice section and logging in with your myACCA credentials.

Selecting questions

To help you plan your revision, we have provided a full topic index which maps the questions to topics in the syllabus (see page vii).

Making the most of question practice

At BPP Learning Media we realise that you need more than just questions and model answers to get the most from your question practice.

- Our **Top tips**, included for certain questions, provide essential advice on tackling questions, presenting answers and the key points that answers need to include.

- We include **marking guides** to show you what the examining team rewards.

- We include **comments from the examining team** to show you where students struggled or performed well in the actual exam

Attempting mock exams

This Kit has four mock exams, including ACCA's Specimen exam 1, the March/June 2021 hybrid exam and the September/December 2021 hybrid exam, all of which have been updated for applicable changes in examinable documents. We strongly recommend that you attempt the mock exams under exam conditions.

Topics to revise

ACCA's examining team consistently warn very strongly against question-spotting and trying to predict the topics that will be included in the exam. Students should not be surprised if the same topic area is examined in two successive sittings. ACCA's examining team regards few areas as off-limits for questions, and all of the syllabus can be tested.

That said, the following areas of the syllabus are very important, and your revision therefore needs to cover them particularly well.

- **Group accounts**: Group accounts will always be examined as part of Section A but may also feature in Section B. You will not be asked to prepare full consolidated financial statements in SBR but do need to be able to prepare extracts from them or key calculations within. You must also be able to explain the accounting treatment, as the marks for numerical aspects will be limited. The group accounts question could feature consolidated statements of cash flows, foreign subsidiaries or changes in group structure, as well as the underlying principles of group accounting, all of which are included in the SBR syllabus.

- **Ethical issues**: Ethical issues will feature in Section A of every exam. It is important that you can analyse ethical issues with regards to the fundamental principles of ACCA's *Code of Ethics and Conduct*.

- **Analysis and appraisal of information** will be tested in Section B. You should not focus only on 'traditional' financial analysis such as ratios. You will need to appraise companies using a range of financial and non-financial information, and from the perspective of different stakeholders.

- An in-depth **knowledge of the *Conceptual Framework*** is required. You are expected to be able discuss the consistency of each examinable IFRS with the *Conceptual Framework*.

- **Developments in Financial Reporting**: You need to be able to discuss the effect of a change or proposed change in accounting standards and other developments, such as the IFRS Practice Statement 2 *Making Materiality Judgements*, including the effect it may have on how stakeholders will analyse the financial statements. You need to read widely to develop your knowledge of current issues, including reading articles published on ACCA's website and looking at real published annual reports.

- More complex IFRS Standards such as IFRS 15 *Revenue from Contracts with Customers* and IFRS 16 *Leases*, as there is significant scope for discussion and justification in more complex standards.

Essential skill areas

There are three areas you should develop in order to achieve exam success in Strategic Business Reporting (SBR). These are:

(1)   Knowledge application
(2)   Specific Strategic Business Reporting skills
(3)   Exam success skills

At the revision and final exam preparation phases **these should be developed together as part of a comprehensive study plan of focused question practice.**

Take some time to revisit the **Specific Strategic Business Reporting skills** and **Exam success skills.** These are shown in the diagram below and followed by tutorial guidance of how to apply them.

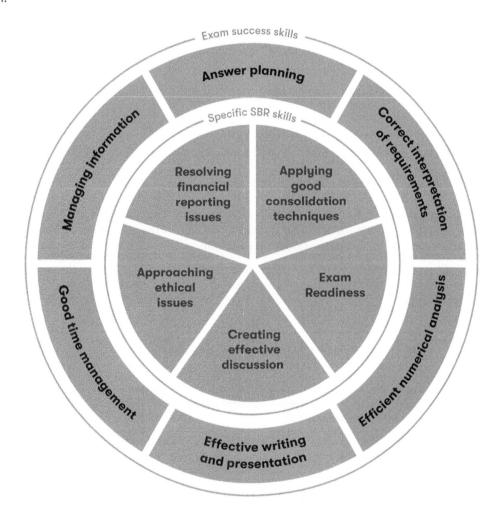

Specific SBR skills

These are the skills specific to SBR that we think you need to develop in order to pass the exam.

In the BPP Strategic Business Reporting Workbook, there are five **Skills Checkpoints** which define each skill and show how it is applied in answering a question. A brief summary of each skill is given below.

Skill 1: Approaching ethical issues

Question 2 in Section A of the exam will require you to consider the **reporting implications** and the **ethical implications** of specific events in a given scenario.

Given that ethics will feature in every exam, it is essential that you master the appropriate technique for approaching ethical issues in order to maximise your mark.

BPP recommends a step-by-step technique for approaching questions on ethical issues:

Step 1   Copy and paste the question requirements to the word processor response option. Work out how many minutes you have to answer the question and make a note of the time under the question requirements.

Step 2   Read the requirements and analyse them. Underline each sub-requirement separately and identify the verb(s). Ask yourself what each sub-requirement means.

Step 3   Read the scenario, identify which IFRS Standard may be relevant, whether the proposed accounting treatment complies with that IFRS Standard. Identify which fundamental principles from the ACCA Code of Ethics are relevant and whether there are any threats to these principles.

Step 4   Prepare an answer plan using key words from the requirements as headings. Ensure your plan makes use of the information given in the scenario.

Step 5   Complete your answer using key words from the requirements as headings.

Skills Checkpoint 1 in the BPP Workbook for Strategic Business Reporting covers this technique in detail through application to an exam-standard question. Consider revisiting Skills Checkpoint 1 and completing the scenario-based question to specifically improve this skill.

Skill 2: Resolving financial reporting issues

Financial reporting issues are highly likely to be tested in both sections of your Strategic Business Reporting exam, so it is essential that you master the skill for resolving financial reporting issues in order to maximise your chance of passing the exam.

The basic approach BPP recommends for resolving financial reporting issues is very similar to the one for ethical issues. This consistency is important because in Question 2 of the exam, both will be tested together.

Step 1   Copy and paste the question requirements to the word processor response option. Work out how many minutes you have to answer the question and make a note of the time under the question requirements.

Step 2   Read the requirements and analyse them. Underline each sub-requirement separately, identify the verb(s) and ask yourself what each sub-requirement means.

Step 3   Read the scenario, identify which IFRS Standard may be relevant and whether the proposed accounting treatment complies with that IFRS Standard.

Step 4   Prepare an answer plan using key words from the requirements as headings. Ensure your plan makes use of the information given in the scenario.

Step 5   Complete your answer, using separate headings for each item in the scenario.

Skills Checkpoint 2 in the BPP Workbook for Strategic Business Reporting covers this technique in detail through application to an exam-standard question. Consider revisiting Skills Checkpoint 2 and completing the scenario based question to specifically improve this skill.

Skill 3: Applying good consolidation techniques

Question 1 of Section A of the exam will be based on the financial statements of group entities, or extracts thereof. Section B of the exam could deal with any aspect of the syllabus so it is also possible that groups feature in Question 3 or 4.

Good consolidation techniques are therefore essential when answering both narrative and numerical aspects of group questions.

Skills Checkpoint 3 focuses on the more challenging technique for correcting errors in group financial statements that have already been prepared.

A step-by-step technique for applying good consolidation techniques is outlined below.

Step 1	Copy and paste the question requirements to the word processor response option. Work out how many minutes you have to answer the question and make a note of the time under the question requirements.
Step 2	Read the requirements and analyse them. Underline each sub-requirement separately and identify the verb(s). Ask yourself what each sub-requirement means.
Step 3	Read the scenario, identify exactly what information has been provided and what you need to do with this information. Identify which consolidation workings/adjustments may be required and which IFRS Standards or parts of the *Conceptual Framework* you may need to explain.
Step 4	Make notes on the group structure. Identify which consolidation working, adjustment or correction to error is required. Do not perform any detailed calculations at this stage.
Step 5	Complete your answer using key words from the requirements as headings. Ensure your explanations refer to underlying accounting concepts and the relevant standards. If you are asked for calculations, perform the calculation first, then explain it.

Skills Checkpoint 3 in the BPP Workbook for Strategic Business Reporting covers this technique in detail through application to an exam-standard question. Consider revisiting Skills Checkpoint 3 and completing the scenario based question to specifically improve this skill.

Skill 4: Creating effective discussion

More marks in your SBR exam will relate to narrative answers than numerical answers. It is very tempting to practise only numerical questions, as they are easy to mark because the answer is right or wrong, whereas narrative questions are more subjective and a range of different answers will be given credit. Even when attempting narrative questions, it is tempting to do a brief answer plan and then look at the answer rather than attempting a full answer. Unless you practise narrative questions in full, to time, you will never acquire the necessary skills to tackle discussion questions.

The basic five steps adopted in Skills Checkpoints 1-3 should also be used in discussion questions. Steps 2 and 4 are particularly important for discussion questions. You will definitely need to spend a third of your time reading and planning. Generating ideas at the planning stage to create a comprehensive answer plan will be the key to success in this style of question. Consideration of the *Conceptual Framework*, ethical principles and the perspective of stakeholders will often help with discursive questions in SBR.

Remember that very few marks are available for just stating relevant knowledge. You must make sure your answers are applied to the scenario given.

A step-by-step technique is outlined below.

Step 1	Copy and paste the question requirements to the word processor response option. Work out how many minutes you have to answer the question and make a note of the time under the question requirements.
Step 2	Read the requirements and analyse them. Underline each sub-requirement separately, identify the verb(s) and ask yourself what each sub-requirement means.

Step 3	Read and analyse the scenario
Step 4	Prepare an answer plan
Step 5	Complete your answer

Skills Checkpoint 4 in the BPP Workbook for Strategic Business Reporting covers this technique in detail through application to an exam-standard question. Consider revisiting Skills Checkpoint 4 and completing the scenario based question to specifically improve this skill.

Skill 5: Exam readiness

Skills Checkpoint 5 gives general advice on being 'exam ready' and focusses on how to make best use of the computer-based exam software.

Consider revisiting Skills Checkpoint 5 in the BPP Workbook for SBR to prepare for your exam.

Exam success skills

Passing the SBR exam requires more than applying syllabus knowledge and demonstrating the Specific SBR skills; it also requires the development of excellent exam technique through question practice.

We consider the following six skills, or exam techniques, to be vital for exam success. These skills were introduced in the BPP Workbook and you can revisit the five Skills Checkpoints in the BPP Workbook for tutorial guidance of how to apply each of the six Exam success skills in your question practice and in the exam.

Aim to consider your performance in all six Exam success skills during your revision stage question practice and reflect on your particular strengths and weaker areas which you can then work on.

Exam success skill 1

Managing information

Questions in the exam will present you with a lot of information. The skill is how you handle this information to make the best use of your time. The key is determining how you will approach the exam and then actively reading the questions.

Advice on developing this skill

Active reading

To avoid being overwhelmed by the quantity of information provided, you must take an active approach to reading each question

Active reading means focussing on the question's requirement first, highlighting key verbs such as 'prepare', 'comment', 'explain', 'discuss', to ensure you answer the question properly. Then read the rest of the question, and as you now have an understanding of what the question requires you to do, you can highlight important and relevant information, and use the scratchpad with the exam software to make notes of any relevant technical information you think you will need.

In the CBE the highlighter tool provided in the toolbar at the top of the screen offers a range of colours:

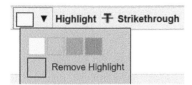

This allows you to choose **different colours to answer different aspects to a question**. For example, if a question asked you to discuss the pros and cons of an issue then you could choose a different colour for highlighting pros and cons within the relevant section of an exhibit.

The **strikethrough function** allows you to delete areas of an exhibit that you have dealt with - this can be useful in managing information if you are dealing with numerical questions because it can allow you to ensure that all numerical areas have been accounted for in your answer.

The CBE also allows you to **resize windows** by clicking and dragging on the bottom right-hand corner of the window.

This functionality allows you to **display a number of windows at the same time**, so this could allow you review:

- the question requirements and the exhibit relating to that requirement, at the same time, or

- the window containing your answer (whether a word processing or spreadsheet document) and the exhibit relating to that requirement, at the same time.

Exam success skill 2

Correct interpretation of the requirements

The active verb used often dictates the approach that written answers should take (eg 'explain', 'discuss', 'evaluate'). It is important you identify and use the verb to define your approach. The Correct interpretation of the requirements skill is correctly producing only what is being asked for by a requirement. Anything not required will not earn marks.

Advice on developing this skill

This skill can be developed by analysing question requirements and applying this process:

Step 1   Read the requirement

Firstly, read the requirement a couple of times slowly and carefully and highlight the active verbs. Use the active verbs to define what you plan to do. Make sure you identify any sub-requirements.

In SBR, the **detailed aspects of a requirement are often embedded in the scenario**. For example, in the scenario, the directors may ask you explain something, and then the requirement will ask you to respond to the director's instruction. Therefore, the initial requirement by itself may not provide a complete understanding of a question's requirement, although it is a useful starting point.

We recommend you copy the requirements into the word processor response option, in order to form the basis of your answer plan. See Exam success skill 3: Answer planning below.

Step 2   Read the rest of the question

By reading the requirement first, you will have an idea of what you are looking out for as you read through the scenario and exhibits. This is a great time saver and means you don't end up having to read the whole question in full twice. You should do this in an active way – see Exam success skill 1: Managing information.

Step 3   Read the requirement again

Read the requirements again to remind yourself of the exact wording before starting your written answer. This will capture any misinterpretation of the requirements or any requirements missed entirely.

It is particularly important to pay attention to any dates you are given in requirements. This is especially the case when, for example, discussing an accounting treatment up to a particular date. No marks will be awarded for discussing the treatment at a different date than that asked for in the requirement.

Exam success skill 3

Answer planning: Priorities, structure and logic

This skill requires the planning of the key aspects of an answer which accurately and completely responds to the requirement.

Advice on developing this skill

We recommend that you plan your answer directly in the word processor response option and then fill out the detail of the plan with your answer. This will save you time spent on creating a separate plan, say in the scratchpad, and then typing up your answer separately - though you could copy and paste between the scratchpad and response option if you wanted to do so.

The easiest way to start your answer plan is to **copy the question requirements to your chosen response option** (eg word processor). This will allow you to ensure that your answer plan addresses all parts of the question requirements. Then, as you **read through the exhibits, you can copy and paste any relevant information into your chosen response option** under the relevant requirement. This approach also has the advantage of making sure your answer is applied to the scenario given, which is crucial in the SBR exam.

Copying and pasting simply involves selecting the relevant information and either right clicking to access the copy and paste functions, or alternatively using Ctrl-C to copy and Ctrl-V to paste.

Exam success skill 4

Efficient numerical analysis

This skill aims to maximise the marks awarded by making clear to the marker the process of arriving at your answer. This is achieved by laying out an answer such that, even if you make a few errors, you can still score subsequent marks for follow-on calculations. It is vital that you do not lose marks purely because the marker cannot follow what you have done.

Advice on developing this skill

This skill can be developed by applying the following process:

Step 1   Use a standard proforma working where relevant

If answers can be laid out in a standard proforma then always plan to do so. This will help the marker to understand your working and allocate the marks easily. It will also help you to work through the figures in a methodical and time-efficient way.

Step 2   Show your workings

Keep your workings as clear and simple as possible and ensure they are cross-referenced to the main part of your answer. Where it helps, provide brief narrative explanations to help the marker understand the steps in the calculation. This means that if a mistake is made then you do not lose any subsequent marks for follow-on calculations.

Step 3	Keep moving!
	It is important to remember that, in an exam situation, it is difficult to get every number 100% correct. The key is therefore ensuring you do not spend too long on any single calculation. If you are struggling with a solution then make a sensible assumption, state it and move on.

You can use the spreadsheet to prepare calculations, if you wish. If you do so, you can make use of formulas to help with calculations, instead of using a calculator. For example, the 'sum' function: =SUM(A1:10) would add all the numbers in spreadsheet cells A1 to A10. You can use the symbol ^ to calculate a number 'to the power of...', eg =1.10^2 calculates 1.10 squared - this is very useful if you need to perform a discounting calculation.

If you use the spreadsheet for calculations, make sure the spreadsheet cell includes your formula and not just the final answer, so that the marker can see what you have done and can award follow-on marks even if you have made a mistake earlier in the calculation.

If you do decide to use a calculator instead, don't just put the final answer into a cell without including your workings - make sure you type up your workings as well and cross refer to them in your final answer.

Exam success skill 5

Effective writing and presentation

Written answers should be presented so that the marker can clearly see the points you are making, presented in the format specified in the question. The skill is to provide efficient written answers with sufficient breadth of points that answer the question, in the right depth, in the time available.

Advice on developing this skill

Step 1	Use headings
	Using the headings and sub-headings from your answer plan will give your answer structure, order and logic. This will ensure your answer links back to the requirement and is clearly signposted, making it easier for the marker to understand the different points you are making. Underlining your headings will also help the marker.

Step 2	Write your answer in short, but full, sentences
	Use short, punchy sentences with the aim that every sentence should say something different and generate marks. Write in full sentences, ensuring your style is professional.

Step 3	Do your calculations first, explanation second
	Questions often ask for an explanation with suitable calculations, the best approach is to prepare the calculation first but present it on the bottom half of the page of your answer. Then add the explanation before the calculation. Performing the calculation first should enable you to explain what you have done.
	In a CBE, this is easy to do - prepare your calculation, then type up your answer above it. If you wish, you can use the word processor to type up narrative discussion and the spreadsheet to prepare any calculations. If you do so, make sure you clearly cross reference to your calculation so the marker can follow what you have done. See Exam success skill 4 - efficient numerical analysis.

Exam success skill 6

Advice on developing this skill

The exam is 3 hours 15 minutes long, which translates to 1.95 minutes per mark. Therefore a 10-mark requirement should be allocated a maximum of 20 minutes to complete your answer before you move on to the next task. At the beginning of a question, work out the amount of time you should be spending on each requirement and write the finishing time next to each requirement on your exam. In a CBE, you could put the time allocation next to the requirements in your answer plan. If you take the approach of spending 10–15 minutes reading and planning at the start of the exam, adjust the time allocated to each question accordingly, eg if you allocate 15 minutes to reading, then you will have 3 hours remaining which is 1.8 minutes per mark.

Keep an eye on the clock

Aim to attempt all requirements, but be ready to be ruthless and move on if your answer is not going as planned. The challenge for many is sticking to planned timings. Be aware this is difficult to achieve in the early stages of your studies and be ready to let this skill develop over time.

If you find yourself running short on time and know that a full answer is not possible in the time you have, consider recreating your plan in overview form and then add key terms and details as time allows. Remember, some marks may be available, for example, simply stating a conclusion which you don't have time to justify in full.

Question Bank

Section 1 – Preparation questions

> **Tutorial note.**
>
> The Section 1 questions are designed to help you prepare for the SBR examination. They are not of a full exam standard but are still very helpful in testing your understanding of key areas of the syllabus. The number of marks and time allocated to each question in this section is for indicative purposes only.

1 Financial instruments   12 mins

(a)   Graben Co purchases a bond for $441,014 on 1 January 20X1. It will be redeemed on 31 December 20X4 for $600,000. The bond is held at amortised cost and carries no coupon.

Required

Calculate the valuation of the bond for the statement of financial position as at 31 December 20X1 and the finance income for 20X1 shown in profit or loss.   (3 marks)

Compound sum of $1: $(1 + r)^n$

Year	2%	4%	6%	8%	10%	12%	14%
1	1.0200	1.0400	1.0600	1.0800	1.1000	1.1200	1.1400
2	1.0404	1.0816	1.1236	1.1664	1.2100	1.2544	1.2996
3	1.0612	1.1249	1.1910	1.2597	1.3310	1.4049	1.4815
4	1.0824	1.1699	1.2625	1.3605	1.4641	1.5735	1.6890
5	1.1041	1.2167	1.3382	1.4693	1.6105	1.7623	1.9254

(b)   Baldie Co issues 4,000 convertible bonds on 1 January 20X2 at par. The bonds are redeemable three years later at a par value of $500 per bond, which is the nominal value.

The bonds pay interest annually in arrears at an interest rate (based on nominal value) of 5%. Each bond can be converted at the maturity date into 30 $1 shares.

The prevailing market interest rate for three year bonds that have no right of conversion is 9%.

Required

Show how the convertible bond would be presented in the statement of financial position at 1 January 20X2.   (3 marks)

Cumulative three year annuity factors:

5%   2.723
9%   2.531

(Total = 6 marks)

2 Leases

20 mins

Sugar Co leased a machine from Spice Co. The terms of the lease are as follows:

Inception of lease	1 January 20X1
Lease term	4 years at $78,864 per annum payable in arrears
Present value of future lease payments	$250,000
Useful life of asset	4 years

Required

(a) Calculate the interest rate implicit in the lease, using the table below. **(3 marks)**

This table shows the cumulative present value of $1 per annum, receivable or payable at the end of each year for n years.

Years	Interest rates		
(n)	6%	8%	10%
1	0.943	0.926	0.909
2	1.833	1.783	1.736
3	2.673	2.577	2.487
4	3.465	3.312	3.170
5	4.212	3.993	3.791

(b) Explain, with suitable workings and extracts from the financial statements, how Sugar Co should account for the lease for the year ended 31 December 20X1. Notes to the accounts are not required. **(7 marks)**

(Total = 10 marks)

3 Defined benefit plan

20 mins

> **BPP note.** In this question, proforma are given to you to help you get used to setting out your answer. You may wish to transfer them to a separate sheet, or alternatively to use a separate sheet for your workings.

Brutus operates a defined benefit pension plan for its employees. The present value of the future benefit obligations and the fair value of its plan assets on 1 January 20X1 were $110 million and $150 million respectively.

The pension plan received contributions of $7 million and paid pensions to former employees of $10 million during the year.

Extracts from the most recent actuarial report shows the following:

Present value of pension plan obligation at 31 December 20X1	$116m
Fair value of plan assets at 31 December 20X1	$140m
Present cost of pensions earned in the period	$11m
Yield on high quality corporate bonds at 1 January 20X1	10%

On 1 January 20X1, the rules of the pension plan were changed to improve benefits for plan members. The actuary has advised that this will cost $10 million.

Required

Prepare extracts from the notes to Brutus' financial statements for the year ended 31 December 20X1 which show how the pension plan should be accounted for. **(10 marks)**

Note. Assume contributions and benefits were paid on 31 December.

NOTES TO THE STATEMENT OF PROFIT OR LOSS AND OTHER COMPREHENSIVE INCOME

Defined benefit expense recognised in profit or loss

	$m
Current service cost	
Past service cost	
Net interest on the net defined benefit asset	———
	≡≡≡

Other comprehensive income (items that will not be reclassified to profit or loss)

Remeasurement of defined benefit plans

	$m
Remeasurement gain on defined benefit obligation	
Remeasurement loss on plan assets	———
	≡≡≡

NOTES TO THE STATEMENT OF FINANCIAL POSITION

Net defined benefit asset recognised in the statement of financial position

	31 December 20X1 $m	31 December 20X0 $m
Present value of pension obligation		
Fair value of plan assets	———	———
Net asset	≡≡≡	≡≡≡

Changes in the present value of the defined benefit obligation

	$m
Opening defined benefit obligation	
Interest on obligation	
Current service cost	
Past service cost	
Benefits paid	
Gain on remeasurement of obligation (balancing figure)	———
Closing defined benefit obligation	≡≡≡

Changes in the fair value of plan assets

	$m
Opening fair value of plan assets	
Interest on plan assets	
Contributions	
Benefits paid	
Loss on remeasurement of assets (balancing figure)	———
Closing fair value of plan assets	≡≡≡

4 Sundry standards   59 mins

(a) Penn has a defined benefit pension plan.

Required

Using the information below, prepare extracts from the statement of financial position and the statement of profit or loss and other comprehensive income for the year ended 31 January 20X8. Ignore taxation.   (10 marks)

   (i)   The opening plan assets were $3.6 million on 1 February 20X7 and plan liabilities at this date were $4.3 million.

   (ii)   Company contributions to the plan during the year amounted to $550,000. The contributions were paid at the start of the year.

   (iii) Pensions paid to former employees amounted to $330,000. These were paid at the start of the year.

   (iv)   The yield on high quality corporate bonds was 8% at 1 February 20X7.

   (v)   On 31 January 20X8, five staff were made redundant, and an extra $58,000 in total was added to the value of their pensions.

   (vi)   Current service costs as provided by the actuary are $275,000.

   (vii) At 31 January 20X8, the actuary valued the plan liabilities at $4.64 million and the plan assets at $4.215 million.

(b) Sion operates a defined benefit pension plan for its employees. Sion has a 31 December year end. The following details relate to the plan.

	$'000
Present value of obligation at 1 January 20X8	40,000
Market value of plan assets at 1 January 20X8	40,000

	20X8	20X9
	$'000	$'000
Current service cost	2,500	2,860
Benefits paid out	1,974	2,200
Contributions paid by entity	2,000	2,200
Present value of obligation at end of the year	46,000	40,800
Market value of plan assets at end of the year	43,000	35,680
Yield on corporate bonds at start of the year	8%	9%

During 20X8, the benefits available under the plan were improved. The resulting increase in the present value of the defined benefit obligation was $2 million as at 31 December 20X8.

Contributions were paid into the plan and benefits were paid out of the plan on the final day of each accounting period.

On 31 December 20X9, Sion divested of part of its business, and as part of the sale agreement, transferred the relevant part of its pension fund to the buyer. The present value of the defined benefit obligation transferred was $11.4 million and the fair value of plan assets transferred was $10.8 million. Sion also made a cash payment of $400,000 to the buyer in respect of the plan.

Required

(i)   Calculate the net defined benefit liability as at the start and end of 20X8 and 20X9 showing clearly any remeasurement gain or loss on the plan each year.

(ii)   Show amounts to be recognised in the financial statements in each of the years 20X8 and 20X9 in respect of the plan.   (15 marks)

(c)   Bed Investment Co entered into a contract on 1 July 20X7 with Em Bank. The contract consisted of a deposit of a principal amount of $10 million, carrying an interest rate of 2.5% per annum and with a maturity date of 30 June 20X9. Interest will be receivable at maturity together with the principal. In addition, a further 3% interest per annum will be payable by Em Bank if the exchange rate of the dollar against the Ruritanian kroner (RKR) exceeds or is equal to $1.15 to RKR 1.

Bed's functional currency is the dollar.

Required

Explain how Bed should account for the above investment in the financial statements for the year ended 31 December 20X7 (no calculations are required).   (5 marks)

(Total = 30 marks)

5 Control   23 mins

(a)   IFRS 10 *Consolidated Financial Statements* focuses on control as the key concept underlying the parent/subsidiary relationship.

Required

Explain the circumstances in which an investor controls an investee according to IFRS 10.   (3 marks)

(b)   Twist holds 40% of the voting rights of Oliver and 12 other investors each hold 5% of the voting rights of Oliver. A shareholder agreement grants Twist the right to appoint, remove and set the remuneration of management responsible for directing the relevant activities. To change the agreement, a two-thirds majority vote of the shareholders is required. To date, Twist has not exercised its rights with regard to the management or activities of Oliver.

Required

Explain whether Twist should consolidate Oliver in accordance with IFRS 10.   (3 marks)

(c)   Copperfield holds 45% of the voting rights of Spenlow. Murdstone and Steerforth each hold 26% of the voting rights of Spenlow. The remaining voting rights are held by three other shareholders, each holding 1%. There are no other arrangements that affect decision-making.

Required

Explain whether Copperfield should consolidate Spenlow in accordance with IFRS 10.   (3 marks)

(d)   Scrooge holds 70% of the voting rights of Cratchett. Marley has 30% of the voting rights of Cratchett. Marley also has an option to acquire half of Scrooge's voting rights, which is exercisable for the next two years, but at a fixed price that is deeply out of the money (and is expected to remain so for that two-year period).

Required

Explain whether either of Scrooge or Marley should consolidate Cratchett in accordance with IFRS 10.   (3 marks)

(Total = 12 marks)

Questions **7**

6 Associate   39 mins

The statements of financial position of J Co and its investee companies, P Co and S Co, at 31 December 20X5 are shown below.

STATEMENTS OF FINANCIAL POSITION AS AT 31 DECEMBER 20X5

	J Co $'000	P Co $'000	S Co $'000
Assets			
Non-current assets			
Freehold property	1,950	1,250	500
Plant and equipment	795	375	285
Investments	1,500	–	–
	4,245	1,625	785
Current assets			
Inventories	575	300	265
Trade receivables	330	290	370
Cash	50	120	20
	955	710	655
	5,200	2,335	1,440
Equity and liabilities			
Equity			
Share capital ($1 ordinary shares)	2,000	1,000	750
Retained earnings	1,460	885	390
	3,460	1,885	1,140
Non-current liabilities			
12% debentures	500	100	–
Current liabilities			
Bank overdraft	560		
Trade payables	680	350	300
	1,240	350	300
	5,200	2,335	1,440

Additional information

(a)   J Co acquired 600,000 ordinary shares in P Co on 1 January 20X0 for $1,000,000 when the accumulated retained earnings of P Co were $200,000.

(b)   At the date of acquisition of P Co, the fair value of its freehold property was considered to be $400,000 greater than its value in P Co's statement of financial position. P Co had acquired the property ten years earlier and the buildings element (comprising 50% of the total value) is depreciated on cost over 50 years.

(c)   J Co acquired 225,000 ordinary shares in S Co on 1 January 20X4 for $500,000 when the retained profits of S Co were $150,000.

(d)   P Co sells goods to J Co at cost plus 25%. J Co held $100,000 of these goods in inventories at 31 December 20X5.

(e)   It is the policy of J Co to review goodwill for impairment annually. The goodwill in P Co was written off in full some years ago. An impairment test conducted at the year end revealed impairment losses on the investment in S Co of $92,000.

(f)   It is the group's policy to value the non-controlling interest at acquisition at fair value. The market price of the shares of the non-controlling shareholders just before the acquisition was $1.65.

Required

Prepare, in a format suitable for inclusion in the annual report of the J Group, the consolidated statement of financial position at 31 December 20X5.   **(20 marks)**

7 Part disposal

> **BPP note.** In this question, proforma are given to you to help you get used to setting out your answer. You may wish to transfer them to a separate sheet or to use a separate sheet for your workings.

Angel Co bought 70% of the share capital of Shane Co for $120,000 on 1 January 20X6. At that date Shane Co's retained earnings stood at $10,000.

The statements of financial position at 31 December 20X8, summarised statements of profit or loss and other comprehensive income to that date and movement on retained earnings are given below.

	Angel Co $'000	Shane Co $'000
STATEMENTS OF FINANCIAL POSITION		
Non-current assets		
Property, plant and equipment	200	80
Investment in Shane Co	120	–
	320	80
Current assets	890	140
	1,210	220
Equity		
Share capital – $1 ordinary shares	500	100
Retained reserves	400	90
	900	190
Current liabilities	310	30
	1,210	220

SUMMARISED STATEMENTS OF PROFIT OR LOSS AND OTHER COMPREHENSIVE INCOME

	$'000	$'000
Profit before interest and tax	100	20
Income tax expense	(40)	(8)
Profit for the year	60	12
Other comprehensive income (not reclassified to P/L), net of tax	10	6
Total comprehensive income for the year	70	18

MOVEMENT IN RETAINED RESERVES

	$'000	$'000
Balance at 31 December 20X7	330	72
Total comprehensive income for the year	70	18
Balance at 31 December 20X8	400	90

Angel Co sells one half of its holding in Shane Co for $120,000 on 30 June 20X8. At that date, the fair value of the 35% holding in Shane was slightly more at $130,000 due to a share price rise. The remaining holding is to be dealt with as an associate. This does not represent a discontinued operation.

No entries have been made in the accounts for the above transaction.

Assume that profits accrue evenly throughout the year.

It is the group's policy to value the non-controlling interest at acquisition fair value. The fair value of the non-controlling interest on 1 January 20X6 was $51.4 million.

Required

(a) Prepare the consolidated statement of financial position, statement of profit or loss and other comprehensive income and a reconciliation of movement in retained reserves for the year ended 31 December 20X8.

(20 marks)

Ignore income taxes on the disposal. No impairment losses have been necessary to date.

PART DISPOSAL PROFORMA

ANGEL GROUP
CONSOLIDATED STATEMENT OF FINANCIAL POSITION
AS AT 31 DECEMBER 20X8 $'000

Non-current assets
Property, plant and equipment
Investment in Shane
                                                          _____

Current assets
                                                          _____
                                                          _____

Equity attributable to owners of the parent
Share capital
Retained earnings
                                                          _____

Current liabilities
                                                          _____
                                                          _____

CONSOLIDATED STATEMENT OF PROFIT OR LOSS AND OTHER COMPREHENSIVE INCOME
FOR THE YEAR ENDED 31 DECEMBER 20X8

                                                          $'000
Profit before interest and tax
Profit on disposal of shares in subsidiary
Share of profit of associate
                                                          _____
Profit before tax
Income tax expense
                                                          _____
Profit for the year
                                                          _____

Other comprehensive income (not reclassified to P/L) net of tax:
Share of other comprehensive income of associate
Other comprehensive income for the year
Total comprehensive income for the year

Profit attributable to:
  Owners of the parent
  Non-controlling interests
                                                          _____
                                                          _____

Total comprehensive income attributable to:
  Owners of the parent
  Non-controlling interests
                                                          _____
                                                          _____

CONSOLIDATED RECONCILIATION OF MOVEMENT IN RETAINED RESERVES

                                                          $'000
Balance at 31 December 20X7
Total comprehensive income for the year
Balance at 31 December 20X8
                                                          _____
                                                          _____

(b) Explain the accounting treatment that would be required if Angel had disposed of 10% of its holding in Shane.

(5 marks)

(Total = 25 marks)

8 Step acquisition   29 mins

SD acquired 60% of the 1 million $1 ordinary shares of KL on 1 July 20X0 for $3,250,000 when KL's retained earnings were $2,760,000. The group policy is to measure non-controlling interests at fair value at the date of acquisition. The fair value of non-controlling interests at 1 July 20X0 was $1,960,000. There has been no impairment of goodwill since the date of acquisition.

SD acquired a further 20% of KL's share capital on 1 March 20X1 for $1,000,000.

The retained earnings reported in the financial statements of SD and KL as at 30 June 20X1 are $9,400,000 and $3,400,000 respectively.

KL sold goods for resale to SD with a sales value of $750,000 during the period from 1 March 20X1 to 30 June 20X1. 40% of these goods remain in SD's inventories at the year-end. KL applies a mark-up of 25% on all goods sold.

Profits of both entities can be assumed to accrue evenly throughout the year.

Required

(a)   Explain the impact of the additional 20% purchase of KL's ordinary share capital by SD on the consolidated financial statements of the SD Group for the year ended 30 June 20X1.

(5 marks)

(b)   Calculate the amounts that will appear in the consolidated statement of financial position of the SD Group as at 30 June 20X1 for:

(i)   Goodwill;
(ii)   Consolidated retained earnings; and
(iii)   Non-controlling interests.

(10 marks)

(Total = 15 marks)

9 Foreign operation   49 mins

> **BPP note.** In this question, proformas for the translation workings are given to assist you with the approach. You will need to also need to draw up proformas for the consolidated financial statements and the remaining group workings.

Standard acquired 80% of Odense SA for $520,000 on 1 January 20X5 when the retained reserves of Odense were 2,500,000 Danish krone.

The financial statements of Standard and Odense for the year ended 31 December 20X6 are as follows:

STATEMENTS OF FINANCIAL POSITION AT 31 DECEMBER 20X6

	Standard $'000	Odense Kr'000
Property, plant and equipment	1,285	4,400
Investment in Odense	520	–
	1,805	4,400
Current assets	410	2,000
	2,215	6,400
Share capital	500	1,000
Retained earnings	1,115	4,300
	1,615	5,300
Loans	200	300
Current liabilities	400	800
	600	1,100
	2,215	6,400

BPP LEARNING MEDIA

STATEMENT OF PROFIT OR LOSS AND OTHER COMPREHENSIVE INCOME

FOR YEAR ENDED 31 DECEMBER 20X6

	Standard $'000	Odense Kr'000
Revenue	1,125	5,200
Cost of sales	(410)	(2,300)
Gross profit	715	2,900
Other expenses	(180)	(910)
Dividend from Odense	40	–
Profit before tax	575	1,990
Income tax expense	(180)	(640)
Profit/Total comprehensive income for the year	395	1,350

STATEMENTS OF CHANGES IN EQUITY FOR THE YEAR 31 DECEMBER 20X6 (EXTRACT FOR RETAINED EARNINGS)

	Standard $'000	Odense Kr'000
Balance at 1 January 20X6	915	3,355
Dividends paid on 31 December 20X6	(195)	(405)
Total comprehensive income for the year	395	1,350
Balance at 31 December 20X6	1,115	4,300

In the year ended 31 December 20X5, Odense's total comprehensive income was 1,200,000 Danish krone. On 31 December 20X5, Odense paid dividends of 345,000 Danish krone.

An impairment test conducted at 31 December 20X6 revealed impairment losses of 148,000 Danish krone relating to Odense's goodwill. No impairment losses had previously been recognised. It is group policy to translate impairment losses at the closing rate.

At the date of acquisition, Standard chose to measure the non-controlling interest in Odense at the proportionate share of the fair value of net assets.

Exchange rates were as follows:

	Kr to $1
1 January 20X5	9.4
31 December 20X5	8.8
Average 20X5	9.1
31 December 20X6	8.1
Average 20X6	8.4

Required

Prepare the consolidated statement of financial position and consolidated statement of profit or loss and other comprehensive income of the Standard Group for the year ended 31 December 20X6 (round your answer to the nearest $'000). **(25 marks)**

TRANSLATION OF ODENSE – STATEMENT OF FINANCIAL POSITION

	Kr'000	Rate	$'000
Property, plant and equipment		X6 CR	
Current assets		X6 CR	
Share capital		HR	
Pre-acquisition retained earnings		HR	
Post-acquisition retained earnings:			
20X5 profit		X5 AR	
20X5 dividend		X5 Actual	
20X6 profit		X6 AR	
20X6 dividend		X6 Actual	
Exchange difference on net assets		Bal. fig.	
Loans		X6 CR	
Current liabilities		X6 CR	

TRANSLATION OF ODENSE – STATEMENT OF PROFIT OR LOSS AND OTHER COMPREHENSIVE INCOME

	Odense Kr'000	Rate (AR)	Odense $'000
Revenue			
Cost of sales			
Gross profit			
Other expenses			
Profit before tax			
Income tax expense			
Profit/Total comprehensive income for the year			

10 Consolidated statement of cash flows   39 mins

> **BPP note.** In this question, proformas are given to you to help you get used to setting out your answer. You may wish to transfer them to a separate sheet, or alternatively to use a separate sheet for your workings.

On 1 September 20X5 Swing Co acquired 70% of Slide Co for $5,000,000 comprising $1,000,000 cash and 1,500,000 $1 shares.

The statement of financial position of Slide Co at acquisition was as follows:

	$'000
Property, plant and equipment	2,700
Inventories	1,600
Trade receivables	600
Cash	400
Trade payables	(300)
Income tax payable	(200)
	4,800

The consolidated statement of financial position of Swing Co as at 31 December 20X5 was as follows:

	20X5 $'000	20X4 $'000
Non-current assets		
Property, plant and equipment	35,500	25,000
Goodwill	1,400	–
	36,900	25,000
Current assets		
Inventories	16,000	10,000
Trade receivables	9,800	7,500
Cash	2,400	1,500
	28,200	19,000
	65,100	44,000
Equity attributable to owners of the parent		
Share capital	12,300	10,000
Share premium	5,800	2,000
Revaluation surplus	350	–
Retained earnings	32,100	21,900
	50,550	33,900
Non-controlling interest	1,750	–
	52,300	33,900
Current liabilities		
Trade payables	7,600	6,100
Income tax payable	5,200	4,000
	12,800	10,100
	65,100	44,000

The consolidated statement of profit or loss and other comprehensive income of Swing Co for the year ended 31 December 20X5 was as follows:

	20X5 $'000
Profit before tax	16,500
Income tax expense	(5,200)
Profit for the year	11,300
Other comprehensive income (not reclassified to P/L)	
Revaluation surplus	500
Total comprehensive income for the year	11,800
Profit attributable to:	
Owners of the parent	11,100
Non-controlling interest	200
	11,300
Total comprehensive income for the year attributable to:	
Owners of the parent	11,450
Non-controlling interest 200 + (500 × 30%)	350
	11,800

Notes

1   Depreciation charged for the year was $5,800,000. The group made no disposals of property, plant and equipment.

2   Dividends paid by Swing Co amounted to $900,000.

It is the group's policy to value the non-controlling interest at its proportionate share of the fair value of the subsidiary's identifiable net assets.

Required

Prepare the consolidated statement of cash flows of Swing Co for the year ended 31 December 20X5. No notes are required. **(20 marks)**

CONSOLIDATED STATEMENT OF CASH FLOWS PROFORMA

STATEMENT OF CASH FLOWS FOR THE YEAR ENDED 31 DECEMBER 20X5

	$'000	$'000
Cash flows from operating activities		
Profit before tax		
Adjustments for:		
Depreciation		
Impairment losses	_____	
Increase in trade receivables (W4)		
Increase in inventories (W4)		
Increase in trade payables (W4)	_____	
Cash generated from operations		
Income taxes paid (W3)	_____	
Net cash from operating activities		
Cash flows from investing activities		
Acquisition of subsidiary, net of cash acquired (W5)		
Purchase of property, plant & equipment (W1)	_____	
Net cash used in investing activities		
Cash flows from financing activities		
Proceeds from issue of share capital		
Dividends paid		
Dividends paid to non-controlling interest (W2)	_____	
Net cash used in financing activities		_____
Net increase in cash and cash equivalents		
Cash and cash equivalents at the beginning of the period		
Cash and cash equivalents at the end of the period		

Workings

1   *Assets*

	Property, plant and equipment $'000	Goodwill $'000
b/d		–
OCI (revaluation)		
Depreciation/Impairment		β
Acquisition of sub/associate		
Cash paid/(rec'd) β	_____	–
c/d	=====	=====

2   *Equity*

	Share capital $'000	Share premium $'000	Retained earnings $'000	Non-controlling interest $'000
b/d				–
P/L				
Acquisition of subsidiary				
Cash (paid)/rec'd β	___	___	___*	___
c/d	=====	=====	=====	=====

*Dividend paid is given in question but working shown for clarity.

3   *Liabilities*

	Tax payable $'000
b/d	
P/L	
Acquisition of subsidiary	
Cash (paid)/rec'd	___ β
c/d	═══

4   *Working capital changes*

	Inventories $'000	Receivables $'000	Payables $'000
Balance b/d			
Acquisition of subsidiary			
Increase/(decrease) (balancing figure)	___	___	___
Balance c/d	___	___	___

5   *Purchase of subsidiary*

	$'000
Cash received on acquisition of subsidiary	
Less cash consideration	
Cash outflow	___ ═══

Note. Only the **cash** consideration is included in the figure reported in the statement of cash flows. The **shares** issued as part of the consideration are reflected in the share capital working (W2) above.

Goodwill on acquisition (to show no impairment):

	$'000
Consideration	
Non-controlling interest	
Net assets acquired	
Goodwill	___ ═══

Section 2 – Exam-standard questions

11 Robby   59 mins

Adapted from P2 June 2012

You work in the finance department of Robby, an entity which has two subsidiaries, Hail and Zinc. Robby has recently appointed two new directors, with limited finance experience, to its board. You have received an email from the finance director, which is shown in **Exhibit 1**.

The following exhibits provide information relevant to the question.

Exhibit 1 – Email from finance director

To: An accountant
From: Finance director
Subject: New directors – help required

Hi, our two new directors are keen to understand the group financial statements. In particular, they want to understand the effect of acquisitions and joint operations on the consolidated accounts.

I am putting together a briefing document for them and would like you to prepare sections for inclusion in the document on goodwill and on joint operations. Please use the acquisitions of Hail and Zinc (**Exhibit 2**) to explain the how the goodwill on acquisition of subsidiaries is accounted for in the group financial statements at 31 May 20X3. Use the gas station joint operation (**Exhibit 3**) to explain what a joint operation is and how we account for it in the group financial statements. Make sure you explain the financial reporting principles that underlie both of these.

Exhibit 2 – Details of acquisitions of Hail and Zinc

Accounting policy: measure non-controlling interests at acquisition at fair value.

(1) **Hail acquisition.** On 1 June 20X2, acquisition of 80% of the equity interests of Hail. The purchase consideration comprised cash of $50 million payable on 1 June 20X2 and *[discount →]* $24.2 million payable on 31 May 20X4. A further amount is payable on 31 August 20X6 if *[contingent consideration ↓ use FV.]* the cumulative profits of Hail for the four-year period from 1 June 20X2 to 31 May 20X6 exceed $150 million. On 1 June 20X2, the fair value of the contingent consideration was measured at $40 million. On 31 May 20X3, this fair value was remeasured at $42 million.

On the acquisition date, the fair value of the identifiable net assets of Hail was $130 million.

The notes to the financial statements of Hail at acquisition disclosed a contingent liability. On 1 June 20X2, the fair value of this contingent liability was reliably measured at $2 million. The non-controlling interest at fair value was $30 million on 1 June 20X2. An appropriate discount rate to use is 10% per annum. *[FV adj. – it is a liability which decrease the assets.]*

(2) **Zinc acquisition.** On 1 June 20X0, acquisition of 5% of the ordinary shares of Zinc. Robby had treated this investment at fair value through profit or loss.

On 1 December 20X2, acquisition of a further 55% of the ordinary shares of Zinc, obtaining control.

Consideration:

	Shareholding %	Consideration $m
1 June 20X0	5	2
1 December 20X2	55	16
	60	18

At 1 December 20X2, the fair value of the equity interest in Zinc before the business combination was $5 million.

The non-controlling interest at fair value was $9 million on 1 December 20X2.

The fair value of the identifiable net assets at 1 December 20X2 of Zinc was $26 million, and the retained earnings were $15 million. The excess of the fair value of the net assets was due to an increase in the value of property, plant and equipment (PPE), which was provisional pending receipt of the final valuations. These valuations were received on 1 March 20X3 and resulted in an additional increase of $3 million in the fair value of PPE at the date of acquisition. This increase does not affect the fair value of the non-controlling interest at acquisition.

At 31 May 20X2 the carrying amount of the investment in Zinc in Robby's separate financial statements was $3 million.

Exhibit 3 – Details of joint operation

joint operation.

Robby holds a 40% share of a natural gas station. No separate entity was set up under the joint operation. Assets, liabilities, revenue and costs are apportioned on the basis of shareholding.

1   The natural gas station cost $15 million to construct, was completed on 1 June 20X2 and is
asset   to be dismantled at the end of its life of ten years. The present value of this dismantling cost to the joint operation at 1 June 20X2, using a discount rate of 5%, was $2 million. *↑PPE ↑provision.*

2   In the year, gas with a direct cost of $16 million was sold for $20 million. Additionally, the joint operation incurred operating costs of $0.5 million during the year.

The revenue and costs are receivable and payable by the other joint operator who settles amounts outstanding with Robby after the year end.

Exhibit 4 – Factoring agreement

Robby held a portfolio of trade receivables with a carrying amount of $4 million at 31 May 20X3. At that date, the entity entered into a factoring agreement with a bank, whereby it transferred the receivables in exchange for $3.6 million in cash. Robby has agreed to reimburse the bank for any shortfall between the amount collected and $3.6 million. Once the receivables have been collected, any amounts above $3.6 million, less interest on this amount, will be repaid to Robby. The directors of Robby believe that these trade receivables should be derecognised.

Required

(a)   Prepare for inclusion in the briefing note to the new directors:

(i)   An explanation, with suitable calculations, of how the goodwill on acquisition of Hail and Zinc should be accounted for in the consolidated financial statements at 31 May 20X3.   (16 marks)

(ii)   An explanation as to the nature of a joint operation and, showing suitable calculations, of how the joint operation should be accounted for in Robby's separate and consolidated statements of financial position at 31 May 20X3. (Ignore retained earnings in your answer.)   (7 marks)

Note. Marks will be allocated in (a) for a suitable discussion of the principles involved as well as the accounting treatment.

(b)   Explain the appropriate accounting treatment of the factoring agreement in the financial statements for the year ended 31 May 20X3, and evaluate this treatment in the context of the *Conceptual Framework for Financial Reporting*.   (7 marks)

(Total = 30 marks)

12 Banana Co   59 mins

SBR September 2018 (amended)

Banana Co is the parent of a listed group of companies which have a year end of 30 June 20X7. Banana Co has made a number of acquisitions and disposals of investments during the current financial year and the directors require advice as to the correct accounting treatment of these acquisitions and disposals.

The following exhibits provide information relevant to the question.

Exhibit 1 – The acquisition of Grape Co

On 1 January 20X7, Banana Co acquired an 80% equity interest in Grape Co. The following is a summary of Grape Co's equity at the acquisition date.

	$m
Equity share capital ($1 each)	20
Retained earnings	42
Other components of equity	8
Total	70

The purchase consideration comprised 10 million of Banana Co's shares which had a nominal value of $1 each and a market price of $6.80 each. Additionally, cash of $18 million was due to be paid on 1 January 20X9 if the net profit after tax of Grape Co grew by 5% in each of the two years following acquisition. The present value of the total contingent consideration at 1 January 20X7 was $16 million. It was felt that there was a 25% chance of the profit target being met. At acquisition, the only adjustment required to the identifiable net assets of Grape Co was for land which had a fair value $5 million higher than its carrying amount. This is not included within the $70 million equity of Grape Co at 1 January 20X7.

Goodwill for the consolidated financial statements has been incorrectly calculated as follows:

	$m
Share consideration	68
Add NCI at acquisition (20% × $70 million)	14
Less net assets at acquisition	(70)
Goodwill at acquisition	12

The financial director did not take into account the contingent cash since it was not probable that it would be paid. Additionally, he measured the non-controlling interest using the proportionate method of net assets despite the group having a published policy to measure non-controlling interest at fair value. The share price of Grape Co at acquisition was $4.25 and should be used to value the non-controlling interest.

Exhibit 2 – Acquisition/disposal of Strawberry Co

Banana Co had purchased a 40% equity interest in Strawberry Co for $18 million a number of years ago when the fair value of the identifiable net assets was $44 million. Since acquisition, Banana Co had the right to appoint one of the five directors on the board of Strawberry Co. The investment has always been equity accounted for in the consolidated financial statements of Banana Co. Banana Co disposed of 75% of its 40% investment on 1 October 20X6 for $19 million when the fair values of the identifiable net assets of Strawberry Co were $50 million. At that date, Banana Co lost its right to appoint one director to the board. The fair value of the remaining 10% equity interest was $4.5 million at disposal but only $4 million at 30 June 20X7. Banana Co has recorded a loss in reserves of $14 million calculated as the difference between the price paid of $18 million and the fair value of $4 million at the reporting date. Banana Co has stated that they have no intention to sell their remaining shares in Strawberry Co and wish to classify the remaining 10% interest as fair value through other comprehensive income in accordance with IFRS 9 *Financial Instruments*.

Exhibit 3 – The acquisition of Melon Co

On 30 June 20X7, Banana Co acquired all of the shares of Melon Co, an entity which operates in the biotechnology industry. Melon Co was only recently formed and its only asset consists of a licence to carry out research activities. Melon Co has no employees as research activities were outsourced to other companies. The activities are still at a very early stage and it is not clear that any definitive product would result from the activities. A management company provides personnel for Melon Co to supply supervisory activities and administrative functions.

Banana Co believes that Melon Co does not constitute a business in accordance with IFRS 3 *Business Combinations* since it does not have employees nor carries out any of its own processes. Banana Co intends to employ its own staff to operate Melon Co rather than to continue to use the services of the management company. The directors of Banana Co have concluded that Melon Co does not meet the definition of a business specified in IFRS 3 and should therefore be treated as an asset acquisition.

Exhibit 4 – The acquisition of bonds

financial asset.

On 1 July 20X5, Banana Co acquired $10 million 5% bonds at par with interest being due at 30 June each year. The bonds are repayable at a substantial premium so that the effective rate of interest was 7%. Banana Co intended to hold the bonds to collect the contractual cash flows arising from the bonds and measured them at amortised cost. *loan*

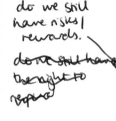

do we still have risks/ rewards.

do we still have the right to repay

On 1 July 20X6, Banana Co sold the bonds to a third party for $8 million. The fair value of the bonds was $10.5 million at that date. Banana Co has the right to repurchase the bonds on 1 July 20X8 for $8.8 million and it is likely that this option will be exercised. The third party is obliged to return the coupon interest to Banana Co and to pay additional cash to Banana Co should bond values rise. Banana Co will also compensate the third party for any devaluation of the bonds.

Required

(a) Draft an explanatory note to the directors of Banana Co, discussing the following:

   (i) How goodwill should have been calculated on the acquisition of Grape Co and show the accounting entry which is required to amend the financial director's error

   (8 marks)

   (ii) Why equity accounting was the appropriate treatment for Strawberry Co in the consolidated financial statements up to the date of its disposal showing the carrying amount of the investment in Strawberry Co just prior to disposal **(4 marks)**

   (iii) How the gain or loss on disposal of Strawberry Co should have been recorded in the consolidated financial statements and how the investment in Strawberry Co should be accounted for after the part disposal **(4 marks)**

   Note. Any workings can either be shown in the main body of the explanatory note or in an appendix to the explanatory note.

(b) Discuss whether the directors are correct to treat Melon Co as an asset acquisition.

   (7 marks)

(c) Discuss how the derecognition requirements of IFRS 9 *Financial Instruments* should be applied to the sale of the bond including calculations to show the impact on the consolidated financial statements for the year ended 30 June 20X7. **(7 marks)**

   (Total = 30 marks)

13 Hill

SBR Specimen exam 2

Hill Co is a public limited company which has investments in two other entities, Chandler Co and Doyle Co. All three entities prepare their financial statements in accordance with International Financial Reporting Standards.

Exhibit 1 - Financial statement extracts

Extracts from the draft individual statements of profit or loss for Hill Co, Chandler Co and Doyle Co for the year ended 30 September 20X6 are presented below.

	Hill Co $m	Chandler Co $m	Doyle Co $m
Profit/(loss) before taxation	(45)	67	154
Taxation	9	(15)	(31)
Profit/(loss) for the period	(36)	52	123

Exhibit 2 - Acquisition of 80% of Chandler Co   *NCI 20%.*

Hill Co purchased 80% of the ordinary shares of Chandler Co on 1 October 20X5. Cash consideration of $150 million has been included when calculating goodwill in the consolidated financial statements. The purchase agreement specified that a further cash payment of $32 million *must be discounted* becomes payable on 1 October 20X7 but no entries have been posted in the consolidated financial statements in respect of this. A discount rate of 5% should be used.

revaluation of PPE. In the goodwill calculation, the fair value of Chandler Co's identifiable net assets was deemed to be $170 million. Of this, $30 million related to Chandler's non-depreciable land. However, on 31 December 20X5, a survey was received which revealed that the fair value of this land was actually only $20 million as at the acquisition date. No adjustments have been made to the goodwill calculation in respect of the results of the survey. The non-controlling interest at acquisition was measured using the proportionate method as $34 million ($170m × 20%).

gross up goodwill - impairment. As at 30 September 20X6, the recoverable amount of Chandler Co was calculated as $250 million. No impairment has been calculated or accounted for in the consolidated financial statements.

Exhibit 3 - Disposal of 20% holding in Doyle Co

On 1 October 20X4, Hill Co purchased 60% of the ordinary shares of Doyle Co. At this date, the fair value of Doyle Co's identifiable net assets was $510 million. The non-controlling interest at acquisition was measured at its fair value of $215 million. Goodwill arising on the acquisition of Doyle Co was $50 million and had not been impaired prior to the disposal date. On 1 April 20X6, Hill disposed of a 20% holding in the shares of Doyle Co for cash consideration of $140 million. At this date, the net assets of Doyle Co, excluding goodwill, were carried in the consolidated financial statements at $590 million.

Significant influence = associate. From 1 April 20X6, Hill Co has the ability to appoint two of the six members of Doyle Co's board of directors. The fair value of Hill Co's 40% shareholding was $300 million at that date.

Exhibit 4 - Convertible bond issue

On 1 October 20X5, Hill Co issued a convertible bond at par value of $20 million and has recorded it as a non-current liability. The bond is redeemable for cash on 30 September 20X7 at par. Bondholders can instead opt for conversion in the form of a fixed number of shares. Interest on the bond is payable at a rate of 4% a year in arrears. The interest paid in the year has been presented in finance costs. The interest rate on similar debt without a conversion option is 10%.

Discount factors:

Year	Discount rate 5%	Discount rate 10%
1	0.952	0.909
2	0.907	0.826

FV consideration   140
FV investment retained   300
net assets   (590)
Goodwill   (50)
loss   (200)

equity account.

Exhibit 5 - Deferred tax asset

Hill Co has made a loss in the year ended 30 September 20X6, as well as in the previous two financial years. In the consolidated statement of financial position it has recognised a material deferred tax asset in respect of the carry-forward of unused tax losses. These losses cannot be surrendered to other group companies. On 30 September 20X6, Hill Co breached a covenant attached to a bank loan which is due for repayment in 20X9. The loan is presented in non-current liabilities on the statement of financial position. The loan agreement terms state that a breach in loan covenants entitles the bank to demand immediate repayment of the loan. Hill Co and its subsidiaries do not have sufficient liquid assets to repay the loan in full. However, on 1 November 20X6 the bank confirmed that repayment of the loan would not be required until the original due date. Hill Co has produced a business plan which forecasts significant improvement in its financial situation over the next three years as a result of the launch of new products which are currently being developed.

Required

Draft an explanatory note to the directors of Hill Co addressing the following:

(a) how goodwill should have been calculated in respect of the investment in Chandler Co. Your answer should include suitable calculations and show the adjustments which need to be made to the consolidated financial statements for this as well as any implications of the
IMPAIRMENT recoverable amount calculated at 30 September 20X6. **(13 marks)**

(b) a calculation of the profit or loss arising from the disposal of the investment in Doyle Co for inclusion in the consolidated financial statements for the year ended 30 September 20X6. **(4 marks)**

(c) how the convertible bond should be accounted for, with suitable calculations, in the consolidated financial statements for the year ended 30 September 20X6. **(5 marks)**

(d) discuss the proposed treatment of Hill's deferred tax asset and the financial reporting issues raised by its loan covenant breach. **(8 marks)**

(Total = 30 marks)

14 Luploid   59 mins

SBR September/December 2019

Luploid Co is the parent company of a group undergoing rapid expansion through acquisition. Luploid Co has acquired two subsidiaries in recent years, Colyson Co and Hammond Co. The current financial year end is 30 June 20X8.

Exhibit 1 - Acquisition of Colyson Co

Luploid Co acquired 80% of the five million equity shares ($1 each) of Colyson Co on 1 July 20X4 for cash of $90 million. The fair value of the non-controlling interest (NCI) at acquisition was $22 million. The fair value of the identifiable net assets at acquisition was $65 million, excluding the following asset. Colyson Co purchased a factory site several years prior to the date of acquisition. Land and property prices in the area had increased significantly in the years immediately prior to 1 July 20X4. Nearby sites had been acquired and converted into residential use. It is felt that, should the Colyson Co site also be converted into residential use, the factory site would have a market value of $24 million. $1 million of costs are estimated to be required to demolish the factory and to obtain planning permission for the conversion. Colyson Co was not intending to convert the site at the acquisition date and had not sought planning permission at that date. The depreciated replacement cost of the factory at 1 July 20X4 has been correctly calculated as $17.4 million.

Exhibit 2 - Impairment of Colyson Co

Colyson Co incurred losses during the year ended 30 June 20X8 and an impairment review was performed. The recoverable amount of Colyson Co's assets was estimated to be $100 million. Included in this assessment was the only building owned by Colyson Co which had been damaged in a storm and impaired to the extent of $4 million. The carrying amount of the net assets of Colyson Co at 30 June 20X8 (including fair value adjustments on acquisition but excluding goodwill) are as follows:

	$m
Land and buildings	60
Other plant and machinery	15
Intangibles other than goodwill	9
Current assets (recoverable amount)	22
Total	106

None of the assets of Colyson Co including goodwill have been impaired previously. Colyson Co does not have a policy of revaluing its assets.

Exhibit 3 - Acquisition of Hammond Co

Luploid Co acquired 60% of the 10 million equity shares of Hammond Co on 1 July 20X7. Two Luploid Co shares are to be issued for every five shares acquired in Hammond Co. These shares will be issued on 1 July 20X8. The fair value of a Luploid Co share was $30 at 1 July 20X7. Hammond Co had previously granted a share-based payment to its employees with a three-year vesting period. At 1 July 20X7, the employees had completed their service period but had not yet exercised their options. The fair value of the options granted at 1 July 20X7 was $15 million. As part of the acquisition, Luploid Co is obliged to replace the share-based payment scheme of Hammond Co with a scheme of its own which has the following details:

Luploid Co issued 100 options to each of Hammond Co's 10,000 employees on 1 July 20X7. The shares are conditional on the employees completing a further two years of service. Additionally, the scheme required that the market price of Luploid Co's shares had to increase by 10% from its value of $30 per share at the acquisition date over the vesting period. It was anticipated at 1 July 20X7 that 10% of staff would leave over the vesting period but this was revised to 4% by 30 June 20X8. The fair value of each option at the grant date was $20. The share price of Luploid Co at 30 June 20X8 was $32 and is anticipated to grow at a similar rate in the year ended 30 June 20X9.

Required

Draft an explanatory note to the directors of Luploid Co, addressing the following:

(a) (i) How the fair value of the factory site should be determined at 1 July 20X4 and why the depreciated replacement cost of $17.4 million is unlikely to be a reasonable estimate of fair value. **(7 marks)**

(ii) A calculation of goodwill arising on the acquisition of Colyson Co measuring the non-controlling interest at:

- fair value;
- proportionate share of the net assets. **(3 marks)**

(b) Discuss the calculation and allocation of Colyson Co's impairment loss at 30 June 20X8 and why the impairment loss of Colyson Co would differ depending on how non-controlling interests are measured. Your answer should include a calculation and an explanation of how the impairments would impact upon the consolidated financial statements of Luploid Co. **(11 marks)**

(c) (i) How the consideration for the acquisition of Hammond Co should be measured on 1 July 20X7. Your answer should include a calculation of the consideration and a discussion of why only some of the cost of the replacement share-based payment scheme should be included within the consideration. **(4 marks)**

(ii) How much of an expense for the share-based payment scheme should be recognised in the consolidated profit or loss of Luploid Co for the year ended 30 June 20X8. Your answer should include a brief discussion of how the vesting conditions impact upon the calculations. **(5 marks)**

Note: Any workings can either be shown in the main body of the explanatory note or in an appendix to the explanatory note.

(Total = 30 marks)

BPP LEARNING MEDIA

15 Sugar Co   59 mins

SBR September/December 2020

At 30 June 20X7, Sugar Co has investments in several associate companies, including Flour Co. On 1 July 20X7 Sugar Co acquired additional shares in Flour Co and obtained control. On 1 October 20X7 Sugar Co also acquired an associate, Butter Co. The group is preparing the consolidated statement of cash flows for the year ended 30 June 20X8.

The following exhibits provide information relevant to the question.

Exhibit 1 - Acquisition of Flour Co

A 40% shareholding in Flour Co was purchased several years ago at a cost of $10 million. This investment gave Sugar Co significant influence in Flour Co. The consideration to acquire an additional three million shares (30% shareholding) in Flour Co on 1 July 20X7 was in two parts:

(i)   cash; and
(ii)   a one for two share exchange when the market price of Sugar Co shares was $6 each.

In Flour Co's individual financial statements, the net assets had increased by $12 million between the two acquisition dates. The carrying amount of Flour Co's net assets on 1 July 20X7 was as follows:

	$'000
Intangible assets (licences and patents)	6,781
Property, plant and equipment	18,076
Cash and cash equivalents	1,234
Other net current assets	9,650
Total net assets carrying amount	35,741

The carrying amounts of the net assets at 1 July 20X7 were equal to the fair values except for land which had a fair value $600,000 above the carrying amount. The Sugar group values non-controlling interests (NCI) at fair value and the share price of Flour Co at 1 July 20X7 was $3.80. This share price should be used to value NCI at that date and to value the initial 40% equity interest in Flour Co.

Goodwill at 1 July 20X7 was correctly calculated as $2,259,000 and has been correctly accounted for in the consolidated statement of financial position.

Exhibit 2 - Asset acquisitions and disposals

Including its purchase of the additional investment in Flour Co which it correctly consolidated from 1 July 20X7, the Sugar group also purchased various assets during the year.

There were no disposals or impairments of intangible assets during the year but amortisation of $3.5 million had been deducted from profit from operations.

The only additions to property, plant and equipment during the year were as a result of the acquisition of Flour Co. The group disposed of some plant and machinery at a loss on disposal of $2 million. Depreciation deducted from the profit from operations was $10 million.

Sugar Co purchased a 25% equity interest in Butter Co on 1 October 20X7 for $5 million cash which gave significant influence. Butter Co paid a dividend in the post-acquisition period and Sugar Co also received dividends from other associates during the year ended 30 June 20X8. Sugar Co did not pay any dividends during the year.

There were no acquisitions of financial assets measured at fair value through profit or loss (FVTPL) during the year but there were disposals which had a carrying amount of $4 million. These were sold at a profit of $500,000 which was included, alongside fair value gains, in investment income in the consolidated statement of profit or loss. The investment income figure also includes dividends received from these investments and any fair value gains or losses recognised on the initial investment in Flour Co.

In addition to the shares issued to purchase Flour Co, Sugar Co issued some ordinary $1 shares for cash during the year ended 30 June 20X8.

Exhibit 3 - Group financial statement extracts

The group's consolidated financial statements have been calculated correctly. Extracts, together with relevant comparative figures at 30 June are provided below:

Consolidated statement of financial position as at 30 June (extracts):

	20X8	20X7
	$'000	$'000
Non-current assets		
Intangible assets	33,456	15,865
Property, plant and equipment	55,124	52,818
Investment in associates	26,328	23,194
Financial assets	3,000	6,000
Equity		
Ordinary share capital ($1 shares)	23,000	20,000
Other components of equity (all share premium)	33,600	18,000
Non-controlling interest	30,152	12,914

Consolidated statement of profit or loss for the year ended 30 June 20X8 (extract):

	$'000
Investment income	3,891
Share of profit from associate companies	15,187
Profit attributable to the non-controlling interest	9,162

Exhibit 4 - Pension scheme

Sugar Co is the only entity of the group which operates a defined benefit pension scheme. The pension scheme obligation increased during the year from $1.175m to $6.368m. The movement on the pension liability represents the service cost component, the net interest component and also the remeasurement component for the year. Sugar Co usually makes cash contributions into the scheme on an annual basis towards the year end. The significant increase in the pension scheme obligation for the year ended 30 June 20X8 was because the contributions to the scheme did not follow normal practice and were instead made in July 20X8. Benefits paid during the year were $2 million in cash.

Required

(a)   Draft an explanatory note to the directors of Sugar Co, addressing how the initial 40% investment in Flour Co and the additional purchase of the equity shares on 1 July 20X7 should be accounted for in the consolidated financial statements (including the statement of cash flows). Using the goodwill figure of $2,259,000, calculate the cash paid to acquire control of Flour Co and include a brief explanation as to how that cash should be accounted for in the consolidated statement of cash flows.   **(10 marks)**

(b)   Prepare extracts of the cash flows generated from

    (i)   investing activities; and

    (ii)   financing activities in the consolidated statement of cash flows for the Sugar group for the year ended 30 June 20X8.

    No explanations are required in part (b).   **(16 marks)**

(c)   Describe the impact, if any, that the defined benefit pension scheme will have on the consolidated statement of cash flows for the Sugar group for the year ended 30 June 20X8 assuming that cash flows from operating activities are calculated by the indirect method.

                    (4 marks)

                    (Total = 30 marks)

BPP
LEARNING
MEDIA

16 Angel   59 mins

Adapted from P2 December 2013

The following draft consolidated financial statements relate to Angel, a public limited company. Angel is a furniture manufacturer which sells its mass-produced goods wholesale to a number of large building contractors with whom it has well established relationships.

Angel's new finance director has explained that he is used to preparing cash flow statements using the direct method and requires some advice on the indirect method as used by his predecessor for the Angel Group.

ANGEL GROUP: EXTRACTS FROM STATEMENT OF FINANCIAL POSITION
AS AT 30 NOVEMBER 20X3

	30 Nov 20X3 $m	30 Nov 20X2 $m
Assets		
Non-current assets		
Property, plant and equipment	475	465
Investment in associate	80	–
Financial assets	215	180
Current assets		
Inventories	155	190
Trade receivables	125	180
Cash and cash equivalents	465	355
	745	725
Current liabilities:		
Trade payables	155	361
Current tax payable	49	138
Total current liabilities	204	499

ANGEL GROUP: EXTRACT FROM STATEMENT OF PROFIT OR LOSS AND OTHER COMPREHENSIVE INCOME FOR THE YEAR ENDED 30 NOVEMBER 20X3

	$m
Revenue	1,238
Cost of sales	(986)
Gross profit	252
Other income	30
Administrative expenses	(45)
Other expenses	(54)
Operating profit	183
Finance costs	(11)
Share of profit of associates	12
Profit before tax	184

The following information relates to the financial statements of the Angel Group:

1 Angel decided to renovate a building which had a carrying amount of $nil at 1 December 20X2. As a result, $3 million was spent during the year on its renovation. On 30 November 20X3, Angel received a cash grant of $2 million from the government to cover some of the renovation cost and the creation of new jobs which had resulted from the use of the building. The grant related equally to both job creation and renovation. The only elements recorded in the financial statements were a charge to revenue for the renovation of the building and the receipt of the cash grant, which has been credited to additions of property, plant and equipment (PPE).

Angel treats grant income on capital-based projects as deferred income.

2   On 1 December 20X2, Angel acquired all of the share capital of Sweety, a manufacturer of bespoke furniture, for cash of $30 million. The fair values of the identifiable assets and liabilities of Sweety at the date of acquisition are set out below. There were no other acquisitions in the period. The fair values in the table below have been reflected in the year end balances of the Angel Group.

	Fair values $m
Property, plant and equipment	14
Inventories	6
Trade receivables	3
Cash and cash equivalents	2
Total assets	25
Trade payables	(5)
Net assets at acquisition	20

3   Angel's property, plant and equipment (PPE) comprises the following.

	$m
Carrying amount at 1 December 20X2	465
Additions at cost including assets acquired on the purchase of subsidiary	80
Gains on property revaluation	8
Disposals	(49)
Depreciation	(29)
Carrying amount at 30 November 20X3	475

Angel has constructed a machine which is a qualifying asset under IAS 23 *Borrowing Costs* and has paid construction costs of $4 million, which has been charged to other expenses. Angel Group paid $11 million in interest in the year, recorded as a finance cost, which includes $1 million of interest which Angel wishes to capitalise under IAS 23. There was no deferred tax implication regarding this transaction.

The proceeds on disposal of PPE were $63 million. The gain on disposal is included in administrative expenses.

Note. Ignore the effects of any depreciation required on the construction costs.

4   Angel purchased a 30% interest in an associate, Digitool, for cash on 1 December 20X2. The associate reported a profit for the year of $40 million and paid a dividend of $10 million out of these profits in the year ended 30 November 20X3.

5   An impairment test carried out at 30 November 20X3 showed that goodwill and other intangible assets were impaired by $26.5 million and $90 million, respectively. The impairment of goodwill relates to 100% owned subsidiaries.

6   The finance costs were all paid in cash in the period.

Required

(a)   (i)   Explain to the finance director why the building renovation has been incorrectly recorded, setting out the correcting entries.   **(4 marks)**

       (ii)   Explain, showing supporting calculations, the adjustments that need to be made to calculate the correct profit before tax figure for inclusion in a consolidated statement of cash flows for the Angel Group for the year ended 30 November 20X3, prepared using the indirect method.   **(4 marks)**

       (iii)   Prepare the cash generated from operations figure for inclusion in a consolidated statement of cash flows for the Angel Group for the year ended 30 November 20X3, using the indirect method, in accordance with the requirements of IAS 7 *Statement of Cash Flows*. For each line item, explain to the finance director of Angel Group the reason for its inclusion in the reconciliation.   **(14 marks)**

BPP
LEARNING
MEDIA

(b) The financial statements of Digitool, the associate (note (iv)) that Angel invested in during the year, were presented to the directors at a recent board meeting, along with non-financial disclosures.

Digitool is a data mining and analysis company that earns revenues by providing business insights such as emerging trends and forecasts to other companies. It has a large number of contracts with new customers that it is building relationships with, and it operates from a single data centre employing 100 high-performing people.

Included within Digitool's annual report is information relating to relationships with customers, emissions levels and the company's investment in human capital. Angel does not make similar disclosures. The directors of Angel have asked its finance director to help them manage their expectations in terms of the financial statements of Digitool and to understand why the
non-financial disclosures provided might be important to a digital company. As a wholesale manufacturing company, the directors of Angel review its gross profit margin, return on capital employed, inventory holding period and receivables collection period.

Required

(i) Identify the key differences that might be expected between the financial statements of Angel and Digitool with references to the key ratios noted by the directors. You do not need to calculate any ratios. (5 marks)

(ii) Discuss why the non-financial disclosures made by Digitool might be important to a digital company. (3 marks)

(Total = 30 marks)

17 Moyes   59 mins

Part (a) adapted from SBR December 2018, part (b) adapted from P2 2015

The following are extracts from the consolidated financial statements of the Moyes group.

GROUP STATEMENT OF PROFIT OR LOSS FOR THE YEAR ENDED 30 SEPTEMBER 20X8

	$m
Revenue	612
Cost of sales	(347)
Gross profit	265
Operating expenses	(123)
Share of profit of associate	67 *investing activities*
Profit before tax	209

GROUP STATEMENT OF FINANCIAL POSITION

	30 September 20X8 $m	30 September 20X7 $m
Inventories	126	165
Trade receivables	156	149
Trade payables	215	197

The following information is also relevant to the year ended 30 September 20X8:

Pension scheme

Moyes operates a defined benefit scheme. A service cost component of $24 million has been included within operating expenses. The remeasurement component for the year was a gain of $3 million. Benefits paid out of the scheme were $31 million. Contributions into the scheme by Moyes were $15 million.

Goodwill

Goodwill was reviewed for impairments at the reporting date. Impairments arose of $10 million in the current year.

Property, plant and equipment

Property, plant and equipment (PPE) at 30 September 20X8 included cash additions of $134 million. Depreciation charged during the year was $99 million and an impairment loss of $43 million was recognised. Prior to the impairment, the group had a balance on the revaluation surplus of $50 million of which $20 million related to PPE impaired in the current year. *[handwritten: non-cash adjustment.]*

Inventory

Goods were purchased for Dinar 80 million cash when the exchange rate was $1:Dinar 5. Moyes had not managed to sell the goods at 30 September 20X8 and the net realisable value at that date was estimated to be Dinar 60 million. The exchange rate at this date was $1:Dinar 6. The inventory has been correctly valued at 30 September 20X8 with the loss resulting from both the exchange difference and impairment correctly included within cost of sales.

Changes to group structure

During the year ended 30 September 20X8, Moyes acquired a 60% subsidiary, Davenport, and also sold all of its equity interests in Barham for cash. The consideration for Davenport consisted of a share for share exchange together with some cash payable in two years. 80% of the equity shares of Barham had been acquired several years ago but Moyes had decided to sell as the performance of Barham had been poor for a number of years. Consequently, Barham had a substantial overdraft at the disposal date. Barham was unable to pay any dividends during the financial year but Davenport did pay an interim dividend on 30 September 20X8.

Discontinued operations

The directors of Moyes wish for advice as to whether the disposal of Barham should be treated as a discontinued operation and separately disclosed within the consolidated statement of profit or loss. There are several other subsidiaries which all produce similar products to Barham and operate in a similar geographical area. Additionally, Moyes holds a 52% equity interest in Watson. Watson has previously issued share options to other entities which are exercisable in the year ending 30 September 20X9. It is highly likely that these options would be exercised which would reduce Moyes' interest to 35%. The directors of Moyes require advice as to whether this loss of control would require Watson to be classified as held for sale and reclassified as discontinued.

Required

[handwritten: +add back non cash items.]

(a) (i)   Draft an explanatory note to the directors of Moyes which should include:

- A calculation of cash generated from operations using the indirect method; and

- An explanation of the specific adjustments required to the group profit before tax to calculate the cash generated from operations.

Note. Any workings can either be shown in the main body of the explanatory note or in an appendix to the explanatory note.   (12 marks)

[handwritten: + dividends .]

(ii)   Explain how the changes to the group structure and dividend would impact upon the consolidated statement of cash flows at 30 September 20X8 for the Moyes group. You should not attempt to alter your answer to Part (a).   (6 marks)

(iii) Advise the directors as to whether Watson should be classified as held for sale and whether both it and Barham should be classified as discontinued operations.

(6 marks)

(b)   Moyes has an equity investment in an entity called Yanong. The directors of Yanong are inexperienced and would like to confirm how some share appreciation rights (SARs) should have been accounted for. The details of the SARs are as follows:

handwritten top: ⅜

handwritten: Grant date · *handwritten: Vesting date*

On 1 October 20X5, Yanong granted 500 share appreciation rights to its 300 managers. All of the rights vested on 30 September 20X7 but they can be exercised from 1 October 20X7 up to 30 September 20X9. At the grant date, the value of each SAR was $10 and it was estimated that 5% of the managers would leave during the vesting period. At 30 September 20X6, the estimate of how many managers would leave during the vesting period remained at 5%. The fair value of the SARs was as follows:

Fair value of SAR

handwritten: = 641,250

	$	
30 September 20X6	9	→ 30/9/x6 = (300 × 95%) × 500 × $9 × ½
30 September 20X7	11	→ 30/9/x7 = (300 × 95%) × 500 × $11 × 2/2
30 September 20X8	12	= 1,567,500

handwritten left: end of 2 yr vesting period.

All of the managers who were expected to leave employment did leave the company as expected before 30 September 20X7. On 30 September 20X8, 60 managers exercised their options, when the intrinsic value of the right was $10.50, and were paid in cash. *handwritten: cash paid.*

The directors of Yanong would like to confirm how the SARs should have been accounted for from the grant date to 30 September 20X8 and whether IFRS 13 *Fair Value Measurement* or IFRS 2 *Share-based Payment* applies.

Required

handwritten: 3 years.

Prepare a briefing note for the directors of Yanong which answers their queries relating to the SARs.

(6 marks)

(Total = 30 marks)

handwritten:
b/d 641,250
P&L 926,250
c/d 1,567,500

18 Hummings Co

59 mins

SBR March 2020

Background

Hummings Co is the parent company of a multinational listed group of companies. Hummings Co uses the dollar ($) as its functional currency. Hummings Co acquired 80% of the equity shares of Crotchet Co on 1 January 20X4 and 100% of Quaver Co on the same date. The group's current financial year end is 31 December 20X4.

The following exhibits provide information relevant to the question.

Exhibit 1 - Crotchet Co: Functional currency

The head office of Crotchet Co is located in a country which uses the dinar as its main currency. However, its staff are located in a variety of other locations. Consequently, half of their employees are paid in dinars and the other half are paid in the currency of grommits. Crotchet Co has a high degree of autonomy and is not reliant on finance from Hummings Co, nor do sales to Hummings Co make up a significant proportion of their income. All of its sales and purchases are invoiced in grommits and therefore Crotchet Co raises most of its finance in grommits. Cash receipts are retained in both grommits and dinars. Crotchet Co does not own a dollar ($) bank account. Crotchet Co is required by law to pay tax on its profits in dinars.

Exhibit 2 - The acquisition of Crotchet Co

Hummings Co paid cash of $24 million for the 80% holding in Crotchet Co on 1 January 20X4. Hummings Co has a policy of measuring non-controlling interests at fair value. The fair value of the non-controlling interests in Crotchet Co on 1 January 20X4 was $6 million. Since Crotchet Co has a range of net assets held domestically and overseas, the fair values of the net assets at acquisition were determined in their local currency. Hence, the fair value of some assets have been determined in dinars and others in grommits. The total fair value of the net assets denominated in grommits at 1 January 20X4 was 43 million grommits. The total fair value of the net assets denominated in dinars at 1 January 20X4 was 50 million dinars.

Excluded from these fair values are several contracts with the customers of Crotchet Co. These contractual relationships prohibit the customers of Crotchet Co from obtaining services from any of the main competitors of Crotchet Co. They have an estimated fair value at 1 January 20X4 of 15 million grommits.

At 31 December 20X4, it was decided to impair goodwill by 30%.

The following is a summary of the exchange rates between the dollar, grommits and dinars at 1 January 20X4 and 31 December 20X4:

1 January 20X4	31 December 20X4
$1:8 grommits	$1:7 grommits
$1:4 dinar	$1:3.5 dinar
1 dinar:2 grommits	1 dinar:2 grommits

Exhibit 3 - The acquisition of Quaver Co

On 1 January 20X4, Hummings Co purchased a 100% equity interest in Quaver Co. Hummings Co made the acquisition with the intention to sell and therefore did not wish to have an active involvement in the business of Quaver Co. Hummings Co immediately began to seek a buyer for Quaver Co and felt that the sale would be completed by 31 October 20X4 at the latest. A buyer for Quaver Co was located in August 20X4 but, due to an unforeseen legal dispute over a contingent liability disclosed in Quaver Co's financial statements, the sale had not yet been finalised as at 31 December 20X4. The sale is expected to be completed in early 20X5.

Exhibit 4 - Impairment of bonds

On 31 December 20X3, Hummings Co purchased $10 million 5% bonds in Stave Co at par value. The bonds are repayable on 31 December 20X6 and the effective rate of interest is 8%. Hummings Co's business model is to collect the contractual cash flows over the life of the asset. At 31 December 20X3, the bonds were considered to be low risk and as a result the 12-month expected credit losses are expected to be $10,000.

[handwritten annotation: financial asset at amortised cost.]

On 31 December 20X4, Stave Co paid the coupon interest, however, at that date the risks associated with the bonds were deemed to have increased significantly. The present value of the repayments for the year ended 31 December 20X5 were estimated to be $462,963 and the probability of default is 3%. At 31 December 20X4, it is also anticipated that no further coupon payments would be received during the year ended 31 December 20X6 and only a portion of the nominal value of the bonds would be repaid. The present value of these cash shortfalls was assessed to be $6,858,710 with a 5% likelihood of default in the year ended 31 December 20X6.

[handwritten annotation: Stage 2 - take full lifetime expected losses.]

Required

Draft an explanatory note to the directors of Hummings Co, addressing the following:

(a)   How the functional currency of Crotchet Co should be determined;   **(5 marks)**

(b)   (i)   How Crotchet Co's customer contracts should be accounted for in the consolidated financial statements of Hummings Co, which are presented in dollars ($), for the year ended 31 December 20X4;   **(4 marks)**

        (ii)   A calculation of the goodwill on acquisition of Crotchet Co (in grommits) and how it would be accounted for in the consolidated statement of financial position of Hummings Co at 31 December 20X4 after translation. Include a brief explanation and calculation of how the impairment and exchange difference on goodwill will impact on the consolidated financial statements;   **(6 marks)**

(c)   How Quaver Co should be accounted for in the consolidated financial statements at 31 December 20X4; and   **(4 marks)**

(d)   A calculation and discussion of how the bonds should be accounted for in the financial statements of Hummings Co as at 31 December 20X3 and for the year ended 31 December 20X4, including any impairment losses.   **(11 marks)**

(Total = 30 marks)

19 Carbise
59 mins

SBR March/June 2019

Carbise is the parent company of an international group which has a presentation and functional currency of the dollar. The group operates within the manufacturing sector. On 1 January 20X2, Carbise acquired 80% of the equity share capital of Bikelite, an overseas subsidiary. The acquisition was not as successful as anticipated and on 30 September 20X6 Carbise disposed of all of its holding in Bikelite. The current year end is 31 December 20X6.

Exhibit 1 - Bikelite trading information

The acquisition of Bikelite Co enabled Carbise Co to access new international markets. Carbise Co transfers surplus work-in-progress to Bikelite Co which is then completed and sold in various locations. Bikelite is based overseas where the domestic currency is the dinar. Staff costs and overhead expenses are all paid in dinars. However, Bikelite also has a range of transactions in a number of other currencies. Approximately 40% of its raw material purchases are in dinars and 50% in the yen. The remaining 10% are in dollars of which approximately half were purchases of material from Carbise. This ratio continued even after Carbise disposed of its shares in Bikelite. Revenue is invoiced in equal proportion between dinars, yen and dollars. To protect itself from exchange rate risk, Bikelite retains cash in all three currencies. No dividends have been paid by Bikelite for several years. At the start of 20X6 Bikelite sought additional debt finance. As Carbise was already looking to divest, funds were raised from an issue of bonds in dinars, none of which were acquired by Carbise.

[Handwritten note in left margin: GW ① Calc in dinar ② Translate to $]

Exhibit 2 - Acquisition of Bikelite

Carbise paid dinar 100 million for 80% of the ordinary share capital of Bikelite on 1 January 20X2. The net assets of Bikelite at this date had a carrying amount of dinar 60 million. The only fair value adjustment deemed necessary was in relation to a building which had a fair value of dinar 20 million above its carrying amount and a remaining useful life of 20 years at the acquisition date. Carbise measures non-controlling interests (NCI) at fair value for all acquisitions, and the fair value of the 20% interest was estimated to be dinar 22 million at acquisition. Due to the relatively poor performance of Bikelite, it was decided to impair goodwill by dinar 6 million during the year ending 31 December 20X5.

Rates of exchange between the $ and dinar are given as follows:

1 January 20X2: *Historic rate*	$1:0.5 dinar
Average rate for year ended 31 December 20X5	$1:0.4 dinar
31 December 20X5:	$1:0.38 dinar
30 September 20X6:	$1:0.35 dinar
Average rate for the nine-month period ended 30 September 20X6	$1:0.37 dinar

Exhibit 3 - Disposal of Bikelite

Carbise sold its entire equity shareholding in Bikelite on 30 September 20X6 for $150 million. Further details relating to the disposal are as follows:

Carrying amount of Bikelite's net assets at 1 January 20X6	dinar 48 million
Bikelite loss for the year ended 31 December 20X6	dinar 8 million
Cumulative exchange gains on Bikelite at 1 January 20X6	$74.1 million
Non-controlling interest in Bikelite at 1 January 20X6	$47.8 million

Required

(a) Prepare an explanatory note for the directors of Carbise which addresses the following issues:

   (i) What is meant by an entity's presentation and functional currency. Explain your answer with reference to how the presentation and functional currency of Bikelite should be determined.
   (7 marks)

(ii)   A calculation of the goodwill on the acquisition of Bikelite and what the balance would be at 30 September 20X6 immediately before the disposal of the shares. Your answer should include a calculation of the exchange difference on goodwill for the period from 1 January 20X6 to 30 September 20X6.   **(5 marks)**

(iii)   An explanation of your calculation of goodwill and the treatment of exchange differences on goodwill in the consolidated financial statements. You do not need to discuss how the disposal will affect the exchange differences.   **(4 marks)**

Note: Any workings can either be shown in the main body of the explanatory note or in an appendix to the explanatory note.

(b)   Explain why exchange differences will arise on the net assets and profit or loss of Bikelite each year and how they would be presented within the consolidated financial statements. Your answer should include a calculation of the exchange differences which would arise on the translation of Bikelite (excluding goodwill) in the year ended 31 December 20X6.

(7 marks)

(c)   (i)   Calculate the group profit or loss on the disposal of Bikelite.   **(3 marks)**

(ii)   Briefly explain how Bikelite should be treated and presented in the consolidated financial statements of Carbise for the year ended 31 December 20X6.   **(4 marks)**

(Total = 30 marks)

20 Bagshot Co   **29 mins**

SBR March 2020

Background

Bagshot Co has a controlling interest in a number of entities. Group results have been disappointing in recent years and the directors of Bagshot Co have been discussing various strategies to improve group performance. The current financial year end is 31 December 20X5.

The following personnel are relevant to the scenario:

Mr Shaw	Head accountant of Bagshot Co
Mrs Dawes	Chief executive of Bagshot Co
Mike Starr	Nephew of Mr Shaw
Mrs Shaw	Wife of Mr Shaw

The following exhibits provide information relevant to the question.

Exhibit 1 – Group restructure

Mr Shaw, an ACCA member, is the head accountant of Bagshot Co. He is not a member of the board of directors. Mrs Dawes, the chief executive of Bagshot Co, is also an ACCA member. During December 20X5, Mrs Dawes revealed plans to Mr Shaw of a potential restructure of the Bagshot group which had been discussed at board meetings. The restructuring plans included a general analysis of expected costs which would be incurred should the restructure take place. These include legal fees, relocation costs for staff and also redundancy costs for a number of employees. One such employee to be made redundant, Mike Starr, is the nephew of Mr Shaw.

Mrs Dawes is insistent that Mr Shaw should include a restructuring provision for all of the expenditure in the financial statements of Bagshot Co for the year ended 31 December 20X5. Mrs Dawes argues that, even if the restructure did not take place exactly as detailed, similar levels of expenditure are likely to be incurred on alternative strategies. It would therefore be prudent to include a restructuring provision for all expenditure. None of the staff other than Mr Shaw have been notified of the plans although Mrs Dawes has informed Mr Shaw that she expects a final decision and public announcement to be made prior to the authorisation of the financial statements.

Exhibit 2 - Mrs Shaw

Mrs Shaw is the wife of Mr Shaw, the head accountant of Bagshot Co. She is not an employee of Bagshot Co and does not know about the proposed restructure. However, Mrs Shaw recently acquired 5% of the equity shares in Bagshot Co. Mr Shaw is considering informing his wife of the proposed restructure so that she can make an informed decision as to whether to divest her shareholding or not. Mr Shaw is concerned that, in the short term at least, the inclusion of any restructuring costs would be harmful to the profitability of Bagshot Co. It is also uncertain as to how the market may react should the restructure take place. It is, however, anticipated that in the long term, shareholder value would be enhanced.

Required

(a) (i) Discuss the appropriate accounting treatment of the restructuring costs in the financial statements of Bagshot Co for the year ended 31 December 20X5.

(6 marks)

(ii) Discuss what is meant by good stewardship of a company and whether the restructure and the recognition of a restructuring provision in the financial statements are examples of good stewardship.

(4 marks)

(iii) Discuss briefly whether Mrs Shaw's acquisition of the equity shares in Bagshot Co should be disclosed as a related party transaction.

(3 marks)

(b) Identify and discuss the ethical issues arising from the scenario which Mr Shaw needs to consider and what actions he should take as a consequence.

(5 marks)

Professional marks will be awarded in part (b) for the clarity of discussion.

(2 marks)

(Total = 20 marks)

21 Calibra Co   39 mins

SBR September/December 2020

Calibra Co operates in the property sector and has invested in new technology, distributed ledgers/blockchain, to trade and to support property transactions. The financial year end of Calibra Co is 31 December 20X8.

The following exhibits provide information relevant to the question.

Exhibit 1 - Apartment blocks

Calibra Co builds apartment blocks which normally take two years to complete from the date of signing the contract. The title and possession, and therefore control, of the apartment blocks pass to the customer upon completion of construction. The price which is payable on completion of each apartment block is $9.55 million. Alternatively, customers can pay $8.5 million cash on the day that the contract is signed. The chief accountant has calculated that this represents an appropriate borrowing rate of 6% for Calibra Co. Calibra Co immediately recognises $8.5 million as revenue if customers pay when they sign the contract.

Exhibit 2 - Chief accountant and Bodoni Co

The chief accountant does not hold a permanent employment contract with Calibra Co. He has applied for the position on a permanent basis and is to be interviewed in the near future. Bodoni Co, a customer of Calibra Co, wanted to take advantage of the $8.5 million reduced price for an apartment block but was having problems with cash flow. The chief accountant therefore allowed Bodoni Co to pay $8.5 million and to delay payment until one month after the contract was signed. In return, Bodoni Co has agreed to provide a good employment reference. The chief accountant of Calibra Co was afraid that he might lose Bodini Co as a customer and referee if he did not agree to the delay in payment.

Exhibit 3 - Distributed ledger technology

Calibra Co has recently used distributed ledger technology/blockchain to sell shares in a property to investors. These digitised transactions are only visible to the authorised parties. The chief accountant publicly supports this technology and is to manage the new system. However, he has private concerns over the reliability of the due diligence carried out on the sale of property shares and the potential violation of local regulations. The directors of Calibra Co want to increase the number of transactions on the distributed ledger by offering digital shares in the whole of the entity's property portfolio. Although the chief accountant has very basic knowledge of distributed ledgers, he has assured the directors that he can facilitate this move. The project has been approved by the board despite the chief accountant's private reservations. The chief accountant has only recently qualified as an accountant and wishes to be employed with Calibra Co on a permanent basis.

Required

(a)   Discuss how Calibra Co should have accounted for the sale of the apartment blocks in accordance with IFRS 15 *Revenue from Contracts with Customers* and IAS 23 *Borrowing Costs*. (5 marks)

(b)   Provide the accounting entries that would be required to record the contractual sale of an apartment block on 1 January 20X8 at the discounted amount over the two-year construction period. (3 marks)

(c)   Discuss the way in which the chief accountant should have acted to ensure that he maintained ethical standards in dealing with the issues described. (10 marks)

Professional marks will be awarded in part (c) for the quality of the ethical discussion. (2 marks)

(Total = 20 marks)

22 Farham   39 mins

SBR September 2018

Background

Farham manufactures white goods such as washing machines, tumble dryers and dishwashers. The industry is highly competitive with a large number of products on the market. Brand loyalty is consequently an important feature in the industry. Farham operates a profit-related bonus scheme for its managers based upon the consolidated financial statements but recent results have been poor and bonus targets have rarely been achieved. As a consequence, the company is looking to restructure and sell its 80% owned subsidiary Newall which has been making substantial losses. The current year end is 30 June 20X8.

Factory subsidence

Farham has a production facility which started to show signs of subsidence since January 20X8. It is probable that Farham will have to undertake a major repair sometime during 20X9 to correct the problem. Farham does have an insurance policy but it is unlikely to cover subsidence. The chief operating officer (COO) refuses to disclose the issue at 30 June 20X8 since no repair costs have yet been undertaken although she is aware that this is contrary to international accounting standards. The COO does not think that the subsidence is an indicator of impairment. She argues that no provision for the repair to the factory should be made because there is no legal or constructive obligation to repair the factory.

Farham has a revaluation policy for property, plant and equipment and there is a balance on the revaluation surplus of $10 million in the financial statements for the year ended 30 June 20X8. None of this balance relates to the production facility but the COO is of the opinion that this surplus can be used for any future loss arising from the subsidence of the production facility. (5 marks)

Sale of Newall

At 30 June 20X8 Farham had a plan to sell its 80% subsidiary Newall. This plan has been approved by the board and reported in the media. It is expected that Oldcastle, an entity which currently owns the other 20% of Newall, will acquire the 80% equity interest. The sale is expected to be complete by December 20X8. Newall is expected to have substantial trading losses in the period up to the sale. The accountant of Farham wishes to show Newall as held for sale in the consolidated financial statements and to create a restructuring provision to include the expected costs of disposal and future trading losses. The COO does not wish Newall to be disclosed as held for sale nor to provide for the expected losses. The COO is concerned as to how this may affect the sales price and would almost certainly mean bonus targets would not be met. The COO has argued that they have a duty to secure a high sales price to maximise the return for shareholders of Farham. She has also implied that the accountant may lose his job if he were to put such a provision in the financial statements. The expected costs from the sale are as follows:

Future trading losses	$30 million
Various legal costs of sale	$2 million
Redundancy costs for Newall employees	$5 million
Impairment losses on owned assets	$8 million

Included within the future trading losses is an early payment penalty of $6 million for a leased asset which is deemed surplus to requirements.   (6 marks)

Required

(a)   Discuss the accounting treatment which Farham should adopt to address each of the issues above for the consolidated financial statements.

Note. The mark allocation is shown against each of the two issues above.

(b)   Discuss the ethical issues arising from the scenario, including any actions which Farham and the accountant should undertake.   (7 marks)

Professional marks will be awarded in this question for the quality of the discussion.   (2 marks)

(Total = 20 marks)

23 Gustoso   39 mins

SBR Specimen exam 2

Gustoso Co is a public limited company which produces a range of luxury food products. It prepares its financial statements in accordance with International Financial Reporting Standards. The directors of Gustoso Co receive a cash bonus each year if reported profits for the period exceed a pre-determined target. Gustoso Co has performed in excess of targets in the year ended 31 December 20X7 but financial forecasts for 20X8 are pessimistic.

Exhibit 1 - Provisions

A new accountant has recently started work at Gustoso Co. She noticed that the provisions balance as at 31 December 20X7 is significantly higher than in the prior year. She made enquiries of the finance director, who explained that the increase was due to substantial changes in food safety and hygiene laws which become effective during 20X8. As a result, Gustoso Co must retrain a large proportion of its workforce. This retraining has yet to occur, so a provision has been recognised for the estimated cost of $2 million. The finance director then told the accountant that such enquiries were a waste of time and would not be looked at favourably when deciding on her future pay rises and bonuses.

Additionally in November 20X7, the board of directors discussed a potential restructure of Gustoso Co. The restructuring plans included an analysis of long term cost savings but, should the restructure take place, there will be significant short term costs which would be necessary. These include professional fees, penalties for cancelling leases and also redundancy costs for a number of employees. Even if the restructure did not take place exactly as planned, alternative plans will need to be explored to ensure Gustoso Co remains a going concern. The finance director has therefore included a restructuring provision, arguing that this is prudent. A final decision and announcements to staff and lessors are likely to be made prior to the authorisation of the financial statements which is expected in April 20X8.

Exhibit 2 - Wheat contract

Gustoso Co purchases significant quantities of wheat on which Gustoso Co records significant profit margins. The price of wheat is volatile and so, on 1 November 20X7, Gustoso Co entered into a contract with a supplier to purchase 500,000 bushels of wheat in June 20X8 for $5 a bushel. The contract can be settled net in cash. Gustoso Co has entered into similar contracts in the past and has always taken delivery of the wheat. By 31 December 20X7 the price of wheat had fallen. The finance director recorded a derivative liability of $0.5 million on the statement of financial position and a loss of $0.5 million in the statement of profit or loss. Wheat prices may rise again before June 20X8. The accountant is unsure if the current accounting treatment is correct but feels uncomfortable approaching the finance director again.

Required

Discuss the ethical and accounting implications of the above situations from the perspective of the accountant. **(18 marks)**

Professional marks will be awarded in this question for the application of ethical principles.

(2 marks)

(Total = 20 marks)

24 Fiskerton   39 mins

SBR December 2018

The following is an extract from the statement of financial position of Fiskerton, a public limited entity as at 30 September 20X8.

	$'000
Non-current assets	160,901
Current assets	110,318
Equity share capital ($1 each)	10,000
Other components of equity	20,151
Retained earnings	70,253
Non-current liabilities (bank loan)	50,000
Current liabilities	120,815

The bank loan has a covenant attached whereby it will become immediately repayable should the gearing ratio (long-term debt to equity) of Fiskerton exceed 50%. Fiskerton has a negative cash balance as at 30 September 20X8. *cash flow is bad.*

Halam property

Lessor accounting

Included within the non-current assets of Fiskerton is a property in Halam which has been leased to Edingley under a 40-year lease. The property was acquired for $20 million on 1 October 20X7 and was immediately leased to Edingley.

The asset was expected to have a useful life of 40 years at the date of acquisition and have a minimal residual value. Fiskerton has classified the building as an investment property and has adopted the fair value model. *incorrect - finance lease.*

The property was initially revalued to $22 million on 31 March 20X8. Interim financial statements had indicated that gearing was 51% prior to this revaluation. The managing director was made aware of this breach of covenant and so instructed that the property should be revalued. The property is now carried at a value of $28 million which was determined by the sale of a similar sized property on 30 September 20X8. This property was located in a much more prosperous area and built with a higher grade of material. An independent professional valuer has estimated the value to be no more than $22 million. The managing director has argued that fair values should be referenced to an active market and is refusing to adjust the financial statements, even though he knows it is contrary to international accounting standards. *unethical*

manipulation

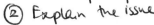

Ethics ① Pick a principle
② Explain the issue
③ Explain the actions.

Sales contract

Fiskerton has entered into a sales contract for the construction of an asset with a customer whereby the customer pays an initial deposit. The deposit is refundable only if Fiskerton fails to complete the construction of the asset. The remainder is payable on delivery of the asset. If the customer defaults on the contract prior to completion, Fiskerton has the right to retain the deposit. The managing director believes that, as completion of the asset is performed over time, revenue should be recognised accordingly. He has persuaded the accountant to include the deposit and a percentage of the remaining balance for construction work in revenue to date.

Required

lease

(a) Discuss how the Halam property should have been accounted for and explain the implications for the financial statements and the debt covenant of Fiskerton. **(7 marks)**

(b) In accordance with IFRS 15 *Revenue from Contracts with Customers*, discuss whether revenue arising from the sales contract should be recognised on a stage of completion basis. **(4 marks)**

(c) Explain any ethical issues which may arise for the managing director and the accountant from each of the scenarios. **(7 marks)**

Professional marks will be awarded in (c) for the quality of the discussion. **(2 marks)**

(Total = 20 marks)

25 Hudson   39 mins

SBR March/June 2019

Background

Hudson has a year end of 31 December 20X2 and operates a defined benefit scheme for all employees. In addition, the directors of Hudson are paid an annual bonus depending upon the earnings before interest, tax, depreciation and amortisation (EBITDA) of Hudson.

Hudson has been experiencing losses for a number of years and its draft financial statements reflect a small loss for the current year of $10 million. On 1 May 20X2, Hudson announced that it was restructuring and that it was going to close down division Wye. A number of redundancies were confirmed as part of this closure with some staff being reallocated to other divisions within Hudson. The directors have approved the restructuring in a formal directors meeting. Hudson is highly geared and much of its debt is secured on covenants which stipulate that a minimum level of net assets should be maintained. The directors are concerned that compliance with International Financial Reporting Standards (IFRS Standards) could have significant implications for their bonus and debt covenants.

Redundancy and settlement costs

Hudson still requires a number of staff to operate division Wye until its final expected closure in early 20X3. As a consequence, Hudson offered its staff two settlement packages in relation to the curtailment of the defined benefit scheme. A basic settlement was offered for all staff who leave before the final closure of division Wye. An additional pension contribution was offered for staff who remained in employment until the final closure of division Wye.

The directors of Hudson have only included an adjustment in the financial statements for those staff who left prior to 31 December 20X2. The directors have included this adjustment within the remeasurement component of the defined benefit scheme. They do not wish to provide for any other settlement contributions until employment is finally terminated, arguing that an obligation would only arise once the staff were made redundant. On final termination, the directors intend to include the remaining basic settlement and the additional pension contribution within the remeasurement component. The directors and accountant are aware that the proposed treatment does not conform to IFRS Standards. The directors believe that the proposed treatment is justified as it will help Hudson maintain its debt covenant obligations and will therefore be in the best interests of their shareholders who are the primary stakeholder. The directors have indicated that, should the accountant not agree with their accounting treatment, then he will be replaced.

Tax losses

The directors of Hudson wish to recognise a material deferred tax asset in relation to $250 million of unused trading losses which have accumulated as at 31 December 20X2. Hudson has budgeted profits for $80 million for the year ended 31 December 20X3. The directors have forecast that profits will grow by 20% each year for the next four years. The market is currently depressed and sales orders are at a lower level for the first quarter of 20X3 than they were for the same period in any of the previous five years. Hudson operates under a tax jurisdiction which allows for trading losses to be only carried forward for a maximum of two years.

Required

(a) Explain why the directors of Hudson are wrong to classify the basic settlement and additional pension contributions as part of the remeasurement component, including an explanation of the correct treatment for each of these items. Also explain how any other restructuring costs should be accounted for. **(8 marks)**

(b) Explain whether a deferred tax asset can be recognised in the financial statements of Hudson in the year ended 31 December 20X2. **(5 marks)**

(c) Identify any ethical issues which arise from the directors' proposed accounting treatments and behaviour. Your answer should also consider the implications for the accountant arising from the directors' behaviour. **(5 marks)**

Professional marks will be awarded in (c) for the quality of the discussion. **(2 marks)**

(Total = 20 marks)

26 Stent   39 mins

September/December 2019

Background

Stent Co is a consumer electronics company which has faced a challenging year due to increased competition. Stent Co has a year end of 30 September 20X9 and the unaudited draft financial statements report an operating loss. In addition to this, debt covenant limits based on gearing are close to being breached and the company is approaching its overdraft limit.

Cash advance from Budster Co

On 27 September 20X9, Stent Co's finance director asked the accountant to record a cash advance of $3 million received from a customer, Budster Co, as a reduction in trade receivables. Budster Co is solely owned by Stent Co's finance director. The accountant has seen an agreement signed by both companies stating that the $3 million will be repaid to Budster Co in four months' time. The finance director argues that the proposed accounting treatment is acceptable because the payment has been made in advance in case Budster Co wishes to order goods in the next four months. However, the accountant has seen no evidence of any intent from Budster Co to place orders with Stent Co. **(4 marks)**

Preference shares

On 1 October 20X8, the CEO and finance director each paid $2 million cash in exchange for preference shares from Stent Co which provide cumulative dividends of 7% per annum. These preference shares can either be converted into a fixed number of ordinary shares in two years' time, or redeemed at par on the same date, at the choice of the holder. The finance director suggests to the accountant that the preference shares should be classified as equity because the conversion is into a fixed number of ordinary shares on a fixed date ('fixed for fixed') and conversion is certain (given the current market value of the ordinary shares). **(4 marks)**

Deferred tax asset

Stent Co includes a deferred tax asset in its statement of financial position, based on losses incurred in the current and the previous two years. The finance director has asked the accountant to include the deferred tax asset in full. He has suggested this on the basis that Stent Co will return to profitability once its funding issues are resolved. **(3 marks)**

Required

(a) Discuss appropriate accounting treatments which Stent Co should adopt for all issues identified above and their impact upon gearing.

Note: The mark allocation is shown against each issue above.

(b) The accountant has been in her position for only a few months and the finance director has recently commented that 'all these accounting treatments must be made exactly as I have suggested to ensure the growth of the business and the security of all our jobs'. Both finance director and accountant are ACCA qualified accountants.

Required

Discuss the ethical issues arising from the scenario, including any actions which the accountant should take to resolve the issues. (7 marks)

Professional marks will be awarded in this question for the application of ethical principles.

(2 marks)

(Total = 20 marks)

27 Calendar Co   49 mins

SBR Specimen exam 2

Calendar Co has a reporting date of 31 December 20X7. It prepares its financial statements in accordance with IFRS Standards. Calendar Co develops biotech products for pharmaceutical companies. These pharmaceutical companies then manufacture and sell the products. Calendar Co receives stage payments during product development and a share of royalties when the final product is sold to consumers. A new accountant has recently joined Calendar Co's finance department and has raised a number of queries.

The following exhibits provide information that is relevant to the question.

Exhibit 1 - Development project

During 20X6 Calendar Co acquired a development project through a business combination and recognised it as an intangible asset. The commercial director decided that the return made from the completion of this specific development project would be sub-optimal. As such, in October 20X7, the project was sold to a competitor. The gain arising on derecognition of the intangible asset was presented as revenue in the financial statements for the year ended 31 December 20X7 on the grounds that development of new products is one of Calendar Co's ordinary activities. Calendar Co has made two similar sales of development projects in the past, but none since 20X0.

Exhibit 2 - Aircraft contract

While searching for some invoices, the accountant found a contract which Calendar Co had entered into on 1 January 20X7 with Diary Co, another entity. The contract allows Calendar Co to use a specific aircraft owned by Diary Co for a period of three years. Calendar Co is required to make annual payments.

On 1 January 20X7, costs were incurred negotiating the contract. The first annual payment was made on 31 December 20X7. Both of these amounts have been expensed to the statement of profit or loss.

There are contractual restrictions concerning where the aircraft can fly. Subject to those restrictions, Calendar Co determines where and when the aircraft will fly, and the cargo and passengers which will be transported.

Diary Co is permitted to substitute the aircraft at any time during the three-year period for an alternative model and must replace the aircraft if it is not working. Any substitute aircraft must meet strict interior and exterior specifications outlined in the contract. There are significant costs involved in outfitting an aircraft to meet Calendar Co's specifications.

Exhibit 3 - Accountant's recommendations

The new accountant has been reviewing Calendar Co's financial reporting processes. She has recommended the following:

- All purchases of property, plant and equipment below $500 should be written off to profit or loss. The accountant believes that this will significantly reduce the time and cost involved in maintaining detailed financial records and producing the annual financial statements.

- A checklist should be used when finalising the annual financial statements to ensure that all disclosure notes required by specific IFRS Standards are included.

Required

(a) The accountant requires advice about whether the accounting treatment of the sale of the development project is correct.   (6 marks)

(b) The accountant requires advice as to the correct accounting treatment of the aircraft contract.   (9 marks)

(c) With reference to the concept of materiality, discuss the acceptability of the accountant's recommendations.

Note. Your answer should refer to IFRS Practice Statement 2: *Making Materiality Judgements*.   (10 marks)

(Total = 25 marks)

28 Digiwire   **49 mins**

SBR September/December 2019 (amended)

Digiwire Co has developed a new business model whereby it sells music licences to other companies which then deliver digital music to consumers.

The following exhibits contain information relevant to the question.

Exhibit 1 - Revenue: sale of three-year licence

Digiwire Co has agreed to sell Clamusic Co, an unlisted technology start-up company, a three-year licence to sell Digiwire Co's catalogue of classical music to the public. This catalogue contains a large selection of classical music which Digiwire Co will regularly update over the three-year period.

As revenue for the three-year licence, Clamusic Co has issued shares to Digiwire Co equivalent to a 7% shareholding. Voting rights are attached to these shares. Digiwire Co received the shares in Clamusic Co on 1 January 20X6, which is the first day of the licence term.

Digiwire Co will also receive a royalty of 5% of future revenue sales of Clamusic Co as revenue for the licence.

Exhibit 2 - Clamusic Co valuation and revenue

On 1 January 20X6, Clamusic Co was valued at between $4–$5 million by a professional valuer who used a market-based approach. The valuation was based on the share price of a controlling interest in a comparable listed company.

For the financial year end of 31 December 20X6, sales of the classical music were $1 million. At 31 December 20X6, a further share valuation report had been produced by the same professional valuer which indicated that Clamusic Co was valued in the region of $6–$7 million.

Exhibit 3 – Investment in FourDee Co

Digiwire Co has agreed to work with TechGame Co to develop a new music platform. On 31 December 20X6, the companies created a new entity, FourDee Co, with equal shareholdings and shares in profit. Digiwire Co has contributed its own intellectual property in the form of employee expertise, cryptocurrency with a carrying amount of $3 million (fair value of $4 million) and an office building with a carrying amount of $6 million (fair value of $10 million). The cryptocurrency has been recorded at cost in Digiwire Co's financial statements. TechGame Co has contributed the technology and marketing expertise. The board of FourDee Co will comprise directors appointed equally by Digiwire Co and TechGame Co. Decisions are made by a unanimous vote.

Exhibit 4 – Debt factor

Digiwire Co is looking at ways to improve its liquidity. One option is to sell some of its trade receivables to a debt factor. The directors are considering two possible alternative agreements as described below:

1   Digiwire Co could sell $4 million of its trade receivables to a factor with the factor advancing 80% of the funds in full and final settlement. The factoring agreement is non-recourse except that Digiwire Co would guarantee that it will pay the factor a further 9% of the balance which is not recovered within six months. Weston believes that its customers represent a low credit risk and so the probability of default is very low. The fair value of the guarantee is estimated to be $5,000.

2   Alternatively, the factor would advance 20% of the $4 million trade receivables sold. Further amounts will become payable to Digiwire Co as the receivables are collected, but are subject to an imputed interest charge so that Digiwire Co receives progressively less of the remaining balance the longer it takes the factor to recover the funds. The factor has full recourse to Digiwire Co for a six-month period after which Digiwire Co has no further obligations and has no rights to receive any further payments from the factor.

Required

(a)   Advise the directors of Digiwire Co on the recognition and measurement of the:

(i)   Clamusic Co shares received as revenue for the sale of the three-year licence and how they should be accounted for in the financial statements for the year ended 31 December 20X6; and

(ii)   royalties which Clamusic Co has agreed to pay as revenue for the sale of the three-year licence in the financial statements for the year ended 31 December 20X6. Your answer to (a)(ii) should demonstrate how it is supported by the *Conceptual Framework for Financial Reporting*   (9 marks)

(b)   Based on IFRS Standards, advise the directors on the following:

(i)   the classification of the investment which Digiwire Co has in FourDee Co;

(ii)   the derecognition of the assets exchanged for the investment in FourDee Co and any resulting gain/loss on disposal in the financial statements of Digiwire Co at 31 December 20X6; and

(iii)   whether the cryptocurrency should be classified as a financial asset or an intangible asset. Your answer should also briefly consider whether fair value movements on the cryptocurrency should be recorded in profit or loss.   (9 marks)

(c)   Explain the financial reporting principles involved in debt factoring and advise how each of the two alternative agreements would affect the financial statements of future years.
          (7 marks)

          (Total = 25 marks)

29 Ecoma Co

49 mins

SBR March 2020

The directors of Ecoma Co consider environmental, social and governance issues to be extremely important in a wide range of areas, including new product development, reputation building and overall corporate strategy. The company is taking a proactive approach to managing sustainability and is actively seeking opportunities to invest in sustainable projects and embed them in their business practices. The company's financial year end is 30 September 20X5.

The following exhibits provide information relevant to the question.

Exhibit 1 - Head office

Ecoma Co is committed to a plan to move its head office to a building which has an energy efficient green roof that acts as a natural temperature controller. The move from the current head office, which is leased, will take place at the company's year end of 30 September 20X5. The new green roof building requires less maintenance than a conventional building and produces oxygen which offsets Ecoma Co's CO_2 emissions. The directors of Ecoma Co believe that the green roof building will save the company $2 million per annum over the useful life of the building. However, over the next two years, it anticipates that the disruption of the move will cause the company to make a loss of $10 million per annum. The company wishes to make a provision of $16 million which comprises the loss to be incurred over the next two years net of the saving created by the green roof.

Meanwhile, the company will have to vacate its currently leased head office building. At 30 September 20X5, the lease has two years to run at a rental of $600,000 per annum payable in advance on 1 October each year. If the lease is cancelled, the full rental is payable on cancellation. The head-lease permits sub-letting and Ecoma Co has sub-let the building for one year from 1 October 20X5 at a rental of $400,000 per annum payable in advance. Ecoma Co estimates that there is a 40% probability that it will be able to extend the sub-lease at the same rental for a second year.

The costs of moving to the green building are estimated at $1 million and the costs of terminating the lease in two years' time are negligible. The pre-tax discount rate is 5%.

Exhibit 2 - Defined benefit pension scheme

Ecoma Co is worried that the poor remuneration package offered to employees is putting the company at risk of reputational damage. Consequently, Ecoma Co changed its pension scheme on 30 September 20X5 to include all of its staff. The benefits accrue from the date of their employment but only vest after two years additional service from 30 September 20X5. The net pension obligation at 30 September 20X5 of $78 million has been updated to include this change. During the year, benefits of $6 million were paid under the scheme and Ecoma Co contributed $10 million to the scheme. These payments had been recorded in the financial statements. The following information relates to the pension scheme:

	$m
Net pension obligation at 30 September 20X5	78
Net pension obligation at 30 September 20X4	59
Service cost for year	18
Past service cost relating to scheme amendment at 30 September 20X5	9
Discount rate at 30 September 20X4	5.5%
Discount rate at 30 September 20X5	5.9%

Required

(a) The current developments in sustainability reporting show that there is a global trend towards more extensive and more meaningful narrative reporting. The improvements in the quality and scope of reporting are driven by both regulatory demands and market demands for transparency. 'Sustainable investing' describes an approach to investment where environmental, social or governance (ESG) factors, in combination with financial considerations, guide the selection and management of investments.

- what is
  sustainability?

- why increased
  demand for
  reporting?

- what do investors
  care about?

Discuss why the disclosure of sustainable information has become an important and influential consideration for investors.

Note. There is no need to refer to any exhibits to answer part (a). **(8 marks)**

(b) (i) Discuss how the $16 million provision associated with Ecoma Co's move to a new head office and the sub-let of its old head office should be accounted for in accordance with IAS 37 *Provisions, Contingent Liabilities and Contingent Assets*.

(6 marks)

(ii) Advise Ecoma Co on the principles of accounting for the pension scheme, including calculations, for the year to 30 September 20X5. **(7 marks)**

(iii) Calculate the impact which the above adjustments in (b)(i) and (ii) will have on profit before tax of $25 million for the year ended 30 September 20X5. Ignore any potential tax implications. **(2 marks)**

Professional marks will be awarded in part (a) for clarity and quality of discussion. **(2 marks)**

(Total = 25 marks)

30 Egin group   49 mins

Part (b) adapted from ACR June 2006

The International Accounting Standards Board (IASB) has been undertaking number of projects to explore how disclosures in IFRS financial reporting can be improved. In 2017, the IASB issued IFRS Practice Statement 2: *Making Materiality Judgements* to provide guidance on the application of materiality to financial statements and in 2018 the IASB amended the definition of materiality to refer to the obscuring of information and change the threshold for materiality influencing users.

Materiality is a matter which has been debated extensively in the context of many forms of reporting, including the International Integrated Reporting Framework. There are difficulties in applying the concept of materiality in practice when preparing the financial statements and it is thought that these difficulties contribute to a disclosure problem, namely, that there is too much irrelevant information in financial statements which often makes it difficult to focus on the relevant information.

Required

① define
materiality
② how its led to
concerns on clarity
+ understanding
③ IFRS practice
stmt 2 .

(a) (i) Discuss the definition of materiality, how the application of the concept of materiality has led to concerns regarding the clarity and understandability of financial statements and briefly discuss the guidance issued in *IFRS Practice Statement 2: Making Materiality Judgements* to address these issues. **(6 marks)**

(ii) Discuss how the concept of materiality would be used in applying the International Integrated Reporting Framework. **(4 marks)**

(b) On 1 June 20X5, Egin, a public limited company, was formed out of the reorganisation of a group of companies which undertake transactions with each other at normal market prices. Egin's directors are reluctant to disclose related party information as they feel that such transactions are a normal feature of business and need not be disclosed.

Under the new group structure, Egin owns 80% of Briars, 60% of Doye, and 30% of Eye. Egin has control over Briars and Doye and exercises significant influence over Eye. The directors of Egin are also directors of Briars and Doye but only one director of Egin sits on the management board of Eye. The management board of Eye comprises six directors. Originally the group comprised five companies but the fifth company, Tang, which was a 70% subsidiary of Egin, was sold on 31 January 20X6. There were no transactions between Tang and the Egin Group during the year to 31 May 20X6. 30% of the shares of Egin are owned by another company, Atomic, which exerts significant influence over Egin. The remaining 40% of the shares of Doye are owned by Spade, which exerts significant influence over Doye.

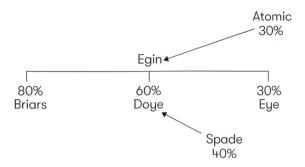

During the current financial year to 31 May 20X6, Doye has sold a significant amount of plant and equipment to Spade at the normal selling price for such items. The directors of Egin have proposed that where related party relationships are determined and sales are at normal selling price, any disclosures will state that prices charged to related parties are made on an arm's length basis.

One of the directors of Briars, who is not on the management board of Egin, owns the whole of the share capital of a company, Blue, that sells goods at market price to Briars. The director is in charge of the production at Briars and also acts as a consultant to the management board of the group.

Required

(i) Discuss why it is important to disclose related party transactions, making reference to the principles in IFRS Practice Statement 2 *Making Materiality Judgements* in your answer. (6 marks)

(ii) Describe the nature of any related party relationships and transactions which exist for the Egin Group, commenting on whether transactions should be described as being at 'arm's length'. (9 marks)

(Total = 25 marks)

31 Alexandra   49 mins

Parts (a) and (c) adapted from P2 June 2012, part (b) adapted from P2 December 2011

Alexandra is a listed group which designs and manages business solutions and infrastructures.

The following exhibits provide information relevant to the question.

Exhibit 1 – Default on loan interest payment

In November 20X0, Alexandra defaulted on an interest payment on an issued bond loan of $100 million repayable in 20X5. The loan agreement stipulates that such default leads to an obligation to repay the whole of the loan immediately, including accrued interest and expenses. The bondholders, however, issued a waiver postponing the interest payment until 31 May 20X1. On 17 May 20X1, Alexandra requested a meeting of the bondholders and agreed a further waiver of the interest payment to 5 July 20X1, when Alexandra was confident it could make the payments. Alexandra classified the loan as long-term debt in its statement of financial position at 30 April 20X1 on the basis that the loan was not in default at the end of the reporting period as the bondholders had issued waivers and had not sought redemption.

Exhibit 2 – Loan provided by Alexandra

Included in the financial assets of Alexandra is a ten-year 7% loan provided to a company external to the group. Alexandra's business model is to collect the contractual cash flows associated the loan. Alexandra has adopted IFRS 9 *Financial Instruments* and the loan asset is currently held at an amortised cost of $31 million. This is net of an allowance at 30 April 20X0 for 12 months' expected credit losses of $2 million. At 30 April 20X1, the borrower was in financial difficulties and its credit rating had been downgraded. Alexandra has assessed that there is now a significant increase in credit risk since initial recognition, however, the asset is not considered to be credit-impaired. Lifetime expected credit losses are $9.9 million. Rather than recognise lifetime expected credit losses, Alexandra now wishes to measure the loan at fair value using current market interest rates. Current market interest rates are 8%.

Exhibit 3 – Related party disclosures

Alexandra has a two-tier board structure consisting of a management and a supervisory board. Alexandra remunerates its board members as follows:

- Annual base salary
- Variable annual compensation (bonus)
- Share options

In the consolidated financial statements, within the related parties note under IAS 24 *Related Party Disclosures*, Alexandra disclosed the total remuneration paid to directors and a total for each of these boards. No further breakdown of the remuneration was provided.

The management board comprises both the executive and non-executive directors. The remuneration of the non-executive directors, however, was not included in the key management disclosures as the board believed the amounts involved to be immaterial. Some members of the supervisory and management boards are of a particular nationality. Alexandra was of the opinion that in that jurisdiction, it is not acceptable to provide information about remuneration that could be traced back to individuals. Consequently, the finance director of Alexandra explained that the board had instructed her to provide the related party information in the annual report in an ambiguous way to prevent users of the financial statements from tracing remuneration information back to specific individuals.

Required

(a) (i) Explain, with reference to the principles of relevant IFRS Standards, the appropriate financial reporting treatment resulting from the default on the interest payment and subsequent waivers (**Exhibit 1**) in Alexandra's financial statements for the year ended 30 April 20X1. **(6 marks)**

(ii) Discuss any potential impact of Alexandra's treatment of the default on the interest payment on the analysis of Alexandra's financial statements by its investors. **(3 marks)**

(b) Explain, with suitable workings, how the ten year 7% loan provided by Alexandra should be accounted for in Alexandra's financial statements for the year ended 30 April 20X1. **(5 marks)**

(c) Explain how the transactions with management described in **Exhibit 3** should be dealt with in Alexandra's financial statements, discussing the application of IFRS Practice Statement 2 *Making Materiality Judgements* and the reasons why this treatment is important to investors. **(11 marks)**

(Total = 25 marks)

32 Yanong   **49 mins**

Part (a) adapted from P2 June 2015

The directors of Yanong, a public limited company, would like advice, with reference to IFRS 13 *Fair Value Measurement*, on the transactions detailed in Exhibits 1 to 3 below. The directors would also like advice regarding the operations to be disposed of detailed in Exhibit 4 below. Yanong prepares its financial statements to 30 April each year.

The following exhibits provide information relevant to the question.

Exhibit 1 - Agricultural vehicles

Yanong owns several farms and also owns a division which sells agricultural vehicles. It is considering selling this agricultural retail division and wishes to measure the fair value of the inventory of vehicles for the purpose of the sale. Three markets currently exist for the vehicles. Yanong has transacted regularly in all three markets. At 30 April 20X5, Yanong wishes to find the fair value of 150 new vehicles, which are identical. The current volume and prices in the three markets are as follows:

Market	Sales price – per vehicle $	Historical volume – vehicles sold by Yanong	Total volume of vehicles sold in market	Transaction costs – per vehicle $	Transport costs to the market – per vehicle $
Europe	40,000	6,000	150,000	500	400
Asia	38,000	2,500	750,000	400	700
Africa	34,000	1,500	100,000	300	600

The directors of Yanong wish to value the vehicles at $39,100 per vehicle as these are the highest net proceeds per vehicle, and Europe is the largest market for Yanong's product.

Exhibit 2 - Biological asset

The company uses quarterly reporting for its farms as they grow short-lived crops such as maize. Yanong planted the maize fields during the quarter to 31 October 20X4 at an operating cost of $10 million. The fields originally cost $20 million. There is no active market for partly grown fields of maize and therefore the directors of Yanong propose to use a discounted cash flow method to value the maize fields. As at 31 October 20X4, the following were the cash flow projections relating to the maize fields:

	3 months to 31 January 20X5 $m	3 months to 30 April 20X5 $m	Total $m
Cash inflows		80	80
Cash outflows	(8)	(19)	(27)
Notional rental charge for land usage	(1)	(1)	(2)
Net cash flows	(9)	60	51

In the three months to 31 January 20X5, the actual operating costs amounted to $8 million and at that date Yanong revised its future projections for the cash inflows to $76 million for the three months to April 20X5. At the point of harvest at 31 March 20X5, the maize was worth $82 million and it was sold for $84 million (net of costs to sell) on 15 April 20X5. In the measurement of fair value of the maize, Yanong includes a notional cash flow expense for the 'rent' of the land where it is self-owned.

Exhibit 3 - Farmland

Yanong uses the revaluation model for its non-current assets. Yanong has several plots of farmland which are unproductive. The company feels that the land would have more value if it were used for residential purposes. There are several potential purchasers for the land but planning permission has not yet been granted for use of the land for residential purposes. However, preliminary enquiries with the regulatory authorities seem to indicate that planning permission may be granted. Additionally, the government has recently indicated that more agricultural land should be used for residential purposes.

The directors of Yanong have also been approached to sell the land for commercial development at a higher price than that for residential purposes.

Exhibit 4 - Disposal of operations

Yanong identified two manufacturing units, North and South, which it had decided to dispose of in a single transaction. These units comprised non-current assets only. One of the units, North, had been impaired prior to 30 April 20X5 and it had been written down to its recoverable amount of $35 million. The criteria in IFRS 5 *Non-current Assets Held for Sale and Discontinued Operations*, for classification as held for sale had been met for North and South at 30 April 20X5. The following information related to the assets of the cash-generating units at 30 April 20X5:

BPP
LEARNING
MEDIA

	Depreciated historical cost $m	Fair value less costs of disposal and recoverable amount $m	Carrying amount under IFRS 5 $m
North	50	35	35
South	70	90	70
	120	125	105

Required

(a) (i) Advise the directors of Yanong as to whether their proposed valuation for the agricultural vehicles would be acceptable under IFRS 13 *Fair Value Measurement*.

(6 marks)

(ii) Advise the directors of Yanong as to how they should have accounted for the biological asset at 31 October 20X4, 31 January 20X5, 31 March 20X5 and when the produce was sold.

(7 marks)

Note. Assume a discount rate of 2% per quarter as follows:

	Factor
3 months to 31 January 20X5	0.980
3 months to 30 April 20X5	0.961

(iii) Advise the directors of Yanong as to how to measure the fair value of the farmland in its financial statements.

(5 marks)

(b) Discuss the accounting treatment required by IFRS Standards of the disposal of the North and South manufacturing units in the financial statements of Yanong at 30 April 20X5.

(7 marks)

Note. Ignore deferred tax.

(Total = 25 marks)

33 Avco   49 mins

Part (a) adapted from P2 June 2014

Avco is a public limited company which has several financial instruments.

The following exhibits provide information relevant to the question.

Exhibit 1 – Share classification

The directors of Avco are reviewing the financial statements of two entities which are acquisition targets, Cavor and Lidan. They have asked for clarification on the treatment of the following financial instruments within the financial statements of the entities.

Cavor has two classes of shares: A and B shares. A shares are Cavor's ordinary shares and are correctly classed as equity. B shares are not mandatorily redeemable shares but contain a call option allowing Cavor to repurchase them. Dividends are payable on the B shares if, and only if, dividends have been paid on the A ordinary shares. The terms of the B shares are such that dividends are payable at a rate equal to that of the A ordinary shares.

Lidan has in issue two classes of shares: A shares and B shares. A shares are correctly classified as equity. Two million B shares of nominal value of $1 each are in issue. The B shares are redeemable in two years' time. Lidan has a choice as to the method of redemption of the B shares. It may either redeem the B shares for cash at their nominal value or it may issue one million A shares in settlement. A shares are currently valued at $10 per share. The lowest price for Lidan's A shares since its formation has been $5 per share.

Exhibit 2 – Debt or equity

At its recent general meeting, a shareholder asked the board to explain how it decides whether certain financial instruments are classified as equity when other seemingly similar financial instruments are classified as debt. The shareholder suggested that the directors do not understand the impact of the classification on investors and their analysis of the financial statements.

Exhibit 3 – Cryptocurrencies

The finance director of Avco has suggested that it invests in cryptocurrencies as part of its investment strategy. The board understands what cryptocurrencies are but has asked the finance director to explain how they would be presented in the financial statements. The finance director has stated that they should be accounted for as financial assets but is unsure if this is consistent with IFRS Standards and the *Conceptual Framework*.

Required

(a) Discuss whether the arrangements regarding the B shares of each of Cavor and Lidan should be treated as liabilities or equity in the financial statements of the respective issuing companies. Your answer should refer to relevant IFRS Standards. **(8 marks)**

(b) (i) Explain to the shareholder the key classification differences between debt and equity under IFRS Standards. **(8 marks)**

(ii) Explain why it is important for entities to understand the impact on investors' analysis of the financial statements of the classification of a financial instrument as debt or equity. **(4 marks)**

(c) Explain to the directors whether the cryptocurrencies should be accounted for as financial assets with reference to relevant IFRS Standards and the *Conceptual Framework*.

(5 marks)

(Total = 25 marks)

34 Lupin   49 mins

Part (a) adapted from ACR December 2005

Lupin is a public limited company with a reporting date of 31 October 20X5.

The following exhibits provide information relevant to the question.

Exhibit 1 – Deferred tax

The directors of Lupin want advice on how the provision for deferred taxation should be calculated for the year ended 31 October 20X5 in the following situations under IAS 12 *Income Taxes*:

1 On 1 November 20X3, the company had granted ten million share options worth $40 million subject to a two-year vesting period. Local tax law allows a tax deduction at the exercise date of the intrinsic value of the options. The intrinsic value of the ten million share options at 31 October 20X4 was $16 million and at 31 October 20X5 was $46 million. The increase in the share price in the year to 31 October 20X5 could not be foreseen at 31 October 20X4. The options were exercised at 31 October 20X5. The directors are unsure how to account for deferred taxation on this transaction for the years ended 31 October 20X4 and 31 October 20X5.

2 Lupin is leasing plant over a five-year period. A right-of-use asset was recorded at the present value of future lease payments of $12 million at the commencement of the lease which was 1 November 20X4. The right-of-use asset is depreciated on a straight-line basis over the five years. The annual lease payments are $3 million payable in arrears on 31 October and the effective interest rate is 8% per annum. The directors have not leased an asset before and are unsure as to the treatment of leases for deferred taxation. The company can claim a tax deduction for the annual lease payments. (You should assume that the IAS 12 recognition exemption for assets and liabilities does not apply in this situation.)

BPP
LEARNING
MEDIA

3   A wholly owned overseas subsidiary, Dahlia, a limited liability company, sold goods costing $7 million to Lupin on 1 September 20X5, and these goods had not been sold by Lupin before the year end. Lupin had paid $9 million for these goods. The directors do not understand how this transaction should be dealt with in the financial statements of the subsidiary and the group for taxation purposes. Dahlia pays tax locally at 30%.

4   Nala, a limited liability company, is a wholly owned subsidiary of Lupin, and is a cash-generating unit in its own right. The carrying amount of the property, plant and equipment of Nala at 31 October 20X5 was $6 million and purchased goodwill was $1 million before any impairment loss. The company had no other assets or liabilities. An impairment loss of $1.8 million had occurred at 31 October 20X5. The tax base of the property, plant and equipment of Nala was $4 million as at 31 October 20X5. The directors wish to know how the impairment loss will affect the deferred tax liability for the year. Impairment losses are not an allowable expense for taxation purposes.

Assume a tax rate of 30%.

Exhibit 2 – Shareholder question

At the last annual meeting, one of Lupin's shareholders raised a question regarding deferred tax to the company's executives. The shareholder stated that he did not understand the concept of deferred tax and did not understand why the accounting standards make adjustments for tax that do not reflect the actual amount of tax paid. He questioned the benefit of the tax reconciliation that is included within the disclosure note as it is too complicated to understand.

The finance director has since suggested that the tax reconciliation could be removed on the grounds that it is difficult to prepare and does not serve its purpose if the users cannot understand it anyway.

Required

① Explain why diff
② Calc DT
③ Where in FS.

(a)   Discuss, with suitable computations, how the situations (i) to (iv) in Exhibit 1 will impact on the accounting for deferred tax under IAS 12 in the consolidated financial statements of Lupin.

       Note. The situations in (i) to (iv) carry equal marks.   (12 marks)

(b)   (i)   In response to the shareholder's statement regarding the concept of deferred tax, discuss the conceptual basis for the recognition of deferred taxation using the temporary difference approach to deferred taxation.   (5 marks)

       (ii)   Discuss the view of the finance director and the shareholder that the tax reconciliation is difficult to understand and comment on the finance director's suggestion that it should not be disclosed. You should refer to the requirements of IFRS Standards, the *Conceptual Framework* and IFRS Practice Statement 2, *Making Materiality Judgements* where relevant.   (4 marks)

                                                                      (Total = 25 marks)

35 Janne   49 mins

Part (a) adapted from P2 June 2013

Janne is a listed real estate company which specialises mainly in industrial property. Investment properties constitute more than 60% of its total assets.

(a)   Janne measures its industrial investment property using the fair value model, and fair value is measured using 'new-build value less obsolescence'. Valuations are conducted by a member of the board of directors. In order to determine the obsolescence, the board member takes account of the age of the property and the nature of its use. According to the board, this method of calculation is complex but gives a very precise result, which is accepted by the industry. There are sales values for similar properties in similar locations available as well as market rent data per square metre for similar industrial buildings.

Required

(i)   Discuss whether the above valuation technique is appropriate, making reference to the principles of relevant IFRSs. **(5 marks)**

(ii)   Discuss Janne's selection of fair value as a measurement basis with reference to the *Conceptual Framework for Financial Reporting*. **(4 marks)**

(b)   Janne has received criticism that its annual report is too detailed, and therefore it is difficult to understand and analyse. In response to the criticism, the managing director has proposed a reduction in disclosures provided in the annual report. This includes, but is not limited to, reducing the accounting policies note, and removing the related party transactions note, which he does not consider important as all transactions are at arm's length. The managing director has recommended that all disclosures that appear irrelevant should be removed.

The finance director has vigorously defended the annual report, stating that all disclosures made are required by IFRSs, even if some of them appear irrelevant. He has confirmed this by using a 'disclosure checklist' provided by a reputable accountancy firm. He is extremely nervous that the changes proposed risk non-compliance with standards and would not improve the relevance or usefulness of the report for investors.

Required

Discuss the implications of the above in relation to Janne's annual report and its usefulness to investors, with reference to IFRS Practice Statement 2 *Making Materiality Judgements*.

(8 marks)

(c)   The managing director has also proposed to report a new performance measure 'adjusted net asset value per share', which is defined as net assets calculated in accordance with IFRS, adjusted for various items and then divided by the total number of shares. This would be presented instead of earnings per share as the managing director believes it is more relevant to investors. This performance measure is disclosed by several companies in the same industry as Janne.

Required

Discuss the benefits and drawbacks to investors of Janne's plan to disclose 'adjusted net asset value per share' instead of earnings per share. **(8 marks)**

(Total = 25 marks)

36 SunChem   **49 mins**

P2 September/December 2015 (amended)

(a)   SunChem trades in the chemical industry. The entity operates one large development and production facility. It has entered into an agreement with a separate entity, Jomaster, under which SunChem will acquire a licence to use Jomaster's technology to manufacture a chemical compound, Volut. The technology has a fair value of $4 million. SunChem cannot use the technology for manufacturing any other compound than Volut. SunChem has not concluded the amount of economic benefits that are likely to flow from Volut, but will use Jomaster's technology for a period of three years. SunChem will have to keep updating the technology in accordance with Jomaster's requirements. The agreement stipulates that SunChem will make a non-refundable payment of $4 million to Jomaster to acquire the licence to use Jomaster's technology.

SunChem is also interested in another compound, Yacton, which is being developed by Jomaster. The compound is in the second phase of development. The intellectual property of compound Yacton has been transferred to a newly formed shell company, Conew, which has no employees. The compound is the only asset of Conew. SunChem is intending to acquire a 65% interest in Conew, which will give it control over the entity and the compound. SunChem will provide the necessary resources to develop Yacton.

Required

Discuss how the above should be dealt with in the financial statements of SunChem under IFRS Standards. **(10 marks)**

(b)   At 30 November 20X6, three people own the shares of SunChem. The finance director owns 60%, and the operations director owns 30%. The third owner is a passive investor who does not help manage the entity. All ordinary shares carry equal voting rights. The husband of the finance director is the sales director of SunChem. Their son is currently undertaking an internship with SunChem and receives a salary of $30,000 per annum, which is normal compensation for the role. Recently, SunChem sold an almost fully depreciated laptop computer to the finance director's son at the going market rate for a laptop of similar make and age.

The finance director and sales director have together set up an investment company, Baleel. They jointly own Baleel and their shares in Baleel will eventually be transferred to their son when he has finished his internship with SunChem.

In addition, on 1 June 20X6 SunChem entered into a five-year maintenance contract with Ocean. Ocean is a new company which is owned and managed by the wife of the operations director. Although the contract with Ocean was more expensive than similar contracts, the board considered that Ocean would provide better service than other companies.

The finance director is of the opinion that none of the above should be disclosed in the financial statements. She believes that it is not relevant to the passive investor, and as she and the operations director are the other two shareholders, they already have all the information they need.

The finance director has heard that that the IASB has issued a new practice statement on materiality. She has not read the practice statement as she doesn't understand what value it can add given that materiality is not a new issue in financial reporting. However, she is concerned that she has missed something mandatory in the practice statement.

Required

(i)   Explain to the finance director the reason the IASB has issued IFRS Practice Statement 2 *Making Materiality Judgements*, a brief summary of the key points contained within it and whether it will give rise to any mandatory requirements.

(4 marks)

(ii)   Advise the finance director on the identification of related parties for the year ending 30 November 20X6. You should refer to IFRS Standards where relevant.   **(5 marks)**

(iii) Explain to the finance director why the company's passive investor may be interested in related party disclosures and comment on the finance director's opinion that the information should not be disclosed. You should refer to IFRS Practice Statement 2 *Making Materiality Judgements* where relevant.   **(6 marks)**

(Total = 25 marks)

37 Kiki Co   49 mins

SBR Specimen exam 2

Kiki Co is a public limited entity. It designs and manufactures children's toys. It has a reporting date of 31 December 20X7 and prepares its financial statements in accordance with IFRS Standards.

The following exhibits provide information that is relevant to the question.

Exhibit 1 - Gift cards

Kiki Co sells $50 gift cards. These can be used when purchasing any of Kiki Co's products through its website.

The gift cards expire after 12 months. Based on significant past experience, Kiki Co estimates that its customers will redeem 70% of the value of the gift card and that 30% of the value will expire unused. Kiki Co has no requirement to remit any unused funds to the customer when the gift card expires unused.

Exhibit 2 - Royalty fee

Kiki Co's best-selling range of toys is called Scarimon. In 20X6 Colour Co, another listed company, entered into a contract with Kiki Co for the rights to use Scarimon characters and imagery in a monthly comic book. The contract terms state that Colour must pay Kiki Co a royalty fee for every issue of the comic book which is sold. Before signing the contract, Kiki Co determined that Colour Co had a strong credit rating. Throughout 20X6, Colour Co provided Kiki Co with monthly sales figures and paid all amounts due in the agreed-upon period. At the beginning of 20X7, Colour Co experienced cash flow problems. These were expected to be short term. Colour Co made nominal payments to Kiki Co in relation to comic sales for the first half of the year. At the beginning of July 20X7, Colour Co lost access to credit facilities and several major customers. Colour Co continued to sell Scarimon comics online and through specialist retailers but made no further payments to Kiki Co.

Exhibit 3 - Property

As a result of rising property prices, Kiki Co purchased five buildings during the current period in order to benefit from further capital appreciation. Kiki Co has never owned an investment property before. In accordance with IAS 40 *Investment Property*, the directors are aware that they can measure the buildings using either the fair value model or the cost model. However, they are concerned about the impact that this choice will have on the analysis of Kiki Co's financial performance, position and cash flows by current and potential investors.

Required

(a) The directors require advice about how revenue from the following sources should be accounted for in the financial statements for the year ended 31 December 20X7:

   (i) gift cards   (6 marks)
   (ii) royalty   (6 marks)

Rel
SoFP
Cash Flow

(b) Discuss the potential impact that the property accounting policy may have on investors' analysis of Kiki Co's financial statements for the year ended 31 December 20X7. Your answer should refer to key financial performance ratios.   (11 marks)

Professional marks will be awarded in Part (b) for clarity and quality of presentation.
                                                                                  (2 marks)

                                                                        (Total = 25 marks)

38 Skizer   49 mins

SBR September 2018 (amended)

Skizer is a pharmaceutical company which develops new products with other pharmaceutical companies that have the appropriate production facilities.

The following exhibits provide information relevant to the question.

Exhibit 1 - Stakes in development projects

When Skizer acquires a stake in a development project, it makes an initial payment to the other pharmaceutical company. It then makes a series of further stage payments until the product development is complete and it has been approved by the authorities. In the financial statements for the year ended 31 August 20X7, Skizer has treated the different stakes in the development projects as separate intangible assets because of the anticipated future economic benefits related to Skizer's ownership of the product rights. However, in the year to 31 August 20X8, the directors of Skizer decided that all such intangible assets were to be expensed as research and development costs as they were unsure as to whether the payments should have been initially recognised as intangible assets. This write off was to be treated as a change in an accounting estimate.

correct if criteria met.

don't write off / capitalise.

> impairment test due to uncertain

incorrect, regardless of whether criteria is met.

Exhibit 2 – Sale of development project

On 1 September 20X6, Skizer acquired a development project as part of a business combination and correctly recognised the project as an intangible asset. However, in the financial statements to 31 August 20X7, Skizer recognised an impairment loss for the full amount of the intangible asset because of the uncertainties surrounding the completion of the project. During the year ended 31 August 20X8, the directors of Skizer judged that it could not complete the project on its own and could not find a suitable entity to jointly develop it. Thus, Skizer decided to sell the project, including all rights to future development. Skizer succeeded in selling the project and, as the project had a nil carrying value, it treated the sale proceeds as revenue in the financial statements. The directors of Skizer argued that IFRS 15 *Revenue from Contracts with Customers* states that revenue should be recognised when control is passed at a point in time. The directors of Skizer argued that the sale of the rights was part of their business model and that control of the project had passed to the purchaser.

Required

[handwritten: → meet the definition / relevant, faithful representation.]

(a) (i)   Explain the criteria in the *Conceptual Framework for Financial Reporting* for the recognition of an asset and discuss whether there are inconsistencies with the criteria in IAS 38 *Intangible Assets*. *[handwritten: ↘ probable, measure reliably in IAS 38]* (8 marks)

(ii) Discuss the implications for Skizer's financial statements for both the years ended 31 August 20X7 and 20X8 if the recognition criteria in IAS 38 for an intangible asset were met as regards the stakes in the development projects above. Your answer should also briefly consider the implications if the recognition criteria were not met. (5 marks)

[handwritten: Should have just expensed]

(iii) Discuss whether the proceeds of the sale of the development project above should be treated as revenue in the financial statements for the year ended 31 August 20X8.

[handwritten: → not recognised as revenue as not part of the business model.] (4 marks)

(b) External disclosure of information on intangibles is useful only insofar as it is understood and is relevant to investors. It appears that investors are increasingly interested in and understand disclosures relating to intangibles. A concern is that, due to the nature of disclosure requirements of IFRS Standards, investors may feel that the information disclosed has limited usefulness, thereby making comparisons between companies difficult. Many companies spend a huge amount of capital on intangible investment, which is mainly developed within the company and thus may not be reported. Often, it is not obvious that intangible assets can be valued or even separately identified for accounting purposes.

The *International Integrated Reporting Framework* may be one way to solve this problem.

Required

(i)   Discuss the potential issues which investors may have with:

- Accounting for the different types of intangible asset acquired in a business combination;

- The choice of accounting policy of cost or revaluation models, allowed under IAS 38 *Intangible Assets* for intangible assets; and

- The capitalisation of development expenditure. (7 marks)

(ii)   Discuss whether integrated reporting can enhance the current reporting requirements for intangible assets. (3 marks)

(Total = 25 marks)

39 Toobasco   49 mins

SBR September 2018

Toobasco is a car retailer. In the reporting of financial information, the directors have disclosed several alternative performance measures (APMs), other than those defined or specified under IFRS Standards.

The following exhibits provide information relevant to the question:

APM = make financial statements more useful.

Exhibit 1 - Alternative Performance Measures (APMs)

The directors have disclosed the following APMs:

1   'Operating profit before extraordinary items' is often used as the headline measure of the Group's performance, and is based on operating profit before the impact of extraordinary items. Extraordinary items relate to certain costs or incomes which are excluded by virtue of their size and are deemed to be non-recurring. Toobasco has included restructuring costs and impairment losses in extraordinary items. Both items had appeared at similar amounts in the financial statements of the two previous years and were likely to occur in future years.

2   'Operating free cash flow' is calculated as cash generated from operations less purchase of property, plant and equipment, purchase of own shares, and the purchase of intangible assets. The directors have described this figure as representing the residual cash flow in the business but have given no detail of its calculation. They have emphasised its importance to the success of the business. They have also shown free cash flow per share in bold next to earnings per share in order to emphasise the entity's ability to turn its earnings into cash.

3   'EBITDAR' is defined as earnings before interest, tax, depreciation, amortisation and rent. EBITDAR uses operating profit as the underlying earnings. In an earnings release, just prior to the financial year end, the directors disclosed that EBITDAR had improved by $180 million because of cost savings associated with the acquisition of an entity six months earlier. The directors discussed EBITDAR at length describing it as 'record performance' but did not disclose any comparable information under IFRS and there was no reconciliation to any measure under IFRS Standards. In previous years, rent had been deducted from the earnings figure to arrive at this APM.

4   The directors have not taken any tax effects into account in calculating the remaining APMs. *why?*

Exhibit 2 - Net Cash from Operating Activities

Toobasco leases vehicles to customers under operating leases and often sells the cars to third parties when the lease ends.

Net cash generated from operating activities for the year ended 31 August 20X8 for the Group is as follows:

Year ended 31 August 20X8	$m
Cash generated from operating activities	345
Income taxes paid	(21)
Pension deficit payments	(33)
Interest paid	(25)
Associate share of profits	12
Net cash generated from operating activities	278

Net cash flows generated from investing activities included interest received of $10 million and net capital expenditure of $46 million excluding the business acquisition described in Exhibit 3 note (iii).

There were also some errors in the presentation of the statement of cash flows which could have an impact on the calculation of net cash generated from operating activities.

BPP
LEARNING
MEDIA

Exhibit 3 - Statement of cash flows potential errors

The directors have provided the following information regarding some potential errors in Net Cash Generated from Operating Activities (exhibit 2):

1   Cars are treated as property, plant and equipment when held under operating leases and when they become available for sale, they are transferred to inventory at their carrying amount. In its statement of cash flows for the year ended 31 August 20X8, cash flows from investing activities included cash inflows relating to the disposal of cars ($30 million).

2   On 1 September 20X7, Toobasco purchased a 25% interest in an associate for cash. The associate reported a profit after tax of $16 million and paid a dividend of $4 million out of these profits in the year ended 31 August 20X8. The directors had incorrectly included a figure of $12 million in cash generated from operating activities as the cash generated from the investment in the associate. The associate was correctly recorded at $23 million in the statement of financial position at 31 August 20X8 and profit for the year of $4 million was included in the statement of profit or loss.

3   Toobasco also acquired a foreign subsidiary during the year ended 31 August 20X8. The statement of cash flows showed a loss of $28 million in net cash inflow generated from operating activities as the effect of changes in foreign exchange rates arising on the retranslation of this overseas subsidiary. The assets and liabilities of the acquired subsidiary had been correctly included in the calculation of the cash movement during the year.

4   During the year to 31 August 20X8, Toobasco made exceptional contributions to the pension plan assets of $33 million but the statement of cash flows had not recorded the cash tax benefit of $6 million.

5   Additionally, Toobasco had capitalised the interest paid of $25 million into property, plant and equipment ($18 million) and inventory ($7 million).

6   Toobasco has defined operating free cash flow as net cash generated by operating activities as adjusted for net capital expenditure, purchase of associate and dividends received, interest received and paid. Any exceptional items should also be excluded from the calculation of free cash flow.

Required

(a)   Advise the directors whether the APMs described would achieve fair presentation in the financial statements.   (10 marks)

(b)   Prepare:

    (i)   An adjusted statement of net cash generated from operating activities to correct any errors above;   (4 marks)

    (ii)   A reconciliation from net cash generated by operating activities to operating free cash flow (as described in Exhibit 3 note (6); and   (4 marks)

    (iii)   An explanation of the adjustments made in parts (b)(i) and (ii) above.   (5 marks)

    Professional marks will be awarded in Part (b) for clarity and quality of discussion.

(2 marks)

(Total = 25 marks)

40 Holls   49 mins

SBR December 2018

The Holls Group is preparing its consolidated financial statements for the year ended 30 November 20X7.

The following exhibits provide information relevant to the question.

Exhibit 1 - Tax rate reconciliation

Holls Group is preparing its financial statements for the year ended 30 November 20X7. The directors of Holls have been asked by an investor to explain the accounting for taxation in the financial statements.

The Group operates in several tax jurisdictions and is subject to annual tax audits which can result in amendments to the amount of tax to be paid.

The profit from continuing operations was $300 million in the year to 30 November 20X7 and the reported tax charge was $87 million. The investor was confused as to why the tax charge was not the tax rate multiplied by the profit from continuing operations. The directors have prepared a reconciliation of the notional tax charge on profits as compared with the actual tax charge for the period.

	$m
Profit from continuing operations before taxation	300
Notional charge at local corporation tax rate of 22%	66
Differences in overseas tax rates	10
Tax relating to non-taxable gains on disposals of businesses	(12)
Tax relating to the impairment of brands	9
Other tax adjustments	14
Tax charge for the year	87

The amount of income taxes paid as shown in the statement of cash flows is $95 million but there is no current explanation of the tax effects of the above items in the financial statements.

Exhibit 2 - Tax rate and deferred tax

The tax rate applicable to Holls for the year ended 30 November 20X7 is 22%. There is a proposal in the local tax legislation that a new tax rate of 25% will apply from 1 January 20X8. In the country where Holls is domiciled, tax laws and rate changes are enacted when the government approves the legislation. The government approved the legislation on 12 November 20X7. The current weighted average tax rate for the Group is 27%. Holls does not currently disclose its opinion of how the tax rate may alter in the future but the government is likely to change with the result that a new government will almost certainly increase the corporate tax rate.

At 30 November 20X7, Holls has deductible temporary differences of $4.5 million which are expected to reverse in the next year. In addition, Holls also has taxable temporary differences of $5 million which relate to the same taxable company and the tax authority. Holls expects $3 million of those taxable temporary differences to reverse in 20X8 and the remaining $2 million to reverse in 20X9. Prior to the current year, Holls had made significant losses.

Required

(a)   IFRS Practice Statement 1 *Management Commentary* provides a broad, non-binding framework for the presentation of management commentary which relates to financial statements which have been prepared in accordance with IFRS Standards. The management commentary is within the scope of the *Conceptual Framework* and, therefore, the qualitative characteristics will be applied to both the financial statements and the management commentary.

— may need to pay new expense
— cost implication.
against — tick box — costly, timely. ✓

(i)   Discuss briefly the arguments for and against issuing IFRS Practice Statement 1 *Management Commentary* as a non-binding framework or as an IFRS Standard.

(4 marks)

TO agree w/ Conceptual framework

(ii)   Discuss how the qualitative characteristics of understandability, relevance and comparability should be applied to the preparation of the management commentary.

(5 marks)

(b)   With reference to the information in Exhibits 1 and 2, explain to the investor the nature of accounting for taxation in financial statements.

Note. Your answer should explain the tax reconciliation, discuss the implications of current and future tax rates, and provide an explanation of accounting for deferred taxation in accordance with relevant IFRS Standards. **(14 marks)**

Professional marks will be awarded in part (b) for clarity and quality of discussion.

(2 marks)

(Total = 25 marks)

41 Crypto   **49 mins**

SBR March/June 2019

Crypto Co trades in the power industry, and owns 45% of the voting shares in Kurran Co.

The following exhibits provide information relevant to the question.

Exhibit 1 - Ownership of Kurran Co

Crypto Co operates in the power industry, and owns 45% of the voting shares in Kurran Co. Kurran Co has four other investors which own the remaining 55% of its voting shares and are all technology companies. The largest of these holdings is 18%. Kurran Co is a property developer and purchases property for its renovation potential and subsequent disposal. Crypto Co has no expertise in this area and is not involved in the renovation or disposal of the property.

The board of directors of Kurran Co makes all of the major decisions but Crypto Co can nominate up to four of the eight board members. Each of the remaining four board members are nominated by each of the other investors. Any major decisions require all board members to vote and for there to be a clear majority. Thus, Crypto Co has effectively the power of veto on any major decision. There is no shareholder agreement as to how Kurran Co should be operated or who will make the operating decisions for Kurran Co. The directors of Crypto Co believe that Crypto Co has joint control over Kurran Co because it is the major shareholder and holds the power of veto over major decisions.

Exhibit 2 - Foreign currency derivative

On 1 April 20X7, Crypto Co, which has a functional currency of the dollar, entered into a contract to purchase a fixed quantity of electricity at 31 December 20X8 for 20 million euros. At that date, the spot rate was 1.25 dollars to the euro. The electricity will be used in Crypto Co's production processes.

Crypto Co has separated out the foreign currency embedded derivative from the electricity contract and measured it at fair value through other comprehensive income (FVTOCI). However, on 31 December 20X7, there was a contractual modification, such that the contract is now an executory contract denominated in dollars. At this date, Crypto Co calculated that the embedded derivative had a negative fair value of 2 million euros.

Required

(a) (i) The directors of Crypto Co would like advice as to whether or not they should account for Kurran Co under IFRS 11 *Joint Arrangements*.   **(6 marks)**

(ii) The directors of Crypto Co would like advice as to whether they should have separated out the foreign currency derivative and measured it at FVTOCI, and how to treat the modification in the contract.   **(5 marks)**

(b) Previous leasing standards have been criticised about the lack of information they required to be disclosed on leasing transactions. These concerns were usually expressed by investors and so IFRS 16 *Leases* was issued in response to these criticisms.

(i) Discuss some of the key changes to financial statements which investors will see when companies apply the lessee accounting requirements in IFRS 16.   **(6 marks)**

(ii) For a company with significant off-balance sheet leases, discuss the likely impact that IFRS 16 will have generally on accounting ratios and particularly on:

• Earnings before interest and tax to interest expense (interest cover);

- Earnings before interest and tax to capital employed (return on capital employed);

- Debt to earnings before interest, tax, depreciation and amortisation (EBITDA).

(6 marks)

Professional marks will be awarded in (b) for clarity and quality of discussion. (2 marks)

(Total = 25 marks)

42 Guidance
49 mins

SBR September/December 2019

Guidance Co is considering the financial results for the year ended 31 December 20X6. The industry places great reliance on the return on equity (ROE) as an indicator of how well a company uses shareholders' funds to generate a profit.

The following exhibits provide information relevant to the question.

Exhibit 1 - Return on equity (ROE)

Guidance Co analyses ROE in order to understand the fundamental drivers of value creation in the company. ROE is calculated as:

$$\text{Return on equity} = \frac{\text{Net profit before tax}}{\text{Sales}} \times \frac{\text{Sales}}{\text{Assets}} \times \frac{\text{Assets}}{\text{Equity}}$$

Guidance Co uses year-end equity and assets to calculate ROE.

The following information in table 1 relates to Guidance Co for the last two years:

	20X5 $m	20X6 $m
Net profit before tax	30	38
Sales	200	220
Assets	250	210
Equity at 31 December	175	100

Exhibit 2 - Special purpose entity (SPE)

During the year ended 31 December 20X6, Guidance Co stated that it had reorganised its assets and set up a SPE. Guidance Co transferred property to the SPE at its carrying amount of $50 million, but had incorrectly charged revaluation surplus with this amount rather than showing the transfer as an investment in the SPE. The property was the SPE's only asset. However, Guidance Co still managed the property, and any profit or loss relating to the assets of the entity was remitted directly to Guidance Co. Guidance Co had no intention of consolidating the SPE.

Exhibit 3 - Miscellaneous transactions

Guidance Co has bought back 25 million shares of $1 for $1.20 per share during the year ended 31 December 20X6 for cash and cancelled the shares. This transaction was deemed to be legal.

Guidance Co also raised loan capital for the first time during the year ended 31 December 20X6 of $20 million in order to help with the buy-back of the company's shares.

Guidance Co had purchased a 25% interest in an associate company on 1 July 20X6 for cash. The investment had cost $15 million and the associate had made profits of $32 million in the year to 31 December 20X6. Guidance Co accounted for the purchase of the associate correctly.

All of these miscellaneous transactions have been accounted for in the financial information for the year ended 31 December 20X6 in table 1 shown in Exhibit 1.

Required

(a) Management's intent and motivation will often influence accounting information. However, corporate financial statements necessarily depend on estimates and judgement. Financial statements are intended to be comparable but their analysis may not be the most accurate way to judge the performance of any particular company. This lack of comparability may be due to different accounting policy choices or deliberate manipulation.

Discuss the reasons why an entity may choose a particular accounting policy where an IFRS Standard allows an accounting policy choice and whether faithful representation and comparability are affected by such choices.

(6 marks)

(b) (i) Discuss the usefulness to investors of the ROE ratio and its component parts provided above and calculate these ratios for the years ended 31 December 20X5 and 20X6. These calculations should be based upon the information provided in table 1 in Exhibit 1. **(5 marks)**

(ii) Discuss the impact that the setting up of the SPE and miscellaneous transactions have had on ROE and its component parts. Given these considerations, adjust table 1 in Exhibit 1 and recalculate the ROE for 20X6 thereby making it more comparable to the ROE of 20X5. **(12 marks)**

Professional marks will be awarded in (b)(i) for clarity and quality of discussion.

(2 marks)

(Total = 25 marks)

43 Handfood Co   49 mins

SBR September/December 2020

Handfood Co is a small and medium-sized enterprise (SME) which has introduced a benefit to encourage employees to remain with the entity. The company's financial year end is 31 December and it prepares its financial statements using IFRS Standards but is interested in understanding the differences between IFRS Standards and the *IFRS for SMEs* Standard

The following exhibit provides information relevant to the question.

Exhibit 1 - Employee benefit

On 1 January 20X2, Handfood Co introduced a benefit to encourage employees to remain in its employment for at least five years. Handfood Co has promised its employees a lump-sum benefit, payable on 1 January 20X7, which is equal to 1% of their salary at 31 December 20X6, provided they remain employed until that date.

The current salaries of employees on 1 January 20X2 are $1.1 million per annum. The directors of Handfood Co have used the following assumptions:

- Salaries for year ended 31 December 20X2 will remain at $1.1 million.

- Salaries should increase by 3% each year from 1 January 20X3.

- There is a 75% probability that all employees will still be employed by Handfood Co at 31 December 20X6.

The discount rate is 5% per year.

Handfood Co recognises actuarial gains and losses in other comprehensive income. Interest is recognised by Handfood Co on an annual basis. Handfood Co uses the projected unit credit method to measure its defined benefit obligation which means that the current service cost is the increase in the present value of the future defined benefit liabilities. The benefit will be payable from the balance on Handfood Co's business bank account at 1 January 20X7.

Present value factors	5%
Periods (years)	
4	0. 823
5	0. 784

Required

It can be argued that small and medium-sized enterprises (SMEs) face financing difficulties because there is serious information asymmetry between SMEs and investors. Information asymmetry, in the context of SMEs, means that the SME has access to relevant information, while the investor suffers from a lack of relevant information. It can be argued that the *IFRS for SMEs* Standard decreases information asymmetry between the entity and investors.

Where SMEs lead in product and service innovation, they can also lead in innovation for integrated reporting. There is a clear, concise and persuasive case for why SMEs and their stakeholders stand to benefit greatly by using integrated reporting.

(a) (i) Discuss the nature of the *IFRS for SMEs* Standard and the principal differences between the *IFRS for SMEs* Standard and full IFRS standards.   **(4 marks)**

   (ii) Discuss the effect that information asymmetry can have on the decision to invest in SMEs.   **(4 marks)**

   (iii) Discuss how integrated reporting could help SMEs better understand and better communicate how they create value to investors.   **(5 marks)**

   Note: you do not need to refer to any information relating to Handfood Co in your answer to part (a).

   Professional marks will be awarded in part (a) for clarity and quality of discussion.

   (2 marks)

(b) (i) Discuss, with suitable calculations, the principles of how Handfood Co should account for the current service cost of its employee benefit for the year ended 31 December 20X2.   **(6 marks)**

   (ii) Discuss the impact on the additional employee benefit for the year ended 31 December 20X3 if Handfood Co were to take into account the following changes in assumptions:

   • an increase in employees' salaries above 3% per annum; and
   • a decrease in the probability of employees leaving the company.

   Note: There is no need to provide any calculations in your answer to (b)(ii).

   (4 marks)

   (Total = 25 marks)

44 Moorland   49 mins

Moorland is a listed entity with several subsidiaries.

The following exhibits provide information relevant to the question.

Exhibit 1 - Operating segments

Tybull is Moorland's only foreign subsidiary and Moorland has always disclosed Tybull as an operating segment within the consolidated financial statements. The directors of Moorland are considering how the company identifies its operating segments and the rationale for disclosing segmental information. In particular, they are interested in whether it is possible to reclassify their operating segments and whether this may impact on the usefulness of segmental reporting for the business. There have been no internal organisational changes at Moorland for the past five years.

Exhibit 2 - Underlying earnings per share

The CEO of Moorland has proposed to report 'underlying earnings per share' in its annual report, calculated by adjusting earnings for various items that are considered to be non-recurring, divided by the weighted average number of ordinary shares outstanding during the period. A similar performance measure is disclosed by several companies in the same industry as Moorland. The CEO believes that presenting underlying earnings per share will aid investors in their analysis of Moorland's performance, and therefore it should be presented prominently. In calculating underlying earnings per share, one item the CEO wishes to exclude from earnings is a large impairment loss relating to the goodwill of a subsidiary. He believes that this cost can be excluded as it is unlikely to reoccur.

Required

(a)   Management commentary is a narrative report that relates to financial statements and is published voluntarily by companies in their annual report.

Describe the principles and objectives of management commentary with reference to IFRS Practice Statement 1 *Management Commentary* and discuss whether the commentary should be made mandatory or whether directors should be free to use their judgement as to what should be included in such a commentary.   (11 marks)

Note. You do not need to refer to any exhibit to answer part (a).

(b)   Advise the directors as to how operating segments are identified and whether they can be reclassified. Include in your discussion whether Tybull should be treated as a separate segment and how it may impact on the usefulness of the information if its results were not separately disclosed in accordance with IFRS 8 *Operating Segments*.   (8 marks)

(c)   Discuss the usefulness to investors of Moorland's plan to report underlying earnings per share, and suggest ways in which the directors could improve its usefulness to investors.

(6 marks)

(Total = 25 marks)

45 Amster   49 mins

P2 December 2017 (amended)

Amster is a group with several subsidiaries.

The following exhibits provide information relevant to the question.

Exhibit 1 - Preference shares

Amster has issued two classes of preference shares. The first class was issued at a fair value of $50 million on 30 November 20X7. These shares give the holder the right to a fixed cumulative cash dividend of 8% per annum of the issue price of each preferred share. The company may pay all, part or none of the dividend in respect of each preference share. If the company does not pay the dividend after six months from the due date, then the unpaid amount carries interest at twice the prescribed rate subject to approval of the management committee. The preference shares can be redeemed but only on the approval of the management committee.

The second class of preference shares was issued at a fair value of $25 million and is a non-redeemable preference share. The share has a discretionary annual dividend which is capped at a maximum amount. If the dividend is not paid, then no dividend is payable to the ordinary shareholders. Amster is currently showing both classes of preference shares as liabilities.

Exhibit 2 - Cash-settled share awards

On 1 December 20X6, Amster granted 250 cash-settled share awards to each of its 1,500 employees on the condition that the employees remain in its employment for the next three years. Cash is payable at the end of three years based on the share price of the entity's shares on that date. During the year to 30 November 20X7, 65 employees left and, at that date, Amster estimates that an additional 115 employees will leave during the following two years. The share price at 30 November 20X7 is $35 per share and it is anticipated that it will rise to $46 per share by 30 November 20X9. Amster has charged the expense to profit or loss and credited equity with the same amount.

Exhibit 3 - Capitalisation table

The capitalisation table of Amster is set out below:

Amster Group – capitalisation table

	30 November 20X7
	$m
Long-term liabilities	81
Pension plan deficit	30
Cumulative preference shares	75
Total long-term liabilities	186
Non-controlling interest	10
Shareholders' equity	150
Total group equity	160
Total capitalisation	346

Required

(a)   When an entity issues a financial instrument, it has to determine its classification either as debt or as equity. The result of the classification can have a significant effect on the entity's reported results and financial position. An understanding of what an entity views as capital and its strategy for capital management is important to all companies and not just banks and insurance companies. There is diversity in practice as to what different companies see as capital and how it is managed.

(i)   Discuss why the information about the capital of a company is important to investors, setting out the nature of the published information available to investors about a company's capital.

Note. Your answer should briefly set out the nature of financial capital in integrated reports.   (8 marks)

(ii)   Discuss the importance of the classification of equity and liabilities under IFRS Standards, with reference to the *Conceptual Framework*, and how this classification has an impact on the information disclosed to users in the statement of profit or loss and other comprehensive income and the statement of financial position.   (6 marks)

Note. You do not need to refer to any exhibit to answer part (a).

(b)   Discuss whether the accounting treatment of the transactions in Exhibit 1 and Exhibit 2 is acceptable under IFRS Standards including any adjustment which is required to the capitalisation table shown in Exhibit 3 and the effect on the gearing and the return on capital employed ratios.   (9 marks)

Professional marks will be awarded in this question for clarity and quality of presentation.

(2 marks)

(Total = 25 marks)

46 Havanna   49 mins

Adapted from P2 December 2013

Havanna is seeking advice on transactions it has entered into in the year ended 30 November 20X3.

The transactions are contained in the following exhibits.

Exhibit 1 - Contracts with sports organisations

Havanna owns a chain of health clubs and has entered into binding contracts with sports organisations, which earn income over given periods. The services rendered in return for such income include access to Havanna's database of members and admission to health clubs, including the provision of coaching and other benefits. These contracts are for periods of between 9 and 18 months. Havanna's accounting policy for revenue recognition is to recognise the contract income in full at the date when the contract is signed. The rationale is that the contracts are binding and at the point of signing the contract, the customer gains access to Havanna's services. The directors are reluctant to change their accounting policy.

Exhibit 2 - Sale of division

In May 20X3, Havanna decided to sell one of its regional business divisions through a mixed asset and share deal. The decision to sell the division at a price of $40 million was made public in November 20X3 and gained shareholder approval in December 20X3. It was decided that the payment of any agreed sale price could be deferred until 30 November 20X5. It is estimated that the cost of allowing the deferred payment is $0.5 million and that legal and other professional fees associated with the disposal will be around $1 million. The business division was identified correctly as 'held for sale' and was presented as a disposal group in the statement of financial position as at 30 November 20X3. At the initial classification of the division as held for sale, its net carrying amount was $90 million. In writing down the disposal group's carrying amount, Havanna accounted for an impairment loss of $30 million which represented the difference between the carrying amount and value of the assets measured in accordance with applicable IFRS Standards.

Exhibit 3 - Sale and leaseback

is at market value

Havanna has decided to sell its main office building to a third party for $5 million and lease it back on a ten-year lease. The current fair value of the property is $5 million and the carrying amount of the asset is $4.2 million. The present value of the future lease payments has been calculated as $3.85 million. The remaining useful life of the building is 15 years. The transaction constitutes a sale in accordance with IFRS 15 *Revenue from Contracts with Customers*.

Havanna's CEO believes this represents a very good deal for Havanna and has told you that the profit on disposal of $0.8 million will help to ensure that the company meets the covenants imposed by the bank in respect of Havanna's interest cover ratio.

Havanna's board of directors would like information about the effect of the introduction of IFRS 16 *Leases*, particularly for its own bank covenants, but also for investors more generally. They have been told that IFRS 16 should be helpful for investors in their analysis of financial statements but are unsure as to why this is the case. MORE COMPARABLE.

Handwritten margin notes (left):

① Remove PPE at CA

② Record ROU asset
CA × $\dfrac{PVFLP}{FV}$

③ lease liability = PVFLP

④ gain/loss for part transferred

total gains = FV − CA

part retained $\dfrac{PVFLP}{FV}$

Required

(a) Advise the directors, with reference to the underlying principles of IFRS 15 *Revenue from Contracts with Customers*, how the revenue in relation to the contracts with sports organisations should be recognised. **(5 marks)**

(b) Advise the directors as how to account for the sale of the division in the financial statements for the year ended 30 November 20X3. **(5 marks)**

(c) In respect of Exhibit 3, prepare a briefing note for the directors which:

  (i) Discusses the key changes to financial statements which investors will see when companies apply the lessee accounting requirements in IFRS 16 *Leases*. **(6 marks)**

  (ii) Explains to the directors how to account for the sale of the main office building at the start of the lease, including any gain on the sale. *Sale and leaseback.* **(5 marks)**

  (iii) Comments on the effect of this transaction Havanna's interest cover ratio. **(2 marks)** *indicator of Risk.*

  Professional marks will be awarded in part (c) of this question for clarity and quality of presentation. **(2 marks)**

Handwritten note (bottom): $\dfrac{\text{profit before tax + interest}}{\text{interest.}}$

(Total = 25 marks)

47 Operating segments   49 mins

Parts (a) and (b) adapted from P2 December 2011, part (c) adapted from P2 June 2010

Accell and Velocity both have queries regarding operating segments.

The following exhibits provide information relevant to the question.

Exhibit 1 - Accell

Accell has three distinct business segments. Management has calculated the net assets, revenue and profit before common costs, which are to be allocated to these segments. However, they are unsure as to how they should allocate certain common costs and whether they can exercise judgement in the allocation process. They wish to allocate head office management expenses; pension expense; the cost of managing properties and interest and related interest-bearing assets. They also are uncertain as to whether the allocation of costs has to conform to the accounting policies used in the financial statements.

Exhibit 2 - Velocity

For the year ended 31 March 20X3, the directors of Velocity, a public limited company operating in the transport sector, identified the following operating segments.

1   Segment 1 local train operations
2   Segment 2 inter-city train operations
3   Segment 3 railway constructions

The finance director has determined that segments 1 and 2 should be aggregated into a single reportable operating segment on the basis of their similar business characteristics, and the nature of their products and services.

The characteristics of each market are as follows:

•   Local train market: the local transport authority awards the contract and pays Velocity for its services; contracts are awarded following a competitive tender process; the ticket prices paid by passengers are set by and paid to the transport authority.

•   Inter-city train market: ticket prices are set by Velocity and the passengers pay Velocity for the service provided.

The managing director is pleased about this as segment 1 has seen a sharp decline in profits during the year, whereas segment 2 has shown improved margins. The managing director doesn't believe that segment information is relevant to investors, he believes that investors simply provide funds and aren't interested in how management derives a return from them.

Required

(a)   Advise the management of Accell on the issues raised in Exhibit 1.   (7 marks)

(b)   (i)   In relation to Velocity in Exhibit 2, discuss whether it is appropriate to aggregate
                 segments 1 and 2 with reference to IFRS 8 *Operating Segments*.   (4 marks)

        (ii)   Discuss, with reference to Velocity, whether the disclosure of segment information is
                 relevant to an investor's appraisal of the financial statements and comment on the
                 managing director's opinion that investors are not interested in how management
                 derives a return from their investment.   (4 marks)

(c)   Explain the factors which encourage companies to disclose social and environmental
        information in their financial statements, briefly discussing whether the content of such
        disclosure should be at the company's discretion.   (8 marks)

Professional marks will be awarded in this question.   (2 marks)

Note. You are not required to refer to any exhibit to answer part (c).

                                                                            (Total = 25 marks)

BPP
LEARNING
MEDIA

48 Cloud   49 mins

P2 December 2015 (amended)

(a)   IAS 1 *Presentation of Financial Statements* defines profit or loss and other comprehensive income. The purpose of the statement of profit or loss and other comprehensive income (OCI) is to show an entity's financial performance in a way which is useful to a wide range of users so that they may attempt to assess the future net cash inflows of an entity. The statement should be classified and aggregated in a manner which makes it understandable and comparable. However, the International Integrated Reporting Council (IIRC) is calling for a shift in thinking more to the long term, to think beyond what can be measured in quantitative terms and to think about how the entity creates value for its owners. Historical financial statements are essential in corporate reporting, particularly for compliance purposes, but it can be argued that they do not provide meaningful information. Preparers of financial statements seem to be unclear about the interaction between profit or loss and OCI especially regarding the notion of reclassification, but are equally uncertain about whether the IIRC's *International Integrated Reporting Framework* (<IR> Framework) constitutes suitable criteria for report preparation.

   Required

   (i)   Describe the current presentation requirements relating to the statement of profit or loss and OCI and discuss the issues surrounding the conceptual basis for the distinction between profit and loss and OCI. Your answer should refer to the requirements of IAS 1 and to the *Conceptual Framework*.   **(6 marks)**

   (ii)   Discuss, with examples, the nature of a reclassification adjustment, any issues surrounding the conceptual basis for reclassification and the arguments for and against allowing reclassification of items from OCI to profit or loss. Your answer should refer to the *Conceptual Framework*.   **(5 marks)**

   (iii) Discuss the principles and key components of the IIRC's *International Integrated Reporting Framework*, and any concerns which could question the <IR> Framework's suitability for assessing the prospects of an entity.   **(8 marks)**

(b)   Cloud, a public limited company, regularly purchases steel from a foreign supplier and designates a future purchase of steel as a hedged item in a cash flow hedge. The steel was purchased on 1 May 20X4 and at that date, a cumulative gain on the hedging instrument of $3 million had been credited to other comprehensive income. At the year end of 30 April 20X5, the carrying amount of the steel was $8 million and its net realisable value was $6 million. The steel was finally sold on 3 June 20X5 for $6.2 million. On a separate issue, Cloud purchased an item of property, plant and equipment for $10 million on 1 May 20X3. The asset is depreciated over five years on the straight-line basis with no residual value. At 30 April 20X4, the asset was revalued to $12 million. At 30 April 20X5, the asset's value has fallen to $4 million. The entity makes a transfer from revaluation surplus to retained earnings for excess depreciation, as the asset is used.

   Required

   Show how the above transactions would be dealt with in the financial statements of Cloud from the date of the purchase of the assets.

   Note. Ignore any deferred taxation effects.   **(6 marks)**

                                                              (Total = 25 marks)

49 Leria Co   49 mins

SBR March 2020

Leria Co is an internationally successful football club. Leria Co is preparing the financial statements for the year ending 31 October 20X5 but is currently facing liquidity problems.

The following exhibits provide information relevant to the question.

Exhibit 1 - Stadium sale/leaseback and improvements

Leria Co has entered into a contract regarding its stadium whereby it will sell the stadium on 30 November 20X6 and immediately lease it back. The directors of Leria Co wish to classify the stadium as a non-current asset 'held for sale' in its financial statements for the year ended 31 October 20X5 as they believe the sale to be highly probable at that date. The sale contract requires the disposal of the stadium for its fair value (market value) of $30 million and for Leria Co to lease it back over 10 years. The present value of the lease payments at market rates on 30 November 20X6 will be $26 million. The market value for a stadium of this type has not changed in several years and is unlikely to change in the near future. The stadium is being depreciated by 5% per annum using the reducing balance method.

In the year to 31 October 20X6, it is anticipated that $2 million will be spent to improve the crowd barriers in the stadium. There is no legal requirement to improve the crowd barriers. Leria Co has incorrectly treated this amount as a reduction of the asset's carrying amount at 31 October 20X5 and the corresponding debit has been made to profit or loss. At 31 October 20X5, the carrying amount of the stadium, after depreciation and deduction of the crowd barrier improvements, is $18 million.

Exhibit 2 - Television programme content rights

Leria Co has its own subscription-based television station. As a result, it has material intangible assets which relate to the content rights associated with the television programmes. The budgeted costs of production are based on the estimated future revenues for the television programme. These costs of production are then capitalised as an intangible asset and called 'contents rights'. The directors of Leria Co believe that the intellectual property in the content rights is consumed as customers view the television programmes. Consequently, Leria Co currently amortises the content rights based upon estimated future revenues from the television programme. For example, if a television programme is expected to generate $8 million of revenue in total and $4 million of that revenue is generated in year 1, then the intangible asset will be amortised by 50% in year 1. However, the industry practice is to amortise the capitalised cost of the programme, less its recoverable amount, over its remaining useful life.

Exhibit 3 - Players' contract costs

Players' registration contract costs are shown as intangible assets and are initially recognised at the fair value of the consideration paid for their acquisition. However, subsequently, players' contracts are often re-negotiated at a cost. Also, players' contracts may contain contingent performance conditions where individual players may be paid a bonus based on their success in terms of goals scored or the success of the football team as a whole. These bonuses represent additional contract costs.

For impairment purposes, Leria Co does not consider that it is possible to determine the value-in-use of an individual player unless the player were to suffer a career threatening injury and cannot play in the team. Players only generate direct cash flows when they are sold to another football club.

Required

(a)   Discuss with reference to International Financial Reporting Standards (IFRS):

   (i)   Whether the directors can classify the stadium as held for sale at 31 October 20X5;

   (ii)   Leria Co's accounting treatment of the crowd barrier improvements at 31 October 20X5; and

   (iii)   The principles of the accounting treatment for the sale and leaseback of the stadium at 30 November 20X6.   (13 marks)

(b)   Discuss:

   (i)   Whether the amortisation of the intangible assets relating to television programme content rights by Leria Co and by the industry are acceptable policies in accordance with IFRS standards; and

   (ii)   How to account for the players' contract costs (including the contingent performance conditions), any impairment which might be required to these non-current assets and whether a player can be considered a single cash generating unit.   (12 marks)

(Total = 25 marks)

50 Corbel Co

49 mins

SBR September/December 2020

Corbel Co trades in the perfume sector. It has recently acquired a company for its brand 'Jengi', purchased two additional brand names, and has announced plans to close its Italian stores. Corbel Co also opened a new store on a prime site in Paris. The current financial year end is 31 December 20X7.

The following exhibits provide information relevant to the question.

Exhibit 1 - Acquisition of Jengi Co

[margin note: Probable future economic benefits.]

On 1 January 20X7, Corbel Co acquired 100% of Jengi Co. Both companies operate in the perfume sector. Corbel Co intends to merge the manufacture of Jengi Co's products into its own facilities and close Jengi Co's manufacturing unit. Jengi Co's brand name is well known in the sector, retailing at premium prices, and therefore, Corbel Co will continue to sell products under the Jengi brand name after its registration has been transferred and its manufacturing units have been integrated. The directors of Corbel Co believe that most of the value of Jengi Co was derived from the brand and there is no indication of the impairment of the brand at 31 December 20X7.

[margin note: in group accounts Show separately if it has a FV.]

[handwritten: → integrated suggests not a separate CGU.]

Exhibit 2 - Acquisition of perfume brands

In addition to now owning the Jengi Co brand, Corbel Co has acquired two other perfume brand names to prevent rival companies acquiring them. The first perfume (Locust) has been sold successfully for many years and has an established market. The second is a new perfume which has been named after a famous actor (Clara) who intends to promote the product. The directors of Corbel Co believe that the two perfume brand names have an indefinite life.

[margin note: could have an indefinite life.]

Exhibit 3 - Plan to close and sell stores

[handwritten: likely finite ~~indeterminate~~.]

Corbel Co approved and announced a plan to close and sell all six Italian stores on 31 December 20X7. The six stores will close after a liquidation sale which will last for three months. Management has committed to a formal plan for the closure of the six stores and has also started an active search for a single buyer for their assets. The stores are being closed because of the increased demand generated by Corbel Co's internet sales.

A local newspaper has written an article suggesting that up to 30 stores may be closed with a loss of 500 jobs across the world, over the next five years. The directors of Corbel have denied that this is the case.

[handwritten: provision]

[margin note: discontinued operations / held for sale.]

Exhibit 4 - Corbel Co's primary store

Corbel Co's primary store is located in central Paris. It has only recently been opened at a significant cost with the result that management believes it will make a loss in the current financial year to 31 December 20X7. This loss-making is not of concern as the performance is consistent with expectations for such a new and expensive store and management believes that the new store will have a positive effect on Corbel Co's brand image.

If impairment testing of the primary store were to be required, then Corbel Co would include the cash flows from all internet sales in this assessment. The goods sold via the internet are sourced from either Corbel Co's central distribution centre or individual stores. Internet sales are either delivered to the customer's home or collected by the customer from the store supplying the goods.

[handwritten notes:]
Impairment indicators.
- performance is not a concern as it is in line with expectations, even though it is loss making.
- no other clear indicators.

value - difficult to value. e.g - brands are unique so difficult to obtain an accurate market value.

→ must be identifiable
↳ e.g. internally generated brands not recognised as not separable.

Required

(a) Describe the main <u>challenges</u> in recognising and measuring intangible assets, such as <u>brands</u>, in the statement of financial position. (5 marks)

(b) Discuss the following accounting issues relating to Corbel Co's financial statements for the year ended 31 December 20X7 in accordance with IFRS standards:

yes. →

(i) Whether the Jengi Co brand name will be accounted for separately from goodwill on acquisition and whether it should be accounted for as a separate cash generating unit after the integration of the manufacturing units; *— write what a CGU is.* (4 marks)

(ii) How to account for intangible assets with an indefinite life and whether the Locust and Clara perfume brand names can be regarded as having an indefinite life; (6 marks)

(iii) How to account for the proposed closure of the six stores and the suggested closure of the remaining stores; and (6 marks)

(iv) Whether the primary store should be tested for impairment at 31 December 20X7 and whether the internet sales can be attributed to this store. (4 marks)

Impairment
test - loss = RA < CA.

→ unethical - manipulation of the accounts to attribute internet sales to this store.

(Total = 25 marks)

51 Fill

49 mins

Fill is a coal mining company that sells its coal on the spot and futures markets.

The following exhibits provide information relevant to the question.

Exhibit 1 - Coal inventory

On the spot market, the coal is traded for immediate delivery and, on the forward market, the coal is traded for future delivery. The inventory is divided into different grades of coal. One of the categories included in inventories at 30 November 20X6 is coal with a low carbon content that is of a low quality. Fill will not process this low quality coal until all of the other coal has been extracted from the mine, which is likely to be in three years' time. Based on market information, Fill has calculated that the three-year forecast price of coal will be 20% lower than the current spot price.

Exhibit 2 - PPE reconditioning costs

At 30 November 20X6, the directors of Fill estimate that a piece of mining equipment needs to be reconditioned every two years. They estimate that these costs will amount to $2 million for parts and $1 million for the labour cost of their own employees. The directors are proposing to create a provision for the next reconditioning which is due in two years' time in 20X8, along with essential maintenance costs. There is no legal obligation to maintain the mining equipment.

As explained in Exhibit 1, it is expected that there will be future reductions in the selling prices of coal which will affect the forward contracts being signed over the next two years by Fill.

Exhibit 3 - The Theta mine

Fill also jointly controls coal mines with other entities. The Theta mine is owned by four participants. Fill owns 28%, and the other three participants each own 24% of the mine. The operating agreement requires any major decisions to be approved by parties representing 72% of the interest in the mine. Fill is considering purchasing one of the participant's interests of 24%.

Required

Advise the directors of Fill on how the following should be dealt with in its financial statements with reference to relevant IFRS Standards and the *Conceptual Framework* where indicated:

(a) Whether the *Conceptual Framework* affects the valuation of inventories and how to calculate the net realisable value of the coal inventory, including the low quality coal. (7 marks)

BPP
LEARNING
MEDIA

(b)   How to treat the reconditioning costs and whether the decline in the price of coal is an impairment indicator. (8 marks)

(c)   Whether the *Conceptual Framework* will affect the decision as to whether Fill controls the mine and whether the acquisition of the interest would be considered a business combination under IFRS Standards. (10 marks)

(Total = 25 marks)

52 Zedtech

49 mins

determine distinct performance obligations:

SBR Mar/Jun 2019 (amended)

Zedtech Co is a software development company which provides data hosting and other professional services. As part of these services, Zedtech Co also securely hosts a range of inventory management software online which allows businesses to manage inventory from anywhere in the world. It also sells hardware in certain circumstances. Zedtech Co sells two distinct software packages: (i) 0inventory and (ii) InventoryX.

The following exhibits provide information relevant to the question.

Exhibit 1 - 0inventory and InventoryX

③ *distinct performance obligations*

Zedtech sells two distinct software packages. The first package, named 0inventory, gives the customer the option to buy the hardware, professional services and hosting services as separate and distinct contracts. Each element of the package can be purchased without affecting the performance of any other element. Zedtech regularly sells each service separately and generally does not integrate the goods and services into a single contract.

hardware and hosting combined revenue recognised together ② *distinct performance obligations.*

With the second package, InventoryX, the hardware is always sold along with the professional and hosting services and the customer cannot use the hardware on its own. The hardware is integral to the delivery of the hosted software. Zedtech delivers the hardware first, followed by professional services and finally, the hosting services. However, the professional services can be sold on a stand-alone basis as this is a distinct service which Zedtech can offer any customer.

Exhibit 2 - New customer ↘*distinct*

Zedtech has decided to sell its services in a new region of the world which is suffering an economic downturn. The entity expects the economy to recover and feels that there is scope for significant growth in future years. Zedtech has entered into an arrangement with a customer in this region for promised consideration of $3 million. At contract inception, Zedtech feels that it may not be able to collect the full amount from the customer and estimates that it may collect 80% of the consideration.

Required

(a)   In the revised 2018 *Conceptual Framework for Financial Reporting* (the *Conceptual Framework*), the accounting model is built on the definitions and principles for the recognition of assets and liabilities.

The 2010 *Conceptual Framework* specified three recognition criteria which apply to all assets and liabilities:

1   the item meets the definition of an asset or a liability; *Same as 2018*

different in new framework

2   it is probable that any future economic benefit associated with the asset or liability will flow to or from the entity; and

3   the asset or liability has a cost or value which can be measured reliably.

However, these definitions were not always consistently applied by the standard setters. The result is that many existing IFRS Standards are inconsistent with the 2010 *Conceptual Framework*.

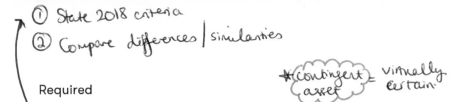

Handwritten annotations at top:
① State 2018 criteria
② Compare differences / similarities

Handwritten: *(contingent asset)* = virtually certain

Required

(i) Discuss and contrast the criteria for the recognition of assets and liabilities as set out in the 2018 *Conceptual Framework* and its predecessor, the 2010 *Conceptual Framework* (given above). *e.g. insurance claim.* **(7 marks)** *Deferred tax asset – probable future profit.*

(ii) Discuss how the recognition of assets and liabilities under IAS 12 *Income Taxes* and IAS 37 *Provisions, Contingent Liabilities and Contingent Assets* are both inconsistent with the definitions in the 2010 *Conceptual Framework* and how certain items recognised in a business combination may not be recognised in the individual financial statements of the group companies. **(6 marks)**

Handwritten left margin: > Contingent liabilities ↓ individual FS ↓ disclosed in a note, no dr/cr.

Handwritten: group ↓ liability is recognised.

Note: you do not need to refer to any exhibit to answer part (a).

(b) (i) Discuss the principles in IFRS 15 *Revenue from Contracts with Customers* which should be used by Zedtech to determine the recognition of its contracts. **(5 marks)**

(ii) Discuss how the sale of both types of inventory and the contract with the new customer should be recognised in the financial statements of Zedtech in accordance with IFRS 15. **(7 marks)**

(Total = 25 marks)

53 Kayte   49 mins

Part (a) SBR December 2018 (amended), Part (b) adapted from P2 December 2014

Kayte has a year end of 31 May. It operates in the shipping industry and owns vessels for transportation.

The following exhibits provide information relevant to the question.

Exhibit 1 - Vessels

Kayte's vessels constitute a material part of its total assets. The economic life of the vessels is estimated to be 30 years, but the useful life of some of the vessels is only 10 years because Kayte's policy is to sell these vessels when they are 10 years old. Kayte estimated the residual value of these vessels at sale to be half of acquisition cost and this value was assumed to be constant during their useful life. Kayte argued that the estimates of residual value used were conservative in view of an immature market with a high degree of uncertainty and presented documentation which indicated some vessels were being sold for a price considerably above carrying amount. Broker valuations of the residual value were considerably higher than those used by Kayte. Kayte argued against broker valuations on the grounds that it would result in greater volatility in reporting.

Kayte keeps some of the vessels for the whole 30 years and these vessels are required to undergo an engine overhaul in dry dock every 10 years to restore their service potential, hence the reason why some of the vessels are sold. The residual value of the vessels kept for 30 years is based upon the steel value of the vessel at the end of its economic life. At the time of purchase, the service potential which will be required to be restored by the engine overhaul is measured based on the cost as if it had been performed at the time of the purchase of the vessel. Normally, engines last for the 30-year total life if overhauled every 10 years. Additionally, one type of vessel was having its funnels replaced after 15 years, but the funnels had not been depreciated separately.

Exhibit 2 - Property

On 1 June 20X1, Kayte acquired a property for $5 million and annual depreciation of $500,000 is charged on the straight-line basis with no residual value. At 31 May 20X3, when accumulated depreciation was $1 million, an impairment loss of $350,000 was recognised, which resulted in the property being valued at its estimated value in use. On 1 October 20X3, as a consequence of a proposed move to new premises, the property was classified as held for sale. At the time of classification as held for sale, the fair value less costs to sell was $3.4 million. At the date of the published interim financial statements, 30 November 20X3, the property market had improved and the fair value less costs to sell was reassessed at $3.52 million and at the year end on 31 May

20X4 it had improved even further, so that the fair value less costs to sell was $3.95 million. The property was sold on 5 June 20X4 for $4 million.

Required

(a)   The 2010 *Conceptual Framework for Financial Reporting* included a probability criterion which specified that in order for an asset or liability to qualify for recognition, it must be probable that any future economic benefit associated with an asset or liability will flow to or from an entity.

Some current accounting standards, which were developed under the 2010 *Conceptual Framework*, have been criticised for not necessarily applying the probability criterion relating to future economic benefits on a consistent basis.

The IASB issued a significantly revised *Conceptual Framework* in 2018. The recognition criteria in the 2018 *Conceptual Framework* no longer include a probability criterion.

Required

Explain how the probability criterion in the 2010 *Conceptual Framework* has not been applied consistently across accounting standards, illustrating your answer with reference to any inconsistencies with the measurement of assets held for sale, provisions and contingent consideration, and discuss how the revised 2018 *Conceptual Framework* may address this issue.   (6 marks)

(b)   (i)   Discuss the financial reporting treatment required by IFRS Standards in the financial statements of Kayte of the issue contained in Exhibit 1.   (12 marks)

       (ii)   Discuss the financial reporting treatment required by IFRS Standards in the financial statements of Kayte of the issue in Exhibit 2.   (7 marks)

(Total = 25 marks)

54 Pensions   49 mins

Part (a) adapted from P2 December 2007, Part (b) adapted from P2 June 2012

(a)   Joydan

Joydan, a public limited company, is a leading support services company which focuses on the building industry. The company would like advice on how to treat certain items under IAS 19 *Employee Benefits*. The company operates the Joydan Pension Plan B which commenced on 1 November 20X6 and the Joydan Pension Plan A, which was closed to new entrants from 31 October 20X6, but which was open to future service accrual for the employees already in the scheme. The assets of the schemes are held separately from those of the company in funds under the control of trustees. The following information relates to the two schemes.

Joydan Pension Plan A

The terms of the plan are as follows.

(i)   Employees contribute 6% of their salaries to the plan.

(ii)   Joydan contributes, currently, the same amount to the plan for the benefit of the employees.

(iii)   On retirement, employees are guaranteed a pension which is based upon the number of years' service with the company and their final salary.

The following details relate to the plan in the year to 31 October 20X7:

	$m
Present value of obligation at 1 November 20X6	200
Present value of obligation at 31 October 20X7	240
Fair value of plan assets at 1 November 20X6	190
Fair value of plan assets at 31 October 20X7	225
Current service cost	20
Pension benefits paid	19
Total contributions paid to the scheme for year to 31 October 20X7	17

Remeasurement gains and losses are recognised in accordance with IAS 19.

Assume that contributions are paid into the plan and pension benefits are withdrawn from the plan on 31 October 20X7.

Joydan Pension Plan B

Under the terms of the plan, Joydan does not guarantee any return on the contributions paid into the fund. The company's legal and constructive obligation is limited to the amount that is contributed to the fund. The following details relate to this scheme:

	$m
Fair value of plan assets at 31 October 20X7	21
Contributions paid by company for year to 31 October 20X7	10
Contributions paid by employees for year to 31 October 20X7	10

The interest rate on high quality corporate bonds for the two plans are:

1 November 20X6	31 October 20X7
5%	6%

The company would like advice on how to treat the two pension plans, for the year ended 31 October 20X7, together with an explanation of the differences between a defined contribution plan and a defined benefit plan.

Required

Prepare a briefing note for the directors of Joydan which includes:

(i)   An explanation of the nature of and differences between a defined contribution plan and a defined benefit plan with specific reference to the company's two schemes.

(8 marks)

(ii)   The accounting treatment for the two Joydan pension plans for the year ended 31 October 20X7 under IAS 19 *Employee Benefits*. (9 marks)

(b)   **William**

William operates a defined benefit pension plan for its employees. Shortly before the year end of 31 May 20X3, William decided to relocate a division from one country to another, where labour and raw material costs are cheaper. The relocation is due to take place in December 20X3. On 13 May 20X3, a detailed formal plan was approved by the board of directors. Half of the affected division's employees will be made redundant in July 20X3, and will accrue no further benefits under William's defined benefit pension plan. The affected employees were informed of this decision on 14 May 20X3. The resulting reduction in the net pension liability due the relocation is estimated to have a present value of $15 million as at 31 May 20X3. Total relocation costs (excluding the impact on the pension plan) are estimated at $50 million.

Required

Advise the directors of William on how to account for the relocation costs and the reduction in the net pension liability for the year ended 31 May 20X3. (8 marks)

(Total = 25 marks)

55 Emcee   49 mins

P2 Mar/Jun 2016 (amended)

Emcee, a public limited company, is a sports organisation which owns several football and basketball teams. It has a financial year end of 31 May 20X6.

(a)   Emcee needs a new stadium to host sporting events which will be included as part of Emcee's property, plant and equipment. Emcee commenced construction of a new stadium on 1 February 20X6, and this continued until its completion which was after the year end of 31 May 20X6. The direct costs were $20 million in February 20X6 and then $50 million in each month until the year end. Emcee has not taken out any specific borrowings to finance the construction of the stadium, but it has incurred finance costs on its general borrowings during the period, which could have been avoided if the stadium had not been constructed. Emcee has calculated that the weighted average cost of borrowings for the period 1 February to 31 May 20X6 on an annualised basis amounted to 9% per annum. Emcee needs advice on how to treat the borrowing costs in its financial statements for the year ended 31 May 20X6.   (6 marks)

(b)   Emcee purchases and sells players' registrations on a regular basis. Emcee must purchase registrations for that player to play for the club. Player registrations are contractual obligations between the player and Emcee. The costs of acquiring player registrations include transfer fees, league levy fees, and player agents' fees incurred by the club. Often players' former clubs are paid amounts which are contingent upon the performance of the player whilst they play for Emcee. For example, if a contracted basketball player scores an average of more than 20 points per game in a season, then an additional $5 million may become payable to his former club. Also, players' contracts can be extended and this incurs additional costs for Emcee.

At the end of every season, which also is the financial year end of Emcee, the club reviews its playing staff and makes decisions as to whether they wish to sell any players' registrations. These registrations are actively marketed by circulating other clubs with a list of players' registrations and their estimated selling price. Players' registrations are also sold during the season, often with performance conditions attached. Occasionally, it becomes clear that a player will not play for the club again because of, for example, a player sustaining a career threatening injury or being permanently removed from the playing squad for another reason. The playing registrations of certain players were sold after the year end, for total proceeds, net of associated costs, of $25 million. These registrations had a net book value of $7 million.

Emcee would like to know the financial reporting treatment of the acquisition, extension, review and sale of players' registrations in the circumstances outlined above.   (11 marks)

(c)   Emcee uses the revaluation model to measure its stadiums. The directors have been offered $100 million from an airline for the property naming rights of all the stadiums for three years. There are two directors who are on the management boards of Emcee and the airline. Additionally, there are regulations in place by both the football and basketball leagues which regulate the financing of the clubs. These regulations prevent capital contributions from a related party which 'increases equity without repayment in return'. The aim of these regulations is to promote sustainable business models. Sanctions imposed by the regulator include fines and withholding of prize monies. Emcee wishes to know how to take account of the naming rights in the valuation of the stadium and the potential implications of the financial regulations imposed by the leagues.   (8 marks)

Required

Discuss how the above events would be shown in the financial statements of Emcee under IFRS Standards.

Note. The mark allocation is shown against each of the three issues above.

(Total = 25 marks)

56 Estoil   49 mins

P2 December 2014 (amended)

(a)   An assessment of accounting practices for asset impairments is especially important in the context of financial reporting quality in that it requires the exercise of considerable management judgement and reporting discretion. The importance of this issue is heightened during periods of ongoing economic uncertainty as a result of the need for companies to reflect the loss of economic value in a timely fashion through the mechanism of asset write-downs. There are many factors which can affect the quality of impairment accounting and disclosures. These factors include changes in circumstance in the reporting period, the market capitalisation of the entity, the allocation of goodwill to cash-generating units, valuation issues and the nature of the disclosures.

Required

Discuss the importance and significance of the above factors when conducting an impairment test under IAS 36 *Impairment of Assets*.   **(15 marks)**

(b)   (i)   Estoil is an international company providing parts for the automotive industry. It operates in many different jurisdictions with different currencies. During 20X4, Estoil experienced financial difficulties marked by a decline in revenue, a reorganisation and restructuring of the business and it reported a loss for the year. An impairment test of goodwill was performed but no impairment was recognised. Estoil applied one discount rate to all cash flows for all cash-generating units (CGUs), irrespective of the currency in which the cash flows would be generated. The discount rate used was the weighted average cost of capital (WACC) and Estoil used the ten-year government bond rate for its jurisdiction as the risk-free rate in this calculation. Additionally, Estoil built its model using a forecast denominated in the functional currency of the parent company. Estoil felt that any other approach would require a level of detail which was unrealistic and impracticable. Estoil argued that the different CGUs represented different risk profiles in the short term, but over a longer business cycle, there was no basis for claiming that their risk profiles were different.

      (ii)   Fariole specialises in the communications sector with three main CGUs. Goodwill was a significant component of total assets. Fariole performed an impairment test of the CGUs. The cash flow projections were based on the most recent financial budgets approved by management. The realised cash flows for the CGUs were negative in 20X4 and far below budgeted cash flows for that period. The directors had significantly raised cash flow forecasts for 20X5 with little justification. The projected cash flows were calculated by adding back depreciation charges to the budgeted result for the period with expected changes in working capital and capital expenditure not taken into account.

Required

Discuss the acceptability of the above accounting practices under IAS 36 *Impairment of Assets*.   **(10 marks)**

(Total = 25 marks)

57 Evolve   49 mins

P2 Sep/Dec 2016 (amended)

(a)   Evolve is a real estate company, which is listed on the stock exchange and has a year end of 31 August. On 21 August 20X6, Evolve undertook a scrip (bonus) issue where the shareholders of Evolve received certain rights. The shareholders are able to choose between:

        (i)   Receiving newly issued shares of Evolve, which could be traded on 30 September 20X6; or

        (ii)   Transferring their rights back to Evolve by 10 September 20X6 for a fixed cash price which would be paid on 20 September 20X6.

In the financial statements at 31 August 20X6, Evolve believed that the criteria for the recognition of a financial liability as regards the second option were not met at 31 August 20X6 because it was impossible to reliably determine the full amount to be paid, until 10 September 20X6. Evolve felt that the transferring of the rights back to Evolve was a put option on its own equity, which would lead to recording changes in fair value in profit or loss in the next financial year. Evolve disclosed the transaction as a non-adjusting event after the reporting period. (9 marks)

(b) At 31 August 20X6, Evolve controlled a wholly owned subsidiary, Resource, whose only assets were land and buildings, which were all measured in accordance with IFRS Standards. On 1 August 20X6, Evolve published a statement stating that a binding offer for the sale of Resource had been made and accepted and, at that date, the sale was expected to be completed by 31 August 20X6. The non-current assets of Resource were measured at the lower of their carrying amount or fair value less costs to sell at 31 August 20X6, based on the selling price in the binding offer. This measurement was in accordance with IFRS 5 *Non-Current Assets Held for Sale and Discontinued Operations*. However, Evolve did not classify the non-current assets of Resource as held for sale in the financial statements at 31 August 20X6 because there were uncertainties regarding the negotiations with the buyer and a risk that the agreement would not be finalised. There was no disclosure of these uncertainties and the original agreement was finalised on 20 September 20X6. (10 marks)

(c) Evolve operates in a jurisdiction with a specific tax regime for listed real estate companies. Upon adoption of this tax regime, the entity has to pay a single tax payment based on the unrealised gains of its investment properties. Evolve purchased Monk whose only asset was an investment property for $10 million. The purchase price of Monk was below the market value of the investment property, which was $14 million, and Evolve chose to account for the investment property under the cost model. However, Evolve considered that the transaction constituted a 'bargain purchase' under IFRS 3 *Business Combinations*. As a result, Evolve accounted for the potential gain of $4 million in profit or loss and increased the 'cost' of the investment property to $14 million. At the same time, Evolve opted for the specific tax regime for the newly acquired investment property and agreed to pay the corresponding tax of $1 million. Evolve considered that the tax payment qualifies as an expenditure necessary to bring the property to the condition necessary for its operations, and therefore was directly attributable to the acquisition of the property. Hence, the tax payment was capitalised and the value of the investment property was stated at $15 million. (6 marks)

Required

Advise Evolve on how the above transactions should be correctly dealt with in its financial statements with reference to relevant IFRS Standards.

Note. The mark allocation is shown against each of the three issues above.

(Total = 25 marks)

58 Gasnature   49 mins

P2 Sep/Dec 2015 (amended)

(a) Gasnature is a publicly traded entity involved in the production and trading of natural gas and oil. Gasnature jointly owns an underground storage facility with another entity, Gogas. Both parties extract gas from offshore gas fields, which they own and operate independently from each other. Gasnature owns 55% of the underground facility and Gogas owns 45%. They have agreed to share services and costs accordingly, with decisions regarding the storage facility requiring unanimous agreement of the parties. The underground facility is pressurised so that the gas is pushed out when extracted. When the gas pressure is reduced to a certain level, the remaining gas is irrecoverable and remains in the underground storage facility until it is decommissioned. Local legislation requires the decommissioning of the storage facility at the end of its useful life. Gasnature wishes to know how to treat the agreement with Gogas including any obligation or possible obligation arising on the underground storage facility and the accounting for the irrecoverable gas. (9 marks)

(b) Gasnature has entered into a ten-year contract with Agas for the purchase of natural gas. Gasnature has made an advance payment to Agas for an amount equal to the total quantity of gas contracted for ten years which has been calculated using the forecasted price of gas. The advance carries interest of 6% per annum, which is settled by way of the supply of extra gas. Fixed quantities of gas have to be supplied each month and there is a price adjustment mechanism in the contract whereby the difference between the forecasted price of gas and the prevailing market price is settled in cash monthly. If Agas does not deliver gas as agreed, Gasnature has the right to claim compensation at the current market price of gas. Gasnature wishes to know whether the contract with Agas should be accounted for under IFRS 9 *Financial Instruments*. (6 marks)

(c) Additionally, Gasnature is finalising its financial statements for the year ended 31 August 20X5 and has the following issues.

(i) Gasnature purchased a major refinery on 1 January 20X5 and the directors estimate that a major overhaul is required every two years. The costs of the overhaul are approximately $5 million which comprises $3 million for parts and equipment and $2 million for labour. The directors proposed to accrue the cost of the overhaul over the two years of operations up to that date and create a provision for the expenditure. (5 marks)

(ii) From October 20X4, Gasnature had undertaken exploratory drilling to find gas and up to 31 August 20X5 costs of $5 million had been incurred. At 31 August 20X5, the results to date indicated that it was probable that there were sufficient economic benefits to carry on drilling and there were no indicators of impairment. During September 20X5, additional drilling costs of $2 million were incurred and there was significant evidence that no commercial deposits existed and the drilling was abandoned. (5 marks)

Required

Discuss, with reference to IFRS Standards, how Gasnature should account for the above agreement and contract, and the issues raised by the directors

Note. The mark allocation is shown against each of the items above.

(Total = 25 marks)

59 Complexity   49 mins

Part (a) adapted from P2 December 2009

(a) Complexity borrowed $47 million on 1 December 20X4 when the market and effective interest rate was 5%. On 30 November 20X5, the company borrowed an additional $45 million when the current market and effective interest rate was 7.4%. Both financial liabilities are repayable on 30 November 20X9 and are single payment notes, whereby interest and capital are repaid on that date.

Complexity's creditworthiness has been worsening. It has entered into an interest rate swap agreement which acts as a hedge against a $2 million 2% bond issue which matures on 31 May 20X6. The directors of Complexity wish to know in which circumstances it can use hedge accounting. In particular, they need advice on hedge effectiveness and whether this can be calculated.

Required

(i) Discuss the accounting for the financial liabilities under IFRS 9 under the amortised cost method, and additionally using the fair value method as at 30 November 20X5. (6 marks)

(ii) Advise Complexity's directors as to the circumstances in which it can use hedge accounting and whether it can calculate hedge effectiveness. (9 marks)

(b)   The type and value of financial instruments that Complexity holds has increased in recent years which has resulted in increased disclosures regarding financial instruments in the financial statements. Complexity's reporting accountant is concerned that the users of the financial statements find financial instruments complicated and has argued that there is no point in providing detailed information in this area as the users will not understand the disclosures.

Required

(i)   Discuss, from the perspective of the users of financial statements, how the measurement of financial instruments under IFRS Standards can create confusion.

(6 marks)

(ii)   Discuss the reporting accountant's view that detailed disclosures in respect of financial instruments do not provide useful information to the users of financial statements.

(4 marks)

(Total = 25 marks)

60 Carsoon   49 mins

P2 Mar/Jun 2017 (amended)

Carsoon Co is a company which manufactures and retails motor vehicles. It also constructs premises for third parties. It has a year end of 28 February 20X7.

(a)   The entity enters into lease agreements with the public for its motor vehicles. The agreements are normally for a three-year period. The customer decides how to use the vehicle within certain contractual limitations. The maximum mileage per annum is specified at 10,000 miles without penalty. Carsoon is responsible for the maintenance of the vehicle and insists that the vehicle cannot be modified in any way. At the end of the three-year contract, the customer can purchase the vehicle at a price which will be above the market value, or alternatively hand it back to Carsoon. If the vehicle is returned, Carsoon will then sell the vehicle on to the public through one of its retail outlets. These sales of vehicles are treated as investing activities in the statement of cash flows.

        The directors of Carsoon wish to know how the leased vehicles should be accounted for, from the commencement of the lease to the final sale of the vehicle, in the financial statements including the statement of cash flows.   (9 marks)

(b)   On 1 March 20X6, Carsoon invested in a debt instrument with a fair value of $6 million and has assessed that the financial asset is aligned with the fair value through other comprehensive income business model. The instrument has an interest rate of 4% over a period of six years. The effective interest rate is also 4%. On 1 March 20X6, the debt instrument is not impaired in any way. During the year to 28 February 20X7, there was a change in interest rates and the fair value of the instrument seemed to be affected. The instrument was quoted in an active market at $5.3 million but the price based upon an in-house model showed that the fair value of the instrument was $5.5 million. This valuation was based upon the average change in value of a range of instruments across a number of jurisdictions.

        The directors of Carsoon felt that the instrument should be valued at $5.5 million and that this should be shown as a Level 1 measurement under IFRS 13 *Fair Value Measurement*. There has not been a significant increase in credit risk since 1 March 20X6, and expected credit losses should be measured at an amount equal to 12-month expected credit losses of $400,000. Carsoon sold the debt instrument on 1 March 20X7 for $5.3 million.

        The directors of Carsoon wish to know how to account for the debt instrument until its sale on 1 March 20X7.   (8 marks)

(c) Carsoon constructs retail vehicle outlets and enters into contracts with customers to construct buildings on their land. The contracts have standard terms, which include penalties payable by Carsoon if the contract is delayed, or payable by the customer, if Carsoon cannot gain access to the construction site.

Due to poor weather, one of the projects was delayed. As a result, Carsoon faced additional costs and contractual penalties. As Carsoon could not gain access to the construction site, the directors decided to make a counterclaim against the customer for the penalties and additional costs which Carsoon faced. Carsoon felt that because a counter claim had been made against the customer, the additional costs and penalties should not be included in contract costs but shown as a contingent liability. Carsoon has assessed the legal basis of the claim and feels it has enforceable rights.

In the year ended 28 February 20X7, Carsoon incurred general and administrative costs of $10 million, and costs relating to wasted materials of $5 million.

Additionally, during the year, Carsoon agreed to construct a storage facility on the same customer's land for $7 million at a cost of $5 million. The parties agreed to modify the contract to include the construction of the storage facility, which was completed during the current financial year. All of the additional costs relating to the above were capitalised as assets in the financial statements.

The directors of Carsoon wish to know how to account for the penalties, counter claim and additional costs in accordance with IFRS 15 *Revenue from Contracts with Customers*.

(8 marks)

Required

Advise Carsoon on how the above transactions should be dealt with in its financial statements with reference to relevant IFRS Standards.

Note. The mark allocation is shown against each of the three issues above.

(Total = 25 marks)

61 Leigh   49 mins

ACR June 2007 (amended)

(a) Leigh, a public limited company, purchased the whole of the share capital of Hash, a limited company, on 1 June 20X6. The whole of the share capital of Hash was formerly owned by the five directors of Hash and under the terms of the purchase agreement, the five directors were to receive a total of three million ordinary shares of $1 of Leigh on 1 June 20X6 (market value $6 million) and a further 5,000 shares per director on 31 May 20X7, if they were still employed by Leigh on that date. All of the directors were still employed by Leigh at 31 May 20X7.

Leigh granted and issued fully paid shares to its own employees on 31 May 20X7. Normally share options issued to employees would vest over a three-year period, but these shares were given as a bonus because of the company's exceptional performance over the period. The shares in Leigh had a market value of $3 million (one million ordinary shares of $1 at $3 per share) on 31 May 20X7 and an average fair value of $2.5 million (one million ordinary shares of $1 at $2.50 per share) for the year ended 31 May 20X7. It is expected that Leigh's share price will rise to $6 per share over the next three years.   Use FV   (10 marks)

(b) On 31 May 20X7, Leigh purchased property, plant and equipment for $4 million. The   Dr PPE 4m
supplier has agreed to accept payment for the property, plant and equipment either in cash or in shares. The supplier can either choose 1.5 million shares of Leigh to be issued in six months' time or to receive a cash payment in three months' time equivalent to the market value of 1.3 million shares. It is estimated that the share price will be $3.50 in three months' time and $4 in six months' time.

[handwritten annotations:]

Counter party has choice ←

need to do split accounting and recognise equity and liability. →

FV share alternative (not given) 4
FV cash alternative   1.3m shares × $3 ($3.9m) Cr liab
Equity   0.1m Cr 0.1m equity.

FV share alternative 50,000 × 2·50
FV cash alternative 40,000 × $3.   recognise expense
    equity   5,000.   for staff cost.

Share based
payment with
choice.
↓
Split accounting.
liability and equity.

Additionally, at 31 May 20X7, one of the directors recently appointed to the board has been granted the right to choose either 50,000 shares of Leigh or receive a cash payment equal to the current value of 40,000 shares at the settlement date. This right has been granted because of the performance of the director during the year and is unconditional at 31 May 20X7. The settlement date is 1 July 20X8 and the company estimates the fair value of the share alternative is $2.50 per share at 31 May 20X7. The share price of Leigh at 31 May 20X7 is $3 per share, and if the director chooses the share alternative, they must be kept for a period of four years.   (9 marks)

(c) Leigh acquired 30% of the ordinary share capital of Handy, a public limited company, on 1 April 20X6. The purchase consideration was one million ordinary shares of Leigh which had a market value of $2.50 per share at that date and the fair value of the net assets of Handy was $9 million. The retained earnings of Handy were $4 million and other reserves of Handy were $3 million at that date. Leigh appointed two directors to the Board of Handy, and it intends to hold the investment for a significant period of time. Leigh exerts significant influence over Handy. The summarised statement of financial position of Handy at 31 May 20X7 is as follows.

	$m
Share capital of $1	2
Other reserves	3
Retained earnings	5
	10
Net assets	10

There had been no new issues of shares by Handy since the acquisition by Leigh and the estimated recoverable amount of the net assets of Handy at 31 May 20X7 was $11 million.
                                    (6 marks)

Required

Discuss with suitable computations how the above share-based transactions should be accounted for in the financial statements of Leigh for the year ended 31 May 20X7.

                                    (Total = 25 marks)

62 Mehran   49 mins

P2 March/June 2016 (amended)

The directors of Mehran, a public limited company, have seen many different ways of dealing with the measurement and disclosure of the fair value of assets, liabilities and equity instruments. They feel that this reduces comparability among different entities' financial statements. They would like advice on how IFRS 13 *Fair Value Measurement* should be applied to several transactions.

(a) Mehran has just acquired a company, which comprises a farming and mining business. Mehran wishes advice on how to place a fair value on some of the assets acquired.

One such asset is a piece of land, which is currently used for farming. The fair value of the land if used for farming is $5 million. If the land is used for farming purposes, a tax credit arises annually, which is based upon the lower of 15% of the fair market value of land or $500,000 at the current tax rate. The current tax rate in the jurisdiction is 20%.

Mehran has determined that market participants would consider that the land could have an alternative use for residential purposes. The fair value of the land for residential purposes before associated costs is thought to be $7.4 million. In order to transform the land from farming to residential use, there would be legal costs of $200,000, a viability analysis cost of $300,000 and costs of demolition of the farm buildings of $100,000. Additionally, permission for residential use has not been formally given by the legal authority and because of this, market participants have indicated that the fair value of the land, after the above costs, would be discounted by 20% because of the risk of not obtaining planning permission.

In addition, Mehran has acquired the brand name associated with the produce from the farm. Mehran has decided to discontinue the brand on the assumption that it will gain increased revenues from its own brands. Mehran has determined that if it ceases to use the brand, then the indirect benefits will be $20 million. If it continues to use the brand, then the direct benefit will be $17 million.

(7 marks)

(b) Mehran wishes to place a fair value on the inventory of the entity acquired. There are three different markets for the produce, which are mainly vegetables. The first is the local domestic market where Mehran can sell direct to retailers of the produce. The second domestic market is one where Mehran sells directly to manufacturers of canned vegetables. There are no restrictions on the sale of produce in either of the domestic markets other than the demand of the retailers and manufacturers. The final market is the export market but the government limits the amount of produce which can be exported. Mehran needs a licence from the government to export its produce. Farmers tend to sell all of the produce that they can in the export market and, when they do not have any further authorisation to export, they sell the remaining produce in the two domestic markets.

It is difficult to obtain information on the volume of trade in the domestic market where the produce is sold locally direct to retailers but Mehran feels that the market is at least as large as the domestic market – direct to manufacturers. The volumes of sales quoted below have been taken from trade journals.

	Domestic market – direct to retailers	Domestic market – direct to manufacturers	Export market
Volume – annual	Unknown	20,000 tonnes	10,000 tonnes
Volume – sales per month	10 tonnes	4 tonnes	60 tonnes
Price per tonne	$1,000	$800	$1,200
Transport costs per tonne	$50	$70	$100
Selling agents' fees per tonne	–	$4	$6

(10 marks)

(c) Mehran owns a non-controlling equity interest in Erham, a private company, and wishes to measure the interest at its fair value at its financial year end of 31 March 20X6. Mehran acquired the ordinary share interest in Erham on 1 April 20X4. During the current financial year, Erham has issued further equity capital through the issue of preferred shares to a venture capital fund.

As a result of the preferred share issue, the venture capital fund now holds a controlling interest in Erham. The terms of the preferred shares, including the voting rights, are similar to those of the ordinary shares, except that the preferred shares have a cumulative fixed dividend entitlement for a period of four years and the preferred shares rank ahead of the ordinary shares upon the liquidation of Erham. The transaction price for the preferred shares was $15 per share.

Mehran wishes to know the factors which should be taken into account in measuring the fair value of their holding in the ordinary shares of Erham at 31 March 20X6 using a market-based approach.

(8 marks)

Required

Discuss the way in which Mehran should measure the fair value the above assets with reference to the principles of IFRS 13 Fair Value Measurement.

Note. The mark allocation is shown against each of the three issues above.

(Total = 25 marks)

63 Ethan

P2 December 2012 (amended)

Ethan, a public limited company, develops, operates and sells investment properties.

(a)   Ethan focuses mainly on acquiring properties where it foresees growth potential, through rental income as well as value appreciation. The acquisition of an investment property is usually realised through the acquisition of the entity, which holds the property.

In Ethan's consolidated financial statements, investment properties acquired through business combinations are recognised at fair value, using a discounted cash flow model as approximation to fair value. There is currently an active market for this type of property. The difference between the fair value of the investment property as determined under the accounting policy, and the value of the investment property for tax purposes results in a deferred tax liability.

Goodwill arising on business combinations is determined using the measurement principles for the investment properties as outlined above. Goodwill is only considered impaired if and when the deferred tax liability is reduced below the amount at which it was first recognised. This reduction can be caused both by a reduction in the value of the real estate or a change in local tax regulations. As long as the deferred tax liability is equal to, or larger than, the prior year, no impairment is charged to goodwill. Ethan explained its accounting treatment by confirming that almost all of its goodwill is due to the deferred tax liability and that it is normal in the industry to account for goodwill in this way.

Since 20X0, Ethan has incurred substantial annual losses except for the year ended 31 May 20X3, when it made a small profit before tax. In year ended 31 May 20X3, most of the profit consisted of income recognised on revaluation of investment properties. Ethan had announced early in its financial year ended 31 May 20X4 that it anticipated substantial growth and profit. Later in the year, however, Ethan announced that the expected profit would not be achieved and that, instead, a substantial loss would be incurred. Ethan had a history of reporting considerable negative variances from its budgeted results. Ethan's recognised deferred tax assets have been increasing year-on-year despite the deferred tax liabilities recognised on business combinations. Ethan's deferred tax assets consist primarily of unused tax losses that can be carried forward which are unlikely to be offset against anticipated future taxable profits.   **(13 marks)**

(b)   Ethan wishes to apply the fair value option rules of IFRS 9 *Financial Instruments* to debt issued to finance its investment properties. Ethan's argument for applying the fair value option is based upon the fact that the recognition of gains and losses on its investment properties and the related debt would otherwise be inconsistent. Ethan argued that there is a specific financial correlation between the factors, such as interest rates, that form the basis for determining the fair value of both Ethan's investment properties and the related debt.   **(7 marks)**

(c)   Ethan has an operating subsidiary, which has in issue A and B shares, both of which have voting rights. Ethan holds 70% of the A and B shares and the remainder are held by shareholders external to the group. The subsidiary is obliged to pay an annual dividend of 5% on the B shares. The dividend payment is cumulative even if the subsidiary does not have sufficient legally distributable profit at the time the payment is due.

In Ethan's consolidated statement of financial position, the B shares of the subsidiary were accounted for in the same way as equity instruments would be, with the B shares owned by external parties reported as a non-controlling interest.   **(5 marks)**

Required

Discuss how the above transactions and events should be recorded in the consolidated financial statements of Ethan.

Note. The mark allocation is shown against each of the three transactions above.

(Total = 25 marks)

82 Strategic Business Reporting (SBR)

BPP
LEARNING
MEDIA

64 Whitebirk

43 mins

P2 December 2010 (amended)

(a)   The main argument for separate accounting standards for small and medium-sized entities is the undue cost burden of reporting, which is proportionately heavier for smaller firms.

Required

Discuss the main differences and modifications to IFRS which the IASB made when it published the *IFRS for Small and Medium-Sized Entities* (IFRS for SMEs), giving specific examples where possible and include in your discussion how the Board has dealt with the problem of defining an SME.   (11 marks)

(b)   Whitebirk has met the definition of a SME in its jurisdiction and wishes to comply with the IFRS for SMEs. The entity wishes to seek advice on how it will deal with the following accounting issues in its financial statements for the year ended 30 November 20X2. The entity already prepares its financial statements under full IFRS Standards.

(i)   Whitebirk purchased 90% of Close, an SME, on 1 December 20X1. The purchase consideration was $5.7 million and the value of Close's identifiable assets was $6 million. Whitebirk has elected to measure the non-controlling interest at acquisition at its fair value of $0.7 million. The life of the goodwill cannot be estimated with any accuracy. Whitebirk wishes to know how to account for goodwill under the IFRS for SMEs.

(ii)   Whitebirk has incurred $1 million of research expenditure to develop a new product in the year to 30 November 20X2. Additionally, it incurred $500,000 of development expenditure to bring another product to a stage where it is ready to be marketed and sold.

(iii)   Whitebirk purchased some properties for $1.7 million on 1 December 20X1 and designated them as investment properties under the cost model. No depreciation was charged as a real estate agent valued the properties at $1.9 million at the year end.

(iv)   Whitebirk has an intangible asset valued at $1 million on 1 December 20X1. The asset has an indefinite useful life, and in previous years had been reviewed for impairment. As at 30 November 20X2, there are no indications that the asset is impaired.

Required

Discuss how the above transactions should be dealt with in the financial statements of Whitebirk, with reference to the IFRS for SMEs.   (11 marks)

(Total = 22 marks)

65 Revenue recognition

49 mins

The exhibits below provide all the information required to answer the question.

Exhibit 1 - Warranties

Premier Co sold a machine to a customer for $196,000, which is the standalone selling price of the machine. The sales contract included a warranty that provides assurance that the machine complies with agreed-upon specifications and will operate as promised for one year from the date of purchase. As the customer represents new business to Premier Co, as an incentive to purchase the machine, Premier Co gave the customer an additional extended warranty, at no extra cost, which guarantees the machine will operate as expected for a further six month period after the standard warranty has elapsed. Six month extended warranties are normally charged at $4,000.

Exhibit 2 - Jewellery sales

Jae Co is a retailer of high-value items of diamond jewellery. A significant proportion of the items available for sale in Jae Co's stores were handmade by Rodia Co.

These items are held under a contractual arrangement with Rodia Co, the terms of which specify that Rodia Co retains the ability to change the selling price of the jewellery, and that Jae Co is required to return any unsold jewellery after a period of nine months. When Jae Co sells an item of jewellery to a customer, legal title to the jewellery passes from Rodia Co to the customer.

Jae Co has paid a significant deposit to Rodia Co in order to hold the jewellery in its stores. This deposit is deducted, on a proportionate basis, from the amount payable to Rodia Co when items are sold or is refunded in full if items are returned. Jae Co is not required to pay in full for the jewellery until it is sold on to a customer.

Exhibit 3 - Right to return sales

Kracker Co sold 100 identical items to a customer for $2,000 each. The items cost Kracker Co $1,600 each to manufacture. The terms of sale are that the customer has the right to return the goods for a full refund within three months. After the three-month period has expired the customer can no longer return the goods and payment becomes immediately due. Kracker Co has entered into transactions of this type with this customer previously and can reliably estimate that no more than 4% of the products are likely to be returned within the three-month period.

Exhibit 4 - Non-refundable fee

Kotta Co has started a community food store which sells food at heavily discounted prices to its members. To become a member, a customer must pay a non-refundable joining fee of $30. On payment of the fee, Kotta Co creates a unique account for the customer and provides the customer with a membership card. The customer can then access the community food store at any time during its opening hours, over a 12 month period. The customer pays for the food they purchase at the time of their visit to the food store.

Required

(a)   Explain the accounting treatment required for each warranty provided by Premier Co and the revenue to be recognised by Premier Co for the sale of the machine in Exhibit 1.

(10 marks)

(b)   Explain how Jae Co and Rodia Co should account for sales under the contractual arrangement made between them as described in Exhibit 2.   (7 marks)

(c)   Explain how Kracker Co should account for the sales transaction described in Exhibit 3 at the date of the sale. You should include relevant journal entries in your answer.   (4 marks)

(d)   Explain how Kotta Co should account for the $30 non-refundable joining fee paid by its customers as described in Exhibit 4.   (4 marks)

(Total = 25 marks)

66 Seltec   49 mins

P2 June 2010 (amended)

Seltec, a public limited company, processes and sells edible oils and uses several financial instruments to spread the risk of fluctuation in the price of the edible oils. The entity operates in an environment where the transactions are normally denominated in dollars. The functional currency of Seltec is the dollar.

(a)   The entity uses forward and futures contracts to protect it against fluctuation in the price of edible oils. Where forwards are used, the company often takes delivery of the edible oil and sells it shortly afterwards. The contracts are constructed with future delivery in mind but the contracts also allow net settlement in cash as an alternative. The net settlement is based on the change in the price of the oil since the start of the contract. Seltec uses the proceeds of a net settlement to purchase a different type of oil or purchase from a different supplier. Where futures are used these sometimes relate to edible oils of a different type and market than those of Seltec's own inventory of edible oil. The company intends to apply hedge accounting to these contracts in order to protect itself from earnings volatility. Seltec has also entered into a long-term arrangement to buy oil from a foreign entity whose currency is the dinar. The commitment stipulates that the fixed purchase price will be denominated in pounds sterling.

Seltec is unsure as to the nature of derivatives and hedge accounting techniques and has asked your advice on how the above financial instruments should be dealt with in the financial statements. (15 marks)

(b)   Seltec has decided to enter the retail market and has recently purchased two well-known brand names in the edible oil industry. One of the brand names has been in existence for many years and has a good reputation for quality. The other brand name is named after a famous film star who has been actively promoting the edible oil as being a healthier option than other brands of oil. This type of oil has only been on the market for a short time. Seltec is finding it difficult to estimate the useful life of the brands and therefore intends to treat the brands as having indefinite lives.

In order to sell the oil, Seltec has purchased two limited liability companies from a company that owns several retail outlets. Each entity owns retail outlets in several shopping complexes. The only assets of each entity are the retail outlets. There is no operational activity and at present the entities have no employees.

Seltec is unclear as to how the purchase of the brands and the entities should be accounted for. (10 marks)

Required

Discuss the accounting principles involved in accounting for the above transactions and how the above transactions should be treated in the financial statements of Seltec.

Note. The mark allocation is shown against each of the two parts above.

(Total = 25 marks)

67 Della Co   49 mins

Della Co has a 31 December reporting date. The following exhibits provide information relevant to the question.

Exhibit 1 – Sale of specialised product

On 30 November 20X0, Della Co sold a specialised product to a Cromer Co for $242,000 in cash on that date. Della Co has the right to cancel the sale and require the return of the product at any time up to and including 31 January 20X1. If Della Co cancels the sale, it must refund Cromer Co the original $242,000 plus $500.

Exhibit 2 - Agreement with Acra Co

Della Co has a contractual agreement with Acra Co, whereby Acra Co holds items of Della Co's product X in its stores for a trial period of 6 months from 1 September 20X1. The items cost $45,000 and have a retail value of $63,000.

Della Co retains the right to set the selling price of the product X. When Acra Co sells one of the items to a customer, legal title passes from Della Co to the customer. At the end of each month, Acra Co must remit amounts to Della Co for items of product X that have been sold.

Acra Co has paid a refundable deposit to hold product X in its stores. The deposit is deducted by Acra Co, on a proportionate basis, from the amounts remitted to Della Co each month. At the end of the trial period Acra Co is required to return any unsold product X to Della Co in return for any remaining deposit.

Exhibit 3 - Hedging arrangement

On 1 January 20X0, Della Co invested in $2 million in 6% bonds, redeemable in 20X9 with a nominal value of £2m. Della Co accounts for the investment at fair value through other comprehensive income. By 31 December 20X0, the fair value of the bonds had increased to $2.5m.

On 1 January 20X1, Della Co decided to protect against the risk of changes in the fair value of the bond caused by future interest rate increases. As a result, on that date it entered into a five-year interest rate swap, in which it would pay a fixed rate and receive a variable rate. The fair value of the swap at inception was nil.

On 31 December 20X1, the fair value of the government bonds had fallen to $1.9m. The fair value of the swap at that date was $0.55m. Della Co is unsure as to hedge accounting techniques and has asked your advice on how the above financial instruments should be dealt with in the financial statements.

Required

(a) Discuss how the sale of the specialised product on 30 November 20X1 should be accounted for in the financial statements of Della Co.   (7 marks)

(b) Discuss how the contractual agreement with Acra Co should be accounted for in the financial statements of Della Co.   (7 marks)

(c) Discuss briefly the requirements for hedge accounting under IFRS 9 *Financial Instruments* and explain how the bonds and the interest rate swap should be accounted for in the financial statements of Della Co at 31 December 20X0 and at 31 December 20X1.

(8 marks)

(Total = 25 marks)

Answer Bank

Section 1 – Preparation questions

1 Financial instruments

(a) STATEMENT OF PROFIT OR LOSS AND OTHER COMPREHENSIVE INCOME

	$
Finance income	
(441,014 × (W1) 8%)	35,281

STATEMENT OF FINANCIAL POSITION

	$
Non-current assets	
Financial asset (441,014 + 35,281)	476,295

Working: Effective interest rate

$$\frac{600,000}{441,014} = 1.3605 \therefore \text{from tables interest rate is 8\%}$$

(b) Compound instrument

	$
Presentation	
Non-current liabilities	
Financial liability component of convertible bond (Working)	1,797,467
Equity	
Equity component of convertible bond (2,000,000 – (Working) 1,797,467)	202,533

Working: Fair value of equivalent non-convertible debt

	$
Present value of principal payable at end of 3 years	1,544,367

$$(4,000 \times \$500 = \$2m \times \frac{1}{(1.09)^3})$$

Present value of interest annuity payable annually in arrears	
for 3 years [(5% × $2m) × 2.531]	253,100
	1,797,467

2 Leases

(a) **Interest rate implicit in the lease**

PV = annuity × cumulative discount factor (CDF)

250,000 = 78,864 × CDF

$$\therefore \text{CDF} = \frac{250,000}{78,864}$$

= 3.170

∴ Interest rate is 10%

(b) At the inception of the lease, Sugar Co recognises a right-of-use asset and a lease liability. The right-of-use asset is measured at the amount of the lease liability, which is the present value of the future lease payments discounted at the rate of interest implicit in the lease, here $250,000. At 31 December, the right-of-use asset is measured at cost less accumulated depreciation: $250,000 – $(250,000/4) = $187,500. The lease liability is measured by increasing the carrying amount to reflect interest on the lease liability and reducing the carrying amount to reflect the lease payments made.

BPP
LEARNING
MEDIA

STATEMENT OF FINANCIAL POSITION AS AT 31 DECEMBER 20X1 (EXTRACT)

	$
Property, plant and equipment	
Right-of-use asset	187,500
Non-current liabilities	
Lease liabilities (W)	136,886
Current liabilities	
Lease liabilities (W) (196,136 – 136,886)	59,250

STATEMENT OF PROFIT OR LOSS AND OTHER COMPREHENSIVE INCOME

FOR THE YEAR ENDED 31 DECEMBER 20X1 (EXTRACT) (PROFIT OR LOSS SECTION)

Depreciation on right-of-use asset	62,500
Finance charges	25,000

Working: Lease liability

		$
Year ended 31 December 20X1:		
1.1.X1	Liability b/d	250,000
1.1.X1 – 31.12.X1	Interest at 10%	25,000
31.12.X1	Instalment in arrears	(78,864)
31.12.X1	Liability c/d	196,136
Year ended 31 December 20X2:		
1.1.X2 – 31.12.X2	Interest at 10%	19,614
31.12.X2	Instalment in arrears	(78,864)
31.12.X2	Liability c/d	136,886

3 Defined benefit plan

NOTES TO THE STATEMENT OF PROFIT OR LOSS AND OTHER COMPREHENSIVE INCOME

Defined benefit expense recognised in profit or loss

	$m
Current service cost	11
Past service cost	10
Net interest on the net defined benefit asset (10% × (110 + 10)) – (10% × 150)	(3)
	18

Other comprehensive income (items that will not be reclassified to profit or loss)

Remeasurement of defined benefit plans

	$m
Remeasurement gain on defined benefit obligation	17
Remeasurement loss on plan assets	(22)
	(5)

NOTES TO THE STATEMENT OF FINANCIAL POSITION

Net defined benefit asset recognised in the statement of financial position

	31 December 20X1 $m	31 December 20X0 $m
Present value of pension obligation	116	110
Fair value of plan assets	(140)	(150)
Net asset	(24)	(40)

Changes in the present value of the defined benefit obligation

	$m
Opening defined benefit obligation	110
Interest on obligation (10% × (110 + 10))	12
Current service cost	11
Past service cost	10
Benefits paid	(10)
Gain on remeasurement through OCI (balancing figure)	(17)
Closing defined benefit obligation	116

Changes in the fair value of plan assets

	$m
Opening fair value of plan assets	150
Interest on plan assets (10% × 150)	15
Contributions	7
Benefits paid	(10)
Loss on remeasurement through OCI (balancing figure)	(22)
Closing fair value of plan assets	140

Tutorial note.

The interest on the defined benefit obligation is calculated on the balance at the start of the year ($110 million) plus the increase in obligation of $10 million due to past service costs. Interest is charged on the increase in obligation due to past service costs because the $10 million given in the question is the present value at the start of the year (if it were the present value at the end of the year, no interest would be required).

4 Sundry standards

Workbook reference. Employee benefits are covered in Chapter 5 of the SBR Workbook, embedded derivatives in covered in Chapter 8.

(a)   NOTES TO THE STATEMENT OF PROFIT OR LOSS AND OTHER COMPREHENSIVE INCOME

Defined benefit expense recognised in profit or loss

	$'000
Current service cost	275
Net interest on the net defined benefit liability (318 − 306)	12
Curtailment cost	58
	345

Other comprehensive income (items that will not be reclassified to profit or loss)

Remeasurement of defined benefit plans

	$'000
Remeasurement loss on defined benefit obligation	(19)
Remeasurement gain on plan assets	89
	70

NOTES TO THE STATEMENT OF FINANCIAL POSITION

Net defined benefit liability recognised in the statement of financial position

	31 January 20X8 $m	31 January 20X7 $'000
Present value of pension obligation	4,640	4,300
Fair value of plan assets	(4,215)	(3,600)
Net liability	425	700

Changes in the present value of the defined benefit obligation

	$'000
Opening defined benefit obligation	4,300
Benefits paid	(330)
Interest on obligation (4,300 – 330) × 8%	318
Curtailment	58
Current service cost	275
Loss on remeasurement through OCI (balancing figure)	19
Closing defined benefit obligation	4,640

Changes in the fair value of plan assets

	$'000
Opening fair value of plan assets	3,600
Contributions	550
Benefits paid	(330)
Interest on plan assets ((3,600 + 550 – 330) × 8%)	306
Gain on remeasurement through OCI (balancing figure)	89
Closing fair value of plan assets	4,215

(b) **Settlement**

(i) *Calculation of net defined benefit liability*

Changes in the present value of the defined benefit obligation 20X8

	$'000
Opening defined benefit obligation (1.1.X8)	40,000
Interest on obligation (40,000 × 8%)	3,200
Current service cost	2,500
Past service cost	2,000
Benefits paid	(1,974)
	45,726
Loss on remeasurement through OCI (bal. fig.)	274
Closing defined benefit obligation (31.12.X8)	46,000

20X9

	$'000
Opening defined benefit obligation (1.1.X9)	46,000
Interest on obligation (46,000 × 9%)	4,140
Current service cost	2,860
Settlement	(11,400)
Benefits paid	(2,200)
	39,400
Loss on remeasurement through OCI (bal. fig.)	1,400
Closing defined benefit obligation (31.12.X9)	40,800

Changes in the fair value of plan assets
20X8

	$'000
Opening fair value of plan assets (1.1.X8)	40,000
Interest on plan assets (40,000 × 8%)	3,200
Benefits paid	(1,974)
Contributions paid	2,000
	43,226
Loss on remeasurement through OCI (bal. fig.)	(226)
Closing fair value of plan assets (31.12.X8)	43,000

	$'000
Opening fair value of plant assets (1.1.X9)	43,000
Interest on plan assets (43,000 × 9%)	3,870
Settlement	(10,800)
Benefits paid	(2,200)
Contributions paid in	2,200
	36,070
Loss on remeasurement through OCI (bal. fig.)	(390)
Closing fair value of plan assets (31.12.X9)	35,680

- During 20X8, there is an improvement in the future benefits available under the plan and as a result there is a past service cost of $2 million, being the increase in the present value of the obligation as a result of the change.

- During 20X9, Sion sells part of its operations and transfers the relevant part of the pension plan to the purchaser. This is a settlement. The overall gain on settlement is calculated as:

	$'000
Present value of obligation settled	11,400
Fair value of plan assets transferred on settlement	(10,800)
Cash transferred on settlement	(400)
Gain	200

(ii) *Financial statements extracts*

STATEMENT OF FINANCIAL POSITION

	20X8 $'000	20X9 $'000
Net defined benefit liability: (46,000 – 43,000)/(40,800 – 35,680)	3,000	5,120

STATEMENT OF PROFIT OR LOSS AND OTHER COMPREHENSIVE INCOME

	20X8 $'000	20X9 $'000
Profit or loss		
Current service cost	2,500	2,860
Past service cost	2,000	–
Gain on settlement	–	(200)
Net interest: (3,200 – 3,200)/(4,140 – 3,870)	–	270
Other comprehensive income		
Remeasurement loss on defined benefit pension plan: (274 + 226)/(1,400 + 390)	500	1,790

(c)   Classification of financial assets

Bed's deposit is a **financial asset**. According to IFRS 9 *Financial Instruments*, financial assets are classified as measured at either **amortised cost or fair value**.

A financial asset is measured at **amortised cost** where:

(i)   The asset is held within a **business model** where the objective is to hold financial assets in order to **collect contractual cash flows**; and

(ii)   The contractual terms of the financial asset give rise on specified dates to **cash flows that are solely payments of principal and interest** on the principal amount outstanding.

All other financial assets are measured at fair value.

Deposit with Em Bank

At first glance, it appears that this deposit **may meet the criteria to be measured at amortised cost** because Bed will receive cash flows comprising the principal amount ($10 million) and interest (2.5%). However, IFRS 9 requires the **cash flows to be consistent with a basic lending arrangement**, where the **time value of money and credit risk** are typically the most significant elements of interest. **Contractual terms** that **introduce exposure to risk or volatility in the contractual cash flows** that is **unrelated** to a basic lending arrangement, such as exposure to changes in exchange rates, **do not give rise to contractual cash flows that are solely payments of principal and interest**.

The **additional 3% interest** Bed will receive if the exchange rate target is reached, exposes Bed to **risk in cash flows** that are **unrelated to a basic lending arrangement** (movement in exchange rates). Therefore, the contract with Em Bank does not give rise to contractual cash flows that are purely payments of principal and interest and as a result, it should not be measured at amortised cost. This type of contract is referred to as a 'hybrid contract'.

This **additional 3%** dependent on exchange rates is an **embedded derivative**. Derivatives embedded within a **host** which is a **financial asset** within the scope of IFRS 9 are **not separated out** for accounting purposes. Instead, the **usual IFRS 9 measurement** requirements should be applied to the entire hybrid contract.

Since the **contract with Em Bank** does **not** meet the criteria to be measured at **amortised cost**, the **entire contract** (including the term entitling Bed to an additional 3% if the exchange rate target is met) should be **measured at fair value through profit or loss**.

5 Control

(a)   IFRS 10 states that an investor **controls** an investee if and only if it has all of the following.

(1)   **Power** over the investee;

(2)   Exposure, or rights, to **variable returns** from its involvement with the investee; and

(3)   The **ability to use its power** over the investee to affect the amount of the investor's returns.

Power is defined as **existing rights that give the current ability to direct the relevant activities of the investee**. There is no requirement for that power to have been exercised.

Relevant activities may include:

- Selling and purchasing goods or services
- Managing financial assets
- Selecting, acquiring and disposing of assets
- Researching and developing new products and processes
- Determining a funding structure or obtaining funding

In some cases assessing power is straightforward, for example, where power is obtained directly and solely from having the majority of voting rights or potential voting rights, and as a result the ability to direct relevant activities.

(b)

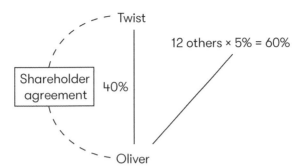

The absolute size of Twist's holding and the relative size of the other shareholdings alone are not conclusive in determining whether the investor has rights sufficient to give it power. However, the fact that Twist has **a contractual right to appoint, remove and set the remuneration of management** is sufficient to conclude that it **has power over Oliver**. The fact that Twist has not exercised this right is not a determining factor when assessing whether Twist has power. In conclusion, Twist does control Oliver, and should consolidate it.

(c)

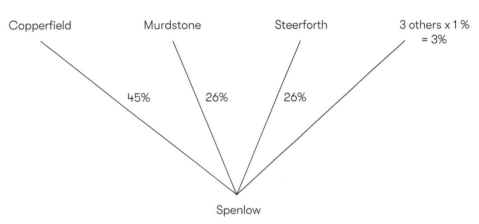

In this case, the size of Copperfield's voting interest and its size relative to the other shareholdings are sufficient to conclude that Copperfield **does not have power**. Only two other investors, Murdstone and Steerforth, would need to co-operate to be able to prevent Copperfield from directing the relevant activities of Spenlow.

(d)

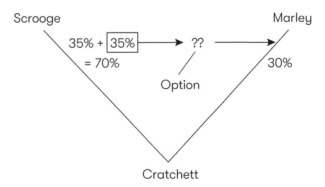

Scrooge holds a majority of the current voting rights of Cratchett, so is likely to meet the power criterion because it appears to have the current ability to direct the relevant activities. Although Marley has currently exercisable options to purchase additional voting rights (that, if exercised, would give it a majority of the voting rights in Cratchett), the terms and conditions associated with those options are such that the options are not considered substantive.

Thus voting rights, even combined with potential voting rights, may not be the deciding factor. Scrooge should consolidate Cratchett.

6 Associate

J GROUP CONSOLIDATED STATEMENT OF FINANCIAL POSITION AS AT 31 DECEMBER 20X5

	$'000
Assets	
Non-current assets	
Freehold property (1,950 + 1,250 + 370 (W7))	3,570
Plant and equipment (795 + 375)	1,170
Investment in associate (W3)	480
	5,220
Current assets	
Inventories (575 + 300 – 20 (W6))	855
Trade receivables (330 + 290))	620
Cash at bank and in hand (50 + 120)	170
	1,645
	6,865
Equity and liabilities	
Equity attributable to owners of the parent	
Issued share capital	2,000
Retained earnings	1,785
	3,785
Non-controlling interests (W5)	890
Total equity	4,675
Non-current liabilities	
12% debentures (500 + 100)	600
Current liabilities	
Bank overdraft	560
Trade payables (680 + 350)	1,030
	1,590
Total liabilities	2,190
	6,865

Workings

1   *Group structure*

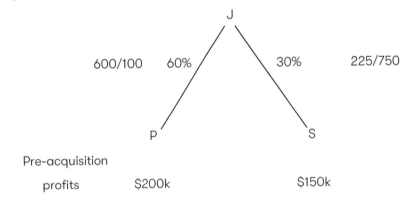

2   Goodwill

	$'000	$'000
Consideration transferred		1,000
NCI (at 'full' FV: 400 × $1.65)		660
Net assets acquired:		
Share capital	1,000	
Retained earnings at acquisition	200	
Fair value adjustment (W7)	400	
		(1,600)
		60
Impairments to date		(60)
Year-end value		–

3   Investment in associate

	$'000
Cost of associate	500.0
Share of post-acquisition retained reserves (W4)	72.0
Less impairment of investment in associate	(92.0)
	480.0

4   Retained earnings

	J Co $'000	P Co $'000	S Co $'000
Retained earnings per question	1,460	885	390
Unrealised profit (W6)		(20)	
Fair value adjustment movement (W6)		(30)	
Retained earnings at acquisition		(200)	(150)
		635	240
P Co: share of post-acquisition retained earnings			
60% × 635	381		
S Co: share of post-acquisition retained earnings			
30% × 240	72		
Goodwill impairments to date			
P Co: 60 (W2) × 60%	(36)		
S Co	(92)		
	1,785		

5   Non-controlling interests

	$'000
NCI at acquisition (W2)	660
NCI share of post-acquisition retained earnings ((W4) 635 × 40%)	254
NCI share of impairment losses ((W2) 60 × 40%)	(24)
	890

6   Unrealised profit on inventories

P Co ⟶ J Co $100k × 25/125 = $20,000

7   *Fair value adjustment table*

	At acquisition $'000	Movement $'000	At reporting date $'000
Land	200		200
Buildings	200	(30)	170 (200 × 34/40)
	400	(30)	370

7 Part disposal

(a)   ANGEL GROUP
CONSOLIDATED STATEMENT OF FINANCIAL POSITION AS AT 31 DECEMBER 20X8

	$'000
Non-current assets	
Property, plant and equipment	200.00
Investment in Shane (W3)	133.15
	333.15
Current assets (890 + 120 (cash on sale))	1,010.00
	1,343.15
Equity attributable to owners of the parent	
Share capital	500.00
Retained reserves (W4)	533.15
	1,033.15
Current liabilities	310.00
	1,343.15

ANGEL GROUP
CONSOLIDATED STATEMENT OF PROFIT OR LOSS AND OTHER COMPREHENSIVE INCOME
FOR THE YEAR ENDED 31 DECEMBER 20X8

	$'000
Profit before interest and tax [100 + (20 × 6/12)]	110.00
Profit on disposal of shares in subsidiary (W6)	80.30
Share of profit of associate (12 × 35% × 6/12)	2.10
Profit before tax	192.40
Income tax expense [40 + (8 × 6/12)]	(44.00)
Profit for the year	148.40
Other comprehensive income (not reclassified to P/L) net of tax [10 + (6 × 6/12)]	13.00
Share of other comprehensive income of associate (6 × 35% × 6/12)	1.05
Other comprehensive income for the year	14.05
Total comprehensive income for the year	162.45
Profit attributable to:	
Owners of the parent	146.60
Non-controlling interests (12 × 6/12 × 30%)	1.80
	148.40
Total comprehensive income attributable to:	
Owners of the parents	159.75
Non-controlling interests (18 × 6/12 × 30%)	2.70
	162.45

ANGEL GROUP
CONSOLIDATED RECONCILIATION OF MOVEMENT IN RETAINED RESERVES

	$'000
Balance at 31 December 20X7 (W5)	373.40
Total comprehensive income for the year	159.75
Balance at 31 December 20X8 (W4)	533.15

Workings

1 *Timeline*

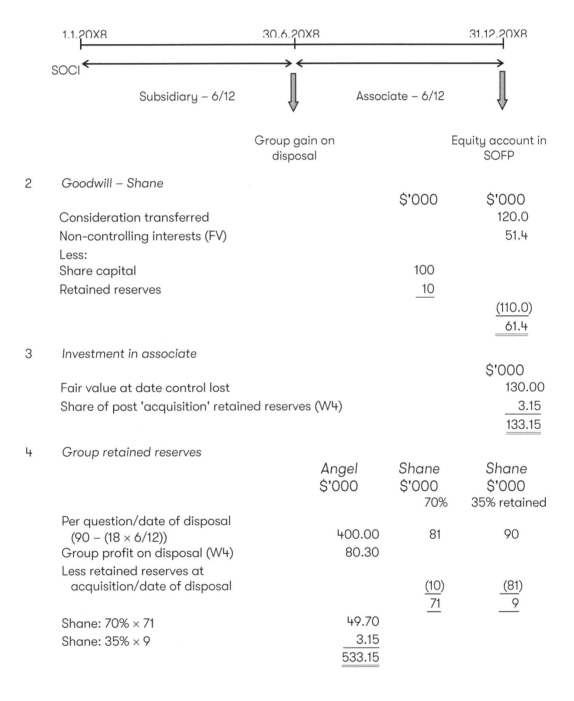

2 *Goodwill – Shane*

	$'000	$'000
Consideration transferred		120.0
Non-controlling interests (FV)		51.4
Less:		
Share capital	100	
Retained reserves	10	
		(110.0)
		61.4

3 *Investment in associate*

	$'000
Fair value at date control lost	130.00
Share of post 'acquisition' retained reserves (W4)	3.15
	133.15

4 *Group retained reserves*

	Angel $'000	Shane $'000 70%	Shane $'000 35% retained
Per question/date of disposal (90 – (18 × 6/12))	400.00	81	90
Group profit on disposal (W4)	80.30		
Less retained reserves at acquisition/date of disposal		(10)	(81)
		71	9
Shane: 70% × 71	49.70		
Shane: 35% × 9	3.15		
	533.15		

5   *Retained reserves b/f*

		Angel $'000	Shane $'000
	Per question	330.0	72
	Less pre-acquisition retained reserves		(10)
		330.0	62
	Shane – Share of post-acquisition ret'd reserves (62 × 70%)	43.4	
		373.4	

6   *Group profit on disposal of Shane*

		$'000	$'000
	Fair value of consideration received		120.0
	Fair value of 35% investment retained		130.0
	Less share of carrying amount when control lost		
	Net assets 190 – (18 × 6/12)	181.0	
	Goodwill (W2)	61.4	
	Less non-controlling interests (W7)	(72.7)	
			(169.7)
			80.3

7   *Non-controlling interests at date of disposal*

	$'000
Non-controlling interest at acquisition (FV)	51.4
NCI share of post-acq'n retained earnings (30% × 71(W4))	21.3
	72.7

(b)   **Angel disposes of 10% of its holding**

If Angel disposes of 10% of its holding in Shane, Shane goes from being a 70% subsidiary to a 60% subsidiary. In other words **control is retained**. No accounting boundary has been crossed, and the event is treated as a transaction between owners.

The accounting treatment is as follows:

Statement of profit or loss and other comprehensive income

(i)   The subsidiary is **consolidated in full** for the whole period.

(ii)   The **non-controlling interest in the statement of profit or loss and other comprehensive income** will be based on percentage before and after disposal, ie time apportion.

(iii) There is **no profit or loss on disposal**.

Statement of financial position

(i)   The **change (increase) in non-controlling interests** is shown as an **adjustment to the parent's equity**.

(ii)   **Goodwill** on acquisition **is unchanged** in the consolidated statement of financial position.

In the case of Angel and Shane you would time apportion the non-controlling interest in the statement of profit or loss and other comprehensive income, giving 30% for the first half the year and 40% for the second half. You would also calculate the adjustment to the parent's equity as follows:

	$'000
Fair value of consideration received	X
Increase in NCI in net assets and goodwill at disposal	(X)
Adjustment to parent's equity	X

8 Step acquisition

(a)   Prior to the acquisition of 20% on 1 March 20X1, **SD already controls KL** with its 60% investment, so **KL is already a subsidiary** and would be fully consolidated. In substance, this is **not an acquisition**. Instead, it is treated in the group accounts as a **transaction between the group shareholders** ie the parent has purchased a 20% shareholding from the non-controlling interests (NCI). No goodwill is calculated on the additional investment.

The value of the NCI needs to be worked out at the date of the additional investment (1 March 20X1), and the **proportion purchased by the parent needs to be removed from NCI**. The difference between the consideration transferred and the amount of the reduction in the NCI is included as an **adjustment to equity**.

KL must be **consolidated** in the group **statement of profit or loss and other comprehensive income** for the **full year** but NCI will be pro-rated with 40% for the first eight months and 20% for the following four months. In the **consolidated statement of financial position**, KL will be **consolidated with a 20% NCI**.

(b)   (i)   Goodwill $1,450,000 (W2)
      (ii)   Group retained earnings $9,843,999 (W3)
      (iii) Non-controlling interests $1,096,001 (W4)

Workings

1   *Group structure*

       SD

	1.7.X0	60%
	1.3.X1	20%
		80%

       KL   Pre-acquisition retained earnings $2,760,000

       Timeline

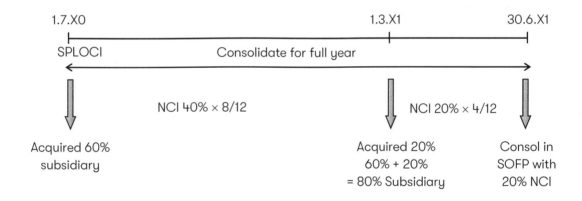

2   *Goodwill (calculated at date when control was originally obtained)*

	$	$
Consideration transferred		3,250,000
NCI at fair value		1,960,000
Less net assets at acquisition:		
Share capital	1,000,000	
Pre-acquisition retained earnings (W1)	2,760,000	
		(3,760,000)
Goodwill		1,450,000

BPP
LEARNING
MEDIA

3   *Consolidated retained earnings*

	SD	KL 60%	KL 80%
	$	$	$
At year end/step acquisition	9,400,000	3,186,667	3,400,000
Unrealised profit (W5)			(60,000)
At acquisition/step acquisition		(2,760,000)	(3,186,667)
		426,667	153,333
Group share (60% × 426,667)	256,000		
(80% × 153,333)	122,666		
Adjustment to parent's equity W6	65,333		
	9,843,999		

KL's retained earnings for the year to 30 June 20X1 (3,400,000 − 2,760,000) = $640,000

KL's retained earnings for the 8 months to 28 February 20X1 (640,000 × 8/12) = $426,667

KL's retained earnings as at 28 February 20X1 (2,760,000 + 426,667) = $3,186,667

4   *Non-controlling interest*

	$
NCI at acquisition	1,960,000
NCI share of post-acquisition retained earnings to 28.2.X1	
(40% × 426,667 (W3))	170,667
	2,130,667
Decrease in NCI on further acquisition (20%/40% × 2,130,667)	(1,065,333)
NCI share of post-acquisition retained earnings to 30.6.X1	
(20% × 153,333 (W3))	30,667
	1,096,001

5   *Provision for unrealised profit*

Intragroup sales by KL $750,000

Mark-up ($750,000 × $\frac{25}{125}$) × 40% = $60,000

(adjust in KL's retained earnings for the period **after** 1 March 20X1)

6   *Adjustment to equity on acquisition of further 20% of KL*

	$
Fair value of consideration paid	(1,000,000)
Decrease in NCI (W4)	1,065,333
Adjustment to equity	65,333

Adjustment would be:

	$	$
Debit (↓) Non-controlling interest	1,065,333	
Credit (↑) Group equity		65,333
Credit (↓) Cash (consideration)		1,000,000

9 Foreign operation

CONSOLIDATED STATEMENT OF FINANCIAL POSITION

	$'000
Property, plant and equipment (1,285 + 543 (W2))	1,828
Goodwill (W4)	240
	2,068
Current assets (410 + 247 (W2))	657
	2,725
Share capital	500
Retained earnings (W5)	1,260
Other components of equity – translation reserve (W8)	98
	1,858
Non-controlling interest (W6)	131
	1,989
Loans (200 + 37 (W2))	237
Current liabilities (400 + 99 (W2))	499
	736
	2,725

CONSOLIDATED STATEMENT OF PROFIT OR LOSS AND OTHER COMPREHENSIVE INCOME

	$'000
Revenue (1,125 + 619 (W3))	1,744
Cost of sales (410 + 274 (W3))	(684)
Gross profit	1,060
Other expenses (180 + 108 (W3))	(288)
Goodwill impairment loss (W4)	(18)
Profit before tax	754
Income tax expense (180 + 76 (W3))	(256)
Profit for the year	498

Other comprehensive income
Items that may subsequently be reclassified to profit or loss

Exchange difference on translating foreign operations (W9)	69
Total comprehensive income for the year	567

Profit attributable to:

Owners of the parent (balancing figure)	466
Non-controlling interests (W7)	32
	498

Total comprehensive income attributable to:

Owners of the parent	525
Non-controlling interests (W7)	42
	567

Workings

1   *Group structure*

Standard

1.1.20X5   80%

Odense   Pre-acquisition retained earnings = 2,500,000 krone

2 Translation of Odense – Statement of financial position

	Kr'000	Rate	$'000	
Property, plant and equipment	4,400	8.1	543	
Current assets	2,000	8.1	247	
	6,400		790	
Share capital	1,000	9.4	106	
Pre-acquisition retained earnings	2,500	9.4	266	
Post-acquisition retained earnings:				
• 20X5 profit	1,200	9.1	132	
• 20X5 dividend	(345)	8.8	(39)	
• 20X6 profit	1,350	8.4	161	470
• 20X6 dividend	(405)	8.1	(50)	
Exchange difference on net assets		Bal fig	78	
	5,300		654	
Loans	300	8.1	37	
Current liabilities	800	8.1	99	
	1,100		136	
	6,400		790	

3 Translation of Odense – statement of profit or loss and other comprehensive income

	Odense Kr'000	Rate	Odense $'000
Revenue	5,200	8.4	619
Cost of sales	(2,300)	8.4	(274)
Gross profit	2,900		345
Other expenses	(910)	8.4	(108)
Profit before tax	1,990		237
Income tax expense	(640)	8.4	(76)
Profit/Total comprehensive income for the year	1,350		161

4 Goodwill

	Kr'000	Kr'000	Rate	$'000
Consideration transferred (520 × 9.4)		4,888		520
Non-controlling interests (3,500 × 20%)		700		74
Share capital	1,000		9.4	
Retained earnings	2,500			
		(3,500)		(372)
		2,088		222
Exchange differences 20X5		–	β	15
At 31.12.X5		2,088	8.8	237
Impairment losses 20X6		(148)	8.1	(18)
Exchange differences 20X6		–	β	21
At 31.12.X6		1,940	8.1	240

5 Consolidated retained earnings

	Standard $'000	Odense $'000
At year end	1,115	470
At acquisition		(266)
		204
Group share of post-acquisition retained earnings (204 × 80%)	163	
Less: impairment losses to date (W4)	(18)	
	1,260	

6   *Non-controlling interests (statement of financial position)*

	$'000
NCI at acquisition (W4)	74
NCI share of post-acquisition retained earnings of Odense (204 (W5) × 20%)	41
NCI share of exchange differences on net assets (78 (W2) × 20%)	16
	131

7   *Non-controlling interests (statement of profit or loss and other comprehensive income)*

	PFY $'000	TCI $'000
Profit/Total comprehensive income for the year (W3)	161	161
Other comprehensive income: exchange differences on net assets (W9)	–	48
	161	209
NCI share	× 20%	× 20%
	= 32	= 42

8   *Consolidated translation reserve*

	$'000
Exchange differences on net assets (78 (W2) × 80%)	62
Exchange differences on goodwill (15 + 21 (W4))	36
	98

9   *Exchange differences*

	$'000
On translation of net assets:	
Closing NA @ CR (W2)	654
Opening NA @ OR (1,000 + 3,355 = 4,355* @ 8.8)	(495)
Less retained profit as translated (PFY – dividends)(161 (W3) – 405 @ 8.1)	(111)
	48
On goodwill (W4)	21
	69

* The opening net assets have been calculated as share capital (from Odense's statement of financial position) plus opening retained earnings (from Odense's statement of changes in equity extract). Alternatively, they could have been calculated as closing net assets less total comprehensive income for the year plus dividends: Kr(5,300,000 – 1,350,000 + 405,000).

Tutorial note.

As Standard chose to measure the non-controlling interest in Odense at the proportionate share of net assets at acquisition, only group goodwill is recognised in the consolidated statement of financial position and therefore, no goodwill is recognised for the non-controlling interests (NCI). Therefore, there are no exchange differences on goodwill relating to NCI. This is why only the exchange differences on net assets (and not the exchange differences on goodwill) are included in the NCI workings ((W6) and (W7)). Since all the recognised goodwill relates to the group, in the consolidated translation reserve working (W8), the exchange differences on goodwill are not multiplied by the group share.

If Standard had measured NCI at fair value at acquisition, both group goodwill and goodwill relating to the NCI would have been recognised. Therefore, in the NCI workings, the exchange differences on goodwill would be included. In the consolidated translation reserve working, the exchange differences on goodwill would be multiplied by the group share (in the same way as the exchange differences on net assets have been treated).

BPP
LEARNING
MEDIA

It might help if you think about the treatment of exchange differences on goodwill as being the same as the treatment for impairment losses on goodwill. So when NCI is measured at the proportionate share of net assets at acquisition, as all of the recognised goodwill relates to the group, all of the impairment losses and exchange differences on goodwill belong to the group so they should be recognised in full in the consolidated retained earnings and translation reserve workings respectively and neither would be included in NCI workings. Whereas for the full goodwill method, impairment losses and exchange differences on goodwill are apportioned between the group (in the retained earnings and translation reserve workings) and the NCI (in the NCI workings).

10 Consolidated statement of cash flows

STATEMENT OF CASH FLOWS FOR THE YEAR ENDED 31 DECEMBER 20X5

	$'000	$'000
Cash flows from operating activities		
Profit before tax	16,500	
Adjustments for:		
Depreciation	5,800	
Impairment losses (W1)	240	
	22,540	
Increase in trade receivables (W4)	(1,700)	
Increase in inventories (W4)	(4,400)	
Increase in trade payables (W4)	1,200	
Cash generated from operations	17,640	
Income taxes paid (W3)	(4,200)	
Net cash from operating activities		13,440
Cash flows from investing activities		
Acquisition of subsidiary net of cash acquired	(600)	
Purchase of property, plant and equipment (W1)	(13,100)	
Net cash used in investing activities		(13,700)
Cash flows from financing activities		
Proceeds from issue of share capital (W2)	2,100	
Dividends paid (W2)	(900)	
Dividends paid to non-controlling interest (W2)	(40)	
Net cash from financing activities		1,160
Net increase in cash and cash equivalents		900
Cash and cash equivalents at the beginning of the period		1,500
Cash and cash equivalents at the end of the period		2,400

Workings

1   Assets

	Property, plant and equipment $'000	Goodwill $'000
b/d	25,000	–
OCI (revaluation)	500	
Depreciation/Impairment	(5,800)	(240) β
Acquisition of sub/associate	2,700	1,640 (W5)
Cash paid/(rec'd) β	**13,100**	–
c/d	35,500	1,400

2   Equity

	Share capital $'000	Share premium $'000	Retained earnings $'000	Non-controlling interest $'000
b/d	10,000	2,000	21,900	–
SPLOCI			11,100	350
Acquisition of subsidiary	1,500	2,500		1,440 (W5)
Cash (paid)/rec'd β	800	1,300	(900)*	(40)
c/d	12,300	5,800	32,100	1,750

*Dividend paid is given in question but working shown for clarity.

3   Liabilities

	Tax payable $'000
b/d	4,000
P/L	5,200
Acquisition of subsidiary	200
Cash (paid)/rec'd	(4,200) β
c/d	5,200

4   Working capital changes

	Inventories $'000	Receivables $'000	Payables $'000
Balance b/d	10,000	7,500	6,100
Acquisition of subsidiary	1,600	600	300
	11,600	8,100	6,400
Increase/(decrease) (balancing figure)	4,400	1,700	1,200
Balance c/d	16,000	9,800	7,600

5   Purchase of subsidiary

	$'000
Cash received on acquisition of subsidiary	400
Less cash consideration	(1,000)
Cash outflow	(600)

Note. Only the **cash** consideration is included in the figure reported in the statement of cash flows. The **shares** issued as part of the consideration are reflected in the share capital working (W2) above.

Goodwill on acquisition (before impairment):

	$'000
Consideration: 55 + 695 (W3) + 120 (W2) + 216	5,000
Non-controlling interest: 4,800 × 30%	1,440
Net assets acquired	(4,800)
Goodwill	1,640

Section 2 – Exam-standard questions

11 Robby

Workbook references. The underlying principles of IFRS 3 are covered in Chapter 11. Business combinations achieved in stages are covered in Chapter 12. Joint operations are covered in Chapter 15 and financial instruments in Chapter 8. The *Conceptual Framework* is covered in Chapter 1.

Top tips. You must make sure that you explain the principles underlying the accounting for goodwill as the marks available for calculations are limited. The examining team is looking for an understanding of the accounting involved and not rote learning of consolidation workings.

In Part (b), you need to evaluate whether the requirements of IFRS 9 relating to the factoring arrangement are in agreement with the *Conceptual Framework*. This kind of evaluation in light of the *Conceptual Framework* is likely to be a feature of questions in the SBR examination, so you need to make sure you are familiar enough with the *Conceptual Framework* to be able to answer questions in this way.

Marking scheme

				Marks
(a)	(i)	Goodwill		
		Explanation of IFRS 3 principles	10	
		Hail – calculation	3	
		Zinc – calculation	3	
				16
	(ii)	Joint operation		
		SOFP	3	
		Explanation – 1 mark per point up to a maximum	4	
				7
(b)		Discussion – 1 mark per point up to a maximum		7
				30

(a) **Sections for inclusion in the finance director's report**

(i) **Goodwill**

IFRS 3 *Business Combinations* requires goodwill to be recognised in a business combination. A business combination takes place when one entity, the acquirer, obtains control of another entity, the acquiree. IFRS 3 requires goodwill to be calculated and recorded as a non-current asset at the acquisition date.

Goodwill is calculated at the acquisition date as the fair value of the consideration transferred by the acquirer plus the amount of any non-controlling interest less the fair value of the net assets of the acquiree. When the business combination is achieved in stages, as is the case for Zinc, the consideration transferred by the acquirer will include any previously held interest in the new subsidiary which must be remeasured to its fair value at the date control is obtained.

Goodwill is not amortised, but instead is tested for impairment at each year end.

Applying these principles, the goodwill on the acquisition of Hail and Zinc for inclusion in the consolidated financial statements at 31 May 20X3 is calculated as follows.

Goodwill related to the acquisition of Hail

Goodwill at acquisition:	$m	$m
Consideration transferred for 80% interest		
Cash payable on 1 June 20X1	50	
Deferred cash consideration ($24.2 million/(1.10)^2)	20	
Contingent consideration	40	
Fair value of non-controlling interest	30	
		140
Fair value of identifiable net assets acquired	130	
Contingent liability	(2)	
		(128)
		12

The immediate, deferred and contingent consideration transferred should be measured at their fair values at the acquisition date.

Deferred consideration

The fair value of the deferred consideration is the amount payable on 31 May 20X4 discounted to its present value at the acquisition date. The requirement to discount to present value is consistent with other standards. The present value should be unwound in the period to 31 May 20X3 which will increase the carrying amount of the obligation and result in a finance cost in profit or loss. The unwinding of the discount does not affect the goodwill calculation as it is based on the amount payable at the date of acquisition.

Contingent consideration

The fair value of the contingent consideration payable should take into account the various milestones set under the acquisition agreement. At the acquisition date the fair value of the contingent consideration is $40 million.

As the contingent consideration will be paid in cash, the amount payable should be remeasured at 31 May 20X3 to its fair value of $42 million. This remeasurement does not affect the goodwill calculation, but the increase in the fair value of the obligation of $2 million should be taken to profit or loss. If the contingent consideration was to be settled in equity, no remeasurement would be required.

Contingent liability

The contingent liability disclosed in Hail's financial statements is recognised as a liability on acquisition in accordance with IFRS 3, provided that its fair value can be reliably measured and it is a present obligation. This is contrary to the normal rules in IAS 37 *Provisions, Contingent Liabilities and Contingent Assets* where contingent liabilities are not recognised but only disclosed.

Conclusion

There is no indication that the goodwill balance is impaired at 31 May 20X3. Thus goodwill of $12 million on acquisition of Hail should be included in the group financial statements at 31 May 20X3.

Goodwill related to the acquisition of Zinc

Substance over form drives the accounting treatment for a subsidiary acquired in stages. The legal form is that shares have been acquired, however, in substance:

(1)   The 5% investment has been 'sold'. Per IFRS 3, the investment previously held is remeasured to fair value at the date control is obtained and a gain or loss reported in profit or loss:

	$m
Fair value of 5% at date control achieved (1 December 20X2)	5
Fair value of carrying amount of 5% per SOFP at 31 May 20X2	(3)
Remeasurement gain (1 June 20X2 to 1 December 20X2)	2

(2)   A subsidiary has been 'purchased'. The previously held 5% investment is effectively re-acquired at fair value, and so goodwill is calculated including the fair value of the previously held 5% investment.

Goodwill	$m	$m
Consideration transferred – for 55%	16	
Fair value of non-controlling interest	9	
Fair value of previously held interest (for 5% at 1 December 20X2)	5	
		30
Fair value of identifiable net assets at acquisition:		
Provisional measurement	26	
Adjustment to fair value of PPE (within measurement period)	3	
		(29)
		1

Fair value of PPE

The fair value of PPE was provisional at the date of acquisition, with an increase of $3 million subsequently identified when the figures were finalised in March 20X3. IFRS 3 permits adjustments to goodwill for adjustments to the fair value of assets and liabilities acquired, provided this adjustment is made within one year of the date of acquisition (the measurement period).

Conclusion

There is no indication that the goodwill balance is impaired at 31 May 20X3. Thus goodwill related to the acquisition of Zinc to be included in the group financial statements at 31 May 20X3 is $1 million.

(ii)   **Joint operation**

Robby has a joint arrangement with another party in respect of the natural gas station. Under IFRS 11 *Joint Arrangements*, a joint arrangement is one in which two or more parties are bound by a contractual arrangement which gives them joint control over the arrangement.

Joint arrangements can either be joint ventures or joint operations. The classification as a joint venture or joint operation depends on the rights and obligations of the parties to the arrangement. It is important to correctly classify the arrangement as the accounting requirements for joint ventures are different to those for joint operations.

IFRS 11 states that a joint arrangement that is not structured through a separate vehicle is a joint operation. In Robby's case, no separate entity has been set up for the joint arrangement, therefore it is a joint operation. Robby has joint rights to the assets and revenue, and joint obligations for the liabilities and costs of the joint arrangement.

BPP
LEARNING
MEDIA

Therefore, Robby, in its capacity as a joint operator, must recognise on a line-by-line basis its own assets, liabilities, revenues and expenses plus its share (40%) of the joint assets, liabilities, revenue and expenses of the joint operation as prescribed by IFRS 11. This treatment is applicable to both the consolidated and separate financial statements of Robby.

The figures are calculated as follows:

Statement of financial position

	$m
Property, plant and equipment:	
1 June 20X2 cost: gas station (15 × 40%)	6.00
dismantling provision (2 × 40%)	0.80
	6.80
Accumulated depreciation: 6.8/10 years	(0.68)
31 May 20X3 carrying amount	6.12
Trade receivables (from other joint operator): 20 (revenue) × 40%	8.00
Trade payables (to other joint operator): (16 + 0.5) (costs) × 40%	6.60
Dismantling provision:	
At 1 June 20X2	0.80
Finance cost (unwinding of discount): 0.8 × 5%	0.04
At 31 May 20X3	0.84

(b) **Accounting treatment**

Trade receivables are financial assets and therefore the requirements of IFRS 9 *Financial Instruments* need to be applied. The main question here is whether the factoring arrangement means that Robby should derecognise the trade receivables from the financial statements.

Per IFRS 9, an entity should derecognise a **financial asset** when:

(1)   The **contractual rights** to the cash flows from the financial asset **expire**; or

(2)   The entity **transfers the financial asset or substantially all the risks and rewards of ownership** of the financial asset to another party.

In the case of Robby, the contractual rights to the cash flows have not expired as the receivables balances are still outstanding and expected to be collected.

In respect of the risks and rewards of ownership, the substance of the factoring arrangement needs to be considered rather than its legal form. Robby has transferred the receivables to the bank in exchange for $3.6 million cash, but remains liable for any shortfall between $3.6 million and the amount collected. In principle, Robby is liable for the whole $3.6 million, although it is unlikely that the default would be as much as this. **Robby therefore retains the credit risk.**

In addition, Robby is entitled to receive the benefit (less interest) of repayments in excess of $3.6 million once the $3.6 million has been collected and therefore retains the potential rewards of full settlement.

Substantially all the risks and rewards of the financial asset **therefore remain with Robby,** and the receivables should **continue to be recognised**. In addition, a **financial liability** should be recognised in respect of the consideration received from the bank.

Conceptual Framework

According to the *Conceptual Framework* derecognition normally occurs when **control** of all or part of an asset is lost.

The requirements for derecognition should aim to **faithfully represent** both:

(a)   Any assets and liabilities retained after derecognition; and

(b)   The change in the entity's assets and liabilities as a result of derecognition.

Meeting both of these aims becomes difficult if the entity disposes of only part of an asset or retains some exposure to that asset. It can be difficult to faithfully represent the legal form (which in this case is the decrease in assets under the factoring arrangement) with the substance of retaining the corresponding risks and rewards.

Because of the difficulties in practice in meeting these two aims, the *Conceptual Framework* does not advocate using a control approach or the risks-and-rewards approach to derecognition in every circumstance. Instead, it describes the options available and discusses what factors the IASB would need to consider when developing Standards.

As such, there appears to be no conflict in principles between the *Conceptual Framework* and the requirements of IFRS 9 for derecognition.

12 Banana Co

Marking scheme

				Marks
(a)	(i)	Application of the following discussion to the scenario:		
		Goodwill and contingent consideration	3	
		Why the existing goodwill valuation is incorrect	4	
		Correcting entry	1	
				8
	(ii)	Application of the following discussion to the scenario:		
		Nature of significant influence	2	
		The equity method of accounting for an associate	1	
		Calculation of the carrying amount of the investment	1	
				4
	(iii)	Calculation of the gain on disposal of Strawberry	2	
		Application of the following discussion to the scenario:		
		Rationale for the calculation of gain on disposal	1	
		Correct treatment of Strawberry after disposal	1	
				4
(b)		Application of the following discussion to the scenario:		
		IFRS 3 definition of a business	3	
		Rationale for inclusion as either an asset acquisition or as a business	4	
				7
(c)		Application of the following discussion to the scenario:		
		Consideration of IFRS 9 principles	4	
		Transfer of rights/conclusion	1	
		Carrying amount of bonds	2	
				7
				30

(a)   Explanatory note to: Directors of Banana Co

        Subject: Consolidation of Grape Co and Strawberry Co

        (i)   Goodwill should be calculated by comparing the fair value of the consideration with the fair value of the identifiable net assets at acquisition. The shares have been correctly valued using the market price of Banana Co at acquisition. Contingent consideration should be included at its fair value which should be assessed taking into account the probability of the targets being achieved as well as being discounted to present value. It would appear reasonable to measure the consideration at a value of $4 million ($16 million × 25%). A corresponding liability should be included within the consolidated financial statements with subsequent remeasurement. This would be adjusted prospectively to profit or loss rather than adjusting the consideration and goodwill.

              The finance director has erroneously measured non-controlling interest using the proportional method rather than at fair value. Although either method is permitted on an acquisition by acquisition basis, the accounting policy of the Banana group is to measure non-controlling interest at fair value. The fair value of the non-controlling interest at acquisition is (20% × $20 million × $4.25) = $17 million.

              Net assets at acquisition were incorrectly included at their carrying amount of $70 million. This should be adjusted to fair value of $75 million with a corresponding $5 million increase to land in the consolidated statement of financial position. Goodwill should have been calculated as follows:

	$m
Fair value of share exchange	68
Contingent consideration	4
Non-controlling interest at acquisition	17
Fair value of identifiable net assets acquired	(75)
Goodwill	14

              The correcting entry required to the consolidated financial statements is:

Debit	Goodwill	$2 million	
Debit	Land	$5 million	
Credit	Non-controlling interest		$3 million
Credit	Liabilities		$4 million

        (ii)   If an entity holds 20% or more of the voting power of the investee, it is presumed that the entity has significant influence unless it can be clearly demonstrated that this is not the case. The existence of significant influence by an entity is usually evidenced by representation on the board of directors or participation in key policy making processes. Banana Co has 40% of the equity of Strawberry Co and can appoint one director to the board. It would appear that Banana Co has significant influence but not control. Strawberry Co should be classified as an associate and be equity accounted for within the consolidated financial statements.

              The equity method is a method of accounting whereby the investment is initially recognised at cost and adjusted thereafter for the post-acquisition change in the investor's share of the investee's net assets. The investor's profit or loss includes its share of the investee's profit or loss and the investor's other comprehensive income includes its share of the investee's other comprehensive income. At 1 October 20X7, Strawberry Co should have been included in the consolidated financial statements at a value of $20.4 million ($18 million + 40% × $50 million − $44 million).

(iii)   On disposal of 75% of the shares, Banana Co no longer exercises significant influence over Strawberry Co and a profit on disposal of $3.1 million should have been calculated.

	$m
Proceeds	19.0
Fair value of retained interest	4.5
Carrying amount of investment in associate (see part (ii))	(20.4)
Gain on disposal	3.1

Banana Co is incorrect to have recorded a loss in reserves of $14 million and this should be reversed. Instead, a gain of $3.1 million should have been included within the consolidated statement of profit or loss. The investment is initially restated to fair value of $4.5 million. Banana Co does not intend to sell their remaining interest and providing that they make an irrecoverable election, they can treat the remaining interest at fair value through other comprehensive income. The investment will be restated to $4 million at the reporting date with a corresponding loss of $0.5 million reported in other comprehensive income.

(b)   Melon Co should only be treated as an asset acquisition if the acquisition fails the definition of a business combination. In accordance with IFRS 3 *Business Combinations*, an entity should determine whether a transaction is a business combination by applying the definition of a business in IFRS 3.

A business combination arises when an acquirer obtains control of a business. According to IFRS 3, a business is an integrated set of activities and assets which are capable of being conducted and managed for the purpose of providing goods or services to customers, generating investment income or generating other income from ordinary activities. A business has inputs and processes which are applied to create outputs.

An input is any economic resource that can be used to create outputs, including tangible and intangible assets such as intellectual property.

A process is any system, standard, protocol, convention or rule that, with inputs, contributes to the creation of outputs.

Outputs are the result of inputs and processes. Outputs provide goods or services to customers, generate investment income such as dividends or interest, or generate other income from ordinary activities.

If an acquired set of activities and assets is generating revenue at the acquisition date, it is considered to have outputs.

It is clear that Melon Co has both inputs and processes. The licence is an input as it is an economic resource within the control of Melon Co which is capable of providing outputs once one or more processes are applied to it. Processes are in place through the research activities, integration with the management company and supervisory and administrative functions performed. The research activities are still at an early stage, so no output is yet obtainable.

To meet the IFRS 3 definition of a business, the acquired set of activities and assets must have   inputs (which Melon Co does) and *substantive* processes that can significantly contribute to the creation of outputs.

To be considered substantive, the acquired process must be essential to convert an acquired input into outputs, and the inputs acquired must include an organised workforce capable of performing the process on other acquired inputs to produce outputs.

Therefore, due to the absence of a substantive process, Melon Co fails the IFRS 3 definition of a business and the directors are correct to treat the purchase of Melon Co as an asset acquisition.

(c)   IFRS 9 *Financial Instruments* requires that a financial asset only qualifies for derecognition once the entity has transferred the contractual rights to receive the cash flows from the asset or where the entity has retained the contractual rights but has an unavoidable obligation to pass on the cash flows to a third party. The substance of the disposal of the bonds needs to be assessed by a consideration of the risks and rewards of ownership.

Banana Co has not transferred the contractual rights to receive the cash flows from the bonds. The third party is obliged to return the coupon interest to Banana Co and to pay additional amounts should the fair values of the bonds increase. Consequently, Banana Co still has the rights associated with the interest and will also benefit from any appreciation in the value of the bonds. Banana still retains the risks of ownership as it has to compensate the third party should the fair value of the bonds depreciate in value.

It would be expected that, if the sale were a genuine transfer of risks and rewards of ownership, then the sales price would be approximate to the fair value of the bonds. It would only be in unusual circumstances such as a forced sale of Banana Co's assets arising from severe financial difficulties that this would not be the case. The sales price of $8 million is well below the current fair value of the bonds of $10.5 million. Additionally, Banana Co is likely to exercise their option to repurchase the bonds.

It can be concluded that no transfer of rights has taken place and therefore the asset should not be derecognised. To measure the asset at amortised cost, the entity must have a business model where they intend to collect the contractual cash flows over the life of the asset. Banana Co maintains these rights and therefore the sale does not contradict their business model. The bonds should continue to be measured at amortised cost in the consolidated financial statements of Banana Co. The value of the bonds at 30 June 20X6 would have been $10.2 million ($10 million + 7% × $10 million – 5% × $10 million). Amortised cost prohibits a restatement to fair value. The value of the bonds at 30 June 20X7 should be $10.414 million ($10.2 million + 7% × $10.2 million – 5% × $10 million). The proceeds of $8 million should be treated as a financial liability and would also be measured at amortised cost. An interest charge of $0.8 million would accrue between 1 July 20X6 and 1 July 20X8, being the difference between the sale and repurchase price of the bonds.

13 Hill

		Marks
(a)	Application of the following discussion to the scenario:	
	• Deferred consideration	2
	• Property, plant and equipment	2
	• NCI	1
	• Goodwill impairment	3
	Goodwill calculations and corrections required	5
		13
(b)	Calculations of:	
	• Profit on disposal	3
	• Treatment as associate	1
		4
(c)	Application of the following discussion to the scenario:	
	• Compound instrument treatment	3
	• Calculation of liability and adjustments	2
		5
(d)	Application of the following discussion to the scenario:	
	• Treatment of deferred tax asset	4
	• Implications of loan covenant breach	4
		8
		30

(a)   **Deferred consideration**

When calculating goodwill, IFRS 3 *Business Combinations* states that purchase consideration should be measured at fair value. For deferred cash consideration, this will be the present value of the cash flows. This amounts to $29 million ($32m × 1/(1.05²) or $32m × 0.907). Goodwill arising on acquisition should be increased by $29 million and a corresponding liability should be recognised:

Debit Goodwill $29 million
Credit Liability $29 million

Interest of $1.5 million ($29m × 5%) should be recorded. This is charged to the statement of profit or loss and increases the carrying amount of the liability:

Debit Finance costs $1.5 million
Credit Liability $1.5 million

Property, plant and equipment (PPE)

During the measurement period IFRS 3 states that adjustments should be made retrospectively if new information is determined about the value of consideration transferred, the subsidiary's identifiable net assets, or the non-controlling interest. The measurement period ends no later than 12 months after the acquisition date.

The survey detailed that Chandler's PPE was overvalued by $10 million as at the acquisition date. It was received four months after the acquisition date and so this revised valuation was received during the measurement period. As such, goodwill at acquisition should be recalculated. As at the acquisition date, the carrying amount of PPE should be reduced by $10 million and the carrying amount of goodwill increased by $10 million:

Debit Goodwill $10 million
Credit PPE $10 million

NCI

The NCI at acquisition was valued at $34 million but it should have been valued at $32 million (($170m – $10m PPE adjustment) × 20%). Both NCI at acquisition and goodwill at acquisition should be reduced by $2 million:

Debit NCI $2 million
Credit Goodwill $2 million

Goodwill

Goodwill arising on the acquisition of Chandler should have been calculated as follows:

	$m
Fair value of consideration ($150m + $29m)	179
NCI at acquisition	32
Fair value of identifiable net assets acquired	(160)
Goodwill at acquisition	51

Goodwill impairment

According to IAS 36 *Impairment of Assets*, a cash-generating unit to which goodwill is allocated should be tested for impairment annually by comparing its carrying amount to its recoverable amount. As goodwill has been calculated using the proportionate method, then this must be grossed up to include the goodwill attributable to the NCI.

	$m	$m
Goodwill	51.0	
Notional NCI ($51m × 20/80)	12.8	
Total notional goodwill		63.8

	$m	$m
Net assets at reporting date:		
Fair value at start of period	160.0	
Profit for period	52.0	
		212.0
Total carrying amount of assets		275.8
Recoverable amount		(250.0)
Impairment		25.8

The impairment is allocated against the total notional goodwill. The NCI share of the goodwill has not been recognised in the consolidated financial statements and so the NCI share of the impairment is also not recognised. The impairment charged to profit or loss is therefore $20.6 million ($25.8m × 80%) and this expense is all attributable to the equity holders of the parent company.

Debit	Operating expenses	$20.6 million	
Credit	Goodwill		$20.6 million

The carrying amount of the goodwill relating to Chandler at the reporting date will be $30.4 million ($51m acquisition − $20.6m impairment).

(b)   **Doyle Co**

Until 1 April 20X6, Doyle Co is a subsidiary of Hill Co and so should be consolidated until that date. The sale of the shares on 1 April 20X6, results in Hill Co losing control over Doyle Co. The goodwill, net assets and NCI of Doyle Co must be derecognised from the consolidated statement of financial position. The difference between the proceeds from the disposal (including the fair value of the shares retained) and these amounts will give rise to a $47 million profit on disposal. This is calculated as follows:

	$m	$m
Proceeds	140	
Fair value of remaining interest	300	
		440
Goodwill at disposal		(50)
Net assets at disposal		(590)
NCI:		
At acquisition	215	
NCI % of post acquisition profit (40% × ($590m − $510m))	32	
NCI at disposal		247
Profit on disposal		47

After the share sale, Hill Co owns 40% of Doyle Co's shares and has the ability to appoint two of the six members of Doyle Co's board of directors. IAS 28 *Investments in Associates and Joint Ventures* states that an associate is an entity over which an investor has significant influence. Significant influence is presumed when the investor has a shareholding of between 20 and 50%. Representation on the board of directors provides further evidence that significant influence exists.

Therefore, the remaining 40% shareholding in Doyle Co should be accounted for as an associate. It will be initially recognised at its fair value of $300 million and accounted for using the equity method. This means that the group recognises its share of the associate's profit after tax, which equates to $24.6 million ($123m × 6/12 × 40%). As at the reporting date, the associate will be carried at $324.6 million ($300m + $24.6m) in the consolidated statement of financial position.

(c) **Convertible bond**

Hill Co has issued a compound instrument because the bond has characteristics of both a financial liability (an obligation to repay cash) and equity (an obligation to issue a fixed number of Hill's own shares). IAS 32 *Financial Instruments: Presentation* specifies that compound instruments must be split into:

- A liability component (the obligation to repay cash); and
- An equity component (the obligation to issue a fixed number of shares).

The split of the liability component and the equity component at the issue date is calculated as follows:

- The liability component is the present value of the cash repayments, discounted using the market rate on non-convertible bonds;
- The equity component is the difference between the cash received and the liability component at the issue date.

The initial carrying amount of the liability should have been measured at $17.9 million, calculated as follows:

Date	Cash flow $m	Discount rate	Present value $m
30 September 20X6	0.8	0.909	0.73
30 September 20X7	20.8	0.826	17.18
			17.91

The equity component should have been initially measured at $2.1 million ($20m – $17.9m). The adjustment required is:

Debit Non-current liabilities $2.1m
Credit Equity $2.1m

The equity component remains unchanged. After initial recognition, the liability is measured at amortised cost, as follows:

1 October 20X5 $m	Finance charge (10%) $m	Cash paid $m	30 September 20X6 $m
17.9	1.8	(0.8)	18.9

The finance cost recorded for the year was $0.8 million and so must be increased by $1.0 million ($1.8m – $0.8m).

Debit Finance costs $1.0m

Credit Non-current liabilities $1.0m

The liability has a carrying amount of $18.9 million as at the reporting date.

(d) **Deferred tax**

According to IAS 12 *Income Taxes*, an entity should recognise a deferred tax asset in respect of the carry-forward of unused tax losses to the extent that it is probable that future taxable profit will be available against which the losses can be utilised. IAS 12 stresses that the existence of unused losses is strong evidence that future taxable profit may not be available. For this reason, convincing evidence is required about the existence of future taxable profits.

IAS 12 says that entities should consider whether the tax losses result from identifiable causes which are unlikely to recur. Hill has now made losses in three consecutive financial years, and therefore significant doubt exists about the likelihood of future profits being generated.

Although Hill Co is forecasting an improvement in its trading performance, this is a result of new products which are currently under development. It will be difficult to reliably forecast the performance of these products. More emphasis should be placed on the performance of existing products and existing customers when assessing the likelihood of future trading profits.

BPP
LEARNING
MEDIA

Finally, Hill Co breached a bank loan covenant and some uncertainty exists about its ability to continue as a going concern. This, again, places doubts on the likelihood of future profits and suggests that recognition of a deferred tax asset for unused tax losses would be inappropriate.

Based on the above, it would seem that Hill Co is incorrect to recognise a deferred tax asset in respect of its unused tax losses.

Covenant breach

Hill Co is currently presenting the loan as a non-current liability. IAS 1 *Presentation of Financial Statements* states that a liability should be presented as current if the entity:

- Settles it as part of its operating cycle;

- Holds the liability primarily for the purpose of trading;

- Is due to settle the liability within 12 months of the reporting date; or

- Does not have the right at the end of the reporting period to defer settlement for at least 12 months after the reporting date.

Hill Co breached the loan covenants before the reporting date but only received confirmation after the reporting date that the loan was not immediately repayable. As per IAS 10 *Events after the Reporting Period*, the bank confirmation is a non-adjusting event because, as at the reporting date, Hill did not have the right to defer settlement of the loan for at least 12 months. IAS 1 is clear that this right only exists if the entity complies with any required conditions at the reporting date, even if compliance is not tested until later. In the statement of financial position as at 30 September 20X6 the loan should be reclassified as a current liability.

Going concern

Although positive forecasts of future performance exist, management must consider whether the breach of the loan covenant and the recent trading losses place doubt on Hill Co's ability to continue as a going concern. If material uncertainties exist, then disclosures should be made in accordance with IAS 1.

14 Luploid

Workbook references. Fair value measurement under IFRS 13 and IAS 36 *Impairment of Assets* are both covered in Chapter 4. The underlying principles of acquisition accounting given in IFRS 3 *Business Combinations* are covered in Chapter 11. Share-based payment is covered in Chapter 10.

Top tips. Question 1 of the real exam will always test group accounting as well as other financial reporting issues. In this question, part (a)(i) required an explanation of how the fair value of a factory site is determined as part of the acquisition of a subsidiary. This required knowledge of IFRS 13. Part (a)(ii) required the calculation of goodwill on acquisition measuring the non-controlling interest (NCI) under both fair value and proportionate share of net assets. The examiner commented that no explanation was needed to support these goodwill calculations, but that some candidates provided an explanation anyway. This explanation would have not gained any marks as it was not required by the question – make sure you read the questions requirements carefully and only provide explanations for calculations if specified.

Part (b) required a discussion and calculation of an impairment loss relating to a subsidiary, including an explanation of how the impairment would differ depending upon the measurement of non-controlling interest. The examiner commented that very few candidates explained the need for grossing-up goodwill when NCI is measured at the proportionate share of net assets. Make sure you review the suggested solution below carefully if you are unsure of the need to gross up goodwill in this way.

Part (c)(i) regarding the share-based payment was tricky - but you should have been able to pick up some marks in this part of the question for discussing the share exchange. With questions like this, if you are unsure, you should have a go at this part of the question, but make sure you don't spend more than the allocated time of 1.95 minutes per mark.

Part (c)(ii) asked for the resulting share-based expense and a discussion of the vesting conditions. The examiner commented that this was not well answered. If you are unsure about share-based payments, go back to your Workbook, Chapter 10, to revise.

Marking scheme

				Marks
(a)	(i)	Application of the following discussion to the scenario:		
		How FV should be determined	5	
		Why depreciation replacement cost is unsuitable	2	
				7
	(ii)	Calculation marks for:		
		Correct FV of net assets	1	
		Correct NCI figures	2	
				3
(b)		Discussion of what constitutes an impairment and CGUs	2	
		Correct calculation of impairment losses for both methods	2	
		Notional goodwill	1	
		Impairment allocation	3	
		Discussion of how and why methods differ	3	
				11
(c)	(i)	Calculation FV of deferred shares	1	
		Calculation of FV of options	1	
		Discussion of the above calculations and Application to the scenario	2	
				4
	(ii)	Calculation share expense	1	
		Application of the following discussion to the scenario:		
		Why expense required	2	
		Vesting conditions	2	
				5
				30

(a) (i) IFRS 13 *Fair Value Measurement* permits a range of valuation methods to estimate fair value including market based, income estimates and a cost-based approach. However, the characteristics of each asset should be considered when determining the most appropriate methodology.

Fair value is defined as the price which would be received to sell an asset or paid to transfer a liability in an orderly transaction between market participants at the measurement date. Fair value is therefore not supposed to be entity specific but rather to be market focused. The estimate consequently should consider what the market would be prepared to pay for the asset.

The market would consider all alternative uses for the assessment of the price which they would be willing to pay. Fair value should therefore be measured by consideration of the highest and best use of the asset. There is a presumption that the current use would be the highest and best use.

The highest and best use of the asset would appear to be as residential property and not the current industrial use. The intentions of Colyson Co are not relevant as fair value is not entity specific. The alternative use would need to be based upon fair and reasonable assumptions. In particular, it would be necessary to ensure that planning permission to demolish the factory and convert into residential properties would be likely. Since several nearby sites have been given such permission, this would appear to be the case.

The fair value of the factory site should be valued as if converted into residential use. Since this cannot be determined on a stand-alone basis, the combined value of the land and buildings is calculated. The $1 million demolition and planning costs should be deducted from the market value of $24 million. The fair value of the land and buildings should be $23 million. The fair value of the identifiable net assets at acquisition are $88 million ($65m + $23m).

Depreciated replacement cost should only be considered as a possible method for estimating the fair value of the asset when other more suitable methods are not available. This may be the case when the asset is highly specialised and market data is therefore limited or unavailable. This is not the case with the factory site. In any case, the rise in value of land and properties particularly for residential use would mean that to use depreciated replacement cost would undervalue the asset. The exit value for the asset, whether it was based on the principal or most advantageous market, would need to be the same as the entry price. Depreciation may not also be an accurate reflection of all forms of obsolescence including physical deterioration. The estimate would need to be adjusted for such factors even where industrial use remained the best use of the asset.

(ii)   Goodwill should be calculated as follows:

	Fair value method $m	Proportional method $m
Consideration	90	90
Non-controlling interest (NCI) at acquisition	22	17.6
Net assets at acquisition	(88)	(88)
Goodwill	24	19.6

NCI at acquisition under proportional method is $17.6 million (20% × $88m).

The fair value of the net assets at acquisition is $88 million as per part a(i) ($65m + $23m).

Tutorial note: Goodwill under the proportional method could also be calculated as:

Consideration	$90m
Less FV of net assets acquired (80% × $88m)	($70.4)m
Goodwill on acquisition	$19.6m

(b)   An impairment arises where the carrying amount of the net assets exceeds the recoverable amount. Where there is a clear indication of impairment, this asset should be reduced to the recoverable amount.

Where the cash flows cannot be independently determined for individual assets, they should be assessed as a cash generating unit. That is the smallest group of assets which independently generate cash flows. Impairments of cash generating units are allocated first to goodwill and then pro rata on the other assets. It should be noted that no asset should be reduced below its recoverable amount.

Fair value method

The overall impairment of Colyson Co is $30 million ($106m + goodwill $24m – $100m). The damaged building should be impaired by $4 million with a corresponding charge to profit or loss. Since $4 million has already been allocated to the land and buildings, $26 million remains. The goodwill should therefore be written off and expensed in the consolidated statement of profit or loss.

Of the remaining $2 million, $1.25 million will be allocated to the plant and machinery (15/(15 + 9) × 2m) and $0.75 million will be allocated to the remaining intangibles (9/(9 + 15) × 2m). As no assets have been previously revalued, all the impairments are charged to profit or loss. $24 million (80% × $30m) will be attributable to the owners of Luploid Co and $6 million to the NCI in the consolidated statement of comprehensive income.

The allocation of the impairment is summarised in this table:

	Original value $m	Impairment $m	Revised CV $m
Land and buildings	60	4	56
Plant and machinery	15	1.25	13.75
Intangibles other than goodwill	9	0.75	8.25
Goodwill	24	24	0
Current assets (at recoverable amount)	22	0	22
Total	130	30	100

Proportionate method

The basic principles and rule for impairment is the same as the fair value method and so $4 million will again first be written off against the land and buildings. The problems arise when performing the impairment review as a cash generating unit. When NCI is measured using the proportional share of net assets, no goodwill is attributable to the NCI since goodwill is not included within the individual net assets of the subsidiary. This means that the goodwill needs to be grossed up when an impairment review is performed so that it is comparable with the recoverable amount. Under the fair value method, the NCI fully represents any premium the other shareholders would be prepared to pay for the net assets and so goodwill does not need to be grossed up.

The goodwill of $19.6 million is grossed up by 100/80 to a value of $24.5 million. This extra $4.9 million is known as notional goodwill. The overall impairment is now $30.5 million ($106m + $24.5m – $100m) of which $4 million has already been allocated. Since the remaining impairment of $26.5 million exceeds the value of goodwill, the goodwill is written down to zero. However, as only $19.6 million goodwill is recognised within the consolidated accounts, the impairment attributable to the notional goodwill is not recognised. Only $19.6 million is deducted in full from the owners of Luploid Co's share of profits since there is no goodwill attributable to the non-controlling interest. The remaining $2 million impairment is allocated between plant and machinery and intangibles (other than goodwill). NCI will be allocated 20% of $6 million ($4m + $2m), ie $1.2 million. Consolidated retained earnings will be charged with 80% of $6 million (ie $4.8 million) plus $19.6 million goodwill impairment (ie $24.4m in total). The allocation of the impairment is summarised in this table:

> **Tutorial note:** Notional goodwill and impairment of notional goodwill does not impact on the consolidated financial statements.

	Original carrying amount $m	Impairment $m	Revised carrying amount $m
Land and buildings	60	4	56
Plant and machinery	15	1.25	13.75
Intangibles other than goodwill	9	0.75	8.25
Goodwill	19.6	19.6	0
(Notional goodwill)	4.9	4.9	0
Current assets (at recoverable amount)	22		22
Total	130.5	30.5	100

(c)   (i)   IFRS 3 *Business Combinations* requires all consideration to be measured at fair value on acquisition of a subsidiary. This will include the deferred shares. Since Luploid Co is obliged to replace the share-based scheme of Hammond Co on acquisition, the replacement scheme should also be included as consideration. There is, however, a post combination service period which means that the portion of the replacement scheme attributable to pre-combination service is the market value of the acquiree award multiplied by the ratio of the portion of the vesting period completed to the greater of the total vesting period or the original vesting period of the acquire award.

The vesting period of the acquiree award had vested and was three years. As there is a two-year post combination vesting period, the total vesting period is five years. Therefore the amount attributable to the pre-combination period (and therefore added to the cost of the investment) should be $15 million × 3/5 = $9 million.

Deferred shares should be measured at the fair value at the acquisition date with subsequent changes in fair value ignored. Luploid Co will issue 2.4 million

(60% × 10m × 2/5) shares as consideration. The market price at the date of acquisition was $30, so the fair value is $72 million. The total consideration should be valued as $81 million (72 + 9).

(ii)   The fair value of the replacement scheme at the grant date is $18 million (100 × 10,000 × 90% × $20). Since $9 million has been allocated to the cost of the investment, the remaining $9 million should be treated as part of the post combination remuneration package for the employees and measured in accordance with IFRS 2 *Share-based Payment*. The fair value at the grant date of the share-based scheme should be expensed to profit or loss over the two-year vesting period. Subsequent changes to the fair value of the shares are ignored.

Luploid Co will need to consider the impact of market and non-market based vesting conditions. The condition relating to the share price of Luploid Co is a market based vesting condition. These are adjusted for in the calculation of the fair value at the grant date of the option. An expense is therefore recorded in the consolidated profit or loss of Luploid Co irrespective of whether the market based vesting condition is met or not. A corresponding credit should be included within equity.

15 Sugar Co

Marking scheme

Marks

(a)   Application of the following discussion to the scenario:

- Treatment as an associate (including FV 40% and share exchange at 1 July 20X7) 5

- FV NCI and identifiable net assets at 1 July 20X7 3

Goodwill calculation and treatment of cash consideration 2

10

		Marks
(b)	Marks for calculations as follows:	
	Acquisition of intangible assets	3
	Proceeds on disposal of PPE	3
	Cash paid for Butter Co	1
	Dividends received from associates	2
	Investment income received	3
	Issue of ordinary shares	2
	Non-controlling interest dividend	2
		16
(c)	Application of the following discussion to the scenario:	
	• Cash flows to include/exclude	2
	• Other elements of defined benefit scheme	2
		4
		30

(a) **Cash paid to acquire Flour Co**

The acquisition of Flour Co is a step acquisition. This means the original 40% equity interest is treated as if it is disposed and then reacquired at fair value. The difference between the carrying amount of the original 40% equity interest and its fair value would be included as a gain within profit or loss. As an associate, the investment would have been accounted for using the equity method and would be valued at $14.8 million as at 1 July 20X7:

	$'000
Cost	10,000
Share of increase in net assets between acquisition dates ($12m × 40%)	4,800
Investment in associate as at 1 July 20X7	14,800

The fair value of the original 40% interest would be $15.2 million (10m × 40% × $3.80) and so gain of $400,000 would be included within profit or loss.

Goodwill will be calculated at 1 July 20X7, the date that control is gained, as the difference between the fair value of the consideration and non-controlling interest and the fair value of the identifiable net assets at acquisition. The consideration must include the fair value of the original 40% equity interest as well as the fair value of the additional consideration.

The fair value of the non-controlling interest at 1 July 20X7 will be $11.4 million (10m × 30% × $3.80).

The fair value of the share exchange will be $9 million (3 million shares acquired × ½ × $6).

Goodwill has been determined to be $2,259,000 which means the cash paid to acquire Flour Co on 1 July 20X7 must be $3 million as follows:

	$'000
Fair value of original 40% equity interest	15,200
Fair value of share exchange	9,000
Fair value of non-controlling interest at acquisition	11,400
Fair value of identifiable net assets at acquisition including FV uplift ($35,741 + $600)	(36,341)
Cash Consideration (balancing figure)	3,000
Goodwill on acquisition per question	2,259

Cash paid to acquire Flour Co will be included within the investing activities of the consolidated statement of cash flows. However, the cash held by Flour Co will now be consolidated so a net outflow arises of $1,766,000 ($3m – $1.234m).

(b) **Extracts from the consolidated statement of cash flows for the Sugar Group year ended 30 June 20X8**

Cash flows from investing activities

	$'000
Net cash paid on acquisition of Flour Co (part (a))	(1,766)
Cash paid to acquire intangible assets (W1)	(12,051)
Proceeds from disposal of property plant and equipment (W2)	4,370
Cash paid on acquisition of Butter Co (given in question)	(5,000)
Dividends received from associates (W3)	2,253
Proceeds from disposal of FVTPL investment ($4m + $0.5m)	4,500
Investment income received (W4)	1,991

Cash flows from financing activities

	$'000
Issue of ordinary shares during the year (W5)	9,600
Dividends paid to the non-controlling interest (W6)	(3,324)

Workings

1 *Intangible assets*

	$'000
Intangible assets b/f	15,865
Goodwill on acquisition of Sugar Co	2,259
Licences and patents on acquisition of Sugar Co	6,781
Amortisation	(3,500)
Cash purchases of intangible assets (balancing figure)	12,051
Intangible assets c/f	33,456

2   *Property, plant and equipment*

	$'000
Property, plant and equipment b/f	52,818
Acquisition of Flour Co (at fair value)	18,676
Depreciation	(10,000)
Carrying amount of disposal (balancing figure)	(6,370)
Property, plant and equipment c/f	55,124

3   *Dividends received from associates*

	$'000
Investment in associates b/f	23,194
Associate profit for the year	15,187
Acquisition of Butter Co	5,000
Step acquisition Sugar Co (part (a))	(14,800)
Dividends received (balancing figure)	(2,253)
Investment in associate c/f	26,328

4   *FV gains recognised in investment income*

	$'000
FVTPL asset b/f	6,000
Carrying amount of disposal	(4,000)
Fair value gains included in investment income (balancing figure)	1,000
FVTPL asset c/f	3,000

	$'000
Investment income per PL	3,891
FV gains on FVTPL investments	(1,000)
Fair value gains on step acquisition	(400)
Profit on disposal of FVTPL	(500)
Investment income received	1,991

Proceeds from the disposal of the FVTPL asset are $4.5 million ($4m + $0.5m)

> **Tutorial note.**
>
> The fair value gain is included within investment income but is not a cash flow and so will be excluded from the consolidated statement of cash flows. In addition there is a $400,000 gain arising upon the step acquisition of Flour Co included within the investment income but isn't a cash flow. The profit on disposal of $0.5 million is also not a cash flow but forms part of the proceeds from the disposal of FVTPL assets within investing activities. Cash proceeds included within the investment income of the group are therefore $1,991,000.

5   Issue of ordinary shares during the year

	$'000
Share capital and share premium b/f ($20m + $18m)	38,000
Share for share exchange (part (a))	9,000
Cash proceeds from issue of shares during the year (balance)	9,600
Share capital and share premium c/f ($23m + $33.6m)	56,600

6   Dividends paid to non-controlling interest

	$'000
Non-controlling interest b/f	12,914
Added on acquisition of Flour Co (part (a))	11,400
Non-controlling interest profit for the year	9,162
Dividends paid to non-controlling interest (balancing figure)	(3,324)
Non-controlling interest c/f	30,152

(c)   The only cash flow that should be recorded in the consolidated statement of cash flows in relation to defined benefit pension schemes are the contributions paid into the scheme. These are typically included within the operating activities of the group statement of cash flows. Since Sugar Co did not make any contributions until after the year-end there will be no cash flows to include in the consolidated statement of cash flows for the year ended 30 June 20X8. The $2 million benefits paid out of the scheme are a cash outflow but they are an outflow of cash from the pension scheme itself, a separate entity, rather than a cash outflow of Sugar Co.

This does not mean that the pension scheme will not have any impact upon the consolidated statement of cash flows of the Sugar group. Since operating activities are being calculated using the indirect method it is necessary to adjust for any items that effect operating profit but are not cash flows. This would include the service cost component which would need to be added back to group profits. Care would also need to be taken in calculating the interest paid in the year. The finance cost charge in the profit and loss would include the net interest charge from unwinding the opening value of the liabilities and the estimated return on the assets. Neither of these are cash flows and so would require adjusting. The remeasurement component is included as part of other comprehensive impact and will not impact on the group statement of cash flows since it is not a cash flow, nor does it impact upon operating profit.

16 Angel

Workbook reference. Group statements of cash flow are covered in Chapter 17. Interpretation of financial statements of different companies is included in Chapter 18.

Top tips. There are many straightforward, non-group aspects to this extracts from consolidated statement of cash flows question, so make sure you don't get bogged down in the information provided at the expense of these. We have set up workings for working capital reconciliations even though the movements are straightforward.

Make sure you allocate enough time to Part (b) – it has eight marks available for fairly straightforward knowledge that is not technically challenging.

Easy marks. These are available for the workings in Part (a)(iii) as well as explanations for the adjustments in Part (a), all of which are straightforward, along with valid points made in Part (b) on the differences between manufacturing and digital companies. The key point with cash flows is to ensure your understanding of the signage of each adjustment is clear, this will be important not only for your workings but also your explanation to the directors.

Marks

(a)	(i)	Building renovation	4
	(ii)	Profit before taxation	4
	(iii)	Cash generated from operations – up to 2 marks per item	14
(b)	(i)	Discussion 1 mark per point to a maximum	5
	(ii)	Discussion 1 mark per point for each non-financial disclosure to a maximum	3

$$\frac{}{\underline{30}}$$

(a)   (i)   **Building renovation**

The building renovation has been incorrectly accounted for because Angel has debited the cash spent to revenue and this needs to be corrected in order to capitalise the correct amount for the enhancement of the asset. The correcting entries are:

Debit	Property, plant and equipment (PPE)	$3m	
Credit	Revenue		$3m

Being capitalisation of renovation of building and correction of charge to revenue

Angel treats grant income on capital-based projects as deferred income so it should not have credited the cash received from the grant to PPE and it needs to be reclassified to deferred income on the statement of financial position. The grant will then be released in line with future depreciation charges so as to recognise the benefit over the same period as the related costs it is intended to compensate. However, the grant of $2 million needs to be split equally between renovation (capital) and job creation (revenue). There do not appear to be any future performance conditions relating to the job creation portion of the grant, so that part may be released immediately to profit and loss at the time the cash has become receivable. The correcting entries for this are:

Debit	Property, plant and equipment (PPE)	$2m	
Credit	Retained earnings – profit or loss		$1m
Credit	Deferred income		$1m

Being correction of treatment of grant income

(ii)   **Adjustments to profit before tax**

Profit before tax needs to be adjusted to take account of:

(1)   The correcting entries for the building refurbishment and grant in Part (a)(i).

(2)   The $4 million construction costs for the machine have been incorrectly charged to other expenses and need to be capitalised as part of property, plant and equipment (information point (iii)).

(3)   The related interest of $1 million which is allowable as part of the cost of the asset under IAS 23 *Borrowing Costs* needs to be capitalised (information point (iii)):

Correcting entries for points (2) and (3) are:

Debit	Property, plant and equipment	$5m	
Credit	Profit or loss		$5m

Being correction of construction costs charged to operating expenses and capitalisation of interest under IAS 23.

Therefore, profit before tax may be adjusted as follows to arrive at a correct figure for inclusion in the cash flow statement:

	$m
Per question	184
Correction of renovation costs and grant (a)(i)	4
Correction of construction costs and interest (a)(ii)	5
	193

(iii)   ANGEL GROUP

EXTRACT FROM STATEMENT OF CASH FLOWS
FOR THE YEAR ENDED 30 NOVEMBER 20X3

	$m
Operating activities	
Profit before tax (Part (a)(ii))	193.0
Adjustments for:	
Profit on sale of property, plant and equipment: (W1)	(14.0)
Depreciation (per question/W2)	29.0
Impairment of goodwill and intangible assets (per question/W3): $26.5m + $90m	116.5
Share of profit of associate (per question/W4)	(12.0)
Interest expense: $11m per question less $1m capitalised ((a)(ii) (W5)	10.0
	322.5
Decrease in trade receivables (W6)	58.0
Decrease in inventories (W6)	41.0
Decrease in trade payables (W6)	(211.0)
Cash generated from operations	210.5

Workings

1   *Profit on sale of property, plant and equipment (PPE)*

	$m
Proceeds from sale of PPE	63
Less carrying amount of PPE disposed	(49)
Profit on sale of property, plant and equipment	14

This amount needs to be deducted from profit before tax because the profit of $14 million is a non-cash credit currently included within profit before tax. The cash proceeds figure of $63 million will be included in the investing activities section.

2   *Depreciation*

The depreciation charge of $29 million which has been deducted in arriving at the profit before tax figure. It is non-cash and must be added back.

3   *Impairment of goodwill and intangible assets*

The impairment charge of $116.5 million, which has been deducted in arriving at the profit before tax figure, is a non-cash movement and, as with depreciation, it must be added back.

4   *Share of profit of associate*

The profit share of $12 million recorded in Angel's profit or loss is again a non-cash figure and should therefore be deducted to arrive at a cash figure related to operations. Any dividend received by Angel from its associate during the year will be included as a cash receipt in the investing activities section of Angel's cash flow statement.

5   *Interest expense*

The interest charge of $10 million (being the $11m paid less the $1m capitalised) is a cash payment. It is reclassified and shown in the cash flow statement below cash generated from operations as a charge to this figure, along with tax, to arrive at a net cash from operating activities figure.

6   *Working capital changes*

	Inventories $m	Trade receivables $m	Trade payables $m
b/d	190	180	361
Acquisition of subsidiary	6	3	5
∴ Increase/(decrease)	(41) β	(58) β	(211) β
c/d	155	125	155

Movements in working capital are brought into the cash generated from operations figure. If the inventories balance has fallen, there is less cash tied up in inventory held and the cash position benefits. The key point here is that Angel acquired a subsidiary, Sweety, during the financial year and gained inventory and trade receivable and payable balances without a related operational movement in cash. Therefore, these amounts must be adjusted when calculating the correct cash flow. The cash payment to acquire Sweety (net of the cash acquired) will be included in the investing activities section of the cash flow statement.

(b)   (i)   **Financial statement differences**

Angel is a wholesale manufacturer and has made an investment gaining significant influence in a digital company. It is important that the stakeholders of Angel, which includes is directors, manage their expectations in terms of the information presented in the financial statements of Digitool. At a high level, as a wholesale manufacturer, Angel will have a significant level of property, plant and equipment (a factory, a distribution warehouse and manufacturing machinery) and it will hold inventories either in the form of finished goods or work in progress. As a result of its long-established relationships with large customers, it would be expected to have a relatively high level of trade receivables. Contrast this with Digitool. Its non-current assets will comprise its data centre and related equipment. Digital companies also frequently invest in research and development relating to new techniques and processes and may therefore have significant capitalised development costs. It would not be expected to have inventory, other than some work in progress relating to any ongoing contracts,

In terms of the ratios commonly reviewed, it is important that ratios are reviewed in the context of the specific entity. It is unlikely that the directors will be able to compare the ratios they regularly review for Angel with equivalent ratios for Digitool. The gross profit margin will not be comparable between the companies. The cost of sales of Digitool will mainly comprise employee costs and therefore its gross profit margin is likely to be higher than that for Angel. Digitool will, however, have additional operating costs relating to research, and advertising and promotion expenditure incurred in generating new customers that Angel is unlikely to have, thus net profit margins may be more comparable. The return on capital employed is likely to be lower for Angel as it has been established for a number of years, has goodwill from its investments in other entities and is heavily capitalised. The inventory holding period is a very important ratio for a manufacturing company but is not relevant for a digital company as it does not hold a physical inventories and any work in progress would be expected to convert to revenue quickly. It is not clear what the credit terms offered to customers are, but given Angel has long-standing contracts with regular customers, it is likely to have a longer receivables collection period than Digitool which has a number of new contracts.

(ii) **Non-financial performance measures**

The non-financial performance measures reported by Digitool are in keeping with expectations for a digital company:

- Relationships with customers – it is essential for companies that do not sell a physical product and instead sell 'business solutions' to their customers to communicate well with their customers to understand their needs and be able to tailor solutions to them. Digitool may report factors such as customer satisfaction scores, the number of individual engagements with their customers in a period or the average number of repeat customers. Although traditional manufacturers must also have a customer focus to keep their products relevant, because Angel produces mass-produced furniture, it is less likely to interact with the final customer.

- Emissions levels – perhaps surprisingly, data centres produce large levels of emissions and digital companies come under the same social and political pressures to reduce emissions as heavy manufacturing companies.

- Investment in human capital – digital companies rely on their staff to be at the cutting edge of technological developments in order to keep them ahead of competitors. Companies compete to attract the best talent and are renowned for having creative working spaces, flexible working conditions and good salaries to ensure they are seen as good places to work. Traditional companies have requirements to pay staff fair rates and must comply with strict health and safety requirements, particularly when operating machinery, but will generally have a more traditional work environment.

17 Moyes

Marking scheme

				Marks
(a)	(i)	Calculation of cash flow generated from operations	6	
		Explanation of the adjustments and use of the scenario	6	
				12
	(ii)	Application of the following discussion to the scenario:		
		• Purchase consideration (shares and deferred cash)	1	
		• Impact on consolidated statement of cash flows of:		
		– Subsidiary acquisition (including dividend)	3	
		– Subsidiary disposal	2	
				6
	(iii)	IFRS 5 definition of discontinued operation and application to the scenario	3	
		Consideration of held for sale and application to the scenario	1	
		Consideration of loss of control and application to the scenario	2	
				6
(b)		Share-based payment		6
				30

(a) (i) Explanatory note to: The directors of Moyes

Subject: Cash generated from operations

	$
Profit before tax	209
Share of profit of associate	(67)
Service cost component	24
Contributions into the pension scheme	(15)
Impairment of goodwill	10
Depreciation	99
Impairment of property, plant and equipment ($43m – $20m)	23
Movement on inventory ($165m – $126m – $6m)	33
Loss on inventory	6
Increase in receivables	(7)
Increase in current liabilities	18
Cash generated from operations	333

Cash flows from operating activities are principally derived from the key trading activities of the entity. This would include cash receipts from the sale of goods, cash payments to suppliers and cash payments on behalf of employees. The indirect method adjusts profit or loss for the effects of transactions of a non-cash nature, any deferrals or accruals from past or future operating cash receipts or payments and any items of income or expense associated with investing or financing cash flows.

The share of profit of associate is an item of income associated with investing activities and so has been deducted. Likewise cash paid to acquire property, plant and equipment is an investing cash flow rather than an operating one. Non-cash flows which have reduced profit and must subsequently be added back include the service cost component, depreciation, exchange losses and impairments. With the impairment of property, plant and equipment, the first $20 million of impairment will be allocated to the revaluation surplus so only $23 million would have reduced operating profits and should be added back. In relation to the pension scheme, the remeasurement component can be ignored as it is neither a cash flow nor an expense to operating profits. Cash contributions should be deducted, though, as these represent an operating cash payment ultimately to be received by Moyes' employees. Benefits paid are a cash outflow for the pension scheme rather than Moyes and so should be ignored.

The movements on receivables, payables and inventory are adjusted so that the timing differences between when cash is paid or received and when the items are accrued in the financial statements are accounted for. Inventory is measured at the lower of cost and net realisable value. The inventory has suffered an overall loss of $6 million
(Dinar 80 million/5 – Dinar 60 million/6). Of this, $2.7 million is an exchange loss (Dinar 80 million/5 – Dinar 80 million/6) and $3.3 million is an impairment loss (Dinar (80 – 60) million/6). Neither of these are cash flows and would be added back to profits in the reconciliation. However, the loss of $6 million should also be adjusted in the movement of the inventory as a non-cash flow. The net effect on the statement of cash flows will be nil.

(ii) When the parent company acquires or sells a subsidiary during the financial year, cash flows arising from the acquisition or disposal are presented within investing activities. In relation to Davenport, no cash consideration has been paid during the current year since the consideration consisted of a share for share exchange and some deferred cash. The deferred cash would be presented as a negative cash flow within investing activities but only when paid in two years' time.

This does not mean that there would be no impact on the current year's statement of cash flows. On gaining control, Moyes would consolidate 100% of the assets and liabilities of Davenport which would presumably include some cash or cash equivalents at the date of acquisition. These would be presented as a cash inflow at the date of acquisition net of any overdrafts held at acquisition. Adjustments would also need to be made to the opening balances of assets and liabilities by adding the fair values of the identifiable net assets at acquisition to the respective balances. This would be necessary to ensure that only the cash flow effects are reported in the consolidated statement of cash flows. Fair value adjustments to assets and liabilities could also have deferred tax effects which would need adjusting so that only cash payments for tax are included within the statement of cash flows. Dividends received by Moyes from Davenport are not included in the consolidated statement of cash flows since cash has in effect been transferred from one group member to another. The non-controlling interest's share of the dividend would be presented as a cash outflow in financing activities.

On the disposal of Barham, the net assets at disposal, including goodwill, are removed from the consolidated financial statements. Since Barham is overdrawn, this will have a positive cash flow effect for the group. The overdraft will be added to the proceeds (less any cash and cash equivalents at disposal) to give an overall inflow presented in investing activities. Care would once again be necessary to ensure that all balances at the disposal date are removed from the corresponding assets and liabilities so that only cash flows are recorded within the consolidated statement of cash flows.

(iii)   IFRS 5 *Non-current Assets Held for Sale and Discontinued Operations* defines a discontinued operation as a component of an entity which either has been disposed of or is classified as held for sale, and:

(i)   Represents a separate major line of business or geographical area of operations;

(ii)   Is a single co-ordinated plan to dispose of a separate major line or area of operations; and

(iii)   Is a subsidiary acquired exclusively for resale.

Both entities would be components of the Moyes group since their operations and cash flows are clearly distinguishable for reporting purposes. Barham has been sold during the year but there appear to be other subsidiaries which operate in similar geographical regions and produce similar products. Little guidance is given as to what would constitute a separate major line of business or geographical area of operations. The definition is subjective and the directors should consider factors such as materiality and relevance before determining whether Barham should be presented as discontinued or not.

To be classified as held for sale, a sale has to be highly probable and the entity should be available for sale in its present condition. At face value, Watson would not appear to meet this definition as no sales transaction is to take place.

IFRS 5 does not explicitly extend the requirements for held for sale to situations where control is lost. However, the International Accounting Standards Board (IASB) has confirmed that in instances where control is lost, the subsidiaries' assets and liabilities should be derecognised. Loss of control is a significant economic event and fundamentally changes the investor – investee relationship. Therefore, situations where the parent is committed to lose control should trigger a reclassification as held for sale. Whether this should be extended to situations where control is lost due to other causes would be judgemental. It is possible therefore that Watson should be classified as held for sale but to be classified as a discontinued operation, Watson would need to represent a separate major line of business or geographical area of operation.

(b)   **Share-based payment**

IFRS 13 applies when another IFRS requires or permits fair value measurements or disclosures about fair value measurements (and measurements, such as fair value less costs to sell, based on fair value or disclosures about those measurements). IFRS 13 specifically excludes transactions covered by certain other standards including share-based payment transactions within the scope of IFRS 2 *Share-based Payment.*

For cash settled share-based payment transactions, the fair value of the liability is measured in accordance with IFRS 2 initially, at each reporting date and at the date of settlement using an option pricing model. The measurement reflects all conditions and outcomes on a weighted average basis, unlike equity settled transactions. Any changes in fair value are recognised in profit or loss in the period. Therefore, the SARs should have been accounted for as follows:

Year	Expense $	Liability $	Calculation	
30 September 20X6	641,250	641,250	$285 \times 500 \times \$9 \times \frac{1}{2}$	Time-apportioned over vesting period. Using the estimated $(300 \times 95\%)$ 285 managers.
30 September 20X7	926,250	1,567,500	$285 \times 500 \times \$11$	Expense is difference between liabilities at 30 September 20X7 and 30 September 20X6
30 September 20X8	97,500	1,350,000	$225 \times 500 \times \$12$	Cash paid is $60 \times 500 \times \$10.50$, ie $315,000. The liability has reduced by $217,500 and therefore the expense is the difference of $97,500

The fair value of the liability is $1,350,000 at 30 September 20X8 and the expense for the year is $97,500.

18 Hummings Co

Workbook references. Foreign operations and functional currency are covered in Chapter 16. Financial instruments are covered in Chapter 8.

Top tips. In part (a) you were required to explain how the functional currency of a subsidiary should be determined. As with all questions in SBR, you must make sure your answer is applied to the scenario given. In part (b)(i), your discussion should have covered both the recognition of the contracts as intangible assets as well as the covering the translation of the assets into the group's presentation currency. In part (b)(ii), make sure you do as the requirement asks - you only need to explain calculations where the requirement asks you to do so. Here the requirement asks you to explain the impact on the group accounts of the impairment and exchange difference on goodwill. It does not ask you to explain the calculation of goodwill, therefore don't waste your time doing this. Part (c) covered the accounting treatment of a subsidiary acquired for resale. With this type of question, a good approach is to explain the relevant requirements of the standard first, then apply those requirements to the scenario to reach a conclusion. Part (d) covered impairment of financial assets. This question was difficult, and the calculation of the loss allowance was particularly hard. In your real exam, you should not overrun on your allocated time for questions which are difficult such as this, ensure you answer as best you can in the time available, and then move on to the next question.

Marks

(a) Application of the following discussion to the scenario:
        Autonomy from parent   2
        Determination of functional currency   3
                                                       5

(b) (i) Application of the following discussion to the scenario:
           Identifiable criteria and recognition   3
           Need to amortise   1
                                                       4

    (ii) Goodwill calculation   4
           Discussion of correct treatment of impairment and
              exchange difference   1
           Recognition of split between shareholders   1
                                                           6

(c) Discussion of asset held for sale criteria   2
    Application of the above discussion to Quaver Co   2
                                                               4

(d) Amortised cost identification   1
    12-month credit loss – discussion   2
                      – calculation   1
    Amortised cost calculation   1
    Explanation lifetime credit losses   3
    Calculation of lifetime credit losses   3
                                                                        11
                                                                       30

(a) The functional currency is the currency of the primary economic environment in which the entity operates. With a foreign acquisition, consideration should be given as to whether Crotchet Co should adopt the same functional currency as its parent, Hummings Co. However, Crotchet Co appears to be largely independent and is not reliant on Hummings Co for either sales or finance. It is not required therefore for Crotchet Co to adopt the same functional currency as Hummings Co. Crotchet Co does not appear to have transactions in dollars or have a dollar bank account and it can be concluded that the dollar should not be their functional currency.

In determining its functional currency, Crotchet Co should consider the currency which mainly influences its sales price of goods and the currency which mainly influences its labour and other costs. This is likely to be the currency which goods are invoiced in and the currency in which costs are settled. The location of the entity's head office is irrelevant except to the extent that it is likely that the costs of running the head office are likely to be settled in the domestic currency. For Crotchet Co, whilst there are a number of transactions in dinars and tax has to be paid in dinars, it appears that the vast majority of their transactions are in grommits. All sales and purchases are invoiced in grommits as well as approximately half of their staff being paid in grommits. Funds for finance are raised in grommits which further suggests that grommits should be chosen as the functional currency of Crotchet Co.

(b) (i) IFRS 3 *Business Combinations* requires the investor to identify all of the investee's identifiable net assets at acquisition. To be identifiable, a customer contract must either be capable of being used or sold separately or it must arise from legal or contractual rights. A reliable estimate of its fair value is also necessary to be recognised as a separate asset rather than subsumed within the goodwill figure. This is the case regardless of whether the contracts had been recognised within the individual financial statements of Crotchet Co or not.

The contracts provide Crotchet Co with a legal right to prevent their customers from obtaining goods and services from their competitors and a reliable estimate of fair value appears to be obtainable. The contracts should be recognised as a separate intangible asset at an initial value of 15 million grommits. This would initially be translated at the spot rate of exchange of $1 to 8 grommits and would be recognised initially in the consolidated financial statements at $1.875 million. The contracts would need to be examined to determine the average unexpired useful life of the contracts and amortised over this period. This would be translated at the average rate of exchange and expensed to consolidated profit or loss. The carrying amount of the contracts would need to be retranslated at the closing rate of exchange of $1 to 7 grommits ($2.143 million) with a corresponding exchange gain recognised within equity.

(ii) Goodwill at 31 December 20X4 would be $8.2 million calculated as follows:

	Grommits (millions)	Ex rate $:grommits	$ (millions)
Consideration ($24m × 8)	192		
NCI at acquisition ($6m × 8)	48		
Net assets at acquisition*	(158)		
Goodwill at 1 January 20X4	82	8	10.25
Impairment (30%)	(24.6)	7	(3.51)
Exchange gain			1.46
	57.4	7	8.2

* Net assets at acquisition are 43 million grommits plus 15 million grommits for the contractual relationships plus 100 million grommits for the dinar assets translated at 1 dinar to 2 grommits (50m × 2).

Goodwill is initially recognised at the spot rate of exchange of $1:8 grommits and so would initially be $10.25 million. The impairment loss of $3.51 million will be expensed against consolidated profit or loss. Goodwill will be retranslated using the closing rate of exchange of $1:7 grommits with the exchange gain of $1.46 million included within other comprehensive income. Since non-controlling interest is valued at fair value, both the impairment and the exchange gain will be apportioned 80/20 between the shareholders of Hummings Co and the non-controlling interest respectively.

(c) It appears as if the acquisition of Quaver Co should be treated as a subsidiary acquired exclusively with a view for resale. The usual criteria for an asset to be classified as held for sale as per IFRS 5 *Non-current Assets Held for Sale and Discontinued Operations* include:

- The sale must be highly probable;

- The sale must be expected to be complete within 12 months;

- The asset must be actively marketed at a reasonable price;

- Management must be committed to a plan of sale and it is unlikely that any significant changes to the plan will be made.

The sale has not taken place within 12 months of acquisition; however, an exception is permitted where the sale is still deemed to be highly probable and the delay was caused by events which were unforeseen and beyond the control of management. The sale is still expected early in 20X5 and the legal dispute was unforeseen, so this exception seems applicable.

It appears clear that management was immediately committed to the sale as Hummings Co did not wish to have active involvement in the activities of Quaver Co. Quaver Co should therefore be treated as a subsidiary acquired exclusively with a view to resale. It should not be consolidated into the Hummings group financial statements. Quaver Co should initially be valued at fair value less costs to sell with any subsequent decreases in fair value less costs to sell taken to consolidated profit or loss. As a subsidiary acquired exclusively for resale, Quaver Co would be classified as a discontinued activity and earnings for the year disclosed separately in the consolidated statement of profit or loss of the Hummings group.

(d)   Since the business model of Hummings Co is to collect the contractual cash flows of the bonds over the life of the asset, the bonds should be measured at amortised cost. All financial assets including amortised cost assets should initially be recognised at fair value. This would be equal to the $10,000,000 paid on acquisition of the bonds.

IFRS 9 *Financial Instruments* requires entities to adopt an expected value approach to the consideration of impairment losses on financial assets. On acquisition, the bonds are considered low risk and are not credit impaired. The bonds would be classified as a stage one financial asset as at 31 December 20X3. This means that Hummings Co should create an expected credit loss equal to 12 months expected credit losses. It is important to appreciate that the 12-month expected credit loss is not the lifetime expected credit loss which an entity will incur which it predicts will default in the next 12 months. The 12-month expected credit loss is defined as a portion of the lifetime expected credit losses which represent the expected credit losses which result from a default within the next 12 months. In effect, the proportion of the lifetime expected credit losses which are expected should a default occur within 12 months are weighted by the probability of a default occurring. Hummings Co should therefore recognise a default allowance of $10,000 as at 31 December 20X3. This will be expensed to profit or loss and a separate allowance created rather than offset against the $10,000,000 bonds. The allowance is, however, netted off the $10,000,000 bond in the statement of financial position of Hummings Co as at 31 December 20X3. The carrying amount of the bonds in the statement of financial position at 31 December 20X3 will be $9.99 million ($10 million – $10,000).

As the bonds are to be measured at amortised cost, the effective rate of interest of 8% will be included in profit or loss and added to the bonds. This is calculated on the initial $10,000,000 and is not affected by the loss allowance of $10,000. The coupon interest of $500,000 ($10,000,000 × 5%) is deducted from the carrying amount of the bonds. This means that the bonds would have a carrying amount of $10,300,000 at 31 December 20X4 before considering the impairment allowance.

B/fwd	Interest 8%	Coupon 5%	C/fwd
$	PL		
10,000,000	800,000	(500,000)	10,300,000

At 31 December 20X4, there has been a significant increase in credit risk. As no actual default has yet occurred, the bonds should be classified as a stage two financial asset. This means that Hummings Co should make an allowance to recognise the lifetime expected credit losses. This is defined as the expected credit losses (cash shortfalls) which result from all possible default events over the expected life of the bonds. An allowance is required equal to the present value of the expected loss in contractual cash flows as weighted by the probability of default. The expected default losses are discounted using the original effective rate of interest of 8%.

Date	Cash flow loss working	PV of default
		$
31 December 20X5	3% × $462,963	13,889
31 December 20X6	5% × $6,858,710	342,936
		356,825

The expected loss allowance should be increased to $356,825 with an expense recorded in profit or loss of $346,825 ($356,825 – $10,000). The loss allowance is deducted directly from the bonds with future interest income recorded on the gross position. The carrying amount of the bonds at 31 December 20X4 would be $9,953,175 ($10,300,000 – $346,825).

19 Carbise

Top tips. In part (a), you must make sure that you apply your knowledge to the scenario given: the examiner's report stated that weaker answers to this question tended to list the factors determining the functional currency, with little application to the scenario. Remember that there are very few marks available for stating knowledge, you must apply your knowledge to the scenario to gain the majority of the marks available.

In questions like this where complex calculations are required, the examiner has advised that you produce your calculation on one sheet of paper and simultaneously explain the calculation on another sheet of paper. This way of producing an answer will help you to explain each part of a calculation as you perform it, enabling you to generate as many marks as possible.

Marking scheme

				Marks
(a)	(i)	Discussion of presentation and functional currency	2	
		Application of the above discussion to the scenario	5	
				7
	(ii)	Calculation of goodwill	2	
		Calculation of the exchange difference on goodwill	3	
				5
	(iii)	Explanation of the goodwill calculation and application to the scenario	2	
		Explanation of the exchange gain and application to the scenario	2	
				4
(b)		Explanation of Bikelite exchange differences	3	
		Calculation of Bikelite exchange differences for y/e 20X6:		
		Translation	3	
		Split between parent and NCI	1	
				7
(c)	(i)	Calculation of group profit or loss on disposal		3
	(ii)	Explanation of the accounting treatment of Bikelite		4
				30

(a)   Explanatory note to: Directors of Carbise

Subject: Foreign subsidiary Bikelite

(i)   The presentation currency is the currency in which the financial statements are presented. IAS 21 *The Effects of Changes in Foreign Exchange Rates* permits an entity to present its individual financial statements in any currency. It would therefore be up to the directors of Bikelite to choose a presentation currency for its individual financial statements. Factors which could be considered include the currency used by major shareholders and the currency in which debt finance is primarily raised.

The functional currency is the currency of the primary economic environment in which the entity operates. Since transactions are initially recorded in an entity's functional currency, the results and financial position would need to be retranslated where this differed to the presentation currency.

When determining the presentation and functional currency of Bikelite, consideration should first be given to whether the functional currency of Bikelite should be the same as Carbise, at least whilst under the control of Carbise. It appears that Bikelite has considerable autonomy over its activities. Despite being acquired to make more efficient use of the surplus inventory of Carbise, purchases from Carbise were only 5% of Bikelite's total purchases. Revenue is invoiced in a range of currencies suggesting a geographically diverse range of customers which, although this allows Carbise access to new international markets, is unlikely to be classified as an extension of the parent's operations. The volume of the transactions involved between Carbise and Bikelite would seem to be far too low to come to this conclusion. Bikelite also appears free to retain cash in a range of currencies and is not obliged to remit the cash to Carbise in the form of dividends. Nor does Bikelite appear to be dependent on financing from Carbise with other investors taking up the bond issue at the start of 20X6. The functional currency of Bikelite does not need to be the same as Carbise.

In choosing its functional currency, Bikelite should consider the following primary factors: the currency which mainly influences the sales price for their goods, the currency of the country whose competitive forces and regulations determine the sales price and also the currency which influences labour, material and overhead costs. The key determinant here is the currency which the majority of the transactions are settled in. Bikelite invoices and is invoiced in a large range of currencies and so it would not be immediately clear as to the appropriate functional currency. Nor is there detail about whether there is a currency in which competitive forces and regulations could be important. We do not know, for example, what currency Bikelite's major competitors invoice in.

Secondary factors including the currency in which financing activities are obtained and the currency in which receipts from operating activities are retained can help guide the entity where it is not immediately clear. In relation to Bikelite, a significant volume of their sales are invoiced in dinars and the majority of their expenses too, given that wages and overheads are also paid in dinars. Funds were raised in dinars from the bond issue and so it would appear that the dinar should probably be the functional currency for Bikelite. It is also possible that Bikelite may lose their autonomy on Carbise's sale of their shares which could have implications for the determination of the functional currency.

(ii) Goodwill in dinars on the acquisition of Bikelite would be dinar 42 million calculated as follows:

	Dinars millions
Consideration	100
FV of NCI	22
Less net assets at acquisition (60 + 20)	(80)
Goodwill at acquisition	42

On acquisition, the goodwill in $ would be (dinar 42m/0.5) $84 million.

Goodwill at 30 September 20X6 would be:

	Dinars millions	Rate	$m
Goodwill at 1 January 20X2	42	0.5	84
Impairment y/e 31 December 20X5	(6)	0.4	(15)
Exchange gain			25.7 (bal)
Goodwill at 31 December 20X5	36	0.38	94.7
Current year exchange gain			8.2 (bal)
Goodwill at 30 September 20X6	36	0.35	102.9

Workings

Dinar impairment of 6 million is translated at the average rate of $1:0.4 dinar = $15 million.

Goodwill at 31 December 20X5 would be translated at last year's closing rate of $1:0.38 dinar = $94.7m.

Goodwill at 31 September 20X6 will be translated at $1:0.35 dinar = $102.9m.

(iii)   On a business combination, goodwill is calculated by comparing the fair value of the consideration plus non-controlling interests (NCI) at acquisition with the fair value of the identifiable net assets at acquisition. Carbise measures NCI using the fair value method. This means that goodwill attributable to the NCI is included within the overall calculation of goodwill. An adjustment of dinar 20 million is required to the property of Bikelite to ensure the net assets at acquisition are properly included at their fair value.

At each year end, all assets (and liabilities) are retranslated using the closing rate of exchange. Exchange differences arising on the retranslation are recorded within equity. Since the non-controlling interest is measured under the fair value method, the exchange difference would be apportioned 80%/20% between the owners of Carbise and the non-controlling interest. Only the current year's exchange difference would initially be recorded within other comprehensive income for the year ended 31 December 20X6 whereas cumulative exchange differences on goodwill at 30 September 20X6 would be recorded within equity.

(b)   The net assets of Bikelite would have been retranslated each year at the closing rate of exchange. There is therefore an exchange difference arising each year by comparing the opening net assets at the opening rate of exchange with the opening net assets at the closing rate of exchange. An additional exchange difference arises through the profit or loss of Bikelite each year being translated at the average rate of exchange in the consolidated statement of comprehensive income. The profit or loss will increase or decrease the net assets of Bikelite respectively which, as is indicated above, will be translated at the closing rate of exchange within the consolidated statement of financial position. As with goodwill, the exchange differences are included within equity with 80% attributable to the shareholders of Carbise and 20% to the NCI. Cumulative exchange differences will be included within the consolidated statement of financial position with just current year differences recorded within other comprehensive income.

The carrying amount of the net assets of Bikelite on 1 January 20X6 was dinar 48 million. The fair value of their opening net assets therefore would be dinar 64 million (dinar 48 + 16/20 × dinar 20 million). Bikelite would only be consolidated for the first nine months of the year since Carbise loses control on 30 September 20X6. Losses per the individual accounts for the year ended 31 December 20X6 were dinar 8 million, so only dinar 6 million would be consolidated. Additional depreciation of dinar 0.75 million (dinar 20m/20 × 9/12) would be charged for the first nine months of the year. Net assets at disposal in dinars would therefore be dinar 57.25 million (dinar 64 − dinar 6.75). The exchange difference arising in the statement of comprehensive income for the year ended 31 December 20X6 would be $13.4 million calculated as follows:

	$m
Opening net assets at opening rate (dinar 64/0.38)	168.4
Loss for 9 months at average rate (dinar 6.75/0.37)	(18.2)
Current year exchange gain (balance)	13.4
Net assets at 30 September 20X6 (dinar 57.25/0.35)	163.6

$10.7 million of the exchange differences are attributed to the shareholders of Carbide (80% × $13.4) and $2.7 million to the NCI.

(c) (i) Group profit or loss on disposal on Bikelite

	$m
Proceeds	150
Net assets at disposal (see (b))	(163.6)
Goodwill at disposal (see (a)(ii))	(102.9)
NCI at disposal	48.5
Exchange gains recycled to profit and loss	76.6
Group profit on disposal	8.6

Workings

Exchange gains at 1 January 20X6 per question are $74.1 million. Current year exchange differences on goodwill are $8.2 million (see (b)(i)) and on the net assets are $13.4 million (see (b)). Cumulative exchange gains at 30 September 20X6 are therefore $95.7 million. On disposal, the parent's share (80%) = $76.6 million should be recycled to profit or loss.

NCI at disposal is calculated as follows:

	$m
NCI at 1 January 20X6 per question	47.8
NCI share of loss to 30 September 20X6 (20% × dinar 6.75m (see (b))/0.37)	(3.6)
NCI share exchange gains for 9 months to 30 September 20X6 (20% × (13.4 + 8.2))	4.3
NCI at 30 September 20X6	48.5

(ii) For the year ended 31 December 20X6, Carbise will consolidate Bikelite for the first nine months of the year up to the date of disposal of the shares and subsequent loss of control. NCI will be calculated on the first nine months of losses. Exchange differences on the translation of the net assets, profits and goodwill in relation to the nine months to 30 September 20X6 will initially be recognised in other comprehensive income classified as gains which will be reclassified subsequently to profit or loss.

On 30 September 20X6, a consolidated profit or loss on disposal will be calculated in the consolidated financial statements of Carbise. In effect, the proceeds are compared to the net assets and unimpaired goodwill not attributable to the non-controlling interest at the disposal date. The cumulative exchange differences on the translation of Bikelite would be reclassified to profit or loss.

Consideration should be given as to whether the disposal of Bikelite would constitute a discontinued operation. For Bikelite to be classified as a discontinued operation, it would need to represent a separate major line of business or geographical area of operations. Since Bikelite was initially acquired by Carbise to gain easier access to international markets, it is likely that the criterion would be met.

20 Bagshot Co

Workbook references. Ethics and related parties are covered in Chapter 2. Restructuring provisions are covered in Chapter 6.

Top tips. In part (a)(i), you were asked to discuss the required accounting treatment of some restructuring costs. Make sure you read the question carefully to address all the points given in the scenario - eg the different types of costs mentioned and the timing of the announcement. Part (a)(ii) was best answered as two sub-requirements: a discussion of what good stewardship means, and then whether the proposed restructuring and accounting for the restructure constituted good stewardship. In part (a)(iii), a good approach would have been to identify the requirements of IAS 24 *Related Party Disclosures* as to the definition of a related party, then apply that definition to the facts of the scenario before reaching your conclusion.

In part (b), as well as discussing the ethical issues, you also needed to discuss the actions Mr Shaw should take. Make sure you cover both of these requirements in your answer. Question 2 of the exam will always feature ethical issues. Two professional marks are available for the application of ethical principles to the scenario given. Quoting ethical guidance will not be enough, you must apply that guidance to the scenario.

Marking scheme

				Marks
(a)	(i)	Discussion of IAS 37 criteria and restructuring expenditure	2	
		Application of the above to the scenario	3	
		Identification of non-adjusting event	1	
				6
	(ii)	Application of the following discussion to the scenario:		
		What is meant by good stewardship	2	
		Examples of good stewardship	2	
				4
	(iii)	Application of the following discussion to the scenario:		
		Control/significant influence criteria	2	
		Recognition of close family member	1	
				3
(b)		Application of the following discussion to the scenario:		
		Intimidation threat	1	
		Insider trading	2	
		Confidentiality	2	
				5
		Professional marks		2
				20

(a) (i) A provision for restructuring costs should only be recognised in the financial statements of Bagshot Co where all of the following criteria are met:

- A reliable estimate can be made of the amount of the obligation;

- It is probable that an outflow of resources embodying economic benefits will be required to settle the obligation;

- There is a present obligation as a result of a past event.

IAS 37 *Provisions, Contingent Liabilities and Contingent Assets* states that it would be extremely rare that no reliable estimate can be made. A best estimate of the expenditure required to settle the present obligation should be provided as at 31 December 20X5 should all criteria be met. In the case of a restructuring provision, this should only include direct expenditure arising from the restructuring and not associated with ongoing activities. Hence the relocation costs would not be included as, although they relate directly to the restructuring, the costs would be classified as an ongoing activity.

An obligation is regarded as probable where the event is more likely than not to occur. It is not clear that the restructuring is probable. Mrs Dawes has indicated that alternative strategies are possible and further clarification would be required to ascertain whether these activities would constitute a restructuring as per IAS 37. Only then may it be determined that a restructuring is indeed probable.

 BPP LEARNING MEDIA

A constructive obligation for restructuring only arises where a detailed formal plan exists and a valid expectation to those affected by the restructuring that it will take place has occurred. A plan is in place but management does not yet appear committed as alternative strategies are possible. It is unlikely therefore that the plan is detailed and specific enough for these criteria to be satisfied. For example, the specific expenditure to be incurred, the date of its implementation and timeframe which should not be unreasonably long must be identified. With alternative strategies available, this does not appear to be the case. Furthermore, Mr Shaw is the only member of staff who has been notified and no public announcement has been made as at the reporting date. Consequently, there is no obligation in existence as at 31 December 20X5 and no provision can be recognised.

Mrs Dawes has identified that a final decision on the restructuring and communication is likely to take place before the financial statements are authorised. This would almost certainly be a material event arising after the reporting date but should be treated as non-adjusting. Accordingly, Bagshot Co should disclose the nature of the restructuring and an estimate of its financial effect but recognition of a restructuring provision is still prohibited.

(ii)   Stewardship is an ethical principle which embodies the responsible planning and management of resources. The directors of Bagshot Co perform a stewardship role in that they are appointed by the shareholders to manage Bagshot Co on their behalf. The directors therefore assume responsibilities to protect the entity's resources from unfavourable effects of economic factors such as price and technological changes and to ensure that Bagshot Co complies with all laws, regulations and contractual obligations. Group results have been disappointing in recent years although no specific causes have been identified. It could be argued, therefore, that the restructure is acting in good faith and reflecting good principles of stewardship. It is anticipated that long-term shareholder value will be enhanced from the proposals.

A second factor of good stewardship is that it is important that investors, both existing and potential, and lenders have reliable and accurate information about the entity's resources so that they can assess how efficiently and effectively the entity's management and governing board have discharged their responsibilities. It is important therefore that the financial statements are transparent, objective and comply fully with International Financial Reporting Standards. Mrs Dawes wants Bagshot Co to include a restructuring provision as at 31 December 20X5 even though no obligation arises. Whilst prudence is a guiding principle when dealing with issues of uncertainty, excessive prudence cannot be justified. As a qualified member of ACCA, it should be apparent to Mrs Dawes that no provision should be recognised and to include one would be misleading to the stakeholders of Bagshot Co.

(iii)   Mrs Shaw's acquisition of the equity shares in Bagshot Co would be deemed a related party transaction if the acquisition enabled her to control or have significant influence over Bagshot Co. A 5% ownership would not give Mrs Shaw control over the operating decisions of Bagshot Co and it is clear she would not be able to control the entity. Significant influence is the power to participate in the financial and operating decisions of the entity. It is presumed that a holding of less than 20% of the voting power is insufficient for significant influence unless this can be clearly demonstrated. Mrs Shaw is unaware of the proposed restructure which would suggest that she does not have a board position. It can be concluded that she does not have control nor significant influence.

Mrs Shaw would be deemed to be a close family member of Mr Shaw. She would therefore be deemed to be a related party if it was concluded that Mr Shaw is a member of key management personnel of Bagshot Co. Mr Shaw is the head accountant of Bagshot Co but it seems highly unlikely that he would be deemed to be key management personnel. There is no evidence that he has authority or responsibility for planning, directing and controlling the activities of Bagshot Co.

Nor does he appear to be a director of the entity. It can be concluded that Mrs Shaw's acquisition of the 5% of the equity in Bagshot Co would not be a related party transaction.

(b) Mr Shaw is facing a number of ethical dilemmas arising from the scenario. Mrs Dawes's insistence that a restructuring provision should be included could constitute an intimidation threat although her motivation for including the provision early is unclear. Mr Shaw is also a qualified member of ACCA and therefore should be aware that the treatment is inconsistent with international accounting standards. Mr Shaw must adhere to the ACCA *Code of Ethics* and prepare financial statements diligently which are objective and fully comply with International Financial Reporting Standards. He must not comply with Mrs Dawes's requests and should politely remind her of her professional responsibilities as a member of ACCA. Non-compliance with accounting standards would be a breach of a range of ethical principles including professional competence, professional behaviour and objectivity. Assuming that Mrs Dawes is aware of the error, her integrity would also be questionable.

Mr Shaw could be accused of insider trading were he to inform his wife of the proposed restructure. Insider trading involves the use of non-publicised information in order to make decisions on financial investments based on the information which others do not yet know about. It is clear that such behaviour would not be ethical since Mrs Shaw would be in an advantageous position to make investment decisions which could impact unfairly on the other shareholders. Insider traders have information which others do not have such that the other stakeholders may act differently and make different decisions should they have been privy to the same information. Such activities are seen as fraudulent and are likely to be in breach of local money laundering regulations.

Mr Shaw has become privy to confidential information regarding Bagshot Co. One of ACCA's key ethical principles is that of confidentiality. Information must not be disclosed to others unless there is a legal or professional right or duty to disclose. Professional accountants must also ensure that they do not use confidential information for their own personal benefit. Mr Shaw has self-interest threats arising both from his wife's ownership of the shares and from his nephew facing potential redundancy. His wife could use the information to consider whether she may wish to sell her 5% ownership interest. Mr Shaw may also feel pressure to inform his nephew of the potential redundancy he may be facing. This may allow his nephew to obtain an unfair advantage over fellow employees by, for example, examining other opportunities in the labour market. Mr Shaw must not disclose the confidential information to his wife or his nephew.

21 Calibra Co

Marking scheme

		Marks
(a)	Application of the following discussion to the scenario:	
	• Revenue IFRS 15	3
	• Borrowing costs IAS 23	2
		5
(b)	Journal entries	3
(c)	Discussion and application of ethical principles to scenario	10
Professional marks		2
		20

BPP
LEARNING
MEDIA

(a) The performance obligation will be satisfied upon the completion of construction which is also when the title, possession and control of the apartment block pass to the customer. The advanced payment represents a significant financing component and IFRS 15 *Revenue from Contracts with Customers* states that where this is the case then revenue is recognised at an amount that reflects the price that a customer would have paid if the customer had paid cash when they transfer the goods to the customer. IFRS 15 also states that the interest rate used should reflect the credit characteristics of the party receiving financing but may be the rate that discounts the nominal amount of the promised consideration to the price that the customer would pay in cash. In this case, the interest rate would be 6%. Using this rate, the cash sales price of $9.55 million can be discounted to $8.5 million. Calibra Co should recognise a liability of $8.5 million and should subsequently accrue interest on this liability balance for two years until it reaches $9.55 million when the performance obligation is satisfied.

The interest should be accounted for in accordance with IAS 23 *Borrowing* Costs as part of the cost of constructing the apartment block. As Calibra Co's business model is based on construction, IAS 23 states that borrowing costs that are directly attributable to the acquisition, construction or production of a qualifying asset form part of the cost of that asset and, therefore, in this case should be included in the cost of inventory production. Other borrowing costs are recognised as an expense.

(b) **Journal entries**

	Dr ($m)	Cr ($m)
Cash	8.5	
Liability		8.5
Records liability on receipt of cash (1/1/X8)		
Inventory: Interest accruing to 31/12/X8	0.51	
Liability		0.51

Interest accruing on liability to 31/12/X8 (6% × 8.5m) included in the costs of inventory

Inventory: Interest accruing to 31/12/X9	0.54	
Liability		0.54

Interest accruing on liability to 31/12/X9 (6% × (8.5 + 0.51)) included in the costs of inventory

Liability	9.55	
Revenue		9.55

Revenue arising on sale of apartment block (per question)

The balance on the contract liability at 31/12/X8 would be $9.55 million (8.5 + 0.51 + 0.54). When control passes to the customer, Calibra Co recognises revenue of $9.55 million.

(c) The chief accountant should not hold himself out as having an understanding of distributed ledgers if he only has a basic knowledge. He should have seen evidence of whether the technology can be scaled up to the requirements of the directors before promising them that he can facilitate the move. Also, he must convince himself that the reliability of the due diligence on the sale of property shares and that local regulations are complied with. In order to maintain integrity, professional accountants must be honest about whether they are comfortable with their knowledge of managing projects such as this. The chief accountant should not manage the project if he has doubts as to his knowledge as there may be significant issues as the project progresses. There may be a need to engage specialist consultancy input from distributed ledger experts. Similarly, the chief accountant should behave in a professional manner and determine whether the data on the distributed ledger breaks any confidentiality principles. He will need to consider the fact that local regulations may be violated and the repercussions thereof. The technology allows resale of the shares in the property and given the chief accountants worries over due diligence, illegal transfers of title ownership could be costly and time consuming to resolve. The chief accountant must also exercise independence of mind and not bow to political pressure from the board even though it may be a high-profile project for the company. He should inform the board of his reservations based upon his opinion and technical knowledge.

One of the main concerns for accounting professionals is the fear of losing objectivity in their judgment due to pressures from clients, employers, or other stakeholders. This occurrence would create a loss of professional identity for the person concerned. Some individuals are more vulnerable to loss of objectivity than others. Young accountants at the beginning of their career could be considered a vulnerable group, as they may be more easily influenced due to a perceived lack of experience and pressures from senior colleagues. The accountant has only just qualified and so might be inexperienced to be in the position of chief accountant. In this case, he has created a self-interest threat as the chief accountant has a personal interest in allowing Bodoni Co to pay the reduced amount one month after the contract for the purchase of the apartment block has been signed, as he wishes a good reference from the client when he applies for the permanent position. The pressure of applying for this position has inappropriately influenced his professional judgement and behaviour. Additionally, there is a threat to the chief accountant's objectivity which stems from a self-interest threat from the fear of losing Bodoni Co as a client which in turn would affect the accountant's chances of securing his position on a permanent basis.

22 Farham

Marking scheme

		Marks
(a)	Application of the following discussion to the scenario:	
	Factory subsidence as an indication of impairment	2
	Fair value	2
	Allocation of impairment loss	1
	Sale of Newall – HFS criteria, valuation and impairment	4
	Required accounting treatment of the expected costs of sale	2
		11
(b)	Discussion of ethical principles	2
	Application of ethical principles to the scenario	5
		7
Professional marks		2
		20

(a) **Factory subsidence**

The subsidence is an **indication of impairment** in relation to the production facility. Consideration would be required to choose a suitable cash-generating unit as presumably the factory would not independently generate cash flows for Farham as a standalone asset. The facility is likely to consist of both the factory and various items of plant and machinery and so it would not be possible to independently measure the cash flows from each of the assets. The recoverable amount of the unit would need to be assessed as the higher of fair value less costs to sell and value in use. Reference to IFRS 13 *Fair Value Measurement* would be required in estimating the fair value of the facility. For example, by considering whether similar facilities have been on the market or recently sold. Value in use would be calculated by estimating the present value of the cash flows generated from the production facility discounted at a suitable rate of interest to reflect the risks to the business. Where the carrying amount exceeds the recoverable amount, an impairment has occurred. Any **impairment loss** is allocated to reduce the carrying amount of the assets of the unit. This will be expensed in profit or loss and cannot be netted off the revaluation surplus as the surplus does not specifically relate to the facility impaired. **No provision for the repair to the factory** should be made because there is no legal or constructive obligation to repair the factory.

Sale of Newall

The disposal of Newall appears to meet the **held for sale criteria**. Management has shown commitment to the sale by approving the plan and reporting it to the media. A probable acquirer has been found in Oldcastle, the sale is highly probable and expected to be completed six months after the year end, well within the 12-month criteria. Newall would be treated as a disposal group since a single equity transaction is the most likely form of disposal. Should Newall be deemed to be a separate major component of business or geographical area of the group, the losses of the group should be presented separately as a discontinued operation within the consolidated financial statements of Farham.

Assets held for sale are valued at the **lower of carrying amount and fair value less costs to sell**. The carrying amount consists of the net assets and goodwill relating to Newall less the non-controlling interest's share. Assets within the disposal group which are not within the scope of IFRS 5 *Assets Held for Sale and Discontinued Operations* are adjusted for in accordance with the relevant standard first. This includes leased assets and it is highly likely that the leased asset deemed surplus to requirements should be written off with a corresponding expense to profit or loss. Any further impairment loss recognised to reduce Newall to fair value less costs to sell would be allocated first to goodwill and then on a pro rata basis across the other non-current assets of the group.

The chief operating officer is wrong to exclude any form of restructuring provision from the consolidated financial statements. The disposal has been communicated to the media and a constructive obligation exists. However, only **directly attributable costs of the restructuring** should be included and not ongoing costs of the business. **Future operating losses** should be excluded as no obligating event has arisen and no provision is required for the impairments of the owned assets as they would have been accounted for on remeasurement to fair value less costs to sell. The legal fees and redundancy costs should be provided for. The early payment fee should also be provided for despite being a future operating loss. This is because the contract is onerous and the losses are consequently unavoidable. A provision is required for $13 million ($2 million + $5 million + $6 million). The $6 million will be offset against the corresponding lease liability with only a net figure being recorded in profit or loss.

(b) **Ethics**

Accountants have a duty to ensure that the financial statements are **fair, transparent and comply with accounting standards**. The accountant appears to have made a couple of mistakes which would be unexpected from a professionally qualified accountant. In particular, the accountant appears unaware of which costs should be included within a restructuring provision and has failed to recognise that there is no obligating event in relation to future operating losses. Accountants must carry out their work with **due care**

and attention for the financial statements to have credibility. They must therefore ensure that their knowledge is kept up to date and that they do carry out their work in accordance with the relevant ethical and professional standards. Failure to do so would be a breach of **professional competence.** The accountant must make sure that they address this issue through, for example, attending regular training and professional development courses.

There are a number of instances which suggest that the chief operating officer is happy to **manipulate** the financial statements for their own benefit. She is not willing to account for an impairment loss for the subsidence despite knowing that this is contrary to IFRSs. She is also unwilling to reduce the profits of the group by properly applying the assets held for sale criteria in relation to Newall nor to create a restructuring provision. All of the adjustments required to ensure the financial statements comply with IFRS will reduce profitability. It is true that the directors do have a responsibility to run the group on behalf of their shareholders and to try to maximise their return. This must not be to the detriment, though, of producing financial statements which are **objective** and **faithfully represent** the performance of the group. It is likely that the chief operating officer is motivated by bonus targets and is therefore unfairly trying to misrepresent the results of the group. The chief operating officer must make sure that she is not unduly influenced by this **self-interest threat.**

The chief operating officer is also acting unethically by threatening to dismiss the accountant should they try to correct the financial statements. It is not clear whether the chief operating officer is a qualified accountant but the ethical principles should extend to all employees and not just qualified accountants. **Threatening and intimidating behaviour** is unacceptable and against all ethical principles. The accountant faces an **ethical dilemma.** They have a duty to produce financial statements which are objective and fair but to do so could mean that they lose their job. The accountant should approach the chief operating officer and remind them of the basic ethical principles and try to persuade them of the need to put the adjustments through the consolidated accounts so that they are fair and objective. Should the chief operating officer remain unmoved, the accountant may wish to contact the ACCA ethical helpline and take legal advice before undertaking any further action.

23 Gustoso

		Marks
Application of the following discussion to the scenario:		
• Provision	3	
• Restructuring	5	
• Contract	3	
		11
Application of the following discussion of ethical issues to the scenario:		
• User expectations	1	
• Nature of errors/bias/intimidation	3	
• Advice to accountant	3	
		7
Professional skills marks		2
		20

BPP
LEARNING
MEDIA

Provision

IAS 37 *Provisions, Contingent Liabilities and Contingent Assets* states that a provision should only be recognised if:

- There is a present obligation from a past event;
- An outflow of economic resources is probable; and
- The obligation can be measured reliably.

No provision should be recognised because Gustoso Co does not have an obligation to incur the training costs. The expenditure could be avoided by changing the nature of Gustoso Co's operations and so it has no present obligation for the future expenditure.

The provision should be derecognised. This will reduce liabilities by $2 million and increase profits by the same amount.

Restructuring

A provision for restructuring costs should only be recognised in the financial statements of Gustoso Co where all of the above IAS 37 criteria are met. However for a restructuring provision to be recognised there are additional requirements per IAS 37. A constructive obligation for restructuring only arises where a detailed formal plan exists and a valid expectation to those affected by the restructuring that it will take place has occurred. Although the Board meeting happened in November 20X7 Gustoso Co does not yet appear committed as other plans are being explored It is unlikely therefore that the plan is detailed and specific enough for these criteria to be satisfied.

In the case of a restructuring provision, this should only include direct expenditure arising from the restructuring and not associated with ongoing activities. Hence the leasing costs would not be included in a restructuring provision however if a decision is made to exit from these leases, it is likely they could meet the requirements of an onerous lease contract in the 20X8 financial statements. Gustoso Co should therefore look to IFRS 16 Leases and carry out an impairment review of the right-of-use assets held under these lease contracts, applying the requirements of IAS 36 *Impairment of Assets*.

As no announcement has been made to staff or lessors as at the reporting date there is no obligation in existence as at 31 December 20X7 and no provision can be recognised for the other costs - professional fees and redundancy costs. However, the finance director has indicated that a final decision on the restructuring and an announcement is likely to take place before the financial statements are authorised in April 20X8. If this constitutes a material event arising after the reporting date it should be treated as a non-adjusting event. Gustoso Co should disclose the nature of the restructuring and an estimate of its financial effect.

Contract

IFRS 9 *Financial Instruments* applies to contracts to buy or sell a non-financial item which can be settled net in cash. Such contracts are usually accounted for as derivatives. However, contracts which are for an entity's 'own use' of a non-financial asset are exempt from the requirements of IFRS 9. The contract will qualify as 'own use' because Gustoso Co always takes delivery of the wheat. This means that it falls outside the scope of IFRS 9 and so the recognition of a derivative is incorrect.

The contract is an executory contract. Executory contracts are not initially recognised in the financial statements unless they are onerous, in which case a provision is required. This particular contract is unlikely to be onerous because wheat prices may rise again. Moreover, the finished goods which the wheat forms a part of will be sold at a profit. As such, no provision is required. The contract will therefore remain unrecognised until Gustoso Co takes delivery of the wheat.

The derivative liability should be derecognised, meaning that profits will increase by $0.5 million.

Ethical implications

The users of Gustoso Co's financial statements, such as banks and shareholders, trust accountants and rely on them to faithfully represent the effects of a company's transactions. IAS 1 *Presentation of Financial Statements* makes it clear that this will be obtained when accounting standards are correctly applied.

The errors made by Gustoso Co overstate liabilities and understate profits. It is possible that these are unintentional errors. However, incentives exist to depart from particular IFRS and IAS standards: most notably the bonus scheme. The bonus target in 20X7 has been exceeded, and so the finance director may be attempting to shift 'excess' profits into the next year in order to increase the chance of meeting 20X8's bonus target. In this respect, the finance director has a clear self-interest threat to objectivity and may be in breach of ACCA's *Code of Ethics and Conduct*.

The accountant is correct to challenge the finance director and has an ethical responsibility to do so. Despite the fact that the finance director is acting in an intimidating manner, the accountant should explain the technical issues to the director. If the director refuses to comply with accounting standards, then it would be appropriate to discuss the matter with other directors and to seek professional advice from ACCA. Legal advice should be considered if necessary. The accountant should keep a record of conversations and actions. Resignation should be considered if the matters cannot be satisfactorily resolved.

24 Fiskerton

Marking scheme

			Marks
(a)	Application of the following discussion to the scenario:		
	• Correct accounting treatment of the lease	3	
	• Implications for the financial statements	2	
	• Implications for the debt covenant	2	
			7
(b)	Consideration of whether it is performance satisfied over time or at a point in time and application to the scenario	3	
	Conclusion and implications for revenue	1	
			4
(c)	Application of the following discussion of ethical issues to the scenario:		
	• Classification of property as investment property	2	
	• Revaluation and manipulation of the debt covenant	3	
	Consideration of the ethical implications and their resolution	2	
			7
Professional			2
			20

(a)   The Halam property should not have been classified as an investment property because it is a finance lease as the lease term is equal to the useful life and its residual value is deemed to be minimal. Edingley should record a right to use asset and Fiskerton should derecognise the property. Fiskerton should instead record a lease receivable equal to the net investment in the lease. The property needs to be removed from investment properties and the fair value gains of $8 million reversed. In any case, the fair value gains were incorrectly calculated since adjustments should have been made for the differences between the Halam building and the one sold due to the different location and quality of the materials between the two buildings. It would appear that $22 million would have been a more accurate reflection of fair value.

The incorrect treatment has enabled Fiskerton to remain within its debt covenant limits. Gearing per the financial extracts is currently around 49.8% (50,000/(10,000 + 20,151 + 70,253)). Fair value gains on investment properties are reported within profit or loss. Retained earnings would consequently be restated to $62.253 million ($70.253m – $8m). Gearing would subsequently become 54.1% (50,000/10,000 + 20,151 + 62,253). Furthermore, retained earnings would be further reduced by correcting for rental receipts.

These presumably have been included in profit or loss rather than deducted from the net investment in the lease. This would in part be offset by interest income which should be recorded in profit or loss at the effective rate of interest. After correcting for these errors, Fiskerton would be in breach of their debt covenants. They have a negative cash balance and would appear unlikely to be able to repay the loan. Serious consideration should therefore be given as to whether Fiskerton is a going concern. It is likely that non-current assets and non-current liabilities should be reclassified to current and recorded at their realisable values. As an absolute minimum, should Fiskerton be able to renegotiate with the bank, the uncertainties surrounding their ability to continue to trade would need to be disclosed.

(b)   At the inception of the contract, Fiskerton must determine whether its promise to construct the asset is a performance obligation satisfied over time. Fiskerton only has rights during the production of the asset over the initial deposit paid. It has no enforceable rights to the remaining balance as construction takes place. Therefore, it would not be able to receive payment for work performed to date. Additionally, Fiskerton has to repay the deposit should it fail to complete the construction of the asset in accordance with the contract. There is a single performance obligation which is only met on delivery of the asset to the customer. Revenue should not be recognised on a stage of completion basis but must be deferred and recognised at a point of time. That is, on delivery of the asset to the customer.

(c)   It is concerning that the property has been incorrectly classified as an investment property. Accountants have an ethical duty to be professionally competent and act with due care and attention. It is fundamental that the financial statements comply with the accounting standards and principles which underpin them. This may be a genuine mistake but even so would not be one expected from a professionally qualified accountant. The financial statements must comply with the fair presentation principles embedded within IAS 1 *Presentation of Financial Statements*.

The managing director appears to be happy to manipulate the financial statements. A self-interest threat arises from the issue over the debt covenants. It is likely that the managing director is concerned about his job security should the bank recall the debt and deem Fiskerton to no longer be a going concern. It appears highly likely that the revaluation was implemented in the interim financial statements to try to maintain a satisfactory gearing ratio. Even more concerning is that the managing director has deliberately overstated the valuation for the year-end financial statements, even though he is aware that it breaches accounting standards. Such deliberate manipulation is contrary to the ethical principles of integrity, professional behaviour and objectivity. It appears that the managing director is trying to defraud the bank by misrepresenting the liquidity of the business to avoid repayment of the loan. This would be in breach of anti-money laundering regulations.

The sales contract is further evidence that the managing director may be attempting to manipulate the financial statements. The proposed treatment will overstate both revenue and assets which would improve the gearing ratio. A governance issue arises from the behaviour of the managing director. It is important that no one individual is too powerful and domineering in running an entity's affairs. An intimidation threat arises from the managing director pressurising the accountant to overstate revenue from the contract. It was also the managing director who implemented the excessive revaluations on the property. It would appear that the managing director is exercising too much power over the financial statements. The accountant must not be influenced by the behaviour of the managing director and should produce financial statements which are transparent and free from bias. Instead, the managing director should be reminded of their ethical responsibilities. The accountant may need to consider professional advice should the managing director refuse to correct the financial statements.

25 Hudson

Workbook references. Ethics are covered in Chapter 2. Employee benefits and pensions are covered in Chapter 5. Deferred tax is covered in Chapter 7. Restructuring provisions are covered in Chapter 6.

Top tips. Question 2 of the exam will always feature a discussion of ethical issues and will have two marks available for the application of ethical principles. In this question, parts (a) and (b) related to the accounting treatment of the issues in the scenario given, and part (c) required a discussion of the ethical issues arising, including actions that the accountant should take.

In this type of question, remember that ethical issues are likely to be interwoven throughout the scenario - you need to be able to spot them. Remember also that you must apply ethical principles to the scenario. Listing out ethical requirements is unlikely to gain you many marks.

Marking scheme

		Marks	
(a)	Application of the following discussion to the scenario:		
	What should be included in the remeasurement component	2	
	Correct treatment of the basic component	2	
	Correct treatment of the additional pension contribution	2	
	Discussion of restructuring costs	2	
			8
(b)	An explanation of temporary differences and asset tax base	3	
	Application of above discussion to the scenario	2	
			5
(c)	Application of the following discussion of accounting issues to the scenario:		
	Termination payments	2	
	Tax losses	1	
	Consideration of the ethical implications and their resolution	2	
			5
	Professional marks		2
			20

(a) The remeasurement component is taken to other comprehensive income and comprises:

- Actuarial gains and losses, such as the return on plan assets which differs from the expected return on the assets included within the net interest figure;

- Changes in the asset ceiling not included within the net interest calculation.

Actuarial gains and losses are sometimes referred to as experience adjustments and arise due to differences between actuarial assumptions and what actually occurred during the period. These will arise in instances such as unexpected movements on interest rates, unexpectedly high or low rates of employee turnover or unexpected increases or decreases in wage growth. The redundancies will create an unusually high level of staff turnover but this should not be treated as part of the remeasurement component. The redundancy will cause the present value of the obligations arising from the defined benefit to decrease. This is classified as a curtailment rather than an experience adjustment to be included within other comprehensive income.

A distinction needs to be made between the basic settlement and the additional pension contribution. The basic settlement is an obligation which Hudson has to pay as compensation for terminating the employee's services regardless of when the employee leaves the entity. IAS 19 Employee Benefits requires such payments to be recognised at the earlier of when the plan of termination is announced and when the entity recognises the associated restructuring costs associated with the closure of Wye.

Hudson should therefore have provided in full for the cost of the basic settlement regardless of whether the staff have left or not. This should be recognised as part of the past service cost in the profit or loss of Hudson for the year ended 31 December 20X2.

The additional pension contribution is only paid to employees who complete service up to the closure of division Wye. Since this is expected in early 20X3, these should be accounted for as a short-term benefit. In effect, the contributions are in exchange for the period of service until redundancy. Hudson should estimate the number of employees who will remain with Hudson until the closure of Wye. The cost of this payment should then be spread over the period of service. Since this should be included within the current service cost, this will have an adverse effect on the profit or loss in both 20X2 and 20X3.

In line with the criteria to recognise any provision, as set out in IAS 37 *Provisions, Contingent Liabilities and Contingent Assets*, an 'obligating event' must have arisen for a restructuring provision and for the associated restructuring costs to be recognised. Furthermore, specific conditions must exist for such an obligating event to have arisen in relation to a restructuring provision:

- a detailed formal plan for the restructuring is in place identifying certain criteria required by the accounting standard; and

- a valid expectation has been created in those affected that the restructuring will be carried out, either by starting to implement the plan or publicly announcing its main features.

In the case of Hudson, a valid expectation has been created because the restructuring has been announced, the redundancies have been confirmed and the directors have approved the restructuring in a formal directors meeting. IAS 37 specifically sets out that a provision cannot be made where only a management or board decision to restructure has been taken as it is not considered that this in itself gives rise to an obligation to restructure. IAS 37 also specifies that only the direct expenditure which is necessary as a result of restructuring can be included in the restructuring provision. This includes costs of making employees redundant and costs of terminating certain leases and other contracts directly as a result of restructuring. However, it specifically excludes costs of retraining or relocating staff, marketing or investment in new systems and distribution networks, as these costs relate to future operations and so do not fall under the definition of a provision. Thus, the costs of ongoing activities such as relocation activities cannot be provided for.

(b) Deferred taxes represent the amounts of income taxes payable or recoverable in future periods in respect of temporary differences.

Temporary differences are differences between the carrying amount of an asset or liability and its tax base. A deferred tax asset arises where the tax base of an asset exceeds the carrying amount. A deferred tax asset can also occur when the tax base of a liability differs from its carrying amount; the eventual settlement of the liability represents a future tax deduction. In relation to unused trading losses, the carrying amount is zero since the losses have not yet been recognised in the financial statements of Hudson. A potential deferred tax asset does arise but the determination of the tax base is more problematic.

The tax base of an asset is the amount which will be deductible against taxable economic benefits from recovering the carrying amount of the asset. Where recovery of an asset will have no tax consequences, the tax base is equal to the carrying amount.

Hudson operates under a tax jurisdiction which only allows losses to be carried forward for two years. The maximum the tax base could be is therefore equal to the amount of unused losses for 20X1 and 20X2 since these only are available to be deducted from future profits.

The tax base though needs to be restricted to the extent that there is a probability of sufficient future profits to offset the trading losses.

The directors of Hudson should base their forecast of the future profitability on reasonable and supportable assumptions. There appears to be evidence that this is not the case. Hudson has a recent history of trading losses and there is little evidence that there will be an improvement in trading results within the next couple of years. The market is depressed and sales orders for the first quarter of 20X3 are below levels in any of the previous five years. It is also likely that Hudson will incur various costs in relation to the restructuring which would increase losses into 20X3 and possibly 20X4. Only directly attributable expenses such as redundancies should be included within a provision and expensed in 20X2 which would increase the current year loss. On-going expenses may be incurred such as retraining and relocating costs but these should only be expensed from 20X3. The forecast profitability for 20X3 and subsequent growth rate therefore appear to be unrealistically optimistic. Given that losses can only be carried forward for a maximum of two years, it is unlikely that any deferred tax asset should be recognised.

(c)   The directors of Hudson are paid a bonus based upon earnings before interest, tax depreciation and amortisation (EBITDA). It is possible therefore, despite the losses, that once these items are adjusted for the directors may receive a bonus. A self-interest threat will arise. The directors have an incentive to manipulate the financial statements in order to try to minimise the losses and maximise profits. Directors have an ethical responsibility to produce financial statements which are fair, objective and a transparent record of the entity's affairs.

There is evidence that the directors are willing to manipulate the financial statements in a way directly contrary to the ethical principles of integrity and objectivity. It is likely that a net expense should be recognised for the termination payments on the assumption that they would exceed the reduction in present value of the obligation from the curtailment. The directors are wishing to recognise this within other comprehensive income rather than profit or loss despite knowing that it is contrary to international accounting standards. This would improve profitability although it would not impact upon net assets due to a corresponding decrease in equity. The directors also have not recognised a restructuring provision despite the terms being communicated to staff. It is possible that this would be treated as an exceptional cost and therefore would not impact on the bonus. It would therefore be useful to examine the precise terms of the contracts in order to assess the potential impact on the bonus. The treatment does, however, at least in the short term, help Hudson to improve their net assets position.

The deferred tax asset is based upon forecasts for too long a period and is also based on unrealistic assumptions. Earnings before interest, tax, depreciation and amortisation will be overstated as a direct consequence. Net assets will also be overstated, helping Hudson to meet its debt covenant obligations.

The directors' explanation for their proposed treatments are not justified. Directors are appointed to run the business on behalf of the company's shareholders who are the primary stakeholder. It will be in the shareholders' interests for the company to be profitable and to maintain net assets within the debt covenant stipulations. However, this should not be at the expense of the credibility and transparency of the financial statements. Deliberate manipulation of financial statements will reduce stakeholders' confidence in the reliability of the financial statements and the accountancy profession as a whole. The directors are deliberating flouting International Financial Reporting Standards (IFRS Standards) to improve their bonus and maintain debt covenant obligations.

The directors' actions with regard to the accountant are contrary to the ethical principles of professional behaviour. It appears that the directors have put the accountant under undue pressure to falsify the financial statements to meet their own needs. An intimidation threat arises from the directors' implying that the accountant would lose their job should they not comply with the directors' instructions.

The accountant would also be bound by the ACCA *Code of Ethics* and must adhere to the same ethical principles. They must not therefore comply with the directors' instructions. The accountant should remind the directors of their obligations to comply with the *Code of Ethics*. Should the accountant feel unable to approach the directors directly, they could consider talking to those charged with governance and, in particular, non-executive directors to explain the situation. The accountant could also seek help from the ACCA ethical helpline and take legal advice. Ultimately, if the situation cannot be resolved, the accountant could consider resigning and seeking employment elsewhere.

26 Stent

Workbook references. Ethics and related party transactions are covered in Chapter 2. Financial instruments are covered in Chapter 8.

Top tips. Question 2 of the exam will always feature a discussion of ethical issues and will have two marks available for the application of ethical principles. In this question, part (a) related to the accounting treatment of the issues in the scenario given as well as the impact on gearing of those accounting treatments. The examiner commented that a surprising number of candidates did not discuss the impact on gearing and therefore missed out on some marks. Make sure you answer each part of a requirement to maximise your score in each question.

Part (b) required a discussion of the ethical issues arising in the scenario. In SBR, ethical issues are likely to go beyond basic accounting errors and could involve personal relationships and pressures that those relationships create - as seen in this question. Be sure to read the question carefully in order to spot these kinds of issues.

Marking scheme

			Marks
(a)	Application of the following discussion to the scenario:		
	Cash advance from related party	4	
	Preference shares: convertible	4	
	Deferred tax asset	3	
			11
(b)	Discussion of ethical principles	2	
	Application of ethical principles to the scenario, and recommended action	5	
			7
	Professional marks		2
			20

(a) Cash advance from Budster Co

Stent Co's finance director also controls Budster Co, the company which has paid a cash advance to Stent Co. International Accounting Standard (IAS) 24 *Related Party Disclosures* requires an entity's financial statements to contain disclosures necessary to draw attention to the possibility that its financial statements may have been affected by the existence of related parties and by transactions and outstanding balances with such parties. Included in the definition of a related party is a person identified as holding significant influence over the entity, or who is a member of the key management personnel of the entity. The finance director, a key management personnel of Stent Co, is a related party. In this case, Stent Co must disclose the nature of the related party relationship as well as information about all transactions and outstanding balances between Stent Co and Budster Co (owned and

BPP LEARNING MEDIA

controlled by the finance director), necessary for users to understand the potential effect of the relationship on the financial statements.

The advance from Budster Co meets the *Conceptual Framework* definition of a liability: Stent Co has a present obligation (legally enforceable as a consequence of a binding contract), the settlement of which involves Stent Co giving up resources embodying economic benefits in order to satisfy the claim. IAS 1 *Presentation of Financial Statements* states that an entity shall not offset assets and liabilities, unless required or permitted by an International Financial Reporting Standard (IFRS). The finance director wants to include the receipt as a credit balance in trade receivables, netting off any amounts owed by Budster Co from trading, with what appears to be a short-term loan. This would result in a misclassification of a current liability under current assets. Offsetting a financial asset and a financial liability is permitted according to IAS 32 *Financial Instruments: Presentation* when, and only when, an entity has a legally enforceable right to set off the recognised amounts and intends either to settle on a net basis, or to realise the asset and settle the liability simultaneously. No such agreement is evident in this case, so Stent Co should report separately both assets and liabilities.

Except when it reflects the substance of the transaction or other event, offsetting detracts from the ability of users both to understand the transactions, other events and conditions which have occurred and to assess the entity's future cash flows. Stent Co would be showing a lower current asset figure and concealing the liability, which if disclosed as a current liability could be included in the debt element of the gearing calculation. Gearing would therefore increase.

Convertible redeemable preference shares

IAS 32 defines an equity instrument as any contract which evidences a residual interest in the assets of an entity after deducting all of its liabilities. An equity instrument has no contractual obligation to deliver cash or another financial asset, or to exchange financial assets or financial liabilities under potentially unfavourable conditions. If settled by the issuer's own equity instruments, an equity instrument has no contractual obligation to deliver a variable number, or is settled only by exchanging a fixed amount of cash or another financial asset for a fixed number of its own equity instruments.

Preference shares which are required to be converted into a fixed number of ordinary shares on a fixed date should be classified as equity (this is known as the 'fixed for fixed' requirement to which the finance director refers). However, a critical feature in differentiating a financial liability from an equity instrument is the existence of a contractual obligation of the issuer either to deliver cash or another financial asset to the holder, or to exchange financial assets or financial liabilities with the holder, under conditions which are potentially unfavourable to the issuer. In this case, Stent Co has issued convertible redeemable preference shares – which makes little commercial sense from the company's perspective, as they offer the holder the benefit of conversion into ordinary shares if share prices rise, and the security of redemption (at the choice of the holder) if share prices fall.

IAS 32 notes that the substance of a financial instrument, rather than its legal form, governs its classification in the entity's statement of financial position. A preference share which provides for mandatory redemption for a fixed or determinable amount at a fixed or determinable future date or gives the holder the right to require the issuer to redeem the instrument at a particular date for a fixed or determinable amount is a financial liability.

Because the preference shares offer the holder the choice of conversion into ordinary shares as well as redemption in two years' time, the terms of the financial instrument should be evaluated to determine whether it contains both a liability and an equity component. Such components are classified separately as compound financial instruments, recognising separately the components of a financial instrument which creates both a financial liability of the entity (a contractual arrangement to deliver cash or another financial asset) and an equity instrument (a call option granting the holder the right, for a specified period of time, to convert it into a fixed number of ordinary shares of the entity).

ANSWERS

In accordance with IFRS 9 *Financial Instruments*, when the initial carrying amount of a compound financial instrument is allocated to its equity and liability components, the equity component is assigned the residual amount after deducting from the fair value of the instrument as a whole the amount separately determined for the liability component. Stent Co would measure the fair value of the consideration in respect of the liability component based on the fair value of a similar liability without any associated equity conversion option. The equity component is assigned the residual amount.

Gearing would increase if the draft financial statements had included the preference shares within equity: the correction would increase non-current debt (the present value of the future obligations) and decrease equity.

Deferred tax asset

In accordance with IAS 12 *Income Taxes*, a deferred tax asset shall be recognised for the carry-forward of unused tax losses to the extent that it is probable that future taxable profit will be available against which the unused tax losses can be utilised.

However, the existence of unused tax losses is strong evidence that future taxable profit may not be available. Therefore, when an entity has a history of recent losses, the entity recognises a deferred tax asset arising from unused tax losses only to the extent that it has convincing evidence that sufficient taxable profit will be available against which the unused tax losses can be utilised. In such circumstances, the amount of the deferred tax asset and the nature of the evidence supporting its recognition must be disclosed. The directors of Stent Co should consider whether it is probable that Stent Co will have taxable profits before the unused tax losses or unused tax credits expire, whether the unused tax losses result from identifiable causes which are unlikely to recur; and whether tax planning opportunities are available to the entity which will create taxable profit in the period in which the unused tax losses or unused tax credits can be utilised. To the extent that it is not probable that taxable profit will be available against which the unused tax losses or unused tax credits can be utilised, the deferred tax asset should not be recognised.

The removal of a deferred tax asset would reduce net assets, and equity. Gearing would therefore increase.

(b)   **Ethical aspects**

The ACCA Rulebook contains the byelaws, regulations and *Code of Ethics and Conduct*, which every ACCA member should follow. The accountant may feel pressured by the finance director's comments on job security given the accountant has only been in her position for a few months. The accountant should comply with the fundamental ethical principles set out in the ACCA Rulebook: to act with integrity, objectivity, professional competence and due care, confidentiality and professional behaviour. The accountant should be mindful of any threats to these fundamental ethical principles. In doing so, the accountant should consider the relevant facts, the ethical issues involved, the fundamental principles which are threatened, whether internal procedures exist which mitigate the threats, and what alternative courses of action could be taken.

In this case, all fundamental ethical principles with the exception of confidentiality appear under threat. The finance director appears to be allowing bias and undue influence from the pressures imposed by debt covenant gearing and overdraft limits into the choice of accounting treatment, rather than following accounting standards. The company is in a precarious position, reporting losses in the year. The finance director should act professionally, in accordance with applicable technical and professional standards, comply with relevant laws and regulations, and avoid any action which discredits the profession.

The finance director faces an advocacy threat by promoting accounting treatments which compromise objectivity. The accountant faces an intimidation threat given the comments from the finance director, who presumably has an influence over career prospects. Assuming the accountant wishes to keep her job, this intimidation threat is also linked to one of self-interest. Before acting, the accountant should speak with the finance director, try to confirm the facts, and discuss the treatment with the finance director and explain the risks of non-compliance: the safeguards of accounting regulations and the sanctions imposed on those professional accountants who do not comply may resolve the issue. A record of conversations and actions should be kept. Stent Co may also have internal procedures which mitigate the threats. It may be that the finance director is not technically up to date, in which case a safeguard would be to undergo continuing professional development. If the finance director refuses to comply with accounting standards, then it would be appropriate to discuss the matter with other directors or an audit committee (if applicable), to seek a solution, then seek professional advice from ACCA, and consider legal advice if necessary. A final consideration for the accountant, if matters cannot be satisfactorily resolved, would be resignation.

27 Calendar Co

		Marks
(a)	Discussion of the principles of relevant standards (IFRS 15, IAS 38, IAS 8)	3
	Application of the principles to Calendar Co	3
		6
(b)	Discussion of IFRS 16 principles of right of control	4
	Application of right of control principles to Calendar Co	5
		9
(c)	Discussion of principles of materiality and reference to Practice Statement 2	4
	Application of principles to PPE purchases by Calendar Co	3
	Application of principles to disclosure checklist use by Calendar Co	3
		10
		25

(a) **Sale of intangible**

IFRS 15 *Revenue from Contracts with Customers* defines revenue as income arising from an entity's ordinary activities. Calendar Co's ordinary activities do not involve selling development projects. In fact, Calendar Co has made no such sales since 20X0. It would seem that Calendar Co's business model instead involves developing products for its customers, who then take over its production, marketing and sale. Stage payments and royalties are the incomes which arise from Calendar Co's ordinary activities and should be treated as revenue.

Based on the above, Calendar Co is incorrect to recognise the gain as revenue. In fact, IAS 38 *Intangible Assets* explicitly prohibits the classification of a gain on derecognition of an intangible asset as revenue.

IAS 38 defines an intangible asset as an identifiable non-monetary asset without physical substance. Intangible assets held for sale in the ordinary course of business are outside the scope of IAS 38 and are instead accounted for in accordance with IAS 2 *Inventories*. The fact that the development project was classified as an intangible asset upon initial recognition further suggests that it was not held for sale in the ordinary course of business.

If the development was incorrectly categorised in the prior year financial statements as an intangible asset, then, as per IAS 8 *Accounting Policies, Changes in Accounting Estimates and Errors*, this should be corrected retrospectively. However, based on the infrequency of such sales, it seems unlikely that the development was misclassified.

(b) **Contract**

IFRS 16 *Leases* says that a contract contains a lease if it conveys the right to control the use of an identified asset for a period of time in exchange for consideration. When deciding if a contract involves the right to control an asset, the customer must assess whether they have:

- The right to substantially all of the identified asset's economic benefits;
- The right to direct the asset's use.

Calendar Co has the right to use a specified aircraft for three years in exchange for annual payments. Although Diary Co can substitute the aircraft for an alternative, the costs of doing so would be prohibitive because of the strict specifications outlined in the contract.

Calendar Co appears to have control over the aircraft during the three-year period because no other parties can use the aircraft during this time, and Calendar Co makes key decisions about the aircraft's destinations and the cargo and passengers which it transports. There are some contractual restrictions which limit the aircraft's use. These restrictions define the scope of Calendar Co's right of use but do not prevent it from having the right to direct the use of the aircraft.

Based on the above, the contract contains a lease. IFRS 16 permits exemptions for leases of less than 12 months or leases of low value. However, this lease contract is for three years, so is not short term, and is for a high value asset so a lease liability should have been recognised at contract inception. The lease liability should equal the present value of the payments yet to be made, using the discount rate implicit in the lease or, where unavailable, the lessee's incremental borrowing rate. A finance cost accrues over the year, which is charged to profit or loss and added to the carrying amount of the lease liability. The year-end cash payment should be removed from profit or loss and deducted from the carrying amount of the liability.

A right-of-use asset should have been recognised at the contract commencement at an amount equal to the initial value of the lease liability plus the initial costs to Calendar Co of negotiating the lease. The right-of-use asset should be depreciated over the lease term of three years and so one year's depreciation should be charged to profit or loss.

(c) **Materiality**

Calendar Co's financial statements should help investors, lenders and other creditors to make economic decisions about providing it with resources. An item is material if omitting, misstating or obscuring it might influence the economic decisions of the users of the financial statements. Materiality is not a purely quantitative consideration; an item can be material if it triggers non-compliance with laws and regulations, or bank covenants. Calendar Co should consider materiality throughout the process of preparing its financial statements to ensure that relevant information is not omitted, misstated or obscured.

Property, plant and equipment (PPE)

IAS 16 *Property, Plant and Equipment* states that expenditure on PPE should be recognised as an asset and initially measured at the cost of purchase. Writing off such expenditure to profit or loss is therefore not in accordance with IAS 16.

According to IAS 8 *Accounting Policies, Changes in Accounting Estimates and Errors*, financial statements do not comply with IFRS Standards if they contain material errors, or errors made intentionally in order to present the entity's financial performance and position in a particular way. However, assuming that the aggregate impact of writing off small PPE purchases to profit or loss is not material, then the financial statements would still comply with IFRS Standards. Moreover, this decision seems to be a practical expedient which will reduce the time and cost involved in producing financial statements, rather than a decision made to achieve a particular financial statement presentation.

If implemented, this policy must be regularly reassessed to ensure that PPE and the statement of profit or loss are not materially misstated.

Disclosure notes

IAS 1 *Presentation of Financial Statements* states that application of IFRS Standards in an entity's financial statements will result in a fair presentation. As such, the use of a checklist may help to ensure that all disclosure requirements within IFRS Standards are fulfilled. However, IAS 1 and IFRS Practice Statement 2 *Making Materiality Judgements* both specify that the disclosures required by IFRS Standards are only required if the information presented is material.

The aim of disclosure notes is to further explain items included in the primary financial statements as well as unrecognised items (such as contingent liabilities) and other events which might influence the decisions of financial statement users (such as events after the reporting period). As such, Calendar Co should exercise judgement about the disclosures which it prepares, taking into account the information needs of its specific stakeholders. This is because the disclosure of immaterial information clutters the financial statements and makes relevant information harder to find.

Calendar Co may also need to disclose information in addition to that specified in IFRS Standards if relevant to helping users understand its financial statements.

28 Digiwire

Workbook references. IFRS 15 on revenue is covered in Chapter 3. IFRS 13 *Fair Value Measurement* is covered in Chapter 4 and IFRS 9 *Financial Instruments* is covered in chapter 8.

Top tips. This question is set in the context of a digital business, something that the examiner has highlighted could be a feature of questions in SBR. The company in the question, Digiwire, sold music licences to other companies who then provide digital music to customers.

Part (a) concerned revenue recognition. In part (a)(ii), you were asked to show how the accounting treatment was supported by the *Conceptual Framework*. The principles in the *Conceptual Framework* are crucial to SBR and are likely to feature in every exam in some way. Therefore, you need to make sure you know the principles in the *Conceptual Framework* and be able to show how those principles support accounting standards, or in some cases, are at odds with accounting standards.

Part (b) included a discussion of whether cryptocurrency can be classified as a financial asset or intangible asset. The examiner report expressed surprise that answers to this question were generally weak given that there is a technical article on Cryptocurrency available on the ACCA website. This highlights the importance of reading the technical articles available - see the exam resources section of the ACCA website.

Part (c) considers debt factoring under IFRS 9. Remember that the substance of the arrangement must be considered.

Marking scheme

			Marks
(a)	(i)	Application of the following discussion to the scenario:	
		• IFRS 15 non-cash consideration and IFRS 13 alternatives to value the shares (including share value calculation at year end)	3
		• IFRS 9 remeasurement gains (including calculation)	2
	(ii)	Application of the following discussion to the scenario:	
		• Revenue recognised over time	2
		• *Conceptual Framework*	2
			9

			Marks
(b)	(i)	Discussion and application of the IFRS 11 requirements to the scenario	2
	(ii)	Discussion of the derecognition of non-monetary assets and application to the scenario	2
		Calculation of carrying amount of the joint venture	1
	(iii)	Discussion of the potential ways in which the cryptocurrency could be accounted for at fair value	4
			9
(c)		IFRS 9 requirements	1
		Agreement 1	4
		Agreement 2	2
			7
			25

(a)   (i)   **Revenue recognition: Clamusic Co shares**

IFRS 15 *Revenue from Contracts with Customers* requires that non-cash consideration received should be measured at the fair value of the consideration received. If fair value cannot be reasonably estimated, the consideration should be measured by reference to the stand-alone selling price of the good or service promised in the contract. The fair value of non-cash consideration may vary. If the non-cash consideration varies for reasons other than the form of the consideration, entities will apply the guidance in IFRS 15 related to constraining variable consideration. However, if fair value varies only due to the form, the variable constraint guidance in IFRS 15 would not apply. In this case, the fair value varies due to the form of the consideration which is equity shares and therefore the variable constraint guidance in IFRS 15 does not apply.

The fair valuation of shares in an unlisted start-up company is problematic. However, IFRS 13 *Fair Value Measurement* gives advice on how to measure unlisted shares. It sets out three approaches: (i) market approach, such as the transaction price paid for identical or similar instruments of an investee; (ii) the income approach, for example, using discounted cash flow; and (iii) the adjusted net asset approach.

In this case, the market approach has been used and the range of fair values is significant based upon the professional valuation report. The range of fair values for a 7% holding of shares would be $280,000 to $350,000 (7% of $4–$5 million) at the date of the contract and $420,000 to $490,000 (7% of $6–$7 million) at the year end. As the fair valuation is based upon a similar listed company and is based upon a controlling interest, a discount on the valuation of the shares should be applied to reflect the lack of liquidity and inability to participate in Digiwire Co's policy decisions. Thus, an estimated value of the shares can be made which takes into account the above facts. This could be the mid-point of $315,000 (($280,000 + $350,000)/2) at the date of the contract and $455,000 (($420,000 + $490,000)/2) at the year end. Digiwire Co would therefore recognise revenue of $315,000 for the receipt of shares from Clamusic Co, as the fair value of non-cash consideration is measured at the contract inception date of 1 January 20X6. This revenue would not be recognised at a point in time but would be recognised over the period of the licence which is three years.

Clamusic Co share valuation at 31 December 20X6

The shares will be recognised at $455,000 (($420,000 + $490,000)/2) at 31 December 20X6. All equity investments in scope of IFRS 9 *Financial Instruments* should be measured at fair value in the statement of financial position, with value changes being recognised in profit or loss. If an equity investment is not held for trading, an entity can make an irrevocable election at initial recognition to measure it at fair value through other comprehensive income (FVTOCI) with only dividend income recognised in profit or loss.

If Digiwire Co elects to present the remeasurements through other comprehensive income (OCI), gains are never recycled through profit or loss. This means that, if the investment in Clamusic Co is successful, when the investment is sold, there will be no profit or loss effect since all gains will already have been recognised in OCI. Thus at the year end, a gain of $140,000 ($455,000 – $315,000) will be recorded in profit or loss or OCI dependent upon any election being made.

(ii)   **Revenue: royalties**

As Digiwire Co retains an active role in the updating and maintenance of a sold licence to ensure its continuing value to the client, revenue would be recognised over the expected length of the contract or related client relationship. An entity must be expected to undertake activities which significantly affect the licence to conclude that revenue is recognised over time. However, reliable measurement of future royalties is not available (see below). Thus, in this case, the revenue would be recognised over the three-year licence based upon the licence agreement. At the year end, however, revenue from royalties can be calculated based upon the sales for the period and it would be $50,000 (5% of $1 million).

The *Conceptual Framework* support

The International Accounting Standards Board has changed the definitions of income and expenses in the *Conceptual Framework* to align with the revised definitions of an asset and a liability. The definition of income encompasses increases in assets or decreases in liabilities which result in increases in equity, other than those relating to contributions from holders of equity claims.

The *Conceptual Framework* also states that an item which meets the definition of an element should only be recognised if it provides users of financial statements with information which is useful. The *Conceptual Framework* defines useful information as: (a) relevant information; and (b) a faithful representation. Relevance may not always be achieved if there is uncertainty over existence or the probability of an inflow of economic benefits is low. Faithful representation will be affected by measurement uncertainty.

Thus, in this case, the royalties cannot be measured with any certainty in the future and should not be recognised until certain. The definitions in the *Conceptual Framework* relating to revenue, recognition and gains are therefore consistent with the approach taken by Digiwire Co.

(b)   (i)   It seems that Digiwire Co and TechGame jointly control FourDee Co and it appears as though the arrangement is a joint venture (IFRS 11 *Joint Arrangements*) as the parties have joint control of the arrangement and have rights to the net assets of the arrangement. Joint control is the contractually agreed sharing of control of an arrangement, which exists only when decisions about the relevant activities require the unanimous consent of the parties sharing control. This is the case with FourDee Co.

A joint venturer recognises its interest in a joint venture as an investment and accounts for that investment using the equity method in accordance with IAS 28 *Investments in Associates and Joint Ventures* unless the entity is exempted.

(ii)   Digiwire Co has exchanged non-monetary assets for its investment in FourDee Co, and thus needs to de-recognise the assets it is contributing to FourDee Co. The carrying amount of $6 million of the property is derecognised but the intellectual property of Digiwire Co has been generated internally and does not have a carrying amount. The cryptocurrency is recorded as an asset in the financial statements of Digiwire Co at $3 million but will be valued at $4 million, its fair value in the financial statements of FourDee Co.

Accordingly, when a joint venturer contributes a non-monetary asset to a joint venture in exchange for an equity interest in the joint venture, the joint venturer recognises a portion of the gain or loss on disposal which is attributable to the other parties to the joint venture (except when the contribution lacks commercial substance). Essentially, Digiwire Co is required by IAS 28 to limit the profit on disposal of its non-monetary assets to 50%. Effectively, Digiwire Co has only disposed of 50% of the asset contributed to the joint venture. Thus, the carrying amount of the joint venture in Digwire Co's financial statements at 31 December 20X6 will be $11.5 million (($6 + $3 carrying amounts derecognised for property and cryptocurrency) + ((4 – 3)/2) + ((10 – 6)/2)). A gain of $2.5 million will be recorded in profit or loss.

(iii) If the cryptocurrency meets the definition of a financial asset, it is possible to measure it at fair value. However, cryptocurrency is not cash or cash equivalents as its value is exposed to significant changes in market value and there is no contractual right to receive either cash or cash equivalents. Therefore, cryptocurrency fails the definition of a financial asset.

If the cryptocurrency is to be recognised as an intangible asset, then the default position would be to measure it at cost. However, there may be an argument to say that there is an active market for the cryptocurrency in which case, it would be possible for it to be measured at fair value. In this case, movements in that fair value would be recognised through other comprehensive income and the gain would not be recycled through profit or loss when the cryptocurrency is realised.

The best way to account for a cryptocurrency would be fair value as that is the value at which the entity will realise their investment or transact in exchange for goods and services. Accounting for cryptocurrency at fair value with movements reflected in profit or loss would provide the most useful information to investors but existing accounting requirements do not appear to permit this.

(c) **Debt factoring**

IFRS 9 *Financial Instruments* requires Digiwire Co to consider the commercial substance rather than the legal form of the debt factoring arrangements. Under IFRS 9, the trade receivables should be derecognised from the financial statements of Digiwire Co when the following conditions are met:

(i) When Digiwire Co has no further rights to receive cash from the factor; and either

(ii) When substantially all of the risks and rewards of ownership relating to the receivables have been transferred to the factor, or if substantially all of the risks and rewards have not been transferred, then

(iii) When Digiwire Co has no further control over the trade receivables

Agreement one

With agreement one, there is a sharing of the risks and rewards of ownership as the factoring is non-recourse except that Digiwire Co retains an obligation to refund the factor 9% of any unrecovered debts. It can be seen, however, that substantially all the risks and rewards of ownership have passed to the factor. The probability of an individual default is low given that there is low credit risk and the factor would suffer the vast majority of the loss arising from any default. Digiwire Co also has no further access to the rewards of ownership as the initial $32 million (80% × $40 million) is in full and final settlement. Furthermore, the factor has assumed full control over the collectability of the receivables. The trade receivables should be derecognised from the financial statements of Digiwire Co and $8 million, being the difference between the amount of the receivables sold and the cash received, should be charged as an irrecoverable debt expense against the profits of Digiwire Co.

The guarantee should be treated as a separate financial liability in accordance with IFRS 9. This would initially be measured at its fair value of $50,000.

Agreement two

The risks and rewards of ownership do not initially pass to the factor in relation to agreement two. The factor has full recourse to Digiwire Co for a six-month period so the irrecoverable debt risk is still with Digiwire Co. Furthermore, Digiwire Co still has the right to receive further cash payments from the factor, the amounts to be received being dependent on when and if the customers pay the factor. Digiwire Co therefore still has the risks associated with slow or non-payment by their customers. The receivables must continue to be recognised in the financial statements with the $0.8 million (20% × $4m) proceeds being treated as a short-term liability due to the factor. The receivables and liability balances would gradually be reduced as the factor recovered the cash from Digiwire Co's receivables which would be adjusted for the imputed interest and expensed in profit or loss.

Following six months the risks and rewards of ownership have passed to the factor and the balances on the loan and the receivables would be offset. The remaining balance following offset within the receivables of Digiwire Co should be expensed in profit or loss as an irrecoverable debt.

29 Ecoma Co

Workbook references. Sustainability reporting is covered in Chapter 18. Provisions are covered in Chapter 6. Pensions are covered in Chapter 5. Leases are covered in Chapter 8.

Top tips. Part (a) required discussion on the disclosure of sustainability and environment, social and governance (ESG) issues and its importance to investors. The examiner's report pointed out that reading the ACCA article on the sustainable development goals (available in the study support resources section of the ACCA website) would have provided good background information for this question. Part (b) looked at the accounting treatment of management responses to sustainability issues. Part (b)(i) included a lease that was onerous. The ACCA suggested solution given below discusses the accounting treatment of this lease as an onerous contract under IAS 37.

However, this accounting treatment only arises on initial application of IFRS 16. This treatment is covered in an ACCA article 'Onerous lease contracts and impairments, and investor issues' (available in the study support resources section of the ACCA website). It is unlikely that you would have been aware of this specific point, but, as with all questions in the SBR exam, marks would have been awarded for sensible discussion of the issues, applying appropriate principles, even if that is different to the suggested solution. The usual treatment of an onerous lease, once IFRS 16 has been applied, is to test the right-of-use asset for impairment under IAS 36 and marks would have been awarded for a discussion of this treatment.

Marking scheme

			Marks
(a)	Discussion of why it is important to investors that companies disclose sustainable information		
	Relevance	2	
	Opportunities	1	
	Valuation models	2	
	Risks	2	
	Screening strategies	1	
			8
(b)	(i) Discussion and application of the following to the scenario:		
	IAS 37 onerous contract	3	
	Future losses	1	
	Provision	2	
			6
	(ii) Discussion and application to scenario of the principles and practice of accounting for the pension scheme	4	
	Calculation of net pension obligation	3	
			7
	(iii) Calculation of the general impact on earnings		2
Professional marks			2
			25

(a)   There is increasing interest by investors in understanding how businesses are developing environmental, social or governance (ESG) goals. The positioning of the ESGs in relation to the overall corporate strategies is information which investors feel is very relevant to the investment decision which in turn will lead to capital being channelled to responsible businesses.

Sustainability practices will not all be equally relevant to all companies and investors' expectations are likely to focus on companies realising their core business activities with financial sustainability as a prerequisite for attracting investment. Because institutional investors have a fiduciary duty to act in the best interests of their beneficiaries, such institutions have to take into account sustainability practices. Companies utilising more sustainable business practices provide new investment opportunities. Investors realise that environmental events can create costs for their portfolio in the form of insurance premiums, taxes and the physical cost related with disasters. Social issues can lead to unrest and instability, which carries business risks which may reduce future cash flows and financial returns.

Investors screen the sustainable policies of companies and factor the information into their valuation models. Investors may select a company for investment based on specific policy criteria such as education and health. Investors may evaluate how successful a company has been in a particular area, for example, the reduction of educational inequality. This approach can help optimise financial returns and demonstrate their contribution to sustainability. Investors increasingly promote sustainable economies and markets to improve their long-term financial performance. However, the disclosure of information should be in line with widely accepted recommendations such as the Global Reporting Initiative (GRI) and the UN Global Compact. Integrated reporting incorporates appropriate material sustainability information equally alongside financial information, thus providing reporting organisations with a broad perspective on risk.

Investors often require an understanding of how the directors feel about the relevance of sustainability to the overall corporate strategy, and this will include a discussion of any risks and opportunities identified and changes which have occurred in the business model as a result.

Investors employ screening strategies, which may involve eliminating companies which have a specific feature, for example, low pay rates or eliminating them on a ranking basis. The latter may be on the basis of companies which are contributing or not to sustainability. Investors will use related disclosures to identify risks and opportunities on which they wish to engage with companies. Investors will see potential business opportunities in those companies which address the risks to people and the environment and those companies which develop new beneficial products, services and investments which mitigate the business risks related to sustainability. Investors are increasingly seeking investment opportunities which can make a credible contribution to the realisation of the ESGs.

(b)   (i)   Ecoma Co cannot make a provision of $16 million as the company cannot make a provision for the future operating losses of $20 million (these are specifically not allowed by IAS 37 *Provisions, Contingent Liabilities and Contingent Assets*), nor take account of the saving of $2 million per annum as no obligation exists. However, the lease represents an onerous contract and an appropriate provision should be made. IAS 37 defines an onerous contract as 'a contract in which the unavoidable costs of meeting the obligations under the contract exceed the economic benefits expected to be received under it.' There are no explicit requirements for entities to 'search' for onerous contracts but it is implicit in the onerous contract principles that reasonable steps should be taken to identify them. If an onerous contract is identified, a provision must be recognised for the best suitable estimate of the unavoidable cost. IAS 37 defines the unavoidable costs under a contract as the least net cost of exiting from the contract, which is the lower of the cost of fulfilling it and any compensation and penalties arising from failure to fulfil it. Before a separate provision for an onerous contract is recognised, an entity recognises any impairment loss which has occurred on assets dedicated to that contract.

The onerous contract should be measured by determining the present value of the unavoidable costs, net of the expected benefits under the contract. The discount rate should be a pre-tax rate which reflects current market assessments of the time value of money and the risks specific to the liability.

In this case, the requirements of the onerous contract must be considered along with the prohibition in IAS 37 of providing for future operating losses. It is important to distinguish between unavoidable costs under an onerous contract, and future operating losses. Future operating losses are not independent of the entity's future actions and do not normally stem from an obligation arising from a past event. A provision for onerous contracts is recognised if the unavoidable costs of meeting the obligations under the contract, or exiting from it, exceed the economic benefits expected to be received under it.

Therefore, the unavoidable cost of the onerous contract should be discounted to 30 September 20X5 is ($600,000 + $600,000/1.05), ie $1,171,429.

The expected benefit of sub-letting the building arising at 30 September 20X5 will be ($400,000 + (40% × 400,000)/1.05), ie $552,381.

A provision of $(1,171,429 – 552,381) $1,619,048 can therefore be made. In addition, a provision of $1 million can be made for the costs of moving to the new head office if it is felt that the cost is unavoidable. This gives a total provision of $1,619,048.

> **Tutorial note:**
>
> IFRS 16 *Leases* says that the right-of-use asset at the date of initial application is adjusted by the amount of any provision for onerous leases recognised in the statement of financial position.

(ii)   At each financial year end, the plan assets and the defined benefit obligation are remeasured. Remeasurement gains and losses are recognised in other comprehensive income.

The statement of profit or loss records the change in the surplus or deficit except for contributions to the plan and benefits paid by the plan and remeasurement gains and losses.

The amount of pension expense to be recognised in profit or loss is comprised of service costs and net interest costs. Service costs are the current service costs, which is the increase in the present value of the defined benefit obligation resulting from employee services in the current period, and 'past-service costs'. Ecoma Co's past-service costs are the changes in the present value of the defined benefit obligation for employee services in prior periods which have resulted from the plan amendment and should be recognised as an expense. IAS 19 *Employee Benefits* requires all past service costs to be recognised as an expense at the earlier of the following dates:

(a)   When the plan amendment or curtailment occurs, and
(b)   When the entity recognises related restructuring costs or termination benefits.

These costs should be recognised regardless of vesting requirements. Thus, the past service cost of $9 million will be recognised at 30 September 20X5.

Net interest on the net defined benefit liability is calculated by multiplying the opening net defined benefit liability by the discount rate at the start of the annual reporting period. Net interest on the net defined benefit liability can be viewed as effectively including theoretical interest income on plan assets.

The table below reflects the change in the net pension obligation for the period. The profit or loss will be charged with the net interest component of $3.2 million and the service cost of $27 million ($18 million + $9 million). OCI will be credited with $1.2 million and this gain cannot be reclassified to profit or loss. Benefits paid have no effect on the net obligation as both plan assets and obligations are reduced by $6 million.

	$m	Charge to
Net pension obligation at 30 September 20X4	59	
Net interest component (5.5% × 59m)	3.2	Profit or loss
Service cost for year	18	Profit or loss
Past service cost relating to plan amendment at 30 September 20X5	9	Profit or loss
Contributions	(10)	Already credited to cash
Remeasurement	(1.2)	To OCI
Net pension obligation at 30 September 20X5	78	

(iii)   Thus profit before tax of $25 million will suffer as the profit available to the ordinary shareholders will be reduced by:

	$m
Onerous contract provision (part (i))	1.6
Net interest component	3.2
Past and current service cost	27
	31.8

Thus, a loss of $6.8 million ($25 million − $31.8 million) will now be reported.

30 Egin Group

Workbook reference. Materiality and IFRS Practice Statement 2 are covered in chapter 20. Integrated Reporting is covered in Chapter 18. Related parties are covered in Chapter 2.

Top tips. This question dealt with materiality as a current issue in part (a). The definition of materiality in part (a)(i) is straightforward, but the consideration of how it could lead to a reduction in clarity and understandability needs more thought. Credit will be given for valid arguments. Integrated reporting has been tested in a number of contexts, here in the context of materiality. You needed to consider how materiality is relevant to the objective of the International Integrated Reporting Framework. The best way to approach Part (b) is to prepare a plan on your exam by adding to the group structure provided any entities or individuals who are not shown as well as any transactions between the entities and individuals involved. Then you need to apply the IAS 24 related party definitions.

Easy marks. The definition of materiality (part (a)(i)) was a good way to earn easy marks. You could also pick up some easy marks in part (a)(i) by having a working knowledge of IFRS Practice Statement 2.

Marking scheme

				Marks
(a)	(i)	Materiality and IFRS Practice Statement 2: 1 mark per well-explained point up to 6 marks	6	
	(ii)	Materiality and integrated reporting: 1 mark per well-explained point up to 4 marks	4	
				10
(b)	(i)	Reasons	4	
		Materiality	2	
				6
	(ii)	Egin Group	5	
		Spade	3	
		Atomic	1	
				9
				25

(a) (i) *Definition of materiality and application of the concept*

Information is **material** if **omitting, misstating or obscuring it** could reasonably be expected to **influence decisions** that primary users make on the basis of financial information about a specific reporting entity.

Materiality is an **entity-specific** aspect of relevance, based on the **nature and/or magnitude** of the items to which it relates in the context of the entity's financial report.

It is therefore **difficult to specify a uniform quantitative threshold** for materiality or predetermine what could be material in a particular situation.

Materiality should ensure that **relevant information is not omitted or mis-stated.** In 2018, the IASB amended the definition of materiality to clarify that relevant information **should not be obscured** by information which is not useful to primary users of financial statements, addressing the issue that too much information can be just as problematic as the omission of information.

The *Conceptual Framework* describes materiality as an **application** by a particular **entity** of the fundamental **qualitative characteristic of relevance.** When an entity is assessing materiality, it is assessing whether the information is relevant to the primary users of its own financial statements. Information relevant for one entity might not be as relevant for another entity.

Although **preparers** may understand the concept of materiality, they may be **less certain about how it should be applied.** Preparers may be **reluctant to filter** out **information which is not relevant** to users as **auditors and regulators may challenge** their reasons for the omissions, particularly where the disclosure is required by an IFRS Standard.

IFRS Practice Statement 2: Making Materiality Judgements

IFRS Practice Statement 2 is **non-mandatory guidance.**

The guidance confirms the general requirement in IAS 1 that an entity need not provide information which is not material:

- The recognition and measurement criteria in an IFRS Standard only need to be applied when **the effect** of applying them is **material.**

- An entity **does not need to make a certain disclosure**, even if that disclosure is part of a list of 'minimum required disclosures' in an IFRS Standard if the information provided by that disclosure requirement is **not material.**

The guidance includes a suggested 4-step process to making materiality judgements which includes identifying potentially material information and assessing whether that information is material.

To assess whether the information is material, preparers should assess whether the information could reasonably be expected to influence primary users. This requires the consideration of both **quantitative** and **qualitative factors.**

Quantitative factors consider the size of the effect of the transaction. These can be assessed with the help of a threshold – eg 5% of profit.

Qualitative factors are characteristics that make information more likely to influence the decisions of primary users, they can be internal or external.

It is usually **more efficient** to assess items from a **quantitative perspective first**: if an item exceeds the quantitative threshold, it is material and no further assessment is required.

As the final part of the 4-step process, the entity should review a complete set of draft financial statements, considering whether all material information has been identified and whether materiality has been considered from a wide perspective and in aggregate.

(ii)   Materiality and the International Integrated Reporting Framework

Integrated reporting takes a broader view of business reporting, emphasising the need for entities to provide information to help investors assess the current shape and performance of the business, the likely effect of management's plans, external issues and opportunities, and the long-term value of a business. Integrated reporting is a process which results in communication, through the integrated report, about how a business creates value over time.

An integrated report is a concise communication about how an organisation's strategy, governance, performance and prospects lead to the creation of value over the short, medium and long term.

Materiality is a guiding principle in the International Integrated Reporting Framework. In the Framework, a matter is considered material if it could substantively affect the organisation's ability to create value over time.

For financial reporting purposes, the nature or extent of an omission or misstatement in the organisation's financial statements determines relevance. Matters which are considered material for financial reporting purposes, or for other forms of reporting, may also be material for integrated reporting purposes if they are of such relevance and importance that they could change the assessments of providers of financial capital with regard to the organisation's ability to create value. Another feature of materiality for integrated reporting purposes is that the definition emphasises the involvement of senior management and those charged with governance in the materiality determination process in order for the organisation to determine how best to disclose its value creation development in a meaningful and transparent way.

(b)   (i)   Why it is important to disclose related party transactions

The directors of Egin are correct to say that related party transactions are a normal feature of business. However, where entities are members of the same group, for example parent and subsidiary, the **financial performance and position of both entities can be affected** by these transactions. An obvious instance of this is where one group company sells goods to another at artificially low prices which can have a detrimental impact on the stakeholders of the selling company.

In the absence of other information, users of the financial statements **assume that a company pursues its interests independently** and undertakes transactions on an **arm's length basis** on terms that could have been obtained in a transaction with a third party.

Knowledge of related party relationships and transactions affects the way in which users assess a company's operations and the risks and opportunities that it faces. Therefore, **details of an entity's controlling party and transactions with related parties should be disclosed.**

It is essential to the **stakeholders' positive view of a company's moral and ethical behaviour** that **controls** are in place to **capture related party disclosures** that are accurate and complete. This serves to **minimise the risk of unethical** or fraudulent **behaviour.**

Materiality judgement

Disclosure of related party transactions, like all other disclosure in financial statements, is subject to the over-arching characteristic of materiality, as is confirmed by IFRS Practice Statement 2: *Making Materiality Judgements.*

The size, nature and context of the related party transaction should be taken into account. A transaction may be small, such that it would be immaterial if it were not with a related party. However, the fact that it is with a related party, which is a qualitative factor, lowers the quantitative threshold for determining if it is material. Ultimately, the entity needs to determine whether disclosing the information could reasonably be expected to influence primary users' decisions. If not, then it is not material and disclosure of that information is not required.

(ii)   Nature of related party relationships

Within the Egin Group

Briars and Doye are related parties of Egin because they are **members of the same group** (both subsidiaries of Egin). For the same reason, as fellow subsidiaries, **Briars and Doye** are also **related parties of each other. Eye is also a related party of Egin** because it is an **associate of Egin**. (Egin has **significant influence** over Eye.)

Briars and Doye are also related parties of Eye. There is only one director in common and IAS 24 states that entities are not necessarily related simply because they have a director (or other member of key management personnel) in common, or because a member of key management personnel of one entity has significant influence over the other entity. However, as **Eye is a member of the same group** that Briars and Doye are members of, they are related.

Although Tang was sold several months before the year end it was a **related party** of the Egin Group until then. Therefore, the related party relationship between Tang and the Egin Group **should be disclosed** even though there were no transactions between them during the period.

Blue is a related party of Briars as a **director of Briars controls it.** Because the director is not on the management board of Egin it is **not clear whether Blue is also a related party of Egin group.** This would depend on whether the director is considered key management personnel at a group level. The director's services as a consultant to the group may mean that a related party relationship exists. The issue would depend on whether this role meant that this person was directing or controlling a major part of the group's activities and resources.

Between Spade and the Egin Group

Spade is a related party of Doye because it exerts **significant influence** over Doye. This means that the **sale** of plant and equipment **to Spade must be disclosed. Egin is not necessarily a related party of Spade** simply because both have an investment in Doye. A related party relationship will only exist if one party **exercises influence** over another **in practice.**

The directors have proposed that disclosures should state that prices charged to related parties are set on an **arm's length basis.** Because the transaction took place **between related parties** by definition it **cannot have taken place on an arm's length basis** and this description cannot be substantiated and would be **misleading.** Doye sold plant and equipment to Spade at **normal selling prices** and this is the information that should be disclosed, provided the terms can be substantiated.

Between Atomic and the Egin Group

Atomic is a related party of Egin because it can exercise **significant influence** over it. Atomic's significant influence over Egin gives it **significant influence over Briars and Doye** as they are controlled by Egin. **Eye is not a related party of Atomic** as Atomic has no ability to exercise control or significant influence over Eye.

31 Alexandra

Marking scheme

				Marks
(a)	(i)	Loan – accounting treatment – 1 mark per point up to	6	
	(ii)	Impact on investors' analysis	3	
				9
(b)		Financial asset		
	•	Classification	3	
	•	Impairment	2	
				5
(c)		Directors remuneration accounting treatment – 1 mark per point up to	4	
		Materiality discussion - 1 mark per point up to	5	
		Importance of disclosure to investors – 1 mark per point up to	2	
				11
				25

(a) (i) **Default on loan**

Under IAS 1 *Presentation of Financial Statements*, a **long-term financial liability** due to be **settled within 12 months** of the year end date should be classified as a **current liability**. Furthermore, a **long-term financial liability** that is payable on **demand** because the entity **breached** a **condition** of its loan agreement should be classified as **current** at the reporting date even if the **lender** has agreed **after the year end**, and **before** the financial statements are **authorised for issue**, **not** to **demand payment** as a consequence of the breach. This is because, at the reporting date, the entity **does not have the right** to defer settlement for at least 12 months after that date.

November 20X0	30 April 20X1	17 May 20X1	Date financial statements approved for issue
Condition of loan agreement breached. Long-term liability becomes payable on demand	Reporting date	Lender agrees not to enforce payment resulting from breach	

However, if the **lender** has **agreed** by the **reporting date** to provide a **period of grace** ending **at least 12 months after the year end** within which the entity can rectify the breach and during that time the lender cannot demand immediate repayment, the liability is classified as **non-current**.

In the case of Alexandra, the waiver was given before the reporting date, but only for the loan to be repaid a month after the reporting date, then a further waiver was agreed, but again only for a few weeks. It would **not therefore be appropriate for Alexandra to classify the bond as long-term debt** in the statement of financial position as at 30 April 20X1.

The fact that Alexandra has defaulted and sought two loan waivers may cast doubt on its ability to continue as a going concern, especially as the loan waivers may not be renewed. If there is uncertainty regarding Alexandra's going concern status, IAS 1 requires Alexandra to disclose these uncertainties. If Alexandra ceases to be a going concern, then the financial statements would need to be prepared on a break-up basis.

(ii) *Impact on investors' analysis*

Alexandra's incorrect presentation of this loan could have a serious impact on investors as they seek to analyse the financial statements. Investors need information to help them assess the prospects for future net cash inflows to an entity. Given that the bond obligation may become repayable immediately in this case, Alexandra's ability to continue as a going concern and be able to generate any future cash flows is clearly at risk.

According to the *Conceptual Framework*, the objective of financial reporting is to provide financial information about the entity that is useful to primary users of the financial statements when making decisions about providing resources to the entity. In Alexandra's case, reporting the loan as non-current is not useful to primary users; it is misleading. In fact, it is materially misleading as it could quite feasibly influence the economic decisions the primary users of Alexandra's financial statements make on the basis of those financial statements.

(b) **Financial asset**

The loan is a financial asset held at amortised cost under IFRS 9 *Financial Instruments*. Alexandra wishes to measure the loan at fair value. However, IFRS 9 states that the classification of an instrument is determined on initial recognition and that reclassifications, which are not expected to occur frequently, are permitted only if the entity's business model changes.

Financial assets are subsequently measured at amortised cost if both of the following apply:

(i) The asset is held within a business model whose objective is to hold the assets to collect the contractual cash flows; and

(ii) The contractual terms of the financial asset give rise, on specified dates, to cash flows that are solely payments of principal and interest on the principal outstanding.

All other financial assets are measured at fair value.

Alexandra's objective (and therefore its business model) for holding the debt instrument has not changed, and so it cannot measure it at fair value but must continue to measure it at amortised cost.

As Alexandra has adopted IFRS 9 *Financial Instruments*, it must apply the standard's forward-looking impairment model. The financial statements must reflect the deterioration in the credit quality of the financial asset in order to provide users with more useful and timely information.

As Alexandra has now determined that the credit risk associated with the asset has increased significantly since initial recognition, it must now increase the allowance for credit losses to reflect lifetime expected credit losses.

Alexandra is required to record the full amount of the increased allowance for credit losses immediately to reflect the impairment. The lifetime expected credit losses should be calculated at the present value of expected cash shortfalls arising from all possible default events over the loan's expected life. . The allowance should be increased to $9.9m, and the increase in the allowance of $7.9m ($9.9m - $2m) should be charged to profit or loss.

Interest revenue relating to the loan should continue to be calculated on the gross carrying amount of the loan as it is not considered to be credit impaired.

(c)   **Directors' remuneration**

IAS 24 *Related Party Disclosures* requires that entities should **disclose** key management personnel compensation **not only in total** but also **for each of the** following **categories:**

- Short-term employee benefits
- Post-employment benefits
- Other long-term benefits
- Termination benefits
- Share-based payment

The remuneration for the directors of Alexandra fits into the categories of 'short-term benefits' (ie salary and bonus) and 'share-based payment' (ie share options).

Only totals for each category need to be disclosed, not the earnings of individual board members, so no cultural protocol will be breached by these disclosures. However, Alexandra is a public limited company, and so local legislation and corporate governance rules may require more detailed disclosure.

Non-executive directors

IAS 24 defines **key management personnel** as those persons having authority and responsibility for planning, directing and controlling the activities of the entity, directly or indirectly, including any director (**whether executive or otherwise**) of that entity. Therefore, Alexandra's non-executive directors are members of Alexandra's key management personnel. The requirements of IAS 24 therefore also apply to the non-executive directors' pay.

Effect of materiality

Practice Statement 2 reaffirms that if information provided by a disclosure is not material, ie that it could not reasonably be expected to influence the decisions primary users make based on the financial statements, then that disclosure need not be made.

This applies equally to related party disclosures as to any other disclosures required by IFRSs, even if they are required under the Standard as 'minimum disclosures'. So in a sense, the finance director is correct – **but** only if the information provided by those related party disclosures is not material.

How the board assesses whether the information is material is important. The boards' assertion that the 'amounts involved are not material' suggests that perhaps they have only considered materiality from a **quantitative perspective.**

Practice Statement 2 suggests it may be efficient to first assess materiality from a quantitative perspective. If an item is considered immaterial from a quantitative perspective, the entity can then consider the presence of any **qualitative factors** and assess materiality from that perspective.

The involvement of related parties is a qualitative factor. The fact that these transactions are with related parties of Alexandra reduces the quantitative threshold that Alexandra should use to determine if the transactions are material.

Sometimes the effect of a qualitative factor can reduce the quantitative threshold to zero – thus the transaction is material despite how small it might be. This is likely to be the case when considering directors' remuneration given that it is such a contentious area.

As such, Alexandra should make the disclosures required under IAS 24, unless they can provide a well-supported argument as to why the information is not material.

Importance of disclosure to investors

Disclosures about related parties are necessary to draw attention to the possibility that the entity's financial position and profit or loss may have been affected by the existence of related parties and by transactions and outstanding balances with such parties.

Director's remuneration disclosures are particularly contentious. Public concern about excessive director remuneration has existed for some time. Investors want to know how much of an entity's income is being spent on its directors and whether this represents good value for money. Given the default on the bond and waivers to postpone interest payments, it is likely that the company would come under criticism if payments to directors were considered particularly high.

The disclosure of individual components of remuneration is important because it could influence the performance of a director – eg a high early termination payment may be seen to be rewarding poor performance.

32 Yanong

> **Workbook references.** Fair value measurement is covered in Chapter 4. **IFRS 5 is included in Chapter 14.**
>
> **Top tips.** The transaction in exhibit 1 required an understanding of the market definitions given in IFRS 13. You are expected to be able to go beyond memorising the valuation inputs. The fair value measurement of the maize (in exhibit 2) was challenging. However, valuation techniques are used extensively in corporate reporting and therefore you must become accustomed to using such techniques in answering questions. Balancing this, the valuation of a non-financial asset (the farmland, exhibit 3) was more straightforward. Exhibit 2 required some knowledge of IAS 41 *Agriculture*, which although not on in the SBR syllabus, is brought forward knowledge from *Financial Reporting*. Do not be put off by this - it is clear from reading the first paragraph of this question that the main focus of the discussion should be on IFRS 13 as per the suggested solution below. IAS 41 would only ever form a very small part of any SBR question. In Part (b) there is no need to spend time giving the IFRS 5 criteria for classification as held for sale, since we are told in the question that these criteria have been met.
>
> **Easy marks.** These are available for identifying which standards apply and outlining the principles applicable, and you will gain these marks whether or not you come to the correct conclusion about the accounting treatment.

Marks

(a) (i) 1 mark per point up to maximum   6

     (ii) 1 mark per point up to maximum   7

     (iii) 1 mark per point up to maximum   5

(b) 1 mark per point up to maximum   7

     $\overline{25}$

(a) (i) **Fair value of agricultural vehicles**

IFRS 13 says that fair value is an exit price in the principal market, which is the market with the highest volume and level of activity. It is not determined based on the volume or level of activity of the reporting entity's transactions in a particular market. Once the accessible markets are identified, market-based volume and activity determines the principal market. There is a presumption that the principal market is the one in which the entity would normally enter into a transaction to sell the asset or transfer the liability, unless there is evidence to the contrary. In practice, an entity would first consider the markets it can access. In the absence of a principal market, it is assumed that the transaction would occur in the most advantageous market. This is the market which would maximise the amount which would be received to sell an asset or minimise the amount which would be paid to transfer a liability, taking into consideration transport and transaction costs. In either case, the entity must have access to the market on the measurement date. Although an entity must be able to access the market at the measurement date, IFRS 13 does not require an entity to be able to sell the particular asset or transfer the particular liability on that date. If there is a principal market for the asset or liability, the fair value measurement represents the price in that market at the measurement date regardless of whether that price is directly observable or estimated using another valuation technique and even if the price in a different market is potentially more advantageous.

The principal (or most advantageous) market price for the same asset or liability might be different for different entities and therefore, the principal (or most advantageous) market is considered from the entity's perspective which may result in different prices for the same asset.

In Yanong's case, Asia would be the principal market as this is the market in which the majority of transactions for the vehicles occur. As such, the fair value of the 150 vehicles would be $5,595,000 ($38,000 − $700 = $37,300 × 150). Actual sales of the vehicles in either Europe or Africa would result in a gain or loss to Yanong when compared with the fair value, ie $37,300. The most advantageous market would be Europe as a net price of $39,100 (after all costs) would be achieved by selling there. Yanong would therefore utilise the fair value calculated by reference to the Asian market as this is the principal market.

IFRS 13 makes it clear that the price used to measure fair value must not be adjusted for transaction costs but should consider transportation costs. Yanong has currently deducted transaction costs in its valuation of the vehicles. Transaction costs are not deemed to be a characteristic of an asset or a liability but they are specific to a transaction and will differ depending on how an entity enters into a transaction. While not deducted from fair value, an entity considers transaction costs in the context of determining the most advantageous market because the entity is seeking to determine the market which would maximise the net amount which would be received for the asset.

(ii) **Accounting treatment of maize**

Where reliable market-based prices or values are not available for a biological asset in its present location and condition, fair value should be measured using a valuation technique. Relevant observable inputs should be maximised whilst unobservable inputs should be minimised. An appropriate valuation technique would be the present value of expected net cash flows from the asset, discounted at a current market-based rate. In the measurement of fair value of growing crops, a notional cash flow expense should be included for the 'rent' of the land where it is owned in order that the value is comparable to an entity which rents its land. The fair value of the biological asset is separate from the value of the land on which it grows.

	3 months to 31 January 20X5 $m	3 months to 30 April 20X5 $m	Total $m
Cash inflows		80	80
Cash outflows	(8)	(19)	(27)
Notional rental charge for land	(1)	(1)	(2)
Net cash flows	(9)	60	51
Discounted at 2%	(8.82)	57.66	48.84

Thus, in the quarterly accounts at 31 October 20X4, the maize fields should be recognised at $68.84 million ($20 million land plus $48.84 million maize). A fair value gain of $48.84 million should be shown in profit or loss less the operating costs of $10 million.

At 31 January, Yanong has revised its projections for cash inflows to $76 million, which means that the net cash flows at that date were projected to be $(76 – 19 – 1) million, ie $56 million. Discounted at 2%, this amounts to $54.9 million. Thus, a fair value gain of $(54.9 – 48.84) million, ie $6.06 million, should be shown in profit or loss together with the actual operating costs of $8 million.

At the point of harvest, on 31 March 20X5, the maize is valued at $82 million which means that a fair value gain of $(82 – 54.9) million, ie $27.1 million, is recognised in profit or loss and the maize is classified as inventory. The actual operating costs for the quarter would also be shown in profit or loss. When the maize is sold, a further profit of $(84 – 82) million, ie $2 million, is made on the sale.

(iii) **Farmland**

A fair value measurement of a non-financial asset takes into account a market participant's ability to generate economic benefits by using the asset in its highest and best use or by selling it to another market participant who would use the asset in its highest and best use. The maximum value of a non-financial asset may arise from its use in combination with other assets or by itself. IFRS 13 requires the entity to consider uses which are physically possible, legally permissible and financially feasible. The use must not be legally prohibited. In this case, Yanong's land for residential development would only require approval from the regulatory authority and that approval seems to be possible, so this alternative use could be deemed to be legally permissible. Market participants would consider the probability, extent and timing of the approval which may be required in assessing whether a change in the legal use of the non-financial asset could be obtained.

Yanong would need to have sufficient evidence to support its assumption about the potential for an alternative use, particularly in light of IFRS 13's presumption that the highest and best use is an asset's current use. Yanong's belief that planning permission was possible is unlikely to be sufficient evidence that the change of use is legally permissible. However, the fact the government has indicated that more agricultural land should be released for residential purposes may provide additional evidence as to the likelihood that the land being measured should be based upon residential value. Yanong would need to prove that market participants would consider residential use of the land to be legally permissible. Provided there is sufficient evidence to support these assertions, alternative uses, for example, commercial development which would enable market participants to maximise value, should be considered, but a search for potential alternative uses need not be exhaustive. In addition, any costs to transform the land, for example, obtaining planning permission or converting the land to its alternative use, and profit expectations from a market participant's perspective should also be considered in the fair value measurement.

If there are multiple types of market participants who would use the asset differently, these alternative scenarios must be considered before concluding on the asset's highest and best use. It appears that Yanong is not certain about what constitutes the highest and best use and therefore IFRS 13's presumption that the highest and best use is an asset's current use appears to be valid at this stage.

(b)   The criteria in IFRS 5 have been met for North and South. As the assets are to be disposed of in a single transaction, North and South together are deemed to be a **disposal group** under IFRS 5.

The disposal group as a whole is **measured as non-current assets held for sale**. Before the manufacturing units are classified as held for sale, impairment is tested for on an individual cash-generating unit basis. Any impairment loss reduces the carrying amount of the non-current assets in the disposal group, the loss being allocated in the order required by IAS 36 *Impairment of Assets*. Once classified as held for sale, the impairment testing is done on a **disposal group basis**.

A disposal group that is held for sale should be measured at the **lower of** it **carrying amount** and **fair value less costs to sell**. Any impairment loss is generally recognised in profit or loss, but if the asset has been measured at a revalued amount under IAS 16 *Property, Plant and Equipment* or IAS 38 *Intangible Assets*, the impairment will be treated as a revaluation decrease.

A **subsequent increase** in fair value less costs to sell may be **recognised** in profit or loss **only to the extent of any impairment previously recognised**. To summarise:

Step 1   Calculate carrying amount under the individual standard, here given as $105 million.

Step 2   Classified as held for sale. Compare the carrying amount ($105m) with fair value less costs to sell ($125m). Measure at the lower of carrying amount and fair value less costs to sell, here $105 million.

Step 3   Determine fair value less costs to sell at the year end (see below) and compare with carrying amount of $105 million.

Yanong has not taken account of the increase in fair value less cost to sell, but only part of this increase can be recognised, calculated as follows.

	$m
Fair value less costs to sell: North	40
Fair value less costs to sell: South	95
	135
Carrying amount	(105)
Increase	30

Impairment previously recognised in North: $15m ($50m – $35m)

Step 4   The change in fair value less cost to sell is recognised but the gain recognised cannot exceed any impairment losses to date. Here the gain recognised is $50m – $35m = $15m

Therefore, **carrying amount can increase** by $15 million to $120 million as loss reversals are limited to impairment losses previously recognised (under IFRS 5 or IAS 36).

33 Avco

Marking scheme

			Marks
(a)		1 mark per point up to maximum	8
(b)	(i)	1 mark per point up to maximum	8
	(ii)	Effects	4
(c)		1 mark per point up to maximum	5
			25

(a)   **Cavor**

B shares

The classification of Cavor's B shares will be made by applying **the principles-based definitions of equity and liability in IAS 32** *Financial Instruments: Presentation*, and considering the **substance,** rather than the legal form of the instrument. 'Substance' here relates only to consideration of the contractual terms of the instrument. Factors outside the contractual terms are not relevant to the classification. The following factors demonstrate that Cavor's B shares are **equity instruments.**

(1)   **Dividends are discretionary** in that they need only be paid if paid on the A shares, on which there is no obligation to pay dividends. Dividends on the B shares will be paid at the same rate as on the A shares, which will be variable.

(2)   Cavor has **no obligation to redeem** the B shares.

Lidan

A financial liability under IAS 32 is **a contractual obligation to deliver cash or another financial asset to another entity.** The contractual obligation may arise from a requirement to make payments of principal, interest or dividends. The contractual obligation may be explicit, but it may be implied indirectly in the terms of the contract.

In the case of Lidan, the **contractual obligation is not explicit**. At first glance it looks as if Lidan has a choice as to how much it pays to redeem the B shares. However, the conditions of the financial instrument are such that the value of the **settlement in own shares is considerably greater than the cash settlement obligation**. The effect of this is that **Lidan is implicitly obliged to redeem the B shares at for a cash amount of $1 per share**. The own-share settlement alternative is uneconomic in comparison to the cash settlement alternative and cannot therefore serve as a means of avoiding classification as a liability.

BPP
LEARNING
MEDIA

IAS 32 states further that where a derivative contract has settlement options, **all of the settlement alternatives must result in it being classified as an equity instrument,** otherwise it is a financial asset or liability.

In conclusion, **Lidan's B shares must be classified as a liability**

(b) (i) **Classification differences between debt and equity**

The distinction between debt and equity in an entity's statement of financial position is not easily distinguishable for preparers of financial statements. Some financial instruments may have features of debt and of equity, which can lead to inconsistency of reporting which can be confusing for the users of financial statements.

IAS 32 requires the **classification to be based on principles** rather than driven by perceptions of users.

IAS 32 defines an **equity instrument** as: 'any contract that evidences a residual interest in the assets of an entity after deducting all of its liabilities' (para. 11). It must first be **established that an instrument is not a financial liability,** before it can be classified as equity.

A key feature of the IAS 32 definition of a financial liability is that it **is a contractual obligation to deliver cash or another financial asset to another entity.** The contractual obligation may arise from a requirement to make payments of principal, interest or dividends. The contractual obligation may be explicit, but it may be implied indirectly in the terms of the contract. An example of a debt instrument is a bond which requires the issuer to make interest payments and redeem the bond for cash.

A financial instrument is an **equity instrument** only if there is no obligation to deliver cash or other financial assets to another entity and if the instrument will or may be settled in the issuer's own equity instruments. An example of an equity instrument is **ordinary shares, on which dividends are payable at the discretion of the issuer.** A less obvious example is preference shares required to be converted into a fixed number of ordinary shares on a fixed date or on the occurrence of an event which is certain to occur.

An instrument may be classified as an equity instrument if it contains a **contingent settlement provision** requiring settlement in cash or a variable number of the entity's own shares **only on the occurrence of an event which is very unlikely to occur** – such a provision is **not considered to be genuine.** If the **contingent payment condition** is **beyond the control of** both the entity and the holder of the instrument, then the instrument is classified as a **financial liability.**

A **contract resulting in the receipt or delivery of an entity's own shares is not automatically an equity instrument.** The classification depends on the so-called **'fixed test'** in IAS 32. A contract which will be settled by the entity receiving or delivering a **fixed number of its own equity instruments in exchange for a fixed amount of cash is an equity instrument.** In contrast, if the **amount of cash or own equity shares to be delivered or received is variable,** then the contract is a **financial liability or asset.**

There are **other factors** which might result in an instrument being **classified as debt.**

(1) Dividends are non-discretionary.

(2) Redemption is at the option of the instrument holder.

(3) The instrument has a limited life.

(4) Redemption is triggered by a future uncertain event which is beyond the control of both the issuer and the holder of the instrument.

Other factors which might result in an instrument being **classified as equity** include the following.

(1) Dividends are discretionary.
(2) The shares are non-redeemable.
(3) There is no liquidation date.

Although IAS 32 establishes principles for presenting financial instruments as liabilities or equity, it is not always easy to apply these principles in practice.

(ii) **Significance of debt/equity classification for the financial statements**

The distinction between debt and equity is very important for users who analyse the financial statements. The classification **can have a significant impact on the entity's reported earnings and gearing ratio**, which in turn can affect investment decisions. Companies may wish to classify a financial instrument as **equity**, in order to give a **favourable impression of gearing,** but this may in turn have a **negative effect** on the perceptions of existing shareholders if it is seen **as diluting existing equity interests**.

The distinction is also relevant in the context of a **business combination** where an entity **issues financial instruments as part consideration, or to raise funds to settle a business combination in cash**. Management is often called upon to **evaluate different financing options**, and in order to do so must **understand the classification rules and their potential effects**. For example, **classification as a liability** generally means that **payments are treated as interest** and charged to profit or loss, and this may, in turn, **affect the entity's ability to pay dividends** on equity shares.

(c) The finance director has suggested that the investment in cryptocurrencies should be recorded as a financial asset. Under IAS 32, a financial asset is 'cash, an equity instrument of another entity or a contractual right to receive cash, an equity instrument or exchange financial instruments on favourable terms' (para. 11). Cryptocurrencies do not meet the definition of cash as they are not generally accepted as legal tender and also do not give a contractual right to receive cash or other instruments. As such, it is not appropriate for Avco to classify the investment as a financial asset.

In the absence of an IFRS Standard covering investments in cryptocurrencies, the directors of Avco should use judgement to develop an appropriate accounting policy in accordance with IAS 8 *Accounting Policies, Changes in Accounting Estimates and Errors*. The directors should consider:

- IFRS Standards dealing with similar issues. As we have discussed, cryptocurrencies do not meet the definition of financial assets and they do not have physical substance and therefore cannot be accounted for as property, plant and equipment or inventories. As cryptocurrencies do not have physical substance, it is likely that IAS 38 *Intangible Assets* is the most appropriate accounting standard to refer to. They also meet the other criteria of IAS 38 as they are identifiable and they are non-monetary (as they do not result in fixed or determinable amounts of money).

- The *Conceptual Framework*. The investment appears to meet the definition of an asset: a present economic resource controlled by the entity as a result of past events. Consideration should be given to the recognition criteria and to other issues such as the measurement basis to apply and how measurement uncertainty may affect that choice given the volatility of cryptocurrencies.

- The most recent pronouncements of other national GAAPs based on a similar conceptual framework and accepted industry practice. The IFRS Interpretations Committee issued an agenda decision in 2019 in which they defined what they meant by a 'cryptocurrency' and concluded that items which met this definition should be treated as intangible assets. The directors should consider whether the investment they hold meets the definition of cryptocurrency as defined in the agenda decision, and if so, should apply the guidance in the agenda decision.

The directors of Avco need to account for the investment in a way which provides **useful** information to the primary users of its financial statements. This means the information provided by the accounting treatment should be **relevant** and should **faithfully represent** the investment.

34 Lupin

Marking scheme

				Marks
(a)	(i)	Share options	4	
	(ii)	Lease plant	4	
	(iii)	Intragroup	4	
	(iv)	Impairment loss	4	
				16
(b)	(i)	Conceptual Framework	2	
		Temporary difference	2	
		Liability	1	
				5
	(ii)	Tax reconciliation discussion	2	
		Omit from disclosures	2	
				4
Total				25

(a) (i) **Share options**

Under IFRS 2 *Share-based Payment* the company **recognises an expense** for the employee services received in return for the share options granted over the vesting period. The related tax deduction **does not arise until the share options are exercised.** Therefore, a **deferred tax asset arises,** based on the difference between the intrinsic value of the options and their carrying amount (normally zero).

At 31 October 20X4 the tax benefit is as follows:

	$m
Carrying amount of share-based payment	–
Less tax base of share-based payment (16/2)	(8)
Temporary difference	(8)

The **deferred tax asset is $2.4 million** (30% × 8). This is recognised at 31 October 20X4 provided that taxable profit is available against which it can be utilised. Because the tax effect of the remuneration expense is greater than the tax benefit, the tax benefit is **recognised in profit or loss.** (The tax effect of the remuneration expense is 30% × $40 million ÷ 2 = $6 million.)

At 31 October 20X5 there is **no longer a deferred tax asset** because the options have been exercised. The **tax benefit receivable is $13.8 million** (30% × $46 million). Therefore, the deferred tax asset of $2.4 million is no longer required.

(ii) **Leased plant**

Under IFRS 16 *Leases*, a **right-of-use asset** and a **lease liability** are recognised.

The lease liability is measured at the **present value of future lease payments** discounted using, if available, the interest rate implicit in the lease. Each instalment payable is allocated partly as interest and partly as repayment of the liability.

The right-of-use asset is measured initially at the amount of the initial measurement of the lease liability, plus certain other direct costs not incurred in this case, such as legal fees. It is depreciated on a straight-line basis over the five years. The **carrying amount** of the right-of-use asset for accounting purposes is the **initial amount of the right-of-use asset less depreciation**.

Tax relief is granted as lease rentals are paid, therefore the tax base of the lease liability is zero as it is calculated as the carrying amount less any future tax-deductible amounts. The tax base of the right-of-use asset is the amount deductible for tax in future, which is zero.

Therefore, at 31 October 20X5 a **net temporary difference** arises as follows:

	$m	$m
Carrying amount in financial statements:		
Asset:		
Right-of-use asset	12.00	
Less depreciation (12/5)	(2.40)	
		9.60
Less lease liability		
Liability at inception of lease	12.00	
Interest (8% × 12)	0.96	
Lease rental	(3.00)	
		(9.96)
		0.36
Less tax base		(0.00)
Temporary difference		0.36

A **deferred tax asset of $108,000** (30% × 360,000) arises.

(iii) **Intra-group sale**

Dahlia has **made a profit of $2 million** on its sale to Lupin. Tax is **payable on the profits of individual companies**. Dahlia is liable for tax on this profit in the current year and will have provided for the related tax in its individual financial statements. However, **from the viewpoint of the group** the profit **will not be realised until the following year**, when the goods are sold to a third party and must be **eliminated** from the consolidated financial statements. Because the group **pays tax before the profit is realised** there is a **temporary difference of $2 million** and a **deferred tax asset of $600,000** (30% × $2 million).

(iv) **Impairment loss**

The impairment loss in the financial statements of Nala **reduces the carrying amount** of property, plant and equipment, but is **not allowable for tax**. Therefore, the **tax base** of the property, plant and equipment **is different from its carrying amount** and there is a **temporary difference**.

Under IAS 36 *Impairment of Assets* the impairment loss is allocated first to goodwill and then to other assets:

	Goodwill $m	Property, plant and equipment $m	Total $m
Carrying amount at 31 October 20X5	1	6.0	7.0
Impairment loss	(1)	(0.8)	(1.8)
	–	5.2	5.2

IAS 12 states that **no deferred tax should be recognised on goodwill** and therefore **only the impairment loss relating to the property, plant and equipment affects the deferred tax position.**

(b) (i) The conceptual basis for accounting for deferred tax is questionable.

On one hand, deferred tax is focused on the statement of financial position, which is in keeping with the *Conceptual Framework*. However, it can be argued that deferred tax assets and liabilities **do not meet the definition of assets and liabilities** under the *Conceptual Framework*. An asset is defined as a **present economic resource** controlled by an entity as a result of past events and a liability is a **present obligation** to transfer economic benefits, again as a result of past events. It is not clear whether deferred tax assets and obligations can be considered present resources or obligations.

IAS 12 *Income Taxes* is based on the idea that **all changes in assets and liabilities** have **unavoidable tax consequences.** Where the recognition criteria in IFRS are different from those in tax law, **the carrying amount of an asset or liability in the financial statements is different from its tax base** (the amount at which it is stated for tax purposes). These differences are known as **temporary differences.**

The practical effect of these differences is that the recognition of the transaction or event occurs in a different accounting period from its tax consequences. For example, unless the accounting depreciation and tax depreciation (capital allowances in the UK) are calculated on exactly the same basis, the amount of accounting depreciation recognised in the financial statements in an accounting period is different to the amount of tax on the same asset in the same period.

Under IAS 12, the tax effects of transactions are recognised in the same period as the transactions themselves, but in practice, tax is paid in accordance with tax legislation when it becomes a legal liability. This is considered another **conceptual weakness** or inconsistency, in that only one liability, that is tax, is being provided for, and not other costs, such as overhead costs that may be associated with the same transaction.

Conclusion

The shareholder is correct to question the basis for providing for deferred tax as there does appear to be some inconsistency between IAS 12 and the *Conceptual Framework*. Nonetheless, Lupin should apply the requirements of IAS 12.

(ii) The tax reconciliation shows how the tax charge in the statement of profit or loss can be reconciled back to the expectation of some users of financial statements that income tax is simply a company's profit before tax multiplied by the applicable tax rate.

It is true that the tax reconciliation can be complicated. This is particularly the case when the tax affairs of the entity are complex. However, this does not mean that the information should be excluded. The *Conceptual Framework* states that excluding information about complex phenomena from financial statements might make the financial statements easier to understand, but it would also make them incomplete and therefore potentially misleading.

The *Conceptual Framework* expects users of financial statements to have a reasonable knowledge of business and economic activities. Lupin should consider whether this is the case for this particular shareholder. However, if several shareholders are complaining about the tax reconciliation, then Lupin could consider including an explanatory note to the tax reconciliation to enable users of the financial statements to fully understand it. While this is not required by IAS 12, IAS 1 requires entities to consider whether additional information should be presented to enable users to understand the impact of transactions or conditions on the entity's financial position or performance.

The fact that the finance director finds the tax reconciliation difficult to prepare is not a valid reason for omitting it. In fact, the finance director's comment raises ethical concerns – is the finance director competent and aware of the requirements of IFRS? The tax reconciliation is a key disclosure required by IAS 12. That is not to say that all disclosures required by an accounting standard must be given – it depends on whether the disclosure is material.

IFRS Practice Statement 2 *Making Materiality Judgements* requires a preparer to make materiality judgements and clarifies that if information provided by a disclosure could not reasonably be expected to influence the decisions users make based on the financial statements, then that disclosure need not be made.

Given that the finance director finds it difficult to prepare the reconciliation suggests that Lupin's tax affairs may be complex and therefore disclosing information about them is unlikely to be immaterial.

35 Janne

> **Workbook references.** Investment property and fair value measurement are covered in Chapter 4. IFRS Practice Statement 2 *Making Materiality Judgements* is covered in Chapter 20. Alternative performance measures are covered in Chapter 18.
>
> **Top tips.** For Part (a)(i) ensure that you relate your answer to the relevant accounting standards, IAS 40 and IFRS 13. The key message is that there is guidance on the measurement of fair value which Janne should have been applying. In Part (a)(ii) requires a discussion of the measurement principles in the *Conceptual Framework* in relation to Janne.
>
> In Part (b) you need to make sure you answer the requirement: relate your answer to Janne's investors and reference the key applicable points of the practice statement. Part (c) covers alternative performance measures which is a key topic for SBR. Again, you need to consider Janne's investors in your answer. Wider reading of articles, particularly those on the ACCA website, will be extremely helpful in being able to answer questions such as those seen here in Parts (b) and (c). The ESMA (European Securities and Markets Authority) Guidelines on Alternative Performance Measures, which are available online, provide another perspective and will be beneficial to read.

Marking scheme

		Marks
(a)	Investment properties discussion – 1 mark per valid point up to	9
(b)	Annual report discussion – 1 mark per valid point up to	8
(c)	Alternative performance measure discussion – 1 mark per valid point up to	8
		25

BPP LEARNING MEDIA

(a) (i) Investment properties

IAS 40 *Investment Property* allows two methods for valuing investment property: the fair value model and the cost model. If the fair value model is adopted, **then the investment property must be valued in accordance with IFRS 13** *Fair Value Measurement*. Fair value is the price that would be received to sell an asset or paid to transfer a liability in an orderly transaction between market participants at the measurement date.

Fair value is a **market-based measurement** rather than specific to the entity, so a company is not allowed to choose its own way of measuring fair value. Valuation techniques must be those which are appropriate and for which sufficient data are available. Entities should maximise the use of relevant **observable inputs** and minimise the use of **unobservable inputs**. The standard establishes a hierarchy for the inputs that valuation techniques use to measure fair value.

Level 1   Quoted prices (unadjusted) in active markets for identical assets or liabilities

Level 2   Inputs other than quoted prices included within Level 1 that are observable for the asset or liability, either directly or indirectly

Level 3   Unobservable inputs for the asset or liability

Although the directors claim that 'new-build value less obsolescence' is accepted by the industry, it **may not be in accordance with IFRS 13**. As investment property is often unique and not traded on a regular basis, fair value measurements are likely to be categorised as Level 2 or Level 3 valuations.

IFRS 13 mentions three valuation techniques: the market approach, the income approach and the cost approach. A market or income approach would usually be more appropriate for an investment property than a cost approach. The 'new-build value less obsolescence' (cost approach) does not take account of the Level 2 inputs such as sales value (market approach) and market rent (income approach). Nor does it take account of reliable estimates of future discounted cash flows, or values of similar properties.

In conclusion, Janne must apply IFRS 13 to the valuation of its investment property, taking account of Level 2 inputs.

(ii) Selection of measurement basis

Janne should ensure that it has given adequate consideration to its particular facts and circumstances in deciding to use fair value as the measurement basis for its investment property.

Applying the principles in the *Conceptual Framework*, Janne should choose a measurement basis should that provides information that is **useful** to the primary users of its financial statements. To be useful, the information must be **relevant** and provide a **faithful representation**.

The relevance of a measurement basis is affected by:

- The characteristics of the asset – eg if information about changes in the value of investment property is important to Janne's primary users, using a cost basis may not provide relevant information.

- How the asset contributes to future cash flows – which in part depends on Janne's business activities.

As investment property makes up 60% of Janne's total assets and assuming that Janne is holding investment property both to obtain rental income and to benefit from increases in value, it would be reasonable to assume that primary users would be very interested in changes in value, suggesting cost may not provide the most relevant information.

However, sometimes the level of **measurement uncertainty** associated with a measurement basis is so high that the information would not be a faithful representation. If significant measurement uncertainty exists through the use of fair value, Janne should consider using cost instead. This principle is also included in IAS 40 as it specifies that if, at recognition, fair value is not expected to be reliably measurable on a continuing basis, cost should be used instead.

(b)   **Annual report**

Too much information in annual reports can be problematic as it can **obscure relevant information** and prevent investors from identifying the key issues that are likely to affect their decisions.

Removing unnecessary information from the annual report is therefore a good idea. However, it must be done carefully to ensure that financial reports still meet their primary objective of providing financial information that is useful to existing and potential investors, lenders and other creditors in making decisions about providing resources to the entity.

Disclosures are prescribed by IFRS and therefore are **not optional**. Management cannot just determine which disclosures appear irrelevant.

However, **materiality** needs to be taken into account when making disclosures. Practice Statement 2 *Making Materiality Judgements* confirms that **disclosure does not need to be made, even when prescribed by an IFRS, if the resulting information presented is not material**.

Although the finance director has used a disclosure checklist and determined that all disclosures made were 'necessary', it is not clear whether an assessment has been made as to whether the disclosures provide information that is material. If not, there is the potential to reduce disclosure in Janne's annual report.

If the information provided by a disclosure could not reasonably be expected to influence the decisions primary users make on the basis of Janne's financial statements, then it is not material and does not need to be disclosed.

Reducing the size of the accounting policy note is a distinct possibility. Only significant accounting policies are required to be disclosed by IAS 1. Determining what constitutes a significant accounting policy requires judgement.

Janne could consider removing the accounting policies which would not affect a user's understanding of the financial statements if they were not disclosed. Accounting policies that require management judgement are likely to be material and if so, should be clearly presented. This is so that investors can see where management judgement has been applied and can assess management's stewardship.

Disclosures required by IAS 24 in relation to related parties are necessary to draw attention to the possibility that an entity's financial position and profit or loss may have been affected by the transactions with related parties. So the managing director is not correct in his assertion that because the transactions are undertaken on terms equivalent to 'arm's length', they are not important to investors.

However, as with other disclosures, they only need to be made if the information provided is material. Related party transactions may be of a relatively small size and therefore considered not material from a **quantitative perspective**. However, Practice Statement 2 considers the fact that the transaction is with a related party to be a **qualitative factor**. A qualitative factor reduces the threshold for assessing whether something is material from a quantitative perspective.

Without considering the transactions more carefully, Janne cannot say that related party transactions are immaterial and need not be disclosed. Conversely, Janne should not assume that just because the transaction is with a related party that it must definitely be disclosed. Janne should apply the guidance provided in Practice Statement 2 in order to make a judgement about what information about related party transactions would be useful to investors and other primary users.

(c) **Additional performance measure**

'Adjusted net asset value per share' (adjusted NAV per share) is an additional performance measure (APM). Entities are increasingly reporting APMs in addition to IFRS performance measures, such as earnings per share, in order to enhance a user's understanding of the financial statements. It is possible for Janne to present this APM, however, it cannot present this measure instead of earnings per share (EPS). EPS is required by IAS 33 which must be applied by listed entities. Therefore, in order to comply with IFRS, EPS and diluted EPS must be presented.

APMs should be provided to enhance the understanding of users of the accounts. Investment properties are likely to form the majority of Janne's assets. Therefore, management will be interested in the increase in the value of those properties and related finance (eg loans), both of which are taken into account in adjusted NAV per share. Disclosing adjusted NAV per share should therefore enhance the understanding of investors as it will allow them to evaluate Janne through the eyes of management. Additionally, as adjusted NAV per share is used by other companies in the same industry, disclosing it should allow investors to more effectively compare the performance of Janne with other companies in the same industry.

However, APMs can also be misleading. Unlike EPS, there is no official definition of adjusted NAV per share, so management can choose what items to include in the 'adjustment'. Therefore, it is open to bias in its calculation as management could decide to only adjust for items that improve the measure. In order to counter the criticisms, management should provide a description of what is included when arriving at adjusted NAV per share and ideally reconcile the information back to the IFRS information included within the financial statements. Similarly, in order to be useful, the basis of the calculation needs to be consistent from year to year, otherwise comparison between years will be inaccurate. Furthermore, different companies may define the same measure in different ways, which reduces the comparability between entities.

Ultimately adjusted NAV per share will only provide useful information to Janne's investors if it is fairly presented. The European Securities and Markets Authority (ESMA) has developed guidelines that address the issues surrounding the use of APMs. The guidelines require appropriate description of APMs, consistency in how the APM is calculated and presented from year to year as well as guidance for presentation, including that APMs should not be presented with more prominence, emphasis or authority than the equivalent IFRS measures, nor should they distract from IFRS disclosures.

It is advisable for Janne's directors to consider this guidance in determining whether to present adjusted NAV per share and how it should be presented. They should also consider whether providing further information in the form of APMs will result in more information being reported in the annual report which they are otherwise attempting to reduce.

36 SunChem

Workbook references. IAS 24 is covered in Chapter 2, IAS 38 in Chapter 4, IFRS 3 in Chapter 11 and IFRS Practice Statement 2 in Chapter 20.

Top tips. Part (a) deals with standards that should be familiar to you, but the issues require in-depth consideration. In particular, you need to consider how IAS 38 and IFRS 3 interact, focusing on the implications of acquiring technology, outlining the fact that the probability recognition criterion is always considered to be satisfied for intangible assets that are acquired separately or in a business combination. You were also expected to discuss that a shell company without employees (and hence without processes required to make it a 'business') is an asset acquisition as opposed to a business combination. Part (b) is on materiality and related parties – identifying the related parties and discussing how such disclosures are useful to investors. You are advised to jot down a plan or diagram of the relationships before launching into your answer.

Easy marks. There are marks for knowing the basics of the standards tested, but those marks will not get you a pass on this question.

			Marks
(a)		1 mark per point up to maximum	10
(b)	(i)	1 mark per point up to maximum	4
	(ii)	1 mark per point up to maximum	5
	(iii)	1 mark per point up to maximum	6
			25

(a) *Intangible asset*

SunChem has purchased a license which gives it the **right** to use Jomaster's technology for a specified period of time in order to manufacture a specific compound. The acquired license meets the definition of an intangible asset as it is:

- **Identifiable** (it arises from the contractual right to use Jomaster's technology for three years);

- **Non-monetary**; and

- Has no physical substance (SunChem has not acquired a physical item of machinery, but instead has acquired the right to use the technology to perform a particular process).

Under IAS 38, an intangible asset should be recognised when

(i) It is probable that the future economic benefits which are attributable to the asset will flow to the entity; and

(ii) The cost of the asset can be measured reliably.

IAS 38 states that the probability recognition criterion is **always considered to be satisfied for intangible assets that are acquired separately** or in a business combination. This is because the price an entity pays to separately acquire an intangible asset will reflect the entity's expectations about the probability of economic benefits flowing to the entity. Put simply, by purchasing the intangible asset, SunChem expects economic benefits to flow from it, even if it is not certain about the timing or amount of those benefits.

Therefore, SunChem should recognise the license as an intangible asset measured at its cost of $4 million. As it has a finite useful life, the license should be **amortised** from the date it is available for use, ie when the manufacturing of the compound begins. The amortisation should be included as an expense in the statement of profit or loss.

At the end of each reporting period, SunChem should assess whether there is any indication that the asset may be **impaired**, and if so, the carrying amount of the asset should be reduced and the impairment loss should be recognised as an expense in profit or loss.

Due to the nature of intangible assets, **subsequent expenditure** will only rarely meet the criteria for being recognised in the carrying amount of an asset. Thus, SunChem should expense its own internal development expenditure, incurred in updating the technology in accordance with Jomaster's requirements, until the criteria for capitalisation in IAS 38 are met and economic benefits are expected to flow to the entity from the capitalised asset.

Acquisition of interest in Conew

SunChem wishes to acquire 65% of the equity of Conew. SunChem must assess whether this acquisition qualifies as a business combination under IFRS 3 *Business Combinations*. A business combination is a transaction in which an entity **obtains control of a business**.

Under IFRS 3, a business consists of **inputs** and **processes applied to those inputs** which have the ability to contribute to the **creation of outputs**.

Conew has an 'input' in that it has an intangible asset. However, Conew does not have any employees, and therefore does not have any processes which could be applied to the intangible asset. Therefore, Conew **does not meet the definition of a business.**

The acquisition of an interest in Conew is therefore an **asset acquisition**, not a business combination, and should be accounted for under IAS 38.

(b)   (i)   **Materiality**

Practice Statement 2 was developed in response to concerns that some companies are unsure how to make judgements concerning materiality. This can result in excessive disclosure of immaterial information while important information can be obscured or even missed out of the financial statements.

This is particularly true for information disclosed in the notes where it appears that some companies use IFRS disclosure requirements as a 'checklist' and therefore provide all disclosures required by a Standard, whether material or not.

Practice Statement 2 is not an IFRS and is therefore **not mandatory** in order to state compliance with IFRS in a financial report.

Key points

- Financial statements are not intended to satisfy the information needs of **all users**, but should provide financial information that is useful to **primary users** (potential and existing investors, lenders and other creditors) in making decisions about providing resources to the entity.

- If the information provided by a disclosure is **not material**, the **entity does not need to make that disclosure.**

- Materiality should be assessed from a **qualitative perspective** as well as a **quantitative perspective**. Practice Statement 2 recommends starting from the quantitative perspective and then applying qualitative factors to further assess immaterial items. The presence of a qualitative factor lowers the quantitative threshold for assessing materiality.

Practice Statement 2 contains a four-step process to help entities make materiality judgements: identify, assess, organise and review.

(ii)   **Related parties**

A person or a close member of that person's family is a **related party** of a reporting entity if that person:

(i)   Has control or joint control over the reporting entity;

(ii)   Has significant influence over the reporting entity; or

(iii)   Is a member of the key management personnel of the reporting entity or of a parent of the reporting entity.

> **Tutorial note.**
>
> You will get very few, if any, marks for writing up the requirements of Standards. The vast majority of marks are available for the application of those requirements to the scenario given. The definition of a related party has been given in this solution for completeness, but you do not need to include this definition in an exam answer.

In SunChem:

- The finance director is a related party, as she owns more than half of the voting power (60%). In the absence of evidence to the contrary, she controls SunChem and is a member of the key management personnel.

- The sales director is also a related party of SunChem as he is a member of the key management personnel and is a close member (spouse) of the family of the finance director.

- Their son is a related party of SunChem as he is a close member (son) of their family.

- The operations director is also a related party as he owns more than 20% of the voting power in SunChem. In the absence of evidence to the contrary, the operations director has significant influence over SunChem and is a member of the key management personnel.

An entity is related to a reporting entity if the entity is controlled or jointly controlled by a person identified as a related party:

- Baleel is a related party because it is controlled by related parties, the finance and sales directors, for the benefit of a close member of their family, ie their son.

- Ocean is a related party because it is controlled by a close family member (spouse) of the operations director (a related party).

In the absence of evidence to the contrary, the third owner of the shares is not a related party. The person is a passive investor who does not appear to exert significant influence over SunChem.

(iii) IAS 24 requires related party disclosures in order to draw attention to the possibility that an entity's financial position and profit or loss may have been affected by the existence of related parties and by transactions and outstanding balances with such parties.

In this case, there is a single investor owning 10% of the shares whose investment may be affected by the related party transactions undertaken.

It is not just investors that are interested in such information. The *Conceptual Framework* states that the objective of financial reports is to provide information that is useful to existing and potential investors, lenders and other creditors of an entity. So it is not just the passive investor that must be considered when determining what to disclose.

Practice Statement 2 clarifies that if information provided by a disclosure could not reasonably be expected to influence the decisions primary users make based on the financial statements, then that disclosure need not be made.

The involvement of related parties is a qualitative factor when assessing materiality. This factor reduces the quantitative threshold and the entity should then go back and re-assess whether the information is material.

In the case of the laptop sold to the son, it is unlikely that this transaction would be material from a quantitative perspective. However, because the transaction is with a related party, the quantitative threshold should be lowered. SunChem should give consideration as to whether disclosing information about this transaction would be useful to its primary users. Given that the transaction is so small and has not reoccurred, it is probably not material.

In the case of the maintenance contract, it may be that the contract is below the quantitative threshold even when this threshold is lowered for the fact that the transaction is with a related party. However, given that the contract is ongoing and that it was awarded to a related party despite being more expensive, suggests that disclosing this information would be useful to primary users.

37 Kiki Co

				Marks
(a)	(i)	Discussion of relevant principles of revenue recognition	2	
		Application to the gift cards issued by Kiki Co	4	
				6
	(ii)	Discussion of relevant principles of revenue recognition	2	
		Application to the royalty income of Kiki Co	2	
		Principle and treatment of the loss allowance	2	
				6
(b)		General implications of the measurement choice	2	
		Investor perceptions re asset base/SOFP	4	
		Investor perceptions re SOPL/performance measures	5	
				11
		Professional		2
				25

(a) (i) **Gift cards**

IFRS 15 *Revenue from Contracts with Customers* says that revenue should be recognised when or as a performance obligation is satisfied by transferring the promised good or service to the customer. When a customer buys a gift card they are pre-paying for a product. Revenue cannot be recognised because the entity has not yet transferred control of an asset and so has not satisfied a performance obligation. As such, cash received in respect of gift cards should be initially recognised as a contract liability.

IFRS 15 refers to a customer's unexercised rights as breakage. The guidance for variable consideration is followed when estimating breakage. In other words, the expected breakage is included in the transaction price if it is highly probable that a significant reversal in the amount of cumulative revenue recognised will not occur once the uncertainty is subsequently resolved. This means that if the company is unable to reliably estimate the breakage amount, then revenue for the unused portion of the gift card is recognised when the likelihood of the customer exercising their remaining rights becomes remote. However, if an entity is able to reliably estimate the breakage amount, then it recognises the expected breakage amount as revenue in proportion to the pattern of rights exercised by the customer.

In relation to Kiki Co, it appears that the amount of breakage can be reliably determined and so this should be recognised in revenue as the gift card is redeemed. For every $1 redeemed, Kiki Co should recognise $1.43 ($1 × 100/70) in revenue.

(ii) **Royalty**

According to IFRS 15, an entity should only account for revenue from a contract with a customer when it meets the following criteria:

- The contract has been approved;
- Rights regarding goods and services can be identified;
- Payment terms can be identified;
- It is probable the seller will collect the consideration it is entitled to.

At inception of the agreement, Kiki Co and Colour Co entered an explicit contract which specified payment terms and conditions. Moreover, Colour Co had a strong credit rating and so payment was probable. As such, it would seem that the above criteria were met. IFRS 15 says that revenue from a usage-based royalty should be recognised as the usage occurs.

Whether a contract with a customer meets the above criteria is only reassessed if there is a significant change in facts and circumstances. In July 20X7, Colour Co lost major customers and sources of finance. As such, it was no longer probable that Kiki Co would collect the consideration it was entitled to. From July 20X7, no further revenue from the contract should be recognised.

According to IFRS 9 *Financial Instruments*, non-payment is an indicator that the outstanding receivables are credit impaired. A loss allowance should be recognised equivalent to the difference between the gross carrying amount of the receivables and the present value of the expected future cash flows receivable from Colour Co. Any increase or decrease in the loss allowance is charged to profit or loss.

(b) Investment properties

In accordance with IAS 40 *Investment Property*, the buildings should be initially measured at cost.

If the cost model is applied, then the buildings will be recognised at cost less accumulated depreciation and impairment losses.

If the fair value model is applied, then the buildings will be remeasured to fair value at each reporting date. Gains and losses on remeasurement are recognised in the statement of profit or loss. No depreciation is charged.

Statement of financial position

Assuming that property prices rise, the fair value model will lead to an increase in reported assets on the statement of financial position. In contrast, investment property measured using the cost model is depreciated, which reduces its carrying amount. This means that the fair value model may make Kiki Co appear more asset-rich. Some stakeholders may place importance on an entity's asset base, as it can be used as security for obtaining new finance. However, reporting higher assets can sometimes be perceived negatively. For example, asset turnover ratios will deteriorate, and so Kiki Co may appear less efficient.

If assets increase, then equity also increases. As such, the fair value model may lead to Kiki Co reporting a more optimistic gearing ratio. This may reduce the perception of risk, encouraging further investment.

Statement of profit or loss

In times of rising prices, the use of the fair value model will lead to gains being reported in the statement of profit or loss. This will increase profits for the period. In contrast, the depreciation charged under the cost model will reduce profits for the period. Therefore, earnings per share, a key stock market and investor ratio, is likely to be higher if the fair value model is adopted.

However, it should be noted that fair values are volatile. In some years, fair value gains may be much larger than in other years. If property prices decline, then the fair value model will result in losses. As such, reported profits are subject to more volatility if the fair value model is adopted. This may increase stakeholders' perception of risk. In contrast, the depreciation expense recorded in accordance with the cost model will be much more predictable, meaning that investors will be better able to predict Kiki Co's future results.

Many entities now present alternative performance measures (APMs), such as EBITDA (earnings before interest, tax, depreciation and amortisation). Other entities present 'underlying profit' indicators, which strip out the impact of non-operating or non-recurring gains or losses (such as the remeasurement of investment properties). Although the use of APMs has been criticised, Kiki Co may consider them to be useful in helping investors to assess underlying business performance through the eyes of management and to eliminate the impact of certain accounting policy choices.

Statement of cash flows

Accounting policy choices have no impact on the operating, investing or financing cash flows reported in the statement of cash flows.

Disclosure

It should be noted that entities using the cost model for investment properties are required to disclose the fair value. Such disclosures enable better comparisons to be drawn between entities which account for investment property under different models.

38 Skizer

				Marks
(a)	(i)	Discussion of the Conceptual Framework and IAS 38 recognition criteria		6
	(ii)	Application of the following discussion to the scenario:		
		20X7 initial assessment of recognition criteria (met/not met), IAS 38 derecognition criteria and potential impairment assessment	2	
		20X8 reclassification as R&D is not a change in estimate and impairment assessment	2	
		If recognition criteria not met	1	
	(iii)	Application of the following discussion to the scenario:		5
		Consideration of Skizer's business model	2	
		The application of IFRS 15 to Skizer	2	
				4
(b)	(i)	Discussion of IFRS 3 recognition of intangible assets and information provided about different intangible assets so that investor adjustments can be made	3	
		Discussion of cost or revaluation under IAS 38 and differences	2	
		Discussion of differences in treatment of R&D and development expenditure	2	
				7
	(ii)	Discussion of measurement choices made in the financial statements	2	
		Consideration of whether IR can supplement financial statements thereby providing more useful information for investors	1	
				3
				25

(a)   (i)   The *Conceptual Framework* defines an asset as a present economic resource **controlled** by the entity as a result of past events. An economic resource is a **right** that has the **potential** to produce economic benefits. Assets should be recognised if they meet the *Conceptual Framework* definition of an asset and such recognition provides users of financial statements with information that is useful (ie it is relevant and results in faithful representation). This is subject to the criteria that the benefits the information provides must be sufficient to justify the costs of providing that information. The wording of the recognition criteria in the *Conceptual Framework* allows for flexibility in how this criteria could be applied by the IASB in amending or developing IFRS Standards.

IAS 38 *Intangible Assets* defines an intangible asset as an identifiable non-monetary asset without physical substance. IAS 38 retains the 2010 *Conceptual Framework* definition of an asset which specifies that future economic benefits are **expected** to flow to the entity. Furthermore IAS 38 requires an entity to recognise an intangible asset, if, and only if:

(a) It is **probable** that the expected future economic benefits that are attributable to the asset will flow to the entity; and

(b) The cost of the asset can be measured reliably.

This requirement applies whether an intangible asset is acquired externally or generated internally. The probability of future economic benefits must be based on reasonable and supportable assumptions about conditions which will exist over the useful life of the asset. The probability recognition criterion is always considered to be satisfied for intangible assets which are acquired separately or in a business combination. If the recognition criteria are not met, IAS 38 requires the expenditure to be expensed when it is incurred.

The *Conceptual Framework* does not prescribe a 'probability criterion', and thus does not prohibit the recognition of assets or liabilities with a low probability of an inflow or outflow of economic benefits. In terms of intangible assets, it is arguable that recognising an intangible asset with a low probability of economic benefits would not be useful to users given that the asset has no physical substance.

The recognition criteria and definition of an asset in IAS 38 are **different** to those in the *Conceptual Framework*. The criteria in IAS 38 are more specific, but arguably do provide information that is relevant and a faithful representation. When viewed in this way, the requirements of IAS 38 in terms of recognition appear to be consistent with the *Conceptual Framework*.

(ii) Skizer should have assessed whether the recognition criteria in IAS 38 were met at the time the entity capitalised the intangible assets. If the recognition criteria were met, then it was not appropriate to derecognise the intangible assets. According to IAS 38, an intangible asset should be derecognised only on disposal or when no future economic benefits are expected from its use or disposal. If there were any doubts regarding the recoverability of the intangible asset, then Skizer should have assessed whether the intangible assets would be impaired. IAS 36 *Impairment of Assets* would be used to determine whether an intangible asset is impaired.

Further, the reclassification of intangible assets to research and development costs does not constitute a change in an accounting estimate. IAS 8 *Accounting Policies, Changes in Accounting Estimates and Errors* states that a change in accounting estimate is an adjustment of the carrying amount of an asset or liability, or related expense, resulting from reassessing the expected future benefits and obligations associated with that asset or liability. However, if Skizer concludes that the intangible assets' carrying amounts exceed their recoverable amounts, an impairment loss should be recognised. The costs of the stakes in the development projects can be determined and will not have been estimated.

If the recognition criteria were not met, then Skizer would have to recognise retrospectively a correction of an error, in accordance with IAS 8.

(iii) Gains arising from the derecognition of an intangible asset cannot be presented as revenue as IAS 38 explicitly forbids it. There is no indication that Skizer's business model is to sell development projects but, rather, it undertakes the development of new products in conjunction with third party entities. Skizer's business model is to jointly develop a product, then leave the production to partners. As Skizer has recognised an intangible asset in accordance with IAS 38, and fully impaired the asset, it cannot argue that it has thereafter been held for sale in the ordinary course of business. Therefore, according to IAS 38, the gain from the derecognition of the intangible asset cannot be classified as revenue under IFRS 15 *Revenue from Contracts with Customers* but as a profit on the sale of the intangible asset.

(b) (i) Under IFRS 3 *Business Combinations*, acquired intangible assets must be recognised and measured at fair value if they are separable or arise from other contractual rights, irrespective of whether the acquiree had recognised the assets prior to the business combination occurring. This is because there should always be sufficient information to reliably measure the fair value of these assets. IFRS 3 requires all intangible assets acquired in a business combination to be treated in the same way in line with the requirements of IAS 38. IAS 38 requires intangible assets with finite lives to be amortised over their useful lives and intangible assets with indefinite lives to be subject to an annual impairment review in accordance with IAS 36.

However, it is unlikely that all intangible assets acquired in a business combination will be homogeneous and investors may feel that there are different types of intangible assets which may be acquired. For example, a patent may only last for a finite period of time and may be thought as having an identifiable future revenue stream. In this case, amortisation of the patent would be logical. However, there are other intangible assets which are gradually replaced by the purchasing entity's own intangible assets, for example, customer lists, and it may make sense to account for these assets within goodwill. In such cases, investors may wish to reverse amortisation charges. In order to decide whether an amortisation charge makes sense, investors require greater detail about the nature of the identified intangible assets. IFRSs do not permit a different accounting treatment for this distinction.

IAS 38 requires an entity to choose either the cost model or the revaluation model for each class of intangible asset. Under the cost model, after initial recognition intangible assets should be carried at cost less accumulated amortisation and impairment losses. Under the revaluation model, intangible assets may be carried at a revalued amount, based on fair value, less any subsequent amortisation and impairment losses only if fair value can be determined by reference to an active market. Such active markets are not common for intangible assets. If an intangible asset is reported using the cost model, the reported figures for intangible assets such as trademarks may be understated when compared to their fair values. Based upon the principle above regarding the different types of intangible asset, it would make sense for different accounting treatments subsequent to initial recognition. Some intangible assets should be amortised over their useful lives but other intangible assets should be subject to an annual impairment review, in the same way as goodwill.

IAS 38 requires all research costs to be expensed with development costs being capitalised only after the technical and commercial feasibility of the asset for sale or use has been established. If an entity cannot distinguish the research phase of an internal project to create an intangible asset from the development phase, the entity treats the expenditure for that project as if it were incurred in the research phase only. There is some logic to the capitalisation of development expenditure as internally generated intangible assets but the problem for investors is disclosure in this area as companies do not have a consistent approach to capitalisation. It is often unclear from disclosures how the accounting policy in respect of research and development was applied and especially how research was distinguished from development expenditure. One of the issues is that the disclosure of relevant information is already contained within IFRSs but preparers are failing to comply with these requirements or the disclosure is insufficient.

Intangible asset disclosure can help analysts answer questions about the innovation capacity of companies and investors can use the disclosure to identify companies with intangible assets for development and commercialisation purposes.

(ii)   Measuring the contribution of intangible assets to future cash flows is fundamental to integrated reporting and will help explain the gaps between the carrying amount, intrinsic and market equity value of an entity. As set out above, organisations are required to recognise intangible assets acquired in a business combination. Consequently, the intangible assets are only measured once for this purpose. However, organisations are likely to go further in their integrated report and disclose the change in value of an intangible asset as a result of any sustainable growth strategy or a specific initiative. It is therefore very useful to communicate the value of intangible assets in an integrated report. For example, an entity may decide to disclose its assessment of the increase in brand value as a result of a corporate social responsibility initiative.

39 Toobasco

			Marks
(a)	Discussion of the comparability of APMs	1	
	Application of the following discussion to the scenario:		
	Extraordinary items	2	
	Free cash flow and its description	2	
	EBITDAR	4	
	Tax effects	1	
			10
(b)	(i) Adjustment of net cash generated from operating activities		4
	(ii) Reconciliation to free cash flow		4
	(iii) Application of the following discussion to the scenario:		
	Purchase and sale of cars	1	
	Purchase of associate	1	
	Foreign exchange losses	1	
	Pension payments	1	
	Interest paid	1	
			5
Professional marks			2
			25

(a) (i) APMs are not defined by IFRS Standards and therefore may not be directly comparable with other companies' APMs, including those in the group's industry. Where the same category of material items recurs each year and in similar amounts (in this example, restructuring costs and impairment losses), the entity should consider whether such amounts should be included as part of underlying profit.

Under IFRS Standards, items cannot be presented as 'extraordinary items' in the financial statements or in the notes. Thus, it may be confusing to users of the APMs to see this term used. It is not appropriate to state that a charge or gain is non-recurring unless it meets the criteria. Items such as restructuring costs or impairment losses should not be labelled as non-recurring where it is misleading. However, the entity can make an adjustment for a charge or gain which they believe is appropriate, but they cannot describe such adjustments inaccurately.

(ii) The deduction of capital expenditures, purchase of own shares and the purchase of intangible assets from the IAS 7 measure of cash flows from operating activities is acceptable as free cash flow does not have a uniform definition. As a result, a clear description and reconciliation showing how this measure is calculated should be disclosed. Entities should also avoid misleading inferences about its usefulness. Free cash flow does not normally represent the residual cash flow available as many entities have mandatory debt service requirements which are not normally deducted from the measure. It would also be misleading to show free cash flow per share in bold alongside earnings per share as they are not comparable.

(iii) When an entity presents an APM, it should present the most directly comparable measure which has been calculated in accordance with IFRS Standards with equal or greater prominence. The level of prominence would depend on the facts and circumstances. In this case, the entity has omitted comparable information from an earnings release which includes APMs such as EBITDAR. Additionally, the entity has emphasised the APM measure by describing it as 'record performance' without an equally prominent description of the measure calculated in accordance with IFRS Standards. Further, the entity has provided a discussion of the APM without a similar discussion and analysis of the same information presented from an IFRS Standards perspective.

The entity has presented EBITDAR as a performance measure; such measures should be reconciled to profit for the year as presented in the statement of comprehensive income. Operating profit would not be considered the best starting point as EBITDAR makes adjustments for items which are not included in operating profit such as interest and tax.

The entity has changed the way it calculates the APM because it has treated rent differently. However, if an entity chooses to change an APM, the change and the reason for the change should be explained and any comparatives restated. A change would be appropriate only in exceptional circumstances where the new APM better achieves the same objectives, perhaps if there has been a change in the strategy. The revised APM should be reliable and more relevant.

(iv)   The entity should provide income tax effects on its APMs depending on the nature of the measures. The entity should include current and deferred income tax expense commensurate with the APM and the APM should not be presented net of tax as income taxes should be shown as a separate adjustment and explained.

(b)   (i)   *Adjustment of net cash generated from operating activities for errors in the statement*

	$m
Net cash generated from operating activities per question	278
Add cash inflows relating to the disposal of cars	30
Effect of changes in foreign exchange rates	28
Reclassification of interest paid	18
Tax credit not recorded	6
	360
Less	
Associate's profit – incorrectly included	(12)
Associate's profit – non-cash flow	(4)
Net cash generated from operating activities	344

(ii)   *Free cash flow reconciliation*

	$m
Net cash generated from operating activities	344
Net capital expenditure	(46)
Purchase of associate	(20)
Dividend received from associate	1
Interest received	10
Interest paid	(18)
Pension deficit payments	27
Free cash flow	298

(iii)   *Purchase and sale of cars*

Toobasco's presentation of cash flows from the sale of cars as being from investing activities is incorrect as cash flows from the sale of cars should have been presented as cash flows from operating activities ($30 million). IAS 16 *Property, Plant and Equipment* (PPE) states that an entity which normally sells items of PPE which are held for rental to others should transfer such assets to inventories at their carrying amount when they cease to be rented and become held for sale. Subsequent proceeds from the sale of such assets should be recognised as revenue in accordance with IFRS 15 *Revenue from Contracts with Customers* and thus shown as cash flows from operating activities.

Purchase of associate

	$m
Balance at 31 August 20X8	23
Less profit for period $16m × 25%	(4)
Add dividend received $4m × 25%	1
Cost of acquisition (cash)	20

Therefore, cash paid for the investment is $20 million, and cash received from the dividend is $1 million.

In order to arrive at the correct figure for net cash generated from operating activities, the incorrect treatment of the profit for the year for the associate must be eliminated ($12 million) and the correct adjustment of $4 million shown in net cash generated by operating activities.

Foreign exchange losses

IAS 7 *Statement of Cash Flows* states that unrealised gains and losses arising from changes in foreign exchange rates are not cash flows. The amounts reported in the statement of cash flows included, in error, the effect of changes in foreign exchange rates arising on the retranslation of its overseas operations. As a consequence, cash generated from operating activities should be increased by $28 million. All exchange differences relating to the subsidiary are taken to a separate component of equity, until disposal of the foreign operation when they are recycled to the statement of profit or loss.

Pension payments

The pension payments are correctly included in operating cash flows. However, they are excluded when calculating free cash flow. As the tax cash benefit has not been included, net cash generated from operating activities will be adjusted for the $6 million and $27 million ($33m – $6m) will be excluded from the free cash flow calculation.

Interest paid

Interest paid which is capitalised into the cost of property, plant, and equipment should be treated as cash flows arising from investing activities whereas interest paid and capitalised into inventory should be classified in the operating section of the statement of cash flows. Thus, there should be a reclassification of interest paid of $18 million from the operating section to the investing activities section.

40 Holls

Marking scheme

				Marks
(a)	(i)	Arguments for and against the non-binding framework		4
	(ii)	• A discussion of understandability, relevance and comparability	3	
		• Application of the above characteristics to management commentary	2	
				5

			Marks
(b)	An explanation of why taxable profits are different from accounting profit		2
	Application of the following explanations to the scenario:		
	• Tax reconciliation		4
	• Tax rates		3
	• Deferred taxation		5
			14
			2
			25

(a) (i) The IFRS Practice Statement *Management Commentary* provides a broad, non-binding framework for the presentation of management commentary. The Practice Statement is not an IFRS. Consequently, entities applying IFRS Standards are not required to comply with the Practice Statement, unless specifically required by their jurisdiction. Furthermore, non-compliance with the Practice Statement will not prevent an entity's financial statements from complying with IFRS Standards.

It can be argued that the International Accounting Standards Board's objectives of enhancing consistency and comparability may not be achieved if the framework is not mandatory. A standard is more likely to guarantee a consistent application of the principles and practices behind the management commentary (MC).

However, it is difficult to create a standard on the MC which is sufficiently detailed to cover the business models of every entity or be consistent with all IFRS Standards. Some jurisdictions take little notice of non-mandatory guidance but the Practice Statement provides regulators with a framework to develop more authoritative requirements.

The Practice Statement allows companies to adapt the information provided to particular aspects of their business. This flexible approach could help generate more meaningful disclosures about resources, risks and relationships which can affect an entity's value and how these resources are managed. It provides management with an opportunity to add context to the published financial information, and to explain their future strategy and objectives without being restricted by the constraints of a standard.

If the MC were a full IFRS Standard, the integration of management commentaries and the information produced in accordance with IFRS Standards could be challenged on technical grounds, as well as its practical merits. In addition, there could be jurisdictional concerns that any form of integration might not be accepted by local regulators.

(ii) The *Conceptual Framework* states that 'an essential quality of the information provided in financial statements is that it is readily understandable by users'. The MC should be written in plain language and a style appropriate to users' needs. The primary users of management commentary are those identified in the *Conceptual Framework*. The form and content of the MC will vary between entities, reflecting the nature of their business, the strategies adopted and the regulatory environment in which they operate. Users should be able to locate information relevant to their needs.

Information has the quality of relevance when it has the capacity to influence the economic decisions of users by helping them evaluate past, present or future events or confirming, or correcting, their past evaluations. Relevant financial information is capable of making a difference to the decision made by users. In order to make a difference, financial information has predictive value, confirmatory value or both. The onus is on management to determine what information is important enough to be included in the MC to enable users to 'understand' the financial statements and meet the objective of the MC. If the entity provides too much information, it could reduce its relevance and understandability. If material events or uncertainties are not disclosed, then users may have insufficient information to meet their needs.

However, unnecessary detail may obscure important information especially if entities adopt a boiler-plate approach. If management presents too much information about, for example, all the risks facing an organisation, this will conflict with the relevance objective. There is no single optimal number of disclosures but it is useful to convey their relative importance in a meaningful way.

Comparability is the qualitative characteristic which enables users to identify and understand similarities and differences amongst items. It is important for users to be able to compare information over time and between entities. Comparability between entities is problematic as the MC is designed to reflect the perspectives of management and the circumstances of individual entities. Thus, entities in the same industry may have different perceptions of what is important and how they measure and report it. There are some precedents on how to define and calculate non-financial measures and financial measures which are not produced in accordance with IFRSs but there are inconsistencies in the definition and calculation of these measures.

It is sometimes suggested that the effectiveness of the overall report may be enhanced by strengthening the links between financial statements and the MC. However, such suggestions raise concerns about maintaining a clear distinction between the financial statement information and other information.

An entity should ensure consistency in terms of wording, definitions, segment disclosures, etc between the financial statements and the MC to improve the understanding of financial performance.

(b) Current tax is based on taxable profit for the year. Taxable profit is different from accounting profit due to temporary differences between accounting and tax treatments, and due to items which are never taxable or tax deductible. Tax benefits such as tax credits are not recognised unless it is probable that the tax positions are sustainable.

The Group is required to estimate the corporate tax in each of the many jurisdictions in which it operates. The Group is subject to tax audits in many jurisdictions; as a result, the Group may be required to make an adjustment in a subsequent period which could have a material impact on the Group's profit for the year.

Tax reconciliation

The tax rate reconciliation is important for understanding the tax charge reported in the financial statements and why the effective tax rate differs from the statutory rate.

Most companies will reconcile the group's annual tax expense to the statutory rate in the country in which the parent is based. Hence the rate of 22% is used in the tax reconciliation. It is important that the reconciliation explains the reasons for the differences between the effective rate and the statutory rate. There should be minimal use of the 'other' category. In this case, the other category is quite significant ($14 million) and there is no explanation of what 'other' constitutes.

One-off and unusual items can have a significant effect on the effective tax rate, but financial statements and notes often do not include a detailed discussion of them. For example, the brand impairment and disposals of businesses should be explained to investors, as they are probably material items. The explanation should include any potential reversal of the treatment.

Some profits recognised in the financial statements are non-taxable such as the tax relating to non-taxable gains on disposals of businesses and in some jurisdictions, taxation relief on impairment losses will not be allowable for taxation. The reasons for these items not being allowed for taxation should be explained to investors.

Tax rates

As the Group is operating in multiple countries, the actual tax rates applicable to profits in those countries are different from the local tax rate. The overseas tax rates are higher than local rates, hence the increase in the taxation charge of $10 million. The local rate is different from the weighted average tax rate (27%) of the Group based on the different jurisdictions in which it operates. Investors may feel that using the weighted tax rate in the reconciliation gives a more meaningful number because it is a better estimate of the tax rate the Group expects to pay over the long term. Investors will wish to understand the company's expected long-term sustainable tax rate so they can prepare their cash flow or profit forecasts.

Information about the sustainability of the tax rate over the long term is more important than whether the rate is high or low compared to other jurisdictions. An adjustment can be made to an investor's financial model for a long-term sustainable rate, but not for a volatile rate where there is no certainty over future performance. For modelling purposes, an understanding of the actual cash taxes paid is critical and the cash paid of $95 million can be found in the statement of cash flows.

Deferred taxation

Provision for deferred tax is made for temporary differences between the carrying amount of assets and liabilities for financial reporting purposes and their value for tax purposes. The amount of deferred tax reflects the expected recoverable amount and is based on the expected manner of recovery or settlement of the carrying amount of assets and liabilities, using the basis of taxation enacted or substantively enacted by the financial statement date.

Deferred tax assets are not recognised where it is more likely than not that the assets will not be realised in the future and reference to IAS 37 *Provisions, Contingent Liabilities and Contingent Assets* is useful in this regard. The evaluation of deferred tax assets' recoverability requires judgements to be made regarding the availability of future taxable income.

Management assesses the available evidence to estimate if sufficient future taxable income will be generated to use the existing deferred tax assets. A significant piece of objective negative evidence evaluated was the loss incurred in the period prior to the period ended 30 November 20X7. Such objective evidence may limit the ability to consider other subjective evidence such as projections for future growth. Deferred taxes are one of the most difficult areas of the financial statements for investors to understand. Thus, there is a need for a clear explanation of the deferred tax balances and an analysis of the expected timing of reversals. This would help investors see the time period over which deferred tax assets arising from losses might reverse. It would be helpful if the company provided a breakdown of which reversals would have a cash tax impact and which would not.

As the proposed tax law was approved, it is considered to be enacted. Therefore, the rate of 25% should be used to calculate the deferred tax liability associated with the relevant items which affect deferred taxation.

At 30 November 20X7, Holls has deductible temporary differences of $4.5 million which are expected to reverse in the next year. In addition, Holls also has taxable temporary differences of $5 million which relate to the same taxable company and the tax authority. Holls expects $3 million of those taxable temporary differences to reverse in 20X8 and the remaining $2 million to reverse in 20X9. Thus a deferred tax liability of $1.25 million ($5 million × 25%) should be recognised and as $3 million of these taxable temporary differences are expected to reverse in the year in which the deductible temporary differences reverse, Holls can also recognise a deferred tax asset for $0.75 million ($3 million × 25%). The recognition of a deferred tax asset for the rest of the deductible temporary differences will depend on whether future taxable profits sufficient to cover the reversal of this deductible temporary difference are expected to arise. Deferred tax assets and liabilities must be recognised gross in the statement of financial position. However, it may be possible to offset the deferred tax assets and the deferred tax liabilities if there is a legally enforceable right to offset the current income tax assets against current income tax liabilities as the amounts relate to income tax levied by the same taxation authority on the same taxable entity.

After the enactment of a new tax law, when material, Holls should consider disclosing the anticipated current and future impact on their results of operations, financial position, liquidity, and capital resources. In addition, Holls should consider disclosures in the critical accounting estimates section of the management commentary to the extent the changes could materially affect existing assumptions used in making estimates of tax-related balances. Changes in tax laws and rates may affect recorded deferred tax assets and liabilities and the effective tax rate in the future.

41 Crypto

Workbook references. IFRS 16 *Leases* is covered in Chapter 9. IFRS 10 is covered in Chapter 11, and IFRS 11 is covered in Chapter 15. IFRS 9 *Financial Instruments* is covered in Chapter 8.

Top tips. There are two professional marks available in this question for clarity and quality of the discussion in part (b). This will be the case for one question in section B of every exam - two professional marks will be available in the question that requires analysis from the perspective of a stakeholder.

Part (a)(i) required advice on the treatment of an investment. The examiner's report stated that many answers to this question were weak - with many candidates focusing on only on IFRS 11, rather than first looking at the issue of control under IFRS 10. Part (a)(ii) was extremely challenging and required advice on the treatment of an embedded derivative contract which was then modified into an executory contract.

Part (b)(i) required a discussion on the key changes from an investor perspective of the application of the lessee accounting requirements in IFRS 16. Remember in this part of your answer to consider the investor and not just state the accounting adjustments required. Part (b)(ii) required a discussion on how IFRS 16 would impact on three accounting ratios and more generally from the financial statements now that previously reported 'off-balance sheet' leases are now on-balance sheet. Ensure you link the effect on each ratio to the change in accounting treatment required under IFRS 16.

Marking scheme

				Marks
(a)	(i)	Discussion of the following accounting issues and application to the scenario:		
		• The definition of control per IFRS 10 and joint control per IFRS 11	3	
		• Power over the investee	3	
				6
	(ii)	Discussion of the following accounting issues and application to the scenario:		
		• IFRS 9 requirements for embedded derivatives and hybrid	3	
		• IFRS 9 requirements for contract modifications	2	
				5
(b)	(i)	Discussion of the IFRS 16 requirements	3	
		Implications for investors	3	
				6
	(ii)	Description of the IFRS 16 impact on accounting numbers	2	
		Impact on the following ratios:		
		• Interest cover	2	
		• ROCE	1	
		• Debt to EBITDA	1	
				6
		Professional marks		2
				25

(a) (i) Before assessing whether an entity has joint control over an arrangement, an entity must first assess whether the parties control the arrangement in accordance with the definition of control in IFRS 10 *Consolidated Financial Statements*. If not, an entity must determine whether it has joint control of the arrangement. IFRS 11 *Joint Arrangements* defines joint control as 'the contractually agreed sharing of control of an arrangement, which exists only when decisions about the relevant activities require the unanimous consent of the parties sharing control'. This means an assessment as to whether any party can prevent any of the other parties from making unilateral decisions without its consent. It must be clear which combination of parties is required to agree unanimously to decisions about the relevant activities of the arrangement. In the case of Kurran Co, there is more than one combination of parties possible to reach the required majority. As a result, Crypto Co does not have joint control.

In addition to the above, Crypto Co does not control Kurran Co because IFRS 10 states that control requires power over the investee which gives the investor the ability to direct the relevant activities. Crypto Co does not have the ability to direct the relevant activities as it can only block decisions and cannot make decisions by itself. Also, there is no shareholder agreement which sets out shareholders' voting rights and obligations and thus the other shareholders can act together to prevent Crypto Co from making decisions in its own interest. Crypto Co does not have joint control as agreement between itself and other board members has to occur for a decision to be made. Therefore, it appears that Kurran Co is an associate of Crypto Co and would apply IAS 28 *Investments in Associates and Joint Ventures*.

(ii) IFRS 9 *Financial Instruments* states that 'any embedded derivative included in a contract for the sale or purchase of a non-financial item that is denominated in a foreign currency shall be separated when its economic characteristics and risks are not closely related to those of the host contract'. Thus, in contrast to the treatment for hybrid contracts with financial asset hosts, derivatives embedded with a financial liability will often be separately accounted for. That is, they must be separated if they are not closely related to the host contract, they meet the definition of a derivative, and the hybrid contract is not measured at fair value through profit or loss (FVTPL).

The contract is a hybrid contract containing a host contract which is an executory contract to purchase electricity at a price of 20 million euros and a non-closely related embedded foreign currency derivative with an initial fair value of zero to buy 20 million euros, sell 25 million dollars. However, the derivative should have been valued at FVTPL and not fair value through other comprehensive income.

At the date of the modification of the contract to the functional currency of Crypto Co, there is a significant change to the contract which will trigger a reassessment of its position under IFRS 9. As the contract no longer has a non-closely related embedded derivative, the entire arrangement will be accounted for prospectively as an executory contract which is outside the scope of IFRS 9. The embedded derivative will be derecognised and it is likely that Crypto Co will have to pay the counterparty 2 million euros in compensation.

(b) (i) IFRS 16 *Leases* introduces a single lessee accounting model and should reduce the number of off-balance sheet leases. Upon lease commencement, a lessee recognises a right-of-use asset and a lease liability. After lease commencement, a lessee measures the right-of-use asset using a cost model less accumulated depreciation and accumulated impairment. The lease liability is initially measured at the present value of the lease payments payable over the lease term, discounted at the rate implicit in the lease if that can be readily determined. Lease liabilities include only economically unavoidable payments.

Investors should bear in mind that some sectors and some companies will be more affected than others. As a result, companies with previous material off-balance sheet leases will report higher assets and financial liabilities. The standard will reduce complexity in financial statements as it should allow comparisons to be made between those companies who lease assets and those who borrow to buy assets.

Investors will no longer have to estimate the assets and liabilities resulting from off-balance sheet leases when calculating ratios as there should be fewer off-balance sheet leases. IFRS 16 will result in more information about leases both on the statement of financial position and in the notes and will provide a more accurate reflection of the economics of leases. The carrying amount of lease assets will typically reduce more quickly than the carrying amount of lease liabilities. This will result in a reduction in reported equity for companies with previous material off-balance sheet leases.

IFRS 16 requires a lessee to disclose lease liabilities separately from other liabilities as a separate line item, or together with other similar liabilities, in a manner which is relevant to understanding the lessee's financial position. A lessee will also split lease liabilities into current and non-current portions, based on the timing of payments.

(ii)   The recognition of an asset which was previously unrecognised will result in a higher asset base, which will affect ratios such as asset turnover. The recognition of a liability which was previously unrecognised will result in higher financial liabilities, which will affect gearing. The recognition of depreciation and interest instead of operating lease expense will result in higher operating profit because interest is typically excluded from operating expenses and will affect performance ratios. Similarly, profit measures which exclude interest and depreciation but previously included operating lease expense, such as EBITDA, will be higher under IFRS 16.

Interest cover: there will be an increase in the earnings measure (ie EBITDA) which will not be proportionate to the increase in interest. The change in the ratio will depend on the characteristics of the lease portfolio.

Return on capital employed: it is likely that ROCE will be lower under IFRS 16 because the increase in operating profit is unlikely to be proportionate to the increase in capital employed.

Debt to EBITDA: ratio of debt to EBITDA is likely to be higher because debt will increase by more than the increase in earnings. Debt will increase because of the fact that lease liabilities will be recognised on the statement of financial position. For companies which have material off-balance sheet leases, IFRS 16 is expected to result in higher profit before interest because a company presents the implicit interest in lease payments for former off-balance sheet leases as part of finance costs. Previously, the entire expense related to off-balance sheet leases was included as part of operating expenses. The size of the increase in operating profit, and finance costs, will depend on the significance of leasing activities to the company.

42 Guidance

Workbook references. The *Conceptual Framework* is covered in Chapter 1. Analysis is covered in Chapter 18. IFRS 10 *Consolidated Financial Statements* is covered in Chapter 11.

Top tips. There are two professional marks available in this question for clarity and quality of the discussion in part (b). This will be the case for one question in section B of every exam - two professional marks will be available in the question that requires analysis from the perspective of a stakeholder.

Part (a) required a discussion of why a reporting entity may choose a particular accounting policy where IFRS allows a choice, and the impact of faithful representation and comparability on the choice. You need to know that faithful representation and comparability are qualitative characteristics of useful information, as described in the *Conceptual Framework*. The *Conceptual Framework* is fundamental to SBR, you must make sure you are familiar with it.

Part (b)(i) required calculation of return on equity ratio (ROE) and discussion on the usefulness to investors of that ratio and its component parts. The examiner commented that some candidates didn't include discussion of the component parts of ROE, despite this being clearly stated in the requirement – make sure you read requirements carefully and ensure you answer each part of each requirement.

BPP LEARNING MEDIA

Part (b)(ii) asked for a discussion of the impact of the accounting transactions in the scenario on the ROE ratio (and its components), and a recalculation of a more comparable ROE between the two years. The examiner commented 'better answers included a description of the impact on each component as well as the ROE (meeting the question's whole requirement) and provided a table in which the original accounting data is adjusted for each transaction'. Remember that laying out your answers clearly helps the marker to see what you have done, enabling them to award you marks more easily.

Marking scheme

				Marks
(a)		Discussion of the issues relating to accounting choice	3	
		Discussion of whether faithful representation and comparability are affected	3	
				6
(b)	(i)	Discussion of the meaning of the return on equity (ROE) and its component parts	3	
		Calculation of ROE for the years ended 31 December 20X5 and 20X6	2	
				5
	(ii)	Application of the following discussion to the scenario:		
		• Transfer of property to SPE	2	
		• Buy back of shares	2	
		• Raising loan capital	2	
		• Purchase of associate	2	
		• Calculation of the impact on ROE and its component parts	4	
				12
		Professional marks		2
				25

(a) Where an IFRS Standard allows an entity an accounting choice, then the financial statements will be influenced and affected by that choice. Management's intent and motivation will influence accounting information. The accounting policy chosen can be driven by self-interest, by a wish to maximise the interests of shareholders, or by a wish to provide information. Where there is flexibility when applying the IFRS Standard, the financial statements can become less comparable. Entities may use the financial choices to increase earnings, and manipulate accounting figures in order to influence contractual outcomes which depend on the accounting figures reported.

Accounting choices exist to provide companies which operate under different business models with the option of utilising an accounting method which best represents their operations. Any accounting choice in IFRS Standards should still result in the financial statements being faithfully represented. A faithful representation means that to the maximum extent possible, the financial statements are complete, neutral and free from error. A faithful representation is affected by the level of measurement uncertainty in the financial statements.

Comparability is one of the four qualitative characteristics which enhances the usefulness of information. Thus, accounting information would be more useful if it can be compared with similar information from other entities, or from the same entity.

However, it is extremely difficult for entities to have 'comparable' financial information. Comparability is crucial to improve financial reporting quality but it can be argued that comparability is made more difficult by the fact that the Board allows entities to choose between alternative measurement bases. Environmental, economic, political, cultural, operational differences could be solved with the existence of accounting choices in the standards, but these choices could be at the cost of comparability, especially if there are internal or external factors influencing the reliable disclosure of an item. A faithful representation might lead to comparability, because it should reflect the characteristics of the asset or liability.

(b) (i) The return on equity (ROE) ratio measures the rate of return which the owners of issued shares of a company receive on their shareholdings in terms of profitability. ROE signifies how good the company is in generating profit on the investment it receives from its shareholders. This metric is especially important from an investor's perspective, as it can be used to judge how efficiently the firm will be able to use shareholder's investment to generate additional revenues.

The net profit margin (net profit/sales) tells how much profit a company makes on every dollar of sales. Asset turnover (sales/assets) ratio measures the value of a company's sales or revenues generated relative to the carrying amount of its assets. The asset turnover ratio can often be used as an indicator of the efficiency with which a company is deploying its assets in generating revenue. The equity ratio indicates the relative proportion that equity is used to finance a company's assets. The equity ratio is a good indicator of the level of leverage used by a company by measuring the proportion of the total assets which are financed by shareholders, as opposed to creditors.

	20X5	20X6
Net profit margin	15%	17.3%
Asset turnover	0.8	1.05
Equity ratio	1.43	2.1
Return on equity	17%	38%

(ii) **Setting up of special purpose entity (SPE)**

IFRS 10 *Consolidated Financial Statements* states that an investor controls a SPE when it is exposed, or has rights, to variable returns from its involvement with the SPE and has the ability to affect those returns through its power over the SPE. This revised definition of control focuses on the need to have both power and variable returns before control is present. Power is the current ability to direct the activities which significantly influence returns. Guidance Co obtains the rewards from the assets transferred and is exposed to the risks. By transferring their assets to a SPE, the asset turnover ratio will be significantly larger. However, the SPE should be consolidated by Guidance Co in its group financial statements and the property included in assets and the charge eliminated from revaluation reserves in its single entity financial statements. The latter will increase shareholder equity.

Miscellaneous transactions

A major concern about using ROE is when a company buys back its shares, it decreases the equity on the statement of financial position and in the case of Guidance Co, its cash and consequently its total assets. As a result, the performance metrics – asset turnover and ROE – will be affected. The ROE figure could produce a misleading indicator as to how well a company is being managed. As the equity portion of ROE shrinks, the ROE metric gets larger. The ROE calculation can become meaningless if a company regularly buys back its shares and thus as a result there may be better metrics for investors to use such as the P/E ratio.

Guidance Co has raised loan capital of $20 million during the period and this amount will not be included in the ROE calculations because ROE is based on assets as opposed to net assets. One company may have a higher ROE than another company simply because it finances the business through loan capital rather than raising equity capital. It can be argued that ROE is not a meaningful measure of performance, as it takes no account of the amount of debt involved in creating profits.

Therefore, return on capital employed may be a better current measure for Guidance Co.

BPP
LEARNING
MEDIA

Guidance Co has included the profit from the purchase of an associate in the current year's figures. If the share of the results of the associate were excluded, this would allow Guidance Co's profitability to result exclusively from Guidance Co's asset base. It could be argued that the full value of the company's reported profit including the associate could distort the analysis of Guidance Co's performance as compared to the last financial year.

There is no need to adjust for the original $15 million investment in the associate because one asset is merely being replaced by another but the total assets remain the same.

Adjusted amounts

		SPE property $m	Shares cancelled $m	Associate $m	Total $m
Profit before tax	38			(4)	34
Sales	220		220		
Assets	210	50	30	290	
Equity	100	50	30	(4)	176

Adjusted calculations

	20X5	20X6 (adjusted)	20X6 (unadjusted)
Net profit margin	15%	15.5%	17.3%
Asset turnover	0.8	0.76	1.05
Equity ratio	1.43	1.65	2.1
ROE	17%	19.3%	38%

It can be seen that if the impact of the transactions in the period were eliminated, then there has been a significant reduction in ROE and its component parts. The buyback of shares and the purchase of the associate were legitimate transactions but they were eliminated in order to determine comparative metrics. The raising of the loan capital was also legitimate but was not adjusted for because ROE is based on assets, not net assets. The transfer of assets to a SPE was contrary to IFRS 10 and would have been reversed in any event. Although financial metrics are intended to enable comparisons between companies, the relative performance of any particular company can be affected by transactions both acceptable and unacceptable under accounting standards.

43 Handfood Co

			Marks
(a)	(i)	Discussion of the *IFRS for SMEs* Standard:	
		Simplifications and omissions	2
		Disclosure	1
		Recognised concepts	1
			4
	(ii)	Discussion of:	
		Information asymmetry issues and investors knowledge	4
	(iii)	Discussion of Integrated Reporting:	
		Better understanding	2
		Better communication	1
		Nature of IR	2
			5

(b)   (i)   Discussion of principles of accounting for additional benefit
              liability/current service cost   4
              Calculation of current service cost 20X2   2
                                                                                   6
      (ii) Discussion of effect of change in assumptions   4
      Professional marks   2
                                                                                   25

(a)   (i)   The principal aim when developing the *IFRS for SMEs* Standard was to provide a
            framework that generated relevant, reliable and useful information and the provision
            of a high quality and understandable accounting standard suitable for SMEs. The
            SMEs Standard itself is self-contained, and incorporates accounting principles based
            on IFRS Standards. It comprises a single standard divided into simplified sections for
            each relevant IFRS Standard but which have also omitted certain IFRS Standards
            such as earnings per share and segmental reporting. In addition, there are certain
            accounting treatments that are not allowable under the SMEs Standard. For
            example, there is no separate guidance for non-current assets held for sale.

            To this end, the SMEs Standard makes numerous simplifications to the recognition,
            measurement and disclosure requirements in full IFRS Standards. Examples of these
            simplifications are:

            •   Intangible assets must be amortised over their useful lives. If the useful life is
                not determinable then it is presumed to be 10 years.

            •   The cost model (investment is measured at cost less any accumulated
                impairment losses) can be used for investments in associates. This model may
                not be used for investments for which there is a published price quotation, in
                which case the fair value model must be applied.

            The disclosure requirements in the SMEs Standard are also substantially reduced
            when compared with those in full IFRS Standards partly because they are not
            considered appropriate for users' needs and for cost-benefit considerations. Many
            disclosures in full IFRS Standards are more relevant to investment decisions in capital
            markets than to the transactions undertaken by SMEs. The SMEs Standard is
            naturally a modified version of full IFRS Standards, and not an independently
            developed standard. It is based on recognised concepts and pervasive principles and
            it will allow easier transition to full IFRS Standards if the SME decides to become a
            public listed entity.

      (ii) The SMEs Standard decreases information asymmetry between the firm and the
            users, because of its recognition, measurement and disclosure requirements.
            However, there are certain facts and information in companies which is not disclosed
            by them to investors under any accounting standards. SMEs have access to all
            relevant information, while investors lack much of the relevant information.
            Unfortunately, lack of relevant information will have an adverse effect on the
            decision-making of the investor. Information related to the SME's credit, project risk
            and benefits are known more by the SME than by the investor giving the SME an
            information advantage. Therefore, investors are in a relatively disadvantaged
            position, and if they, for example, are financial institutions, they will raise lending
            rates to reduce potential risk of credit losses or may not invest at all. The more
            incomplete and the less transparent the information from the SME, the higher will be
            the risk related to the investment and the higher will be the return that the investor
            requires. The access to investment by SMEs could be determined by the quality of
            financial statements, information asymmetry and perceived risk. Quality financial
            statements reduce the level of information asymmetry which reduces perceived risk.

(iii) Integrated reporting could help SMEs better understand and better communicate how they create value. It can provide a roadmap for SMEs to consider the multiple capitals that make up its value creation. An integrated report represents a more complete corporate report which will help SMEs understand their business so they can implement a business model that will help them grow. SMEs use a range of resources and relationships to create value. An integrated reporting approach helps SMEs build a better understanding of the factors that determine its ability to create value over time. Integrated thinking helps SMEs gain a deeper understanding of the mechanics of their business. This will help them assess the strengths of their business model and spot any deficiencies. These will create a forward-looking approach and sound strategic decision making.

Some SMEs have few tangible assets and operate in a virtual world. As such, conventional accounting will fail to provide a complete picture as to its ability to create value. Capitals, such as employee expertise, customer loyalty, and intellectual property, will not be accounted for in the financial statements which are only one aspect of an SME's value creation. As a result, SME stakeholders can be left with insufficient information to make an informed decision.

Integrated reporting will include key financial information but that information is alongside significant non-financial measures and narrative information. Integrated reporting can help fulfil the communication needs of financial capital and other stakeholders and can optimize reporting.

(b) (i) Handfood Co should recognise a liability for its obligations as a result of the additional employee benefit net of plan assets. The treatment for these payments is similar to a defined benefit pension scheme, but the difference is that any actuarial gains or losses are recognised immediately and not in other comprehensive income as Handfood Co does at present. Any service costs, net interest and remeasurements should all be recognised in profit or loss. In this case, Handfood Co is going to pay the benefit out of cash and therefore there will be no plan assets. Handfood Co will recognise the net annual change in that liability during the five year period as the service cost. The company will measure the benefit liability at the present value of its obligations at the reporting date. This amount is the estimated amount of benefit that employees have earned in return for their service in the current and prior periods, including benefits that are not yet vested. The benefit is based on future salaries, and therefore the projected unit credit method requires an entity to measure its defined benefit obligations on a basis that reflects estimated future salary increases. The components of the cost of the additional benefit will be recognised in profit or loss which includes the current service cost.

For the year ended 31 December 20X2

Handfood Co recognises a current service cost expense of $7,700 in profit or loss as set out below:

	$'000
Expected final salary $1.1 million × (1.03)^4	1,238
Benefit for the current year (1% × $1.238 million)	12.4
Adjusted benefit for the current year (75% × $12,400)	9.3
Current service cost (($9,300 × 0.823) discounted at 5% over 4 years)	7.7

This figure will be unwound each year and the movement recorded as the current service cost (in so far as no other changes to the assumptions are made).

(ii) An increase in employees' salaries above 3% per annum and a decrease in the probability of employees leaving the company would have the same effect on the additional benefit liability. The changes in the assumptions would both increase the benefit liability (discounted) at 31 December 20X3. This would in turn increase the current service cost for the year in profit or loss as the benefit payable on 1 January

20X7 will have increased as will the number of employees to whom the benefit will be payable.

Interest, which is calculated on the opening balance of the benefit obligation, will not be affected by the changes in assumptions. It will be charged to profit or loss at $385 ($7,700 × 5%). Actuarial gains or losses arise when the assumptions change. In this case because of the changes in assumptions, an actuarial loss will arise because of the increase in benefits payable and the obligation and this will be charged to profit or loss.

44 Moorland

Workbook reference. Chapter 18: Interpretation of financial statements for different stakeholders.

Top tips. Part (a) requires knowledge of the purpose of a management commentary and the requirements of IFRS Practice Statement 1. If you struggled with this, go back and revise the content in Chapter 18.

Part (c) covers alternative performance measures which is a key topic for SBR. You need to consider Moorland's investors in your answer. Wider reading of articles, particularly those on the ACCA website, will be extremely helpful in being able to answer questions such as this. The ESMA (European Securities and Markets Authority) Guidelines on Alternative Performance Measures and IOSCO's (International Organisation of Securities Commissions) Statement on Non-GAAP Financial Measures, both available online, provide another perspective and will be beneficial to read.

Easy marks. Some marks are available for the principles of IFRS 8 in part (b).

(a)   The purpose of the management commentary is to provide a context for interpreting a company's **financial position, performance and cash flows**. According to IFRS Practice Statement 1 *Management Commentary*, the principles and objectives of a Management Commentary (MC) are as follows:

    (i)   To provide **management's view** of the entity's performance, position and progress
    (ii)   To **supplement and complement** information presented in the financial statements

To align with these principles, an MC should include **forward-looking information**, and all information provided should possess the **qualitative characteristics** described in the *Conceptual Framework*.

Practice Statement 1 says that to meet the objective of management commentary, an entity should include information that is essential to an understanding of:

    (i)   The **nature of the business**

    (ii)   Management's **objectives and its strategies** for meeting those objectives

    (iii)   The entity's most significant **resources, risks and relationships**

    (iv)   The **results** of operations and **prospects**

    (v)   The critical **performance measures and indicators** that management uses to evaluate the entity's performance against stated objectives

The arguments for a mandatory MC are largely to do with content and comparability. It is argued that a mandatory MC will make it easier for companies themselves to judge what is required in such a report and the required standard of reporting, thereby making such reports more **robust, transparent and comparable**. If an MC is not mandatory then there may be **uncertainty** as to content and the possibility of **misinformation**. There is also the risk that, without a mandatory MC, directors may take a **minimalist approach** to disclosure which will make the MC less useful and the information to be disclosed will be in hands of senior executives and directors.

However, the **arguments against** a mandatory MC are that it could **stifle the development of the MC as a tool** for communication and may lead to a **checklist approach** to producing it. It is argued that a mandatory MC is not required as market forces and the needs of investors should lead to companies feeling the pressure to provide a useful and reliable report. The IASB decided to issue a Practice Statement rather than an IFRS and to leave it to regulators to decide who would be required to publish a management commentary. This approach avoids the **adoption hurdle**, ie that the perceived cost of applying IFRSs might increase, which could otherwise dissuade jurisdictions/countries not having adopted IFRSs from requiring its adoption, especially where requirements differ significantly from existing national requirements.

(b) **Operating segment**

IFRS 8 *Operating Segments* describes an operating segment as a component of an entity:

(1) Which engages in business activities from which it may earn revenues and incur expenses;

(2) Whose operating results are regularly reviewed by the entity's chief operating decision-maker to make decisions about resources to be allocated to the segment and assess its performance;

(3) For which discrete financial information is available.

There is a considerable amount of subjectivity in how an entity may apply these criteria to its choice of operating segments. Usually an operating segment would have a segment manager who maintains regular contact with the chief operating decision-maker to discuss operating activities, financial results, forecasts or plans for the segment. Therefore, segment managers could have overall responsibility for a particular product, service line or geographical area and so there could be considerable overlap in how an entity may apply the criteria. In such situations the directors of Moorland should consider the core principles of the standard. Information should be disclosed to enable users of its financial statements to evaluate the nature and financial effects of the business activities in which it engages and the economic environments in which it operates.

Since Tybull is the only foreign subsidiary, it is likely that separate disclosure is necessary so that users can better assess the performance of Tybull and its significance to the group. The directors should consider whether there are other segments which exhibit similar long-term financial performance and similar economic characteristics to Tybull. In such circumstances it is possible to aggregate the operating segments into a single segment. For example, the segments should have products of a similar nature and similar methods to distribute their products. The segments should also have similar types of customer, production processes and regulatory environment. The directors of Moorland would need to assess whether such aggregation would limit the usefulness of the disclosures for the users of the financial statements. For example, it would no longer be possible to assess the gross margins and return on capital employed for Tybull on an individual basis, without referring to its individual financial statements.

Operating segments can be reclassified where an entity changes its internal organisational structure. As Tybull has not changed its organisational structure, it is unlikely that it would be able to argue for a reclassification of its operating segments. Should the directors of Moorland decide to reclassify the operating segments and combine Tybull with other segments, IAS 8 *Accounting Policies, Changes in Accounting Estimates and Errors* would need to be applied. A retrospective adjustment would be required to the disclosures and the change would need to be justified. An entity should only change its policy if it enhances the reliability and relevance of the financial statements. This would appear unlikely given the circumstances.

(c) **Underlying earnings per share**

Underlying earnings per share (underling EPS) is an alternative performance measure (APM). APMs should be provided to enhance the understanding of users of the accounts.

However, APMs can be misleading. Unlike earnings per share, which is defined in IAS 33 *Earnings per Share*, there is no official definition of underlying EPS, so management can choose what items to include or exclude in the underlying earnings. Therefore, it is open to bias in its calculation as management could decide to only adjust for items that improve the measure. Furthermore, different companies may define the measure in different ways, which reduces the comparability between entities.

The CEO's wish to exclude impairment on goodwill from the calculation of earnings on the basis that it is unlikely to reoccur is also misleading to investors. An impairment loss on goodwill could quite feasibly re-occur in the future as it is at least partly dependent on circumstances outside of Moorland's control, such as the state of the economy. Therefore, it could be argued that excluding the impairment loss would make the measure of underlying earnings per share less useful to investors.

The CEO wishes to present underlying EPS 'prominently'. It is not clear what is meant by this comment, however, Moorland should ensure that it complies with the requirements of IAS 33 regarding the calculation and presentation of this alternative EPS. IOSCO's (International Organisation of Securities Commissions) Statement on Non-GAAP Financial Measures recommends that APMs are not presented more prominently than GAAP measures, or in a way that confuses or obscures GAAP measures.

Ultimately underlying earnings per share will only provide useful information to Moorland's investors if it is fairly presented.

Moorland could improve the usefulness of underlying EPS by:

- Including an appropriate description of how the measure is calculated

- Ensuring that the calculation of underlying EPS is consistent year on year and that comparatives are presented

- Explaining the reasons for presenting the measure, why it is useful for investors and for what purpose management may use it

- Presenting a reconciliation to the most directly reconcilable measure in the financial statements, for example EPS calculated in accordance with IAS 33

- Not excluding items from underlying EPS that could legitimately reoccur in the future, such as impairment losses on goodwill

45 Amster

Workbook references. Financial instruments are covered in Chapter 8. The *Conceptual Framework* is covered in Chapter 1.

Top tips. This question might have alarmed you as you might not have seen a capitalisation table before. However, you must be prepared to encounter disclosures such as this, which are a common feature of published financial statements and useful to investors. You should be able to work out that it requires adjusting in the same way as a statement of financial position would be. For (a)(ii), you need to think about the principles around debt and equity classification for financial instruments and try and relate this to the definitions in the *Conceptual Framework*.

Marking scheme

			Marks
(a)	(i)	1 mark per point up to maximum	8
	(ii)	1 mark per point up to maximum	6
(b)		1 mark per point up to maximum	9
		Professional marks	2
			25

(a) (i) Importance of information concerning an entity's capital

Essentially there are two classes of capital reported in financial statements, namely debt and equity. However, debt and equity instruments can have different levels of right, benefit and risks. Hence, the details underlying a company's capital structure are absolutely essential to assessing the prospects for changes in a company's financial flexibility, and ultimately, its value.

For investors who are assessing the risk profile of an entity, the management and level of an entity's capital is an important consideration. Disclosures about capital are normally in addition to disclosures required by regulators as their reasons for disclosure may differ from those of the International Accounting Standards Board (IASB). The details underlying a company's capital structure are essential to the assessment of any potential change in an entity's financial standing.

Investors have specific but different needs for information about capital depending upon their approach to their investment in an entity. If their approach is income based, then shortage of capital may have an impact upon future dividends. If ROCE is used for comparing the performance of entities, then investors need to know the nature and quantity of the historical capital employed in the business. Some investors will focus on historical invested capital, others on accounting capital and others on market capitalisation.

Published information

As an entity's capital does not relate solely to financial instruments, the IASB has included these disclosures in IAS 1 *Presentation of Financial Statements* rather than IFRS 7 *Financial Instruments: Disclosures*. Although IFRS 7 requires some specific disclosures about financial liabilities, it does not have similar requirements for equity instruments.

As a result, IAS 1 requires an entity to disclose information which enables users to evaluate the entity's objectives, policies and processes for managing capital. This objective is obtained by disclosing qualitative and quantitative data. The former should include narrative information such as what the company manages as capital, whether there are any external capital requirements and how those requirements are incorporated into the management of capital. The IASB decided that there should be disclosure of whether the entity has complied with any external capital requirements and, if not, the consequences of non-compliance.

Besides the requirements of IAS 1, IFRS *Practice Statement 1: Management Commentary* suggests that management should include forward-looking information in the commentary when it is aware of trends, uncertainties or other factors which could affect the entity's capital resources. Additionally, some jurisdictions refer to capital disclosures as part of their legal requirements.

In addition to the annual report, an investor may find details of the entity's capital structure where the entity is involved in a transaction, such as a sale of bonds or equities. It can be seen that information regarding an entity's capital structure is spread across several documents including the management commentary, the notes to financial statements, interim financial statements and any document required by securities regulators.

Integrated reporting

The capitals identified by the International Integrated Reporting Council (IIRC) are: financial capital, manufactured capital, intellectual capital, human capital, social and relationship capital, and natural capital. Together, they represent stores of value which are the basis of an organisation's value creation. Financial capital is broadly understood as the pool of funds available to an organisation. This includes both debt and equity finance. This description of financial capital focuses on the source of funds, rather than its application which results in the acquisition of manufactured or other forms of capital. Financial capital is a medium of exchange which releases its value through conversion into other forms of capital. It is the pool of funds which is available to the organisation for use in the production of goods or the provision of services obtained through financing, such as debt, equity or grants, or generated through operations or investments.

(ii) Whether an instrument is classified as either a financial liability or as equity is important as it has a direct effect on an entity's reported results and financial position. The critical feature of a liability is that, under the terms of the instrument, the issuer is or can be required to deliver either cash or another financial asset to the holder and it cannot avoid this obligation. An instrument is classified as equity when it represents a residual interest in the issuer's assets after deducting all its liabilities. If the financial instrument provides the entity an unconditional discretion, the financial instrument is equity.

IAS 32 *Financial Instruments Presentation* sets out the nature of the classification process but the standard is principle based and sometimes the outcomes are surprising to users. IAS 32 focuses on the contractual obligations of the instrument and considers the substance of the contractual rights and obligations. The variety of instruments issued by entities makes this classification difficult with the application of the principles occasionally resulting in instruments which seem like equity being accounted for as liabilities. Recent developments in the types of financial instruments issued have added more complexity to capital structures with the resultant difficulties in interpretation and understanding.

Equity and liabilities are classified separately in the statement of financial position. The *Conceptual Framework* distinguishes the two elements by the obligation of the entity to deliver cash or other economic resources from items which create no such obligation. The statement of profit or loss and other comprehensive income (OCI) includes income and expenses arising from liabilities which is interest and, if applicable, remeasurement and gain or loss on settlement. The statement does not report as income or expense any changes in the carrying amount of the entity's own equity instruments but does include expenses arising from the consumption of services which fall under IFRS 2 *Share-based Payment*. IFRS 2 requires a valuation of the services consumed in exchange for the financial liabilities or equity instruments.

In the statement of financial position, the carrying amount of many financial liabilities changes either with the passage of time or if the liability is remeasured at fair value. However, the amount reported for classes of equity instruments generally does not change after initial recognition except for non-controlling interest.

Liability classification typically results in any payments on the instrument being treated as interest and charged to earnings. This may in turn affect the entity's ability to pay dividends on its equity shares depending upon local legislation.

Equity classification avoids the negative impact which liability classification has on reported earnings, gearing ratios and debt covenants. It also results in the instrument falling outside the scope of IFRS 9 *Financial Instruments*, thereby avoiding the complicated ongoing measurement requirements of that standard.

(b) In the case of the first class of preference shares, even though there are negative consequences of not paying dividends on the preferred shares as agreed contractually, the company can avoid the obligation to deliver cash. The preferred shares do have redemption provisions but these are not mandatory and are at the sole discretion of the management committee and therefore the shares should be classified as equity.

In the case of the second class, the contractual term requires no dividend to be paid to ordinary shareholders if a payment is not made on the preferred shares. In this case, as Amster can avoid the obligation to settle the annual dividend, the shares are classified as equity. Thus $75 million should be transferred from liabilities to equity.

IFRS 2 *Share-based Payment* states that cash settled share-based payment transactions occur where goods or services are paid for at amounts which are based on the price of the company's equity instruments. The expense for cash settled transactions is the cash paid by the company and any amounts accrued should be shown as liabilities and not equity. Therefore, Amster should remove the following amount from equity and show it as a liability.

Expense for year to 30 November 20X7 is:

(1,500 – 180 employees × 250 awards × $35) × $\frac{1}{3}$ = $3.85 million

As a result of the adjustments to the financial statements, Amster's gearing ratio will be lowered significantly as the liabilities will drop from 53.8% of total capitalisation to 33.2% of total capitalisation. However, the ROCE may stay the same even though there is an increase in shareholders equity as total capitalisation has not changed. However, this will depend upon the definition used by the entity for capital employed.

Amster Group – capitalisation table

	30 November 20X7	Adjustment	30 November 20X7
	$m	$m	$m
Long-term liabilities	81	3.85	84.85
Pension plan deficit	30		30.00
Cumulative preference shares	75	(75)	–
Liabilities	186		114.85
Non-controlling interest	10		10.00
Shareholders equity	150	(75 – 3.85)	221.15
Group equity	160		231.15
Total capitalisation	346		346.00

46 Havanna

Workbook references. Revenue recognition is covered in Chapter 3, IFRS 5 *Non-current Assets Held for Sale and Discontinued Operations* in Chapter 14 and sale and leaseback in Chapter 9.

Top tips. Revenue recognition is an area in which preparers of accounts may wish to interpret the standard in such a way as to present the results in a favourable light. In Part (a), you need to explain why the proposed treatment is unacceptable, not just state that it is.

Part (b), which tests IFRS 5, requires clear, logical thinking: there are two potential impairments, the first in calculating the adjusted carrying amount of the disposal group at the time of classification as held for sale, and then again on comparison of this adjusted carrying amount with fair value less costs to sell.

Part (c)(i) requires you to demonstrate wider reading on the impact of IFRS 16. For part (c)(ii), the difficulty with sale and leaseback often lies with identifying whether the transfer of the asset constitutes a sale but here the question actually states that the transaction constitutes a sale so you just need to explain why the directors' understanding is incorrect and advise on the correct accounting treatment in the context of the scenario.

Marking scheme

			Marks
(a)	Revenue recognition – 1 mark per point to a maximum		5
(b)	IFRS 5 explanation – 1 mark per point to a maximum		5
(c)	(i)	Key changes to financial statements from IFRS 16 – 1 mark per point to a maximum	6
	(ii)	Sale and leaseback – 1 mark per point to a maximum	5
	(iii)	Effect on interest cover – 1 mark per point to a maximum	2
	Professional marks		2
			25

(a) Contracts with sports organisations

Havanna has treated the services provided under the contracts as a single performance obligation satisfied at a point in time, when the customer signs the contract.

However, there are **potentially at least three separate performance obligations** in the form of the different services provided by Havanna to the sports organisations. These are access to Havanna's database of members, admission to health clubs and provision of coaching (and other benefits).

Under IFRS 15, Havanna is providing a **series of distinct services** that are **substantially the same** and have the **same pattern of transfer** to the customer.

This is the case because both of the following criteria are met:

(1) Each distinct service in the series **meets the criteria to be a performance obligation satisfied over time** (ie when the customer simultaneously receives and consumes the benefits provided by the entity). This is the case with all three of the services offered by Havanna to the sports organisations.

(2) **The same method** would be used to **measure the entity's progress towards complete satisfaction of the performance obligation** to transfer each distinct service in the series to the customer. This is the case for Havanna as the most appropriate measure would be a time-based measure as Havanna has an obligation to provide their services on a continuous basis over the 9 to 18-month contract.

Therefore, Havanna's services qualify as a series of distinct goods and services that are substantially the same which should be grouped together as a **single performance obligation** which is satisfied over time.

For performance obligations satisfied over time, IFRS 15 requires an entity to recognise revenue over time by measuring progress towards complete satisfaction of that performance obligation.

Havanna should recognise revenue on a **straight-line basis over the period of the contract** rather than when the customer signs the contract.

(b) **Sale of division**

The division to be sold meets the criteria in IFRS 5 *Non-current Assets Held for Sale and Discontinued Operations* to be classified as held for sale and has been classified as a **disposal group** under IFRS 5.

A disposal group that is held for sale should be measured at the **lower of** its **carrying amount** and **fair value less costs to sell**. Immediately before classification of a disposal group as held for sale, the entity must recognise impairment in accordance with applicable IFRS. Any impairment loss is generally recognised in profit or loss, but if the asset has been measured at a revalued amount under IAS 16 *Property, Plant and Equipment* or IAS 38 *Intangible Assets*, the impairment will be treated as a revaluation decrease.

Once the disposal group has been **classified as held for sale**, any further **impairment loss** will be based on the **difference between the adjusted carrying amounts and the fair value less cost to sell**. The impairment loss (if any) will be **recognised in profit or loss**. For assets carried at fair value prior to initial classification, the requirement to deduct costs to sell from fair value will result in an immediate charge to profit or loss.

Havanna has calculated the impairment as $30 million, being the difference between the carrying amount at initial classification and the value of the assets measured in accordance with IFRS. However, applying the treatment described above:

Step 1   Calculate carrying amount under applicable IFRS: $90m – $30m = $60m

Step 2   Classified as held for sale. Measure at the lower of the adjusted carrying amount under applicable IFRS ($60m) and fair value less costs to sell of $38.5 million ($40m expected sales prices less expected costs of $1.5m). Therefore, an additional impairment loss of $21.5 million is required to write down the carrying amount of $60 million to the fair value less costs to sell of $38.5 million.

(c) **Briefing note for directors**

(i) *Key changes investors will see as a result of IFRS 16*

IFRS 16 has brought all lease obligations (with limited exemptions for short-term leases and low value assets) on to the statement of financial position because on lease commencement, a lessee recognises a right-of-use asset and a corresponding lease liability.

Under IAS 17, lessees only recognised an asset and liability in respect of leases that met the definition of a finance lease. Leases that were not classified as finance leases were therefore 'off-balance sheet'. This made investor analysis of financial statements more difficult as investors had to estimate the assets and liabilities resulting from off-balance sheet leases when calculating ratios.

IFRS 16 will reduce complexity in financial statements as it should allow comparisons to be made between those companies who lease assets and those who borrow to buy assets.

The requirement to recognise right-of-use assets and lease liabilities under IFRS 16 will result in more information about leases both on the statement of financial position and in the notes and will provide a more accurate reflection of the impacts of lease arrangements on an entity's financial statements.

The carrying amount of lease assets will typically reduce more quickly than the carrying amount of lease liabilities. This will result in a reduction in reported equity for companies with previous material off-balance sheet leases.

IFRS 16 requires a lessee to disclose lease liabilities separately from other liabilities as a separate line item, or together with other similar liabilities, in a manner which is relevant to understanding the lessee's financial position. A lessee will also split lease liabilities into current and non-current portions, based on the timing of payments.

Investors should bear in mind that some sectors and some companies will be more affected than others. As a result, companies with previous material off-balance sheet leases will report higher assets and financial liabilities.

(ii) *Sale and leaseback*

This is a sale and leaseback transaction which should be accounted for in accordance with IFRS 16 *Leases*. IFRS 16 requires an **initial assessment** to be made regarding **whether** the **transfer constitutes a sale,** here we are told the **IFRS 15 criteria have been met.**

Havanna should **derecognise the carrying amount** of the asset ($4.2m) and **recognise a right-of-use asset** at the proportion of the previous carrying amount that relates to the right-of-use asset retained.

A **gain or loss** should then be recognised in relation to the **rights transferred** to the buyer-lessor. Although there is a gain to be recognised in profit or loss, this will not be the $0.8 million (being sales price of $5m – carrying amount of $4.2m) the CEO has calculated.

Havanna should also recognise a **lease liability** at the present value of the future lease payments of $3.85 million.

The right-of-use asset at the start of the leaseback should be calculated as:

Carrying amount × present value of future lease payments/Fair value

= $4.2m × $3.85m/$5m = $3,234,000.

Havanna should only recognise the amount of gain that relates to the rights transferred. The gain on sale of the building is $800,000 ($5,000,000 – $4,200,000), of which:

($800,000 × $3.85m/$5m) = $616,000 relates to the rights retained.

The balance, $184,000 ($800,000 – $616,000), relates to the rights transferred to the buyer and should be recognised as a gain.

At the start of the lease Havanna should account for the transaction as follows:

	Debit $	Credit $
Cash	5,000,000	
Right-of-use asset	3,234,000	
Building		4,200,000
Lease liability		3,850,000
Gain on rights transferred		184,000
	8,234,000	8,234,000

The **right-of-use asset** should be **depreciated over ten years** (being the shorter of the lease term and the remaining useful life of the asset). The **gain will be recognised in profit or loss** and the **lease liability** will be **increased** each year by the **interest charge** and **reduced by the lease payments**.

(iii) *Effect on interest cover*

The interest cover ratio in its most simple form is an entity's earnings before interest and tax divided by its interest expense for the period. In stating that the transaction will help to ensure that the interest cover covenant will be met, the CEO has failed to take into account the additional finance cost that will arise as a result of the lease liability.

Furthermore, earnings will be increased by the gain on the rights transferred of $0.184 million, but this is far less than the $0.8 million gain expected by the CEO. More information would be required as to the interest payable on the lease in order to quantify whether the interest cover will indeed improve as a result of the sale and leaseback.

47 Operating segments

Workbook references. The topics in this question are covered in Chapter 18.

Top tips: Parts (a) and (b) require you to apply the criteria in IFRS 8 to two different companies. In (a) you need to consider the allocation of common costs to operating segments and explain how those costs differ to amounts in the financial statements because IFRS 8 is based on internally reported information. In (b) you need to determine whether the company was correct in aggregating two reportable segments (there is plenty of information in the scenario to suggest otherwise) and consider how investors use segmental information in their appraisal of companies. Part (c) considers the disclosure of social and environmental information in financial statements.

Easy marks. There are some easy marks for definitions in Part (b).

Marking scheme

		Marks
(a)	Accell – allocation of common costs – discussion 1 mark per point to a maximum of 7 marks. Points may include:	
	Impact on profit/net assets of allocation	1
	IFRS 8 guidance on allocation	1
	Suggested basis for allocation for each cost in scenario	3
	Differing amounts in segment report to financial statements	2
		7

			Marks
(b)	(i)	Velocity – application of IFRS 8:	
		Criteria for aggregation	1
		Customer base/risk	2
		Conclusion	1
			4
	(ii)	Velocity – discussion of investor appraisal and segments:	
		Used to determine cash flows	1
		Aggregation less useful	1
		Conclusion	1
		Ethics	1
			4
(c)	1 mark per relevant well-explained point		8
Professional marks			2
			25

(a) **Accell – allocation of common costs under IFRS 8**

If operating segment disclosure is to fulfil a useful function, costs need to be appropriately assigned to segments. Centrally incurred expenses and central assets can be significant, and the basis chosen by an entity to allocate such costs **can therefore have a significant impact** on the financial statements. In the case of Accell, head office management expenses, pension expenses, the cost of managing properties and interest and related interest-bearing assets could be material amounts, whose misallocation could mislead users.

IFRS 8 **does not prescribe a basis** on which to allocate common costs, but it does require that that basis should be **reasonable**. For example, it would not be reasonable to allocate the head office management expenses to the most profitable business segment to disguise a potential loss elsewhere. Nor would it be reasonable to allocate the pension expense to a segment with no pensionable employees.

A reasonable basis on which to allocate common costs for Accell might be as follows:

(i) **Head office management costs.** These could be allocated on the basis of revenue or net assets. Any allocation might be criticised as arbitrary – it is not necessarily the case that a segment with a higher revenue requires more administration from head office – but this is a fairer basis than most.

(ii) **Pension expense.** A reasonable allocation might be on the basis of the number of employees or salary expense of each segment.

(iii) **Costs of managing properties.** These could be allocated on the basis of the value of the properties used by each business segment, or the type and age of the properties (older properties requiring more attention than newer ones).

(iv) **Interest and interest-bearing assets.** These need not be allocated to the same segment – the interest receivable could be allocated to the profit or loss of one segment and the related interest-bearing asset to the assets and liabilities of another. IFRS 8 calls this asymmetrical allocation.

The **amounts reported under IFRS 8 may differ from those reported in the financial statements** because IFRS 8 requires the information to be presented on the same basis as it is reported internally, even if the accounting policies are not the same as those of the consolidated financial statements. For example, segment information may be reported on a cash basis rather than an accruals basis or different accounting policies may be adopted in the segment report when allocating centrally incurred costs if necessary for a better understanding of the reported segment information.

IFRS 8 requires **reconciliations** between the segments' reported amounts and those in the consolidated financial statements. Entities must disclose the nature of such differences, and of the basis of accounting for transactions between reportable segments.

(b) (i) Velocity – operating segments

IFRS 8 *Operating Segments* requires operating segments to be reported separately if they exceed at least one of certain quantitative thresholds. An entity can choose to aggregate two or more operating segments into a single operating segment **before** applying the quantitative thresholds if those operating segments have **similar economic characteristics**, and the segments are similar in **all** of the following aggregation criteria:

(i)   The nature of the products and services
(ii)   The nature of the production process
(iii) The type or class of customer for their products or services
(iv)   The methods used to distribute their products or provide their services
(v)   If applicable, the nature of the regulatory environment.

Operating segments can also be aggregated if, after applying the quantitative thresholds, no operating segments are found to be reportable, in order to produce a reportable segment. This can only be done if the operating segments have **similar economic characteristics**, and the segments are similar in a **majority** of the above aggregation criteria.

Management have a choice as to whether to aggregate operating segments that meet the aggregation criteria. But in making that choice, management must consider the core principle of IFRS 8 which is to provide useful information to users in evaluating the business.

Velocity has aggregated segments 1 and 2, but this aggregation may not be permissible under IFRS 8. While the products and services are similar, the **customers for those products and services are different**. Therefore, the third aggregation criteria has not been met.

In the local market, the decision to award the contract is in the hands of the local authority, which also sets prices and pays for the services. The **company is not exposed to passenger revenue risk**, since a contract is awarded by competitive tender.

By contrast, in the inter-city train market, the **customer ultimately determines whether a train route is economically viable** by choosing whether or not to buy tickets. Velocity sets the ticket prices, but will be influenced by customer behaviour or feedback. The **company is exposed to passenger revenue risk**, as it sets prices which customers may or may not choose to pay.

It is possible that the fifth criteria, regulatory environment, is not met, since the local authority is imposing a different set of rules to that which applies in the inter-city market.

In conclusion, the two segments have different economic characteristics and so **should be reported as separate segments** rather than aggregated.

(ii) Relevance to investor analysis

Contrary to the managing director's views, IFRS 8 provides information that makes the financial statements more useful to investors. The objective of financial statements is to provide financial information to primary users (not just investors) which enables them to make decisions about providing resources to the entity.

In making those decisions, investors and creditors consider the returns they are likely to make on their investment. This requires assessment of the amount, timing and uncertainty of the future cash flows of Velocity as well as of management's stewardship of Velocity's resources. How management derives profit is therefore relevant information to an investor.

Inappropriately aggregating segments reduces the usefulness of segment disclosures to investors. IFRS 8 requires information to be disclosed that is not readily available elsewhere in the financial statements, therefore it provides additional information which aids an investor's understanding of how the business operates and is managed.

BPP
LEARNING
MEDIA

In Velocity's case, if the segments are aggregated, then the increased profits in segment 2 will hide the decreased profits in segment 1. However, the fact profits have sharply declined in segment 1 would be of interest to investors as it may suggest that future cash flows from this segment are at risk.

The fact that the director was pleased at the aggregation of the segments raises concern that perhaps Velocity is trying to conceal facts from investors. The reasons for this should be investigated further to determine if there is any unethical practice taking place.

(c)   Social and environmental information

There are a number of factors which encourage companies to disclose social and environmental information in their financial statements. **Public interest** in corporate social responsibility has increased in recent years and in an age where society is increasingly aware of the impact of both individual and business decisions on the climate, environment and sustainability, it remains a key area of focus for reporting accountants.

Although financial statements are intended for present and potential investors, lenders and other creditors, there is recognition that companies have a responsibility to **a number of different stakeholders**. These include **customers, employees and the general public**, all of whom are **potentially interested** in the way in which a company's operations affect the natural environment and the wider community. These stakeholders can have a **considerable effect on a company's performance.** As a result, most companies now take positive steps to build a **reputation for social and environmental responsibility.** Therefore, the disclosure of environmental and social information is essential.

It is also generally accepted that **corporate social responsibility is actually an important part of an entity's overall performance.** Responsible practice in areas such as reduction of damage to the environment and fair recruitment practices **increase shareholder value.** Companies that act responsibly and make social and environmental disclosures are **perceived as better investments** than those that do not.

Another factor is **commitments by governments** to achieve, for example, climate change targets or to meet Sustainable Development Goals by 2030 and the pressure placed on companies to make a positive contribution towards achieving such targets. Although there are **no IFRS Standards** that specifically require environmental and social reporting, it may be required by **company legislation** and **stock exchange requirements.** There are now a number of **awards for environmental and social reports** and high-quality disclosure in financial statements. These provide further encouragement to disclose information.

At present companies are normally able to disclose **as much or as little information as they wish in whatever manner that they wish.** This causes a number of **problems.** Companies tend to disclose information **selectively** and it is difficult for users of the financial statements to **compare the performance of different companies.** However, there are **good arguments** for continuing to allow companies a certain amount of freedom to determine the information that they disclose. If detailed rules are imposed, **companies are likely to adopt a 'checklist' approach** and will **present information in a very general and standardised way,** so that it is of very little use to stakeholders.

48 Cloud

Marking scheme

			Marks
(a)	(i)	1 mark per point up to maximum	6
	(ii)	1 mark per point up to maximum	5
	(iii)	1 mark per point up to maximum	8
(b)		1 mark per point up to maximum	6
			25

(a) (i) **Current presentation requirements**

IAS 1 requires the presentation of either one combined statement of profit or loss and other comprehensive income (SPLOCI) or two separate statements, the statement of profit or loss (SPL) and the statement of comprehensive income.

Separate disclosure is required of those items of other comprehensive income (OCI) which would be reclassified to profit or loss and those items of OCI which would never be reclassified to profit or loss, along with the related tax effects of each category.

Conceptual basis

The conceptual basis for what should be classified as OCI is not clear. This has led to an **inconsistent use of OCI in IFRS**.

Opinions vary but there is a feeling that **OCI has become a home for anything controversial** because of a lack of clear definition of what should be included in the statement.

Many users are thought to ignore OCI, as the changes reported are not caused by the operating flows used for predictive purposes. It is also difficult for users to understand the concept of OCI as opposed to profit or loss which, although subject to accounting standards, is an easier notion to grasp.

The definitions of profit and loss and OCI in IAS 1 are not particularly helpful in understanding the conceptual basis:

- Profit or loss is the total of all items of income and expenses except those items of income or expense which are recognised in OCI

- OCI comprises items of income and expense that are not recognised in profit or loss as required or permitted by other IFRSs

The IASB has been asked to define what financial performance is, clarify the meaning and importance of OCI and how the distinction between profit or loss and OCI should be made in practice. Many stakeholders were hoping that the *Conceptual Framework* as revised in 2018 would answer these questions, but the matter has not been adequately addressed.

The revised *Conceptual Framework* identifies the SPL as the **primary source** of information about an entity's performance and states that in principle, therefore, all income and expenses are included in it.

However, it goes on to say that in developing IFRSs the IASB may include income or expenses **arising from a change in the current value of an asset or liability as OCI** when they determine it provides more relevant information or a more faithful representation.

So although there is more guidance on what constitutes OCI, the conceptual basis for it is still not clear.

(ii)   **Reclassification adjustments**

Reclassification adjustments are **amounts reclassified to profit or loss in the current period which were recognised in OCI in the current or previous periods.**

Items which may be reclassified include foreign currency gains on the disposal of a foreign operation and realised gains or losses on cash flow hedges.

Items which may not be reclassified are changes in a revaluation surplus under IAS 16 *Property, Plant and Equipment*, and actuarial gains and losses on a defined benefit plan under IAS 19 *Employee Benefits*.

However, the notion of reclassification and when or which OCI items should be reclassified is not clear. The revised *Conceptual Framework* (2018) states that in principle, OCI is recycled to profit or loss in a future period when doing so results in the provision of more relevant information or a more faithful representation. While providing more guidance than the previous *Conceptual Framework*, the conceptual basis for when OCI should be reclassified is not clear.

Arguments for and against reclassification

It is argued that reclassification protects the integrity of profit or loss and **provides users with relevant information about a transaction which occurred in the period**. Additionally, it can **improve comparability** where IFRSs permits similar items to be recognised in either profit or loss or OCI.

Those against reclassification argue that the **recycled amounts add to the complexity of financial reporting**, may lead to earnings management and the reclassification adjustments may not meet the definitions of income or expense in the period as the change in the asset or liability may have occurred in a previous period.

(iii)   **Integrated Reporting**

The <IR> Framework establishes **principles** and **concepts** which govern the overall content of an integrated report. This enables each company to set out its own integrated report rather than adopting a checklist approach.

The integrated report aims to provide an insight into the company's resources and relationships (known as **capitals**) and how the company interacts with the external environment and the capitals to create value. These capitals can be financial, manufactured, intellectual, human, social and relationship, and natural capital but companies need not adopt these classifications.

Integrated reporting is built around the following key components:

(1) Organisational overview and the external environment under which it operates

(2) Governance structure and how this supports its ability to create value

(3) Business model

(4) Risks and opportunities and how they are dealing with them and how they affect the company's ability to create value

(5) Strategy and resource allocation

(6) Performance and achievement of strategic objectives for the period and outcomes

(7) Outlook and challenges facing the company and their implications

(8) The basis of presentation needs to be determined including what matters are to be included in the integrated report and how the elements are quantified or evaluated

An integrated report should provide insight into the **nature and quality of the organisation's relationships** with its **key stakeholders**, including how and to what extent the organisation understands, takes into account and responds to their **needs and interests**. The report should be consistent over time to enable comparison with other entities.

'Value' depends upon the individual company's own perspective. It can be shown through movement of capital and can be defined as **value created for the company or for others**. An integrated report should not attempt to quantify value, as assessments of value are left to those using the report.

An integrated report does not contain a statement from those 'charged with governance' acknowledging their responsibility for the integrated report. This may undermine the reliability and credibility of the integrated report.

There has been discussion about whether the <IR> Framework constitutes suitable criteria for report preparation and for assurance. There is a degree of uncertainty as to measurement standards to be used for the information reported and how a preparer can ascertain the completeness of the report. The IIRC has stated that the prescription of specific measurement methods is beyond the scope of a principles-based framework.

The <IR> Framework contains information on the principles-based approach and indicates that there is a need to include quantitative indicators whenever practicable and possible. Additionally, consistency of measurement methods across different reports is of paramount importance. There is outline guidance on the selection of suitable quantitative indicators.

There are additional concerns over the ability to assess future disclosures, and there may be a need for confidence intervals to be disclosed. The preparation of an integrated report requires judgement but there is a requirement for the report to describe its basis of preparation and presentation, including the significant frameworks and methods used to quantify or evaluate material matters. Also included is the disclosure of a summary of how the company determined the materiality limits and a description of the reporting boundaries.

A company should consider how to describe the disclosures without causing a significant loss of competitive advantage. The entity will consider what advantage a competitor could actually gain from information in the integrated report, and will balance this against the need for disclosure.

(b) At 30 April 20X5, Cloud should write down the steel, in accordance with IAS 2 *Inventories*, to its net realisable value of $6 million, therefore reducing profit by $2 million. Cloud should reclassify an equivalent amount of $2 million from equity to profit or loss. Thus there is no net impact on profit or loss from the write down of inventory. The gain remaining in equity of $1 million will affect profit or loss when the steel is sold. Therefore, on 3 June 20X5, the gain on the sale of $0.2 million with be recognised in profit or loss, and the remaining gain of $1 million will be transferred to profit or loss from equity.

As regards the property, plant and equipment, at 30 April 20X4, there is a revaluation surplus of $4 million being the difference between the carrying amount of $8 million ($10 million − $2 million) and the revalued amount of $12 million. This revaluation surplus is recognised in other comprehensive income.

At 30 April 20X5 the asset's value has fallen to $4 million and the carrying amount of the asset is $9 million ($12 million − $3 million). The entity will have transferred $1 million from revaluation surplus to retained earnings, being the difference between historical cost depreciation of $2 million and depreciation on the revalued amount of $3 million. The revaluation loss of $5 million will be charged first against the revaluation surplus remaining in equity of ($4 million − $1 million), ie $3 million and the balance of $2 million will be charged against profit or loss.

IAS 1 requires an entity to present a separate statement of changes in equity showing amongst other items, total comprehensive income for the period, reconciliations between the carrying amounts at the beginning and the end of the period for each component of equity, and an analysis of other comprehensive income.

49 Leria Co

Workbook references. Non-current assets held for sale are covered in Chapter 14. Sale and leaseback is covered in Chapter 9. Intangible assets are covered in Chapter 4.

Top tips. This question was set in the context of a football club, however industry-specific knowledge was not required. Part (a) contained three separate sub-requirements, all related to the treatment of the football stadium. Part (a)(i) required careful application to the scenario of the requirements of IFRS 5 for assets held for sale relating to the date of the sale agreement. In part (a)(ii), you were told in the scenario that the company's accounting treatment for the crowd barriers was incorrect, so that gave you a starting point for the discussion. Part (a)(iii) covered the sale and leaseback. This is where you should have spent most of your time in part (a) as there was lots to discuss. Part (b)(i) was tricky if you were not aware of the rebuttable presumption in IAS 38 that that basing amortisation on revenue, for which the intangible is used, is inappropriate, unless both use and revenue are highly correlated. However, if you were not aware of this, you could have described the principles underlying amortisation and developed your answer from there. Part b(ii) required a discussion of the accounting treatment of the players' contract costs, including contingent performance conditions, the possible need for impairment and whether a player can be considered a single cash generating unit (CGU).

Marking scheme

			Marks
(a)	Discussion and application of the following to the scenario:		
	(i) Held for sale guidance under IFRS 5	3	
	(ii) Accounting treatment barrier improvements	3	
	(iii) Sale and leaseback principles	4	
	Accounting treatment sale and leaseback	3	
			13
(b)	Discussion and application of the following to the scenario:		
	Potential amortisation of the intangible asset	5	
	Performance conditions and contract costs	5	
	Value-in-use of an individual player/CGU	2	
			12
			25

(a) (i)   IFRS 5 *Non-current Assets Held for Sale and Discontinued Operations* addresses the accounting for assets which are classified as held for sale. IFRS 5 requires a non-current asset to be classified as held for sale if its carrying amount will be recovered principally through a sale transaction rather than through its continuing use. It must be available for immediate sale in its present condition, and its sale must be highly probable within 12 months of classification as held for sale. The standard only foresees an exemption to this rule if the sale is delayed by events or circumstances which are beyond the entity's control, which is unlikely to be the case in this instance. Leria Co has entered into a firm sales commitment but the sale will occur after the 12-month threshold. Therefore, the stadium cannot be classified as held for sale. Additionally, a sale and leaseback transaction is outside the scope of IFRS 5 and is covered by IFRS 16 *Leases*.

(ii) The $2 million to be spent on crowd barrier improvements to the stadium should not be treated as an impairment of the asset's carrying amount at 31 October 20X5. There is no present obligation (legal or constructive) as a result of a past event and there is no probable payment. Leria Co may decide not to carry out the improvements, especially as the stadium is going to be sold and then subsequently leased back. Therefore the $2 million should be added back to the carrying amount of the stadium and a corresponding credit made to profit or loss.

(iii) A sale and leaseback transaction occurs where an entity transfers an asset to another entity and leases that asset back from the buyer/lessor. The first required criteria of IFRS standards is to determine whether a sale has occurred. Under IFRS 16, an entity must apply the IFRS 15 *Revenue from Contracts with Customers* requirements to determine when a performance obligation is satisfied. If it is concluded that the transfer of an asset is not a sale, then the seller/lessee will continue to recognise the transferred asset. In this event, a financial liability and financial asset will be recognised under IFRS 9 *Financial Instruments*. In this case, it seems that a sale will occur on 30 November 20X6 because of the binding sale commitment. If the fair value of the sale consideration equals the asset's fair value, and the lease payments are at market rates, there is no need to adjust the sales proceeds under IFRS 16.

Leria Co should follow IFRS 15 to account for the sale and then apply IFRS 16 to account for the lease. Thus, Leria Co should account for the sale and leaseback as follows:

- Derecognise the underlying asset.

- Recognise the sale at fair value.

- Recognise only the gain/loss which relates to the rights transferred to buyer/lessor.

- Recognise a right-of-use asset as a proportion of the previous carrying amount of the underlying asset.

- Recognise a lease liability.

Leria Co should account for the sale and leaseback at 30 November 20X6 as follows:

Carrying amount of stadium is $(18 + 2) million =	$20 million
Less Depreciation for year to 31 October 20X6 $(20 × .05) million	($1 million)
Depreciation for November 20X6 $(20 − 1) × .05)/12) million	($0.08 million)
	$18.92 million

Present value of lease/fair value of asset = $26m/$30 × 100% = 86.67%
The right-of-use asset recorded will be 86.67% × $18.92 = $16.4 million.

The gain on disposal is limited to the gain on the portion of the asset sold recognising that Leria has retained an interest in the asset. It will be reported in the statement of profit or loss.

(b) (i)   Leria Co's accounting policy to base the amortisation of the intangible asset for content rights on revenue stemming from the rights seems reasonable and systematic. However, IAS 38 *Intangible Assets* sets out a rebuttable presumption that amortisation based on revenue generated by an activity which includes the use of an intangible asset is not appropriate. This presumption can be overcome when it can be demonstrated that revenue and the consumption of the economic benefits of the intangible asset are highly correlated. The intellectual property embodied in the television programmes will generate cash flows through the television channel subscriptions and the estimated revenues for a television programme determine the amount to be spent on producing the television programme. Therefore, revenue reflects a proxy for the pattern of consumption of the benefits received. Revenue and consumption of the economic benefits of the intangible asset seem highly correlated and therefore a revenue-based amortisation method seems appropriate.

The industry practice method is also acceptable and conceptually sound as it is based on an analysis of the remaining useful life of the programme and the recoverable amount. Such an approach does not contradict IAS 38's prohibition on revenue-based amortisation because it is not based on direct matching of revenue and amortisation. The useful life of an asset is required to be reassessed in accordance with IFRS Standards at least at each financial year end. Where this results in a change in estimate, this is will be accounted for prospectively from the date of reassessment.

IAS 38 also states that if a pattern of amortisation cannot be measured reliably, the straight-line method must be used.

(ii)   When a player's contract is signed, management should make an assessment of the likely outcome of performance conditions. Contingent consideration will be recognised in the players' initial registration costs if management believes the performance conditions will be met in line with the contractual terms. Periodic reassessments of the contingent consideration should be made. Any contingent amounts which the directors of Leria Co believe will be payable should be included in the players' contract costs from the date management believes that the performance conditions will be met. Any additional amounts of contingent consideration not included in the costs of players' registrations will be disclosed separately as a commitment. Amortisation of the costs of the contract will be based upon the length of the player's contract.

The costs associated with the renegotiation of a playing contract should be added to the residual balance of the players' contract costs at the date of signing the contract extension. The revised carrying amount should be amortised over the remaining renegotiated contract length. Where a player sustains a career threatening injury and is removed from the playing team, the carrying amount of the individual would be assessed against the best estimate of the individual's fair value less any costs to sell and an impairment charge made in operating expenses reflecting any loss arising.

It is unlikely that any individual player can be a separate single cash generating unit (CGU) as this is likely to be the playing squad. Also, it is difficult to determine the value-in-use of an individual player in isolation as players cannot generate cash flows on their own unless via a sale.

50 Corbel Co

			Marks
(a)	Listing of major challenges		
	1 mark per point up to maximum		5
(b)	Discussion and application of the following to the scenario:		
	(i)	Treatment of brand on acquisition	2
		Allocation of brand to CGU	2
			4
	(ii)	Intangible assets with indefinite life principles (IAS 38)	2
		Application to scenario	4
			6
	(iii)	NCA held for sale-principles	3
		Application to scenario	3
			6
	(iv)	Impairment principles	2
		Impairment of primary store	2
			4
			25

(a) There are many challenges in recognising and measuring intangible assets such as brands in the statement of financial position.

Many intangible assets are not frequently traded on a stand-alone basis and therefore very often there is no active market for them which makes arriving at a valuation more difficult. Additionally, many intangible assets are unique and therefore it is not easy to identify and assess their value. Valuation methods are often complex and subjective and the measurement is more subjective when the intangible assets are not based on legally enforceable rights. In some cases, the acquirer does not intend to use the intangible assets (for example, Corbel has acquired the brands for defensive reasons) and this raises issues with regards to arriving at a value. Finally, determining the useful life of intangible assets can be subjective.

Generally, the reason for the omission from the financial statements of intangible assets has been due to a perceived lack of a link between their costs and estimating future revenue. In addition, the difficulties in ascertaining cost or valuation figures for intangibles and a focus on reliability over relevance when disclosing asset information have meant that internally generated intangibles have not usually been recognised. However, the importance of intangibles is reflected in the increasing proportion of a company's market value being attributable to the existence of intangibles.

Intangible assets are not physical assets that can be easily recognised. In some cases, perceptions may clash and what may seem like an intangible asset to one party may appear not so to another.

(b) (i) The Jengi brand will generate future economic benefits by increasing sales volumes and by the potential of premium prices. Control over these potential future benefits is achieved by the registration of the brand. The registration also satisfies the requirement to identify the intangible asset separately from goodwill and estimate its fair value.

IAS 36 *Impairment of Assets* defines a cash generating unit (CGU) as the smallest identifiable group of assets that generates cash inflows that are largely independent of the cash inflows from other assets or other groups of assets. However, brands are typically not a separate CGU under IFRS. The brand would be tested for impairment together with the associated manufacturing facilities. The brand would be separately identified and valued, and should be allocated to each of Corbel Co's cash generating units that are expected to benefit from the synergies of the combination. IAS 36 recognises that sometimes there is no basis for allocating the brand to an individual CGU that is not arbitrary, so it permits it to be allocated to a group of CGUs. However, each CGU must represent the lowest level within the entity that is monitored for internal management purposes and not be larger than an operating segment.

(ii) Intangible assets have an indefinite useful life when there is no foreseeable limit to the period over which, based on an analysis of all relevant factors, the asset is expected to generate net cash inflows for the entity (IAS 38 *Intangible Assets*). An intangible asset with an indefinite useful life should not be amortised. IAS 36 *Impairment of Assets*, requires an entity to test an intangible asset with an indefinite useful life for impairment by comparing its recoverable amount with its carrying amount:

(a) annually, and
(b) whenever there is an indication that the intangible asset may be impaired.

The useful life of an intangible asset that is not being amortised should be reviewed each period to determine whether events and circumstances continue to support an indefinite useful life assessment for that asset. If they do not, the change in the useful life assessment from indefinite to finite should be accounted for as a change in an accounting estimate in accordance with IAS 8 *Account Policies, Changes in Estimates and Errors*.

Corbel Co should consider various factors to determine whether the brand names can be considered to have a useful life. These will include the extent to which Corbel Co is prepared to support the brand and the extent to which the brand has long-term potential and has had proven success. Perfume is often subject to market and fashion trends and therefore, an assessment of how resistant the brands are to change should be made. Also Corbel Co has purchased the brands as a defensive measure to prevent rival companies acquiring them. Therefore, there may be a doubt as to the support that Corbel Co may be prepared to give to the brands.

The Locust perfume has been sold successfully in the market for many years and could be deemed to have an indefinite life. The Clara perfume is linked to the popularity of the actor and therefore, it is difficult to assess whether the brand has an indefinite life as it is likely to be dependent upon the longevity of the popularity of the actor. In the case of the Clara perfume, it is difficult to state that the brand will have an indefinite life. Thus, Clara is likely to have a finite life.

(iii) IFRS 5 *Non-current Assets Held for Sale and Discontinued Operations* states that immediately before classifying a disposal group as held for sale, the carrying amounts of the assets and liabilities within the group are measured in accordance with the applicable IFRS standards. After classification as held for sale, disposal groups are measured at the lower of carrying amount and fair value less costs to sell. Impairment must be considered both at the time of classification as held for sale and subsequently after classification. The six stores should be accounted for as a discontinued operation as they represent a component of Corbel Co and are a separate geographical area of operations. The approval and announcement of a plan to close the six Italian stores is an indication that the assets attributable to the discontinuing operation may be impaired. In addition, the six stores would be classified as a 'disposal group' which is a group of assets that, an entity intends to dispose of in a single transaction. The measurement basis required for non-current assets classified as held for sale is applied to the group as a whole, and any resulting impairment loss reduces the carrying amount of the non-current assets in the disposal group in the order of allocation required by IAS 36. Additionally, there may be a need to provide for the additional costs of closure such as redundancy costs, under IAS 37 *Provisions, Contingent liabilities and Contingent Assets*.

At the end of each reporting period, an entity is required to assess whether there is any indication that an asset may be impaired, ie its carrying amount may be higher than its recoverable amount. IAS 36 has a list of external and internal indicators of impairment. If there is an indication that an asset may be impaired, then the asset's recoverable amount must be calculated. Whenever there is an indication of impairment, the entity estimates the recoverable amount of the asset and records an impairment if the recoverable amount is lower than the carrying amount.

Although there has been a local newspaper article that Corbel Co is to shut 30 stores with a loss of 500 jobs across the world over the next five years, there has been no formal announcement by Corbel Co and therefore, until there has been formal plans drawn up to close the additional stores there should be no provisions made for the stores potential closure and loss of jobs. It is feasible that the closure of the additional 24 stores will not take place, and there is no constructive obligation unless there is at least a detailed formal plan. The directors have denied the fact that the additional stores will be closed.

(iv) As stated in (a)(ii), an entity needs to assess at the end of each reporting period whether there is any indication that an asset may be impaired. An indication of impairment is whether the performance of the asset is worse than expected. As the primary store is performing in line with expectations, it would appear that at present, there is no indication of impairment and therefore no impairment test is required. Additionally, if Corbel Co feels that the primary store benefits all the other stores from a brand perspective, it may be appropriate to treat the store as a corporate asset and allocate its cost to the other stores for impairment testing. The amount of internet sales included in any impairment assessment of the primary store will depend on the quantity of sales that are sourced directly from it. Where Internet sales are sourced from a central warehouse or another store, the cash inflows should be excluded from the primary store's impairment assessment and included in the appropriate CGU.

51 Fill

		Marks
(a)	A discussion of potential measurement basis, NRV and relevant Standards	3
	Application of IAS 2 to the scenario	4
		7
(b)	A discussion of IAS 16 and application to the scenario	4
	A discussion of IAS 36 and application to the scenario	4
		8

		Marks
(c)	A discussion of control in the *Conceptual Framework* and other relevant Standards	4
	A discussion of a business combination per IFRS 3	2
	Application of the above discussions to the scenario	4

$$\frac{10}{25}$$

(a) Inventories should be valued at the lower of cost and net realisable value. The *Conceptual Framework* acknowledges a variety of measurement bases including historical cost, current cost, value-in-use and fair value. Historical cost is consistent with the cost valuation in IAS 2 *Inventories*, however value in use and fair value are not:

- Value-in-use requires the use of the present value of future cash flows.

- Fair value is a market-based measurement, not an entity-specific measurement. When determining fair value, the assumptions used are those that market participants would use when pricing the asset, this would not take into consideration entity-specific factors like the cost needed to complete an asset and sell it.

The *Conceptual Framework* is not a Standard and does not override the requirements of a Standard, therefore in order to determine NRV, the directors would need to refer to IAS 2.

IAS 2 defines NRV as the estimated selling price in the ordinary course of business less the costs of completion and costs of sale.

NRV is an entity-specific measure which should be determined on the basis of conditions which existed at the date of the statement of financial position.

To estimate NRV, Fill should take into consideration future price movements if they provide information about the conditions at the reporting date. However, normally these movements would reflect changes in the market conditions after that date and therefore would not affect the calculation of NRV.

The NRV will be based upon the most reliable estimate of the amounts which will be realised for the coal.

Fill should calculate the NRV of the low carbon coal using the forecast market price based upon when the inventory is expected to be processed and realised. The forecast market price should be adjusted for the time value of money (where this is material) and for processing and selling costs to give a reasonable estimate of NRV.

Future changes in the forecast market price or the processing and sale of the low carbon coal may result in adjustments to the NRV. As these adjustments are changes in estimates, IAS 8 *Accounting Policies, Changes in Accounting Estimates and Errors* will apply with the result that such gains and losses will be recognised in the statement of profit or loss in the period in which they arise.

> **Tutorial note.**
>
> The year-end spot price will provide good evidence of the realisable value of the inventories at the year end. The forward contract price may be appropriate if the company has an executory contract to sell coal at a future date. However, if the company does not have an executory contract, but instead a financial instrument under IFRS 9 *Financial Instruments* or an onerous contract recognised as a provision under IAS 37 *Provisions, Contingent Liabilities and Contingent Assets*, the forward contract price is unlikely to be used to calculate NRV.

(b)   IAS 16 *Property, Plant and Equipment* (PPE) requires an entity to recognise in the carrying amount of PPE the cost of replacing part of such an item. When each major inspection is performed, its cost is recognised in the carrying amount of the item of PPE as a replacement if the recognition criteria are satisfied. Any remaining carrying amount of the cost of a previous inspection is derecognised. The costs of performing a major reconditioning are capitalised if it gives access to future economic benefits. Such costs will include the labour and materials costs ($3 million) of performing the reconditioning. However, costs which do not relate to the replacement of components or the installation of new assets, such as routine maintenance costs, should be expensed as incurred.

It is not acceptable to accrue the costs of reconditioning equipment as there is no legal or apparent constructive obligation to undertake the reconditioning. As set out above, the cost of the reconditioning should be identified as a separate component of the mine asset at initial recognition and depreciated over a period of two years. This will result in the same amount of expense being recognised as the proposal to create a provision.

IAS 36 *Impairment of Assets* says that at the end of each reporting period, an entity is required to assess whether there is any indication that an asset may be impaired. IAS 36 has a list of external and internal indicators of impairment. If there is an indication that an asset may be impaired, then the asset's recoverable amount must be calculated.

Past and future reductions in selling prices may indicate that the future economic benefits which relate to the asset have been reduced. Mining assets should be tested for impairment whenever indicators of impairment exist. Impairments are recognised if a mine's carrying amount exceeds its recoverable amount. However, the nature of mining assets is that they often have a long useful life. Commodity prices can be volatile but downward price movements are more significant if they are likely to persist for longer periods. In this case, there is evidence of a decline in forward prices. If the decline in prices is for a significant proportion of the remaining expected life of the mine, this is more likely to be an impairment indicator. It appears that forward contract prices for two years out of the three years of the mine's remaining life indicate a reduction in selling prices. Based on market information, Fill has also calculated that the three-year forecast price of coal will be 20% lower than the current spot price (Part (a) of question).

Short-term market fluctuations may not be impairment indicators if prices are expected to return to higher levels. However, despite the difficulty in making such assessments, it would appear that the mining assets should be tested for impairment.

(c)   The *Conceptual Framework* states that an entity controls an economic resource if it has the present ability to direct the use of the economic resource and obtain the economic benefits that may flow from it. An entity has the ability to direct the use of an economic resource if it has the right to deploy that economic resource in its activities. Although control of an economic resource usually arises from legal rights, it can also arise if an entity has the present ability to prevent all other parties from directing the use of it and obtaining the benefits from the economic resource. For an entity to control a resource, the economic benefits from the resource must flow to the entity instead of another party.

Although the *Conceptual Framework* gives some guidance on the definition of control, existing IFRS Standards also provide help in determining whether Fill controls the mine and therefore should account for it as a business combination:

- IFRS 10 *Consolidated Financial Statements* states that an investor controls an investee when it is exposed, or has rights, to variable returns from its involvement with the investee and has the ability to affect those returns through its power over the investee.

- IFRS 15 *Revenue from Contracts with Customers* lists indicators of the transfer of control of an asset to a customer. One of the indicators is that the customer has the significant risks and rewards of ownership of the asset which is basically exposure to significant variations in the amount of economic benefits.

A business combination is defined in IFRS 3 *Business Combinations* as a transaction or other event in which an acquirer obtains control of one or more businesses. A business is further defined as 'an integrated set of activities and assets that is capable of being conducted and managed for the purpose of providing goods or services to customers, generating investment income or generating other income from ordinary activities.' Thus the producing mine represents a business and Fill now owns a majority of the interest in the business.

However, this is not a business combination as Fill does not have the ability to affect decisions unless another participant agrees to vote with Fill. Although Fill will control 52% of the mine, it cannot direct the use of the economic resource unless one of the other participants agrees with an operating decision proposed by Fill and approval is given by 72% of participants. However, Fill can prevent the other parties from directing the use of the mine if the purchase goes ahead, because the other two parties cannot make an operating decision without Fill's consent. Prior to the purchase of the additional investment, the approval of decisions required agreement by 72% of the participating interests. A joint control situation existed between the entities. Following the additional purchase, there is still a joint control situation as Fill's interest does not meet the 72% threshold. Therefore, the transaction will be treated as an asset acquisition and no goodwill will arise on the acquisition.

52 Zedtech

			Marks	
(a)	(i)	Discussion of recognition per previous *Conceptual Framework*	2	
		Discussion of the revised *Conceptual Framework* approach to recognition	2	
		Comparison and contrast	3	
				7
	(ii)	Discussion of IAS 12 recognition criteria	2	
		Discussion of IAS 37 recognition criteria	2	
		Discussion of recognition in business combinations	2	
				6
(b)	(i)	Discussion of the collectability of consideration	2	
		Discussion of performance obligations	3	
				5
	(ii)	Application of the above principles to:		
		0inventory	2	
		InventoryX	3	
		Collectability assessment	2	
				7
				25

(a) (i) Existing IFRS Standards did not consistently apply the recognition criteria included in the 2010 *Conceptual Framework* and thus the revised 2018 *Conceptual Framework* sets out new principles for the recognition in the financial statements. The revised 2018 *Conceptual Framework* defines recognition as the process of capturing for inclusion in the financial statements an item which meets the definition of an element. Assets and liabilities are both elements of the financial statements, along with equity, income and expenses. This approach requires recognition decisions to be made by reference to the qualitative characteristics of useful financial information.

The revised 2018 *Conceptual Framework* requires that the elements of financial statements should be recognised if it provides users of financial statements with information that is useful, ie with:

- **Relevant** information about the element
- A **faithful representation** of the element

Recognition is subject to **cost constraints**: the benefits of the information provided by recognising an element should justify the costs of recognising that element.

Recognition may not provide relevant information where it is uncertain whether an asset exists, or is separable from goodwill, or whether a liability exists and where there is only a low probability that an inflow or outflow of economic benefits will occur. Additionally, if the level of measurement uncertainty is so high that the resulting information has little relevance, then recognition should not occur. The IASB decided that the revised 2018 *Conceptual Framework* should not contain a 'probability criterion', which means that there may be recognition of assets or liabilities with a low probability of an inflow or outflow of economic benefit.

(ii)   According to IAS 12 *Income Taxes*, deferred tax liabilities are recognised for all taxable temporary differences, with three exceptions. However, deferred tax assets are only recognised to the extent that it is **probable** that taxable profit will be available against which the deductible temporary differences can be utilised. Thus, the standard applies a probability threshold to deferred tax assets but not to liabilities.

Although the 2010 *Conceptual Framework* gave the same threshold for recognition of assets and liabilities, IAS 37 *Provisions, Contingent Liabilities and Contingent Assets* requires the recognition of assets when they are virtually certain but for liabilities when they are probable, defined as more likely than not. IAS 37 also requires the recognition of liabilities for constructive obligations. Thus, the definition of an obligation under IAS 37 can often be broader than in other standards, for example, IAS 32 *Financial Instruments: Presentation*. IAS 37 includes a probable outflow threshold for the recognition of provisions but the recognition threshold does not apply to obligations which normally fall within the scope of IAS 37 when they are acquired as part of a business combination.

IFRS 3 *Business Combinations* requires recognition of the contingent liabilities of a subsidiary irrespective of their probability. IFRS 10 *Consolidated Financial Statements* requires recognition at fair value of contingent consideration to be received for a business which is disposed of, even if the inflow is not probable. Thus, these items are recognised under IFRS 3/IFRS 10 when they arise from a business combination, whereas they are not recognised in the normal course of business.

(b)   (i)   IFRS 15 *Revenue from Contracts with Customers* states that an entity must first identify the contract with the customer and as part of that identification, the entity has to determine whether it is probable that the consideration which the entity is entitled to in exchange for the goods or services will be collected. An assessment of collectability is included as one of the criteria for determining whether a contract with a customer exists.

IFRS 15 states that the entity must identify the performance obligations in the contract. Once an entity has identified the contract with a customer, it evaluates the contractual terms and its customary business practices to identify all the promised goods or services within the contract and determine which of those promised goods or services will be treated as separate performance obligations. An entity will have to decide whether the obligations are distinct or part of a series of distinct goods and services which are substantially the same and have the same pattern of transfer to the customer. A good or service is distinct if the customer can benefit from the good or service on its own.

(ii)   Technology entities often enter into transactions involving the delivery of multiple goods and services.

As regards 0inventory, it seems that all of the individual goods and services in the contract are distinct because the entity regularly sells each element of the contract separately and is not providing the significant service of integrating the goods and services. Also, as the customer could purchase each good and service without significantly affecting the other goods and services purchased, there is no dependence upon individual elements of the service. Thus hardware, professional services and hosting services should each be accounted for as separate performance obligations.

Regarding InventoryX, the professional services are distinct because Zedtech frequently sells those services on a stand-alone basis.

However, the hardware is always sold in a combined contract with the professional and hosting services and the customer cannot use the hardware on its own. As a result, the hardware is not distinct and because the hardware is integral to the delivery of the hosted software, the hardware and hosting services should be accounted for as one performance obligation while the professional services, which are distinct, would be a separate performance obligation.

When performing the collectability assessment, Zedtech only considers the customer's ability and intention to pay the expected consideration when due. Zedtech has entered into an arrangement and does not expect to collect the full contractual amount such that the contract contains an implied price concession. Therefore, Zedtech needs to assess the collectability of the amount to which it expects to be entitled, rather than the stated contractual amount. Zedtech assesses whether collectability is probable, whether the customer has the ability and intent to pay the estimated transaction price. Zedtech will determine that the amount to which it expects to be entitled is $2.4 million and performs the collectability assessment based on that amount, rather than the contractual price of $3 million.

53 Kayte

> **Workbook references.** The *Conceptual Framework* and interim financial reporting are covered in chapter 1. IAS 16 is covered in Chapter 4. IFRS 5 is covered in Chapter 13.
>
> **Top tips.** Part (a) required you to discuss the probability recognition criterion in the 2010 Conceptual Framework. Don't be put off by the fact this is the 2010 Conceptual Framework, as the relevant part of it has been given in the question. The question told you which standards to discuss – make sure you address what it asks for. Part (b)(i) covered the application of IAS 16 and was demanding, indicative of what could be asked in an SBR exam on topics covered in your earlier studies.
>
> **Easy marks.** There were some easy marks available in part (a) for stating the recognition criteria in the 2018 Conceptual Framework. In part (b)(ii) you should have been able to apply the IFRS 5 accounting treatment for non-current assets held for sale even if you were unfamiliar with IAS 34.

Marking scheme

				Marks
(a)		Inconsistent application of the probability criterion (one per example)	3	
		Changes to the recognition criteria in 2018 *Conceptual Framework*	3	
				6
(b)	(i)	Vessels sold after 10 years	5	
		Vessels kept for 30 years	5	
		Funnels	2	
				12

		Marks
(ii)	Interim follow same accounting policies as for annual financial statements	1
	Measure asset at lower of carrying amount and fair value less costs to sell	1
	1.10.20X3: Recognise impairment loss of $100,000	1
	1.12.20X4: Reverse impairment loss of $120,000 as less than cumulative impairment losses to date of $45,000	1
	31.5.20X4: Can only recognise $330,000 of the $430,000 increase in fair value less costs to sell (up to remaining cumulative impairment losses to date)	1
	5.6.20X4: Recognise gain on disposal	1
	Gain on disposal is non-adjusting event after the reporting period	1
		$\frac{7}{25}$

(a)   **Probability criterion**

Different accounting standards use different levels of probability to discuss when assets and liabilities should be recognised in the financial statements.

For example:

- Economic benefits from property, plant and equipment and intangible assets need to be **probable** to be recognised; but to be classified as held for sale, the sale has to be **highly probable**.

- Under IAS 37 *Provisions, Contingent Liabilities and Contingent Assets*, a provision should be **probable** to be recognised, but uncertain assets on the other hand would have to be **virtually certain** to be disclosed. This could lead to a situation where two sides of the same court case have two different accounting treatments despite the likelihood of payout being identical for both parties.

- Contingent consideration is recognised in the financial statements **regardless of the level of probability**. Rather the fair value is adjusted to reflect the level of uncertainty of the contingent consideration.

The 2018 *Conceptual Framework* requires an item to be recognised in the financial statements if:

(a)   The item meets the definition of an **element** (asset, liability, income, expense or equity); and

(b)   Recognition of that element provides users of the financial statements with information that is **useful**, ie with:

- **Relevant** information about the element
- A **faithful representation** of the element

While this will not remove the inconsistencies in recognition criteria that currently exist across IFRS Standards, it does provide a basis for the IASB to consider when developing new IFRS Standards and revising existing IFRS Standards.

Furthermore, the new criteria may mean that more assets and liabilities with a low probability of inflow or outflow of economic resources are likely to be recognised. The criteria also allow for IFRS Standards to contain recognition criteria that may be considered inconsistent, but this may be a necessary consequence of providing the most useful information.

ANSWERS

(b) (i) **Vessels**

Vessels sold at ten years old

Kayte's estimate of the residual life of these vessels is **based on acquisition cost.** This is **unacceptable** under IAS 16 *Property, Plant and Equipment.* IAS 16 defines residual value as:

> 'The estimated amount that an entity would currently obtain from disposal of the asset, after deducting the estimated costs of disposal, if the asset were already of the age and in the condition expected at the end of its useful life.'
>
> (para. 6)

IAS 16 requires that property, plant and equipment must be depreciated so that its depreciable amount is allocated on a systematic basis over its useful life. Depreciable amount is the cost of an asset less its residual value. IAS 16 stipulates that the **residual value must be reviewed at least each financial year-end** and, if expectations differ from previous estimates, any change is accounted for prospectively as a change in estimate under IAS 8 *Accounting Policies, Changes in Accounting Estimates and Errors.*

Kayte's model implies that the residual value of the vessels remains constant through the vessels' useful life. However, the **residual value should be adjusted,** particularly as the date of sale approaches and the residual value approaches proceeds of disposal less costs of disposal at the end of the asset's useful life.

Following IAS 16, if the residual value is greater than an asset's carrying amount, the depreciation charge is zero until such time as the residual value subsequently decreases to an amount below the asset's carrying amount. The residual value should be the value at the reporting date as if the vessel were already of the age and condition expected at the end of its useful life. Depreciable amount is affected by an increase in the residual value of an asset because of past events, but not by expectation of changes in future events, other than the expected effects of wear and tear.

The **useful life of the vessels (10 years) is shorter than the total life (30 years)** so it is the residual value at the end of the 10-year useful life that must be established.

Vessels kept for 30 years

Kayte **correctly uses a residual value for these vessels based upon the scrap value of steel.** The depreciable amount of the vessels is therefore the cost less the scrap value of steel, and the vessels should be depreciated over the 30-year period.

The engine is a significant part of the asset and should be depreciated separately over its useful life of ten years until the date of the next overhaul. The cost of the overhaul should be capitalised (a necessary overhaul is not considered a day-to-day servicing cost) and any carrying amount relating to the engine before overhaul should be derecognised. Generally, however, the depreciation of the original amount capitalised in respect of the engine will be **calculated to have a carrying amount of nil when the overhaul is undertaken.**

Funnels

The funnels should be identified as significant parts of the asset and depreciated across their useful lives of 15 years. As this has not occurred, it will be necessary to **determine what the carrying amount would have been had the funnels been initially separately identified.** The initial cost of the funnels can be determined by reference to replacement cost, and the associated depreciation charge determined using the rate for the vessel (over 30 years). There will therefore be a significant carrying amount to be written off at the time the replacement funnels are capitalised.

(ii)   **Property**

IAS 34 requirement

In accordance with IAS 34 *Interim Financial Reporting*, an entity must apply the same accounting policies in its interim financial statements as in its annual financial statements. Measurements should be made on a 'year to date' basis. Kayte's interim financial statements are for the six months to 30 November 20X3.

Kayte must apply the provisions of IFRS 5 *Non-Current Assets Held for Sale and Discontinued Operations* to the valuation of the property.

Application of IFRS 5

In accordance with IFRS 5, an asset held for sale should be measured at the **lower of** its **carrying amount** and **fair value less costs to sell**. Immediately before classification of the asset as held for sale, the entity must recognise impairment in accordance with applicable IFRS. Any impairment loss is generally recognised in profit or loss, but if the asset has been measured at a revalued amount under IAS 16 or IAS 38 the impairment will be treated as a revaluation decrease. **Once** the asset has been **classified as held for sale**, any **impairment loss** will be based on the **difference between the adjusted carrying amounts and the fair value less cost to sell**. The impairment loss (if any) will be **recognised in profit or loss**.

A **subsequent increase** in fair value less costs to sell may be **recognised** in profit or loss **only to the extent of any impairment previously recognised**. To summarise:

Step 1   Calculate carrying amount under the applicable accounting standard, here IAS 16:

Depreciation of $500,000 per year implies a useful life of ten years, of which eight years are remaining at 1 June 20X3. Depreciation must then be charged for the four months to 1 October 20X3, the date of classification as held for sale is calculated on the carrying amount net of the impairment loss incurred on 31 May 20X3, over the remaining useful life of eight years:

$$\frac{\$5m\,cost - \$1m\,accumulated\,depreciation - \$0.35m\,impairment}{8\text{-}year\,remaining\,useful\,life} \times 4/12$$

= $152,083 (rounded to $0.15 million)

So the carrying amount at 1 October 20X3 is $5m – $1m – $0.35m – $0.15m = $3.5 million

Step 2   Classified as held for sale. Compare the carrying amount ($3.5 million) with fair value less costs to sell ($3.4 million). Measure at the lower of carrying amount and fair value less costs to sell, here $3.4 million, giving an initial write-down of $100,000. Cease depreciation.

Step 3   Determine fair value less costs to sell at the date of the interim financial statements, 1 December 20X3, here given as $3.52 million and compare with carrying amount of $3.4 million. This gives a gain of $120,000.

The impairment previously recognised is: $350,000 + $100,000 = $450,000. The gain of $120,000 is less than this, and may therefore be credited to profit or loss, and the property is carried at $3.52 million.

Step 4   On 31 May 20X4, fair value less costs to sell is $3.95 million. The change in fair value less cost to sell is recognised but the gain recognised cannot exceed any impairment losses to date. Impairment losses to date are $350,000 + $100,000 – $120,000 = $330,000, and this is less than the change in fair value less costs to sell of $430,000 ($3.95m – $3.52m). This restricted gain of $330,000 is recognised, and the property is carried at $3.85 million ($3.52m + $330,000).

BPP
LEARNING
MEDIA

Answers   **239**

54 Pensions

Marking scheme

				Marks
(a)	Joydan	(i)	Explanation	8
		(ii)	A scheme	7
			B scheme	2
(b)	William		Provision for relocation costs	4
			Curtailment (past service cost) of defined benefit pension plan	4
				25

(a)   Briefing note for the directors of Joydan

(i)   Defined contribution plans and defined benefit plans

With **defined contribution** plans, the employer (and possibly, as here, current employees too) pay regular contributions into the plan of a given or 'defined' amount each year. The contributions are invested, and the size of the post-employment benefits paid to former employees depends on how well or how badly the plan's investments perform. If the investments perform well, the plan will be able to afford higher benefits than if the investments performed less well.

The B scheme is a defined contribution plan. The employer's liability is limited to the contributions paid.

With **defined benefit** plans, the size of the post-employment benefits is determined in advance, ie the benefits are 'defined'. The employer (and possibly, as here, current employees too) pay contributions into the plan, and the contributions are invested. The size of the contributions is set at an amount that is expected to earn enough investment returns to meet the obligation to pay the post-employment benefits. If, however, it becomes apparent that the assets in the fund are insufficient, the employer will be required to make additional contributions into the plan to make up the expected shortfall. On the other hand, if the fund's assets appear to be larger than they need to be, and in excess of what is required to pay the post-employment benefits, the employer may be allowed to take a 'contribution holiday' (ie stop paying in contributions for a while).

The **main difference** between the two types of plans lies in **who bears the risk**: if the employer bears the risk, even in a small way by guaranteeing or specifying the return, the plan is a defined benefit plan. A defined contribution scheme must give a benefit formula based solely on the amount of the contributions.

A defined benefit scheme may be created even if there is no legal obligation, if an employer has a practice of guaranteeing the benefits payable.

The A scheme is a defined benefit scheme. Joydan, the employer, guarantees a pension based on the service lives of the employees in the scheme. The company's liability is not limited to the amount of the contributions. This means that the employer bears the investment risk: if the return on the investment is not sufficient to meet the liabilities, the company will need to make good the difference.

(ii) **Accounting treatment: B scheme**

No assets or liabilities will be recognised for this defined contribution scheme, other than current liabilities to reflect amounts due to be paid to the pension scheme at year end. The **contributions** paid by the company of $10 million will be **charged to profit or loss**. The contributions paid by the employees will not be a cost to the company but will be adjusted in calculating employee's net salary.

Accounting treatment: A scheme

The accounting treatment is as follows:

STATEMENT OF PROFIT OR LOSS AND OTHER COMPREHENSIVE INCOME NOTES

Expense recognised in profit or loss for the year ended 31 October 20X7

	$m
Current service cost	20.0
Net interest on the net defined benefit liability (10 – 9.5)	0.5
Net expense	20.5

Other comprehensive income: remeasurement of defined benefit plans (for the year ended 31 October 20X7)

	$m
Remeasurement gains or losses on defined benefit obligation	(29.0)
Remeasurement gains or losses on plan assets (excluding amounts in net interest)	27.5
	(1.5)

STATEMENT OF FINANCIAL POSITION NOTES

Amounts recognised in statement of financial position

	31 October 20X7 $m	1 November 20X6 $m
Present value of defined benefit obligation	240	200
Fair value of plan assets	(225)	(190)
Net liability	15	10

Change in the present value of the defined benefit obligation

	$m
Present value of obligation at 1 November 20X6	200
Interest on obligation: 5% × 200	10
Current service cost	20
Benefits paid	(19)
Loss on remeasurement through OCI (balancing figure)	29
Present value of obligation at 31 October 20X7	240

Change in the fair value of plan assets

	$m
Fair value of plan assets at 1 November 20X6	190.0
Interest on plan assets: 5% × 190	9.5
Contributions	17.0
Benefits paid	(19.0)
Gain on remeasurement through OCI (balancing figure)	27.5
Fair value of plan assets at 31 October 20X7	225.0

(b)   Relocation costs and reduction to net pension liability

A **provision for restructuring** should be recognised in respect of the relocation of the provision during the year ended 31 May 20X3 in accordance with IAS 37 *Provisions, Contingent Liabilities and Contingent Assets*. This is because William's board of directors authorised a **detailed formal plan** for the relocation shortly before the year end (13 May 20X3) and William has **raised a valid expectation in affected employees** that it will carry out the restructuring by informing them of the main features of the plan. As the relocation is due to take within two months of the year end (July 20X3), the time value of money is likely to be immaterial. Therefore, no discounting is required and a provision should be recognised at the estimated relocation costs of $50 million. This assumes that the $50 million relocation costs are only direct expenditures arising from the restructuring which are necessarily entailed by the restructuring and are not associated with the ongoing activities of William. Specifically, the restructuring provision should not include costs relating to the relocation of continuing staff.

The reduction in the net pension liability as a result of the employees being made redundant and no longer accruing pension benefits is a **curtailment** under IAS 19 *Employee Benefits*. IAS 19 defines a curtailment as occurring when an entity significantly reduces the number of employees covered by a plan. It is **treated as a type of past service costs**. The past service cost may be negative (as is the case here) when the benefits are withdrawn so that the present value of the defined benefit obligation decreases. IAS 19 requires the past service cost to be **recognised in profit or loss** at the earlier of:

- When the plan curtailment occurs; and
- When the entity recognises the related restructuring costs.

Here the restructuring costs (and corresponding provision) are recognised in the year ended 31 May 20X3 and the plan curtailment will not take place until after the year end in July 20X3 when the employees are made redundant. Therefore, the reduction in the net pension liability and corresponding income in profit or loss should be recognised at the earlier of these two dates, ie when the restructuring costs are recognised in the year ended 31 May 20X3.

Both the relocation costs and income from the reduction in the net pension liability are likely to require **separate disclosure** in the statement of profit or loss and other comprehensive income or in the notes to the accounts per IAS 1 *Presentation of Financial Statements* due to their materiality.

55 Emcee

Workbook references. IAS 38 *Intangible Assets*, IAS 23 *Borrowing Costs* and IFRS 13 *Fair Value Measurement* are covered in Chapter 4. IFRS 5 *Non-current Assets Held for Sale and Discontinued Operations* is covered in Chapter 14 and IAS 24 *Related Party Disclosures* in Chapter 2.

Top tips. This is a multi-standard question in which the three parts are independent. You should scan read all parts of the question and attempt the part you feel most comfortable with first. The issues covered are borrowing costs (Part (a)), intangible assets, non-current assets held for sale and impairment of assets (Part (b)) and fair value measurement and related party transactions (Part (c)). The recommended approach is to discuss the general principles of the relevant standards and then apply them to the scenario. Part (b) is broken down into four elements so ensure you provide an answer to each.

Easy marks. No parts of this question are particularly easy – the main way to get the marks is to break down the scenario into its constituent parts and make sure you deal with each relevant standard.

		Marks
(a)	Discussion of IAS 23 requirements and calculation of capitalised interest – 1 mark per point to a maximum	6
(b)	Discussion of IAS 38 recognition requirements, applicability of IFRS 5 and impairment under IAS 36 – 1 mark per point to a maximum	11
(c)	Discussion of IFRS 13 and IAS 24 – 1 mark per point to a maximum	8
		25

(a) **Borrowing costs**

IAS 23 *Borrowing Costs* requires borrowing costs incurred on acquiring or constructing an asset to be **capitalised** if the asset takes a substantial period of time to be prepared for its intended use or sale. Borrowing costs should be capitalised during construction and include the costs of general borrowings which would have been avoided if the expenditure on the asset had not occurred. The general borrowing costs are determined by applying the weighted average of the borrowing costs applicable to the general pool

The weighted average carrying amount of the stadium during the period is:

$(20 + 70 + 120 + 170)m/4$, that is $95 million.

The capitalisation rate of the borrowings of Emcee during the period of construction is 9% per annum, therefore the total amount of borrowing costs to be capitalised is the weighted average carrying amount of the stadium multiplied by the capitalisation rate.

That is ($95m \times 9\% \times 4/12$) $2.85 million.

(b) **Players' registrations**

Acquisition

IAS 38 Intangible Assets states that an entity should recognise an intangible asset where it is probable that future economic benefits will flow to the entity and the cost of the asset can be measured reliably. Therefore, the **costs** associated with the acquisition of players' registrations should be **capitalised at the fair value of the consideration payable**. Costs would include transfer fees, league levy fees, agents' fees incurred by the club and other directly attributable costs. Costs also **include the fair value of any contingent consideration**, which is primarily payable to the player's former club with associated league levy fees, once payment becomes probable. Subsequent reassessments of the amount of contingent consideration payable would be also included in the cost of the player's registration. The estimate of the fair value of the contingent consideration payable requires management to assess the likelihood of specific performance conditions being met, which would trigger the payment of the contingent consideration. This assessment would be carried out on an individual player basis. The additional amount of contingent consideration potentially payable, in excess of the amounts included in the cost of players' registrations, would be disclosed. Amounts capitalised would be fully amortised over the period covered by the player's contract.

Extension

Where a playing contract is extended, any **costs associated with securing the extension are added to the unamortised carrying amount** at the date of the extension and the revised carrying amount is amortised over the remaining revised contract life.

Sale of registrations

Player registrations would be classified as assets held for sale under IFRS 5 Non-Current Assets Held for Sale and Discontinued Operations when their **carrying amount is expected to be recovered principally through a sale** transaction and a sale is considered to be highly probable. Additionally, the registrations should be actively marketed by Emcee, which it appears that they are. It would appear that in these circumstances that management is committed to a plan to sell the registration, that the asset is available for immediate sale, that an active programme to locate a buyer is initiated by circulating clubs. IFRS 5 requires that it is unlikely that the plan to sell the registrations will be significantly changed or withdrawn. In order to fulfil the last criteria of IFRS 5, it may be prudent to only class these registrations as held for sale where unconditional offers have been received prior to a period end.

However, because of the subjectivity involved, in the case of player registrations these assets would be stated at the lower of the carrying amount and fair value less costs to sell, as the carrying amount will already be stated in accordance with IFRSs.

Gains and losses on disposal of players' registrations would be determined by comparing the fair value of the consideration receivable, net of any transaction costs, with the carrying amount and would be recognised in profit or loss within profit on disposal of players' registrations. Where a part of the consideration receivable is contingent on specified performance conditions, this amount is recognised in profit or loss when the conditions are met.

The player registrations disposed of, subsequent to the year end, for $25 million, with an associated net book value of $7 million, would be disclosed as events after the reporting date.

Impairment review

IAS 36 Impairment of Assets states that entities should annually **test their assets for impairment**. An asset is impaired if its carrying amount exceeds its recoverable amount which is the higher of the asset's fair value less costs of disposal and its value in use. It is difficult to determine the value in use of an individual player in isolation as that player (unless via a sale or insurance recovery) cannot generate cash flows on his own. Whilst any individual player cannot really be separated from the single cash-generating unit (CGU), being the basketball or football team, there may be certain circumstances where a player is taken out of the CGU, when it becomes clear that they will not play for the club again. If such circumstances arise, the **carrying amount of the player should be assessed against the best estimate of the player's fair value less any costs to sell and an impairment charge made in profit or loss**, which reflects any loss arising.

(c) **Valuation of stadiums**

IFRS 13 *Fair Value Measurement* would value the stadiums at the **price which would be received to sell the asset in an orderly transaction between market participants** at the measurement date. The price would be the one which **maximises the value of the asset** or the group of assets using the principal of the highest and best use. The price would essentially use Level 2 inputs which are inputs other than quoted market prices included within Level 1 which are observable for the asset or liability, either directly or indirectly. Property naming rights present complications when valuing property. The status of the property dictates its suitability for inviting sponsorship attached to its name. It has nothing to do with the property itself but this can be worth a significant amount. Therefore, Emcee could **include the property naming rights in the valuation** of the stadiums and write it off over three years.

IAS 24 *Related Party Disclosures* sets out the criteria for two entities to be treated as related parties. Such criteria include being members of the same group or where a person or a close member of that person's family is related to a reporting entity if that person has control or joint control over the reporting entity. IAS 24 deems that parties are not related simply because they have a director or key manager in common. In this case, there are **two directors in common** and it appears as though the **entities are not related**. However, the regulator will need to establish whether the **sponsorship deal is a related party transaction** (RPT) for the purpose of the financial control provisions. There would need to be demonstrated that the airline may be expected to influence, or be influenced by, the club or a related party of the club. If the deal is deemed to be an RPT, the regulator will consider whether the sponsorship is at fair value.

56 Estoil

> **Workbook reference.** Impairment is covered in Chapter 4 of your Workbook.
>
> **Top tips.** IAS 36 is brought forward knowledge from earlier studies, however, in SBR the depth of discussion required is greater, and the scenario requires more thought. Part (a) required a discussion of factors to take account of in conducting an impairment test. There are five factors provided in the question and you should use these as headings under which to structure your answer. The discussion required drew on your financial management knowledge (eg WACC).
>
> **Easy marks.** There are no obvious easy marks in this question.

Marking scheme

			Marks
(a)	Changes in circumstances	3	
	Market capitalisation	2	
	Allocating goodwill	2	
	Valuation issues	6	
	Disclosures	2	
			15
(b)	Discount rate	5	
	Cash flow forecast	5	
			10
			25

(a) Entities must determine, **at each reporting date,** whether there are any indications that impairment has occurred. Indicators of impairment may be internal or external. The following factors need to be considered when conducting an impairment test under IAS 36 *Impairment of Assets.*

    (i)   **Changes in circumstances in the reporting period**

        Circumstances may change due to internal factors, for example matters as physical damage, adverse changes to the methods of use of the asset, management restructuring and over-estimation of cash flows, and external factors, such as **adverse changes** in the **markets** or **business** in which the asset is used, or adverse changes to the **technological, economic or legal environment** of the business.

        If such indicators come to light between the date of the impairment test and the end of the next reporting period, **more than one impairment test may be required** in the accounting period. In addition, tests for impairment of goodwill and some other intangible assets may be performed at any time during the accounting period, provided it is performed at the same time each year. Not all goodwill is tested at the year end – some entities test it at an interim period. Should impairment indicators arise after the annual impairment test has been performed, it may be necessary to test goodwill for impairment again at the year end.

        A possible indicator of impairment is volatility in the market, for example, sharp changes in commodity prices may cause the assets of mining and energy companies to be impaired. In such cases, the assets affected should be tested in the interim period.

BPP LEARNING MEDIA

(ii)   **Market capitalisation**

A strong indicator of impairment is when the **carrying amount** of an entity's assets exceeds the entity's **market capitalisation,** suggesting that the entity is overvalued. However, there **may not be a direct correlation** between the market capitalisation and the impairment loss arising from a lower return generated on the entity's assets –the market may have taken other factors into account. The discrepancy does, however, **highlight the need for the entity to examine its cash-generating units, and possibly to test goodwill for impairment**. The reason for the shortfall must be examined and understood, even though IAS 36 does not require a formal reconciliation between an entity's market capitalisation, its fair value less costs to sell and its value in use.

(iii)   **Allocating goodwill to cash-generating units**

Goodwill arising on an acquisition is required to be allocated to each of the acquirer's cash-generating units (CGUs), or to a group of CGUs, that are expected to benefit from the synergies of the combination. If **CGUs are subsequently revised or operations disposed of, IAS 36 requires goodwill to be reallocated, based on relative values, to the units affected.**

The difficulty with this is that IAS 36 **does not give guidance as to what is meant by relative value.** While **fair value less costs to sell** (FVLCS) could be used, this is not mandated by the standard. However, the entity may still need to carry out a valuation process on the part retained. **Value in use** (VIU) is a possibility, but the measure needs to be one that can be applied equally to both the part retained and the part disposed of. VIU has the obvious problem that it will be much the same as FVLCS for the operations disposed of, but there could be significant differences between VIU and FVLCS for the part retained. Alternatively, there could be reasonable ways of estimating relative value by using an **appropriate industry or business surrogate**, for example revenue, profits, industry KPIs.

(iv)   **Valuation issues**

The basic principle of IAS 36 is that an asset should be carried at no more than its recoverable amount, that is the amount to be recovered through use or sale of the asset. If an **asset's value is higher than its recoverable amount,** an **impairment loss** has occurred. The impairment loss should be **written off** against profit or loss for the year.

The **recoverable amount is defined** as the **higher of the asset's fair value less costs of disposal** and the asset's **value in use.** Measuring both of these requires the use of **estimates and assumptions,** some of which **may be problematic.**

(1)   **Fair value less costs of disposal** is defined as the price that would be received to sell the asset in an orderly transaction between market participants at the measurement date under current market conditions, net of costs of disposal. IAS 36 gives a 'hierarchy of evidence' for this, with 'price in a binding sale agreement' at the top, only likely to be available if the asset is held for sale, and allowing, in the absence of any active market, estimates based on **a discounted cash flow (DCF) model, which may not be reliable.**

(2)   Determining the types of **future cash flows which should be included in the measurement of VIU can also be difficult.** Under IAS 36 an asset or CGU must be tested in its current status, not the status that management wishes it was in or hopes to get it into in the near future. Therefore, the standard requires VIU to be measured at the net present value of the future cash flows the entity expects to derive from the asset or CGU in its current condition over its remaining useful life. This means that it is not appropriate to take account of management plans for enhancing the performance of the asset or CGU, even though these may bring about an increase in value.

(3) While the cash flows used in testing for impairment are specific to the entity, the **discount rate is supposed to appropriately reflect the current market assessment of the time value of money and the risks specific to the asset or cash-generating unit**. When a specific rate for an asset or cash-generating unit is not directly available from the market, which is usually the case, the discount rate to be used is a surrogate. An estimate should be made of a **pre-tax rate that reflects the current market assessment of the time value of money and the risks specific to the asset** that have **not been adjusted** for in the estimate of future cash flows. According to IAS 36, this rate is the return that the investors would require if they chose an investment that would generate cash flows of amounts, timing and risk profile equivalent to those that the entity expects to derive from the assets.

Rates that should be considered are the entity's weighted average cost of capital (WACC), the entity's incremental borrowing rate or other market rates. The objective must be to obtain a rate which is sensible and justifiable.

(4) The test is further complicated by the **impact of taxation**. IAS 36 requires that VIU be measured using pre-tax cash flows and a pre-tax discount rate, but WACC is a post-tax rate, as are most observable equity rates used by valuers.

(5) There is a need for **consistency in determining the recoverable amount and carrying amount which are being compared**. For example, in the case of pensions, there can be significant differences between the measurement basis of the pension asset or (more likely) liability and the cash flows that relate to pensions.

(6) IAS 36 requires that **corporate assets** must be allocated to a cash-generating unit on a 'reasonable and consistent basis, but does not expand on this.

(v) **Disclosures**

With regard to the impairment loss recognised in respect of each cash-generating unit, IAS 36 would disclosure of:

(1) The amount of the loss
(2) The events and circumstances that led to the loss
(3) A description of the impairment loss by class of asset

It is **no defence** to maintain that this information was **common knowledge in the market**. The disclosures are still needed.

(b) (i) **Discount rate**

Estoil has **not complied with IAS 36** *Impairment of Assets* in its use of one discount rate for all cash-generating units (CGUs) regardless of the currency of the country in which the cash flows are generated. IAS 36 requires that **future cash flows must be estimated in the currency in which they will be generated** and then discounted using a discount rate appropriate for that currency. The present value thus calculated must be **translated using the spot exchange rate at the date of the value in use calculation.**

The currency in which the estimated cash flows are denominated has an impact on many of the inputs to the weighted average cost of capital (WACC) calculation, including the risk-free interest rate. **Estoil was incorrect in using the ten-year government bond rate for its own jurisdiction** as the risk-free rate because government bond rates differ between countries due to different expectations about future inflation, and so there may be a discrepancy between the expected inflation reflected in the estimated cash flows and the risk-free rate.

IAS 36 requires that the **discount rate should appropriately reflect the current market assessment of the time value of money and the risks specific to the asset or cash-generating unit.** Applying one discount rate for all the CGUs does not achieve this. The WACC of the CGU or of the company of which the CGU is currently part should generally be used to determine the discount rate. The company's WACC may only be used for all CGUs if the risks associated with the individual CGUs do not materially diverge from the remainder of the group, and this is **not evident** in the case of Estoil.

(ii)   Cash flow forecasts

IAS 36 requires that any cash flow projections are based upon **reasonable and supportable assumptions** over a maximum period of five years unless it can be proven that longer estimates are reliable. The assumptions should **represent management's best estimate of the range of economic conditions expected to obtain over the remaining useful life of the asset.** Management must also assess the reasonableness of the assumptions by examining the reasons for any differences between past forecasted cash flows and actual cash flows. **The assumptions that form the basis for current cash flow projections must be consistent with past actual outcomes.**

Fariole has **failed to comply** with the requirements of IAS 36 in the preparation of its cash flow forecasts. Although the realised cash flow **forecasts for 20X4 were negative** and well below projected cash flows, **the directors significantly increased budgeted cash flows for 20X5.** This increase was **not justified**, and casts doubts on Fariole's ability to budget realistically.

IAS 36 requires estimates of future cash flows to include:

(1)   Projections of cash inflows from the continuing use of the asset

(2)   Projections of cash outflows which are necessarily incurred to generate the cash inflows from continuing use of the asset

(3)   Net cash flows to be received (or paid) for the disposal of the asset at the end of its useful life

Forecast cash outflows must include those relating to the day-to-day servicing of the asset. This will **include future cash outflows needed to maintain the level of economic benefits expected to be generated by the asset in its current condition.** Fariole has not taken into account expected changes in working capital and capital expenditure, but it is very likely that investments in working capital and capital expenditure would be necessary to maintain the assets of the CGUs in their current condition.

In conclusion, the **cash flow forecasts used by Fariole are not in accordance with** IAS 36.

57 Evolve

Workbook references. IAS 32 *Financial Instruments: Presentation* and IFRS 9 *Financial Instruments* are covered in Chapter 8. IFRS 5 *Non-current Assets Held for Sale and Discontinued Operations* is covered in Chapter 14. IAS 16 *Property, Plant and Equipment* and IAS 40 *Investment Property* are covered in Chapter 4 and IAS 12 *Income Taxes* in Chapter 7.

Top tips. Part (a) is tricky. It asks how the potential payment of cash in the future to equity shareholders should be classified. It had to be classified as a financial liability as there was a contractual obligation to deliver cash as a result of a put option to sell the rights back to the company. An event after the reporting period provided additional evidence of the valuation and should therefore be treated as an adjusting event. Part (b) is more mainstream. The directors had not classified the assets of a subsidiary as held for sale, even though the IFRS 5 criteria were met, on the grounds that they did not have a binding agreement to sell. However, this is not required for a sale to be considered 'highly probable' under IFRS 5, and so the assets should have been classified as held for sale. Part (c) required consideration of three issues. First, a gain arising where a subsidiary which was purchased at less than the market value of its sole asset should not be treated as a bargain purchase because this treatment is only available for a business combination, and the substance of the transaction was the purchase of an asset rather than a business combination. Second, the company wishes to use the cost model, the asset should have been recorded at cost, even if this is less than market value, so the potential gain should not have been recorded in profit or loss or added to the cost of the asset. Third, the deferred tax liability arising on the difference from market value should not be capitalised as it is not linked to bringing the asset to the condition necessary for its operations,

Easy marks. There are no easy marks in this question. Marks are not as difficult to earn in Part (b), as opposed to Parts (a) or (c).

		Marks
(a)	1 mark per point up to maximum	9
(b)	1 mark per point up to maximum	10
(c)	1 mark per point up to maximum	6
		25

(a) **Obligation to purchase own equity instruments**

A financial liability for the present value of the maximum amount payable to shareholders should be recognised in the financial statements as of 31 August 20X6. At 31 August 20X6, the rights are equivalent to a written put option because they represent for Evolve a purchase obligation which gives shareholders the right to sell the entity's own equity instruments for a fixed price. The fundamental principle of IAS 32 *Financial Instruments: Presentation* is that a financial instrument should be classified as either a financial liability or an equity instrument according to the substance of the contract, not its legal form, and the definitions of financial liability and equity instrument. IAS 32 states that a contract which contains an entity's obligation to purchase its own equity instruments gives rise to a financial liability, which should be recognised at the present value of its redemption amount. IAS 32 also states that a contractual obligation for an entity to purchase its own equity instruments gives rise to a financial liability for the present value of the redemption amount even if the obligation is conditional on the counterparty exercising a right to redeem, as is the case with the scrip issue of Evolve.

Evolve had set up the conditions for the share capital increase in August 20X6 and, therefore, the contract gave rise to financial liabilities from that date and Evolve should have recognised a financial liability for the present value of the maximum amount payable to shareholders in its financial statements for the year ended 31 August 20X6. A non-adjusting event under IAS 10 *Events After the Reporting Period* is an event after the reporting period which is indicative of a condition which arose after the end of the reporting period. However, it could be argued that the transferring of the free allocation rights back to Evolve is in fact an adjusting event as it is an event after the reporting period which provides further evidence of conditions which existed at the end of the reporting period.

(b) **Classification as held for sale**

The non-current assets of Resource should have been presented as held for sale in the financial statements, in accordance with IFRS 5 *Non-current Assets Held for Sale and Discontinued Operations*, as at 31 August 20X6. IFRS 5 states that the appropriate level of management must be committed to a plan to sell the asset for the sale to be probable. Evolve's acceptance of a binding offer in August 20X6 and the publication of this information indicated a high probability of sale. Despite the uncertainties surrounding the sale, the transaction remained highly probable at 31 August 20X6. IFRS 5 requires an entity to classify a non-current asset as held for sale if its carrying amount will be recovered principally through sale rather than through continuing use.

IFRS 5 does not require the existence of a binding sales agreement in order to classify a non-current asset as held for sale but only a high probability of its occurrence. The acceptance of an offer by Evolve indicates that the transaction met the criteria to be classified as held for sale at 31 August 20X6. The finalisation of the agreement on 20 September 20X6 only confirmed the situation existing at 31 August 20X6. Further, Evolve cannot apply IFRS 5 measurement criteria without classifying the item as held for sale in its statement of financial position particularly as a profit or impairment may arise when using such criteria. IFRS 5 also states that immediately before the initial classification of the asset as held for sale, the carrying amount of the asset should be measured in accordance with applicable IFRSs. This was already the case as regards the non-current assets of Resource.

Other criteria which indicate that the non-current assets should be shown as held for sale include the fact that a buyer for the non-current assets has been found, the sale occurred within 12 months of classification as held for sale, the asset was actively marketed for sale at a sales price which has been accepted, and despite the uncertainties at 31 August 20X6, events after the reporting period indicate that the contract was not significantly changed or withdrawn. The fact that the information regarding the uncertainties was not publicly disclosed is irrelevant.

Thus, as the non-current assets met the criteria to be classified as held for sale, they should have been measured and presented as such in the financial statements. Assets classified as held for sale must be presented separately on the face of the statement of financial position.

(c)   **Investment property**

IFRS 3 *Business Combinations* must be applied when accounting for business combinations, but does not apply where the acquisition is not of a business. In this case, the acquisition was essentially that of an asset and therefore the measurement requirements of IFRS 3 would not apply.

IAS 40 *Investment Property* states that the cost of an investment property comprises its purchase price and any directly attributable expenditure, such as professional fees for legal services. IAS 16 *Property, Plant and Equipment* states that the cost of an item of PPE comprises any cost directly attributable to bringing the asset to the condition necessary for it to be capable of operating in the manner intended by management. Hence if Evolve wishes to use the cost basis for accounting for the investment property, the potential gain should not have been recorded in profit or loss or added to the cost of the asset.

Evolve should have recognised the tax payment as an expense in the statement of profit or loss and other comprehensive income. Administrative and other general overhead costs are not costs of an item of PPE according to IAS 16. The specific fiscal treatment and the tax to be paid were not linked to bringing the asset to the condition necessary for its operations, as the asset would have been operational without the tax. As such, the tax is a cost linked to the activity of Evolve and should be accounted for as an expense in accordance with IAS 12 *Income Taxes* and included in the profit or loss for the period, unless that tax arises from a transaction recognised outside profit or loss.

58 Gasnature

Workbook references. IFRS 9 *Financial Instruments* is covered in Chapter 8, IFRS 11 *Joint Arrangements* in Chapter 15 and IAS 10 *Events after the Reporting Period* in Chapter 6.

Top tips. Part (a) is a good example of applying mainstream syllabus topics (IAS 16) to an unusual situation ('irrecoverable gas'). Part (b) on 'own use' contracts has come up before, and the case could be argued either way. There were marks available for dealing with fundamental principles of whether the contract is a financial contract or an executory contract. If the arguments seem complex, the good news is that there are only six marks for this part of the question, and you can make up the marks in Part (c), which is more mainstream.

Easy marks. Part (c) is relatively straightforward, and you should by now be familiar with the IFRS 11 criteria for distinguishing joint ventures from joint operations.

			Marks
(a)	1 mark per point up to maximum		9
(b)	1 mark per point up to maximum		6
(c)	(i)	1 mark per point up to maximum	5
	(ii)	1 mark per point up to maximum	5
			25

(a) **Joint arrangement**

The classification of a joint arrangement as a joint operation or a joint venture depends upon the rights and obligations of the parties to the arrangement (IFRS 11 *Joint Arrangements*). A joint arrangement occurs where two or more parties have joint control. The contractually agreed sharing of control of an arrangement exists only when decisions about the relevant activities require the unanimous consent of the parties sharing control. The structure and form of the arrangement determines the nature of the relationship. However, regardless of the purpose, structure or form of the arrangement, the classification of joint arrangements depends upon the parties' rights and obligations arising from the arrangement. A joint arrangement which is not structured through a separate vehicle is a joint operation. In such cases, the contractual arrangement establishes the parties' rights and obligations. A joint operator accounts for the assets, liabilities, revenues and expenses relating to its involvement in a joint operation in accordance with the relevant IFRSs. The arrangement with Gogas is a joint operation as there is no separate vehicle involved and they have agreed to share services and costs with decisions regarding the platform requiring unanimous agreement of the parties. Gasnature should recognise its share of the asset as property, plant and equipment.

Under IAS 16 *Property, Plant and Equipment* (PPE), the cost of an item of property, plant and equipment includes the initial estimate of the present value of dismantling and removing the item and restoring the site on which it is located. IAS 37 *Provisions, Contingent Liabilities and Contingent Assets* contains requirements on how to measure decommissioning, restoration and similar liabilities. Where the effect of the time value of money is material, the amount of a provision should be the present value of the expenditures expected to be required to settle the obligation. Thus costs incurred by an entity in respect of obligations for dismantling, removing and restoring the site on which an item of property, plant and equipment is located are recognised and measured in accordance with IAS 16 and IAS 37. Gasnature should recognise 55% of the cost of decommissioning the underground storage facility. However, because Gasnature is a joint operator, there is also a contingent liability for 45% of the decommissioning costs and there is a possible obligation for the remainder of the costs depending on whether some uncertain future event occurs, that is Gogas goes into liquidation and cannot fund the decommissioning costs. Therefore Gasnature, should also disclose a contingent liability relating to the Gogas's share of the obligation to the extent that it is contingently liable for Gogas's share.

IAS 16 states that property, plant and equipment are tangible items which:

(i) Are held for use in the production or supply of goods or services, for rental to others, or for administrative purposes; and

(ii) Are expected to be used during more than one period.

Thus Gasnature should classify and account for its share of the irrecoverable gas as PPE. The irrecoverable gas is necessary for the storage facility to perform its function. It is therefore part of the storage facility and should be capitalised as a component of the storage facility asset. The irrecoverable gas should be depreciated to its residual value over the life of the storage facility. However, if the gas is recoverable in full when the storage facility is decommissioned, then depreciation will be recorded against the irrecoverable gas component only if the estimated residual value of the gas decreases below cost during the life of the facility. When the storage facility is decommissioned and the cushion gas extracted and sold, the sale of the irrecoverable gas is accounted for as the disposal of an item of PPE in accordance with IAS 16 and the gain or loss recognised in profit or loss. The natural gas in excess of the irrecoverable gas which is injected into the facility should be treated as inventory in accordance with IAS 2 *Inventories*.

(b) **Contract with Agas**

IFRS 9 *Financial Instruments* applies to those contracts to buy or sell a non-financial item which can be settled net in cash with the exception of contracts which are held for the purpose of the receipt or delivery of a non-financial item in accordance with the entity's expected purchase, sale or usage requirements (own use contract). In other words, it will result in physical delivery of the commodity, in this case the extra gas. Contracts which are for an entity's 'own use' are exempt from the requirements of IFRS 9. Such a contract can be irrevocably designated as measured at fair value through profit or loss even if it was entered into for the above purpose. This designation is available only at inception of the contract and only if it eliminates or significantly reduces a recognition inconsistency (sometimes referred to as an 'accounting mismatch') which would otherwise arise from not recognising that contract because it is excluded from the scope of IFRS 9. There are various ways in which a contract to buy or sell a non-financial item can be settled net in cash or another financial instrument or by exchanging financial instruments. These include the following:

(i) When the terms of the contract permit either party to settle it net in cash

(ii) When the ability to settle net in cash is not explicit in the terms of the contract, but the entity has a practice of settling similar contracts net in cash

(iii) When, for similar contracts, the entity has a practice of taking delivery of the underlying and selling it within a short period after delivery, for the purpose of generating a profit

(iv) When the non-financial item which is the subject of the contract is readily convertible to cash

A written option to buy or sell a non-financial item which can be settled net in cash is within the scope of IFRS 9. Such a contract cannot be entered into for the purpose of the receipt or delivery of the non-financial item in accordance with the entities expected purchase, sale or usage requirements. Contracts to buy or sell a non-financial item, such as a commodity, which can be settled net in cash or another financial instrument, or by exchanging financial instruments, are within the scope of IFRS 9. They are accounted for as derivatives. A level of judgement will be required in this area as net settlements caused by unique events beyond management's control may not necessarily prevent the entity from applying the 'own use' exemption to all similar contracts.

The contract entered into by Gasnature with Agas seems to be an own use contract which falls outside IFRS 9 and therefore would be treated as an executory contract. However, it could be argued that the contract is net settled because the penalty mechanism requires Agas to compensate Gasnature at the current prevailing market price. Further, if natural gas is readily convertible into cash in the location where the delivery takes place, the contract could be considered net settled. Additionally, if there is volume flexibility, then the contract could be regarded as a written option, which falls within the scope of IFRS 9.

However, the contract will probably still qualify as 'own use' as long as it has been entered into and continues to be held for the expected counterparties' sales/usage requirements. Additionally, the entity has not irrevocably designated the contract as measured at fair value through profit or loss, thus adding weight to the 'own use' designation.

(c) (i) It is not acceptable to accrue the costs of the overhaul. The entity does not have a constructive obligation to undertake the overhaul. Under IFRS, costs related to major inspection and overhaul are recognised as part of the carrying amount of property, plant and equipment if they meet the asset recognition criteria in IAS 16 *Property, Plant and Equipment*. The major overhaul component will then be depreciated on a straight-line basis over its useful life (ie over the period to the next overhaul) and any remaining carrying amount will be derecognised when the next overhaul is performed. Costs of the day-to-day servicing of the asset (ie routine maintenance) are expensed as incurred. Therefore, the cost of the overhaul should have been identified as a separate component of the refinery at initial recognition and depreciated over a period of two years. This will result in the same amount of expense being recognised in profit or loss over the same period as the proposal to create a provision.

(ii) Since there were no indicators of impairment at the period end, all costs incurred up to 31 August 20X5 amounting to $5 million should remain capitalised by the entity in the financial statements for the year ended on that date. However, if material, disclosure should be provided in the financial statements of the additional activity during the subsequent period which determined the exploratory drilling was unsuccessful. This represents a non-adjusting event as defined by IAS 10 *Events After the Reporting Period* as an event which is indicative of a condition which arose after the end of the reporting period. The asset of $5 million and additional drilling costs of $2 million incurred subsequently would be expensed in the following year's financial statements.

59 Complexity

Workbook references. Financial instruments are covered in Chapter 8.

Top tips. This is a largely discursive question relating to financial instruments, focusing on the perceived problems with accounting for financial instruments. It requires understanding of IFRS 9 and IFRS 13, as well as an awareness of current issues around financial instruments.

Easy marks. The calculation is a good source of easy marks as it is straightforward. And there are marks for bookwork – listing the problems of complexity and advantages of fair value.

Marking scheme

			Marks	
(a)	(i)	Identical payment	2	
		Carrying amount	2	
		Fair value	2	
				6
	(ii)	Hedging discussion	5	
		Effectiveness discussion	4	
				9
(b)	(i)	1 mark per point up to maximum	6	
	(ii)	1 mark per point up to maximum	4	
				10
				25

(a) (i) IFRS 9 *Financial Instruments* requires an entity to value its financial liabilities at **amortised cost** with an option to designate them as measured at **fair value through profit or loss** if it reduces or eliminates an accounting mismatch or because a group of liabilities is managed and its performance evaluated on a fair value basis. The accounting treatment applied will impact on how the initial and new loans are measured and at what carrying amount they are presented within the financial statements.

The carrying amounts under the amortised cost and fair value methods are calculated as follows:

Amortised cost

Using amortised cost, both the initial loan and the new loan result in **single payments that are almost identical** on 30 November 20X9:

Initial loan: $47m × 1.05 for 5 years = $59.98m

New loan: $45m × 1.074 for 4 years = $59.89m

However, the **carrying amounts at 30 November 20X5 will be different:**

Initial loan: $47m + ($47m × 0.05) = $49.35m

New loan: $45m

Fair value

If the two loans were carried at fair value, both **the initial loan and the new loan would have the same carrying amount,** and be carried at $45 million at 30 November 20X5. This is because both loans result in a single repayment of $59 million on 30 November 20X9 and so are effectively worth the same amount. As the second loan was obtained on 30 November 20X5, the fair value of a loan with repayment of $59 million on 30 November 20X9 must be the amount borrowed at the market rate on that date, ie $45 million. There would be a net profit of $2 million, made up of the interest expense of $47m × 5% = $2.35m and the unrealised gain of $49.35m − $45m = $4.35m.

(ii) **Hedge accounting**

IFRS 9 *Financial Instruments* allows hedge accounting but only if **all** of the following **conditions** are met.

(i) The hedging relationship consists **only of eligible hedging instruments and eligible hedged items.**

(ii) There must be **formal documentation** (including identification of the hedged item, the hedging instrument, the nature of the risk that is to be hedged and how the entity will assess the hedging instrument's effectiveness in offsetting the exposure to changes in the hedged item's fair value or cash flows attributable to the hedged risk).

(iii) The hedging relationship meets all of the IFRS 9 hedge effectiveness criteria.

IFRS 9 defines **hedge effectiveness** as the degree to which changes in the fair value or cash flows of the hedged item attributable to a hedged risk are offset by changes in the fair value or cash flows of the hedging instrument. The directors of Complexity have asked whether hedge effectiveness can be calculated. IFRS 9 uses an **objective-based assessment** for hedge effectiveness, under which the following criteria must be met.

(i) There is an **economic relationship** between the hedged item and the hedging instrument, ie the hedging instrument and the hedged item have values that generally move in the opposite direction because of the same risk, which is the hedged risk;

(ii) The **effect of credit risk does not dominate the value** changes that result from that economic relationship, ie the gain or loss from credit risk does not frustrate the effect of changes in the underlying item on the value of the hedging instrument or the hedged item, even if those changes were significant; and

(iii) The **hedge ratio of the hedging relationship** (quantity of hedging instrument vs quantity of hedged item) is the same as that resulting from the quantity of the hedged item that the entity **actually hedges** and the quantity of the hedging instrument that the entity **actually uses** to hedge that quantity of hedged item.

(b) (i) IFRS 9 *Financial Instruments* provides a model for the classification and measurement of financial instruments that is based on principles and the entity's underlying business model. Many users find financial instruments to be complex often due to the nature of the financial instruments themselves and the **many different ways in which they can be measured**. The measurement method depends on:

(1) The **applicable financial reporting standard.** A variety of IFRS Standards apply to the measurement of financial instruments. For example, financial assets may be measured using consolidation for subsidiaries (IFRS 10), the equity method for associates and joint ventures (IAS 28 and IFRS 11) or IFRS 9 for most other financial assets.

(2) The **categorisation of the financial instrument.** IFRS 9 classifies financial assets as measured at **amortised cost, fair value through profit or loss or fair value through other comprehensive income** A financial asset may only be classified as measured at amortised cost if the object of the business model in which it is held is to collect contracted cash flows and its contractual terms give rise on specified dates to cash flows that are solely payments of principal and interest. Financial liabilities are generally accounted for at amortised cost but may be accounted for under the fair value model as was shown in (a)(i).

(3) Whether **hedge accounting** has been applied. As was discussed in (a)(ii), hedge accounting is **complex**, for example when cash flow hedge accounting is used, gains and losses may be split between profit or loss for the year and other comprehensive income (items that may subsequently be reclassified to profit or loss). In addition, there may be mismatches when hedge accounting applies reflecting the underlying mismatches under the non-hedging rules.

Some measurement methods use an estimate of **current value, and others use historical cost.** Some include impairment losses, others do not.

The different measurement methods for financial instruments creates a number of **problems for preparers and users** of accounts:

(1) The treatment of a particular instrument **may not be the best**, but may be determined by other factors.

(2) Gains or losses resulting from different measurement methods may be combined in the same line item in the statement of profit or loss and other comprehensive income. **Comparability** is therefore compromised.

(3) Comparability is also affected when it is **not clear** what measurement method has been used.

(4) It is **difficult to apply the criteria** for deciding which instrument is to be measured in which way. As new types of instruments are created, the criteria may be applied in ways that are not consistent.

(ii)   The accountant's suggestion that information relating to financial instruments is too complex to disclose is not a good enough reason to avoid making disclosures in the financial statements. IFRS 7 *Financial Instruments: Disclosure* requires extensive disclosures that will enable the users of financial statements to better understand the quantitative effects of financial instruments (the numbers within the financial statements) and to evaluate the nature and extent of risks that arise from financial instruments and how Complexity manages those risks. That is not to say that all information relating to financial instruments needs to be disclosed and it is important that the accountant focuses on making material disclosures only.

Practice Statement 2 clarifies that if information provided by a disclosure could not reasonably be expected to influence the decisions users make based on the financial statements, then that disclosure need not be made. The assessment of materiality needs to be made from a quantitative perspective first and then any qualitative factors should be considered.

The reporting accountant should not view the requirements of IFRS 7 as a prescriptive list of items that must be disclosed. They must apply judgement to assess what requires disclosure and present it in a manner that will be of benefit to the users of the financial statements.

60 Carsoon

Workbook references. Leases are covered in Chapter 9, financial instruments in Chapter 8 and revenue in Chapter 3. Fair value is covered in Chapter 4.

Top tips. Allocate your time appropriately across this three-part question. The parts are independent of each other so you should scan read all parts and attempt the one you feel most comfortable with first. The key to Part (a) is to understand that Carsoon is the lessor, not the lessee and therefore the distinction between finance leases and operating leases applies. Part (b) asks you to advise on measurement issues for a financial instrument. The calculation is straightforward if you have understood the principles; if not, you would be advised to briefly state the measurement principles of IFRS 13 as far as you can and move on quickly to another part of the question. Part (c) of the question, on contractual revenue, is challenging as it gets into the specific detail of IFRS 15, but it is a topical area you should be familiar with. Ensure you breakdown your response to cover each element.

Easy marks. Part (a) contains generous marks for using the information in the question to explain how to classify Carsoon's vehicle leases in the context of IFRS 16. Parts (b) and (c) are more challenging but Part (c) contains some easy marks if you know that the general administration costs and the wasted materials costs should be expensed.

		Marks
(a)	Classification of lease as operating lease not finance lease, accounting requirements for lease payments and assets and cash flow implications – 1 mark per point up to maximum	9
(b)	Type of financial asset, IFRS 13 requirements, account for financial asset – 1 mark per point up to maximum	8
(c)	Discuss each of penalties, counter claim and additional costs 1 mark per point up to maximum	8
		25

(a)   Under IFRS 16 *Leases*, **Carsoon is a lessor** and must classify each lease as an operating or finance lease. A lease is classified as a finance lease if it transfers substantially all of the risks and rewards incidental to ownership of the underlying asset. All other leases are classified as operating leases. Classification is made at the inception of the lease. Whether a lease is a finance lease or an operating lease depends on the **substance of the transaction** rather than the form.

In this case, the **leases are operating leases**. The lease is unlikely to transfer ownership of the vehicle to the lessee by the end of the lease term as the option to purchase the vehicle is at a price which is higher than fair value at the end of the lease term. The lease term is not for the major part of the economic life of the asset as vehicles normally have a length of life of more than three years and the maximum unpenalised mileage is 10,000 miles per annum. Additionally, the present value of the minimum lease payments is unlikely to be substantially all of the fair value of the leased asset as the price which the customer can purchase the vehicle is above market value, hence the lessor does not appear to have received an acceptable return by the end of the lease. Carsoon also stipulates the maximum mileage and maintains the vehicles. This would appear to indicate that the risks and rewards remain with Carsoon.

Carsoon should account for the leased vehicles as property, plant and equipment (PPE) under IAS 16 *Property, Plant and Equipment* and depreciate them taking into account the expected residual value. The rental payments should go to profit or loss on a straight-line basis over the lease term. Where an item of PPE ceases to be rented and becomes held for sale, it should be transferred to inventory at its carrying amount. The proceeds from the sale of such assets should be recognised as revenue in accordance with IFRS 15 *Revenue from Contracts with Customers*.

IAS 7 *Statement of Cash Flows* states that payments from operating activities are primarily derived from the principal revenue-producing activities of the entity. Therefore, they generally result from the transactions and other events which enter into the determination of profit or loss. Therefore, cash receipts from the disposal of assets formerly held for rental and subsequently held for sale should be treated as cash flows from operating activities and not investing activities.

(b)   For financial assets which are debt instruments measured at fair value through other comprehensive income (FVOCI), both amortised cost and fair value information are relevant because debt instruments in this measurement category are held for both the collection of contractual cash flows and the realisation of fair values. Therefore, debt instruments measured at FVOCI are measured at **fair value** in the **statement of financial position**. In **profit or loss**, interest revenue is calculated using the **effective interest rate method**. The fair value gains and losses on these financial assets are recognised in other comprehensive income (OCI). As a result, the difference between the total change in fair value and the amounts recognised in profit or loss are shown in OCI. When these financial assets are derecognised, the cumulative gains and losses previously recognised in OCI are reclassified from equity to profit or loss. Expected credit losses (ECLs) do not reduce the carrying amount of the financial assets, which remains at fair value. Instead, an amount equal to the ECL allowance which would arise if the asset were measured at amortised cost is recognised in OCI.

The fair value of the debt instrument therefore needs to be ascertained at 28 February 20X7. IFRS 13 *Fair Value Measurement* states that Level 1 inputs are unadjusted quoted prices in active markets for identical assets or liabilities which the entity can access at the measurement date. In-house models are alternative pricing methods which do not rely exclusively on quoted prices. It would seem that a **Level 1 input is available**, based upon activity in the market and further that, because of the active market, there is no reason to use the in-house model to value the debt.

Therefore, the accounting for the instrument should be as follows:

Initial measurement

The bonds will be initially recorded at $6 million and interest of $0.24 million will be received and credited to profit or loss.

BPP
LEARNING
MEDIA

Subsequent measurement

At 28 February 20X7, the bonds will be valued at $5.3 million, which recognises 12-month credit losses and other reductions in fair value. The loss of $0.7 million will be charged as an impairment loss of $0.4 million to profit or loss, representing the 12-month expected credit losses and $0.3 million to OCI. When the bond is sold for $5.3 million on 1 March 20X7, the financial asset is derecognised and the loss in OCI ($0.3 million) is reclassified to profit or loss. Also, the fact that the bond is sold for $5.3 million on 1 March 20X7 illustrates that this should have been the fair value on 28 February 20X7.

(c)   IFRS 15 *Revenue from Contracts with Customers* specifies how to account for costs incurred in fulfilling a contract which are not in the scope of another standard. Costs to fulfil a contract which is accounted for under IFRS 15 are divided into those which give rise to an asset and those which are expensed as incurred. Entities will recognise an asset when costs incurred to fulfil a contract meet certain criteria, one of which is that the costs are expected to be recovered.

For costs to meet the 'expected to be recovered' criterion, they need to be either explicitly reimbursable under the contract or reflected through the pricing of the contract and recoverable through the margin.

The penalty and additional costs attributable to the contract should be considered when they occur and Carsoon should have included them in the total costs of the contract in the period in which they had been notified.

As regards the counter claim for compensation, Carsoon accounts for the claim as a contract modification in accordance with IFRS 15. The modification does not result in any additional goods and services being provided to the customer. In addition, all of the remaining goods and services after the modification are not distinct and form part of a single performance obligation. Consequently, Carsoon should account for the modification by updating the transaction price and the measure of progress towards complete satisfaction of the performance obligation. However, on the basis of information available, it is possible to consider that the counter claim had not reached an advanced stage, so that claims submitted to the client should not be included in total revenues.

When the contract is modified for the construction of the storage facility, an additional $7 million is added to the consideration which Carsoon will receive. The additional $7 million reflects the stand-alone selling price of the contract modification. The construction of the separate storage facility is a distinct performance obligation and the contract modification for the additional storage facility is accounted for as a new contract which does not affect the accounting for the existing contract. Therefore, the contract is a performance obligation which has been satisfied as assets are only recognised in relation to satisfying future performance obligations. General and administrative costs cannot be capitalised unless these costs are specifically chargeable to the customer under the contract. Similarly, wasted material costs are expensed where they are not chargeable to the customer. Therefore, a total expense of $15 million will be charged to profit or loss and not shown as assets.

61 Leigh

Workbook reference. Share-based payments are covered in Chapter 10. Associates are covered in Chapter 11.

Top tips. This was a difficult question which dealt with several share-based payment transactions. However, not all such transactions were dealt with by a single accounting standard. Part (a) dealt with the cost of a business combination and the issue of shares as purchase consideration. It also dealt with shares given to employees as remuneration. The events are dealt with under the separate accounting standards IFRS 2 and IFRS 3. Part (b) dealt with the purchase of property, plant and equipment, and the grant of rights to a director when there is a choice of settlement. This part of the question was quite technically demanding. Part (c) dealt with the issue of shares to acquire an associate and the subsequent accounting for the associate.

Easy marks. It is difficult to identify easy marks for this question.

		Marks
(a)	Hash	7
	Employees	3
(b)	Property, plant and equipment	5
	Director	4
(c)	Handy	6
		25

(a) **Shares issued to the directors**

The 3 million $1 shares issued to the directors **on 1 June 20X6** as part of the **purchase consideration** for Hash are accounted for under **IFRS 3** *Business Combinations* rather than under IFRS 2 *Share-based Payment*. This is because they are not remuneration or compensation, but simply part of the purchase price of the company. The cost of the business combination will be the total of the fair values of the consideration given by Leigh plus any attributable costs. The total fair value here is $6 million, of which $3 million is share capital and $3 million is share premium.

The **contingent consideration** – 5,000 shares per director to be received on 31 May 20X7 if the directors are still employed by Leigh – may, however, be seen as compensation and thus fall to be treated under IFRS 2. The fact that the additional payment of shares is **linked to continuing employment** suggests that it is a compensation arrangement, and therefore **IFRS 2 will apply**.

Under IFRS 2, the fair value used is that at the **grant date,** rather than when the shares vest. The market value of each share at that date is $2. (Three million shares are valued at $6 million.) So the total value of the compensation is $5 \times 5,000 \times \$2 = \mathbf{\$50,000}$.

The $50,000 is charged to profit or loss with a corresponding increase in equity.

Shares issued to employees

These shares are remuneration and are **accounted for under IFRS 2.**

The fair value used is that at the **date of issue,** as the grant date and issue date are the same, **that is, $3 per share**. Because the shares are given as a bonus they vest immediately and are presumed to be consideration for past services.

The total of $3 million would be changed to profit or loss and included in equity.

(b) **Purchase of property, plant and equipment**

Under IFRS 2, the purchase of property, plant and equipment would be treated as a share-based payment in which the counterparty has a **choice of settlement,** in shares or in cash. Such transactions are **treated as cash-settled** to the extent that the entity has incurred a **liability**. It is treated as the issue of a compound financial instrument, with a debt and an equity element.

Similar to IAS 32 *Financial Instruments: Presentation*, IFRS 2 requires the **determination of the liability element and the equity element**. The fair value of the equity element is the fair value of the goods or services (in this case the property) less the fair value of the debt element of the instrument. The fair value of the property is $4 million (per question). The share price of $3.50 is the expected share price in three months' time (assuming cash settlement). The fair value of the liability component at 31 May 20X7 is its present value: 1.3 million × $3 = $3.9m.

The journal entries are:

Debit	Property, plant and equipment	$4m	
Credit	Liability		$3.9m
Credit	Equity		$0.1m

In three months' time, the debt component is remeasured to its fair value. Assuming the estimate of the future share price was correct at $3.50, the liability at that date will be 1.3 million × $3.5 = $4.55m. An adjustment must be made as follows:

Debit	Expense (4.55 – 3.9)	$0.65m	
Credit	Liability		$0.65m

Choice of share or cash settlement

The share-based payment to the new director, which offers a choice of cash or share settlement, is also treated as the issue of a compound instrument. In this case, the **fair value of the services is determined by the fair value of the equity instruments given**. The fair value of the equity alternative is $2.50 × 50,000 = $125,000. The cash alternative is valued at 40,000 × $3 = $120,000. The **difference** between these two values – $5,000 – is deemed to be the **fair value of the equity component**. At the settlement date, the liability element would be measured at fair value and the method of settlement chosen by the director would determine the final accounting treatment.

At 31 May 20X7, the accounting entries would be:

Debit	Profit or loss – directors' remuneration	$125,000	
Credit	Liability		$120,000
Credit	Equity		$5,000

In effect, the director surrenders the right to $120,000 cash in order to obtain equity worth $125,000.

(c) ### Investment in Hardy

The investment in Hardy should be treated as an **associate under** IAS 28 *Investments in Associates and Joint Ventures*. Between 20% and 50% of the share capital has been acquired, and significant influence may be exercised through the right to appoint directors. Associates are accounted for as cost plus post acquisition change in net assets, **generally cost plus share of post-acquisition retained earnings**. The cost is the fair value of the shares in Leigh exchanged for the shares of Handy. However, negative goodwill arises because the fair value of the net assets of Hardy exceeds this. The negative goodwill must be added back to determine the cost to be used for the carrying amount, and, following a reassessment, credited to profit or loss (Dr Cost 0.2, Cr P/L 0.2).

	$m
Cost: 1m × $2.50	2.5
Add back negative goodwill: (2.5 + (9 × 70% 'NCI') – 9)	0.2
	2.7
Post-acquisition profits: (5 – 4) × 30%	0.3
Carrying amount at 31 May 20X7	3.0

Note. The 0.2 is not part of post-acquisition retained earnings. It is adjustment to the original cost to remove the negative goodwill.

Because negative goodwill has arisen, the investment must be **impairment tested**. A comparison must be made with the estimated recoverable amount of Hardy's net assets. The investment must not be carried above the recoverable amount:

Recoverable amount at 31 May 20X7: $11m × 30% = $3.3m

The recoverable amount is above the carrying amount, so the investment at 31 May 20X7 will be shown at $3 million.

62 Mehran

Marking scheme

		Marks
(a)	1 mark per point up to maximum	7
(b)	1 mark per point up to maximum	10
(c)	1 mark per point up to maximum	8
Maximum		25

(a) **Land and brand name**

IFRS 13 *Fair Value Measurement* requires the fair value of a non-financial asset to be measured based on its highest and best use from a market participant's perspective. This requirement does not apply to financial instruments, liabilities or equity. The highest and best use takes into account the use of the asset which is physically possible, legally permissible and financially feasible. The highest and best use of a non-financial asset is determined by reference to its use and not its classification and is determined from the perspective of market participants. It does not matter whether the entity intends to use the asset differently. IFRS 13 allows management to presume that the current use of an asset is the highest and best use unless market or other factors suggest otherwise.

In this case, the agricultural land appears to have an alternative use as market participants have considered its use for residential purposes. If the land zoned for agricultural use is currently used for farming, the fair value should reflect the cost structure to continue operating the land for farming, including any tax credits which could be realised by market participants. Thus, the fair value of the land if used for farming would be $(5 + (20% of 0.5))$ million, ie $5.1 million.

If used for residential purposes, the value should include all costs associated with changing the land to the market participant's intended use. In addition, demolition and other costs associated with preparing the land for a different use should be included in the valuation. These costs would include the uncertainty related to whether the approval needed for changing the usage would be obtained, because market participants would take that into account when pricing value of the land if it had a different use. Thus, the fair value of the land if used for residential purposes would be $(7.4 - 0.2 - 0.3 - 0.1)$ million × 80%, ie $5.44 million. Therefore, the value of the land would be $5.44 million on the highest and best use basis. In this situation, the presumption that the current use is the highest and best use of the land has been overridden by the market factors which indicate that residential development is the highest and best use. A use of an asset need not be legal at the measurement date, but it must not be legally prohibited in the jurisdiction.

BPP
LEARNING
MEDIA

In the absence of any evidence to the contrary, Mehran should value the brand on the basis of the highest and best use. The fair value is determined from the perspective of a market participant and is not influenced by the Mehran's decision to discontinue the brand. Therefore, the fair value of the brand is $17 million.

(b)   **Fair value of inventory**

IFRS 13 sets out the concepts of principal market and most advantageous market. Transactions take place in either the principal market, which is the market with the greatest volume and level of activity for the inventory, or in the absence of a principal market, the most advantageous market. The most advantageous market is the market which maximises the amount which would be received to sell the inventory, after taking into account transaction costs and transportation costs. The price used to measure the inventory's fair value is not adjusted for transaction costs although it is adjusted for transport costs. The principal market is not necessarily the market with the greatest volume of activity for the particular reporting entity. The principle is based upon the importance of the market from the participant's perspective. However, the principal market is presumed to be the market in which the reporting entity transacts, unless there is evidence to the contrary. In evaluating the principal or most advantageous markets, IFRS 13 restricts the eligible markets to only those which can be accessed at the measurement date. If there is a principal market for the asset or liability, IFRS 13 states that fair value should be based on the price in that market, even if the price in a different market is higher. It is only in the absence of the principal market that the most advantageous market should be used. An entity does not have to undertake an exhaustive search of all possible markets in order to identify the principal or most advantageous market. It should take into account all information which is readily available.

There is a presumption in the standard that the market in which the entity normally transacts to sell the asset or transfer the liability is the principal or most advantageous market unless there is evidence to the contrary.

In this case, the greatest volume of transactions is conducted in the domestic market – direct to manufacturers. There is no problem with obtaining data from trade journals but the problem for Mehran is that there is no data to substantiate the volume of activity in the domestic market – direct to retailers even though Mehran feels that it is at least 20,000 tonnes per annum. The most advantageous market is the export market where after transport and transaction costs the price per tonne is $1,094.

	Domestic market – direct to retailers $	Domestic market – direct to manufacturers $	Export market $
Price per tonne	1,000	800	1,200
Transport costs per tonne	50	70	100
Selling agents' fees per tonne	–	4	6
Net price per tonne	950	726	1,094

It is difficult to determine a principal market because of the lack of information. It could be argued that the domestic market – direct to manufacturers has the highest volume for the produce, and is therefore the principal market by which Mehran should determine fair value of $730 ($800 – $70). However, because of the lack of information surrounding the domestic market – direct to retailers, the principal or most advantageous market will be presumed to be the market in which Mehran would normally enter into transactions which would be the export market. Therefore, the fair value would be $1,100 ($1,200 – $100) per tonne.

(c)   Investment in Erham

Measuring the fair value of individual unquoted equity instruments which constitute a non-controlling interest in a private company falls within the scope of IFRS 9 *Financial Instruments* in accordance with the principles set out in IFRS 13. There is a range of commonly used valuation techniques for measuring the fair value of unquoted equity instruments and income approaches as well as the adjusted net asset method are acceptable. IFRS 13 states that fair value is a market-based measurement, although it acknowledges that in some cases observable market transactions or other market information might not be available. IFRS 13 does not contain a hierarchy of valuation techniques nor does it prescribe the use of a specific valuation technique for meeting the objective of a fair value measurement. However, IFRS 13 acknowledges that, given specific circumstances, one valuation technique might be more appropriate than another. The market approach takes a transaction price paid for an identical or a similar instrument in an investee and adjusts the resultant valuation. The transaction price paid recently for an investment in an equity instrument in an investee which is similar, but not identical, to an investor's unquoted equity instrument in the same investee would be a reasonable starting point for estimating the fair value of the unquoted equity instrument.

Mehran would take the transaction price for the preferred shares and adjust it to reflect certain differences between the preferred shares and the ordinary shares. There would be an adjustment to reflect the priority of the preferred shares upon liquidation.

Mehran should acknowledge the benefit associated with control. This adjustment relates to the fact that Mehran's individual ordinary shares represent a non-controlling interest whereas the preferred shares issued reflect a controlling interest. There will be an adjustment for the lack of liquidity of the investment which reflects the lesser ability of the ordinary shareholder to initiate a sale of Erham relative to the preferred shareholder. Further, there will be an adjustment for the cumulative dividend entitlement of the preferred shares. This would be calculated as the present value of the expected future dividend receipts on the preferred shares, less the present value of any expected dividend receipts on the ordinary shares. The discount rate used should be consistent with the uncertainties associated with the relevant dividend streams.

Mehran should review the circumstances of the issue of the preferred shares to ensure that its price was a valid benchmark. Mehran must, however, use all information about the performance and operations of Erham which becomes reasonably available to it after the date of initial recognition of the ordinary shares up to the measurement date. Such information can have an effect on the fair value of the unquoted equity instrument at 31 March 20X6. In addition, Mehran should consider the existence of factors such as whether the environment in which Erham operates is dynamic, or whether there have been changes in market conditions between the issue of the preferred shares and the measurement date.

63 Ethan

Workbook references. Deferred tax is covered in Chapter 7. Investment property, impairment and fair value are covered in Chapter 4, and financial instruments in Chapter 8.

Top tips. In Part (a), you should focus on IFRS 13. Part (b) required application of the fair value option in IFRS 9 *Financial Instruments*. The option is used where such application would eliminate or significantly reduce a measurement or recognition inconsistency between the debt liabilities and the investment properties to which they were related in this question. In Part (c), candidates needed to recognise that, in classifying the B shares as equity rather than as a liability, the entity had not complied with IAS 32 *Financial Instruments: Presentation*. There were pointers to the shares being classified as a liability, in particular the fact that entity was obliged to pay an annual cumulative dividend on the B shares and did not have discretion over the distribution of such dividend.

Easy marks. There are no obviously easy marks in this question.

ANSWERS

BPP
LEARNING
MEDIA

		Marks
(a)	Fair value of investment properties	13
(b)	Fair value option – IFRS 9	7
(c)	B shares of subsidiary	5
		25

(a) Fair value of investment properties

The **fair value** of an asset is the price that would be received to sell an asset or paid to transfer a liability in an orderly transaction between market participants at the measurement date (IFRS 13 *Fair Value Measurement*). IFRS 13 states that valuation techniques must be those which are appropriate and for which sufficient data are available. Entities should maximise the use of relevant **observable inputs** and minimise the use of **unobservable inputs**. The standard establishes a three-level hierarchy for the inputs that valuation techniques use to measure fair value.

Level 1	Quoted prices (unadjusted) in active markets for identical assets or liabilities that the reporting entity can access at the measurement date
Level 2	Inputs other than quoted prices included within Level 1 that are observable for the asset or liability, either directly or indirectly, eg quoted prices for similar assets in active markets or for identical or similar assets in non-active markets or use of quoted interest rates for valuation purposes
Level 3	Unobservable inputs for the asset or liability, ie using the entity's own assumptions about market exit value

Although an active market exists for Ethan's investment properties, Ethan uses a discounted cash flow model to measure fair value. This is **not in accordance with IFRS 13**. As the fair value hierarchy suggests, IFRS 13 favours Level 1 inputs, that is market-based measures, over unobservable (Level 3) inputs such as discounted cash flows.

Goodwill and deferred tax

If the **fair value** of the investment properties **is not measured correctly** in accordance with IFRS 13, this means that the **deferred tax liability** on investment properties **may also be incorrect**. In addition, as goodwill is calculated as consideration transferred less fair value of net assets, **goodwill may be incorrect**. This is because deferred tax is calculated on the difference between the carrying amount of the asset and its tax base. So if the carrying amount is incorrect, the deferred tax will be incorrect. The goodwill calculation uses the fair value of **all** net assets, not just the investment properties and the related deferred tax liability, so it is **incorrect to use an increase in the deferred tax liability** as the **basis** for assessing whether goodwill is impaired.

The reasoning behind Ethan's approach is that as the deferred tax liability decreases, the fair value of net assets increases, thereby decreasing goodwill. However, this method of determining whether goodwill is impaired **does not accord with IAS 36** *Impairment of Assets*. IAS 36 requires that goodwill should be **reviewed for impairment annually** for any indicators of impairment, which may be internal or external, and are not confined to changes in the deferred tax liability. Where it is not possible to measure impairment for individual assets, the loss should be measured for a **cash-generating unit.**

The **recoverable amount** is **defined** as the **higher** of:

(i)   The **asset's fair value less costs to sell**. This is the price that would be received to sell the asset in an orderly transaction between market participants at the measurement date under current market conditions, net of costs of disposal.

(ii)   The asset's **value in use**. This is the present value of estimated future cash flows (inflows minus outflows) generated by the asset, including its estimated net disposal value (if any) at the end of its useful life.

If an **asset's carrying amount** is **higher than its recoverable amount**, an **impairment loss** has occurred. The impairment loss should be **written off against profit or loss** for the year, and the corresponding credit (write-off) applied first to goodwill, then to the investment properties, then to other assets pro-rata.

Deferred tax assets on losses

In theory, unused tax losses give rise to a deferred tax asset. However, IAS 12 *Income Taxes* states that **deferred tax assets should only be recognised to the extent that they are regarded as recoverable.** They should be regarded as recoverable to the extent that on the basis of all the evidence available it is **probable that there will be suitable taxable profits against which the losses can be recovered.** It is unlikely that future taxable profits of Ethan will be sufficient to realise all of the tax loss because of:

(i)   The announcement that a substantial loss will be incurred this year instead of the expected profit

(ii)   Considerable negative variances against budgets in the past

Consequently, **Ethan should not recognise the deferred tax asset.**

(b)   **IFRS 9 fair value option**

Generally under IFRS 9 *Financial Instruments*, the debt issued to finance its investment properties would be accounted for using **amortised cost**, while the properties themselves are at fair value. This is an **accounting mismatch,** that is a recognition or measurement inconsistency between the debt liability and the asset to which it relates. The asset and liability, and the gains and losses arising on them, would be measured on different bases.

The IFRS 9 **fair value option** allows an entity to **designate a liability at initial recognition as being at fair value through profit or loss** if using this option would **eliminate or significantly reduce** an accounting mismatch. Ethan has argued that the basis of measurement of the debt and the investment properties is **similar**, particularly as regards **interest rates.** This argument holds good in respect of the interest, and so the **fair value option would be allowed.**

However, IFRS 9 stipulates that if a liability is designated as being at fair value through profit or loss, **changes in the fair value that are due to changes in the liability's credit risk must be recognised directly in other comprehensive income** rather than profit or loss. Such **changes may not be re-classified** to profit or loss in subsequent years, although a **reserves transfer** is permitted from other components of equity to retained earnings. On the other hand, **if changes in the fair value attributable to the credit risk** of the liability **create or enlarge an accounting mismatch in profit or loss,** then all fair value movements are **recognised in profit or loss.**

(c)   **B shares of subsidiary**

Ethan's accounting treatment of the B shares (as equity instruments) does not comply with IAS 32 *Financial Instruments: Presentation*. The IAS 32 definition of a financial liability includes any liability that is **a contractual obligation to deliver cash or another financial asset to another entity.** A financial instrument may only be classified as an equity instrument rather than a liability if the instrument does not include an obligation to deliver cash or other financial asset to another entity, or to exchange financial instruments with another entity under conditions that are potentially unfavourable.

In the **subsidiary's books**, the B shares would be treated as a **financial liability**. They contain an **obligation** to deliver cash in the form of a fixed dividend. The dividend is cumulative and must be paid whether or not the subsidiary has sufficient legally distributable profits when it is due, and so **the subsidiary cannot avoid this obligation**.

In the **consolidated financial statements**, the B shares would also be treated as a financial liability, **the intragroup element of this liability (70%) would cancel against the investment in B shares in the parent's (Ethan's) statement of financial position**. The shares **owned by external parties would not cancel**; they would remain **a financial liability**. It **is incorrect to treat them as non-controlling interest** because they are **not equity**.

64 Whitebirk

Marking scheme

			Marks
(a)		Subjective assessment including professional	11
(b)	(i)	Business combination	4
	(ii)	Research and development expenditure	3
	(iii)	Investment property	2
	(iv)	Intangible	2
			22

(a)   **Modifications to reduce the burden of reporting for SMEs**

The IFRS for SMEs has **simplifications** that reflect the needs of users of SMEs' financial statements and cost-benefit considerations. It is designed to facilitate financial reporting by small and medium-sized entities in a number of ways:

(i)   It provides significantly **less guidance** than full IFRS. A great deal of the guidance in full IFRS would not be relevant to the needs of smaller entities.

(ii)   Many of the **principles** for recognising and measuring assets, liabilities, income and expenses in full IFRSs are **simplified**. For example, goodwill and intangibles are always amortised over their estimated useful life (or ten years if it cannot be estimated). Research and development costs must be expensed. With defined benefit pension plans, all actuarial gains and losses are to be recognised immediately in other comprehensive income. All past service costs are to be recognised immediately in profit or loss. To measure the defined benefit obligation, the projected unit credit method must be used.

(iii) Where full IFRSs allow accounting policy choices, the IFRS for SMEs **allows only the easier option**. Examples of alternatives not allowed in the IFRS for SMEs include: revaluation model for intangible assets and property, plant and equipment, proportionate consolidation for investments in jointly-controlled entities and choice between cost and fair value models for investment property (measurement depends on the circumstances).

(iv) **Topics not relevant** to SMEs are **omitted**: earnings per share, interim financial reporting, segment reporting, insurance and assets held for sale.

(v) Significantly **fewer disclosures** are required.

(vi) The standard has been written in **clear language** that can easily be translated.

The above represents a considerable reduction in reporting requirements – perhaps as much as 90% – compared with listed entities. Entities will naturally wish to use the IFRS for SMEs if they can, but **its use is restricted**.

The restrictions are **not related to size**. There are several disadvantages of basing the definition on size limits alone. Size limits are **arbitrary** and **different limits are likely to be appropriate in different** countries. Most people believe that SMEs are **not simply smaller versions of listed entities,** but differ from them in more fundamental ways.

The most important way in which SMEs differ from other entities is that they are **not usually publicly accountable**. Accordingly, there are **no quantitative thresholds** for qualification as a SME; instead, the scope of the IFRS is determined by a **test of public accountability**. The IFRS is suitable for all entities except those whose securities are publicly traded and financial institutions such as banks and insurance companies.

Another way in which the use of the IFRS for SMEs is restricted is that **users cannot cherry pick** from this IFRS and full IFRS. If an entity adopts the IFRS for SMEs, it **must adopt it in its entirety**.

(b) (i) **Business combination**

IFRS 3 *Business Combinations* allows an entity to measure non-controlling interests at acquisition at either fair value or at the proportionate share of the acquiree's net assets. The IFRS for SMEs **only allows non-controlling interests to be measured at the proportionate share of the acquiree's net assets**. This avoids the need for SMEs to determine the fair value of the non-controlling interests when undertaking a business combination.

In addition, IFRS 3 requires goodwill to be tested annually for impairment. The IFRS for SMEs **requires goodwill to be amortised instead**. This is a much simpler approach and the IFRS for SMEs specifies that if an entity is unable to make a reliable estimate of the useful life, it is presumed to be ten years, simplifying things even further.

Goodwill on Whitebirk's acquisition of Close will be calculated as:

	$'000
Consideration transferred	5,700
Non-controlling interest: 10% × $6m	600
	6,300
Less fair value of identifiable net assets acquired	(6,000)
Goodwill	300

This goodwill of $0.3 million will be amortised over ten years, that is $30,000 per annum.

(ii)   Research and development expenditure

The IFRS for SMEs requires all internally generated research and development expenditure to be **expensed through profit or loss**. This is simpler than full IFRS – IAS 38 *Intangible Assets* requires internally generated assets to be capitalised if certain criteria (proving future economic benefits) are met, and it is often difficult to determine whether or not they have been met.

Whitebirk's total expenditure on research ($0.5m) and development ($1m) must be written off to profit or loss for the year, giving a charge of $1.5 million.

(iii)   Investment property

Investment properties must be held at fair value through profit or loss under the IFRS for SMEs where their fair value can be measured without undue cost or effort, which appears to be the case here, given that an estate agent valuation is available. Consequently, a gain of $0.2 million ($1.9m – $1.7m) will be reported in Whitebirk's profit or loss for the year.

(iv)   Intangible asset

IAS 36 *Impairment of Assets* requires annual impairment tests for indefinite life intangibles, intangibles not yet available for use and goodwill. This is a complex, time-consuming and expensive test.

The IFRS for SMEs only requires impairment tests where there are indicators of impairment. In the case of Whitebirk's intangible, there are no indicators of impairment, and so an impairment test is not required.

In addition, IAS 38 *Intangible Assets* does not require intangible assets with an indefinite useful life to be amortised. In contrast, under the IFRS for SMEs, all intangible assets must be amortised. If the useful life cannot be established reliably, it must not exceed ten years.

65 Revenue recognition

Workbook references. Revenue recognition is covered in Chapter 3 and provisions are covered in Chapter 6.

Top tips. This question mainly covered the accounting treatment for revenue given in IFRS 15 *Revenue from Contracts with Customers*. In part (a) Premier Co has issued two warranties, the 'standard' warranty should be accounted for under IAS 37 as a provision. However, the additional warranty is a separate performance obligation (as it offers an additional service to the customer that is usually paid for) and is therefore accounted for under IFRS 15. In part (b), Rodia Co appears to have entered into a consignment arrangement with Jae Co. In part (c), the customer has a right of return, as such Kracker Co must only recognise revenue related to items it does not expect to be returned and must recognise a refund liability and an asset in relation to the items expected to be returned. In part (d), Kotta Co must assess whether the non-refundable up-front fee relates to the transfer of a promised good or service, if so, then it is a separate performance obligation. However, in this case it appears that the actions associated with the fee are administrative in nature, and therefore are not a separate performance obligation. The fee should therefore be recognised as the access to the food store is provided.

Remember that in SBR, the situations presented will rarely be straightforward, the examiner is looking for you to present a discussion: draw out the relevant principles from the Standard and then apply them to the scenario to identify the most appropriate accounting treatment.

		Marks
(a)	Warranties	10
(b)	Consignment arrangement	7
(c)	Right of return	4
(d)	Non-refundable fee	4
		25

(a) **Warranties**

Standard warranty

The warranty that provides assurance that the machine complies with agreed-upon specifications and will operate as promised one year from the date of purchase is a standard warranty at no cost to the customer.

Therefore, it should be accounted for in accordance with IAS *37 Provisions, Contingent Liabilities and Contingent Assets.* Premier Co should recognise a provision if there is a present obligation as a result of a past event and the amount can be measured reliably.

Premier Co has a present obligation as a result of providing a warranty with each sale of the machine. The probability of paying out on an individual warranty will likely be low. However, Premier Co should consider all standard warranties provided for this machine together as they are similar obligations. When considered together, it may mean the probability of payout becomes more likely than not.

Premier Co can use an expected value approach to reliably estimate the amount of the provision.

Additional warranty

IFRS 15 *Revenue from Contracts with Customers* specifies that if the customer has the option to purchase a warranty separately, the warranty is a distinct service and should be accounted for as a separate performance obligation. In this case, the additional warranty has been given as an incentive to a new customer. As the customer would usually have the option to purchase the warranty separately for $4,000, it should be treated as a separate performance obligation.

Sale of the machine

There are two performance obligations: the sale of the machine and the provision of the extended warranty service. The transaction price of $196,000 should be allocated to the two performance obligations in accordance with their standalone selling prices:

Performance obligation	Stand-alone selling price $	% of total	Transaction price allocated $
Machine	196,000	98%	192,080
Extended warranty	4,000	2%	3,920
Total	200,000	100	196,000

Revenue of $192,080 from the sale of the machine should be recognised when control of the machine is transferred to the customer, which is likely to be on delivery. Revenue of $3,920 should be recognised over the period in which the service related to the extended warranty is provided. On sale of the machine, a contract liability of $3,920 should be recognised in relation to the extended warranty.

BPP
LEARNING
MEDIA

(b)   **Consignment arrangement**

This transaction appears to be a consignment arrangement. Per IFRS 15, a consignment arrangement exists when a product is delivered to another party for sale to end customers, but the other party does not obtain control of the product.

IFRS 15 includes the following indicators that an arrangement is a consignment arrangement between an entity and a dealer:

(i)   The product is controlled by the entity until a specified event occurs, such as the sale of the product to a customer of the dealer or until a specified period expires;

(ii)   The entity is able to require the return of the product or transfer the product to a third party (such as another dealer); and

(iii) The dealer does not have an unconditional obligation to pay for the product (although it might be required to pay a deposit).

In this case, the jewellery must be returned to Rodia Co after nine months if it is not sold, but it is not clear whether Rodia Co can require the jewellery to be returned at a date earlier than that. Jae Co does not have an unconditional obligation to pay for the jewellery because, even though Jae Co has to pay a deposit, it can return unsold products after nine months in exchange for a refund.

In terms of control of the jewellery, it seems that Rodia Co retains control of the jewellery until sale to the final customer because as it can change the selling price of the jewellery and it retains legal tile over it (and therefore could use it as security against a loan for example) until it is sold to the end customer.

The arrangement therefore appears to be a consignment arrangement and control of the jewellery remains with Rodia Co. As such, revenue for the sale of each item of jewellery should not be recognised by Rodia Co or by Jae Co until the item of jewellery has been sold to the end customer. Each item of jewellery should remain in the inventories balance of Rodia Co until it is sold to the end customer.

(c)   **Right of return**

When the customer has a right to return products, the transaction price contains a variable element because the aggregate amount of revenue recognised by Kracker Co will vary. Kracker Co should therefore only recognise revenue to the extent that it is highly probable that a significant reversal in the amount of revenue recognised will not occur when the uncertainty is resolved, ie when the right of return period expires. Kracker Co reliably estimates that no more than 4% of goods of goods will be returned, so it is highly probable that goods sold for $192,000 (96 × $2,000) will not reverse.

For the items expected to be returned, Kracker Co should not recognise any revenue, instead it should recognise a refund liability for $8,000 ($200,000 − $192,000) as a current liability, and an asset representing the items expected to be returned for $6,400 (4% × 100 × $1,600), shown as a right of return asset under current assets.

The journal entries required at the date of sale are:

Dr Trade receivable	$200,000	
Cr Revenue		$192,000
Cr Refund liability		$8,000
Dr Cost of sales (β)	$153,600	
Dr Right of return asset	$6,400	
Cr Inventory (100 × $1,600)		$160,000

The refund liability should be reassessed and updated at each reporting date. The right of return asset should be assessed for recoverability at each reporting date.

(d)   **Non-refundable fee**

IFRS 15 requires an entity to assess whether a non-refundable up-front fee paid by a customer relates to the transfer of a promised good or service.

In this case, when a customer becomes a member, Kotta Co must set up a customer's account and issue them with a membership card. However, this appears to be an administrative task rather than a good or service transferred to the customer. IFRS 15 states that administrative tasks do not transfer a good or service to the customer and are not performance obligations.

Instead, the non-refundable fee is an advance payment for access to the community food store over the 12 month period. Kotta Co should recognise a contract liability on receipt of the fee, and then recognise the fee as revenue over the 12 month period, as the access to the food store is provided to the customer. As the customer can access the store at any time during the 12 month period, Kotta Co will need to determine the most appropriate way of allocating the revenue over the 12 month period. The most straightforward method may be a straight-line basis, if this is a suitable approximation for how customers use their access to the food store.

66 Seltec

> **Workbook references.** Financial instruments are covered in Chapter 7, intangible assets in Chapter 3, and business combinations in Chapters 10 to 16.
>
> **Top tips.** Part (a) of this question will likely have seemed daunting on first reading as it was 15 marks on a topic that a lot of students find difficult: financial instruments. However, as the directors of Seltec were unsure as to the nature of derivatives and hedge accounting techniques, this gives you a clue that there are marks available for presenting relevant knowledge of these topics: the definition of a derivative, the requirements for hedge accounting, the definitions and differences between a fair value hedge and a cash flow hedge and the definition of an embedded derivative. If you were unsure of these definitions, it is worth learning them as there will always be some marks available in an exam question for relevant knowledge, particularly when the topic is challenging.
>
> In part (b), you need to think carefully about what constitutes a business combination. You should apply the guidance in IFRS 3, which is essentially an application of the substance over form principle.
>
> **Easy marks.** These are available for the basic principles of intangible assets.

Marking scheme

			Marks
(a)	Hedge accounting	5	
	Futures	5	
	Embedded derivative	5	
			15
(b)	Brands	5	
	Business combinations	5	
			10
			25

(a)   Financial instruments

Derivatives

IAS 32 *Financial Instruments: Presentation* and IFRS 9 *Financial Instruments* define a **derivative** as a financial instrument or other contract that has all three of the following characteristics.

(i)   Its value changes in response to the change in a specified interest rate, financial instrument price, commodity price, foreign exchange rate, index of prices or rates, credit rating or credit index, or other variable (sometimes called the 'underlying').

(ii)   It requires no initial net investment or an initial net investment that is smaller than would be required for other types of contracts that would be expected to have a similar response to changes in market factors.

(iii) It is settled at a future date.

A contract is **not considered to be a derivative where its purpose is to take physical delivery** in the normal course of business, unless the entity has a practice of settling the contracts on a net basis.

In the case of Seltec, while the company often takes physical delivery of the edible oil, it does so only to sell shortly afterwards, and usually settles on a net basis. Thus the **contracts will be considered to be derivative** contracts rather than contracts for purchase of inventory. Derivatives are accounted for at fair value through profit or loss, unless hedge accounting applies.

Hedge accounting

The rules on hedge accounting are set out in IFRS 9. Before a hedging relationship qualifies for hedge accounting, **all** of the following **conditions** must be met.

(i)   The hedging relationship consists **only of eligible hedging instruments and eligible hedged items.**

(ii)   There must be **formal documentation** (including identification of the hedged item, the hedging instrument, the nature of the risk that is to be hedged and how the entity will assess the hedging instrument's effectiveness in offsetting the exposure to changes in the hedged item's fair value or cash flows attributable to the hedged risk).

(iii) The hedging relationship meets all of the following hedge effectiveness criteria

(1)   There is an **economic relationship** between the hedged item and the hedging instrument, ie the hedging instrument and the hedged item have values that generally move in the opposite direction because of the same risk, which is the hedged risk;

(2)   The **effect of credit risk does not dominate the value** changes that result from that economic relationship, ie the gain or loss from credit risk does not frustrate the effect of changes in the underlyings on the value of the hedging instrument or the hedged item, even if those changes were significant; and

(3)   The **hedge ratio of the hedging relationship** (quantity of hedging instrument vs quantity of hedged item) is the same as that resulting from the quantity of the hedged item that the entity **actually hedges** and the quantity of the hedging instrument that the entity **actually uses** to hedge that quantity of hedged item.

There are two kinds of hedging that Seltec may consider: fair value hedging and cash flow hedging.

A **fair value hedge** is a hedge of the exposure to changes in the fair value of a recognised asset or liability, or an identified portion of such an asset or liability, that is attributable to a particular risk and could affect profit or loss. The **gain or loss** resulting from re-measuring the hedging instrument at fair value is **recognised in profit or loss**. The gain or loss on the hedged item attributable to the **hedged risk** should **adjust the carrying amount** of the hedged item and be **recognised in profit or loss**.

A **cash flow hedge**: a hedge of the exposure to variability in cash flows that:

(i) Is attributable to a particular risk associated with a recognised asset or liability (such as all or some future interest payments on variable rate debt) or a highly probable forecast transaction (such as an anticipated purchase or sale); and that

(ii) Could affect profit or loss.

The portion of the gain or loss on the hedging instrument that is determined to be an **effective** hedge must be accounted for in a cash flow reserve and **recognised in other comprehensive income (items that may subsequently be reclassified to profit or loss)** and transferred to profit or loss when the hedged item is recognised in profit or loss. The **ineffective portion** of the gain or loss on the hedging instrument must be **recognised in profit or loss**.

The rules for cash flow hedges are particularly restrictive because it is difficult to isolate and measure the cash flows attributable to the specific risks for the non-financial items. Cash flow hedging results in higher volatility in earnings, so, provided the documentation and other requirements are met, **Seltec may prefer to use fair value hedging**. Seltec must take into account all changes in the price of edible oil of all types and geographical locations that it processes and sells and these must be compared with the changes in the value of the future. The hedge will be ineffective if the contracts have different prices. However, a hedge does not need to be fully effective, and hedge accounting may still be used provided the criteria above are met.

Embedded derivative

Certain contracts that are not themselves derivatives (and may not be financial instruments) include derivative contracts that are 'embedded' within them. These non-derivatives are called **host contracts** IFRS 9 defines an embedded derivative as a derivative instrument that is combined with a non-derivative host contract to form a single hybrid instrument. Some of the cash flows of the instrument vary in a way that is similar to a stand-alone derivative.

Ordinary derivatives must be accounted for at fair value in the statement of financial position with changes recognised through profit or loss.

IFRS 9 treatment

Where the host contract is a financial asset within the scope of the IFRS 9, the classification and **measurement rules of the standard are applied to the entire hybrid contract**. However, in this case the contract is a financial liability, not a financial asset within the scope of IFRS 9. Accordingly, the following rules apply:

The embedded derivative must be **separated from its host contract** and accounted for as a derivative, provided the following conditions are met.

(i) The economic characteristics and risks of the embedded derivative are not closely related to the economic characteristics and risks of the host contract.

(ii) A separate instrument with the same terms as the embedded derivative would meet the definition of a derivative.

(iii) The hybrid (combined) instrument is not measured at fair value with changes in fair value recognised in the profit or loss (a derivative embedded in a financial asset or financial liability need not be separated out if the entity holds the combined instrument at fair value through profit or loss).

If the embedded derivative is separated from its host contract, the **host contract is accounted for under the applicable IFRS**. A contract denominated in a foreign currency contains an embedded derivative unless:

(i) The foreign currency denominated in the contract is the currency of one of the parties to the contract.

(ii) The foreign currency is that commonly used in the market in which such transactions take place.

(iii) The foreign currency is that in which the related goods or services are denominated in routine commercial transactions.

In the case of Seltec, **none of the above three exceptions apply**. Seltec's trade in edible oil is generally in dollars, not pounds sterling, the pound is not the functional currency of either party, and it is not the currency normally used in transactions in the business environment in which Seltec operates. Finally, the economic characteristics and risks of the embedded derivative are not closely related to the economic characteristics and risks of the host contract, since changes in the price of oil and currency fluctuations have different risks.

In conclusion, IFRS 9 would treat Seltec's contracts as containing an embedded derivative. The currency derivative must be accounted for at fair value through profit or loss.

(b) **Intangible assets**

An entity should **assess** the useful life of an intangible asset, which may be **finite or indefinite**. An intangible asset has an indefinite useful life when there is **no foreseeable limit** to the period over which the asset is expected to generate net cash inflows for the entity.

Seltec wishes to treat both brands as having indefinite useful lives. However, this may not be appropriate, and there are certain factors that need to be considered:

(i)   Does the brand have long-term potential? The first brand has a proven track record, but the second, named after a famous film star, may last only as long as the film star's popularity, which will not be indefinite.

(ii)   Is Seltec committed to supporting the brand? In the case of the first, it is, but the second is a relatively new product, and it is not clear that Seltec is in for the long haul.

If, as is likely, the **useful life of the second brand is considered to be finite**, its cost less residual value should be amortised on a systematic basis over its useful life, using the straight-line method as an approximation if the pattern of benefits cannot be determined reliably.

The **first brand**, which is correctly said to have an **indefinite useful life**, should not be amortised. Its useful life should be reviewed at each reporting period to determine whether the assessment of the useful life as indefinite is still applicable. If not, the change, from indefinite to finite would be accounted for as a change in accounting estimate as per IAS 8 *Accounting Policies, Changes in Accounting Estimates and Errors*. It should also be tested for impairment annually in accordance with IAS 36 *Impairment of Assets*, and otherwise accounted for like the second brand.

Purchase of entities

IFRS 3 *Business Combinations* defines a business combination as 'a transaction or event in which an acquirer obtains control of one or more businesses. A business is defined as an integrated set of activities and assets that is capable of being conducted and managed for the purpose of providing goods or services to customers, generating investment income (such as dividends or interest) or generating other income from ordinary activities'. This is essentially an application of the substance over form principle.

IFRS 3 provides additional guidance as to whether an entity is a business. To qualify as a business, an entity must have at a minimum an **input** and a **substantive process** that together significantly contribute to the **ability to create an output**.

The two limited liability companies **do not have any substantive processes** at acquisition as they do not have any operational activity nor any employees (and so have no 'organised workforce' as specified in the application guidance to IFRS 3). **As such, they do not meet the IFRS 3 definition of a business** and the acquisition is not a business combination.

In substance, Seltec has purchased two assets (the two retail units) and the acquisition **should be treated as an asset acquisition**.

67 Della Co

Marking scheme

	Marks
(a) Repurchase agreement	7
(b) Consignment arrangement	7
(c) Hedge accounting	8
	25

(a) Repurchase agreement

Della Co has entered into a repurchase agreement with Cromer Co because it has the right to cancel the sale and require return of the product at any point up to 31 January 20X1.

In accordance with IFRS 15 *Revenue from Contracts with Customers*, because Della Co has the right to repurchase the specialised product, Cromer Co does not obtain control of the product, even though it has physical possession of it, because it is limited in its ability to direct the use of the asset and to obtain substantially all of the remaining benefits from the asset. Therefore, Della Co cannot recognise any revenue on the date of the sale.

IFRS 15 specifies instead that:

- if the repurchase price is less than the original selling price, the transaction should be accounted for as a lease in accordance with IFRS 16 *Leases*

- if the repurchase price is the same or greater than the original selling price, the transaction should be accounted for as a financing arrangement.

The repurchase price for Della Co is $500 higher than the original selling price, therefore it should be treated as a financing arrangement.

On the date of the sale, Della Co should not recognise any revenue and should not derecognise the specialised product, but should instead recognise a financial liability for $242,000 for the amount received from Cromer Co. Della Co should also recognise an interest expense for $500 over the two months to 31 January 20X1, which increases the liability.

On 31 January 20X1, if the contract is not cancelled, Della Co should derecognise the liability and recognise revenue of $242,500.

(b) Consignment arrangement

This transaction appears to be a consignment arrangement. A consignment arrangement exists when a product is delivered to another party for sale to end customers, but the other party does not obtain control of the product.

IFRS 15 includes the following indicators that an arrangement is a consignment arrangement between an entity and a dealer:

(i) the product is controlled by the entity until a specified event occurs, such as the sale of the product to a customer of the dealer or until a specified period expires;

(ii) the entity is able to require the return of the product or transfer the product to a third party (such as another dealer); and

(iii) the dealer does not have an unconditional obligation to pay for the product (although it might be required to pay a deposit).

IFRS 15 defines control as the ability to direct the use of and to obtain substantially all the remaining benefits from the asset. From the information provided, product X appears to be controlled by Della Co until it is sold to the end customer because Della Co can dictate the selling price and legal title passes directly from Della Co to the end customer and does not transfer to Acra Co at any point.

Acra Co does not have an unconditional obligation to pay for the product, only amounts relating to items of product X that have been sold must be remitted to Della Co, and any remaining deposit at the end of the six-month period is refundable. Furthermore, Acra Co is required to return any unsold product at the end of the six-month trial period.

It therefore seems that this is a consignment arrangement. As such, any items of product X that are still held by Acra Co should be retained in the inventory balance of Della Co until they are sold to end customers. Della Co should only recognise revenue relating to product X on products which Acra Co has sold on to end customers.

Any remaining amount of the deposit paid by Acra Co is refundable on return of any unsold goods at the end of the trial period and should be recognised by Della Co as a current liability.

(c) Hedge accounting

At 31 December 20X0, the interest rate swap had not been arranged and therefore the fair value gain of $500,000 on the investment in bonds should be accounted for through other comprehensive income. The finance income of $120,000 ($2m × 6%) should be recorded in profit or loss. The journal entries would be:

Debit Financial asset (bond)	$500,000	
Debit Bank/cash	$120,000	
Credit Finance income		$120,000
Credit Other comprehensive income		$500,000

On 1 January 20X1, Della Co entered into a hedging arrangement. In order to apply hedge accounting, IFRS 9 requires that all of the following conditions are met:

(i) The hedging relationship consists **only of eligible hedging instruments and eligible hedged items.**

(ii) There must be **formal documentation** which includes identification of the hedged item and hedging instrument and the nature of the risk.

(iii) The hedging relationship meets all of the following hedge effectiveness criteria

    (1)   There is an **economic relationship** between the hedged item and the hedging instrument, ie the hedging instrument and the hedged item have values that generally move in the opposite direction because of the same risk, which is the hedged risk;

    (2)   The **effect of credit risk does not dominate the value** changes that result from that economic relationship, ie the gain or loss from credit risk does not frustrate the effect of changes in the underlyings on the value of the hedging instrument or the hedged item, even if those changes were significant; and

    (3)   The **hedge ratio of the hedging relationship** (quantity of hedging instrument vs quantity of hedged item) is the same as that resulting from the quantity of the hedged item that the entity **actually hedges** and the quantity of the hedging instrument that the entity **actually uses** to hedge that quantity of hedged item.

Assuming that all of this is in place and that the hedge effectiveness criteria are met, Della Co can apply the hedge accounting requirements of IFRS 9. As Della Co is hedging the risk that the fair value of the bond will change, it has entered into a fair value hedge.

The investment in bonds is the hedged item and the interest rate swap (a derivative) is the hedging instrument.

At 31 December 20X1, the interest rate swap should be recognised as a financial asset with a fair value of $550,000 and a gain of $550,000 should be recognised through profit or loss:

Debit Financial asset (swap)	$550,000	
Credit Profit or loss		$550,000

The fair value loss of $600,000 ($2.5m - $1.9m) on the investment in bonds should then be recognised in profit or loss, rather than in other comprehensive income, to reflect the hedging relationship.

The interest income of $120,000 on the bonds should be recognised as finance income through profit or loss.

The required journal entries are:

Debit Profit or loss	$600,000	
Debit Bank/cash	$120,000	
Credit Finance income		$120,000
Credit Financial asset (bond)		$600,000

ACCA

Strategic Business Reporting (International)

Mock Examination 1

Questions	
Time allowed	3 hours 15 minutes
This exam is divided into two sections	
Section A	BOTH questions are compulsory and MUST be attempted
Section B	BOTH questions are compulsory and MUST be attempted

DO NOT OPEN THIS EXAM UNTIL YOU ARE READY TO START
UNDER EXAMINATION CONDITIONS

Section A – BOTH questions are compulsory and MUST be attempted

1 Joey

Joey, a public limited company, operates in the media sector. Joey has two subsidiaries: Margy and Hulty.

The following exhibits provide information relevant to the question.

Exhibit 1 - Draft statements of financial position

The draft statements of financial position at 30 November 20X4 are as follows:

	Joey $m	Margy $m	Hulty $m
Assets			
Non-current assets			
Property, plant and equipment	3,295	2,000	1,200
Investments in subsidiaries			
Margy	1,675		
Hulty	700		
	5,670	2,000	1,200
Current assets	985	861	150
Total assets	6,655	2,861	1,350
Equity and liabilities			
Share capital	850	1,020	600
Retained earnings	3,340	980	350
Other components of equity	250	80	40
Total equity	4,440	2,080	990
Total liabilities	2,215	781	360
Total equity and liabilities	6,655	2,861	1,350

Exhibit 2 - Acquisition of Margy

On 1 December 20X1, Joey acquired 30% of the ordinary shares of Margy for a cash consideration of $600 million when the fair value of Margy's identifiable net assets was $1,840 million. Joey has equity accounted for Margy up to 30 November 20X3. Joey's share of Margy's undistributed profit amounted to $90 million and its share of a revaluation gain amounted to $10 million for the period 1 December 20X1 to 30 November 20X3.

On 1 December 20X3, Joey acquired a further 40% of the ordinary shares of Margy for a cash consideration of $975 million and gained control of the company. The cash consideration paid has been added to the equity accounted balance for Margy at 1 December 20X3 to give the carrying amount at 30 November 20X4.

At 1 December 20X3, the fair value of Margy's identifiable net assets was $2,250 million. The excess of the fair value of the net assets over their carrying amount at that date is due to an increase in the value of non-depreciable land and a contingent liability. At 1 December 20X3, the fair value of the equity interest in Margy held by Joey before the business combination was $705 million and the fair value of the non-controlling interest of 30% was assessed as $620 million. The retained earnings and other components of equity of Margy at 1 December 20X3 were $900 million and $70 million respectively. It is group policy to measure the non-controlling interest at fair value. The goodwill that arises the acquisition of Margy has been tested for impairment and is not considered impaired.

Contingent liability

On 1 December 20X3, Joey included in the fair value of Margy's identifiable net assets, an unrecognised contingent liability with a fair value of $6 million in respect of a warranty claim in progress against Margy, considered to have been measured reliably. In March 20X4, there was a revision of the estimate of the liability to $5 million. The amount has met the criteria to be recognised as a provision in current liabilities in the financial statements of Margy and the revision of the estimate is deemed to be a measurement period adjustment.

Fair value of buildings

Buildings with a carrying amount of $200 million had been included in the fair value of Margy's identifiable net assets at 1 December 20X3. The buildings have a remaining useful life of 20 years at 1 December 20X3 and are depreciated on the straight-line basis. However, Joey had commissioned an independent valuation of the buildings of Margy which was not complete at 1 December 20X3 and therefore not considered in the fair value of the identifiable net assets at the acquisition date. The valuations were received on 1 April 20X4 and resulted in a decrease of $40 million in the fair value of property, plant and equipment at the date of acquisition. This decrease does not affect the fair value of the non-controlling interest at acquisition and has not been entered into the financial statements of Margy.

Exhibit 3 - Acquisition of Hulty

On 1 December 20X3, Joey acquired 80% of the equity interests of Hulty, a private entity, in exchange for cash of $700 million, gaining control of Hulty from that date. Because the former owners of Hulty needed to dispose of the investment quickly, they did not have sufficient time to market the investment to many potential buyers. The fair value of the identifiable net assets was $960 million. Joey determined that the fair value of the 20% non-controlling interest in Hulty at that date was $250 million. Joey reviewed the procedures used to identify and measure the assets acquired and liabilities assumed and to measure the fair value of both the non-controlling interest and the consideration transferred. After that review, Hulty determined that the procedures and resulting measures were appropriate. The retained earnings and other components of equity of Hulty at 1 December 20X3 were $300 million and $40 million respectively. The excess in fair value is due to an unrecognised franchise right, which Joey had granted to Hulty on 1 December 20X2 for five years. At the time of the acquisition, the franchise right could be sold for its market price. It is group policy to measure the non-controlling interest at fair value.

Goodwill arising on the acquisition of Hulty has been tested for impairment and is not considered impaired.

Exhibit 4 - Property for sale

From 30 November 20X3, Joey carried a property in its statement of financial position at its revalued amount of $14 million in accordance with IAS 16 *Property, Plant and Equipment*. Depreciation is charged at $300,000 per year on the straight-line basis. In March 20X4, the management decided to sell the property and it was advertised for sale. On 31 March 20X4, the sale was considered to be highly probable and the criteria for IFRS 5 *Non-current Assets Held for Sale and Discontinued Operations* were met. At that date, the property's fair value was $15.4 million and its value in use was $15.8 million. Costs to sell the property were estimated at $300,000. On 30 November 20X4, the property was sold for $15.6 million. The transactions regarding the property are deemed to be material and no entries have been made in the financial statements regarding this property since 30 November 20X3 as the cash receipts from the sale were not received until December 20X4.

Exhibit 5 - Share options

The Joey Group has granted to the employees of Margy and Hulty, some of whom are considered key management personnel, options over its own shares as at 7 December 20X4. The options vest immediately. Joey is not proposing to make a charge to the subsidiaries for these options.

Joey does not know how to account for this transaction.

Exhibit 6 - Foreign currency loan

Joey took out a foreign currency loan of 5 million dinars at a fixed interest rate of 8% on 1 December 20X3. The interest is paid at the end of each year. The loan will be repaid after two years on 30 November 20X5. The interest rate is the current market rate for similar two-year fixed interest loans.

Joey is unsure how to account for the loan and related interest.

The average currency exchange rate for the year is not materially different from the actual rate.

Exchange rates:	$1 = dinars
1 December 20X3	5.0
30 November 20X4	6.0
Average exchange rate for year ended 30 November 20X4	5.6

Required

(a) (i) Explain, showing relevant calculations and with reference to IFRS 3 *Business Combinations*, how the goodwill balance in Joey's consolidated financial statements at 30 November 20X4 should be calculated. **(10 marks)**

(ii) Explain how the transaction described in Exhibit 4 should be accounted for in Joey's consolidated financial statements at 30 November 20X4. **(6 marks)**

(iii) Prepare, showing required calculations, an extract from Joey's consolidated statement of financial position showing the group retained earnings at 30 November 20X4. **(4 marks)**

(b) Explain to Joey how the share options should be dealt with in the subsidiaries' financial statements and Joey's consolidated financial statements, and advise on any disclosures that may be required to ensure external stakeholders are aware of the transaction.

(5 marks)

(c) Explain to Joey how to account for the foreign currency loan and related interest in its individual financial statements for the year ended 30 November 20X4. **(5 marks)**

(Total = 30 marks)

2 Ramsbury

39 mins

The directors of Ramsbury, a public limited company which manufactures industrial cleaning products, are preparing the consolidated financial statements for the year ended 30 June 20X7. In your capacity as advisor to the company, you become aware of the issues described in the following exhibits.

Exhibit 1 - Loan to director

In the draft consolidated statement of financial position, the directors have included in cash and cash equivalents a loan provided to a director of $1 million. The loan has no specific repayment date on it but is repayable on demand. The directors feel that there is no problem with this presentation as IFRS Standards allow companies to make accounting policy choices, and that showing the loan as a cash equivalent is their choice of accounting policy.

Exhibit 2 - Pension scheme amendment

On 1 July 20X6, there was an amendment to Ramsbury's defined benefit pension scheme whereby the promised pension entitlement was increased from 10% of final salary to 15%. A bonus is paid to the directors each year which is based upon the operating profit margin of Ramsbury. The directors of Ramsbury are unhappy that there is inconsistency on the presentation of gains and losses in relation to pension scheme within the consolidated financial statements. Additionally, they believe that as the pension scheme is not an integral part of the operating activities of Ramsbury, it is misleading to include the gains and losses in profit or loss. They therefore propose to change their accounting policy so that all gains and losses on the pension scheme are recognised in other comprehensive income. They believe that this will make the financial statements more consistent, more understandable and can be justified on the grounds of fair presentation. Ramsbury's pension scheme is currently in deficit.

Required

Discuss the ethical and accounting implications arising from the scenario, with reference to IFRS Standards.

(18 marks)

Professional marks will be awarded in this question for the application of ethical principles.

(2 marks)

(Total = 20 marks)

Section B – BOTH questions are compulsory and MUST be attempted

3 Klancet

Klancet is a public limited company operating in the pharmaceuticals sector. The company is seeking advice on several financial reporting issues.

The following exhibits provide information relevant to the question.

Exhibit 1 - Segment reporting

Klancet produces and sells its range of drugs through three separate divisions. In addition, it has two laboratories which carry out research and development activities.

In the first laboratory, the research and development activity is funded internally and centrally for each of the three divisions. It does not carry out research and development activities for other entities. Each of the three divisions is given a budget allocation which it uses to purchase research and development activities from the laboratory. The laboratory is directly accountable to the division heads for this expenditure.

The second laboratory performs contract investigation activities for other laboratories and pharmaceutical companies. This laboratory earns 75% of its revenues from external customers and these external revenues represent 18% of the organisation's total revenues.

The performance of the second laboratory's activities and of the three separate divisions is regularly reviewed by the chief operating decision maker (CODM). In addition to the heads of divisions, there is a head of the second laboratory. The head of the second laboratory is directly accountable to the CODM and they discuss the operating activities, allocation of resources and financial results of the laboratory.

The managing director does not think IFRS 8 provides information that is useful to investors. He feels it just adds more pages to financial statements that are already very lengthy. The finance director partially agrees with the managing director and believes that the IASB's practice statement on materiality confirms his opinion that not all the disclosure requirements in IFRS 8 are necessary.

Exhibit 2 - Drug development

Klancet is collaborating with Retto, a third party, to develop two existing drugs owned by Klancet.

Project 1

In the case of the first drug, Retto is simply developing the drug for Klancet without taking any risks during the development phase and will have no further involvement if regulatory approval is given. Regulatory approval has been refused for this drug in the past. Klancet will retain ownership of patent rights attached to the drug. Retto is not involved in the marketing and production of the drug. Klancet has agreed to make two non-refundable payments to Retto of $4 million on the signing of the agreement and $6 million on successful completion of the development.

Project 2

Klancet and Retto have entered into a second collaboration agreement in which Klancet will pay Retto for developing and manufacturing an existing drug. The existing drug already has regulatory approval. The new drug being developed by Retto for Klancet will not differ substantially from the existing drug. Klancet will have exclusive marketing rights to the drug if the regulatory authorities approve it. Historically, in this jurisdiction, new drugs receive approval if they do not differ substantially from an existing approved drug.

The contract terms require Klancet to pay an upfront payment on signing of the contract, a payment on securing final regulatory approval, and a unit payment of $10 per unit, which equals the estimated cost plus a profit margin, once commercial production begins. The

cost-plus profit margin is consistent with Klancet's other recently negotiated supply arrangements for similar drugs.

BPP
LEARNING
MEDIA

Required

(a) (i)   Advise the managing director, with reference to IFRS 8 *Operating Segments*, whether the research and development laboratories should be reported as two separate operating segments. **(6 marks)**

      (ii)   Discuss the managing director's view that IFRS 8 does not provide useful information to investors. **(5 marks)**

      (iii)   Discuss whether the finance director is correct in his opinion about IFRS 8. You should briefly refer to Practice Statement 2 *Making Materiality Judgements* in your answer. **(4 marks)**

      Professional marks will be awarded in Part (a) for clarity and quality of presentation.

      (2 marks)

(b)   Prepare notes for a presentation to the managing director of Klancet as to how to account for the contracts with Retto in accordance with IFRS Standards. **(8 marks)**

(Total = 25 marks)

4 Jayach

Jayach is a public limited company with a reporting date of 30 November 20X2.

The following exhibits provide information relevant to the question.

Exhibit 1 - Fair values

Asset traded in different markets

Jayach carries an asset that is traded in different markets. The asset has to be valued at fair value under IFRS Standards. Jayach currently only buys and sells the asset in the Australasian market. The data relating to the asset are set out below.

Year to 30 November 20X2	Asian market	European market	Australasian market
Volume of market – units	4 million	2 million	1 million
Price	$19	$16	$22
Costs of entering the market	$2	$2	$3
Transaction costs	$1	$2	$2

Decommissioning liability

Additionally, Jayach had acquired an entity on 30 November 20X2 and is required to fair value a decommissioning liability. The entity has to decommission a mine at the end of its useful life, which is in three years' time. Jayach has determined that it will use a valuation technique to measure the fair value of the liability. If Jayach were allowed to transfer the liability to another market participant, then the following data would be used.

Input	Amount
Labour and material cost	$2 million
Overhead	30% of labour and material cost
Third party mark-up – industry average	20%
Annual inflation rate	5%
Risk adjustment – uncertainty relating to cash flows	6%
Risk-free rate of government bonds	4%
Entity's non-performance risk	2%

Exhibit 2 - Investment in iCoin

Jayach has recently employed a new managing director. The managing director has convinced the board that an investment in a new cryptocurrency, iCoin, would generate excellent capital gains. Consequently, Jayach purchased 50 units of iCoin for $250,000 on 20 December 20X1. The finance director has expressed concern about how to report this investment in Jayach's 31 December 20X1 financial statements. Given the lack of an accounting standard for such investments, he sees no alternative but to include it as a cash equivalent. As the amount invested is less than the quantitative threshold Jayach has used to assess materiality, he is not planning to provide any further information about the investment in the financial statements.

Exhibit 3 - Email from shareholder

The directors of Jayach have received an email from its majority shareholder.

To: Directors of Jayach
From: A Shareholder
Re: Measurement

I have recently seen an article in the financial press discussing the 'mixed measurement approach' that is used by lots of companies. I hope this isn't the case at Jayach because 'mixed' seems to imply 'inconsistent'? Surely it would be better to measure everything in the same way? I would appreciate it if you could you provide further information at the next annual general meeting on measurement bases, covering what approach is taken at Jayach and why, and the potential effect on investors trying to analyse the financial statements.

Required

(a) Discuss, with relevant computations, how Jayach should measure the fair value of the asset traded in different markets and the decommissioning liability in accordance with IFRS 13 *Fair Value Measurement*. **(11 marks)**

(b) (i) In the absence of a specific accounting standard on cryptocurrencies, discuss how Jayach should determine how to account for the investment in iCoin under IFRS Standards. **(4 marks)**

(ii) Discuss the finance director's decision not to provide any further disclosures about the investment in the financial statements, making reference to IFRS Practice Statement 2 *Making Materiality Judgements*. **(4 marks)**

(c) Prepare notes for the directors of Jayach which discuss the issues raised in the shareholder's email in Exhibit 3. You should refer to the *Conceptual Framework* where appropriate in your answer. **(6 marks)**

(Total = 25 marks)

Answers

DO NOT TURN THIS PAGE UNTIL YOU HAVE
COMPLETED THE MOCK EXAM

Section A

1 Joey

Workbook references. Basic groups and the principles of IFRS 3 are covered in Chapter 11. Step acquisitions are covered in Chapter 12. IFRS 5 is covered in Chapter 14. Share-based payment is covered in Chapter 10. IAS 21 is covered in Chapter 16.

Top tips. For step acquisitions, it is important to understand the transaction – here you have an associate becoming a subsidiary, so the goodwill calculation for Margy needs to include the fair value of the previously held investments. Remember to discuss the principles rather than just working through the calculations. The examiner has stated that a candidate will not be able to pass the SBR exam on numerical elements alone. The other goodwill calculation is very straightforward, the only unusual aspect being that it is a gain on a bargain purchase.

Don't skimp on parts (b) and (c) – there are five marks available.

Easy marks. There are some easy marks available in Part (a) for the standard parts of calculations of goodwill and retained earnings. The calculations in part (c) should also be relatively easy.

Marking scheme

				Marks
(a)	(i)	Goodwill		
		Calculation	4	
		Discussion – 1 mark per point up to maximum	6	
	(ii)	Asset held for sale		
		Calculation	3	
		Discussion – 1 mark per point up to maximum	3	
	(iii)	Retained earnings	4	
				20
(b)	Subjective assessment of discussion – 1 mark per point up to maximum		5	
(c)	Calculation		3	
	Discussion		2	
				10
				30

(a)   (i)   **Goodwill**

IFRS 3 *Business Combinations* requires goodwill to be recognised in a business combination. A business combination takes place when one entity, the acquirer, obtains control of another entity, the acquiree. IFRS 3 requires goodwill to be calculated and recorded at the acquisition date. Goodwill is the difference between the consideration transferred by the acquirer, the amount of any non-controlling interest and the fair value of the net assets of the acquiree at the acquisition date. When the business combination is achieved in stages, as is the case for Margy, the previously held interest in the now subsidiary must be remeasured to its fair value.

Applying these principles, the goodwill on the acquisition of Hulty and Margy should be calculated as follows:

	Hulty		Margy	
	$m	$m	$m	$m
Consideration transferred		700		975
Non-controlling interest (at fair value)		250		620
Fair value of previously held equity interest (Note (1))				705
Less fair value of net assets at acquisition				
Share capital	600		1,020	
Retained earnings	300		900	
Other components of equity	40		70	
Fair value adjustments:				
Land (Note (2) and W1)	–		266	
Contingent liability (Note (3))	–		(6)	
Franchise right (W1)	20		–	
		(960)		(2,250)
Gain on bargain purchase (Note (4))		(10)		50
Measurement period adjustments:				
Add decrease in FV of buildings (Note (5))				40
Contingent liability: $6m – $5m (Note (3))				(1)
Goodwill				89

Notes

(1)   Margy is a business combination achieved in stages, here moving from a 30% owned associate to a 70% owned subsidiary on 1 December 20X3. Substance over form dictates the accounting treatment as, in substance, an associate has been disposed of and a subsidiary has been purchased. From 1 December 20X3, Margy is accounted for as a subsidiary of Joey and goodwill on acquisition is calculated at this date. IFRS 3 requires that the previously held investment is remeasured to fair value and included in the goodwill calculation as shown above. Any gain or loss on remeasurement to fair value is reported in consolidated profit or loss.

(2)   IFRS 3 requires the net assets acquired to be measured at their fair value at the acquisition date. The increase in the fair value of Margy's net assets (that are not the result of specific factors covered in Notes (3) and (5) below) is attributed to non-depreciable land.

(3)   In accordance with IFRS 3, contingent liabilities should be recognised on acquisition of a subsidiary where they are a present obligation arising as the result of a past event and their fair value can be measured reliably (as is the case for the warranty claims) even if their settlement is not probable. Contingent liabilities after initial recognition must be measured at the higher of the amount that would be recognised under IAS 37 *Provisions, Contingent Liabilities and Contingent Assets* and the amount initially recognised under IFRS 3.

(4)   As the goodwill calculation for the acquisition of Hulty results in a negative value, this is a gain on a bargain purchase and should be recorded in profit or loss for the year attributable to the parent. Before doing so, Joey must review the goodwill calculation to ensure that it has correctly identified all of the assets acquired and all of the liabilities assumed, along with verifying that its measurement of the consideration transferred and the non-controlling interest is appropriate. Joey has completed this exercise and thus it is appropriate to record the negative goodwill and related profit.

(5) As a result of the independent property valuation becoming available during the measurement period, the carrying amount of property, plant and equipment as at 30 November 20X4 is decreased by $40 million less excess depreciation charged of $2 million ($40m/20 years), ie $38 million. This will increase the carrying amount of goodwill by $40 million as IFRS 3 allows the retrospective adjustment of a provisional figure used in the calculation of goodwill at the acquisition date where new information has become available about the circumstances that existed at the acquisition date. Depreciation expense for 20X4 is decreased by $2 million.

Workings

1 *Hulty: Fair value adjustments*

	At acq'n 1 Dec 20X3	Movement (over 4 years)	At year end 30 Nov 20X4
	$m	$m	$m
Franchise: 960 – (600 + 300 + 40)	20	(5)	15

2 *Margy: Fair value adjustments*

	At acq'n 1 Dec 20X3	Movement (reduced dep'n)	At year end 30 Nov 20X4
	$m	$m	$m
Land: 2,250 – (1,020 + 900 + 70) + 6*	266	–	266
Property, plant and equipment	(40)	2	(38)

*Contingent liability

(ii) **Asset held for sale**

At 31 March 20X4, the criteria in IFRS 5 *Non-current Assets Held for Sale and Discontinued Operations* have been met, and the property should be classified as held for sale. In accordance with IFRS 5, an asset held for sale should be measured at the **lower of** its **carrying amount** and **fair value less costs to sell**. Immediately before classification of the asset as held for sale, the entity must recognise any impairment in accordance with the applicable IFRS. Any impairment loss is generally recognised in profit or loss. The steps are as follows:

Step 1 Calculate carrying amount under applicable IFRS, here IAS 16 Property, Plant and Equipment:

At 31 March 20X4, the date of classification as held for sale, depreciation to date is calculated as $300,000 × 4/12 = $100,000. The carrying amount of the property is therefore $13.9 million ($14.0 – $0.1m). The journal entries are:

Debit	Profit or loss	$0.1m	
Credit	Property, plant and equipment (PPE)		$0.1m

The difference between the carrying amount and the fair value at 31 March 20X4 is material, so the property is revalued to its fair value of $15.4 million under IAS 16's revaluation model:

Debit	PPE ($15.4m – $13.9m)	$1.5m	
Credit	Other comprehensive income		$1.5m

Step 2 Consider whether the property is impaired by comparing its carrying amount, the fair value of $15.4 million, with its recoverable amount. The recoverable amount is the higher of value in use (given as $15.8 million) and fair value less costs to sell ($15.4m – $3m = $15.1m.) The property is not impaired because the recoverable amount (value in use) is higher than the carrying amount (fair value). No impairment loss is recognised.

Step 3 Classify as held for sale and cease depreciation under IFRS 5. Compare the carrying amount ($15.4 million) with fair value less costs to sell ($15.1 million). Measure at the lower of carrying amount and fair value less costs to sell, here $15.1 million, giving an initial write-down of $300,000.

Debit	Profit or loss	$0.3m	
Credit	PPE		$0.3m

Step 4 On 30 November 20X4, the property is sold for $15.6 million, which, after deducting costs to sell of $0.3 million gives a profit or $0.2 million.

Debit	Receivables	$15.3m	
Credit	PPE		$15.1m
Credit	Profit or loss		$0.2m

(iii) **Retained earnings**

JOEY GROUP

CONSOLIDATED STATEMENT OF FINANCIAL POSITION AS AT 30 NOVEMBER 20X4 (EXTRACT)

	$m
Retained earnings (W1)	3,451.7

Workings

1 *Group retained earnings*

	Joey $m	Hulty $m	Margy $m
At year end	3,340.0	350	980
FV adjustment: dep'n reduction (part (a)(i) W2)			2
FV adjustment: franchise amortisation (part (a)(i) W1)		(5)	
Liability adjustment (6 − 1)* (part (a)(i))			5
Gain on bargain purchase (part (a)(i))	10.0		
Profit on derecognition of associate (W2)	5.0		
Asset held for sale: (0.2 − 0.1 − 0.3) (part (a)(ii))	(0.2)		
At acquisition		(300)	(900)
		45	87

Group share:

Hulty: 80% × 45	36.0
Margy: 70% × 87	60.9
	3,451.7

* The warranty claim provision of $5 million in Margy's financial statements must be reversed on consolidation to avoid double counting. This is because the contingent liability for this warranty claim was recognised in the consolidated financial statements on acquisition of Margy.

2 *Profit on derecognition of 30% associate*

	$m
Fair value of previously held equity interest at date control obtained (per question/((a) (i))	705
Carrying amount of associate: 600 cost + 90 (post-acq'n RE) + 10 (post acq'n OCE)	(700)
Profit	5

(b)   **Share-based payment**

This arrangement will be governed by IFRS 2 *Share-based Payment*, which includes within its scope **transfers of equity instruments of an entity's parent in return for goods or services**. Clear guidance is given in the Standard as to **when to treat group share-based payment transactions as equity settled and when to treat them as cash settled.**

To determine the accounting treatment, the group entity receiving the goods and services must **consider its own rights and obligations as well as the awards granted**. The amount recognised by the group entity receiving the goods and services will not necessarily be consistent with the amount recognised in the consolidated financial statements.

Group share-based payment transactions **must be treated as equity settled** if either of the following apply:

(i)   The entity **grants rights to its own equity instruments**.
(ii)   The entity has **no obligation to settle** the share-based payment transactions.

Treatment in consolidated financial statements

Because the group receives all of the services in consideration for the group's equity instruments, the transaction is treated as **equity settled**. The fair value of the share-based payment at the grant date is **charged to profit or loss over the vesting period with a corresponding credit to equity**. In this case, the options vest immediately on the grant date, the employees not being required to complete a specified period of service and the services therefore being presumed to have been received. The fair value will be taken by reference to the market value of the shares because it is deemed not normally possible to measure directly the fair value of the employee services received.

Treatment in subsidiaries' financial statements

The subsidiaries do not have an obligation to settle the awards, so the grant is treated as an **equity settled** transaction. The fair value of the share-based payment at the grant date is **charged to profit or loss over the vesting period with a corresponding credit to equity**. The parent, Joey, is compensating the employees of the subsidiaries, Margy and Hulty, with no expense to the subsidiaries, and therefore the **credit in equity is treated as a capital contribution**. Because the shares vest immediately, the expense recognised in Margy and Hulty's statement of profit or loss will be the full cost of the fair value at grant date.

IAS 24 disclosures

Some of the employees are considered **key management personnel** and therefore IAS 24 *Related Party Disclosures* should be applied. IAS 24 requires disclosure of the related party relationship, the transaction and any outstanding balances at the year end date. Such disclosures are required in order to provide sufficient information to the users of the financial statements about the potential impact of related party transactions on an entity's profit or loss and financial position.

IAS 24 requires that an entity discloses key management personnel compensation in total and for several categories, of which share-based payments is one. IFRS Practice Statement 2 *Making Materiality Judgements* confirms that disclosures required in IFRSs need only be made if the information provided by the disclosure is **material**. Some related party transactions may be assessed as immaterial and therefore not disclosed. That said, the remuneration of key management personnel is of great interest to investors and it would be difficult to see how it could be considered immaterial.

(c)   **Foreign currency loan**

On 1 December 20X3

On initial recognition (at 1 December 20X3), the loan is measured at the transaction price translated into the functional currency (the dollar), because the interest is at a market rate for a similar two-year loan. The loan is translated at the rate ruling on 1 December 20X3.

Debit	Cash 5m ÷ 5	$1m	
Credit	Financial liability (loan payable)		$1m

Being recognition of loan

Year ended 30 November 20X4

Because there are no transaction costs, the effective interest rate is 8%. Interest on the loan is translated at the average rate because this is an approximation for the actual rate

Debit	Profit or loss (finance cost): 5m × 8% ÷ 5.6	$71,429	
Credit	Financial liability (loan payable)		$71,429

Being recognition of finance costs for the year ended 30 November 20X4

On 30 November 20X4

The interest is paid and the following entry is made, using the rate on the date of payment of $1 = 6 dinars

Debit	Financial liability (loan payable) 5m × 8% ÷ 6	$66,667	
Credit	Cash		$66,667

Being recognition of interest payable for the year ended 30 November 20X4

In addition, as a monetary item, the loan balance at the year-end is translated at the spot rate at the year-end: 5m dinars ÷ 6 = $833,333. This gives rise to an exchange gain of £1,000,000 – $833,333 = $166,667.

The exchange gain on the interest paid of $71,429 – $66,667 = $4,762 is added to the exchange gain on retranslation of the loan of $166,667. This gives a total exchange gain of $4,762 + $166,667 = $171,429.

2 Ramsbury

Marking scheme

	Marks
Accounting issues 1 mark per point to a maximum	9
Ethical issues 1 mark per point to a maximum	9
Professional marks	2
	20

Treatment of loan to director

The directors have included the loan made to the director as part of the cash and cash equivalents balance. It may be that the directors have misunderstood the definition of cash and cash equivalents, believing the loan to be a cash equivalent. IAS 7 *Statement of Cash Flows* defines cash equivalents as short-term, highly liquid investments that are readily convertible to known amounts of cash and which are subject to an insignificant risk of changes in value. However, the loan is not in place to enable Ramsbury to manage its short-term cash commitments, it has no fixed repayment date and the likelihood of the director defaulting is not known. The classification as a cash equivalent is therefore inappropriate.

It is likely that the loan should be treated as a financial asset under IFRS 9 *Financial Instruments*. Further information would be needed, for example, is the $1 million the fair value? A case could even be made that, since the loan may never be repaid, it is in fact a part of the director's remuneration, and if so should be treated as an expense and disclosed accordingly. In addition, since the director is likely to fall into the category of key management personnel, related party disclosures under IAS 24 *Related Party Disclosures* are likely to be necessary.

The treatment of the loan as a cash equivalent is in **breach of the two fundamental qualitative characteristics** prescribed in the IASB's *Conceptual Framework for Financial Reporting*, namely:

(i)   **Relevance.** The information should be disclosed separately as it is relevant to users.

(ii)   **Faithful representation.** Information must be **complete, neutral** and **free from error**. Clearly this is not the case if a loan to a director is shown in cash.

The treatment is also in breach of the *Conceptual Framework's* key **enhancing qualitative characteristics:**

(i)   **Understandability.** If the loan is shown in cash, it hides the true nature of the practices of the company, making the financial statements less understandable to users.

(ii)   **Verifiability.** Verifiability helps assure users that information faithfully represents the economic phenomena it purports to represent. It means that different knowledgeable and independent observers could reach consensus that a particular depiction is a faithful representation. The treatment does not meet this benchmark as it reflects the subjective bias of the directors.

(iii)   **Comparability.** For financial statements to be comparable year-on-year and with other companies, transactions must be correctly classified, which is not the case here. If the cash balance one year includes a loan to a director and the next year it does not, then you are not comparing like with like.

In some countries, loans to directors are **illegal**, with directors being personally liable. Even if this is not the case, there is a potential **conflict of interest** between that of the director and that of the company, which is why separate disclosure is required as a minimum. Directors are responsible for the financial statements required by statute, and thus it is their responsibility to put right any errors that mean that the financial statements do not comply with IFRS. There is generally a legal requirement to maintain proper accounting records, and recording a loan as cash conflicts with this requirement.

In obscuring the nature of the transaction, it is possible that the directors are **motivated by personal interest**, and are thus failing in their duty to act honestly and ethically. There is potentially a self-interest threat to the fundamental principles of the ACCA *Code of Ethics and Conduct*. If one transaction is misleading, it casts doubt on the credibility of the financial statements as a whole.

In conclusion, the treatment is problematic and **should be rectified**.

Ethical implications of change of accounting policy

IAS 8 *Accounting Policies, Changes in Accounting Estimates and Errors* only permits a change in accounting policy if the change is: (i) required by an IFRS or (ii) results in the financial statements providing reliable and more relevant information about the effects of transactions, other events or conditions on the entity's financial position, financial performance or cash flows. A retrospective adjustment is required unless the change arises from a new accounting policy with transitional arrangements to account for the change. It is possible to depart from the requirements of IFRS but only in the extremely rare circumstances where compliance would be so misleading that it would conflict with the overall objectives of the financial statements. Practically this override is rarely, if ever, invoked.

ANSWERS

IAS 19 *Employee Benefits* requires all gains and losses on a defined benefit pension scheme to be recognised in profit or loss except for the remeasurement component relating to the assets and liabilities of the plan, which must be recognised in other comprehensive income. So, current service cost, past service cost and the net interest cost on the net defined benefit liability must all be recognised in profit or loss. There is no alternative treatment available to the directors, which, under IAS 8, a change in accounting policy might be applied to move Ramsbury to. The directors' proposals cannot be justified on the grounds of fair presentation. The directors have an ethical responsibility to prepare financial statements which are a true representation of the entity's performance and comply with all accounting standards.

There is a clear self-interest threat arising from the bonus scheme. The directors' change in policy appears to be motivated by an intention to overstate operating profit to maximise their bonus potential. The amendment to the pension scheme is a past service cost which must be expensed to profit or loss during the period the plan amendment has occurred, ie immediately. This would therefore be detrimental to the operating profits of Ramsbury and depress any potential bonus.

Additionally, it appears that the directors wish to manipulate other aspects of the pension scheme such as the current service cost and, since the scheme is in deficit, the net finance cost. The directors are deliberately manipulating the presentation of these items by recording them in equity rather than in profit or loss. The financial statements would not be compliant with IFRS, would not give a reliable picture of the true costs to the company of operating a pension scheme and this treatment would make the financial statements less comparable with other entities correctly applying IAS 19. Such treatment is against ACCA's *Code of Ethics and Conduct* fundamental principles of objectivity, integrity and professional behaviour. The directors should be reminded of their ethical responsibilities and must be dissuaded from implementing the proposed change in policy.

The directors should be encouraged to utilise other tools within the financial statements to explain the company's results such as drawing users attention towards the cash flow where the cash generated from operations measure will exclude the non-cash pension expense and if necessary alternative performance measures such as EBITDA could be disclosed where non-cash items may be consistently stripped out for comparison purposes.

Section B

3 Klancet

Workbook references. Segment reporting is covered in Chapter 18. Intangible assets are covered in Chapter 4. Financial instruments are covered in Chapter 8. IFRS Practice Statement 2 *Making Materiality Judgements* is covered in Chapter 20.

Top tips. In Part (a)(i), on segment reporting, the key was to argue that the second laboratory met the definition of an operating segment, while the first one did not. In Part (a)(ii) you should consider why segmental information is useful to investors – why would they want this information? What makes this information particularly useful to investors? Part (a)(iii) requires an awareness of current issues in financial reporting, in this case IFRS Practice Statement 2 *Making Materiality Judgements*. It is crucial that you read widely while studying SBR as questions on current issues will definitely feature in your exam.

In Part (b) the key issue was whether the costs could be capitalised as development expenditure, which was the case for the latter, but not the former.

Easy marks. These are available for discussing the principles and quantitative thresholds of IFRS 8 in Part (a).

Marking scheme

			Marks
(a)	(i)	Requirements of IFRS 8 – 1 mark per point up to maximum	6
	(ii)	Usefulness of IFRS 8 – 1 mark per point up to maximum	5
	(iii)	Materiality – 1 mark per point up to maximum	4
(b)		Notes for presentation – 1 mark per point up to maximum	8
Professional marks (Part (a))			2
			25

(a) (i) **Segment reporting**

IFRS 8 *Operating Segments* states that an operating segment is a component of an entity which engages in business activities from which it may earn revenues and incur costs. In addition, discrete financial information should be available for the segment and these results should be regularly reviewed by the entity's chief operating decision maker (CODM) when making decisions about resource allocation to the segment and assessing its performance.

Other factors should be taken into account, including the nature of the business activities of each component, the existence of managers responsible for them, and information presented to the board of directors.

According to IFRS 8, an operating segment is one which meets any of the following quantitative thresholds:

(i) Its reported revenue is 10% or more of the combined revenue of all operating segments.

(ii) The absolute amount of its reported profit or loss is 10% or more of the greater, in absolute amount, of (1) the combined reported profit of all operating segments which did not report a loss and (2) the combined reported loss of all operating segments which reported a loss.

(iii) Its assets are 10% or more of the combined assets of all operating segments.

As a result of the application of the above criteria, the first laboratory will not be reported as a separate operating segment. The divisions have heads directly accountable to, and maintaining regular contact with, the CODM to discuss all aspects of their division's performance. The divisions seem to be consistent with the core principle of IFRS 8 and should be reported as separate segments. The laboratory does not have a separate segment manager and the existence of a segment manager is normally an important factor in determining operating segments. Instead, the laboratory is responsible to the divisions themselves, which would seem to indicate that it is simply supporting the existing divisions and not a separate segment. Additionally, there does not seem to be any discrete performance information for the segment, which is reviewed by the CODM.

The second laboratory should be reported as a separate segment. It meets the quantitative threshold for percentage of total revenues and it meets other criteria for an operating segment. It engages in activities which earn revenues and incurs costs, its operating results are reviewed by the CODM and discrete information is available for the laboratory's activities. Finally, it has a separate segment manager.

(ii) Contrary to the managing director's views, IFRS 8 provides information that makes the financial statements more relevant and more useful to investors. IFRS financial statements are highly aggregated and may prevent investors from understanding the many different business areas and activities that an entity is engaged in. IFRS 8 requires information to be disclosed that is not readily available elsewhere in the financial statements, therefore it provides additional information which aids an investor's understanding of how the business operates and is managed.

IFRS 8 uses a 'management approach' to report information on an entity's segments and results from the point of view of the decision makers of the entity. This allows investors to examine an entity 'though the eyes of management' – to see the business in the way in which the managers who run the business on their behalf see it. This provides investors with more discrete information on the business segments allowing them to better assess the return being earned from those business segments, the risks that are associated with those segments and how those risks are managed. The more detailed information provides investors with more insight into an entity's longer term performance.

The requirement to disclose information that is actually used by internal decision makers is an important feature of IFRS 8, but is also one of its main criticisms. The fact that the reporting does not need to be based on IFRS makes it difficult to make comparisons with information that was reported in prior periods and with other companies in the sector. The flexibility in reporting can make it easier to manipulate what is reported. IFRS 8 disclosures are often most useful if used in conjunction with narrative disclosures prepared by the directors of the company, such as the Strategic Review in the UK.

(iii) The finance director's opinion that 'not all the disclosure in IFRS 8 is necessary' could be interpreted to mean that he believes he can pick and choose which disclosure requirements he feels are necessary and which he believes are not.

This is not correct. IAS 1 Presentation of Financial Statements requires all standards to be applied if fair presentation is to be achieved. Directors cannot choose which parts of standards they do or do not apply.

However, as confirmed by Practice Statement 2, if the information provided by a disclosure is immaterial and it therefore cannot reasonably be expected to influence the decisions of primary users of the financial statements, then that disclosure does not need to be made.

If the finance director is suggesting that the information provided about Klancet by some of the disclosures required by IFRS 8 are not material, then assuming that the information is indeed immaterial, he would be correct in stating that those disclosures are not necessary.

The directors should apply the principles given in Practice Statement 2 to review how they have made materiality judgements in their financial reporting. It may be that their current financial report is very lengthy because they include information that is not material.

> **Tutorial note.** Consideration of the ethical issues was not part of the question requirement, however, it is clear both directors appear reluctant to give the disclosures required by IFRS 8 which raises concern. If the finance director is not aware that he cannot pick and choose requirements from IFRS Standards, then his professional competence may be called into question. If he is aware of this, and an assessment of whether the disclosures are material has not been done, or has been done inappropriately, then it may be that the directors are trying to hide an issue which should be considered in more detail.

(b)   **Development of drugs**

Notes for presentation to the managing director

1   **Criteria for recognising as an asset**

IAS 38 *Intangible Assets* requires an entity to recognise an intangible asset, whether purchased or self-created (at cost) if, and only if, it is **probable** that the future economic benefits which are attributable to the asset will flow to the entity and the cost of the asset can be **measured reliably**.

2   **Internally generated intangible assets**

The recognition requirements of IAS 38 apply whether an intangible asset is acquired externally or generated internally. IAS 38 includes additional recognition criteria for internally generated intangible assets.

Development costs are capitalised only after technical and commercial feasibility of the asset for sale or use have been established. This means that the entity must intend and be able to complete the intangible asset and either use it or sell it and be able to demonstrate how the asset will generate future economic benefits, in keeping with the recognition criteria.

If an entity cannot distinguish the research phase from the development phase of an internal project to create an intangible asset, the entity treats the expenditure for that project as if it were incurred in the research phase only.

The price which an entity pays to acquire an intangible asset reflects its expectations about the probability that the expected future economic benefits in the asset will flow to the entity.

3   **Project 1**

Klancet owns the potential new drug, and Retto is carrying out the development of the drug on its behalf. The risks and rewards of ownership remain with Klancet.

By paying the initial fee and the subsequent payment to Retto, Klancet does not acquire a separate intangible asset. The payments represent research and development by a third party, which need to be expensed over the development period provided that the recognition criteria for internally generated intangible assets are not met.

Development costs are capitalised only after technical and commercial feasibility of the asset for sale or use have been established. This means that the entity must intend and be able to complete the intangible asset and either use it or sell it and be able to demonstrate how the asset will generate future economic benefits. At present, this criterion does not appear to have been met as regulatory authority for the use of the drug has not been given and, in fact, approval has been refused in the past.

4   Project 2

In the case of the second project, the drug has already been discovered and therefore the costs are for the development and manufacture of the drug and its slight modification. There is no indication that the agreed prices for the various elements are not at fair value. In particular, the terms for product supply at cost plus profit are consistent with Klancet's other supply arrangements.

Therefore, Klancet should capitalise the upfront purchase of the drug and subsequent payments as incurred, and consider impairment at each financial reporting date. Regulatory approval has already been attained for the existing drug and therefore there is no reason to expect that this will not be given for the new drug. Amortisation should begin once regulatory approval has been obtained. Costs for the products have to be accounted for as inventory using IAS 2 *Inventories* and then expensed as costs of goods sold as incurred.

4 Jayach

Workbook references. Fair value measurement under IFRS 13 is covered in Chapter 4. The *Conceptual Framework* is covered in Chapter 1, IAS 8 in Chapter 2 and Practice Statement 2 in Chapter 20.

Top tips. Fair value measurement affects many aspects of financial reporting. Part (a) requires application of IFRS 13 to the valuation of assets and liabilities. Ensure that you provide explanations to support your workings. Part (b) looks at an investment in cryptocurrency for which there is no specific accounting standard. Don't panic if you see such a question in your exam. Sensible points which apply the principles of IAS 8 and the *Conceptual Framework* will gain marks. Part (c) considers the topic of measurement from a wider perspective. Make sure you relate your answer to the email given in the question. Remember that the examiner has recommended that you read widely, including technical articles and real financial reports, to support your learning.

Easy marks. Credit will be given for textbook knowledge in Part (a).

Marking scheme

			Marks
(a)	1 mark per point up to maximum of	6	
	Calculations	5	
			11
(b)	(i) 1 mark per point up to maximum of	4	
	(ii) 1 mark per point up to maximum of	4	
			8
(c)	1 mark per point up to maximum of		6
			25

(a)   **Fair value of asset**

YEAR TO 30 NOVEMBER 20X2

	Asian market	European market	Australasian market
Volume of market – units	4m	2m	1m
	$	$	$
Price	19	16	22
Costs of entering the market	(2)	(2)	–
Potential fair value	17	14	22
Transaction costs	(1)	(2)	(2)
Net profit	16	12	20

Notes

1   Because Jayach currently buys and sells the asset in the Australasian market, the **costs of entering that market** are not incurred and therefore **not relevant**.

2   Fair value is **not adjusted for transaction costs**. Under IFRS 13, these are not a feature of the asset or liability, but may be taken into account when determining the most advantageous market.

3   The **Asian market is the principal market** for the asset because it is the market with the greatest volume and level of activity for the asset. If information about the Asian market is available and Jayach can access the market, then Jayach should base its fair value on this market. Based on the Asian market, the **fair value of the asset would be $17**, measured as the price that would be received in that market ($19) less costs of entering the market ($2) and ignoring transaction costs.

4   If **information** about the Asian market is **not available**, or if Jayach **cannot access the market**, Jayach must measure the fair value of the asset using the price in the **most advantageous market**. The most advantageous market is the market that maximises the amount that would be received to sell the asset, after taking into account both transaction costs and usually also costs of entry, which is the net amount that would be received in the respective markets. The most advantageous market here is therefore the **Australasian market**. As explained above, costs of entry are not relevant here, and so, based on this market, the **fair value would be $22**.

It is assumed that market participants are independent of each other and knowledgeable, and able and willing to enter into transactions.

Fair value of decommissioning liability

Because this is a business combination, Jayach must measure the liability at fair value in accordance with IFRS 13, rather than using the best estimate measurement required by IAS 37 *Provisions, Contingent Liabilities and Contingent Assets*. In most cases there will be no observable market to provide pricing information. If this is the case here, Jayach will use **the expected present value technique** to measure the fair value of the decommissioning liability. If Jayach were contractually committed to transfer its decommissioning liability to a market participant, it would conclude that a market participant would use the inputs as follows, arriving at a **fair value of $3,215,000**.

Input	Amount $'000
Labour and material cost	2,000
Overhead: 30% × 2,000	600
Third party mark-up – industry average: 2,600 × 20%	520
	3,120
Inflation adjusted total (5% compounded over three years):	
$3,120 \times 1.05^3$	3,612
Risk adjustment – uncertainty relating to cash flows: 3,612 × 6%	217
	3,829
Discount at risk-free rate plus entity's non-performance risk	
(4% + 2% = 6%): $3,829/1.06^3$	3,215

(b)   (i)   It isn't appropriate for Jayach to classify the investment as a cash equivalent purely because it is unsure of how else to account for it. In the absence of an IFRS covering investments in cryptocurrencies, the directors of Jayach should use judgement to develop an appropriate accounting policy.

In developing the policy, IAS 8 *Accounting Policies, Accounting Estimates and Errors* requires that the directors consider:

(1)   IFRSs dealing with similar issues. For example, the specific facts and circumstances could lead Jayach to conclude that the investment is an intangible asset accounted for under IAS 38 *Intangible Assets*.

(2)   The *Conceptual Framework*. The investment appears to meet the definition of an asset: a present economic resource controlled by the entity as a result of past events. Consideration should be given to the recognition criteria and to other issues such as the measurement basis to apply and how measurement uncertainty may affect that choice given the volatility of cryptocurrencies.

(3)   The most recent pronouncements of other national GAAPs based on a similar conceptual framework and accepted industry practice. This is sparse. The Australian Accounting Standards Board have concluded that standard setting activity on cryptocurrencies should be undertaken by the IASB.

Fundamentally, the directors need to account for the investment in a way which provides **useful** information to the primary users of its financial statements. This means the information provided by the accounting treatment should be **relevant** and should **faithfully represent** the investment.

(ii)   The finance director's decision to not provide any further disclosure about the investment in iCoin is questionable.

The objective of Jayach's financial report is to provide financial information which is useful to its primary users in making decisions about providing resources to Jayach. Practice Statement 2 re-affirms the principle in IFRS that information that is not material does not need to be disclosed in the financial statements. However, whether this information is material should be properly assessed.

Practice Statement 2 recommends that assessment of materiality should be performed with reference to both quantitative factors and qualitative factors. So far, the finance director has only considered quantitative factors, but qualitative factors should be considered. For example, the fact that this investment not the usual type of investment made by Jayach is a qualitative factor. The presence of a qualitative factor lowers the quantitative threshold below what would otherwise be used – so in this case, the investment could be material.

Furthermore, the investment is risky because cryptocurrencies are highly volatile. If it is Jayach's plan to invest in more cryptocurrencies in the future, or even to accept cryptocurrencies as payment, then this investors are likely to consider this important. Depending on their risk appetite, investors may consider the investment too risky and therefore inappropriate, and may be concerned about the potential future impact should Jayach decide to invest more in such currencies.

Part of the decision-making that primary users make on the basis of financial statements involves assessing management's stewardship of Jayach's resources. Some investors may consider this not to be good stewardship, given the risk involved.

(c)   A 'mixed measurement' approach means that a company selects a different measurement basis (eg historical cost or current value) for its various assets and liabilities, rather than using a single measurement basis for all items. The measurement basis selected should reflect the type of entity and sector in which it operates and the business model that the entity adopts.

Some investors have criticised the mixed measurement approach because they think that if different measurement bases are used for assets and liabilities, the resulting totals can have little meaning or lack relevance.

However, a single measurement basis may not provide the most relevant information to users. A particular measurement basis may be easier to understand, more verifiable and less costly to implement. Therefore, a mixed measurement approach is not 'inconsistent' but can actually provide more relevant information for stakeholders.

The *Conceptual Framework* confirms that the IASB uses a mixed measurement approach in developing standards. The measurement methods included in standards are those which the IASB believes provide the most relevant information and which most faithfully represent the underlying transaction or event. It seems that most investors feel that this approach is consistent with how they analyse financial statements. The problems of mixed measurement appear to be outweighed by the greater relevance achieved.

Jayach prepares its financial statements under IFRSs, and therefore applies the measurement bases permitted in IFRSs. IFRSs adopt a mixed measurement basis, which includes current value (fair value, value in use, fulfilment value and current cost) and historical cost.

When an IFRS allows a choice of measurement basis, the directors of Jayach must exercise judgement as to which basis will provide the most useful information for its primary users. Furthermore, when selecting a measurement basis, the directors should consider measurement uncertainty. The *Conceptual Framework* states that for some estimates, a high level of measurement uncertainty may outweigh other factors to such an extent that the resulting information may have little use.

ANSWERS

ACCA

Strategic Business Reporting (International)

Mock Examination 2

Questions	
Time allowed	3 hours 15 minutes
This exam is divided into two sections	
Section A	BOTH questions are compulsory and MUST be attempted
Section B	BOTH questions are compulsory and MUST be attempted

DO NOT OPEN THIS EXAM UNTIL YOU ARE READY TO START
UNDER EXAMINATION CONDITIONS

Section A – BOTH questions are compulsory and MUST be attempted

1 Kutchen Co

Kutchen Co is a listed company which acquired two subsidiaries, House Co and Mach Co, during the year ended 31 December 20X6. Niche Co is a third subsidiary that was both acquired and disposed of during the same period. Kutchen Co has also restructured one of its business segments during the year ended 31 December 20X6.

The following exhibits provide information that is relevant to the question.

Exhibit 1 - Acquisition of House (70%)

On 1 June 20X6, Kutchen Co acquired 70% of the equity interests of House Co. The purchase consideration comprised 20 million shares of $1 of Kutchen Co at the acquisition date and a further 5 million shares on 31 December 20X7 if House Co's net profit after taxation was at least $4 million.

The market price of Kutchen Co's shares on 1 June 20X6 was $2 per share and that of House Co's shares was $4.20 per share. It is felt that there is a 20% chance of the profit target being met.

In accounting for the acquisition of House Co, the finance director did not take into account the non-controlling interest (NCI) in the goodwill calculation. He determined that a gain on a bargain purchase of $8 million arose on the acquisition of House Co, being the purchase consideration of $40 million less the fair value of the identifiable net assets of House Co acquired on 1 June 20X6 of $48 million. This valuation was included in the group financial statements in Exhibit 6.

After the directors Kutchen Co discovered the error, they decided to measure the NCI at fair value at the date of acquisition. The fair value of the NCI in House Co was to be based upon quoted market prices at acquisition. House Co had issued share capital of $1 each, totaling $13 million at 1 June 20X6 and there has been no change in this amount since acquisition.

Exhibit 2 - Mach Co initial acquisition (80%)

On 1 January 20X6, Kutchen Co acquired 80% of the equity interests of Mach Co, a privately owned entity, for a consideration of $57 million. The consideration comprised cash of $52 million and the transfer of non-depreciable land with a fair value of $5 million. The carrying amount of the land at the acquisition date was $3 million and the land has only recently been transferred to the seller of the shares in Mach Co and is still carried at $3 million in the group financial statements at 31 December 20X6.

At the date of acquisition, the identifiable net assets of Mach Co had a fair value of $55 million. Mach Co had made a profit for the year attributable to ordinary shareholders of $3.6 million for the year to 31 December 20X5.

The directors of Kutchen Co wish to measure the non-controlling interest at fair value at the date of acquisition but had again omitted NCI from the goodwill calculation. The NCI is to be measured at fair value using a public entity market multiple method. The directors of Kutchen Co have identified two companies which are comparable to Mach Co and which are trading at an average price to earnings ratio (P/E ratio) of 21. The directors have adjusted the P/E ratio to 19 for differences between the entities and Mach Co, for the purpose of fair valuing the NCI. The finance director has determined that a bargain purchase of $3 million arose on the acquisition of Mach Co being the cash consideration of $52 million less the fair value of the net assets of Mach Co of $55 million. This gain on the bargain purchase had been included in the group financial statements in Exhibit 6.

Exhibit 3 - Acquisition and disposal of Niche Co (80%)

Kutchen Co had purchased an 80% interest in Niche Co for $40 million on 1 January 20X6 when the fair value of the identifiable net assets was $44 million. The partial goodwill method had been used to calculate goodwill and an impairment of $2 million had arisen in the year ended 31 December 20X6. The holding in Niche Co was sold for $50 million on 31 December 20X6. The carrying amount of Niche Co's identifiable net assets other than goodwill was $60 million at the date of sale. Kutchen Co had carried the investment in Niche at cost. The finance director calculated that a gain arose of $2 million on the sale of Niche Co in the group financial statements being the sale proceeds of $50 million less $48 million being their share of the identifiable net assets at the date of sale (80% of $60 million). This was credited to retained earnings.

Exhibit 4 - Business segment restructure

Kutchen Co has decided to restructure one of its business segments. The plan was agreed by the board of directors on 1 October 20X6 and affects employees in two locations. In the first location, half of the factory units were closed on 1 December 20X6 and the affected employees' pension benefits have been frozen. Any new employees will not be eligible to join the defined benefit plan. After the restructuring, the present value of the defined benefit obligation in this location is $8 million. The following table relates to location 1.

Value before restructuring	Location 1 $m
Present value of defined benefit obligation	(10)
Fair value of plan assets	7
Net pension liability	(3)

In the second location, all activities have been discontinued. It has been agreed that employees will receive a payment of $4 million in exchange for the pension liability of $2.4 million in the unfunded pension scheme.

Kutchen Co estimates that the costs of the above restructuring excluding pension costs will be $6 million. Kutchen Co has not accounted for the effects of the restructuring in its financial statements because it is planning a rights issue and does not wish to depress the share price. Therefore, there has been no formal announcement of the restructuring.

Exhibit 5 - Mach Co subsequent acquisition of 20%

When Kutchen Co acquired the majority shareholding in Mach Co, there was an option on the remaining non-controlling interest (NCI), which could be exercised at any time up to 31 March 20X7. On 31 January 20X7, Kutchen Co acquired the remaining NCI in Mach Co. The payment for the NCI was structured so that it contained a fixed initial payment and a series of contingent amounts payable over the following two years.

The contingent payments were to be based on the future profits of Mach Co up to a maximum amount. Kutchen Co felt that the fixed initial payment was an equity transaction. Additionally, Kutchen Co was unsure as to whether the contingent payments were either equity, financial liabilities or contingent liabilities.

After a board discussion which contained disagreement as to the accounting treatment, Kutchen Co is preparing to disclose the contingent payments in accordance with IAS 37 Provisions, Contingent Liabilities and Contingent Assets. The disclosure will include the estimated timing of the payments and the directors' estimate of the amounts to be settled.

Exhibit 6 - Group statement of financial position

Group statement of financial position as at 31 December 20X6

Assets	$
Non-current assets	
Property, plant and equipment	365
Goodwill	-
Intangible assets	23
	388
Current assets	133
Total assets	521
Equity and liabilities	
Share capital of $1 each	63
Retained earnings	56
Other components of entity	26
Non-controlling interest	3
	148
Non-current liabilities	101
Current liabilities	
Trade payables	272
	373
Total liabilities	521

Required

(a) Explain to the directors of Kutchen Co, with suitable workings, how goodwill should have been calculated on the acquisition of House Co and the initial acquisition of Mach Co showing the adjustments which need to be made to the consolidated financial statements to correct any errors by the finance director. (10 marks)

(b) Explain, with suitable calculations, how the gain or loss on the sale of Niche Co should have been recorded in the group financial statements. (5 marks)

(c) Discuss, with suitable workings, how the pension scheme should be dealt with after the restructuring by Kutchen Co of its business segment and whether a provision for restructuring should have been made in the financial statements for the year ended 31 December 20X6. (7 marks)

(d) Advise Kutchen Co on the difference between equity and liabilities, and on the proposed accounting treatment of the contingent payments on the subsequent acquisition of 20% of Mach Co. (8 marks)

(Total = 30 marks)

2 Abby Co   39 mins

The accountant of Abby Co is concerned about the disclosure of trading that has occurred between Abby Co and a company that a director of Abby Co is associated with. This director is also attempting to influence how the accountant should account for two issues associated with the consolidated financial statements. The following exhibits provide information relevant to Abby Co.

Exhibit 1 - Related party transactions

The accountant has discovered that the finance director of Abby Co has purchased goods from a company, Arwight Co, which one of the director's jointly owns with his wife and the accountant believes that this purchase should be disclosed. However, the director refuses to disclose the transaction as in his opinion it is an 'arm's length' transaction. He feels that if the transaction is disclosed, it will be harmful to business and feels that the information asymmetry caused by such non-disclosure is irrelevant as most entities undertake related party transactions without disclosing them. Similarly, the director felt that competitive harm would occur if disclosure of operating segment profit or loss was made. As a result, the entity only disclosed a measure of total assets and total liabilities for each reportable segment.

When preparing the financial statements for the recent year end, the accountant noticed that Arwight Co has not paid an invoice for several million dollars and it is significantly overdue for payment. It appears that the entity has liquidity problems and it is unlikely that Arwight Co will pay. The accountant believes that a loss allowance for trade receivables is required. The finance director has refused to make such an allowance and has told the accountant that the issue must not be discussed with anyone within the trade because of possible repercussions for the credit worthiness of Arwight Co.

Exhibit 2 - Subsidiary fair value adjustments

Additionally, when completing the consolidated financial statements, the director has suggested that there should be no positive fair value adjustments for a recently acquired subsidiary and has stated that the accountant's current position is dependent upon following these instructions. The fair value of the subsidiary is $50 million above the carrying amount in the financial records. The reason given for not fair valuing the subsidiary's net assets is that goodwill is an arbitrary calculation which is meaningless in the context of the performance evaluation of an entity.

Exhibit 3 - Goodwill impairment calculation

Finally, when preparing the annual impairment tests of goodwill arising on other subsidiaries, the director has suggested that the accountant is flexible in the assumptions used in calculating future expected cash flows, so that no impairment of goodwill arises. He has specifically suggested that the accountant should use a discount rate which reflects risks for which future cash flows have been adjusted. He has indicated that he will support a salary increase for the accountant if he follows his suggestions.

Required

Discuss the ethical and accounting implications of the director's suggestions from the perspective of the reporting accountant.   (18 marks)

Professional marks will be awarded in question 2 for the application of ethical principles.
                                                                                        (2 marks)

                                                                             (Total = 20 marks)

Section B – BOTH questions are compulsory and MUST be attempted

3 Africant Co   49 mins

Africant Co owns several farms and also owns a division which sells agricultural vehicles. It is considering selling this agricultural retail division and wishes to measure the fair value of the inventory of vehicles for the purpose of the sale. The directors are also considering several options to value some farmland that the company owns. Finally, the directors are preparing for a forthcoming meeting with shareholders and thinking about questions they might be asked regarding a mixed measurement approach for assets and liabilities.

The following exhibits provide information relevant to the question.

Exhibit 1 - Vehicles

Three markets currently exist for the vehicles. Africant Co has transacted regularly in all three markets.

At 31 December 20X5, Africant Co wishes to find the fair value of 150 new vehicles, which are identical. The current volume and prices in the three markets are as follows:

Market	Sales price per vehicle $	Historical volume – vehicles sold by Africant Co	Total volume of vehicles sold in the market	Transaction costs per vehicle $	Transport cost to market per vehicle $
Europe	40,000	6,000	150,000	500	400
Asia	38,000	2,500	750,000	400	700
Africa	34,000	1,500	100,000	300	600

Africant Co wishes to value the vehicles at $39,100 per vehicle as these are the highest net proceeds per vehicle, and Europe is the largest market for Africant Co's product.

The directors of Africant Co are unclear about the principles behind the valuation of the new vehicles and also whether their valuation would be acceptable under IFRS 13 *Fair Value Measurement*.

Exhibit 2 - Land

Africant Co uses the revaluation model for its non-current assets. Africant Co has several plots of farmland which are unproductive. The company directors of Africant Co believe that the land would have more value if it were used for residential purposes. There are several potential purchasers for the land but planning permission has not yet been granted for use of the land for residential purposes. However, preliminary enquiries with the regulatory authorities seem to indicate that planning permission may be granted. Additionally, the government has recently indicated that more agricultural land should be used for residential purposes.

Africant Co has also been approached to sell the land for commercial development at a higher price than that for residential purposes and understands that fair value measurement of a non-financial asset takes into account a market perspective. The directors of Africant Co are unclear about what is meant by a 'market perspective' and how to measure the fair value of the land in its financial statements.

Exhibit 3 - Mixed measurement approach

Africant Co is about to hold its annual general meeting with shareholders and the directors wish to prepare for any potential questions which may be raised at the meeting. There have been discussions in the media over the fact that the most relevant measurement method should be selected for each category of assets and liabilities. This 'mixed measurement approach' is used by many entities when preparing financial statements. There have also been comments in the media about the impact that measurement uncertainty and price volatility can have on the quality of financial information.

Required

(a) Advise Africant Co on the appropriate accounting treatment of (i) its vehicles and (ii) its land with reference to relevant International Financial Reporting Standards.

(i)	Vehicles	(8 marks)
(ii)	Land	(7 marks)

(b) Discuss the impact which the mixed measurement approach may have on the analysis of financial statements by investors. (8 marks)

Professional marks will be awarded in Part (b) for clarity and quality of presentation. (2 marks)

(Total = 25 marks)

4 Rationale Co

The directors of Rationale Co are reviewing the published financial statements of the group which include performance measures, such as 'underlying profit'. This information is additional to that which is required by IFRS Standards.

The following exhibit provides information relevant to the question.

Exhibit 1 - Financial statement extract

The following is an extract of information to be found in the financial statements.

Year ended	$m	31 December 20X6 $m	31 December 20X5 $m
Net profit/(loss) before taxation and after the items set out below		(5)	38
Net interest expense		10	4
Depreciation		9	8
Amortisation of intangible assets		3	2
Impairment of property	10		
Insurance recovery	(7)		
		3	
Debt issue costs		2	
Share-based payment		3	1
Restructuring charges		4	
Impairment of acquired intangible assets		6	8

The directors use 'underlying profit' to comment on its financial performance. Underlying profit is a measure normally based on earnings before interest, tax, depreciation and amortisation (EBITDA). However, the effects of events which are not part of the usual business activity are also excluded when evaluating performance.

The following items were excluded from net profit to arrive at 'underlying profit'. In 20X6, Rationale Co had to write off a property due to subsidence and the insurance recovery for this property was recorded but not approved until 20X7, when the company's insurer concluded that the claim was valid. In 20X6, Rationale Co considered issuing loan notes to finance an asset purchase, however, the purchase did not go ahead. Rationale Co incurred costs associated with the potential issue and so these costs were expensed as part of net profit before taxation. The directors of Rationale Co felt that the share-based payment was not a cash expense and that the value of the options was subjective. Therefore, the directors wished to exclude the item from 'underlying profit'. Similarly, they wish to exclude restructuring charges incurred in the year, and impairments of acquired intangible assets.

Required

(a) (i) Discuss the possible concerns where an entity may wish to disclose information that is in addition to that required by IFRS standards in its financial statements and whether the *Conceptual Framework for Financial Reporting (2018)* helps in determining the boundaries for disclosure. **(8 marks)**

(ii) Discuss the use and the limitations of the proposed calculation of 'underlying profit' by Rationale Co.

Note. Your answer should include a comparative calculation of underlying profit for the years ended 31 December 20X5 and 20X6. **(9 marks)**

(b)   The directors of Rationale Co are confused over the nature of a reclassification adjustment.

Discuss, with examples, the nature of a reclassification adjustment and the arguments for and against allowing reclassification of items to profit or loss.

Note. A brief reference should be made in your answer to the *Conceptual Framework for Financial Reporting (2018)*.

(8 marks)

(Total = 25 marks)

Answers

DO NOT TURN THIS PAGE UNTIL YOU HAVE
COMPLETED THE MOCK EXAM

Section A

1 Kutchen Co

			Marks
(a)	Application of the following discussion to the scenario:		
	• Contingent consideration	2	
	• NCI	2	
	• Fair value of assets acquired	2	
	Goodwill calculations and corrections required	4	
			10
(b)	Application of the following discussion to the scenario:		
	• Proceeds	1	
	• Carrying amount of the assets disposed of	2	
	Calculation of the gain/loss on disposal of Niche Co	2	
			5
(c)	Application of the following discussion to the scenario:		
	• Present value and past service cost	2	
	• Calculation of SOPL effect	3	
	• Consideration of a restructuring provision	2	7
(d)	Application of the following discussion to the scenario:		
	• Definition of a liability and IAS 32 (liability vs equity)	2	
	• Definition of equity	2	
	• Consideration of contingent payments of Mach Co	4	
			8
			30

(a) Goodwill on the acquisition of House Co and Mach Co should have been calculated as follows.

House Co

	$m	$m
Fair value of consideration for 70% interest	42.00	
Fair value of non-controlling interest	16.38	58.38
Fair value of identifiable net assets acquired		(48.00)
Goodwill		10.38

Tutorial note

The goodwill calculation should be done in the **spreadsheet response option**, in which you can make use of a formula to add up the calculation:

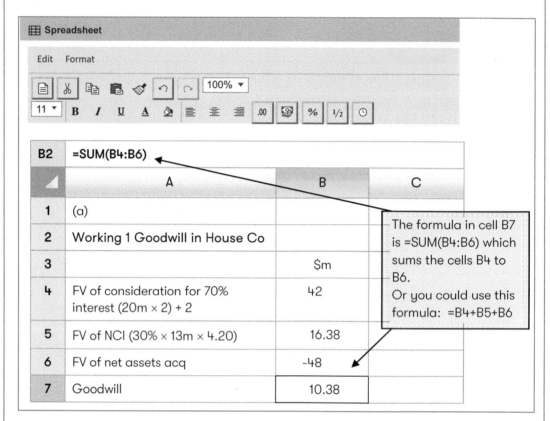

Remember to **cross reference to your working** from your narrative answer. You could say something like 'Refer to Working 1 in the spreadsheet for the goodwill working'.

Contingent consideration should be valued at fair value and will have to take into account the various milestones set under the agreement. The expected value is (20% × 5 million shares) 1 million shares × $2, ie $2 million. There will be no remeasurement of the fair value in subsequent periods because the amount is settled in equity. If this were a liability, there would be remeasurement. The contingent consideration will be shown in OCE. The fair value of the consideration is therefore 20 million shares at $2 plus $2 million (above), ie $42 million.

The fair value of the NCI is 30% × 13 million × $4.20 = $16.38 million.

The finance director has not taken into account the fair value of the NCI in the valuation of goodwill or the contingent consideration. If the difference between the fair value of the consideration, NCI and the identifiable net assets is negative, the resulting gain is a bargain purchase in profit or loss, which may arise in circumstances such as a forced seller acting under compulsion. However, before any bargain purchase gain is recognised in profit or loss, and hence in retained earnings in the group statement of financial position, the finance director should have undertaken a review to ensure the identification of assets and liabilities is complete, and that measurements appropriately reflect consideration of all available information.

The adjustment to the group financial statements would be as follows:

Debit	Goodwill	$10.38 million	
Debit	Profit or loss	$8 million	
Credit	NCI		$16.38 million
Credit	OCE		$2 million

Mach Co

Net profit of Mach Co for the year to 31 December 20X5 is $3.6 million. The P/E ratio (adjusted) is 19. Therefore, the fair value of Mach Co is 19 × $3.6 million, ie $68.4 million. The NCI has a 20% holding; therefore, the fair value of the NCI is $13.68 million.

	$m	$m
Fair value of consideration for 80% interest ($52m + $5m)	57.00	
Fair value of non-controlling interest	13.68	70.68
Fair value of identifiable net assets acquired		(55.00)
Goodwill		15.68

The land transferred as part of the purchase consideration should be valued at its acquisition date fair value of $5 million and included in the goodwill calculation. Therefore, the increase of $2 million over the carrying amount should be shown in retained earnings.

Debit	PPE	$2 million	
Credit	Retained earnings		$2 million

The adjustment to the group financial statements would be as follows:

Debit	Goodwill	$15.68 million	
Debit	Retained earnings	$3 million	
Credit	NCI		$13.68 million
Credit	PPE		$5 million

Total goodwill is therefore $(15.68 + 10.38) million, ie $26.06 million.

(b) **Niche Co**

The finance director had calculated that a gain arose of $2 million on the sale of Niche Co in the group financial statements being the sale proceeds of $50 million less $48 million which is their share of the identifiable net assets at the date of sale (80% of $60 million). However, the calculation of the gain or loss on sale should have been the difference between the carrying amount of the net assets (including any unimpaired goodwill) disposed of and any proceeds received. The calculation of net assets will include the appropriate portion of cumulative exchange differences and any other amounts recognised in other comprehensive income and accumulated in equity. Additionally, the loss on sale should have been reported as a loss in profit or loss attributable to the parent.

The gain on the sale of Niche Co should have been recorded as follows:

	$m
Gain/(Loss) in group financial statements on sale of Niche Co	
Sale proceeds	50.0
Less	
Share of identifiable net assets at date of disposal (80% × $60 million)	(48.0)
Goodwill $(40m – (80% of $44m) – impairment $2m)	(2.8)
Loss on sale of Niche Co recognised in group profit or loss	(0.8)

(c) After restructuring, the present value of the pension liability in location 1 is reduced to $8 million. Thus, there will be a negative past service cost in this location of $(10 – 8) million, ie $2 million. As regards location 2, there is a settlement and a curtailment as all liability will be extinguished by the payment of $4 million. Therefore, there is a loss of $(2.4 – 4) million, ie $1.6 million. The changes to the pension scheme in locations 1 and 2 will both affect profit or loss as follows:

Location 1

Debit	Pension obligation	$2m	
Credit	Retained earnings		$2m

Location 2

Debit	Pension obligation	$2.4m	
Debit	Retained earnings	$1.6m	
Credit	Current liabilities		$4m

IAS 37 *Provisions, Contingent Liabilities and Contingent Assets* states that a provision for restructuring should be made only when a detailed formal plan is in place and the entity has started to implement the plan, or announced its main features to those affected. A board decision is insufficient. Even though there has been no formal announcement of the restructuring, Kutchen Co has started implementing it and therefore it must be accounted for under IAS 37.

A provision of $6 million should also be made at the year end.

(d) The *Conceptual Framework* defines a liability as a present obligation, arising from past events for which there is an expected outflow of economic benefits. IAS 32 *Financial Instruments: Presentation* establishes principles for presenting financial instruments as liabilities or equity. IAS 32 does not classify a financial instrument as equity or financial liability on the basis of its legal form but on the substance of the transaction. The key feature of a financial liability is that the issuer is obliged to deliver either cash or another financial asset to the holder. An obligation may arise from a requirement to repay principal or interest or dividends.

In contrast, equity has a residual interest in the entity's assets after deducting all of its liabilities. An equity instrument includes no obligation to deliver cash or another financial asset to another entity. A contract which will be settled by the entity receiving or delivering a fixed number of its own equity instruments in exchange for a fixed amount of cash or another financial asset is an equity instrument. However, if there is any variability in the amount of cash or own equity instruments which will be delivered or received, then such a contract is a financial asset or liability as applicable.

The contingent payments should not be treated as contingent liabilities but they should be recognised as financial liabilities and measured at fair value at initial recognition. IAS 37 *Provisions, Contingent Liabilities and Contingent Assets* excludes from its scope contracts which are executory in nature, and therefore prevents the recognition of a liability. Additionally, there is no onerous contract in this scenario.

Contingent consideration for a business must be recognised at the time of acquisition, in accordance with IFRS 3 *Business Combinations*. However, IFRSs do not contain any guidance when accounting for contingent consideration for the acquisition of a NCI in a subsidiary. The contract for contingent payments does meet the definition of a financial liability under IAS 32. Kutchen Co has an obligation to pay cash to the vendor of the NCI under the terms of a contract. It is not within Kutchen Co's control to be able to avoid that obligation. The amount of the contingent payments depends on the profitability of Mach Co, which itself depends on a number of factors which are uncontrollable. IAS 32 states that a contingent obligation to pay cash which is outside the control of both parties to a contract meets the definition of a financial liability which shall be initially measured at fair value. Since the contingent payments relate to the acquisition of the NCI, the offsetting entry would be recognised directly in equity.

2 Abby Co

	Marks
Application of the following discussion of accounting issues to the scenario:	
• Related party transactions	2
• Competitive harm exemptions	2
• Impairment of financial assets	2
• Fair value adjustments	2
• Goodwill impairment review	2
Application of the following discussion of ethical issues to the scenario:	
• Potential breaches	4
• Advice to accountant	4
	18
Professional	2
	20

Related parties

The objective of IAS 24 *Related Party Disclosures* is to ensure that an entity's financial statements contain the disclosures necessary to draw attention to the possibility that its financial position and profit or loss may have been affected by the existence of related parties and by transactions and outstanding balances with such parties.

If there have been transactions between related parties, there should be disclosure of the nature of the related party relationship as well as information about the transactions and outstanding balances necessary for an understanding of the potential effect of the relationship on the financial statements. The director is a member of the key management personnel of the reporting entity and the entity from whom the goods were purchased is jointly controlled by that director. Therefore, a related party relationship exists and should be disclosed.

Operating segments

IFRS 8 *Operating Segments* requires an entity to report financial and descriptive information about its reportable segments. Reportable segments are operating segments or aggregations of operating segments which meet specified criteria.

IFRS 8 does not contain a 'competitive harm' exemption and requires entities to disclose the financial information which is provided by the chief operating decision maker (CODM). The management accounts reviewed by the CODM may contain commercially sensitive information, and IFRS 8 might require that information to be disclosed externally.

Under IFRS 8, firms should provide financial segment disclosures which enable investors to assess the different sources of risk and income as management does. This sensitive information would also be available for competitors. The potential competitive harm may encourage firms to withhold segment information.

However, this is contrary to IFRS 8 which requires information about the profit or loss for each reportable segment, including certain specified revenues and expenses such as revenue from external customers and from transactions with other segments, interest revenue and expense, depreciation and amortisation, income tax expense or income and material non-cash items.

Impairment of financial assets

Areas such as impairments of financial assets often involve the application of professional judgement. The director may have received additional information, which has allowed him to form a different opinion to that of the accountant. The matter should be discussed with the director to ascertain why no provision is required and to ask whether there is additional information available.

However, suspicion is raised by the fact that the accountant has been told not to discuss the matter. Whilst there may be valid reasons for this, it appears again that the related party relationship is affecting the judgement of the director.

Fair value adjustments

Positive fair value adjustments increase the assets of the acquired company and as such reduce the goodwill recognised on consolidation. However, the majority of positive fair value adjustments usually relate to items of property, plant and equipment.

As a result, extra depreciation based on the net fair value adjustment reduces the post-acquisition profits of the subsidiary. This has a negative impact on important financial performance measures such as EPS. Therefore, by reducing fair value adjustments it will improve the apparent performance of new acquisitions and the consolidated financial statements.

Accountants should act ethically and ignore undue pressure to undertake creative accounting in preparing such adjustments. Guidance such as IFRS 3 *Business Combinations* and IFRS 13 *Fair Value Measurement* should be used in preparing adjustments and professional valuers should be engaged where necessary.

Impairment tests

In measuring value in use, the discount rate used should be the pre-tax rate which reflects current market assessments of the time value of money and the risks specific to the asset.

The discount rate should not reflect risks for which future cash flows have been adjusted and should equal the rate of return which investors would require if they were to choose an investment which would generate cash flows equivalent to those expected from the asset.

By reducing the impairment, it would have a positive impact on the financial statements. The offer of a salary increase is inappropriate and no action should be taken until the situation is clarified. Inappropriate financial reporting raises issues and risks for those involved and others associated with the company. Whilst financial reporting involves judgement, it would appear that this situation is not related to judgement.

Ethical issues

There are several potential breaches of accounting standards and unethical practices being used by the director. The director is trying to coerce the accountant into acting unethically.

IAS 1 requires all IFRS Standards to be applied if fair presentation is to be obtained. Directors cannot choose which standards they do or do not apply.

It is important that accountants identify issues of unethical practice and act appropriately in accordance with ACCA's *Code of Ethics*. The accountant should discuss the matters with the director. The technical issues should be explained and the risks of non-compliance explained to the director. If the director refuses to comply with accounting standards, then it would be appropriate to discuss the matter with others affected such as other directors and seek professional advice from ACCA. Legal advice should be considered if necessary.

An accountant who comes under pressure from senior colleagues to make inappropriate valuations and disclosures should discuss the matter with the person suggesting this. The discussion should try to confirm the facts and the reporting guidance which needs to be followed.

Financial reporting does involve judgement but the cases above seem to be more than just differences in opinion. The accountant should keep a record of conversations and actions and discuss the matters with others affected by the decision, such as directors. Additionally, resignation should be considered if the matters cannot be satisfactorily resolved.

Section B

3 Africant Co

			Marks	
(a)	(i)	Discussion of the principles of IFRS 13	4	
		Application of the IFRS 13 principles to Africant Co	4	
				8
	(ii)	Market perspective and highest and best use	4	
		Application of highest and best use to Africant Co	3	
				7
(b)		Single vs mixed measurement and investor issues	2	
		Examples	2	
		Investor issues re uncertainty	2	
		Investor issues re price volatility	2	
				8
		Professional		2
				25

(a) (i)   IFRS *13 Fair Value Measurement* says that fair value is an exit price in the principal market, which is the market with the highest volume and level of activity. It is not determined based on the volume or level of activity of the reporting entity's transactions in a particular market.

Once the accessible markets are identified, market-based volume and activity determines the principal market. There is a presumption that the principal market is the one in which the entity would normally enter into a transaction to sell the asset or transfer the liability, unless there is evidence to the contrary.

In practice, an entity would first consider the markets it can access. In the absence of a principal market, it is assumed that the transaction would occur in the most advantageous market. This is the market which would maximise the amount which would be received to sell an asset or minimise the amount which would be paid to transfer a liability, taking into consideration transport and transaction costs.

In either case, the entity must have access to the market on the measurement date. Although an entity must be able to access the market at the measurement date, IFRS 13 does not require an entity to be able to sell the particular asset or transfer the particular liability on that date.

If there is a principal market for the asset or liability, the fair value measurement represents the price in that market at the measurement date regardless of whether that price is directly observable or estimated using another valuation technique and even if the price in a different market is potentially more advantageous.

The principal (or most advantageous) market price for the same asset or liability might be different for different entities and therefore, the principal (or most advantageous) market is considered from the entity's perspective which may result in different prices for the same asset.

In Africant Co's case Asia is the principal market as this is the market in which the majority of transactions for the vehicles occur. As such, the fair value of the 150 vehicles would be $5,595,000 ($38,000 – $700 = $37,300 × 150). Actual sales of the vehicles in either Europe or Africa would result in a gain or loss to Africant Co when compared with the fair value, ie $37,300. The most advantageous market would be Europe where a net price of $39,100 (after all costs) would be gained by selling there and the number of vehicles sold in this market is at its highest. Africant Co would therefore utilise the fair value calculated by reference to the Asian market as this is the principal market.

The IASB decided to prioritise the price in the most liquid market (ie the principal market) as this market provides the most reliable price to determine fair value and also serves to increase consistency among reporting entities.

IFRS 13 makes it clear that the price used to measure fair value must not be adjusted for transaction costs, but should consider transportation costs.

Africant Co has currently deducted transaction costs in its valuation of the vehicles. Transaction costs are not deemed to be a characteristic of an asset or a liability but they are specific to a transaction and will differ depending on how an entity enters into a transaction.

While not deducted from fair value, an entity considers transaction costs in the context of determining the most advantageous market because the entity is seeking to determine the market which would maximise the net amount which would be received for the asset.

(ii)   A fair value measurement of a non-financial asset takes into account a market participant's ability to generate economic benefits by using the asset in its highest and best use or by selling it to another market participant who would use the asset in its highest and best use.

The maximum value of a non-financial asset may arise from its use in combination with other assets or by itself.

IFRS 13 requires the entity to consider uses which are physically possible, legally permissible and financially feasible. The use must not be legally prohibited. For example, if the land is protected in some way by law and a change of law is required, then it cannot be the highest and best use of the land.

In this case, Africant Co's land for residential development would only require approval from the regulatory authority and as that approval seems to be possible, then this alternative use could be deemed to be legally permissible. Market participants would consider the probability, extent and timing of the approval which may be required in assessing whether a change in the legal use of the non-financial asset could be obtained.

Africant Co would need to have sufficient evidence to support its assumption about the potential for an alternative use, particularly in light of IFRS 13's presumption that the highest and best use is an asset's current use.

Africant Co's belief that planning permission was possible is unlikely to be sufficient evidence that the change of use is legally permissible. However, the fact the government has indicated that more agricultural land should be released for residential purposes may provide additional evidence as to the likelihood that the land being measured should be based upon residential value. Africant Co would need to prove that market participants would consider residential use of the land to be legally permissible.

Provided there is sufficient evidence to support these assertions, alternative uses, for example, commercial development which would enable market participants to maximise value, should be considered, but a search for potential alternative uses need not be exhaustive.

In addition, any costs to transform the land, for example, obtaining planning permission or converting the land to its alternative use, and profit expectations from a market participant's perspective should also be considered in the fair value measurement.

If there are multiple types of market participants who would use the asset differently, these alternative scenarios must be considered before concluding on the asset's highest and best use.

It appears that Africant Co is not certain about what constitutes the highest and best use and therefore IFRS 13's presumption that the highest and best use is an asset's current use appears to be valid at this stage.

(b)   A measurement basis must be selected for each element recognised in the financial statements. The *Conceptual Framework* describes the characteristics of historical cost and current value (including fair value) measurement bases and when it may be appropriate to use each basis.

Some investors may be in favour of a **single measurement basis** for all recognised assets and liabilities arguing that the resulting totals and subtotals can have little meaning if different measurement methods are used.

Similarly, they may argue that profit or loss may lack relevance if it reflects a combination of flows based on historical cost and of value changes for items measured on a current value basis.

However, the majority of investors would tend to prefer that the most **relevant measurement method** is selected for each category of assets and liabilities. This is known as a **mixed measurement** approach and is consistent with how investors analyse financial statements.

The *Conceptual Framework* requires selection of a measurement basis that provides the most useful information to primary users, subject to the cost constraint. Therefore, it supports a mixed measurement basis as consideration of these factors is likely to result in the selection of different measurement bases for different items.

The problems of mixed measurement are outweighed by the **greater relevance achieved** if the most relevant measurement basis is used for each class of assets and liabilities. The mixed measurement approach is reflected in the most recently issued standards. For example IFRS 9 *Financial Instruments* requires the use of cost in some cases and fair value in other cases. While IFRS 15 *Revenue from Contracts with Customers* essentially applies cost allocation.

Most accounting measures of assets and liabilities are uncertain and require estimation. While some measures of historical cost are straightforward as it is the amount paid or received, there are many occasions when the measurement of cost can be uncertain. In particular, recoverable cost, for which impairment and depreciation estimates are required.

In a similar vein, while some measures of fair value can be easily observed because of the availability of prices in an actively traded market (a so-called 'Level 1' fair value), others inevitably rely on management estimates and judgements ('Level 2' and 'Level 3').

High measurement uncertainty may mean that the measurement basis selected does not produce a faithful representation of the entity's financial position and financial performance. In such cases, selecting a slightly less relevant measurement basis but with less measurement uncertainty may provide more useful information to investors.

If a relevant measure of an asset or liability value is volatile, this should not be hidden from investors. To conceal its volatility would decrease the usefulness of the financial statements. Of course, such volatile gains and losses do need to be clearly presented and disclosed, because their predictive value may differ from that provided by other components of performance.

4 Rationale Co

(a) (i) There is no specific guidance on the disclosure of additional information which is not specifically required by an IFRS Standard. IFRS Standards require an entity to disclose additional information which is relevant to an understanding of the entity's financial position and financial performance.

A company may disclose additional information where it is felt that its performance may not be apparent from its financial statements prepared under IFRS Standards. A single standardised set of financial statements can never provide sufficient information to understand an entity's position or performance. Additional information can help users understand management's view of what is important to the entity and the nature of management's decisions.

However, there are concerns relating to the disclosure of additional information:

- Such information may not readily be derived or reconciled back to the financial statements.

- There may be difficulty comparing information across periods and between entities because of the lack of a standardised approach.

- The presentation of additional information may be inconsistent with that defined or specified in IFRS Standards and the entity may present an excessively optimistic picture of an entity's financial performance.

- Non-IFRS information may make it difficult to identify the complete set of financial statements, including whether the information is audited or not.

- Non-IFRS information may be given undue prominence or credibility merely because of its location within the financial statements.

Disclosure boundaries are not specifically defined in IFRS Standards, but they do derive from the objective of financial statements. According to the *Conceptual Framework*, the objective of financial statements is to provide financial information about an entity's assets, liabilities, equity, income and expenses which is useful to users of financial statements in assessing the prospects for future net cash inflows to the entity and in assessing management's stewardship of the entity's resources. As a result, financial statements provide information about an entity's assets, liabilities and equity which existed at the end of the reporting period and about income and expenses which arose during the reporting period. It is directed at users who provide resources to the reporting entity but lack the ability to compel the entity to provide them with the information which they need. The *Conceptual Framework* limits the range of addressees of general-purpose financial statements to existing or potential investors, lenders and other creditors. The *Conceptual Framework* acknowledges that general-purpose financial statements may not provide information which serves all users' needs.

(ii)   The directors of Rationale Co are utilising a controversial figure for evaluating the company's performance. Depreciation and amortisation are non-cash expenses related to assets which have already been purchased and they are expenses which are subject to judgement or estimates based on experience and projections. The company, by using EBITDA, is attempting to show operating cash flow since the non-cash expenses are added back.

EBITDA can often be misused and manipulated. It can be argued that because the estimation of depreciation, amortisation and other non-cash items is vulnerable to judgement error, the profit figure can be distorted but by focusing on profits before these elements are deducted, a truer estimation of cash flow can be given. However, the substitution of EBITDA for conventional profit fails to take into account the need for investment in fixed capital items.

There can be an argument for excluding non-recurring items from the net profit figure. Therefore, it is understandable that the deductions for the impairment of property, the insurance recovery and the debt issue costs are made to arrive at 'underlying profit'. However, IAS 1 *Presentation of Financial Statements* states that 'an entity shall present additional line items, headings and subtotals in the statements presenting profit and loss and other comprehensive income when such presentation is relevant to an understanding of the entity's financial performance' (para. 55). This paragraph should not be used to justify presentation of underlying, adjusted and pre-exceptional measures of performance on the face of the statement of profit or loss. The measures proposed are entity specific and could obscure performance and poor management.

Stock-based compensation may not represent cash but if an entity chooses to pay equity to an employee that affects the value of equity, no matter what form that payment is in and therefore it should be charged as employee compensation. It is an outlay in the form of equity. There is therefore little justification in excluding this expense from net profit. Restructuring charges are a feature of an entity's business and they can be volatile. They should not be excluded from net profit because they are part of corporate life. Severance costs and legal fees are not non-cash items.

Impairments of acquired intangible assets usually reflect a weaker outlook for an acquired business than was expected at the time of the acquisition, and could be considered to be non-recurring. However, the impairment charges are a useful way of holding management accountable for its acquisitions. In this case, it seems as though Rationale Co has not purchased wisely in 20X6.

It appears as though Rationale Co wishes to disguise a weak performance in 20X6 by adding back a series of expense items. EBITDA, although reduced significantly from 20X5, is now a positive figure and there is an underlying profit created as opposed to a loss. However, users will still be faced with a significant decline in profit whichever measure is disclosed by Rationale Co. The logic for the increase in profit is flawed in many cases but there is a lack of authoritative guidance in the area. Many companies adopt non-financial measures without articulating the relationship between the measures and the financial statements.

Year ended	31 December 20X6 $m	31 December 20X5 $m
Net profit/(loss) before taxation and after the items set out below	(5)	38
Net interest expense	10	4
Depreciation	9	8
Amortisation of intangible assets	3	2
EBITDA	17	52
Impairment of property	10	
Insurance recovery	(7)	–
Debt issue costs	2	–
EBITDA after non-recurring items	22	52
Share-based payment	3	1
Restructuring charges	4	
Impairment of acquired intangible assets	6	8
Underlying profit	35	61

Tutorial note

The recalculation of underlying profit is best answered using the **spreadsheet response option,** in which you can make use of formulas to add up the columns:

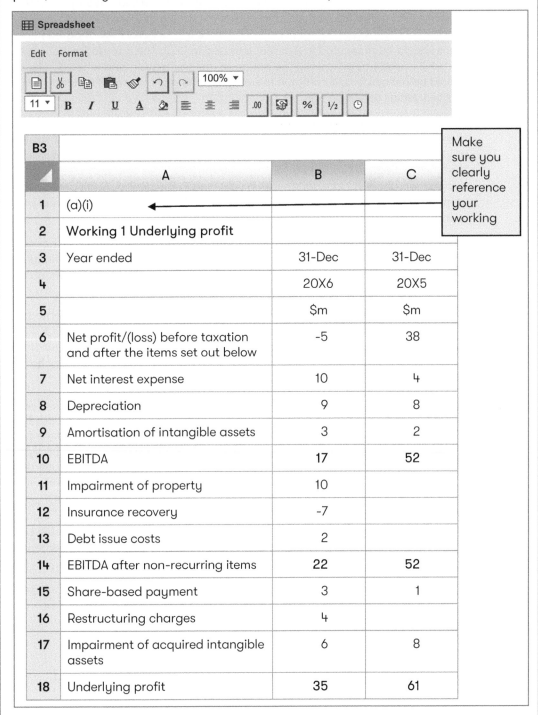

	A	B	C
1	(a)(i)		
2	**Working 1 Underlying profit**		
3	Year ended	31-Dec	31-Dec
4		20X6	20X5
5		$m	$m
6	Net profit/(loss) before taxation and after the items set out below	-5	38
7	Net interest expense	10	4
8	Depreciation	9	8
9	Amortisation of intangible assets	3	2
10	EBITDA	17	52
11	Impairment of property	10	
12	Insurance recovery	-7	
13	Debt issue costs	2	
14	EBITDA after non-recurring items	22	52
15	Share-based payment	3	1
16	Restructuring charges	4	
17	Impairment of acquired intangible assets	6	8
18	Underlying profit	35	61

Make sure you clearly reference your working

Remember to **clearly label your working.**

(b)   Reclassification adjustments are amounts recycled to profit or loss in the current period which were recognised in OCI in the current or previous periods. An example of items recognised in OCI which may be reclassified to profit or loss are foreign currency gains on the disposal of a foreign operation and realised gains or losses on cash flow hedges. Those items which may not be reclassified are changes in a revaluation surplus under IAS 16 *Property, Plant and Equipment*, and actuarial gains and losses on a defined benefit plan under IAS 19 *Employee Benefits*. However, there is a general lack of agreement about which items should be presented in profit or loss and in OCI. The interaction between profit or loss and OCI is unclear, especially the notion of reclassification and when or which OCI items should be reclassified. A common misunderstanding is that the distinction is based upon realised versus unrealised gains.

There are several arguments for and against reclassification. If reclassification ceased, then there would be no need to define profit or loss, or any other total or subtotal in profit or loss, and any presentation decisions can be left to specific IFRS Standards. It is argued that reclassification protects the integrity of profit or loss and provides users with relevant information about a transaction which occurred in the period. Additionally, it can improve comparability where IFRS Standards permits similar items to be recognised in either profit or loss or OCI.

Those against reclassification argue that the recycled amounts add to the complexity of financial reporting, may lead to earnings management and the reclassification adjustments may not meet the definitions of income or expense in the period as the change in the asset or liability may have occurred in a previous period.

The lack of a consistent basis for determining how items should be presented has led to an inconsistent use of OCI in IFRS. Opinions vary but there is a feeling that OCI has become a home for anything controversial because of a lack of clear definition of what should be included in the statement. Many users are thought to ignore OCI, as the changes reported are not caused by the operating flows used for predictive purposes.

Chapter 7 of the *Conceptual Framework* contains guidance on reclassification. There is a presumption that if income and expenses are included in OCI in one period, that they will be reclassified in some future period when doing so enhances the relevance of the information or provides more faithful representation in that period. The presumption can be rebutted if there is no clear basis for identifying the period in which the reclassification would enhance the relevance of the information in the statement of profit or loss. This may indicate that the income or expense should not have been included in OCI originally. It can be argued that reclassification adjustments do not meet the definition of income and expenses in the period they occur and, therefore, those adjustments should be acknowledged as items which do not fulfil the definition of income and expense.

Tutorial note.

This part of the answer is best done in the word processor response option. Remember to use key text from the requirement as headings to break up your answer.

(b)   **Nature of a reclassification adjustment**

Reclassification adjustments are amounts recycled to profit or loss in the current period that were recognised in other comprehensive income (OCI) in a previous period.

The Conceptual Framework states that there is a presumption that if income or expenses are included in OCI in one period they will be recycled to OCI in a future period when doing so provides more relevant information or a more faithful representation in that period.

This presumption can be rebutted if there is no clear basis for identifying the period in which the reclassification would enhance the relevance of the information.

Examples

- Foreign currency gains on the disposal on a foreign operation
- Realised gains or losses on cash flow hedges

Arguments for allowing reclassification

Some people argue that reclassification protects the integrity of profit or loss and provides users with relevant information about a transaction that occurred in the period.

Arguments against allowing reclassification

There is no clear basis in the Conceptual Framework as to when a gain or loss is presented in OCI instead of in profit or loss and when a gain/loss can be recycled.

This means that there is inconsistency between IFRS Standards as to when an item is presented in OCI and when items are recycled.

For example, revaluation gains on property, plant and equipment are recognised in OCI but are not reclassified when the item is disposed, but foreign currency gains on foreign operations previously recognised in OCI are recycled when the foreign operation is disposed of.

It can be argued that reclassification results in increased complexity of financial statements and so make it harder for users of financial statements to understand. The increased complexity could also make it easier for preparers to misclassify amounts in order to manage earnings.

ANSWERS

ACCA

Strategic Business Reporting (International)

Mock Examination 3

Questions	
Time allowed	3 hours 15 minutes
This exam is divided into two sections	
Section A	BOTH questions are compulsory and MUST be attempted
Section B	BOTH questions are compulsory and MUST be attempted

DO NOT OPEN THIS EXAM UNTIL YOU ARE READY TO START
UNDER EXAMINATION CONDITIONS

Section A – BOTH questions are compulsory and MUST be attempted

1 Columbia Co

Columbia Co is the parent of a listed group which operates within the telecommunications industry. During the year ended 31 December 20X5 Columbia Co acquired a new subsidiary and made adjustments to its pension scheme. The group's current year end is 31 December 20X5.

The following exhibits provide information relevant to the question.

Exhibit 1 - Acquisition of Peru Co

Brazil Co is a competitor of Columbia Co. On 1 July 20X5 both Brazil Co and Columbia Co acquired 50% of the 5 million ordinary $1 shares of Peru Co. The consideration paid by Columbia Co consisted of cash of $8 per share and also a 1 for 20 share exchange when the market price of Columbia Co's shares was $10 each. Brazil Co also paid $8 per share for their interest but did not issue any shares to the original shareholders of Peru Co. The ordinary shares of Peru Co have one voting right each.

Following the acquisition, Columbia Co had the contractual right to appoint 60% o the board of Peru Co with the remaining 40% appointed by Brazil Co. Brazil Co has veto rights over any amendments to the articles of incorporation and also over the appointment of auditors. Brazil Co and Columbia Co each appointed one member to Peru Co's senior management team. It is the senior manager appointed by Columbia Co who makes the key decisions regarding the development of Peru Co's new technologies, its principal revenue stream, the markets that it will operate in and how it is financed. The senior manager appointed by Columbia Co also provides a supervisory role and has the right to request that significant activities get board approval, such as imposing restrictions on Peru Co from undertaking activities that would significantly increase credit risk.

Exhibit 2 - Peru Co: net assets at 1 July 20X5

The net assets of Peru Co reported in the individual financial statements had a carrying amount of $32 million on 1 July 20X5. However, on the acquisition of Peru Co, the directors of Columbia Co discovered the following:

On 1 January 20X5 Peru Co acquired 6 million 6% coupon bonds for $6 million in an unquoted company at par ($1). Bond interest is paid annually on 31 December. Due to a premium on redemption the effective rate of interest was 8%. Peru Co has a business model to collect the contractual cash-flows from the bonds and therefore measures them at amortised cost. Columbia Co holds similar unquoted assets but has a business model whereby they may either collect the contractual cash-flows or sell the asset. Bonds with a similar risk profile for a similar quoted company were trading at $2 per bond on 1 July 20X5. A discount of 30% is considered reasonable to reflect the difference in liquidity of the two types of bonds.

One of the identifiable intangible assets of Peru Co at acquisition was a brand. The brand had a carrying amount of $4 million on 1 July 20X5. Columbia Co has a similar branded product and is therefore planning to discontinue the trade of Peru Co's branded product with immediate effect. The future cash-flows from the Peru Co's product post-acquisition are therefore considered to be $nil. If the trade of the branded product were to be sold to a competitor in order to continue the trade, it is estimated that it could be sold for around $5 million.

Peru Co has several technical support service contracts for which there are outstanding performance obligations at 1 July 20X5. Included in contract liability (deferred income) at this date is a balance of $2.8 million in respect of these contracts. It is estimated that these contracts will cost $1.7 million for Peru co (and any other market participants) to complete. A mark-up of 30% is considered reasonable for this type of contract.

Columbia Co has a policy of measuring the non-controlling interest at fair value.

Exhibit 3 - Columbia Co: pension scheme

Columbia Co has, for many years, operated a defined benefit pension scheme. At 1 January 20X5 the fair value of the pension scheme assets were estimated to be $260 million and the present value of the pension scheme liabilities were $200 million. The total of the present value of future refunds and reductions in future contributions (asset ceiling) was $20 million at 1 January 20X5.

This table provides details of the scheme for the year ended 31 December 20X5 when there was a curtailment to the scheme.

Discount rate on good quality corporate bonds: 5%

	$(millions)
Current service cost	30
Cash contributions	21
Benefits paid during the year	25
Scheme curtailment (31 December 20X5)	28
Payment to employees as settlement for curtailment (paid 31 December 20X5)	16

At 31 December 20X5 the fair value of the pension scheme assets were estimated to be $242 million and the present value of the pension scheme liabilities were $195 million. The total of the present value of future refunds and reductions in future contributions (asset ceiling) was $25 million at 31 December 20X5.

Columbia Co intends all new employees to be offered a defined contribution rather than a defined benefit pension scheme. Contributions of $0.5 million were paid into a defined contribution scheme for new employees over the last 3 months of the year.

Required

Draft an explanatory note to the directors of Columbia Co to address the following issues:

(a)   (i)   whether Columbia Co should be considered the acquirer in a business combination with Peru Co;   (9 marks)

      (ii) a calculation of goodwill at 1 July 20X5, explaining how fair values of both the consideration and the net assets have been determined; and   (11 marks)

(b)   how the defined benefit and the defined contribution pension schemes should be accounted for in the year ended 31 December 20X5.   (10 marks)

(Total = 30 marks)

2 Bismuth Co

Bismuth Co is a mining company. Investors in Bismuth Co receive earnings from mining projects as a return on their investment. The year end is 31 December 20X7.

The following exhibits provide information relevant to the question.

Exhibit 1 - Impairment testing of mines

At 31 December 20X7, Bismuth Co owns mines which have a carrying amount of $200 million. The company has committed itself to decommissioning its mines at the end of their useful life (five years or less) and has created a decommissioning provision of $53 million. However, the directors are unsure how the decommissioning provision will impact on the impairment testing of the mines. At the end of the useful life of a mine, its reusable components will be dismantled and sold.

The following information relates to the decommissioning of the mines at 31 December 20X7:

	$ million
Carrying amount of decommissioning provision	53
Present value of future cash inflows from:	
sale of reusable components at decommission date (inflows)	20
sale of mining output from 31 December 20X7 to decommission date (inflows)	203
operating costs from 31 December 20X7 to decommission date (outflows)	48

Exhibit 2 - Class A and B shares

Bismuth Co has issued two classes of shares, class A and class B, in exchange for a cryptocurrency, Bitcoin. Both types of shares permit the holder to vote and give an entitlement to 'rewards'. Bismuth Co has discretion over whether 'rewards' are payable on class A and class B shares. Bitcoin can be readily converted into cash in Bismuth Co's jurisdiction.

Class A shares are redeemable at par in the event of Bismuth Co obtaining a listing on a formal stock exchange which is highly probable. On listing, Bismuth Co has a choice as to the method of redemption either:

(i)   cash to the value of 1 Bitcoin per 1000 class A shares, or
(ii)   shares to the value of 2 Bitcoins per 1000 class A shares.

Note. 1 Bitcoin equates to approximately $12,000

The share settlement option, option (ii) above, would involve exchanging class A shares for the equivalent number of class B shares. Class B shares have never fluctuated in value.

Bismuth Co is not compelled to redeem the class B shares but these shares do contain an option allowing Bismuth Co to repurchase them. However, if within two years, Bismuth Co fails to exercise its call option on the class B shares, it must pay an additional reward to the holders of class B shares.

Exhibit 3 - Blockchain technology

Bismuth Co plans to implement Blockchain technology to store all of its data relating to its mines, trading and to certify the ethical sourcing of all its raw materials. The chief accountant, Ms Pleasant, is currently developing a blockchain technology that will be filed for patent. Ms Pleasant has only recently taken up the post and has discovered that work done at her previous employer, Gypsam Co, is relevant to the project. If Ms Pleasant discloses this information, it will compromise a patent process at Gypsam Co but will consolidate her position as chief accountant in Bismuth Co. When she left the employment of Gypsam Co, she signed a confidentiality agreement but the clauses were not clear or specific about what information could be shared and with whom.

Ms Pleasant has significant knowledge of Blockchain technology but the finance director, Mr Fricklin has limited knowledge of it or the new business model that Bismuth Co is trying to develop. Mr Fricklin has told her that there is no need to spend a significant amount of time creating a technology to ethically source materials. Ms Pleasant is worried about Mr Fricklin's lack of technical and legal knowledge as she feels that it will affect the development of the technology. In addition, some of the data concerning ethically sourced materials has gone missing and she thinks that Mr Fricklin has erased the data to try and sabotage the project. Mr Fricklin has told the Board of Directors that he has an 'in depth knowledge' of the technology.

Required

(a)   Discuss, with suitable calculations, whether Bismuth Co should recognise an impairment loss for the mines.   (5 marks)

(b)   Discuss whether the class A and B shares should be classified as either equity or liability in accordance with IAS 32 *Financial Instruments: Presentation*.   (5 marks)

(c)   Discuss the ethical issues raised by the implementation of the blockchain technology for both the chief accountant and the finance director, including any appropriate actions which should be considered to resolve these issues.   (8 marks)

Professional marks will be awarded in part (c) for the quality of the discussion.   (2 marks)

(Total = 20 marks)

Section B – BOTH questions are compulsory and MUST be attempted

3 Sitka Co

Sitka Co is a software development company which operates in an industry where technologies change rapidly. Its customers use the cloud to access the software and Sitka Co generates revenue by charging customers for the software license and software updates. It has recently disposed of an interest in a subsidiary, Marlett Co, and purchased a controlling interest in Billing Co. The year end of the company is 31 December 20X7

The following exhibits provide information relevant to the question.

Exhibit 1 - Software contract and updates

On 1 January 20X7, Sitka Co agreed a four-year contract with Cent Co to provide access to licence Sitka Co's software including customer support in the form of monthly updates to the software.

The total contract price is $3 million for both licensing the software and the monthly updates. Sitka Co licenses the software on a stand-alone basis for between $1 million and $2 million over a four-year period and regularly sells the monthly updates separately for $2.5 million over the same period. The software can function on its own without the updates. Although, the monthly updates improve its effectiveness, they are not essential to its functionality. However, because of the rapidly changing technology in the industry, if Cent Co does not update the software regularly, the benefits of using the software would be significantly reduced. In the year to 31 December 20X7, Cent Co has only updated the software on two occasions. Cent Co must access the software via the cloud and does not own the rights to the software.

Exhibit 2 - Part-disposal of Marlett Co

Sitka Co prepares separate financial statements in accordance with IAS 27 Separate Financial Statements. At 31 December 20X6, it held a 60% controlling equity interest in Marlett Co and accounted for Marlett Co as a subsidiary. In its separate financial statements, Sitka Co had elected to measure its investment in Marlett Co using the equity method. On 1 July 20X7, Sitka Co disposed of 45% of its equity interest in Marlett Co for $10 million and lost control. At the date of disposal, the carrying amount of Marlett Co in its separate financial statements was $12 million. After the partial disposal, Sitka Co does not have joint control of, or significant influence over Marlett Co and its retained interest of 15% is to be treated as an investment in an equity instrument.

At 1 July 20X7, the fair value of the retained interest of 15% in Marlett Co was $3.5 million. Sitka Co wishes to recognise any profit or loss on the disposal of the 45% interest in other comprehensive income.

Exhibit 3 - Acquisition of Billing Co

Sitka Co has acquired two assets in a business combination with Billing Co. The first asset is 'Qbooks' which is an accounting system developed by Billing Co for use with the second asset which is 'Best Cloud' software. The directors of Sitka Co believe that the fair value of the assets is higher if valued together rather than individually. If the assets were to be sold, there are two types of buyers that would be interested in purchasing the assets. One buyer group would be those who operate in the same industry and have similar assets. This group of buyers would eventually replace Qbooks with their own accounting system which would enhance the value of their assets. The fair values of the individual assets in the industry buyer group would be $30 million for Qbooks and $200 million for 'Best Cloud', therefore being $230 million in total.

Another type of buyer is the financial investor who would not have a substitute asset for Qbooks. They would licence Qbooks for its remaining life and commercialise the product. The indicated fair values for Qbooks and Best Cloud within the financial investor group are $50 million and $150 million, being $200 million in total.

Required

(a)　(i)　Discuss whether the four-year software contract with Cent Co is a single performance obligation in accordance with IFRS 15 *Revenue from Contracts with Customers* including how the revenue from the contract would be accounted for in Sitka Co's financial statements for the year ended 31 December 20X7. Your answer should include whether the revenue should be recognised at a point in time or over time.
(8 marks)

　　(ii)　Discuss briefly why the right to receive access to Sitka Co's software is unlikely to be accounted for as an intangible asset or a lease in Cent Co's financial statements.
(4 marks)

(b)　Discuss and demonstrate how the disposal of 45% interest and the retained interest of 15% in Marlett Co should be accounted for in the separate financial statements of Sitka Co at the date of disposal.
(9 marks)

(c)　Discuss how the two assets acquired on the acquisition of Billing Co should be valued in accordance IFRS 13 *Fair Value Measurement*.
(4 marks)

(Total = 25 marks)

4 Colat Co   49 mins

Colat Co manufactures aluminium products and operates in a region that has suffered a natural disaster on 1 November 20X7. There has been an increase in operating costs as the company had to replace a regional supplier with a more costly international supplier. The year-end of Colat Co is 31 December 20X7.

The following exhibits provide information relevant to the question.

Exhibit 1 - Non-current assets

As a result of the natural disaster, the share price of Colat Co has declined as a significant amount of non-current assets were destroyed, including the manufacturing facility. In addition, Colat Co has suffered reputational damage resulting in a decline in customer demand.

The non-current assets of Colat Co that were destroyed had a carrying amount of $250 million on 31 October 20X7 and the fair value of these non-current assets was $280 million based on an independent appraisal shortly before that date. In addition, Colat Co determined that a power plant will have to be closed and decommissioned earlier than previously expected. The remaining useful life of the power plant has reduced from 25 years to 8 years. Non-current assets are valued using the cost model.

Exhibit 2 - Other natural disaster consequences

Environmental damage and government compensation

Colat Co has, in the past, repaired minor environmental damage that it has caused but it has never suffered a natural disaster on this scale. There is no legal obligation for Colat Co to repair and restore damage caused by the disaster as this will be the responsibility of the government.

The government announced on 1 December 20X7 that there would be compensation of $50 million available to repair the environmental damage only and that companies should apply for the compensation by 31 December 20X7. By 1 March 20X8, when the financial statements were approved, Colat Co had only received an acknowledgement of their application but no approval.

Hedge of commodity price risk in aluminium

Colat Co hedges commodity price risk in aluminium and such transactions were classified as 'highly probable' in accordance with IFRS 9 *Financial Instruments*. However, the purchases which were considered highly probable prior to the natural disaster, are no longer expected to occur.

Potential insurance policy proceeds

Colat Co's insurance policy provides compensation for losses based on the fair value of non-current assets, any temporary relocation costs estimated at $2 million and any revenue lost during the two-month period from 1 November 20X7. At 31 December 20X7, it is unclear which events and costs are covered by insurance policies and significant uncertainty exists as to whether any compensation will be paid. Before the financial statements were approved, it was probable that the insurance claim for the loss of the non-current assets would be paid but no further information was available about other insured losses.

The insurance policy does not cover environmental damage which is the responsibility of the government.

Required

Investors need to understand a variety of factors when making an investment decision. The nature of the companies in which they are looking to invest is an important consideration, as is the need to incorporate sustainability factors into investment decisions.

(a)   Discuss why sustainability has become an important aspect of the investors' analysis of companies.

   Note. There is no requirement to refer to any exhibit when answering part (a).

(4 marks)

Professional marks will be awarded in part (a) for clarity and quality of discussion.

(2 marks)

(b)   Discuss any events affecting Colat Co which might indicate that an impairment test ought to be conducted in accordance with IAS 36 Impairment of Non-Current Assets.   (3 marks)

(c)   Discuss how the following should be accounted for in the financial statements for the year ended 31 December 20X7:

   (i)   the destruction of the non-current assets and decommissioning of the power plant;

(4 marks)

   (ii)   the cost of repairing the environmental damage and the potential receipt of government compensation;   (4 marks)

   (iii) the hedge of the commodity price risk in aluminium; and   (4 marks)

   (iv)   the potential insurance policy proceeds.   (4 marks)

(Total = 25 marks)

Answers

DO NOT TURN THIS PAGE UNTIL YOU HAVE
COMPLETED THE MOCK EXAM

Section A

1 Columbia Co

			Marks	
(a)	(i)	Definition of control	1	
		Application of the following to the scenario:		
		Voting rights	2	
		Governance structure	2	
		Key management	2	
		Premium on consideration	2	
				9
	(ii)	IFRS 13 discussion	2	
		Application of IFRS 13 to the following:		
		– Bonds	2	
		– Brand	2	
		– Deferred income	2	
		Goodwill calculation	3	
				11
(b)		Discussion of defined benefit scheme and asset ceiling	4	
		Defined benefit calculations	5	
		Discussion of the defined contribution scheme	1	
				10
				30

(a) (i) An acquirer is the entity which has assumed control over another entity. In accordance with IFRS 10 *Consolidated Financial Statements*, an investor controls an investee where it has:

- Power over the investee;
- Exposure or rights to variable returns from its involvement with the investee;
- The ability to use its power over the investee to affect the amount of the investor's returns.

There are a significant number of factors to consider when determining which entity should be treated as the acquirer. The first factor to consider is the consideration transferred for the relative share of ownership. It may look at first that Columbia Co and Brazil Co have undertaken a joint venture where the two parties share control over the investee. This is because both Columbia Co and Brazil Co have paid an equal amount of $8 per share. Additionally, Columbia Co and Brazil Co have each obtained 50% of the equity interests and have equal voting rights of one vote per share. Both entities satisfy the criteria for rights to a variable return. However, a joint venture relies upon there being joint control over all the key operating and financing decisions of the entity. The scenario does not indicate that unanimous consent is required because decision-making responsibilities appear to be split between Columbia Co and Brazil Co.

A second factor to consider is who has the rights to appoint the majority of the governing body. Columbia Co can appoint 60% of the board suggesting they may be the acquirer. It is true that Brazil Co does have additional rights in terms of the power to veto amendments to the articles of incorporation and the appointment of auditors. In the assessment of control, it is important to consider whether these rights give Brazil Co power over the investee and whether it can use this power to affect their return. In this assessment, it is important to distinguish between substantive

BPP LEARNING MEDIA

ANSWERS

rights and protective rights. Only rights which are substantive are said to give the investor control. These rights are more likely to be considered protective since they appear to prohibit changes in the activities of the investee which Brazil Co does not agree with rather than give Brazil Co power. Additionally, these are not rights which would allow Brazil Co to affect the profitability of Peru Co and subsequently their return. Protective rights do not prevent Columbia Co from obtaining control.

A similar argument can be applied to the appointment of the senior managers. The entity which has the right to appoint the majority of the senior management team is more likely to be the acquirer. Whilst each entity can appoint one senior manager each, the rights of the senior management appointed by Brazil Co appear to be protective while all key decisions are made by the senior manager appointed by Columbia Co. The rights of the senior manager appointed by Columbia Co therefore appear substantive including requesting board approval for significant activities. They have the rights over decisions affecting the key revenue earning capabilities of Peru Co including technological development, markets to operate it and ways of raising finance. Thus, Columbia Co has power over the investee and these rights enable them to affect their return.

Further evidence that Columbia Co is the acquirer is reflected by the share issue which Columbia paid as additional consideration. To obtain control, it is often the case that the acquirer has to pay a premium on acquisition for their equity interests. Columbia Co has in effect had to pay additional consideration equal to $1.25 million (50% × $5 million × 1/20 × $10) despite each investor acquiring 50% of the equity shares. It can be concluded that Columbia is the acquirer in a business combination and that Brazil Co, in effect, is the non-controlling interest.

(ii) Goodwill at acquisition should be calculated as follows:

	$ millions	$ millions
Consideration		
- Cash (5m shares × 50% × $8)	20	
- Shares (5m shares × 50%/20 × $10)	1.25	21.25
Add fair value of non-controlling interest at acquisition (5m shares × 50% × $8)		20
Less net assets at acquisition – per question:	32	
Fair value adjustment – bonds (see below)	2.16	
Fair value adjustment – brand (see below)	1	
Fair value adjustment – deferred income (see below)	0.59	
		(35.75)
Goodwill at acquisition		5.5

Fair value per IFRS 13 *Fair Value Measurement* defines fair value as the price paid which would be received to sell an asset or paid to transfer a liability in an orderly transaction between market participants at the measurement date. This means that fair value is not entity specific but rather should take into account a market participant's ability to generate economic benefits by using the asset in its highest and best use or by selling it to another market participant who would use the asset in its highest and best use. Goodwill should be measured by deducting the fair value of the identifiable net assets at acquisition from the fair value (including any non-controlling interest) of the consideration paid.

In terms of the consideration paid by Columbia Co for the acquisition of Peru Co, the fair value of the cash paid will be equal to face value. Columbia Co has paid $8 per share for their 50% equity interest resulting in a cash consideration of $20 million (50% × 5 million × $8). The most reliable evidence of fair value is where an observable price for an identical asset or liability is traded on an active market. The fair value of Columbia Co's equity should therefore be measured using the market price of their own shares at the acquisition date of $10 per share. This results in a fair value measurement of $1.25 million (50% × 5 million × 1/20 × $10) for the share for share exchange.

Since the non-controlling interest is also to be measured at fair value and Brazil Co paid $8 per share for their 50% equity interest, this will have a fair value of $20 million.

In assessing the fair value of the identifiable net assets at acquisition, it is important that the net assets of Peru Co are measured using the same accounting policies of the group. Since Columbia Co has similar bonds where their business model is to either collect the cash flows or to sell, the bonds should be measured at their acquisition date fair values and treated as a fair value through other comprehensive income investment rather than amortised cost. The carrying amount of the bonds in the individual financial statements of Peru Co on 1 July 20X5 would be $6.24 million ($6 million + (6/12 × $6 million × 8%)). Since the bonds are in an unquoted company and an active market for an identical asset is not observable, it appears reasonable to use the market value for a similar asset as adjusted for differences in their liquidity. The bonds would have a fair value of $8.4 million (6 million × $2 × 70%). A fair value uplift to the net assets of Peru Co of $2.16 million ($8.4 million − $6.24 million) is required.

The fair value of the brand has to be determined in accordance with its highest and best use for market participants. Since it is not entity specific, the intention by Columbia Co to discontinue the brand is not relevant unless it is what other market participants would also do with the brand. Since it is estimated that a competitor would be prepared to pay $5 million to continue the trade of the brand, this is not the case. The highest and best use of the brand from a market perspective would appear to be continue the trade at a value of $5 million. A $1 million increase is required to the fair value of the brand.

The deferred income must be measured from the market's perspective. Since the market would expect to incur direct and incremental costs of $1.7 million in the performance of their obligations, the fair value should be determined by adding the 30% mark-up to this estimate. The fair value of the deferred income should be $2.21 million ($1.7 million × 130/100). This will result in a decrease in the liabilities at acquisition and therefore an increase in the net assets of Peru Co equal to $590,000 ($2.8 million − $2.21 million).

(b) Where a defined benefit pension scheme is in surplus, IAS 19 *Employee Benefits* requires the surplus to be measured as the lower of:

- The surplus in the plan; and

- The present value of the economic benefits in the form of refunds from the plan or reductions in the future combinations (known as the asset ceiling).

At 1 January 20X5, the surplus of the scheme is $60 million ($260 million − $200 million) but the asset ceiling is only $20 million, so the defined benefit pension asset would have been restricted to $20 million. Interest on the opening asset would therefore be adjusted and only $1 million (5% × $20 million) interest income will be recorded in profit or loss for the year. The cash contributions of $21 million should be added to the scheme assets, benefits paid of $25 million are deducted from both the scheme's assets and the scheme's liabilities and the current service cost of $30 million is charged to profit or loss.

IAS 19 states that an entity must first determine any past service cost arising from a gain or loss on settlement without considering the effect on the asset ceiling. A gain therefore should be recognised in the profit or loss of Columbia Co on the settlement equal to $12 million ($28 million − $16 million). The pension scheme surplus at 31 December 20X5 is summarised as follows.

	Assets $ millions	Liabilities $ millions	Net plan asset before ceiling adjustment $ millions	Ceiling adjustment $ millions	Net plan asset after ceiling adjustment $ millions
Balance 1 January 20X5	260	200	60	(40)	20
Net interest at 5%	13	10	3	(2)	1
Cash contributions	21		21		21
Benefits paid	(25)	(25)			
Current service cost		30	(30)		(30)
Curtailment and settlement	(16)	(28)	12		12
Total at 31 December 20X5	253	187	66	(42)	24

Tutorial note: Candidates are not required to produce this table in its entirety and the detail provided here is for tutorial purposes only.

The actuary has valued the scheme as a surplus of $47 million ($242 million – $195 million) immediately after the curtailment which would result in a remeasurement loss of $19 million ($66 million – $47 million) on 31 December 20X5. However, the effect of the asset ceiling is that the pension scheme would only be recognised at a value of $24 million following the curtailment (see table above). Since the scheme is valued at the lower of the surplus of the scheme and the present value of the economic benefits in the form of refunds from the plan or reductions in the future combinations, the scheme will be restated to $25 million. A net gain of $1 million ($25 million – $24 million) will be recognised in other comprehensive income.

The pension scheme asset should be included in the financial statements of Columbia Co at $25 million (the lower of $25 million and $47 million).

With a defined contribution scheme, it is the employee who undertakes all of the risk should the pension plan not perform to expectations. Columbia Co would have no obligations further to their contributions into the scheme. This means that provided the correct contributions have been paid into the scheme, no asset or liability would be recognised within their statement of financial position. The cash contributions of $0. 5 million are instead recognised as an expense in profit or loss.

2 Bismuth Co

			Marks
(a)	Discussion and application of IAS 36 principles to scenario	3	
	Calculation of impairment	2	
			5
(b)	Discussion and application of IAS 32 principles to scenario	3	
	Contractual obligation discussion	2	
			5
(c)	Discussion of the following key ethical principles and application to the scenario:		
	– Confidentiality	3	
	– Competence	3	
	– Whistleblowing	2	
			8
	Professional marks		2
			20

(a)   Most liabilities are ignored when calculating recoverable amounts in impairment testing. However, certain liabilities, such as decommissioning liabilities, cannot be separated from the related assets.

IAS 36 *Impairment of Assets* requires the carrying amount of a recognised liability to be deducted from both the carrying amount of a cash generating unit (CGU) and the amount determined using the value-in-use (VIU). The recoverable amount of the asset should be determined using the VIU model in IAS 36.

The amount of the decommissioning provision is used to calculate the net recoverable amount by deducting it from the VIU amount. The net recoverable amount is then compared to the carrying amount of the CGU which should be adjusted to include the decommissioning provision in accordance with IAS 37 *Provisions, Contingent Liabilities and Contingent Assets*.

Cash flow projections should be based on reasonable and supportable assumptions, the most recent budgets and forecasts, and extrapolation for periods beyond budgeted projections. IAS 36 presumes that budgets and forecasts should not go beyond five years; for periods after five years, extrapolation should be used from the earlier budgets. In this case, the mines have a useful life of five years or less and, therefore, the cash flow projections can be used in the impairment testing.

At 31 December 20X7	$ millions
Present value of future cash inflows from the sale of components for re-use	20
Present value of future cash inflows from sale of mining output	203
Present value of future cash outflows from operating the mines	(48)
Carrying amount of decommissioning provision	(53)
Recoverable amount (NPV of cash flows)	122
Carrying amount of mines	200
Carrying amount of decommissioning provision	(53)
Net carrying amount of mines	147

The recoverable amount is less than the carrying amount and, hence, there is an impairment charge of $25 million ($147 million − $122 million).

(b)   IAS 32 *Financial Instruments: Presentation* states that a financial instrument is a financial liability if it provides that, on settlement, the entity will deliver either:

(i)   cash or another financial asset; or

(ii)   its own shares whose value is determined to exceed substantially the value of the cash or other financial asset.

Bismuth Co has discretion over whether 'rewards' are payable on class A shares and class B shares. The rewards are essentially a dividend paid on the investment. This would seem to indicate that both instruments should be classified as equity. The Bitcoin can be readily converted into cash in Bismuth Co's jurisdiction and therefore can be treated in the same way as legal tender or cash (also known as fiat money).

The possibility of Bismuth Co listing on a stock exchange is a contingent settlement provision. Bismuth Co is able to avoid listing shares on a stock exchange if it so chooses but is unlikely to do so, as the listing is deemed to be highly probable. Thus, the class A shares will be classified as a liability because the value of the share settlement of 1,000 class A instruments at 2 Bitcoin substantially exceeds that of the 'cash' settlement option of 1 Bitcoin for the same number of instruments and Bismuth Co is implicitly obliged to redeem the instruments for a 'cash' amount of 1 Bitcoin.

If Bismuth Co fails to exercise its call option on the class B shares, it must transfer an additional reward to the holder. An obligation must be established through the terms and conditions of the financial instrument. Anything outside the contractual terms is not relevant to the classification process in accordance with IAS 32. Therefore, the potential failure to exercise the call option does not affect the classification of class B shares as equity as there is no unavoidable contractual obligation to pay the reward or to call the instrument. Also, if the call option is not exercised, the reward payable will only constitute

ANSWERS

an increase in the dividend rate and not a redemption of the class B shares. Hence the class B shares constitute equity shares.

(c)   Ms Pleasant is in a difficult position as regards information gained at a previous employer. In general, she should respect the confidentiality of information acquired as a result of professional and business relationships and therefore, not disclose any such information to third parties without proper and specific authority, unless there is a legal or professional right or duty to disclose. In addition, she should not use the information for her personal advantage. However, the situation will depend upon the nature of the confidentiality agreement with her previous employer. This agreement may have been made in order to protect commercially sensitive information and to prevent her from sharing such information with Bismuth Co. However, if the agreement is not clear or specific, then it will be left up to the ethical conscience of Ms Pleasant as to whether she should disclose the information. The purpose of the agreement is to prevent the disclosure of this type of sensitive information and the chief accountant's ethical conscience should prevail. In addition, the confidentiality agreement may be legally binding.

Opportunities and challenges presented by technology, and new business models, require an evolving level of digital literacy by accountants. Accountants should provide relevant, decision-useful analysis to ensure that the right technological applications are adopted in the best interests of the business. New business models present opportunities for professional accountants to provide relevant advice on regulatory matters. This development requires a growing set of competencies. These competencies relate to not only financial matters but also social impact assessment, environmental accounting or other non-financial capital valuation techniques. Mr Fricklin is obviously not aware of the importance of the entity being environmentally aware as he has told the chief accountant not to worry about ethically sourced material data. Professional accountants need to expand their competency areas to include digital and social awareness. The fundamental principle of professional competence and due care requires that a professional accountant only undertake significant tasks for which the professional accountant has, or can obtain, sufficient specific training or experience. A professional accountant should not intentionally mislead an employer as to the level of expertise or experience possessed such as is the case with Mr Fricklin who has told the board that he has 'in depth knowledge' of the technology.

Ms Pleasant is in a difficult position as regards the competence and sabotage of the project by Mr Fricklin, as an act of 'whistleblowing' can cause a conflict of interest between the personal, organisational and societal spheres. This conflict stems from the way in which a whistle-blower is viewed. The chief accountant could be viewed as someone sharing knowledge of misconduct for the benefit of others or as someone who is acting 'disloyal' to their superior. Ms Pleasant will be torn between loyalty to Mr Fricklin and her own moral commitment.

As long as her motivations are sound and she is confident in the system and her knowledge, she should not hesitate to relay such information as she is helping to create an environmentally aware project which will enhance the company's business.

3 Sitka Co

| Marking scheme |

			Marks
(a)	(i)	Discussion and application of the following to the scenario:	
		IFRS 15	2
		Updates of software	3
		Single performance obligation	1
		Revenue allocated over time	1
		Cannot use residual value	1
			8

			Marks

(ii) Discussion and application of the following to the scenario:

IAS 38	2	
IFRS 16	1	
Service contract	1	
		4

(b) Discussion and application of the following to the scenario:

IAS 27	2	
IFRS 9	3	
IAS 28	2	
Calculation of profit or loss	1	
Principles of OCI	1	
		9

(c) Discussion and application of the following to the scenario:

IFRS 13 highest and best use	2	
Grouping of fair values	2	
		4
		25

(a) (i) IFRS 15 *Revenue from Contracts with Customers* states that goods or services which are promised to a customer are distinct if both of the following criteria are met:

(a) the customer can benefit from the good or service either on its own or together with other resources; and

(b) the entity's promise to transfer the good or service to the customer is separately identifiable from other promises in the contract.

The updates are integral to Cent Co's ability to derive benefit from the licence during the four-year contract, because the entity works in an industry in which technologies change rapidly. The determination of whether licence and updates are separate performance obligations requires judgement. In this case, the updates improve the effectiveness of software without being essential However, for the updates to be combined with the licence, they should fundamentally change the functionality of the software or be essential to its functionality.

Although the software can function on its own without updates, the benefits of using the software would be significantly reduced. The frequency of the monthly updates indicates that they are essential to the effective operation of the software. However, Sitka Co should consider not only the frequency but also whether Cent Co accepts the updates. Updates are made available every month but Cent Co has only updated its software on two occasions which seems to indicate that the software is functional without updates.

To conclude, the benefit which Cent Co could obtain from the licence over the four-year term without the updates would be significantly reduced, the contract to grant the licence and to provide the expected updates is, in effect, a single promise to deliver a combined item to Cent Co. As Cent Co simultaneously receives and consumes the benefits of the entity's performance as it occurs, the performance obligation is satisfied over time. As the contract is a single promise, the revenue of $3 million will be allocated over the four-year time period. Sitka Co should disclose the method used to recognise revenue together with the judgements used to determine the timing of the satisfaction of performance obligations, in the financial statements for the year ended 31 December 20X7. It should not and cannot allocate $2.5 million to the monthly updates and the residual amount of $0.5 million to the licence of software as this does not faithfully reflect the stand-alone selling price of the software.

Note. If the conclusion was that the software could function without updates (since they are not essential to functionality, and Cent Co has only updated twice which could indicate the software is functional without updates), then two performance obligations would be identified and the contract price allocated to each performance obligation. This approach to an answer, if well argued, would have been given credit.

(ii)   Cent Co pays fees to Sitka Co to access and use its software. The recognition criteria for an intangible asset in accordance with IAS 38 *Intangible Assets* are identifiability, control over a resource and existence of future economic benefits. These need to be considered when determining whether an intangible asset is created. The current arrangement with Sitka Co is likely to satisfy the identifiability and existence of future economic benefits criteria, but it is questionable whether the control criterion is satisfied. IAS 38 states that 'an entity controls an asset if the entity has the power to obtain the future economic benefits flowing from the underlying resource and to restrict the access of others to those benefits'. Cent Co does not own the rights to the software at any time.

Thus, Cent Co should not recognise an intangible asset because Cent Co does not control the resource.

The contract is not a lease contract in accordance with IFRS 16 *Leases* as Cent Co does not have the right to direct the use of an asset by having decision-making rights to change how and for what purpose the asset is used throughout the four-year contract. At 1 January 20X7, the contract gave Cent Co only the right to receive access to Sitka Co's software in the future and is therefore a service contract which is expensed over the four-year period.

(b)   IAS 27 *Separate Financial Statements* requires an entity which prepares separate financial statements to account for investments in subsidiaries, joint ventures and associates either:

–   at cost

–   in accordance with IFRS 9 *Financial Instruments*

–   using the equity method as described in IAS 28 *Investments in Associates and Joint Ventures*.

After the partial disposal, Marlett Co is not a subsidiary, joint venture or associate of Sitka Co but is an investment in an equity instrument. Therefore, IFRS 9 is used to account for the retained interest. Investments in equity instruments should be measured at fair value. However, IFRS 9 also states that an entity can make an irrevocable election at initial recognition to present subsequent changes in fair value in other comprehensive income. This can only occur if the investment is neither held for trading nor contingent consideration. In this case, Sitka Co could make such an election at 1 July 20X7. IAS 28 specifies how an entity should account for a transaction which results in discontinuing the use of the equity method because the investment ceases to be an associate or joint venture but retaining an interest which is a financial asset. Here the entity recognises in profit or loss any difference between:

(i)   the fair value of the retained interest and any proceeds from disposing of a part interest in the associate or joint venture; and

(ii)   the carrying amount of the investment at the date the equity method is discontinued.

Thus, Sitka Co would make a profit of $(10 + 3.5 – 12) million, i.e. $1.5 million. This applies regardless of whether the entity elects to present in OCI subsequent changes in fair value of the retained interest. Sitka Co should only present any difference in OCI to subsequent changes in fair value which arise after initial recognition. Such a difference is not a result of a change in fair value but instead results from a change in the measurement basis of the retained interest when an entity loses control of an investee. The difference also meets the definition of income or expenses in the *Conceptual Framework for Financial Reporting* (2018).

(c)   IFRS 13 *Fair Value Measurement* states that the fair value of an asset is the price which would be received to sell an asset or paid to transfer a liability in an orderly transaction between market participants at the measurement date. However, IFRS 13 also uses the concept of the highest and best use which is the use of a non-financial asset by market participants which would maximise the value of the asset or the group of assets and liabilities within which the asset would be used. The fair values of the two assets would be determined based on the use of the assets within the buyer group which operates in the industry. The fair value of the asset group of $230 million is higher than the asset group for the financial investor of $200 million. The use of the assets in the industry buyer group does not maximise the fair value of the assets individually but it maximises the fair value of the asset group. Thus, even though Qbooks would be worth $50 million to the financial investors, its fair value for financial reporting purposes is $30 million as this is the value placed upon Qbooks by the industry buyer group.

4 Colat Co

Marking scheme

				Marks
(a)	Discussion of: Integration of sustainability issues		4	
				4
(b)	Discussion of impairment indicators		2	
	Conclusion		1	
				3
(c)	(i)	Discussion and application to scenario: Derecognition of NCA	1	
		Change in accounting for decommissioning	3	
				4
	(ii)	Discussion and application to scenario of liability for environmental damage	2	
		Government grant	2	
				4
	(iii)	Discussion and application to scenario: Hedged transaction	2	
		Accounting treatment	2	
				4
	(iv)	Discussion and application to scenario: Contingent asset	2	
		Disclosure	2	
				4
	Professional marks			2
				25

(a)   Sustainability has become an increasingly crucial aspect of investing. There is a growing recognition that sustainability can have a significant effect on company financial performance. Investors are increasingly integrating consideration of sustainability issues and metrics into their decision-making. Investors require a better understanding of the wider social and environmental context in which the business operates. This creates a greater trust and credibility with investors and a reduced risk of investors using inaccurate information to make decisions about the company.

Investors have shown an appetite for products which recognise and reflect the relationship between their investments and social and environmental conduct. Investors need to completely understand the nature of the companies in which they are looking to invest and need to incorporate material sustainability factors into investment decisions. They need to understand whether there are material risks or opportunities connected with sustainability factors which do not appear in traditional financial reports.

Their materiality will differ from sector to sector, industry to industry. Sustainability is often unique to the sector. This analysis can be the deciding factor between otherwise identical companies. If the company is viewed poorly based on its sustainability performance, it could lead to a non-investment decision. The increasing availability of data from companies offers the opportunity for rating and ranking analysis, as well as observing trends. These advances have led to the quantitative application of sustainability data in investment analysis and decision making. Companies need a greater knowledge of investor needs and perspectives to help make reporting more relevant to investors and to clearly communicate the financial value of the company's sustainability efforts.

(b)   If Colat Co determines that the events resulting from a natural disaster have triggered impairment indicators, an impairment test must be performed in accordance with IAS 36 *Impairment of Assets* for the respective assets and/or cash-generating units. In this instance, a decline in customer demand has taken place because of the damage in reputation resulting from the disaster. Also, the share price of Colat Co has declined which again may indicate that the carrying amount of the entity's net assets is higher than its market capitalisation. Finally, damage to the manufacturing facility is a direct indicator and the increase in operating costs resulting from the replacement of a supplier in the region with an international supplier is an indirect indicator. The increase in costs as an indicator of impairment depends on the significance and duration of the expected change. Short-term, temporary disruptions are not necessarily indicative of an impairment for assets with a long-term remaining useful life. As a result of the above impairment indicators, an impairment test must be performed in accordance with IAS 36.

(c)   (i)   The destruction of a non-current asset (NCA) results in the derecognition of that asset as opposed to an impairment as there will be no future economic benefits expected either from its use or disposal. Therefore, the NCA of $250 million would be derecognised. As regards the decommissioning of the power plant, IAS 37 *Provisions, Contingent Liabilities and Contingent Assets* requires that a liability is recognised as soon as the obligation arises, which will normally be at commencement of operations. Similarly, IAS 16 *Property, Plant and Equipment* requires the initial cost of an item of property, plant and equipment to include an estimate of the amount of the costs to dismantle and remove the item and restore the site on which it is located. As regards the change in the useful life of the power plant, the present value of the decommissioning liability will increase because of the shorter period over which cash flows are discounted. This increase is added to the carrying amount of the asset, which is tested for impairment. The remaining carrying amount is depreciated prospectively over the following eight years.

        (ii)   Colat Co has, in the past, put right minor environmental damage which it has caused but it has never been involved in a natural disaster on this scale and there is no legal obligation. A constructive obligation for the environmental costs will only result in the recognition of a provision if there is an established pattern of past practice, published policies or a specific current statement that Colat Co will pay for the damage. In this case, the entity has not indicated to other parties that it will accept certain responsibilities and as a result, it has not created a valid expectation. IAS 37 states that a provision should be recognised only when there is a present obligation resulting from past events. The future expected costs would not meet the definition of a provision as there is no legal obligation nor a constructive obligation. In the case of the natural disaster, Colat Co is not at fault and therefore there will be no obligation to correct the environmental damage which may be put right by the government.

                IAS 20 *Accounting for Government Grants and Disclosure of Government Assistance* states that a government grant is recognised only when there is reasonable assurance that the entity will comply with any conditions attached to the grant and the grant will be received. A grant receivable as financial support should be recognised as income in the period in which it is receivable. In this case, Colat Co has only received acknowledgement of its application for a grant on 1 March 20X8 and, therefore, there is no reasonable assurance that the grant will be received. Further, it is not probable that the grant will be received and it should not be disclosed in the financial statements.

(iii)   Prior to the disaster, Colat Co hedges commodity price risk in aluminium and such transactions constituted 'highly probable' hedged transactions in cash flow hedges under IFRS 9 *Financial Instruments*. However, the purchases which were considered highly probable prior to the natural disaster are now not expected to occur. Colat Co should follow hedge accounting principles up until the date of the natural disaster and then should cease hedge accounting. As the forecast transaction is no longer expected to occur, Colat Co should reclassify the accumulated gains or losses on the hedging instrument from other comprehensive income into profit or loss as a reclassification adjustment.

(iv)   IAS 37 does not permit the recognition of contingent assets. Accordingly, an insurance recovery asset can only be recognised if it is determined that the entity has a valid insurance policy which includes cover for the incident and a claim will be settled by the insurer. The recognition of the insurance recovery will only be appropriate when its realisation is virtually certain, in which case the insurance recovery is no longer a contingent asset. Decisions about the recognition and measurement of losses are made independently of those relating to the recognition of any compensation which might be receivable. It is not appropriate to take potential proceeds into account when accounting for the losses. The potential receipt of compensation should be assessed continually to ensure that it is appropriately reflected in the financial statements. The asset and the related income are recognised in the period in which it is determined that a compensation will be received which means reviewing the situation after the end of the reporting period and before the date of approval of the financial statements.

In this case, as it appears probable that the insurance claim for the loss of the non-current assets would be paid and as this information was received before the financial statements were approved, the potential proceeds ($280 million) should be disclosed in the financial statements for the year ended 31 December 20X7. There would be no disclosure of the insurance recovery related to the relocation costs or the lost revenue as the recovery is not virtually certain. The insurance policy does not cover environmental damage which is the responsibility of the government.

ACCA

Strategic Business Reporting (International)

Mock Examination 4

Questions	
Time allowed	3 hours 15 minutes
This exam is divided into two sections	
Section A	BOTH questions are compulsory and MUST be attempted
Section B	BOTH questions are compulsory and MUST be attempted

DO NOT OPEN THIS EXAM UNTIL YOU ARE READY TO START
UNDER EXAMINATION CONDITIONS

Section A – BOTH questions are compulsory and MUST be attempted

1 Chuckle Co

Chuckle Co has an equity interest in a number of entities including Grin Co. Chuckie Co has recently acquired additional equity in Grin Co and the directors of Chuckie Co are unsure as to how this may impact upon their consolidated financial statements. The year end is 31 March each year.

The following **exhibits** provide information relevant to the question.

Exhibit 1 – Initial acquisition of Grin Co

On 1 April 20X2, Chuckle Co acquired 30% of the equity shares of Grin Co. The consideration consisted of $100 million cash. The carrying amount of the net assets of Grin Co on 1 April 20X2 were $286 million which was the same as their fair value. Since then, Grin Co has been correctly treated as an associate in the consolidated financial statements of Chuckle Co.

The remaining 70% of the equity of Grin Co at 1 April 20X2 is owned by a few other investors, none of which own more than 10% of the equity of Grin Co. Analysis shows that all shareholders have voted independently in the past. Chuckle Co and Grin Co share some key management personnel.

Exhibit 2 - Subsequent acquisition of Grin Co

Chuckle Co acquired a further 18% of Grin Co's equity on 1 April 20X6. The consideration for the further 18% of the equity shares of Grin Co on 1 April 20X6 was $66 million in cash. The fair value of the original 30% equity interest was $127 million at 1 April 20X6. The carrying amount of the net assets of Grin Co on 1 April 20X6 was $348 million which included some land which had been revalued upwards by $15 million and correctly accounted for on 1 April 20X5.

Deferred tax at 20% had also been correctly accounted for on this gain in the individual statement of financial position of Grin Co as at 31 March 20X6. The rest of the increase in the net assets of Grin Co since acquisition was solely due to profits. Grin Co paid no dividends during this period.

The remaining 52% of the equity of Grin Co at 1 April 20X6 is owned by a few other investors, none of which own more than 10% of the equity of Grin Co.

On 1 April 20X6, Chuckle Co also acquired some share options in Grin Co exercisable any time until 31 March 20X7. The exercise price of the options at 1 April 20X6 was just above the market price of Grin Co's shares. Grin Co has been profitable for a number of years and the share price has been on an upwards trend which is expected to continue. Chuckle Co would increase its ownership to 60% should it exercise its rights. It is believed that there would be additional cost savings should the additional shares be acquired as decisions at board level could be made more efficiently.

Exhibit 3 - Fair value of net assets of Grin Co

The carrying amounts of the net assets of Grin Co on 1 April 20X6 were as follows:

	$ millions
Non-current assets	355
Current assets	214
Deferred tax	(16)
Other liabilities	(205)
Total	348

Included within the non-current assets was the land which had been previously revalued upwards by $15 million (Exhibit 2) on 1 April 20X5. The carrying amount of this land at 1 April 20X5 and 20X6 was $50 million but its fair value was assessed to be $60 million at 1 April 20X6.

Current assets include finished goods with a cost of $84 million. The fair value of these goods is $131 million.

On 1 April 20X6, the directors of Chuckle Co also identified that Grin Co had an internally generated database of customers who were likely to be interested in purchasing their products. Although there were no contractual or legal rights associated with this database, a professional expert has estimated that competitors of Grin Co would be prepared to pay $5 million for this database. Grin Co has not recognised the database as an asset within their individual financial statements.

The current rate of tax is 20%. This rate should be applied to any fair value adjustments deemed necessary.

Chuckle Co has a policy of measuring the non-controlling interest as the proportionate share of the net assets.

Required

Draft an explanatory note to the directors of Chuckie Co to address the following issues:

(a) (i)   why it was correct to initially classify Grin Co as an associate, as opposed to a subsidiary, on 1 April 20X2;   (4 marks)

(ii)   how Grin Co should be accounted for as an associate using equity method in the consolidated statement of financial position of Chuckie Co at 31 March 20X6. Your answer should also explain how the revaluation of the land at 1 April 20X5 was accounted for (exhibit 2) and include all relevant calculations; and   (5 marks)

(iii) whether the classification of Chuckie Co's investment in Grin Co should change on 1 April 20X6.   (5 marks)

(b) On the assumption that Chuckle Co obtains control on 1 April 20X6, explain:

(i)   how the fair value of the non-current and current assets at acquisition (including any deferred tax adjustments) should be calculated; and   (8 marks)

(ii)   how goodwill/gain on bargain purchase should be calculated at 1 April 20X6. Your discussion should include a brief description of the accounting treatment arising from the additional purchase of the 18% equity in Grin Co.   (8 marks)

(Total = 30 marks)

2 Agency Group

The Agency Group manufactures products for the medical industry. They have been suffering increased competition and therefore have sold a license to distribute an existing product and have also developed a new product which they hope will improve their market reputation. They have recently employed an ACCA student accountant. The year end is 31 December 20X7.

The following **exhibits** provide information relevant to the question.

Exhibit 1 – Ethical issues and foreign exchange

On 1 October 20X7, the finance director, Ms Malgun, a financial accountant, recruited Mr Raavi as an ACCA student accountant on a temporary employment contract which can be terminated by either party without reason. Mr Raavi has found it difficult to find employment and therefore accepted the risk attached to the employment contract. However, the jurisdiction has laws which protect employees from termination due to discrimination. Mr Raavi has been told by Ms Malgun that there has been a global slowdown in business and that the biggest uncertainty is customer demand. She has therefore impressed upon Mr Raavi that the company profitability targets are based upon achieving 30% higher net profit than their nearest competitors. Ms Malgun is partly remunerated through profit related pay.

Ms Malgun has been under significant pressure from the board of directors to meet performance targets and would normally prepare the year-end financial statements. However, for the current year end, she has delegated this task to Mr Raavi.

Mr Raavi has included in profit or loss the foreign exchange gains arising on the re-translation of a foreign subsidiary which is held for sale. Mr Raavi has emailed Ms Malgun informing her of the accounting treatment. Although Ms Malgun is an expert in IFRS® standards, she did not comment on this incorrect accounting treatment of the foreign exchange gains.

After the financial statements had been published, Ms Malgun disciplined Mr Raavi for the incorrect accounting treatment of the foreign exchange gains. However, despite this, she is prepared to make his employment contract permanent.

Exhibit 2 – Sale of licence

On 1 January 20X7, Agency Co granted (sold) Kokila Co a licence with no end date to sell a headache product (Headon) in South America. Agency Co has retained the rights to sell Headon in the rest of the world. The South American market's relative value compared to the rest of the world is 20%. The manufacturing process used to produce Headon is not specialised and several other entities could also manufacture it for Kokila Co. Kokila Co will purchase Headon directly from Agency Co at cost plus 50%. The product has been sold for many years.

On 1 January 20X7, Kokila Co made an up-front payment of $15 million and will make an additional payment of $3 million when South American sales exceed $35 million. Agency Co had correctly capitalised development costs for Headon as an intangible asset at a carrying amount of $30 million.

Exhibit 3 – Drug development

Agency Co is developing a biosimilar product for the treatment of a particular medical condition. A biosimilar product is one which is highly similar to another which has already been given regulatory approval. The existing approved product's (Xudix) patent is expiring and Agency Co has applied to the government for regulatory approval of its new product. The submission includes an analysis which compares Xudix to Agency Co's proposed product in order to demonstrate biosimilarity. The government has reviewed the analysis and allowed Agency Co to undertake initial medical trials. Agency Co feels that the trials are going well. The product is used in the treatment of a very specific condition which affects only a small group of people, and Agency Co has decided to develop this product for reputational reasons. A person using the product will only pay a notional amount for the product if it is proven to be effective.

Required

(a)   (i)   Discuss the appropriateness of Mr Raavi's accounting treatment of the foreign exchange gains on the re-translation of the foreign subsidiary which is held for sale.
(3 marks)

(ii)   Discuss any ethical issues raised by Ms Malgun's actions regarding her management of Mr Raavi. (6 marks)

(b)   Discuss how the granting (sale) of the licence to Kokila Co should be accounted for by Agency Co on 1 January 20X7. (5 marks)

(c)   Discuss the accounting treatment of the costs incurred to date in developing the biosimilar drug. (4 marks)

Professional marks will be awarded in part (a)(ii) for the quality of the discussion.   (2 marks)

(Total = 20 marks)

Section B – BOTH questions are compulsory and MUST be attempted

3 Stem Co

Stem Co is a manufacturing company and is considering providing cars for its senior management. It has also entered into an agreement with two other companies to develop a new technology through a separate legal entity, Emphasis Co. The financial year end of Stem Co is 31 December 20X7.

The following **exhibits** provide information relevant to the question.

Exhibit 1 – Company cars

On 1 January 20X7, Stem Co is considering providing company cars for its senior management and is comparing three options.

Option 1

The cars can be leased for a period of four years starting on 1 January 20X7. The cars have a total market value of $75,274 on this date. The lease requires payments of $1,403 on a monthly basis for the duration of the lease term of which $235 is a servicing charge. Stem Co wishes to show the servicing charge as a separate line item in profit or loss.

At the end of the four-year period, there is no option to renew the lease or purchase the cars, and there is no residual value guarantee. The interest to be charged for the year ended 31 December 20X7 is correctly calculated at $2,274 based upon the implicit interest rate in the lease. The net present value of the lease payments over four years is $50,803 excluding the service charge.

Option 2

The cars can be purchased for $75,274 with a 100% bank loan. The cars would be purchased on 1 January 20X7 and held for four years. The estimated residual value is $29,753. Monthly service costs would still be $235 per month. The loan would be repayable in four annual instalments commencing 1 January 20X8. Assume that an average annual percentage rate on a loan is 5%.

Option 3

A final alternative is to lease the cars with a 12-month agreement on 1 January 20X7 with no purchase option. The cost would be $1,900 per month in advance including servicing charge. Stem Co would take advantage of the short-term lease exemption under IFRS 16 *Leases*.

Other relevant information

The profit before tax and before accounting for any of the three options for cars is likely to be $100,000 for the year ended 31 December 20X7. Stem Co depreciates cars over a four-year period using straight line depreciation.

Exhibit 2 - Emphasis Co

On 1 January 20X7, Stem Co has contributed cash to a new legal entity, Emphasis Co, and holds an interest of 40%. The other two companies contributing have retained equity interests of 40% and 20%, respectively. The purpose of the entity is to share risks and rewards in developing a new technology. The holders of a 40% interest can appoint three members each to a seven-member board of directors. All significant decisions require the unanimous consent of the board. The holder of the 20% interest can appoint only one board member and can only participate in the significant decisions of the entity through the board. There are no related parties.

Stem Co contributed cash of $150,000 to Emphasis Co. The entity will use the cash invested by Stem Co to gain access to new markets and to develop new products. At 1 January 20X7, the carrying amount of the net assets contributed by the three companies was $310,000 but the fair value of the net assets contributed was $470,000.

Required

(a) Explain, with suitable calculations, the impact of the three alternative company car options on:

- earnings before interest, tax, depreciation and amortisation (EBITDA);
- profit before tax; and
- the statement of financial position for the year ended 31 December 20X7.

Note: Candidates should refer to IFRS 16 *Leases* where appropriate. **(13 marks)**

(b) (i) Discuss briefly principles of the equity method of accounting and whether it is a more relevant measurement basis that cost or fair value for an investment in an associate company.

Note: There is no need to refer to any exhibit when answering part (b)(i). **(4 marks)**

(ii) Discuss why Stem Co's investment in Emphasis Co should be classified as a joint venture and how Stem Co should account for its interest at 1 January 20X7 in accordance with IAS 28 *Investments in Associates and Joint Ventures*.

Note: Candidates should show any relevant entries required in the accounting records of Stem Co. **(8 marks)**

(Total = 25 marks)

4 Symbal Co

Symbal Co develops cryptocurrency funds and is a leading authority on crypto investing. Symbal Co specialises in Initial Coin Offerings ('ICO') that raises funds from investors in the form of cash or a crypto asset such as Bitcoin.

The year end of Symbal Co is 31 March 20X7.

The following **exhibits** provide information relevant to the question.

Exhibit 1– Development costs

The diagram below illustrates how the ICO is used by Symbal Co.

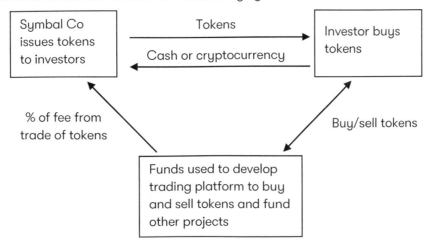

Note: The terms token and coin mean the same and investors are often referred to as supporters.

An ICO issues tokens to investors for cryptocurrency or cash. For each ICO, Symbal Co establishes a separate payment platform on which the investors can trade the tokens. These tokens do not represent an ownership interest in the entity. Symbal Co promises to produce gains for investors from trading the tokens on the platform and in return, the company takes a percentage of the profit as a fee.

As at 31 March 20X7, Symbal Co has incurred significant cost in promoting the issue of the ICO tokens, and developing the trading platform for dealing with the purchase and sale of the ICO tokens. These costs have been met from its own capital and expensed to profit or loss. Symbal Co will earn revenue from supporting the purchase and sale of tokens.

Exhibit 2 - ICO arrangements

Occasionally, Symbal Co enters into pre-sale agreements to raise funding from selected investors prior to a public sale of tokens. Symbal Co has entered into a pre-sale agreement with an investor which entitles the investor to a 10% discount on the price for tokens compared to other investors at the time of the ICO. On 1 March 20X7, the investor paid Symbal Co $1 million in cash. The issue date of the ICO is 30 April 20X7. The cash is only refundable if the ICO is abandoned before 30 April 20X7 because the minimum funding level of $9 million has not been achieved.

Once the tokens are issued, ICO investors can readily convert them into cash or cryptocurrencies on Symbal Co's platform but they do not entitle the holder to future goods and services from Symbal Co other than supporting the purchase and sale of tokens. The inflows received for tokens are used by Symbal Co to fund the future development of the payment platform and other projects.

In order to induce investment in the ICO, Symbal Co has made a commitment to the holders of tokens to pay a single payment of 10% of any annual profit for the year ended 31 March 20X8. The holders do not have any other rights such as redemption of their tokens or any residual interest in the assets of Symbal Co.

The ICO raised $10 million on 30 April 20X7.

Exhibit 3 – Tokens granted to directors

Symbal Co sometimes does not issue all the tokens from an ICO to investors but retains some to use to reward their employees. On 1 March 20X7, Symbal Co granted tokens to its five directors from the issue on 30 April 20X7. The award vests on 31 March 20X7 to directors who were in Symbal Co's employment at 31 March 20X7. The tokens give the directors the right to receive a car of their choice up to a value of $50,000 at any time in the next 12 months to 31 March 20X8 if they remain as directors of Symbal Co. All five directors were still with Symbal Co on 31 March 20X7.

Required

(a) Explain the principles of good disclosure which should be used to inform investors regarding the company's holding of crypto assets.

> Note: there is no need to refer to any exhibit when answering part (a). **(6 marks)**

> Professional marks will be awarded in part (a) for clarity and quality of discussion.
> **(2 marks)**

(b) Advise whether the various development and promotional costs related to the ICO can be accounted for as an intangible asset at 31 March 20X7. **(5 marks)**

(c) Discuss how the receipt of $1 million cash in the pre-sale agreement should be accounted for in the financial statements for the year ended 31 March 20X7 and how the $10 million raised in the ICO should be accounted for in the financial statements for the year ended 31 March 20X8. **(6 marks)**

(d) Discuss why the granting of the tokens to the five directors should be accounted for in accordance with IAS 19 *Employee Benefits* rather than IFRS 2 *Shared-based Payment* in the financial statements for the year ended 31 March 20X7. **(6 marks)**

(Total = 25 marks)

Answers

DO NOT TURN THIS PAGE UNTIL YOU HAVE
COMPLETED THE MOCK EXAM

Section A

1 Chuckle Co

				Marks
(a)	(i)	Discussion of control (IFRS 10 and other factors) v significant influence and application to the scenario		4
	(ii)	Discussion of equity accounting and application to the scenario	2	
		– Calculation of investment in associate	2	
		– Calculation of reserves	1	5
	(iii)	Application of the following discussion to the scenario:		
		– Acquisition of 18% equity	2	
		– Share options	3	5
(b)	(i)	Discussion and calculation of the following FV adjustments:		
		– Land and DT	2	
		– Inventory and DT	3	
		– Customer list	3	8
	(ii)	Application of the following discussion to the scenario:		
		– Piecemeal acquisition	3	
		– Gain on step acquisition calculation	1	
		– Impact on revaluation gain	1	
		– Goodwill calculation	3	8
				$\underline{30}$

(a) (i) Significant influence is the ability to participate in the financial and operating policy decisions of the investee but is not control or joint control over these policies.

IFRS 10 *Consolidated Financial Statements* states that an investor controls an investee only if the investor has all of the following:

- power over the investee;

- exposure to or rights to variable returns from its involvement with the investee; and

- the ability to use its power over the investee to affect the amount of the investor's returns.

Control is presumed to exist where the investor has a majority of the voting rights of the investee. This would usually give the investor the ability to direct the relevant activities, ie the activities which significantly affect the investee's returns. An ownership of 50% or less of the voting rights does not necessarily preclude an investor from obtaining control.

Prior to 1 April 20X6, Chuckle Co only owned 30% of the equity and no share options. Where an investor has a significant minority, close consideration should be given as to whether the voting rights alone or whether a combination of factors is deemed sufficient to obtain power. Chuckle Co and Grin Co do share some key management personnel which can sometimes be evidence of control. However, there has been no clear past voting pattern suggesting that Chuckle Co is unable to directly influence the economic decisions of the other investors. With only 30% of the equity and no additional potential rights, it would appear that Chuckle Co was only able to exercise significant influence rather than control. It can be concluded that it was correct to classify Grin Co as an associate.

(ii)   Grin Co is an associate and would have been accounted for using the equity method in the consolidated financial statements of Chuckle Co. The initial investment is measured at cost and the carrying amount is increased to recognise the investors' share of the profits and other comprehensive income after the date of acquisition. One line would be included within non-current assets, investment in associate which at 31 March 20X6 would be valued at $118.6 million ($100m + (30% × ($348m − $286m))).

The revaluation gain of $15 million would be recorded within other components of equity and deferred tax at 20% of $3 million would be netted off within equity in the individual financial statements of Grin Co. In the consolidated financial statements Chuckle Co should include $3.6 million (30% of the net gain of $12 million ($15m × 80%)) within other components of equity. As the remaining increase in net assets is due to profits (i.e. $50 million ($348m − $286m − $12m)), Chuckle Co should include $15 million (30% × $50m) within consolidated retained earnings.

(iii)   The acquisition of the extra 18% of the equity on 1 April 20X6 would now unquestionably make Chuckle Co a significant minority investor. No other investor owns more than 10% of the equity so Chuckle Co owns a much higher proportional share (48%). Where the other shareholdings are owned by a large number of unconnected, dispersed holders, it would be clear that power has been obtained. However, the other shares are owned by just a few other investors which is unlikely to be considered a large, dispersed group of unconnected shareholders.

Potential voting rights should be considered in the assessment of control. For these to be included in the assessment, the rights should be substantive. That would usually mean that they are currently exercisable and have an exercise price which is below the market price of the shares so that they are 'in the money'. In that sense it is worthwhile for the investor to acquire the extra shares. In the case of Chuckle Co, they own share options that are currently exercisable but not in the money. This is because the exercise price is above the share price of Grin Co. However, it can be seen that they are only just out of the money. In addition, the share price of Grin Co is expected to increase and cost savings are expected from a further acquisition of shares. It seems therefore that the share options would be deemed to be substantive. Since exercising these options would enable Chuckle Co to obtain a 60% shareholding, it can be concluded that Chuckle Co is able to exercise power over Grin Co from 1 April 20X6. Grin Co should be reclassified from an associate to a subsidiary at this date.

(b)   (i)   It is necessary for the calculation of goodwill that Chuckle Co measures the identifiable assets acquired and the liabilities assumed at their acquisition date fair values. IFRS 13 *Fair value Measurement* should be considered in the assessment of the fair values. It has been identified that the fair value of the land is $10 million above carrying amount. The valuation should be representative of the amount which market participants would be willing to sell the asset or transfer the liability in an orderly transaction under current market conditions.

The increase in value of $10 million will create an additional taxable temporary difference. In effect, the carrying amount of the land is increased by $10 million with no alteration to the tax base. An additional deferred tax liability arises at the acquisition date of $2 million. Since the deferred tax is an identifiable liability at the acquisition, it should be recognised on acquisition with a corresponding increase in net assets of $8 million ($10m − $2m).

Finished goods should be valued at their estimated sales price less the sum of the costs of disposal and a reasonable profit allowance for the selling effort of the acquiring entity. The fair value of the finished goods is $131 million and so a fair value adjustment of $47 million ($131m − $84m) is required. This creates a further taxable temporary difference in the consolidated financial statements of Chuckle Co with a corresponding deferred tax liability at 20% of $9.4 million.

It is correct that the database as an internally generated intangible asset is not recognised in the individual financial statements of Grin Co. On acquisition, Chuckle Co should recognise the database as a separate intangible asset from goodwill in the consolidated financial statements providing that the database satisfies the criteria for recognition as an intangible asset and a reliable estimate of the fair value can be determined. Although there are no contractual or legal rights associated with the database, the database still appears to be identifiable as it could be sold separately to Grin Co's competitors. The professional expert's valuation of $5 million would appear to provide a reliable estimate of fair value. The database should therefore be recognised in the consolidated financial statements at $5 million with a further increase to the deferred tax liability at 20% equal to $1 million.

(ii)   The additional purchase of the 18% equity would constitute a piecemeal or step acquisition. Goodwill will be calculated as the amount by which the fair value of the consideration exceeds the fair value of the identifiable net assets on acquisition. Chuckle Co must therefore remeasure its previously held equity interest in Grin Co at its acquisition fair value and recognise the resulting gain or loss in profit or loss. The previously held equity interest would have a carrying amount of $118.6 million (part (b)). The fair value is $127 million, so a gain of $8.4 million is recognised in the consolidated statement of profit or loss. Goodwill will be calculated including both the fair value of the original consideration and the fair value of the additional consideration.

The previous revaluation gain (net of deferred tax) which was included within other comprehensive income should be recognised on the same basis as would be required if Chuckle Co had disposed directly of the previously held equity interest. Since gains on revaluation are not reclassified to profit or loss on disposal, $3.6 million (see part (a) (ii)) should be transferred from the revaluation surplus of the group to retained earnings on 1 April 20X6.

Goodwill will be calculated as follows:

	$m	$m
Consideration of 18% holding		66.0
Fair value of original 30% holding		127.0
Non-controlling interest at acquisition (397.6 × 52%)		206.8
Less net assets at acquisition:		
Net assets per question	348.0	
Fair value adjustment land	10.0	
Subsequent deferred tax	(2.0)	
Fair value adjustment inventory	47.0	
Subsequent deferred tax	(9.4)	
Database	5.0	
Subsequent deferred tax	(1.0)	
		(397.6)
Goodwill on acquisition of Grin Co		2.2

2 Agency Co

			Marks
(a)	(i)	Discussion of appropriateness of the accounting policy	3
	(ii)	Application and discussion of ethical principles to scenario which includes:	
		Employment contract	
		Accounting policy and profit related pay	
		Time pressures	
		Competition	
		Less severe discipline	6

(b)	Discussion of key principles of IFRS 15 and relate to scenario	2	
	Derecognition of intangible asset and IAS 38	2	
	Calculation of gain	1	5

(c)	Setting out principles for capitalisation	1	
	Application of principles to scenario	3	4

	Professional marks		2
			20

(a) (i)   IAS 21 *The Effects of Changes in Foreign Exchange Rates* requires gains and losses to be reclassified from equity to the statement of profit or loss (SOPL) as a reclassification adjustment. When a group has a foreign subsidiary, a group exchange difference will arise on the re-translation of the subsidiary's goodwill and net assets. In accordance with IAS 21, such exchange differences are recognised in other comprehensive income (OCI) and so accumulate in other components of equity (OCE). On the disposal of the subsidiary, IAS 21 requires that the net cumulative balance of group exchange differences be reclassified from equity to the SOPL as a reclassification adjustment. Mr Raavi should not have included the exchange gains arising on the re-translation of the foreign subsidiary in the SOPL as it is currently only held for sale. When the subsidiary is then sold, the gains accumulated in OCE may be reclassified to profit or loss.

     (ii) Although Mr Raavi is a student accountant, he is bound by the same ethical codes as a qualified accountant. Mr Raavi is employed on the basis that either he or Agency Co can choose to terminate his employment for no reason. Even though the jurisdiction has laws which protect such employees from termination due to discrimination, it can be argued that the ability to terminate employment benefits the employer more than the employee. Thus, a primary issue is whether this type of employment contract is fair to the employee and whether it can result in unethical behaviour.

     It can be argued that fear of termination acts as a motivation for Mr Raavi to act unethically and that this type of employment has provided Mr Raavi with an opportunity as he had struggled to be employed. It is arguable whether fear of losing his job is an effective motivator for Mr Raavi. Also, allowing employees to be arbitrarily dismissed amounts to treating them with very little respect. The employer's ability to terminate a contract without reason undermines Mr Raavi's potential to set and achieve goals for himself. Mr Raavi's ability to terminate employment without cause, on the other hand, has comparatively little effect on the company's ability to set and achieve its goals.

Competitive markets are more likely to see unethical behaviour especially if unethical behaviour benefits the organisation. Accountability can have a major influence on ethical behaviour. People may behave unethically if they do not have responsibility for their actions. Mr Raavi is only an ACCA student accountant and therefore would not bear the ultimate responsibility for the inaccurate accounting for foreign exchange gains. Ms Malgun obviously knew that the accounting was inaccurate but because it benefited the company and helped the performance targets, she was prepared to overlook it. Also, this can be an unintended consequence of performance related pay as Ms Malgun is partly remunerated through profit related pay. However, in order to preserve her position, she disciplined Mr Raavi after the financial statements had been published, thus displaying a lack of integrity and professional values in her dealings with Mr Raavi and stakeholders.

Ms Malgun should not have left the preparation of the year-end financial statements to Mr Raavi as he is a student accountant and has only been with the company for 3 months. She has significant experience and expertise in their preparation. Work pressure can influence ethical behaviour. Difficult performance goals and time pressure make unethical behaviour more likely. When employees are under pressure, this not only affects their wellbeing and motivation, but also their behaviour. Ms Malgun is an expert in IFRS standards and should have ensured that she allocated some time to assist Mr Raavi in the preparation of the year-end financial statements. It is the responsibility of both Ms Malgun and Mr Raavi to engage in fair and accurate reporting with regard to the truthfulness of the data they provide as well as its completeness. It is ethically important for accountants to present the financial information in a way which is clear and honest.

Competition can influence unethical behaviour. Individuals are more inclined to engage in unethical behaviour when their organisation is in competition with other organisations or they have been given targets which have to be met. When unethical behaviour leads to a gain for a company, managers choose less severe disciplinary measures for their employees. Thus, although Ms Malgun knew of the error in the financial statements, she only reprimanded Mr Raavi after the financial statements had been published and even then, she then offered him a full-time contract instead of his current temporary contract.

(b) Agency Co had correctly capitalised development costs for Headon at a carrying amount of $30 million. IAS 38 *Intangible Assets* states that an intangible asset, in this case a proportion of the development costs, may be derecognised on disposal or when no future economic benefits are expected from its use or disposal. The gain or loss arising on derecognition is the difference between the net proceeds and the carrying amount of the asset. Gains are not classified as revenue. The amount of gain or loss arising from the derecognition will be affected by the determination of the transaction price with reference to IFRS 15 *Revenue from Contracts with Customers*.

In assessing whether an entity's promises to transfer goods or services to the customer are separately identifiable, the objective of IFRS 15 is to determine whether the nature of the promise is to transfer each of those goods or services individually or, instead, to transfer a combined item.

Kokila Co can benefit from the licence without Agency Co's manufacturing service because there are other entities which can provide the manufacturing service. Therefore, Agency Co's promises to grant the licence and to provide the manufacturing service are separately identifiable.

The consideration for the licence comprises the up-front payment of $15 million and a variable consideration of $3 million. Initially, only the up-front payment will be recognised as proceeds together with the gain on the disposal of the South American development costs. The variable consideration will be recognised in SOPL when it occurs, i.e. when South American sales exceed $35 million. The performance obligation needs to be satisfied before the payment is recognised.

Judgement is required to determine the portion of the carrying amount of the intangible asset to derecognise, relative to the amount retained. Therefore, a gain is recognised on disposal of the South American development costs of $9 million ($15m – ($30m × 20%)).

(c) Development costs are capitalised as an intangible asset if certain criteria in IAS 38 are met. There is no definitive starting point for the capitalisation of internal development costs and, therefore, Agency Co must use its judgement, based on the facts and circumstances of each product. A strong indication that Agency Co has met all of the IAS 38 criteria arises when regulatory approval is issued for the biosimilar drug as it proves the technical feasibility of the asset. This is often the most difficult criterion to demonstrate.

Another criterion to be met is that the asset should generate probable future economic benefits and demonstrate the existence of a market, or the usefulness of the asset if it is to be used internally. At present, this criteria has not been met as the product is aimed at a small group of people who will only pay a notional amount if it is an effective product.

In addition, regulatory approval has only been applied for, and there is a concern over the limited market and revenue stream. Thus, the costs are unlikely to meet the capitalisation criteria and all costs to date will be written off to profit or loss.

3 Stem Co

Marking scheme

				Marks
(a)	Discussion and application of principles to scenario:			
	IFRS 16 *Leases*		3	
	Purchasing cars		2	
	12-month leases		2	
	Impact on EBITDA and profit		3	
	SOFP		3	13
(b)	(i)	Discussion of key principles of equity accounting:		
		Nature	2	
		Cost	1	
		Fair value	1	4
	(ii)	Discussion of key principles of joint venture accounting including a well argued conclusion	5	
		Discussion of bargain purchase	2	
		Accounting for bargain purchase	1	8
				25

(a) **Option 1 Leased for a four-year period**

At 1 January 20X7, a right-of-use asset and lease liability of $50,803 would be recognised according to IFRS 16 *Leases*. The annual lease component of the lease payments is $14,016 (12 × $1,403 - $235) and the service component is $2,820 (12 × $235). At 31 December 20X7, operating expenses will comprise the service component of $2,820, and depreciation of $12,701 ($50,803/4). An interest expense of $2,274 will be recognised as a finance cost. The lease liability recognised will be $50,803 less the annual payments of $14,016 plus the interest element of $2,274 ie $39,061. The closing lease liability will be split between its non-current and current liability in the statement of financial position. IFRS 16 requires a company to recognise interest on lease liabilities separately from depreciation of lease assets.

Option 2 Purchased on 1 January 20X7

If the cars were purchased on 1 January 20X7, then depreciation would be charged of $11,380 ($75,274 - $29,753 = $45,521/4 = $11,380) and interest of $3,763 ($75,274 x 5%) would also be charged. The cars would have to be serviced at a cost of $2,820.

Option 3 Leased on a 12-month agreement

Instead of applying the recognition requirements of IFRS 16, a lessee may elect to account for lease payments as an expense on a straight-line basis over the lease term for the following two types of leases:

(i)   leases with a lease term of 12 months or less and containing no purchase options; and

(ii)   leases where the underlying asset has a low value.

The effect of applying the IFRS 16 exemption would be that neither an asset nor a liability will be recognised and therefore it will not affect the statement of financial position. Neither a right of use asset nor lease liability will be recognised if this exemption is applied. Instead, an expense will be recognised in the statement of profit or loss.

The cost of the short-term lease would be included in operating expenses at $22,800 (12 × $1,900).

It can be seen that the impact on EBITDA is greatest if 12-month leases are chosen. This is because the cost is shown in operating expenses. Additionally, profit before tax is lower under this option. EBITDA does not include lease interest when IFRS 16 is used and thus is naturally higher.

There will be no effect on EBITDA if Kayte Co leases or buys the cars and, further, the impact on profit before tax is minimal with profit being lower if Kayte Co purchases the cars.

If 12-month leases are chosen, then there will be no recognition of an asset for the cars which will result in a higher asset base for the four-year lease/purchase of cars, which will affect ratios such as asset turnover. Similarly, a liability will not be recognised in the case of the 12-month lease which will mean higher financial liabilities for the four-year lease/purchase, which will affect financial leverage (gearing).

The carrying amount of the leased cars will typically reduce more quickly than the carrying amount of lease liabilities. This is because, in each period of the lease, the leased car is depreciated on a straight-line basis, and the lease liability is reduced by the amount of lease payments made and increased by the interest which reduces over the life of the lease. Consequently, although the amounts of the lease asset and lease liability are the same at the start and end of the lease, the amount of the asset would typically be lower than that of the liability throughout the lease term. This will result in a further reduction in reported equity as compared to 12-month leases. This will be similar to the effect on reported equity which arises from financing the purchase of the cars through a loan.

	Lease over 4 years ($)	Purchase with loan ($)	12-month leases ($)
Profit before accounting for cars	100,000	100,000	100,000
Service cost	(2,820)	(2,820)	
Operating expense			(22,800)
EBITDA	97,180	97,180	77,200
Depreciation	(12,701)	(11,380)	
Interest	(2,274)	(3,763)	
Profit before tax	82,205	82,037	77,200
PPE	38,102 (50,803-12,701)	63,894 (75,274-11,380)	0
Lease/Loan Liability	39,061	79,039 (75,274+3,763)	0

(b) (i) The equity method is a measurement method and not a consolidation method, as the equity-accounted entity remains as a single line in the investor's statement of financial position and IFRS Standards consolidation is based on the existence of control. Equity accounting is a measurement method for investments where there is 'significant influence' and recognises an associate's profits which have not been received and could not be successfully demanded. The equity method provides better information than that provided by cost, but it can be argued that where investments are listed, then there is no reason not to use fair value. The equity method is likely to be better than cost because cost is in isolation an uninformative basis for decision-making. However, if an investment is listed, then its fair value would be easier to establish and more intuitively appealing than the numbers derived from the equity method. If the associate is unlisted, then there might be questions about the verifiability of fair value. However, even then, there appears to be no reason why the equity method should be preferred to IFRS 13 *Fair Value Measurement*.

(ii) The following are the characteristics of a joint venture:

- Joint ventures are joint arrangements which are structured through a separate vehicle which confers legal separation between the joint venture and the assets and liabilities in the vehicle.

- The entity must be under the joint control of the venturers, which is the contractually agreed sharing of control of an arrangement, which exists only when decisions about the relevant activities require the unanimous consent of the parties sharing control.

- The venturers must be able to exercise joint control of the entity.

- The purpose of the entity must be consistent with the definition of a joint venture.

Emphasis Co is a joint venture. Its activities are conducted through a separate legal entity and the parties participating in the decision making, exercise control through their equity investments. This control is determined by the ability to appoint board members. This means that the significant decisions require the unanimous consent of all of the parties. The company holding 20% of the equity can only appoint one board member but does have the ability to prevent the remaining companies from making significant decisions without its consent.

Each party to the joint venture (or each 'joint venturer') recognises an investment, which is accounted for using the equity method in accordance with IAS 28 *Investments in Associates and Joint Ventures*.

According to IAS 28, where an investor's investment is less than their share of the fair value of the identifiable net assets acquired, this results in a gain to the investor and is referred to as a bargain purchase. IAS 28 states that on the acquisition of the investment in an entity, any difference (whether positive or negative) between the cost of acquisition and the investor's share of the fair values of the net identifiable assets of the entity is accounted for like goodwill in accordance with IFRS 3 *Business Combinations*. Thus, any excess fair value of the identifiable net assets over the cost of the equity method investment would be recognised as a bargain purchase gain in earnings on the investment date, which is consistent with the accounting for bargain purchases in business combinations.

However, bargain purchases are rare. Therefore, before recognising a gain on a bargain purchase, Stem Co should reassess whether it has correctly identified all of the assets acquired and all of the liabilities assumed as part of the investment, in order to ensure that all identifiable assets or liabilities are properly recognised. In addition, Stem Co should reconsider and challenge all valuations to verify that the identifiable net assets are properly measured. Stem Co should try to understand why the other parties would contribute assets of higher value than those contributed by Stem Co. Usually, investors act in an economically rational manner. There may be strategic reasons for such actions. For example, Stem Co may have specialised knowledge of the industry. Also, the fair value of the net identifiable assets of the Emphasis Co may have increased before the finalisation of the agreement.

Stem Co contributed cash of $150,000 to Emphasis Co. The carrying amount of the net assets contributed by the investors was $310,000 but the fair value of the net assets contributed was $470,000 .Therefore, Stem Co's share of the fair value of the identifiable assets of Emphasis Co is 40% of $470,000, ie $188,000 .This exceeds the contribution of $150,000.Once Stem Co has reassessed whether it has correctly identified all of the assets acquired and all of the liabilities assumed as part of its investment in Emphasis Co, Stem Co will record the investment at $188,000 and will record a gain of $38,000 ($188-$150)000.

Dr	Investment in Emphasis Co	$188,000	
Cr	Cash		$150,000
Cr	Profit or loss		$38,000

4 Symbal Co

			Marks
(a)	Discussion of key principles of disclosure for crypto assets		6
(b)	Discussion of: Principles of IAS 38 Application to scenario	2 3	5
(c)	Application of the following discussion to the scenario of: Pre-sale agreement/IAS 32 ICO and profit entitlement	3 3	6
(d)	Discussion of key principles of the award – IAS 19/IFRS 2 Accounting for the award	3 3	6
	Professional marks		2
			25

(a)   There is significant interest in crypto assets with implications for both new and traditional investors. There is a growing need for clarity regarding the accounting and related disclosures relating to these new investments. The general disclosure principles which should be used to help investors can include that the disclosures should be entity-specific as information tailored to an entity's own circumstances is more useful than generic information which is readily available outside the financial statements. Thus, detailed information concerning the company's holding of crypto assets and Initial Coin Offerings (ICO) should be disclosed. The company's involvement in ICO's or other issues of crypto assets should be described as simply and directly as possible without a loss of material information and without unnecessarily increasing the length of the financial statements. Additionally, the information disclosed should be organised in a way which highlights important matters which includes providing disclosures in an appropriate order and emphasising the important matters within them. It is important that the terms of an ICO are disclosed so that investors can determine the rights associated with it.

The information about crypto assets should be linked when relevant to other information in the financial statements or to other parts of the annual report to highlight relationships between pieces of information and improve navigation through the financial statements. Commodity broker-traders holding crypto-assets as inventory at fair value less costs to

BPP
LEARNING
MEDIA

sell, in addition to the general IAS 2 *Inventories* requirements, will need to disclose the carrying amount of such inventories carried at fair value less costs to sell. In addition, IFRS 13 *Fair value measurement* disclosure requirements for recurring fair value measurements would also apply. The information about crypto assets should be provided in a way which optimises comparability among entities and across reporting periods without compromising the usefulness of the information. Holders of crypto assets classified as intangible assets under IAS 38 *Intangible Assets* will need to disclose, by class, a reconciliation between the opening and closing carrying amounts, whether the useful life is assessed as indefinite, and, if so, the reasons supporting the indefinite useful life assessment, and a description of individually material holding.

Finally, the proper application of materiality is key to determining what information to disclose. The judgmental nature of materiality assessments could lead to entities omitting useful information concerning crypto assets from the financial statements. Similarly, difficulties in exercising judgement around materiality could contribute to 'disclosure overload'.

(b) If the costs do not satisfy the requirements of IAS 38 they are recognised as expenses. The costs satisfy the requirements for recognition of intangible assets if, and only if, it is probable that the future economic benefits which are attributable to the asset will flow to the entity and the cost of the asset can be measured reliably. The probability of future economic benefits must be based on reasonable and supportable assumptions about conditions which will exist over the life of the asset.

In making the decision on recognition of the costs incurred, Symbal Co should evaluate whether after the issue of the tokens, it is still capable of controlling the trading platform and whether it may reasonably expect future economic benefits from the token holders. It is important to know whether Symbal Co will be able to get future economic benefits from token holders by providing them with future services other than another issue of tokens.

If costs incurred will not ensure further economic benefits, they should be immediately recognised as an expense in profit or loss. In this case, Symbal Co promises to produce gains for investors from trading the tokens on the platform and in return, the company takes a percentage of the profit as a fee. Thus, the company can reasonably expect further economic benefits after the issue of tokens. The costs may be recognised as an intangible asset and amortised over the useful life of these assets. However, IAS 38 states that an entity should expense promotional activity costs when incurred. Thus, these costs should be excluded from the intangible asset.

If during future reporting periods new circumstances are revealed, which indicate that there may be no more future economic benefits, then the value of the intangible asset would be impaired and written down.

(c) **Year ended 31 March 20X7**

The success of the ICO is not within the control of Symbal Co as the ICO can be abandoned if the minimum fundraising level of $9 million is not reached. Neither does the investor have the right to be repaid $1 million in cash prior to 30 April 20X7. However, on the basis that the occurrence of a successful ICO is beyond the control of the entity, the agreement contains a financial obligation, because it represents a contractual obligation to deliver cash or another financial asset to another entity if the ICO does not occur by 30 April 20X7. At 31 March 20X7, the $1 million is viewed as a financial liability of Symbal Co in accordance with IAS 32 *Financial Instruments: Presentation* at initial recognition.

Year ended 31 March 20X8

At 30 April 20X7, the funds paid by the holders of tokens of $10 million have the one-off right to 10% of profits from the year ended 31 March 20X8 but they do not have the right to their redemption or residual interest in the assets. Due to this reason, the company should not record any inflows as a financial liability or equity but record them as income by the following accounting entry.

Dr	Bank	$10 million	
Cr	Other financial income		$10 million

Also at 30 April 20X7, the liability of $1 million recorded for the pre-sale agreement will be reversed and recorded as income.

Initially, at 30 April 20X7, the commitment to the holders of tokens to pay 10% of annual profits for the year ended 31 March 20X8 is considered by Symbal Co to be a contingent liability. IAS 37 *Provisions, Contingent Liabilities and Contingent Assets* defines a contingent liability as a possible obligation depending on whether some uncertain future event occurs. The recognition of the liability depends on whether there are annual profits. Therefore, a liability should be recognised if the company earns profits during the reporting period to 31 March 20X8. Symbal Co will recognise a financial liability to the holders of tokens and an expense to profit or loss.

The tokens are not equity instruments as they do not have a residual interest in the assets of the entity after deducting all of its liabilities and they have a contractual obligation to deliver cash.

(d) When assessing the accounting treatment of such arrangements, an entity should consider the characteristics of the ICO tokens generated. Equity is the residual interest in the assets of an entity after deducting all of its liabilities. Unless the ICO tokens meet the definition of equity, the arrangements would not meet the definition of a share-based payment arrangement in accordance with IFRS 2 *Share-based Payment*. Instead, they would fall within the scope of IAS 19 *Employee Benefits* as a non-cash employee benefit. IAS 19 can then be used to determine the recognition, as well as the measurement, of the employee benefit.

The tokens do not meet the definition of the equity of Symbal Co as they do not grant the directors a residual interest in the net assets of the Symbal Co. Therefore, the arrangements do not meet the definition of a share-based payment arrangement in accordance with IFRS 2. Instead, it is a non-cash short term employee benefit. Short-term employee benefits are those expected to be settled wholly before twelve months after the end of the annual reporting period during which employee services are rendered. The substance of the arrangement is an exchange of employee services for the tokens.

The arrangement includes a condition that the directors should be in employment at 31 March 20X7. Symbal Co should recognise a liability and short-term employee benefit expense at 31 March 20X7.

Symbal Co would measure the amount that it expects to pay by using the fair value of the tokens to be delivered to the employees, or by using the estimated cost of the goods or services which it expects to deliver in the future. This amount would be (5 x $50,000) $250,000.

Thus, at 31 March 20X7

Dr	Employee costs	$250,000	
Cr	Short-term employee benefit liability		$250,000